Introduction to International Political Economy

David N. Balaam

Department of Politics and Government

Michael Veseth

*Department of Economics
and Director of the Political Economy Program*

University of Puget Sound

IN COLLABORATION WITH FACULTY
OF THE POLITICAL ECONOMY PROGRAM
UNIVERSITY OF PUGET SOUND

Prentice Hall, Upper Saddle River, New Jersey 07458

Library of Congress Cataloging-in-Publication Data

Balaam, David N.
    Introduction to international political economy / by David Balaam,
Michael Veseth in collaboration with Faculty of the political
economy program, University of Puget Sound.
      p. cm.
    Includes bibliographical references and index.
    ISBN 0–13–149592–5
    1. International economic relations.   I. Veseth, Michael.
II. Title.
HF1359.B33   1996
337—dc20
                                      95–34435
                                           CIP

Acquisitions editor: Jennie Katsaros
Editorial/production supervision: Darrin Kiessling
Interior design: Terry O'Brien
Copy editor: Dorian Hastings
Cover design: Wendy Alling Judy
Buyer: Bob Anderson

© 1996 by Prentice-Hall, Inc.
Simon & Schuster/A Viacom Company
Upper Saddle River, New Jersey 07458

Printed in the United States of America
10 9 8 7 6 5 4 3 2

ISBN 0-13-149592-5

Prentice-Hall International (UK) Limited, *London*
Prentice-Hall of Australia Pty. Limited, *Sydney*
Prentice-Hall Canada Inc., *Toronto*
Prentice-Hall Hispanoamericana, S.A., *Mexico*
Prentice-Hall of India Private Limited, *New Delhi*
Prentice-Hall of Japan, Inc., *Tokyo*
Simon & Schuster Asia Pte. Ltd., *Singapore*
Editora Prentice-Hall do Brasil, Ltda., *Rio de Janeiro*

Contents

Preface

... the ideas of economists and political philosophers, both when they are right and when they are wrong, are more powerful than is commonly understood. Indeed the world is ruled by little else. Practical men, who believe themselves to be quite exempt from any intellectual influences, are usually the slaves of some defunct economist. Madmen in authority, who hear voices in the air, are distilling their frenzy from some academic scribbler of a few years back.

John Maynard Keynes,
The General Theory of Employment, Interest, and Money
(*New York: Harcourt Brace Jovanovich, 1964*), *p. 383*

The ideas, questions, issues, and problems that we study in International Political Economy (IPE) are increasingly important. It is hard to make sense of a newspaper, a business investment, or a government policy without an understanding of the theories, institutions, and relationships found in IPE. It is difficult, in other words, to understand our everyday lives without some understanding of IPE, so deeply are we now touched by international relations and global events.

We believe that IPE is so important that all college students need to understand it in a fundamental way. Our conviction is that it is possible to present this material in simple ways that retain the complexity of the global issues and intellectual problems we address, but without making the discussion fit only for graduate students. Our aim is to provide educational materials that will allow "beginners" (college freshmen and sophomores) to go from zero-to-sixty in IPE in a single semester. Our hope is that these students will become excited about IPE and become life-long-learners—and become better citizens and more knowledgeable individuals in the process.

The book begins with five chapters designed to set out some basic tools for studying IPE. Chapter 1 introduces the fundamental idea of IPE and then tries to motivate the complexity inherent in IPE, giving a peek at the final goal. We will begin with relatively simple tools and ideas, then add layers and detail to make IPE real. Chapters 2, 3, and 4 then explore three ways of looking at IPE that have been powerful forces in history and remain influential in today's world: Mercantilism, Liberalism, and Marxism or Structuralism. Chapter 5 introduces a method, Rational Choice Analysis, that is particularly useful in understanding some IPE questions and events.

The second section of the text examines the web of relationships or structures that tie nations and their citizens together. As a student sitting at your desk, you are linked to people and places around the world in a number of ways, which you need to understand if you are to make good personal, business, and social choices. Chapter 6 looks at production and international trade. Chapter 7 looks at the monetary linkages that bind us together. Chapters 8, 9, and 10 examine, respectively, the debt connections, the security structure, and the ties created by knowledge and technology.

At the end of the first ten chapters, then, you should be able to imagine yourself as part of the IPE and how you are linked to states and markets around the globe. You should have a fundamental understanding of how the linkages are made and an appreciation of the theories and perspectives that interpret these structures and guide our understanding of them.

The second half of the book looks at specific topics and problems in IPE that are essential to a sound understanding of the world today. Chapters 11 through 14 look at issues and events that are usually associated with the industrial nations of the "North." We examine the European Union, the controversy over NAFTA, the IPE of Japan, and the problems of the formerly Communist countries making the transition to another form of political economy.

Problems and issues generally associated with the less developed countries of the "South" are discussed in chapters 15 to 17. These chapters look at the dilemma of LDCs and NICs, the nature of the multinational corporation, and the IPE of oil and energy.

Finally, the last three chapters examine global problems. The global environment and the food crisis are discussed. The very last chapter looks at the global problems of the United States. This chapter should help our U.S. readers to place themselves within the IPE and help them to make some sense of where the United States is going in the global IPE and how it will affect them.

In addition to this text, we worked with Prentice-Hall to produce three other valuable educational tools: (1) an Introductory IPE Reader, with short edited readings keyed to this text, which adds depth and breadth to the material here; (2) The Prentice-Hall–New York Times IPE Supplement, which presents recent articles and opinion pieces from the pages of the *New York Times*, keyed to chapters in this text; and (3) The Prentice Hall–ABC News IPE video library, which contains "ABC News," "Nightline," and other video clips keyed to the topics in this text. We hope that most readers of this text will also have access to these other resources, although the textbook is in fact self-contained and can be read easily without the use of these other refrences.

At the University of Puget Sound, where we teach, every student takes a course in IPE, or something similar, in their sophomore year. We have written this text to help our students and to help ourselves serve their needs. We hope you find it a valuable educational resource.

This textbook is truly a cooperative effort. We have benefited from the contributions and support of many persons, students, colleagues, family, and friends. We are especially grateful, to our colleagues in the Political Economy Program who have contributed directly to this work by writing chapters in their fields of expertise.

We would like to stress, however, that all these chapters benefited from the collaborative efforts of everyone involved in this project, giving the text a coherent voice and unified approach. We want to thank you all for your hard work, help, constructive criticism, and continuing support.

We also want to acknowledge the debt we owe to David Calleo and Susan Strange, who helped get the IPE program at the University of Puget Sound off to a good start, and to the Hewlett Foundation grant that made their visits possible. Thanks go, as well, to the reviewers, who read the entire book and provided constructive criticism, and to our friends and colleagues who did the same: Michael Carey, Dan Pearson, Richard Hill, and Stephen Newlin. We also want to thank our students, who struggled through the early drafts of these chapters in good spirits and provided many useful comments.

Finally, we owe debts we can never repay to our families and to our mentors. We love you.

David Balaam and Michael Veseth

Part I

Perspectives on International Political Economy

What is international political economy? The first chapter of this book answers this logical question, stressing the fundamental nature of IPE and its multidimensional character. The chapters that follow in part I will broaden and deepen this basic understanding. Chapters 2 through 4 are the core chapters of part I, presenting ideas that are used everywhere in the text. These chapters explore the history of IPE through a discussion of the three main IPE viewpoints or perspectives—namely, mercantilism, liberalism, and structuralism. This discussion will provide students with a basic vocabulary and some theoretical tools that are useful in understanding any IPE issue. These chapters will also help students see more clearly the roots of IPE in the past and its relevance to the contemporary world. The first part of the text concludes with chapter 5, which presents the rational-choice view of IPE, a particular method of analysis that is often employed by political economists.

1
What Is International Political Economy?

OVERVIEW

What is international political economy? Chapter 1 answers this question both in general, using social science concepts, and in particular, through concrete examples that illustrate important ideas.

In simple terms, we define IPE as the study of a fundamental tension between and dynamic interaction of two spheres of life, which we can variously call "society and individuals," "politics and economics," or "states and markets." Any way you say it, political economy is about the lines that both connect and divide national interest from individual self-interest.

The main case study presented in this chapter looks at the tension between the United States and China regarding two sets of issues—international trade and human rights—that are brought together in the international political economy. The purpose of this case study is not so much to inform the reader about this specific issue as to provide a concrete example for use in thinking generally about IPE.

U.S. IS TO MAINTAIN TRADE PRIVILEGES FOR CHINA'S GOODS

WASHINGTON, May 26—President Clinton's decision to renew China's trade benefits was the culmination of a titanic clash between America's global economic interests and its self-image as the world's leading advocate of human rights. In the end, economic interests won the day.

The New York Times, Friday, 27 May 1994[1]

International political economy dominated the front page of *The New York Times* and most other newspapers in the United States on May 27, 1994. The issue was complex but clearly important. President Bill Clinton had to choose between two conflicting national interests. The economic interests of both China and the United States would be best served by granting Chinese goods favorable entry into the U.S. market, a condition termed **most favored nation** (MFN) status (see the case study, page 10). China, however, had a record of violating human rights as they are defined by Western culture. It was long-standing U.S. policy to deny MFN status to nations that violate human rights standards.

President Clinton's dilemma was an example of the tension between economics and politics, two spheres of human life that often intersect. In making his choice, President Clinton had to take into account the many types of interactions between China and the U.S., and the impacts they have on other nations. He had, as well, to weigh historical factors and consider deep cultural differences. In the end, President Clinton chose to extend MFN trade privileges to China, satisfying some economic and political interests, despite China's lack of progress on human rights.

Sometimes international political economy makes the front page, as it did here, but it is *always* in the news. We live in a rapidly changing world, where everyday concerns are increasingly global. As interdependence grows, economic issues are increasingly political in their nature and impact, and political issues are increasingly economic.

It is necessary to understand something about IPE if one is to comprehend the nature of many of today's events, their impact on us as nations, businesses, and individuals, and their consequences for the future. The IPE of MFN trade status for China, for example, will affect profoundly the lives of millions of Americans and many more millions in China and other countries. Such important information can no longer be ignored by intelligent people seeking to understand broadly the world they live in and their place in it.

What is IPE? Why should it be studied? How? This book is an introduction to IPE, written to help you understand the issues, forces, and problems that characterize today's interdependent world and to help you appreciate where you fit into the picture. This chapter gets you started by outlining the basics of IPE, using the China MFN decision as a case study to illustrate IPE's power and importance.

One way to understand the basics of IPE is to pick apart its name. It is first, therefore, *international,* meaning it deals with issues that cross national borders and with relations between and among nation-states.

IPE is secondly *political* in that it involves the use of state power to make decisions about who gets what, when, and how in a society. Politics is a process of collective choice, drawing in competing interests and values of different actors, including individuals, groups, businesses, and political parties. The political process is complex and multilayered, involving nation-states, bilateral relations among nation-states, and many international organizations, regional alliances, and global agreements.

Lastly, IPE is about the *economy* or economics, which means that it deals with how scarce resources are allocated to different uses and distributed among individuals through the decentralized market process. Economic analysis and political analysis often look at the same questions, but economic analysis focuses less on issues of power and national interest and more on issues of income and wealth and individual interest. Political economy, therefore, combines these two ways of looking at the world in order to grasp more fully society's fundamental nature.

The issue of China's MFN is thus typically IPE in its nature, since this issue deals with U.S. government policies that affect both commerce and social values in the United States and China. IPE is a social science based on the set of problems, issues, and events where I, P, and E intersect, connect, or overlap, creating a rich pattern of interactions. In today's world, this is a growing and increasingly fascinating set of questions to study.

FIRST PRINCIPLES: STATES AND MARKETS

The world is a complicated place, characterized at all levels by elements of interdependence. We depend on one another in many ways and at many levels. Human existence is, therefore, filled with elements of tension, boundaries where differing and sometimes conflicting interests, points of view, or value systems come into contact with one another. It is the purpose of the humanities and the social sciences to im-

---

WHY STUDY INTERNATIONAL POLITICAL ECONOMY?

Why should a person study international political economy? We give three brief answers: because it is interesting, because it is important, and because it is useful.

IPE is interesting. To paraphrase Samuel Johnson, a person who is bored with IPE is bored with life! IPE is all about life and the many actions and interactions that connect human beings around the globe. The study of IPE is the opportunity to study some of the most interesting issues and questions in the world.

IPE is important. IPE makes the front pages every day because IPE events affect us all as citizens of the world, residents of particular nation-states, and daily participants in systems of markets that are increasingly global in nature. IPE events affect us all and it is important that we understand them and see how we connect to and can influence global affairs.

Finally, *IPE is useful.* Public and private employers increasingly seek out individuals who can think broadly and critically, who can understand complex and dynamic systems, and who can appreciate the impact of social conditions and alternative values. Employers, in short, seek out those who can understand the international and global context of human activity today. IPE is the social science that most directly addresses these needs.

prove our understanding of the human condition by analyzing the causes of these tensions and their consequences—how they are resolved. Political economy contributes to this work by focusing on particular tensions that have traditionally been of interest to social scientists.

Since it is useful, especially at the start, to use a simple vocabulary to discuss new ideas, let us agree to think about political economy as *the field of study that analyzes the problems and questions arising from the parallel existence and dynamic interaction of "state" and "market" in the modern world.*[2]

The interactions that define political economy can be described in many ways. To a certain extent, political economists focus on the fundamental conflict between the interests of the *individual* and the broader interests of the *society* in which that individual exists. To put this another way, political economy is the study of the tension between the **market**, where individuals engage in self-interested activities, and the **state**, where those same individuals undertake collective action that is—or should be—in the national interest or in the interest of a more broadly defined community or "society." In short, political economy looks at the fundamental tension between *economics* and *politics*.

The state is the realm of collective action and decision. By *state* we usually mean political institutions of the modern nation-state, a geographic region with a relatively coherent system of government that extends over that region. The nation-state is a legal entity that has a well-defined territory and population, with a government capable of exercising sovereignty. France, for example, means the territory of France, the people of France, and the government of France and its policies, depending on context.[3] We should, however, also consider the state more broadly, as the domain of collective or political behavior that takes place at many levels. The European Union (EU), for example, is not a nation-state; it is an organization of nation-states. Yet to the extent the EU makes choices or policies that affect the entire group of nations and their citizens, it demonstrates the properties of a state.

The market is the realm of individual actions and decisions. By *market* we usually mean the economic institutions of modern capitalism. The market is the sphere of human action dominated by individual self-interest and conditioned by the forces of competition. Although a market is sometimes a geographical location (such as the New York Stock Exchange or the Pike Place Market in Seattle), it is more often a *force*. That is, the force of the market motivates and conditions individual human behavior. Individuals are driven by the motive of self-interest, for example, to produce and supply scarce goods and services or to seek out bargain products or high-wage jobs. They are driven by the market force of competition to make products better, or cheaper, or more attractive.

Society contains both state and market elements, and states and markets therefore generally reflect the history, culture, and values of their social systems. We define political economy this way, knowing that states and markets are complicated systems of social organization, which exist within a broader society (see figure 1–1).

The parallel existence of states (politics) and markets (economics) creates a fundamental tension that characterizes political economy. States and markets do not always conflict, but they do overlap to such a degree that their fundamental

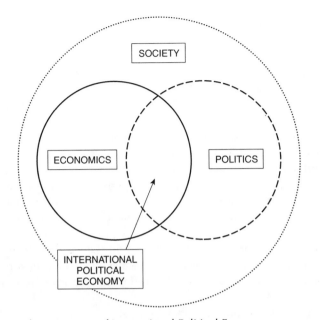

FIGURE 1–1   The Geometry of International Political Economy

tension is apparent. The tensions created by their differing interests or values can be resolved in different ways at different times, but the underlying conflicts remain and reappear throughout human history. The interaction of states and markets is *dynamic*, which means it changes over time. In particular, states influence markets and markets influence states, constantly changing the pattern of interests and values that political economists study.

WEALTH AND POWER: THE TENSION BETWEEN STATES AND MARKETS

What is the nature of the interaction between states and markets? Why does their parallel existence and dynamic interaction often create tensions? Where are the boundary lines drawn? States and markets embrace different basic values. They work in different ways to achieve different ends. They necessarily intersect and overlap, creating the subject we will study here.

Economists like to say that markets "allocate and distribute scarce resources." Markets are a highly decentralized and individualistic way to decide how scarce resources are used (allocation) and who gets them (distribution). Markets let the "invisible hand" of individual action make resource decisions. Decisions that affect resource use influence the creation of wealth and its distribution both within nations and among nations. There are ways other than markets of making choices about scarce resources. In command economies, like the Soviet Union before 1989, allocation and distribution choices were made by the state, based on the government's notion of national interest.

Political scientists often say that states "allocate and distribute power." Power is the ability to affect or determine outcomes. Hans Morgenthau defined power as the ability to control the minds and actions of others.[4] In its sphere of influence, a state may be said to be in the business of choosing where the power of collective action is used (allocation) and who gets to use it (distribution). Elections are all about the allocation and distribution of power. Elections are one way the state determines who has power and how it is used.

Since the exercise of power generally affects the allocation and distribution of resources, politics (power) and economics (wealth) are thoroughly intertwined. States and markets interact because the boundary between what happens to wealth (the sphere of the market) and what happens to power (the sphere of the state) is sometimes ambiguous and constantly shifting. People who can command resources in our society have power, so the market necessarily influences actions of the state. People who command power in our society can influence how and where resources go. A strict distinction between states and markets is therefore really arbitrary and artificial. If markets are yellow and states are blue, then most of the world is made up of the various shades of green that reflect the many degrees of relative influence of state and market forces.

When states and markets have similar goals or are driven by similar interests and values, their interactions tend to be relatively uncontroversial. It is more typically the case, however, that the motives of states and markets differ. Markets typically reflect the values and interests of the individuals that comprise them. Both buyers and sellers are typically self-interested; they take actions that they perceive will make them better off. Thus, workers try to negotiate the highest wages they can, subject to working conditions and other factors, in order to increase their command of scarce resources (food, clothing, housing, education, etc.). In the same way, employers find it in their interest to pay the lowest wages they can, subject to other concerns such as worker loyalty and workforce stability, so as to increase their profits and thus their own ability to command scarce resources. The outcome of the market reflects whatever compromise that is reached between the often-opposing individual interests.

States also reflect social values, but in a very different way. In a market, an individual's voice is heard loudly or softly or not at all based on the value of the resources that person commands. The state engages in collective action—its laws, wars, and rules affect everyone—while the market is based on individual actions. How well the collective choices of the state reflect the general will and public interest depends on a large number of factors, such as voting rights, representation rules, and the nature of political institutions in a country. In the United States, we employ an extremely complicated system of public choice, with a president, Congress, the Supreme Court, and a great many state and local government agencies.

It is difficult to know to what extent any particular law or action follows the general will. But it is easy to predict that the state's reaction to a particular problem will generally differ from the market's reaction to it. A business manager is likely to be removed if her performance is persistently inefficient and unprofitable. A political leader may be more likely to be removed for being uncompassionate or unfair.

One problem with markets that is often noted is that no one negotiates with the public interest in mind.[5] That is, in the process of satisfying individual interests, the market may allocate and distribute resources (and therefore power) in ways that are not in the general interest of the population or that is different from the way the state would make these choices. In fact, states can sometimes be manipulated by a small group of "elites" or by the economic forces of special interests. Public interest can be sacrificed on the altar of narrow private interest.

A value that markets strongly hold is efficiency, the ability to use and distribute resources (and hence power) effectively and with little waste. The motivation of private self-interested action and the economy of decentralized decision making tend to promote efficiency. A value that states strongly hold is fairness (variously termed *equity* or *equality*) and state power is often used to promote fairness. Relations between and among individuals can be unfair or unequal if the power that individuals can exercise (either through states or markets) is unequally distributed.[6]

One value that both states and markets strongly hold is security. Security is a basic human need that we have both as individuals and collectively. Sometimes the need for security drives states and markets in the same direction. At other times, however, these two spheres conflict. Farmers in both the United States and in the European Union desire greater economic security, for example, and so demand subsidy payments from their governments. These subsidies, however, create problems on international food markets, which bring the states into conflict with one another, lessening security on this level.

To summarize, states and markets embody different *values* (such as efficiency versus fairness), they employ different *means* (decentralized markets and voluntary bargains versus collective action and force) and they therefore have different *goals*. It is unsurprising, therefore, that a tension exists along the fault lines between states and markets. The controversy over human rights in China and the granting of MFN status to Chinese goods is just one example of the way that the pressure between differences in values and means creates the tensions that define IPE.

THE DYNAMIC NATURE OF STATE-MARKET INTERACTION

What makes IPE an especially interesting field of study is the dynamic nature of the interaction of states and markets. People live simultaneously in a state and in a variety of markets, confronting at once the constraints of wealth and power. It is not surprising, therefore, that change in one sphere of existence evokes change in the other. This dynamic interaction means that IPE is always in a state of transition. Cycles of change are transposed upon evolutionary paths. There is always something familiar, and always something new.

Changes in the state's domain—power—necessarily affects the individuals in the economy. In South Africa, for example, the decision to abandon apartheid and to increase the power of blacks in government rule necessarily also impacts the status of black people in the market. Their ability to command resources, earn incomes, and accumulate wealth will surely change as their political power increases. It may be some years before the full outline of the consequences of these interactions are clear.

Likewise, changes in the market's domain—wealth—necessarily affect the allocation and distribution of state power. In China, for example, changes in the economy have helped galvanize forces for political change in the state. In an attempt to improve the living standards of their people, Chinese leaders have introduced free market forces into some areas of China's economy. Free markets, profits, and private enterprise are seen as a way to speed growth.

The rise of self-interest in the market, however, has created problems for China's state. Individuals who follow the beacon of self-interest in the market may be less willing to be guided by the light of social interest as revealed through state policies. The 1989 Tianamen Square confrontation between state forces and members of the democracy movement in China illustrate vividly the tensions that exist between these changes in the two spheres of life. This fault line between individual interest and state power is seen as well in the most favored nation issue with which this chapter began.

CASE STUDY: THE UNITED STATES, CHINA, AND THE MFN ISSUE

When a nation is granted most favored nation (MFN) status by the United States, its products can enter the vast U.S. marketplace on equal footing with those from other nations. Although MFN is often referred to as "preferential treatment," it means, in fact, that your goods are treated as well (or as badly) as those from most other countries in terms of U.S. trade policy. Of course, being denied MFN means that imports from a country may face additional barriers to trade, which discourages their purchase and use. This is important to people in both countries in the case of China.

Open access to the U.S. market means greater sales, higher incomes, and more jobs to workers and businesses in China. If China did not have MFN status, its products would be less competitive in the United States. Many U.S. businesses also have a stake in China's MFN status. Some U.S. businesses want access to inexpensive Chinese raw materials and semi-finished items to use in the production of their own products. Other U.S. firms want to invest in China or have already done so. These investments will pay higher returns if the U.S. market is open to Chinese goods. Other U.S. businesses plan to export goods to China, and believe that the Chinese market is likely to be more open to their products if the U.S. market remains open to goods from China.

Based on this information, it is tempting to conclude that "the market" favors granting MFN status to China. Such a statement is accurate in the sense that markets, which value efficiency, tend to operate best when there are fewer restrictions, which is what MFN provides. This conclusion is wrong, however, in the sense that not all market participants necessarily favor more U.S. trade with and investment in China. In particular, there are firms and workers in the U.S. who stand to lose if there is greater competition with Chinese goods. In the same way, more trade with China would mean less trade with other countries, which affects producers there.

Business interests in the U.S. that favored increased trade and investment with China were well organized in 1994. President Clinton's decision to grant MFN status to China thus represented a "victory" for these market-affiliated groups. But the decision was not an easy one because of the fundamental tension between market forces and state interests. While the market values efficiency, the U.S. state puts higher value on human

Continued

CASE STUDY: THE UNITED STATES, CHINA, AND THE MFN ISSUE, *continued*

rights, or at least this was the point of tension on this issue. China's commitment to Western-style human rights is suspect for several reasons that entered into the political debate over President Clinton's decision.

A *Financial Times* article listed a number of concerns that the U.S. "state" had regarding China's behavior. "Mr. Clinton called on China to release political prisoners, to recognize Tibet's 'distinctive cultural heritage,' to permit international radio and television broadcasts into China and follow humane practices in the use of prison labour. He said he wanted Chinese progress on nuclear non-proliferation and eliminating trade barriers" (*Financial Times*, 29/30 May 1993, p. 3).

Underlying these remarks, of course, is the fact that China's state has long been organized according to fundamentally different principles than the United States (communist state/market versus market/democracy) and the still vivid memory of the 1989 Tianamen Square massacre. China's history, culture, and the nature of its social system are fundamentally different from Western countries such as the United States, which may account in part for the difference in state values and behavior here. The conflict remains, however, and this necessarily colors the political and economic relations among these nations.

Clearly, there is a strong temptation to use the MFN issue as a way to employ market pressure to change the Chinese state. In the end, however, President Clinton chose to "de-link" MFN and human rights—granting China MFN status despite its lack of progress in human rights. The economic costs of imposing trade barriers on China was high, it was said, and many believed the MFN "stick" too weak to force China to reform its political and social system.

The Economist, an influential British newsweekly, took a strong stand in favor of open trade with China in a leading editorial titled "China Belongs to Me" (29 May 1993, pp. 13–14). "How should China be treated: with fear or favour?" it asked. The answer was clear: Western nations should do all they can to draw China into the world market system. "China's rush to capitalism is also a rush to individual liberty: a chance to choose not just fancy clothes and fast cars but how to live, where to live, and who to be ruled by. China remains a repressive place. . . . But economic reform is passing power from central governments to the provinces, and from repressive institutions to individual enterprises."

This idea—that states and markets are ultimately ruled by the same principles—is a controversial one. Does competition and individual choice in the market lead to freedom and respect for individual rights in the state? Or is the direction of causation the other way round—does democracy create capitalism? Or are these two issues fundamentally *un*related? These are questions that have puzzled moral philosophers for centuries.

Fang Lizhi, a refugee from Chinese oppression, is less optimistic about the free market's ability to transform the communist state. He writes that

> While we can note with satisfaction the political collapse of communist regimes in Eastern Europe during the last few years, and the economic collapse of the communist regime in China during the same period, we cannot be wholly optimistic. The critical problem is that the state-run enterprises will remain a curb to economic development. Without political reform and changes in property rights, these dinosaurs will not be transformed; and, as long as the current leaders are alive, we cannot expect significant political change. . . . China will be deadlocked in a political and economic paradox, a possible result of which will be (to a greater or lesser degree) chaos ("China: Since 1989," *Common Knowledge* [Spring 1993]: 7).

Continued

CASE STUDY: THE UNITED STATES, CHINA, AND THE MFN ISSUE, *continued*

Fang paints a dismal but realistic picture. Economic reform needs political change to be successful. But changes in political systems often need the backing of successful economic reforms. These two sets of transformations could unite into a virtuous cycle of change and growth. Or they could spiral down into a tangled and chaotic wreck. Which will it be?

The dynamic relationship between changes in markets and changes in states is an increasingly important issue in the world today. All around the world, states and markets are changing. This is obviously true in places like Russia and the former Yugoslavia, where old patterns of state-market relationships have been abandoned to a great extent. But many other nations face these changes to a lesser or perhaps just a different extent. India, the European Community, the United States, and other countries are now redefining or reconsidering, in fundamental ways, the nature of state-market interactions.

The Economist, for its part, sees clearly the answer to this complex, uncertain, and puzzling problem. "Capitalism and economic growth will not guarantee the Chinese people their human rights. But they do make abusing them steadily harder. The transfer of power to the market and to the individual, and away from the state and the party, offers a billion people the best possible chance of better lives. After all, tomorrow's China belongs to them." (*The Economist*, "China Belongs to Me," 29 May 1993, 13–14).

WHAT IS *INTERNATIONAL* POLITICAL ECONOMY?

> Political Economy is the intellectual discipline that investigates the rich interface between economics and politics. International political economy is the extention of that investigation to the international sphere.[7]

Political economy is clearly not the only way to study or understand the fault lines that define human geography, but it is a particularly interesting and useful one. This study becomes distinctly international when it focuses on the aspects of state-market relations that extend beyond the borders of a single nation-state, becoming international, regional, or global in nature.

Perhaps the clearest definition of *international* political economy comes from Professor Susan Strange, who helped establish the modern study of IPE at the London School of Economics and Politics. Professor Strange has written that IPE

> concerns the social, political, and economic arrangements affecting the global systems of production, exchange, and distribution and the mix of values reflected therein. Those arrangements are not divinely ordained, nor are they the fortuitous outcome of blind chance. Rather they are the result of human decisions taken in the context of manmade institutions and sets of self-set rules and customs.[8]

Several elements of this definition are worthy of note. This definition of IPE gives equal weight to social, political, and economic arrangements and stresses that IPE is not just the study of institutions or organizations, but also of the *values* they reflect. States and markets are connected by "global systems of production, exchange, and distribution," which this book terms the *structures* of the international political economy. IPE therefore looks at the ways that the states and markets of the world are connected to one another and the arrangements or structures that have evolved to connect them. These arrangements reflect culture, history, and values. They change—and will continue to change in the future.

While Professor Strange's definition seems to focus narrowly on economic connections (production, exchange, and distribution), in fact these terms have broader intent and meaning. While it is true that goods and services get produced, exchanged, and distributed, this is also true about other aspects of life, such as power and status. The arrangements that IPE studies are the arrangements of lives, with particular emphasis on their global character. Some persons, like some nations, are wealthier than others, are more powerful than others, or have higher status or greater authority than others. These conditions are the result of the global structures or arrangements that produce, exchange, and distribute social, political, and economic resources. These IPE structures provide a useful framework for the analysis of IPE problems.

IPE is thus a multidimensional study: States and markets and their tensions and interactions give IPE its basic substance and form, but we also must look deeper and perceive the textures of their global social, political, and economic arrangements and the colors produced by the values they reflect. Let us look briefly, therefore, at the "arrangements" or global structures of IPE, and then at the "values" or different perspectives that dominate IPE debate.

THE STRUCTURES OF INTERNATIONAL POLITICAL ECONOMY

The international political economy is a network of bargains between and among states (that deal in power) and markets (that deal in wealth). These bargains determine the production, exchange, and distribution of wealth and power. Bargains can take many forms. Some are formal agreements, signed, ratified, and enforced. Other bargains are merely conventions, understandings, or rules of thumb. These bargains tend to be far less formal, but just as important.[9]

Some IPE bargains reflect what Professor Strange calls *relational power*, which is the power of one player to get another player to do something (or not do it). This is power as most of us normally think of it. Increasingly, however, what is important in IPE according to Professor Strange, is *structural power*, which she defines as "the power to shape and determine the *structures* of the global political economy within which other states, their political institutions, their economic enterprises and (not least) their scientists and other professional people have to operate."[10] In a sense, these structures are the institutions, arrangements, and the "rules of the game" that govern the behavior of states and markets in the international political economy, which together produce, exchange, and distribute wealth and power. The four global structures are: security, production, finance, and knowledge.[11]

The Security Structure

Security—from natural forces or, more important, from the threats and actions of others—is perhaps the most basic human need. When one person or group provides security for another (or contributes to that security), a **security structure** is created. The nature of this security structure depends on the kind of bargain that is struck among its participants. The security structure has been an important defining force in IPE in the twentieth century. The nature of a nation's production, finance, and knowledge of structural relationships during the Cold War depended critically on its status as a member of either the Soviet bloc (the Warsaw Pact nations and their allies), the U.S.-centered NATO bloc, or the group of nonaligned states.

The nature of the security structure was a contributing factor in the debate over China's MFN status in 1994. Sometimes China has been thought of as a threat to U.S. security interests, at other times it has been seen as a part of a trilateral balance of power along with the U.S. and the Soviet Union. Until the late 1970s, all trade with China was forbidden for national security reasons. Although the ban on China trade is gone, it is clear that fear, uncertainty, and doubt remain regarding what threat, if any, China represents to the United States. This security question tempers to some degree relations between the U.S. and China in all areas.

The Production Structure

"A **production structure** can be defined as the sum of all arrangements determining what is produced, by whom and for whom, by what methods and on what terms. It is people at work, and the wealth they produce by working."[12] Production is the act of creating value and wealth, and wealth is nearly always linked to power. The issue of who produces what for whom on what terms, therefore, lies at the heart of international political economy. Recent decades have seen dramatic changes in the production structure, with production of certain high-value items such as automobiles shifting from the United States to Japan and now to other countries, such as Korea, Mexico, Brazil—and possibly China. These structural changes affect the distribution of wealth and power in the world and, therefore, impact the other structures of IPE.

The Finance Structure

The **finance structure** is perhaps the most abstract set of linkages between and among nations. One way to describe the finance structure is to say that it is the pattern of money flows between and among nations. That is, this structure defines who has access to money, how, and on what terms. This definition's simplicity covers up two important points. First, we are not really interested in money so much as in what money can buy—scarce resources. So the finance structure is really a description of how certain resources are allocated and distributed between and among nations. In this respect, money is a means, not an end.

Second, we are at this point mostly interested in money to the extent that it creates an obligation between people or states. This occurs in several ways. For example, sometimes money moves from one nation to another in the form of loans, which must be repaid. At other times the money movement is in the form of direct investment, where a foreigner gains control directly over the use of resources by, say, purchasing a factory or a farm. Financial bargains create obligations, which join the interests of different nations. The nature of these obligations, and their effects, are important elements of IPE.

The Knowledge Structure

It is often said that knowledge is power. Knowledge is wealth, too, for those who can use it effectively. Who has knowledge and how it is used is therefore an important factor in IPE. Nations with poor access to knowledge in the form of industrial technology, scientific discoveries, medical procedures, or instant communications, for example, find themselves at a disadvantage relative to others. Increasingly in the world today, the bargains made in the security, production, and finance structure depend on access to knowledge in its several forms.

It may be difficult to overestimate the importance of the **knowledge structure** in the world today. Indeed, Robert Reich has written an influential book that envisions the future as a world where wealth and power are determined more by knowledge than by any other single factor.[13] One reason China desired MFN status in 1994 was that it hoped that increased economic interaction with the United States would give it greater access to industrial technology. In the 1990s, technology determines in large measure a nation's place in the production structure. To move up in the international division of labor, China needed to accelerate its acquisition of science, technology, and know-how from abroad.

VALUES AND VIEWPOINTS: THEORETICAL PERSPECTIVES ON IPE

Finally, there are a variety of theories that attempt to describe how states and nations should interact (normative theories) or how they really do behave (positive theories). These theories are like lenses that we can use to view and interpret the international political economy. They are also important in the history of IPE. Indeed, in many respects the history of international relations is a competition for dominance among opposing IPE theoretical perspectives.

The theories of IPE are not just abstract academic scribblings; they guide the thoughts and actions of men and women in all sorts of ways and so shape and condition the world. If we want to understand how people think about and behave within the spheres that define IPE, we must understand these theories.

Different people give different names to the main IPE theories, a problem that results from the "wide open spaces" that are also the strength of IPE. The three main IPE theories are often broadly termed:

- *Mercantilism*, or economic nationalism, which looks at IPE issues mainly in terms of national interest. Mercantilism is the IPE perspective that is most closely associated with political science, especially the political philosophy of *realism*.

- **Liberalism**, or economic liberalism, which looks at IPE issues mainly in terms of individual interests. Liberalism is most closely associated with the system of markets that are the study of economists.
- **Structuralism,** or **Marxism** or Marx-Leninism, which looks at IPE issues mainly in terms of class interests. Structuralism is most closely associated with the methods of analysis employed by many sociologists.

It would be a mistake to try to summarize or simplify these perspectives here, so the next three chapters will examine them in historical terms. Also, we will explore their development and their relationship to one another. These theories are important because they provide us with a frame of reference as we try to understand IPE and reconcile its many dimensions.

It is useful, in fact, to think of these IPE theories as "points of view" or "perspectives" because they really are exactly that. All IPE theories look at the same world of international problems, issues, and events. But each approaches it from a different angle, and so sees the multidimensional form in a different light. Each viewpoint reveals some aspects particularly well, but may cast a shadow on other important points.

While many authors approach IPE from a single point of view that they feel is most revealing or useful for the problems they want to consider, this book takes a firmly multidimensional stand. Most IPE problems, like most aspects of human existence, can best be understood if a variety of viewpoints are considered, not just one, reducing the chance of overlooking some important aspect. It is often true, however, that a given situation can be most revealingly understood from a particular perspective. Thus, while we encourage the consideration of many perspectives, we emphasize the right and obligation of individuals to make their own judgments about which view (or combination of perspectives) is best.

IPE IN PERSPECTIVE

International political economy is both the past and the future of social science. It is the past because it represents a return to the origins of social science, before the study of human social behavior became fragmented into the discrete fields of economics, political science, sociology, history, and philosophy. It is the future because, in today's complex world, most important social problems clearly have an international or multinational aspect that is best understood through an integrated study drawing on a variety of tools and perspectives, not just one.

In an academic world full of fences that enclose disciplines and limit interaction, IPE represents a return to the idea of "a vast, wide open range where anyone interested in the behavior of men and women in society could roam just as freely as the deer and the antelope. There were no fences or boundary-posts to confine the historians to history, the economists to economics. Political scientists had no exclusive rights to write about politics, nor sociologists to write about social relations."[14] Rowland Maddock put it slightly differently: "In short, international political economy is not a tightly defined and exclusive discipline with a well-established methodology. It is more a set of issues, which need investigating and which tend to be ignored by the more established disciplines, using whatever tools are at hand."[15]

IPE does not replace the separate social science disciplines, it unites them into a fence-free, wide-open field, better to serve the needs of our complex society. IPE attempts to understand the world of human interaction in a comprehensive fashion, which is an ambitious undertaking but a necessary one for the people who live in the world and for future leaders who will have to deal with its economic, political, and social problems.

JURASSIC IPE

In 1993, millions of people around the world read Michael Crichton's book *Jurassic Park* or saw the Steven Spielberg movie of the same name. Interestingly, most of them thought the story was about dinosaurs. But *Jurassic Park* was really all about international political economy.

The story of *Jurassic Park*, for readers who somehow missed the movie or the media blitz, is about a biotechnology firm that discovers how to recover dinosaur DNA from amber-entombed prehistoric blood-sucking insects. The company takes over an island off the coast of Costa Rica and creates a theme park filled with real live dinosaurs that have been cloned from the dinosaur DNA. Soon, however, the dinosaurs get out of control and kill nearly everyone (except the kids, of course) and the Costa Rican air force comes to bomb the island back into the Jurassic Age, killing all the dinosaurs, except maybe Barney and a few other escapees, just in case *Jurassic Park II* is ever produced.

You can see why people would become confused about this story and mistake it for a tale of dinosaurs. It really is about IPE, however (this is clearer in the book than the movie, admittedly). It really is about the fundamental tension and dynamic interaction of states and markets on the international level.

Why did the biotechnology company choose to make dinosaurs instead of more useful items, like life-saving drugs? The answer, made clear in the book, is that the prices of high-tech drugs are regulated by the government in an attempt to control medical costs and make the drugs available to a wide group of users. This limited the profit potential for bio-tech research in socially *useful* fields—the conflict between social values and private profit was clear. So the firm spent millions creating dinosaurs because dinosaurs (and entertainment generally) were unregulated. The conflict between private profit and social values only appeared as the prehistoric critters began to threaten people's lives.

Why was Jurassic Park built in Costa Rica? It surely wasn't the case that the Costa Ricans were the park's target market. Rather, Costa Rican citizens provided relatively inexpensive labor. Of course, a less developed country was chosen because its government was unlikely to impose many regulations on what happened on the island. Less developed countries have very low income levels compared to ours and often value jobs and incomes over environmental regulations or safety standards. Also, Costa Rica was chosen because of its climate.

Foreign investment is not uniformly welcomed by less developed countries (LDCs). Some LDCs are suspicious that foreign investment generates one-sided gains and ends up exploiting the country, its people, and natural resources. Costa Rica, however, has a history of positive relations with the United States, and has experienced relatively good results from foreign investment. Costa Rica has a stable democratic system of

Continued

JURASSIC IPE, *continued*

government and fairly open markets. So Costa Rica would be on the shortlist of any investment project of this type.

Professor Strange believes that, in looking at any IPE story, it is useful to ask *cui bono?*—Latin for "who benefits?" Asking this question always pushes one from description to analytical thought. Who stood to benefit from Jurassic Park? Most people who are asked this question about *Jurassic Park* see an uneven pattern of gains. Costa Rica stood to gain a bit, due to the foreign investment and jobs that the theme park would have created (in the end, however, they certainly lost from the dino-disaster). The rich American, European, and Japanese visitors to Jurassic Park would have gained. The park was an expensive but unique experience that they would have enjoyed, had it worked as planned. They would have gained just as visitors to Disney World gain. Of course, Jurassic Park was a much more expensive attraction than Disney World, so these gains would have been concentrated among the world's wealthiest 1 percent.

The biggest gains from a successful Jurassic Park would have gone to the businesses that produced it and their multinational investors. They would have earned far greater profit than if they had devoted the same resources and effort to finding a cure for cancer or a treatment for heart problems. (So maybe it's O.K. that the dinosaurs ate them.)

Michael Crichton's story presents a view of IPE where gains flow from the poor to the rich. This is one of three important perspectives on IPE that we will discuss in upcoming chapters, and it is the right answer to the question *cui bono?* under many, but not all, circumstances.

Who *really* benefited from *Jurassic Park?* If you apply Michael Crichton's ideas, you must answer that the real gainers were Crichton, Spielberg, and the investors that backed the book and the movie that so many people paid so much money to read or view. And that's no dinosaur story.

A READER'S GUIDE TO "ISMS"[16]

- *Capitalism*   A social and economic system that features private ownership of the means of production and the use of markets to make allocation and distribution decisions.
- *Communism*   The final stage of the dialectic described by Marx: feudalism, capitalism, the dictatorship of the proletariat, communism. Under communism, the state will "wither away," and economic life will be organized to achieve "from each according to his abilities, to each according to his needs."
- *Imperialism*   A social and economic system among nations that is uneven or asymmetric in the sense that wealth and power tend to flow from the dependent nations to the imperial nation.
- *Liberalism*   The IPE perspective that free markets and minimal state interference is the most desirable system of political economy. Capitalism is one variant of liberalism.
- *Mercantilism*   This IPE perspective stresses the importance of state power in the creation of national wealth. The state is seen as the focus of the process that creates wealth and power.
- *Marxism*   This IPE perspective focuses on the relationship between the owners of the means of production and the workers, who are all seen in historical context. Marxism stresses the idea of class and the nature of class exploitation.
- *Socialism*   A social and economic system in which the means of production are collectively owned and equality is given a high priority. There are various forms of socialism, from Marxism to the social-democrat systems of Western Europe, but all share a belief in the necessity for collective intervention in economic affairs.

DISCUSSION QUESTIONS

1. Define the terms "state" and "market" and give examples of "state actions" and "market actions." Is the line between state and market clean and clear, or is it sometimes hard to determine? What is the relationship between politics and the state and economics and the market?

2. International political economy is sometimes defined as the set of questions and issues arising from the parallel existence and dynamic interaction of states and markets. Find an example of a current event that should properly be considered part of IPE (newspapers and newsmagazines are good sources for this information). How do state-market tensions and interactions figure in these events?

3. How do states and markets differ in their values and goals and the means with which they seek to achieve their goals? Discuss this question both in general and with respect to the current event topic in Question 2.

4. How does the U.S.-China MFN issue illustrate the concepts presented in this chapter? Identify state and market interests, the tension between economics and politics, and the dynamic interaction of states and markets in this example. Which force seems to be stronger in this case: state or market? How is an understanding of history and culture useful in understanding this issue?

SUGGESTED READINGS

Kenneth E. Boulding. "Is Economics Necessary?" and "The Relations of Economic, Political, and Social Systems." In *Beyond Economics: Essays on Society, Religion and Ethics.* Ann Arbor: University of Michigan Press, 1970.

"China Belongs to Me." *The Economist,* 29 May 1993, 13–14.

Milton Friedman. Especially chap. 1 in *Capitalism and Freedom.* Chicago: University of Chicago Press, 1982.

Robert Gilpin. Especially chapter 1 in *The Political Economy of International Relations.* Princeton, NJ: Princeton University Press, 1987.

Miles Kahler. "The International Political Economy." *Foreign Affairs* 69 (Fall 1990): 139–152.

Susan Strange, ed. *Paths to International Political Economy.* London: George Allen & Unwin, 1984.

———. *States and Markets: An Introduction to International Political Economy.* New York: Basil Blackwell, 1988.

NOTES

1. Thomas L. Friedman, "U.S. Is to Maintain Trade Privileges for China's Goods," *The New York Times,* 27 May 1994, 1.

2. This is the definition used by Robert Gilpin in his influential book, *The Political Economy of International Relations* (Princeton, NJ: Princeton University Press, 1987), 8.

3. The issue of what constitutes a nation or nation-state is of more than academic interest. A nation is more than a territorial government. The residents of a nation share something in common that gives them a distinct collective identity, giving meaning to the concept of *national interest* and substance to the vigorous pursuit of national interest, which we often call *nationalism.* Walter Bagehot, a nineteenth century British po-

litical economist, observed of the nation that "We know what it is when you do not ask us, but we cannot very quickly explain or define it." Nations, states, and nationalism are clearly important concepts, even if they are hard to pin down. Many people in the world feel strongly their national identity. National interest and the problems caused by its vigorous and sometimes violent pursuit have plagued the twentieth century.

4. Cited in Charles P. Kindleberger, *Power and Money* (New York: Basic Books, 1970), 55.

5. As we will see later, the public interest may be represented through the force of the market's "invisible hand." Economic liberals believe that, in a wide range of situations, the compromise that is reached in the market between opposing self-interests is ultimately also a reflection of the public interest.

6. These are not the only values that states and markets may hold, as will be discussed later. It is also true that markets value efficiency and states value fairness to much different degrees, at different times and different places.

7. Rowland Maddock, "The Global Political Economy," in John Bayless and N. J. Rengger, eds., *Dilemmas of World Politics* (New York: Oxford University Press, 1992), 107.

8. Susan Strange, *States and Markets: An Introduction to International Political Economy* (New York: Basil Blackwell, 1988), 18.

9. The Cold War was a period when the U.S. and the U.S.S.R. behaved according to a highly unstable "bargain"—not to launch an unprovoked "first-strike" nuclear attack. This agreement was backed only by the reality of "mutually assured destruction" (MAD). Only in recent years have formal agreements started to replace the balance of terror as the organizing principle of nuclear weapons policy.

10. See Susan Strange, *States and Markets*, 24–25.

11. See Susan Strange, *States and Markets*, ch. 3–6.

12. Susan Strange, *States and Markets*, 62.

13. Robert B. Reich, *The Work of Nations* (New York: Alfred A. Knopf, 1991).

14. Susan Strange, ed., *Paths to International Political Economy* (London: George Allen & Unwin, 1984), ix.

15. Rowland Maddock, "The Global Political Economy," 108.

16. See Rupert Pennant-Rea and Bill Emmott, *Pocket Economist*, 2nd ed. (London: Basil Blackwell, 1987) and Graham Bannock, R. E. Baxter, and Evan Davis, *Dictionary of Economics* (London: Hutchinson, 1987).

2

Wealth and Power: Mercantilism and Economic Nationalism

OVERVIEW

Mercantilism was the first important coherent international political economy perspective. It grew out of developments related to the rise of nation-states on the European continent beginning around the seventeenth century. Mercantilist ideas have evolved over the centuries in response to the development of other theories of international political economy, namely liberalism and structuralism, and as the international political economy itself has changed. This chapter looks at classical mercantilism in its historical context, then examines the evolution and development of subsets of concepts and ideas associated with mercantilism including economic nationalism, neomercantilism, realism, and statism.

In the past, the term *mercantilism* accounted for the desire of states to generate trade surpluses to increase their wealth. To the extent that wealth enhanced a state's military power by producing or purchasing weapons, it enhanced national security as well. Mercantilism is also the name given to a historical period when the major European powers colonized much of the "New World." As it did earlier, neomercantilism today accounts for the compulsion of states to use the economy to generate wealth but also to adopt a variety of protectionist trade, investment, and other policies to sustain that wealth and condition the behavior of other states.

Neomercantilism remains a potent force, often manifested in protectionist policies some states adopt to counter the benign neomercantilist policies of other nations. Given the compulsion of nation-states to think or act on the basis of the national interest, policymakers will continue to be guided by mercantilist tendencies.

Anglo-American *theory* instructs Westerners that economics is by nature a "positive sum game" from which all can emerge as winners. Asian *history* instructs many Koreans, Chinese, Japanese, and others that economic competition is a form of war in which some win and others lose. To be strong is much better than to be weak; to give orders is better than to take them. By this logic, the way to be strong, to give orders, to have independence and control, is to keep in mind the difference between "us" and "them." This perspective comes naturally to Koreans (when thinking about Japan), or Canadians (when thinking about the United States), or Britons (when thinking, even today, about Germany), or to Chinese or Japanese (when thinking about what the Europeans did to their nations).[1]

James Fallows (1994)

Our economic rights are leaking away. . . . If we want to recover these rights . . . we must quickly employ state power to promote industry, use machinery in production, give employment to the workers of the nation.[2]

Sun Yat-sen (1920)

Mercantilism is an approach to IPE one needs to understand because it accounts for one of the basic compulsions of all nation-states—to create wealth and power in order to enhance independence and national security. Mercantilism is at once an old and a new phenomenon. It is as old as there have been armies and war. And it is as new as morning newspaper reports recounting the latest trade dispute between, for instance, the United States and Japan.

Typically, mercantilism is defined somewhat narrowly in terms of state efforts to promote exports and limit imports, thereby generating trade surpluses to create wealth and power.[3] Yet the idea of mercantilism connotes more than a trade objective. This chapter covers three different ways in which the term *mercantilism* is used: to describe a period of history; as a philosophical outlook about the state's role in the economy; and the state's use of a variety of economic tools and policies to defend the nation and protect its industries.

Mercantilism can refer to the sixteenth through mid-nineteenth century practice of states pursuing supremacy over one another by accumulating gold and silver bullion, colonizing developing regions of the world, and trying to generate trade surpluses. In the emerging competing nation-state system of Western and Central

Europe, governments added to their military arsenals a variety of economic instruments and policies to protect themselves and/or groups within their jurisdiction. Since then, a variety of terms have become synonymous with the idea of mercantilism: namely, economic nationalism, realism, neomercantilism, and statism. These terms connote the different ways states employ wealth and power to protect their industries and an assortment of other national interests.

THE INTELLECTUAL ROOTS OF MERCANTILISM

As a philosophical outlook, mercantilism describes the state's role in the economy. One of the founding fathers of the United States, Alexander Hamilton, was an early proponent of mercantilism. In his report on manufacturing to the first Congress in terms that are familiar today, Hamilton argued for trade protection and a strong role for the state in promoting domestic industries. To successfully industrialize, Hamilton said, the United States should adopt protectionist trade policies that would help its industries compete with the more mature "bounty" (an export subsidy) assisted industries of other nations. Hamilton wrote:

> It is well known . . . that certain nations grant bounties on the exportation of particular commodities, to enable their own workmen to undersell and supplant all competitors in the countries to which those commodities are sent. Hence the undertakers of a new manufacture have to contend not only with the natural disadvantages of a new undertaking, but with the gratuities and remunerations which other governments bestow. To be enabled to contend with success, it is evident that the interference and aid of their own government are indispensable.[4]

The case Hamilton made for mercantilism is similar to the case the nineteenth century political economist Friedrich List made with respect to Germany at the time. List's mercantilism links the national interest to state promotion of industry (as opposed to trade) and short-term sacrifice for future gain. He also believed that state action was needed, in this case to promote ***productive power*** in the form of education, technology, and industry. According to List, "The *power of producing* is . . . infinitely more important than *wealth* itself."[5] List goes on to argue that

> The prosperity of a nation is not . . . greater in proportion in which it has amassed more wealth . . . but in the proportion in which it has more *developed its powers of production*. . . . [Yet] the nation must sacrifice and give up a measure of material prosperity in order to gain culture, skill, and powers of united production; it must sacrifice some present advantage in order to insure itself future ones. . . . A nation capable of developing a manufacturing power, if it makes use of the system of protection, thus acts quite in the same spirit as that landed proprietor did who by the sacrifice of some material wealth allowed some of his children to learn a production trade.[6]

List offered many reasons why manufacturing and not agriculture was a more desirable basis for national wealth and power. List's argument that manufacturing developed greater human skills and opportunities is still popular today. He wrote:

> If we regard manufacturing occupations as a whole, it must be evident at the first glance that they develop and bring into action an incomparably greater variety and higher type of mental qualities and abilities than agriculture does. . . . Manufactures are at once the offspring, and at the same time the supporters and the nurses, of science and the arts.[7]

The writings of Hamilton and List incorporate a spirit of patriotic ***economic nationalism*** to the extent that they emphasize the state's use of the economy to do what is in the nation's best interest. Their views tie together the important notions of national interest, a positive role for the state in the economy, and sacrifice for future gain. Taken together, many regard them as some of the key ingredients found in the classical prescription for nation building. Indeed, Robert Reich writes that "the idea that the citizens of a nation shared responsibility for their economic well-being was a natural outgrowth of this budding patriotism."[8]

This kind of patriotic political economy is still found everywhere in the world today. Many officials in less developed countries (LDCs) as yet view the development and nation-building processes as one of "catching up" to the Western industrialized nations. In so doing, quite often they look to the state to promote domestic industries and/or to protect their "infant" industries against the more mature industries and protectionist policies of the industrialized nations. Likewise, in contrasting Japan and the newly industrialized countries (NICs) to the United States and other industrialized nations, the economist Lester Thurow has recently written about Japan that "The Japanese secret is to be found in the fact that they have tapped a universal human desire to build, to belong to an empire, to conquer neighboring empires, and to become the world's economic power."[9] At some level or another, these are the emotions that drive mercantilism.

Finally, the term *neomercantilism* accounts for the variety of ways that states in today's increasingly interdependent international political economy attempt to create political and economic advantages for its industries and counter the advantages other states give their industries. Some use the term neomercantilism pejoratively. For example, economic liberals usually oppose state policies that enhance domestic welfare by promoting trade surpluses at the expense of consumers and other countries. Others, however, view a range of economic-nationalist–driven activities less critically—as a natural phenomenon. Robert Gilpin characterizes the relationship of the state (politics) to the market (economy) as producing contradictory tendencies. In Gilpin's words:

> Whereas powerful market forces in the form of trade, money and foreign investment tend to jump national boundaries, to escape political control, and to integrate societies, the tendency of government is to restrict, to channel, and to make economic activities serve the perceived interests of the state and of powerful groups within it. The logic of the market is to locate economic activities where they are most productive and profitable; the logic of the state is to capture and control the process of economic growth and capital accumulation.[10]

Today, neomercantilists would argue that to accumulate and maintain their wealth and power, states are tempted to intervene in and influence developments in their domestic economies but also in the international economy. Neomercantilists also agree with *realists* that in an international system where there is no single sovereign to guarantee the security of the nation-state, the state is necessarily involved in a struggle to benefit as much as it can from market forces and transactions, for the sake of national security.

THE MERCANTILIST PERIOD OF HISTORY

The period from the sixteenth through the eighteenth centuries is designated as the period of mercantilism, when the major (most powerful) European states explored, conquered, and colonized large tracts of the New World in search of gold, silver, and other precious metals. The mercantilist period corresponds to the deepening entrenchment of the *nation-state* as the major sovereign political actor on the European continent. A *nation* is a collection of people who, on the basis of ethnic background, language, and history, define themselves as members of an extended political community.[11] The *state* is a legal entity, theoretically free of external interference, that monopolizes the means of physical force in society and that exercises sovereignty (final political authority) over the population of a well-defined territory.[12]

The modern nation-state merges social-psychological and political phenomena into a single actor above which there is no higher sovereign in the international state system. Nation-states as we think of them today first appeared in Europe in the fifteenth century. Soon after Venice and other Italian city-states, together with Portugal, Spain, the Netherlands (the Dutch United Provinces), France, England, and a number of weaker powers, formed a system of states and fought long wars with one another. To help pay for their wars, these states tried to accumulate trade surpluses by promoting exports and limiting imports. Currency earned from trade helped them purchase gold and silver bullion, much of it imported from the New World, which was added to the monarch's treasury. Because commerce and exploration were so important, the Dutch, Spanish, and British all competed with one another to build ships and rule the seas. Seapower became as important, if not more so, than land-based military power. Commerce-generated wealth enhanced the nation's power, which the major powers believed ultimately made them more secure in relation to one another.[13] Economic gains by one state were perceived by competing states as losses, conferring on mercantilism a zero-sum disposition to account for heavy state competition for resources that generated wealth and power.

The mercantilist period coincides with what Marxists and others structuralists refer to as *classical imperialism*, when stronger nations ventured overseas in search of gold and other precious metals. Conquered territories became colonies and provided their mother countries with raw materials and labor. As was the case of the American colonies that had to purchase and pay a tax on British tea, colonies were often forced to purchase some of the mother country's value-added products. And many were forbidden to produce semi-manufactured or manufactured goods of their own that competed with the products of the mother country. At home, many states adopted policies to complement their colonial practices. States emphasized exported goods because they were cheaper to ship and often earned high prices in foreign markets. Many absolute rulers of the period limited spending for imported goods and used treasury funds to encourage the production of goods for export. For example, King Louis XIV's minister, Jean-Baptiste Colbert (1619–1683), imported shipbuilders from Holland to build ships, built seaports, financed road construction, and provided tax exemptions and subsidies to exporters of some of France's most expensive items such as silk, tapestries, and glassware.

For over three centuries, mercantilism helped concentrate wealth and power into the hands of a few European nations. For better or for worse, increasing trade between European powers and their colonies helped entrench economic interdependence (interconnectedness) among them. The stronger European powers gradually settled down into a relatively stable military balance of power among themselves.

In the late eighteenth century, mercantilism receded in influence corresponding to, among other things, the increasing popularity of economic liberal ideas associated with Adam Smith and David Ricardo (see chapters 3 and 6). Smith and Ricardo preached to English policymakers, academics, and businessmen the benefits of free trade and a laissez-faire (hands off) role for the state in the economy. Liberalism's popularity paralleled at least three significant developments in Europe. First, England ascended to the position of hegemon—dominant economic and military power—in the European state system. British maritime power shifted from one of support of one continental power to that of helping maintain a balance of power among the European nations. Second, the industrial revolution took place first in England, which gave it an advantage over its continental competitors in producing goods at cheaper prices. Third and finally, at this juncture of history, the absolute power of the monarch was weakened. A number of European monarchs were gradually compelled to share power with relatively democratic bodies such as a parliament. Spurred on by the French Revolution and Napoleonic wars, the eighteenth through twentieth centuries experienced a change: the overriding economic and political goals of states gradually shifted from increasing the power of the monarchy and merchant class to improving the well-being of an entire nation's population. More often, governments contracted with the people to provide for their security and welfare in exchange for their financial support of state institutions and loyalty to the fatherland.[14] Nationalistic feelings spread throughout the continent and became another driving force behind the state's desire to influence developments in the economy.

ECONOMIC NATIONALISM

From the late eighteenth to mid-nineteenth centuries, mercantilism remained popular for some continental states that tried to overcome their economic and industrial "backwardness" and make themselves more competitive with Great Britain. As economies became truly national in scope (rather than merely local or regional), many states adopted a variety of protectionist measures to enhance citizen welfare. In the United States, Alexander Hamilton's views[15] about the necessity for a strong central government found favor with those who looked for employment opportunities in manufacturing, with businesses that wanted to attract foreign capital, and with public officials who desired a more secure and independent nation. As we noted at the beginning of this chapter, Hamilton felt that a strong manufacturing and industrial base for the nation required an active state along with trade protection for U.S. infant industries and agriculture. In addition to export subsidies to make U.S. goods more competitive abroad, Hamilton only reluctantly favored the use of tariffs to limit imports.

After the U.S. Civil War, the ideas of the German Friedrich List became synonymous with an economic nationalist outlook and a justification for mercantilist policies. List attacked Smith's and Ricardo's liberal idea that all nations could gain from trade if governments did not regulate it excessively and industries produced items for which the nation had a comparative advantage. List persuasively argued that liberals wrongly assumed there to be a "cosmopolitical" world composed of relatively equally powerful nations that agreed with one another to share the benefits of trade.[16] List argued that in the real world, as the economy shifted from an agricultural to an industrial base, states had to protect domestic industries in order to catch up with lead states. Great Britain was politically and economically much stronger than other nations. Its lead in developing industrial revolution technology conferred on it the advantage of its industries being able to produce goods cheaper than continental industries. From the perspective of Great Britain's competitors, British free-trade policies were an attempt to thwart the continent's economic growth and industrial development.

Economic depression in the late nineteenth century stimulated a second wave of imperialism, when most of Europe and the United States went abroad in search of cheap labor, access to less costly sources of labor and raw materials, and new markets for their manufactured products. The major powers forced Japan to open its doors to Western trade and colonized parts of China and other parts of Asia, along with most of central and southern Africa.

In the 1930s, the Great Depression spread throughout the world. Raw material producers such as Brazil and Chile were hit especially hard.[17] In response to weakening demand for industrial goods and manufactured products, the industrialized nations erected relatively high tariff walls to slow imports. They also adopted other protectionist measures to insulate their national economic recovery efforts from the dislocating effect of the Depression and to counter the protectionist trade policies of other nations. The Great Depression helped weaken Britain's political and economic power. As a reflection of economic nationalism, Germany and Japan responded to the Depression, in part, by adopting aggressive territorial expansionist measures to complement their state-supported industrial policies and programs. Spiraling protectionism driven by intense political and economic nationalism in the Depression years is often cited as a major factor contributing to World War II.

THE ROAD TO POSTWAR NEOMERCANTILISM

Neomercantilism connotes more than just another round of mercantilist practices after World War II. It accounts for a qualitative change in the international political economy generated by international economic interdependence. At the end of the war until the early 1970s, the United States, in cooperation with its allies, attempted to liberalize the international economic system. However, security considerations and state efforts to generate and sustain economic growth raised doubts about the benefits of excessively liberal domestic and international economic policies. Growing international economic interdependence made it increasingly difficult for states to insulate themselves from one another's policies. Likewise, the line between domestic and international economic problems blurred, making it difficult for state officials to sustain let alone generate economic growth while trying to manage the economy. Under these circumstances, states yet again found it necessary to develop and employ even more sophisticated protectionist trade, monetary, investment, and other economic policies that were not overtly, but nonetheless decidedly, mercantilist and economic nationalist in character.

As the Cold War went on, the United States found it increasingly difficult to reconcile its foreign economic policy objectives of liberalizing the international political economy with its national security objective of containing international communism. In many instances, the United States acted in a mercantilist fashion when, for example, it used its trade and foreign aid as another weapon in the battle against communism. Saving the Western European economies from communism was the primary motivation behind Marshall Plan aid to Western Europe in the late 1940s. In 1952, the United States went so far as to make it illegal for its corporations to trade with the Soviet Union and its allies. It also encouraged its allies to do the same. During the Cold War with the Soviet Union, the United States also agreed to accept the European Union's (EU) protectionist trade barriers as part of a "bargain"[18] it made with the new Community (as it was then referred to) (see chapter 9). In exchange, the United States gained bases in Western Europe to station its forces along the East-West border. The United States also went out of its way to help farmers in the General Agreement on Tariffs and Trade (GATT) member countries gain an exemption from GATT's trade rules that sought to liberalize trade policies and practices. Since then, industrialized nations have been reluctant to expose their farmers to international commodity trade competition for any number of reasons, including the desire to maintain food security, the political influence of commodity groups and their lobbies, and state strategic interests. To this day, agricultural trade remains one of the world trade system's most protected items.

In the late 1960s, the U.S.–West European political bargain gradually came unstuck when the West European economies recovered and a glut of U.S. dollars inflated their economies. The U.S. acted unilaterally to make the dollar nonconvertible to gold and imposed a 10 percent surcharge across the board on Japanese imports to the United States. U.S. and West European views about the Soviet threat gradually changed. West European states increasingly wanted to trade with the Soviet Union. Many of those who have studied this period argue that underlying shifts in the economic and security structures of the international political economy (see chapter 9) were precipitated by a leveling of wealth and power among the major powers.[19] Ironically, this situation did not enhance cooperation among the allies as much as it intensified their political and economic rivalries.

By the early 1970s, U.S. officials clearly regarded the United States hegemonic responsibilities and obligations as too costly. Many came to doubt whether the effort to liberalize the international political economy of the West would survive the un-willingness of a hegemon to sustain it.[20] Many U.S. allies felt that cooperation with the hegemon imposed unacceptable costs for their economies in the form of na-tional economic adjustments and the loss of political sovereignty. In 1973 and again in 1979, the Organization of Petroleum Exporting Countries (OPEC) raised the price of oil. Western industrialized nations became more dependent on trade to earn income to pay for their high energy bills. Global economic interdependence was pushing and pulling states in two directions at once, but the balance of liberal and mercantilist policies and practices was tipping in favor of the nation first.

As more nations defined their security interests in terms of protecting their domestic industries, they sought newer more sophisticated but also less intensively economic nationalist ways. Several developments set the tone for the kind of pro-tectionist policies that were to become synonymous with neomercantilism. The first was the economic recovery and increasing power of Japan. After the war, Japan adopted a carefully thought-out, mercantilistic strategy of running a trade surplus to finance its industrial recovery and development. Officials from the Ministry of Trade and Industry (MITI) worked closely with corporate officials and Liberal Democratic Party (LDP) members to guide the development of Japan's economy. Certain industries were chosen for government subsidies and other forms of sup-port to make them more competitive with U.S. and European firms.

Japan's export-led industrial economic growth strategy was adopted by a num-ber of other Asian NICs, the most successful of whom were the "Four Asian Tigers": Hong Kong, Singapore, Taiwan, and South Korea, which experienced rapid eco-nomic growth in the 1970s and 1980s. Their success has been attributed to state in-tervention in and guidance of the economy (see chapter 15). A state-guided economy that employs protectionist trade policies has also become popular in many other LDCs such as Brazil. Many LDCs have made a conscious attempt to grow their way out of their "underdeveloped" status by generating a trade surplus. As in the case of Japan, the state selects industries for government production and export assistance, while competitive imports are discouraged.

Postwar neomercantilism was also driven by a second development: the glob-alization of multinational corporate activity. Many states increasingly found it in their interest to adopt policies that linked multinational corporation (MNC) investment to national economic objectives (see chapter 16). To enhance the economic com-petitiveness of their industries, many states became increasingly dependent on MNCs for information and technology. Likewise, MNCs became dependent on states to fos-ter the kind of stable political environment in which they could efficiently and ef-fectively operate.

MERCANTILISM AS ECONOMIC MANAGEMENT: STATISM

Another development that contributed to the growing use of neomercantilist policies was *statism*. Because states have some amount of influence over economic activity, and because they influence market forces to some degree, political arrangements are the foundation upon which both domestic and international markets function. Statism refers to the continuation but also intensification of an earlier trend of states subordinating economic policies to political objectives. Communist states come closest to this ideal. In relatively open economies, states allow markets a good deal of leeway in setting prices for goods. On the other hand, in relatively closed economies, states severely restrict markets and set prices according to some ideological or nationalist objective.

In the 1970s and 1980s the state increasingly took on more responsibility for providing "wealth and welfare" benefits to its citizens. In order to better macro- and micromanage their economies, the industrialized states became less willing to allow market forces to determine their policy objectives and shape the size of their public programs. In response to the demands of domestic groups, but also in response to increasing international economic interdependence, protectionist trade, finance, and monetary policies proliferated. Many states felt compelled more than ever to resort to using a variety of neomercantilist policies and measures to insulate and protect their economies and certain industries. Many of these industries employed large numbers of people or occupied strategic positions in the economy—that is, they made military weapons or items some of the major powers did not want to be dependent on importing from other nations. Likewise during the 1970s and 1980s, aside from some of the NICs who adopted the Japanese export-led growth model, the states of many developing nations adopted a variety of protectionist measures in response to intensive domestic pressure on their governments to manage the economy (see chapter 15).

MERCANTILISM AND REALISM: COMPLEMENTARY PHILOSOPHIES

Because mercantilism accounts for some of the ways that politics, power, and the state affect the economy and markets, many of its tenets necessarily complement those of *political realism*, the dominant *weltanschauung* (worldview) of most world leaders and foreign policy officials since World War II.[21] Quite often the ideas of mercantilists and realists have been lumped together. In many ways, these two approaches incorporate some of the same assumptions, yet in some ways they differ. A brief sketch of realism reveals that many of the forces that drive the international political economy and generate economic nationalism are the same conditions that compel states to seek security for themselves and groups within their jurisdiction.

For realists, as for mercantilists, the nation-state is the primary actor in an international system because it is the highest unit of sovereign political authority. One of the tenets of realism is that the international system of nation-states is constantly on the brink of anarchy given that conflicting national interests force states into competition with one another for limited amounts of resources. Power is the ultimate arbiter of conflict. Power stems from natural resources, geographic location, and national characteristics and traits that go into the production of wealth and military weapons and other national capabilities. For realists, the capabilities of states and the global distribution of power determine the manner in which rival states deal with one another in a self-help international state system. State competition results in a zero-sum game where relative gains for one state may be perceived as absolute losses by other states. Both realists and neomercantilists today assume that measures taken to enhance the security of one state necessarily detract from the security of others because of the relatively fixed amount of power resources in the world.

One slight difference between realists and modern neomercantilists is the stress realists put on military instruments and similar state capabilities to render the state secure. When push comes to shove, realists feel strongly that military power and capabilities are crucial if a state is to either defend itself against the aggressive tendencies of other states or, if necessary, overcome its enemies. On the other hand, mercantilists and economic nationalists stress not only that conflict is economically driven, but that a viable economy is essential if a state is to be able to purchase the weapons necessary to secure itself. The tension between the pursuit of wealth and the pursuit of power by the state is usually settled in favor of one or the other from time to time, or both simultaneously. Jacob Viner's often cited dictum that "wealth and power are each proper ultimate ends of national policy"[22] has become the credo of most economic nationalist and neomercantilist public officials. Furthermore, in an international system where a state must ultimately rely on itself for security, the economy remains one of several instruments the state uses to accomplish a variety of domestic and foreign policy objectives.

For most modern neomercantilists, the capacity of the nation-state to generate wealth is as important as its capacity to produce military weapons. Industrial capacity (including defense industries) benefit the state in at least three ways. First, it generates military weapons and defense-related technologies and products. Second, the effects of industrial production spill over into other parts of the national political economy, generating jobs and stimulating the production of consumer goods such as computers and laser technology. Finally, a nation's industrial capacity increases its self-sufficiency and political autonomy, to the extent that the nation does not become dependent on external sources of raw materials for security, or on imports to satisfy consumer demands.

For both realists and neomercantilists, state competition and the unequal distribution of the world's resources generates dependence of states on other states. Those who supply needed manufactured products or agricultural commodities usually view their capacity and the resultant dependence of other states as something positive that contributes to their power and security. On the other hand, states reliant on external sources of resources usually view their dependence as the equivalent of vulnerability or even a security threat should the supplier ever decide to cut off the client state.

A classic example of both zero-sum relations and the impact of dependency on state wealth and power is the dependency of the West on OPEC oil in the early 1970s. In 1973, OPEC embargoed oil shipments to the United States and the Netherlands and reduced oil shipments to the rest of the world by 25 percent. The resultant increase in the price of oil and transfer of massive amounts of currency to oil-rich countries was thought to have economically weakened the West and made OPEC a political economic power with which to reckon (see chapter 17).

For realists and neomercantilists, then, interdependencies are not always symmetrical (felt equally) among all states. Some states are more dependent on, and thus vulnerable to, the actions and power of other states.[23] Ideally, only complete self-sufficiency would make a nation-state politically and economically secure. In the real world, however, states are constantly trying to minimize their dependence on others while fostering conditions that make others dependent on them.

CONTEMPORARY ECONOMIC NATIONALISM AND NEOMERCANTILISM

From a mercantilist perspective, liberal institutions and processes have not been able to overcome the compulsion of states to realize wealth and security at one another's expense. Nation-states today are more competitive than ever. The degree of political and economic interdependence in the international political economy is much greater and certainly more multidimensional than it was up until World War II. Since the early 1970s, economic growth has been harder to achieve and sustain in nearly all regions of the world. The number of nation-states has more than tripled from approximately 60 at the end of World War II to roughly 185 in 1995. Most countries find it difficult to accept the political, social, and dislocating economic effects and costs of adjustment associated with economic recessions and uneven growth rates.

To enhance their autonomy, security, and wealth, many states continue to employ a variety of instruments to limit their dependency on other nations while promoting a favorable trade balance and adding to their power capabilities. To help us understand the nature of economic competition among nation-states today in a neomercantilist international setting, Robert Gilpin makes a useful distinction between benign and malevolent mercantilism. Malevolent mercantilism is a more hostile version of economic warfare and expansionary economic policies associated with the practices of such countries as Nazi Germany and imperial Japan. Malevolent nations employ a variety of measures to expand their territorial base and/or political and economic influence beyond what is regarded as reasonable to protect themselves. Benign mercantilism is more defensive in nature; "it attempts to protect the economy against untoward economic and political forces."[24]

Many LDCs use a variety of neomercantilist policies such as import quotas to restrict trade with the industrialized nations. In some cases, though, the objective is more than generating a trade surplus. Quite often, motives include attempts to limit what LDC officials believe to be the neoimperial practices of the industrialized nations. Likewise, limiting the dependence of Northern industrialized nations on Southern developing nations for such items as minerals and strategic raw materials is another important objective of Northern nations served by neomercantilist policies.

Much of the motivation behind defensive neomercantilism today, then, stems from reaction to the protectionist policies adopted by other states. Because economic growth has slowed and been so difficult to generate and maintain, states everywhere have felt compelled to adopt measures to assist certain groups in consideration of national economic objectives. Economic nationalists and neomercantilists today are likely to argue that an assortment of protectionist policies are justified on the basis of countering the protectionist policies of other nations, such as Japan or the EU who use subsidies to generate a surplus trade balance or as part of a state strategy to support select industries.[25] In an international political economy that is not dominated by a hegemon as much as it was in the early postwar years, many nations feel even more strongly about, but also have the opportunity to counter, the economic and political challenges of other nations whose trade and investment policies not only disrupt their economy but also politically threaten what is perceived to be the nation's political autonomy.

As during the mercantilist period of history, in order to protect themselves many governments still emphasize a favorable trade balance to complement other efforts to manage the economy. Many nations employ export subsidies to lower the price of goods, making them more attractive to importers. The United States routinely subsidizes its agricultural exports, it claims, to counter the subsidies the EU uses to increase its share of agriculture export markets. Likewise, a number of other strategies have been developed in the recent past to limit spending for imports. Even though GATT negotiations have successfully limited import tariffs on industrial products, many nations still impose import quotas on incoming goods. These quotas specify the quantity of a particular product that can be sold locally. For instance, the United States uses import quotas to limit the amount of sugar its consumers can buy from abroad that would compete with U.S. sugar producers. Still another mechanism to limit imports that has been used more often recently is the export quota or "gentlemen's agreement" of an exporter to "voluntarily" restrict sales of one product in another country. Other barriers to imports include an array of nontariff barriers (NTBs). Quite often, a series of complex government regulations pertaining to health and safety standards, licensing and labeling requirements, and domestic content requirements block either the sales or distribution of imported goods (see chapter 6).

Still other measures states routinely use to assist select industries include loans, regional infrastructure development programs, investment promotions, and even direct public ownership of certain industries. Many governments also help certain companies market their products overseas. The embassies of most developed countries employ officials whose responsibility is to monitor national political economic conditions and assess potential impact on the businesses of their home country.

Some states continue to look with favor at the Japanese export-led growth model and have adopted an industrial policy whereby the state, in close cooperation with corporate executives and party leaders, chooses which industries are most likely to be successful in international markets and, thus, which ones will receive state assistance. **Strategic trade practices** of the industrialized nations incorporate efforts to purposefully shift comparative advantage in favor of certain industries and nations (see chapter 6).

Based on the success Japan and the EU have had, many experts feel that an industrial policy complemented by strategic trade measures would help the United States regain its competitive trade status.[26] President Clinton's leading economic advisor, Laura Tyson, has argued that the United States should adopt these practices because U.S. industries find it exceedingly difficult to be competitive without state assistance—for superconductor research and development,[27] in an international environment where states are consciously adopting measures to make their industries more competitive (see chapter 6).

Still another version of neomercantilism that is being practiced with more frequency is **industrial espionage**. Many states and/or national industries have engaged in efforts to acquire information and technology through clandestine activities.

CASE STUDY: ESPIONAGE

Since the end of the Cold War, espionage—the business of spying and gathering secret intelligence—has not disappeared, as some expected it might, but has shifted its focus from *military* security to *economic* security. As nations find themselves drawn into more intensive economic competition in an international political economy marked by increasing international economic interdependence, so many of the industrialized nations have looked to industrial espionage as another tactic for states and businesses to use to acquire information and technology.

The end of the Cold War produced a large number of agents in the West and in the former Soviet Union who already had established contact networks and were well versed in the art of spying and intelligence gathering. A number of businesses have sprung up, mainly in the industrialized countries, who specialize in providing industries and governments with intelligence, counterintelligence, and security services.

The U.S. Federal Bureau of Investigation (FBI) is currently "investigating instances of foreign intelligence services stealing U.S. information on robotics, high-tempered materials, advanced ceramics and biogenetics."[28] The FBI estimates that in the United States alone, some thirty nations conduct economic spying. Twenty of those nations, including Japan, France, England, Canada, Germany, South Korea, Sweden, and Israel, have been considered to be allies of the United States. Just some of the practices governments (including the United States) have been accused of are: electronic eavesdropping, bugging hotel facilities and the flights of executives of large companies such as Boeing, IBM, NCR, and Texas Instruments; attempting to bribe U.S businessmen with intelligence-trained prostitutes; infiltrating congressional offices and even the White House; organizing spy networks in conjunction with foreign military or national security and intelligence operations; recruiting spies in the U.S. military; and monitoring database networks of large companies. China has set up three institutes to monitor intelligence. Japan has an economic espionage school, while the Germans have a computer-hacking school in Frankfurt.

Most experts on the subject of industrial espionage estimate that approximately 75 percent of commercial intelligence is acquired rather easily through computers, publications, and research or business journals. "In the information age, there's very little that an adversary can't dig up with a computer."[29] On the other hand, many companies are known to ward off spies and their clandestine practices with such counterintelligence methods as filing false patents for inventions.

Since the end of the Cold War, international conflict has centered more on economic competition than on traditional high-security issues. Recently, the CIA has been accused by France of bribing French officials to gain information on France's position on trade talks. A question raised by the act of, for instance, using a class of first graders

Continued

CASE STUDY: ESPIONAGE, *continued*

to slip a spy into an industrial plant is the intent behind the practice. Is it malevolent or merely defensive mercantilism? Answering this question may have become very difficult given the globalization of industrial production and business that has accompanied an increase in the number, size, and influence of multinational corporations. While states have been reluctant to regulate these international business enterprises, in the mind of both state and private business officials, state security has become tied up in the economic success of national and multinational corporate enterprises.

CONCLUSION

This chapter has revealed at least three sources of motivation behind the mercantilist practices of nation-states in the international political economy today. First, mercantilism and economic nationalism originated in the protective role states play in the modern international system of nation-states. Second, practices of imperialism and colonialism had as one of their sources the drive for national wealth and power. Liberalism was merely another instrument used by the hegemonic states, Great Britain and later the United States, to increase their wealth and power at the expense of weaker powers. For mercantilists and economic nationalists, liberalization of the international political economy, if a worthy state objective, proved difficult to realize. Third and finally, states continue to intervene in their economies for the sake of creating wealth and military power.

Responsibilities and objectives related to increasing and maintaining state wealth and power have proliferated since World War II due to the growing interdependence of nations and globalization of the international political economy. Today, economic "statecraft" has proven to be a complicated task that befuddles politicians and academics alike.[30] As states and national industries become more dependent on external sources of revenue and markets, states and industries feel more vulnerable to developments in the international political economy, necessitating some form of protection. National trade, finance, aid, monetary, and corporate investment policies and programs continue to necessitate state efforts to manage a vast network of interactions and interdependencies.

Of the three ideological perspectives most often used to explain IPE, namely mercantilism, liberalism, and structuralism, mercantilism is the oldest and arguably the most powerful. If List were still around, he would likely argue that as long as states are the final source of political (sovereign) authority, the economy and markets cannot be divorced from the effects politics and the state have on them. States can be expected to use the economy as a means to generate more wealth and power. List would also likely argue that free trade is a myth. Liberalism is merely another instrument used especially by a hegemonic state to protect itself by undermining its political and economic competitors. Moreover, mercantilists believe that liberals are naive to expect the goal of liberalizing the international political economy to be easily achieved—or, for that matter, even worthy of achievement.

For mercantilists, the difference between a liberal and mercantilistic international political economy is no longer a difference in kind, but in degree. Liberalization requires that states find it in their interest to overcome "beggar-thy-neighbor" policies (the tendency to gain at the disadvantage of other states) and cooperate with one another. Or, liberalization may require that a hegemonic power impose liberal institutions and practices on the international political economy. It is simply politically and economically easier to protect certain industries and pass the burden of economic adjustment on to other nations than it is to make those adjustments necessary within one's own national political economic system. Most practices associated with modern-day neomercantilism, then, are a second-best solution to the problem of nation-state conflict and competition for power and limited resources.

Whether or not neomercantilism can be overcome is a matter that concerns many experts and officials. Its (liberal) critics believe that it works to the detriment of all nations, that it generates more protectionism and makes it hard for market forces to properly influence prices as well as consumer and government decisions. In an international environment where security interests have broadened to include economic interests, a vicious cycle of protectionism begets defensive reaction when governments adopt protectionist measures to defend themselves and their businesses from one another. Then again, those who view economic nationalism as the norm, and not an aberration in the modern international political economy, are usually not as pessimistic about neomercantilism. Many modern day neomercantilists and realists believe that nations, like people, are aggressive and value security above all else. So long as nations behave this way, the international political economy will exhibit high levels of mercantilist behavior.

DISCUSSION QUESTIONS

1. After reading the chapter, define and discuss the different ways the term mercantilism has come to be used.
2. Outline some of the many motives for mercantilism in the international political economy. Be specific and give examples from the reading.
3. Compare early forms of mercantilism to more recent forms (neomercantilism). What do they have in common by way of motive? Policies that states use to protect themselves? How do they differ? Be specific. Give examples from the reading.
4. Explain what Balaam and Veseth meant when they said that "for mercantilism, the difference between a liberal and mercantilist international political economy is no longer a difference in kind, but in degree."

SUGGESTED READINGS

James Fallows. *More Like Us: Putting America's Native Strengths and Traditional Values to Work to Overcome the Asian Challenge.* Boston: Houghton-Mifflin, 1990.
————. *Looking at the Sun.* New York: Pantheon, 1994.

Alexander Hamilton. "Report on Manufactures." In George T. Crane and Abla Amawi, eds., *The Theoretical Evolution of International Political Economy: A Reader*. New York: Oxford University Press, 1991.

Eli F. Heckscher. *Mercantilism*, rev. ed., 2 vols. New York: Macmillan, 1955.

Robert Kuttner. *The End of Laissez-Faire*. New York: Knopf, 1991.

Friedrich List. *The National System of Political Economy*. New York: Augustus M. Kelley, 1966.

Robert B. Reich. *The Work of Nations*. New York: Knopf, 1991.

Lester Thurow. *Head to Head: The Coming Economic Battle Among Japan, Europe, and America*. New York: William Morrow, 1992.

Jacob Viner. "Power Versus Plenty as Objectives of Foreign Policy in the Seventeenth and Eighteenth Centuries." *World Politics* 1 (October 1948).

John Zysman and Laura Tyson. *American Industry in International Competition: Government Policies and Corporate Strategies*. Ithaca, NY: Cornell University Press, 1983.

NOTES

1. James Fallows, *Looking at the Sun* (New York: Pantheon, 1994), 231.
2. Sun Yat-sen (1920), cited in Robert Reich, *The Work of Nations* (New York: Knopf, 1991), 30.
3. See, for example, the "Mercantilism" entry of Randy Epping, *A Beginner's Guide to the World Economy* (New York: Vintage Books, 1992), 139.
4. Alexander Hamilton, "Report on Manfactures," in George T. Crane and Abla Amawi, eds., *The Theoretical Evolution of International Political Economy: A Reader* (New York: Oxford University Press, 1991), 42.
5. Friedrich List, *The National System of Political Economy* (New York: Augustus M. Kelley, 1966).
6. Ibid., 144–145. Italics and emphasis is ours.
7. Ibid., 199–200.
8. Reich, *The Work of Nations*, 18.
9. Lester Thurow, *Head to Head: The Coming Economic Battle Among Japan, Europe, and America* (New York: William Morrow, 1992.), 118.
10. Robert Gilpin, *The Political Economy of International Relations* (Princeton, NJ: Princeton University Press, 1987), 11.
11. The concepts of *nation* and *nationalism* are the focus of the classic work by Hans Kohn, *The Idea of Nationalism* (New York: Macmillan, 1944), and E. J. Hobsbawm, *Nations and Nationalism Since 1780*, 2nd ed. (Cambridge, England: Cambridge University Press, 1992).
12. The classic definition of the state is Max Weber's, which emphasizes its administrative and legal qualities. See Max Weber, *The Theory of Social and Economic Organization* (New York: The Free Press, 1947), 156.
13. For a detailed history of mercantilism, see Eli F. Heckscher, *Mercantilism*, rev. ed., in 2 vols. (New York: Macmillan, 1955).
14. There is a good deal of literature available that discusses the shift in the nature of the state and its relationship to society. See, for example, Roger King, *The State in Modern Society: New Directions in Political Sociology* (Chatham, NJ: Chatham House Publishers, 1986).
15. For a detailed account of Hamilton's works see J. C. Hamilton, ed., *The Works of Alexander Hamilton* (New York: 1850–1851).
16. List, *The National System of Political Economy*, 119–132.
17. For an overview of the Great Depression, see Sidney Pollard, ed., *Wealth and Poverty: An Economic History of the Twentieth Century* (New York: Oxford University Press, 1990).
18. Benjamin J. Cohen, "The Revolution in Atlantic Economic Relations: A Bargain Comes Unstuck," in Wolfram F. Hanrieder, ed., *The United States and Western Europe: Political, Economic and Strategic Perspectives* (Cambridge, MA: Winthrop, 1974), 106–133.

19. This is the one of the themes of David Calleo's many works. See his *Beyond American Hegemony: The Future of the Western Alliance* (New York: Basic Books, 1987).

20. Charles Kindleberger, among others, makes this argument. See his *The International Economic Order: Essays on Financial Crises and International Public Goods* (Cambridge, MA: MIT Press, 1988).

21. There are a variety of subdivisions within realist thought. Two of the classic works in the field are Hans Morgenthau, *Politics Among Nations: The Struggle for Power and Peace* (New York: Alfred Knopf, any edition) and Kenneth Waltz, *Theory of International Politics* (Reading, MA: Addison-Wesley, 1979).

22. Jacob Viner, "Power Versus Plenty as Objectives of Foreign Policy in the Seventeenth and Eighteenth Centuries," *World Politics* 1 (October 1948), 2.

23. Robert Keohane and Joseph S. Nye, Jr., *Power and Interdependence* (Boston: Little, Brown, 1977).

24. Gilpin, *The Political Economy of International Relations*, 33.

25. See, for example, John Zysman and Laura Tyson, *American Industry in International Competition: Government Policies and Corporate Strategies* (Ithaca, NY: Cornell University Press, 1983).

26. See, for example, Zysman and Tyson, *American Industry in International Competition*.

27. Laura Tyson, "As Economists Snipe, Adviser Gets to Work," *The New York Times*, 15 March 1993, A.8.

28. See "Cold War Spies Turn Their Skills to Corporate Data," *The Seattle Times*, 13 June 1993.

29. Ibid.

30. For a sophisticated discussion of the problems associated with economic statecraft, see David A. Baldwin, *Economic Statecraft* (Princeton, NJ: Princeton University Press, 1985).

3

"Laissez-Faire, Laissez-Passer": The Liberal IPE Perspective

OVERVIEW

This chapter outlines the liberal perspective on international political economy, linking today's rise of the liberal view to its historical roots. We trace liberalism from eighteenth century France, through nineteenth century England, to today's world of the twentieth century. Along the way we listen to the words of some of the most famous political economists, Adam Smith, David Ricardo, and John Maynard Keynes, and to some noteworthy practitioners of political economy, such as Václav Havel. This chapter contains an unusual number of direct quotes from the works of these authors because the grace and power of their writing is irresistible.

Liberalism, like many other terms we use in IPE, suffers from something of a personality disorder. The same set of letters means different things in different contexts. In the United States today, for example, a "liberal" is generally one who believes in a strong and active state role in society, helping the poor and solving social problems. It is ironic, therefore, that liberalism, as we will study it here, means almost (but not exactly) the opposite of this.

Liberals, in the classical sense used here, fear the heavy hand of government and seek to liberate the individual from state oppression. Liberals believe in the guiding influence of free markets. In other words, liberals have much in common with people who are now called "conservatives" in the U.S. and other countries.

Liberalism arose and evolved in reaction to important trends and events in the real world. In plotting liberalism's path from its origins to the present day, we will necessarily pause to consider the events that shaped this point of view. A case study of the Corn Laws will illustrate the political economy of liberalism in the context of nineteenth century Britain.

This chapter also introduces the important notion of hegemony. A hegemon is a rich, powerful nation that organizes the IPE. Britan was hegemon in the nineteenth century, and the United States in the twentieth century. Is a hegemon necessary? What are its motives? These are critical questions in IPE today.

Though my heart may be left of centre, I have always known that the only economic system that works is a market economy, in which everything belongs to someone—which means that someone is responsible for everything. It is a system in which complete independence and plurality of economic entities exist within a legal framework, and its workings are guided chiefly by the laws of the marketplace. This is the only natural economy, the only kind that makes sense, the only one that can lead to prosperity, because it is the only one that reflects the nature of life itself. The essence of life is infinitely and mysteriously multiform, and therefore it cannot be contained or planned for, in its fullness and variability, by any central intelligence.

The attempt to unite all economic entities under the authority of a single monstrous owner, the state, and to subject all economic life to one central voice of reason that deems itself more clever than life itself, is an attempt against life itself. It is an extreme expression of the hubris of modern man, who thinks that he understands the world completely—that he is the apex of creation and is therefore competent to run the whole world; who claims that his own brain is the highest form of organized matter and has not noticed that there is a structure infinitely more complex, of which he himself is merely a tiny part: this is, nature, the universe, the order of Being.[1]

Václav Havel (1992)

Václav Havel's elegant words praise the market and condemn the state. The market is natural, the essence of life, while the state is arrogant and monstrous. In this essay, Havel's state was, of course, the rigid and authoritarian communist regime that fused state and market in his native Czechoslovakia before 1989. For Havel, then, the market represents the individual freedom that the communist state denied.

If you listen carefully, you might hear an echo as you read Havel's text aloud. It is the echo of François Quesnay (1694–1774), leader of a group of French philosophers called the Physiocrats or "les Économistes." Quesnay condemned government interference in the market, holding that, with few exceptions, it brought harm to society. The Physiocrats' motto was "Laissez-faire, laissez-passer," meaning "let be, let pass" but said in the spirit of "Hands off! Leave us alone!"

The echo reappears in the writings of Adam Smith (1723–1790), a Scottish contemporary of Quesnay, who is generally regarded as the father of modern economics. Compare these lines from Smith's *The Wealth of Nations* (1776) with the views of Václav Havel printed above. Speaking of the free individual, the *entrepreneur*, Smith said that

> Every Individual is continually exerting himself to find out the most advantageous employment for whatever capital he can command. It is his own advantage, indeed, and not that of society, which he has in view. But the study of his own advantage naturally, or rather necessarily, leads him to prefer that employment which is most advantageous to society.[2]
>
> The Statesman, who should attempt to direct private people in what manner they ought to employ their capitals, would not only load himself with a most unnecessary attention, but assume an authority which could safely be trusted, not only to no single person, but to no council or senate whatever, and which would nowhere be so dangerous as in the hands of a man who had folly and presumption enough to fancy himself fit to exercise it.[3]

Adam Smith and Václav Havel explore common themes in these brief passages. On one hand, they display respect, admiration, almost affection for the market. It is Smith's "invisible hand" and Havel's "essence of life." The other side of this love of market is a distaste for the state, or at least for the abusive potential of the state. Smith's state is dangerous and untrustworthy. Havel's is arrogant and "monstrous." Smith and Havel share affection for the same market, the "laissez-faire" world of individual initiative, private ownership, and limited government interference, but their fear and loathing are directed toward very different sorts of states.

The state that Smith argued against in 1776 was the mercantilist state of the eighteenth century, a strong state established on the principle that the national interest is best served when state power is used to create wealth, which produces even more power. For Adam Smith, the individual freedom of the marketplace represented the best alternative to abusive state power. As we look around the world today, we see that many nations are seeking to replace restrictive, mercantilist systems of political economy with new regimes that put more stress on market and less on state control. India and Mexico are just two examples of nations that look to market reforms to stimulate economic growth and raise living standards. Even China is using the market to infuse its political economy with the spirit of individual initiative.

The state that Havel criticized in 1992 was the communist state that dominated Czechoslovakia (and other Soviet bloc nations) from the end of World War II until 1989. This communist state engulfed the market, replacing most market activities with rigid and centralized state planning. The state owned the shops and factories and natural resources, for the most part, and ordered their use in ways that fit the planners' notion of the national interest. This centralized state-market system was powerful, but it proved to be terribly inefficient in its ability to create wealth. In embracing the marketplace, then, Havel seeks both to gain individual freedom from state power and also to gain prosperity through the market's flexibility and dynamism.

Today's news is filled with stories of the transition from rigid communist state to flexible free markets. The states of the former Soviet Union, including Russia, and former members of the Warsaw Pact, including Hungary, Poland, East Germany, and the Czech and Slovak republics, are all moving toward greater emphasis on markets and less stress on state control. Taken together, over half of all the human beings on earth are now coming to terms with the liberal ideas of Quesnay, Adam Smith, Havel, and others of their stripe. We are living in the time of a great market surge. By all appearances, this is the liberal hour.

ROOTS OF THE LIBERAL PERSPECTIVE

Liberalism is "a simple, dramatic philosophy. Its central idea is liberty under the law."[4] The liberal perspective sees individuals and states in a decidedly different light from the mercantilist perspectives discussed in the last chapter. The liberal point of view reveals clearly some parts of political economy that mercantilists miss, but necessarily loses other valuable insights in the shadows.

The liberal perspective focuses on the side of human nature that is peaceful and cooperative, competitive in a constructive way, and guided by reason, not emotion. To the extent that individuals and states behave in this way, the liberal perspective holds. Although liberals believe that people are fundamentally self-interested, they do not see this as a disadvantage because they think that broad areas of society are set up in such a way that competitors can all gain, through peaceful and cooperative actions. This contrasts with the mercantilist view, which dwells on the side of human nature that is more aggressive, combative, and suspicious.

While the cooperative side of human nature is highlighted by the liberal perspective, it tends to focus on the abusive aspects of the state. Indeed, it might not be too strong to consider liberalism as an antistate school of thought. Early liberals condemned the abuses of state authority and promoted reforms, such as democratic systems of government, that weakened central power while promoting individual liberty. The dual nature of liberal thought—embracing individual liberty and wary of state abuses—is fundamental to liberalism and can be seen clearly in the earlier quotations from Smith and Havel.

It is easy to imagine why one might fear state abuses; one need only read the U.S. Declaration of Independence to gain an appreciation of this side of liberalism. But it may be more difficult to appreciate the liberal tendency to view individual actions as cooperative and constructive, not competitive and destructive. In the jargon of political economy, liberals think that society is a **positive-sum game**. In a positive-sum game, everyone can potentially get more out of a bargain than they put in. Love is one example of a positive-sum game, and market exchanges of goods or services that are mutually advantageous are another. If you prefer apples to pears, and I prefer pears to apples, then we can swap fruit and both potentially benefit from the exchange. Mercantilists, on the other hand, tend to view life as a **zero-sum game**, where gains by one person or group necessarily come at the expense of others. Poker is one example of a zero-sum game, and dividing up a pizza pie is another. If one gets more, someone else gets less.

Liberals view the fundamental tension between state and market as a conflict between coercion and freedom, authority and individual rights, autocratic dogma and rational logic. Appalled by the abuses of church and state authority dating from feudal days, the early liberals saw a kind of salvation in individual freedom, voluntary association, and rational thought. The market, in their view, was an admirable distillation of the values and characteristics that they advocated.

The liberal view, then, comes down heavily on the side of the market when choosing sides between state and market, a fundamental tension that characterizes political economy. A free market is just one element of the liberal view (democratic government is another), but it is a very important one.

The liberal perspective on political economy is perhaps best summarized by the phrase **laissez-faire** or "let be." Free individuals are best equipped to make social choices. Liberalism is, in short, very conservative, as we understand liberal and conservative politics today. The role of the state is to perform the limited number of tasks that individuals cannot perform by themselves, such as establishment of a basic legal system, assurance of national defense, and coining money. People sometimes talk about liberalism as "classical liberalism" to differentiate it from the "modern liberalism" of today.

The liberal view of human nature shows up in Adam Smith's writings. He believed in the cooperative, constructive side of human nature, and gave it the famous name, the "invisible hand."

> He generally, indeed, neither intends to promote the public interest, nor knows how much he is promoting it. By preferring the support of domestic to that of foreign industry, he intends only his own security; and by directing that industry in such a manner as its own produce may be of the greatest value, he intends only his own gain, and he is in this, as in many other cases, led by an invisible hand to promote an end which was no part of his intention. Nor is it always the worse for the society that it was no part of it. By pursuing his own interest he frequently promotes that of society more effectually than when he really intends to promote it. I have never known much good done by those who affected to trade for the public good.[5]

It is clear that Smith sees people working in harmony, even when they are competing for the same customers or products. For the most part, then, the Smith's liberal philosophy sees no need for the heavy hand of the state in individual and market activities. Indeed, as we have seen, Smith was suspicious of the motives and methods of those who would use state power in the "public interest."

Some writers paint Adam Smith as unrealistic in his optimistic view of human nature, but he was no romantic Pollyanna. Smith knew that any individual or group that gains power also gains the potential to abuse it. This is true even in the market. Smith wrote that "People of the same trade seldom meet together, even for merriment and diversion, but the conversation ends in a conspiracy against the public, or in some contrivance to raise prices."[6]

Adam Smith has been quoted frequently in these pages; it would be hard to overstate the importance of his writings and his ideas in the development of political economy. Smith's works struck the right note at the right time, and so gained a measure of respect and influence that is rare. It is important, however, to think of both sides of Smith's writings when considering the liberal view. It is not so much that liberals such as Adam Smith love wealth, perhaps, than that they fear and loathe power. The fact that a liberal looks favorably on the market, where power tends to be widely dispersed, and unfavorably on the state's concentrated power, simply reflects this point of view.[7]

THE LIBERAL VIEW OF INTERNATIONAL RELATIONS

The liberal view of human nature extends to an analysis of international affairs. Liberals tend to focus on the domain where nation-states show their cooperative, peaceful, constructive natures through harmonious competition. International trade is therefore seen as mutually advantageous, not a cutthroat competition for wealth and power. What is true about individuals is true about states, in this view. Or, as Smith wrote, "What is prudence in the conduct of every family, can scarce be folly in that of a great kingdom. If a foreign country can supply us with a commodity cheaper than we ourselves can make it, better buy it of them with some part of the produce of our industry, employed in a way in which we have some advantage."[8]

Liberals like Smith generally opposed most state restrictions on free international markets. The tariffs that mercantilists saw as tools for concentrating wealth and distilling power, for example, were condemned by Smith: "Such taxes, when they have grown up to a certain height, are a curse equal to the barrenness of the earth and the inclemency of the heavens. . . ."[9]

David Ricardo (1772–1823) followed Smith in adopting the liberal view of international affairs. Ricardo was a true *political* economist who pursued successful careers in business, economics, and as a member of Parliament. Ricardo was a particular champion of free trade, which made him part of the minority in Britain's Parliament in his day. Ricardo opposed the **Corn Laws** (see the Case Study, page 45), which restricted agricultural trade. This passage shows Ricardo's liberal point of view on trade issues:

> Under a system of perfectly free commerce, each country naturally devotes its capital and labour to such employments as are most beneficial to each. The pursuit of individual advantage is admirably connected with the universal good of the whole. By stimulating industry, by rewarding ingenuity, and by using most efficaciously the peculiar powers bestowed by nature, it distributes labour most effectively and most economically: while, by increasing the general mass of productions, it diffuses general benefit, and binds together, by one common tie of interest and intercourse, the universal society of nations throughout the civilized world.[10]

A close reading of Ricardo's words throws new light on the liberal perspective on IPE. Free commerce makes nations efficient, and efficiency is a quality that liberals value almost as highly as freedom. Individual success is "admirably connected" with "universal good"—no conflict among people or nations is envisioned here. The free international market stimulates industry, encourages innovation, and creates a "general benefit" by raising production.

Most important, perhaps, is the notion that it "binds together, by one common tie of interest and intercourse" the nations of the world. In other words, free individual actions in the production, finance, and knowledge structures create such strong ties of mutual advantage among nations that the security tie is irrelevant, or nearly so. The nations of the world become part of a "universal society" united, not separated, by their national interests.

CASE STUDY: BRITAIN'S CORN LAWS

Britain's Parliament enacted the Corn Laws in 1815, soon after the defeat of Napoleon ended the long years of war. The Corn Laws were a system of tariffs and regulations that restricted food imports into Great Britain. The battle over the Corn Laws, which lasted from their inception until they were finally removed in 1846, is a classic IPE case study in the conflict between liberalism and mercantilism, market and state.

Why would Britain seek to limit imports of food from the United States and other countries? The "official" argument was that Britain needed to be self-sufficient in food, and the Corn Laws were a way to assure that it did not become dependent on uncertain foreign supplies. This sort of argument carried some weight at the time, given Britain's wartime experiences (although Napoleon never attempted to cut off food supplies to Great Britain).

There were other reasons for Parliament's support of the Corn Laws, however. Parliament was constituted along different lines in the nineteenth century. The right to vote was not universal, and members of Parliament were chosen based on rural landholdings, not the distribution of population. The result was that Parliament represented the largely agricultural interests of the landed estates, which were an important source of both power and wealth in the seventeenth and eighteenth centuries. The growing industrial cities and towns, which were increasingly the engine of wealth in the nineteenth century, were not represented in Parliament to a proportional degree.

Seen in this light, it is clear that the Corn Laws were in the economic interests of the members of Parliament and their allies. They were detrimental, however, to the rising industrial interests in two ways. First, by forcing food prices up, the Corn Laws indirectly forced employers to increase the wages they paid workers. This increased production costs and squeezed profits. Second, by reducing Britain's imports from other countries, the Corn Laws indirectly limited Britain's manufactured exports to these markets. The United States, for example, counted on sales of agricultural goods to Britain to generate the cash to pay for imported manufactured goods. Without agricultural exports, the U.S. couldn't afford as many British imports.

The industrialists embraced the liberal view of IPE, that free markets and minimal state interference were in the nation's interest. (It was clearly in their interest to do so!) Adam Smith's ghost was repeatedly summoned to support their assaults. David Ricardo, the liberal political economist, grew wealthy enough from his financial affairs

Continued

CASE STUDY: BRITAIN'S CORN LAWS, *continued*

to acquire landholdings and a seat in Parliament, from which he railed against the Corn Laws.

Clearly, the industrialists favored repeal of the Corn Laws, but they lacked the political power to achieve their goal. The Parliamentary Reform Act of 1832, however, revised the system of parliamentary representation in Britain, reducing the power of the landed elites, who had previously dominated the government, and increasing the power of representatives of the emerging industrial centers. This Reform Act began the political process that eventually abolished the Corn Laws by weakening their political base of support.

The Corn Laws were repealed in 1846, in an act of high political drama, which changed the course of British policy for a generation. While this act is often seen as the triumph of liberal views over old-fashioned mercantilism, it is perhaps better seen as the victory of the masses over the agricultural oligarchy. Britain's population had grown quickly during the first half of the nineteenth century, and agricultural self-sufficiency was increasingly difficult, even with rising farm productivity. Crop failures in Ireland (the potato famine) in the 1840s left Parliament with little choice. It was either repeal the Corn Laws or face famine, death, and food riots.

The repeal of the Corn Laws was accompanied by a boom in the Victorian economy. Cheaper food and bigger export markets fueled a rapid short-term expansion of British economy. Britain embraced a liberal view of trade for the rest of the century. Given Britain's place in the global political economy as the "workshop of the world," liberal policies were the most effective way to build national wealth and power. Other nations, however, felt exploited or threatened by Britain's power, and adopted mercantilist policies in self-defense.

The Corn Laws illustrate the dynamic interaction of state and market. Changes in the wealth-producing structure of the economy (from farm to industry, from country to city) eventually led to a change in the distribution of state power. The transition was not smooth, however, and took a long time, important points for us to remember as we consider states and markets in transition today.

J. S. MILL AND THE EVOLUTION OF THE LIBERAL PERSPECTIVE

It is tempting to stop here with our discussion of the liberal perspective. A view of IPE that says, basically, "Hands off the market" is easy to memorize and apply. And there are political economists today who adopt what is fundamentally this classical liberal view of state-market relations. But political economy is a dynamic field, and the liberal view has evolved over the years as the nature of state-market interaction has changed. The liberal view today is more complex and interesting, a set of variations on Adam Smith's powerful tune, not an endless repetition of it.

A critical person in the intellectual development of liberalism was John Stuart Mill (1806–1873).[11] Mill inherited the liberalism of Smith and Ricardo, as transmitted by his father, the political economist James Mill. His textbook, *Principles of Political*

Economy with Some of Their Applications to Social Philosophy (1848) more or less defined liberalism for half a century.

Mill held that liberalism had been an important *destructive* force in the eighteenth century—it was the intellectual foundation of the revolutions and reforms that weakened central authority and strengthened individual liberty in the United States and in Europe. This was an important accomplishment, in Mill's view, but he wanted more. Mill wanted a philosophy of social progress that was "moral and spiritual progress rather than the mere accumulation of wealth."[12] He proposed, therefore, that the state should take limited and selective action to supplement the market, correcting for market failures or weaknesses better to achieve social progress.

Mill believed that the state should "laissez-faire" in most but not all areas of life. He advocated limited state action in some areas, such as educating children and assisting the poor, where individual initiative might be inadequate in promoting social welfare. In general,

> Mill advocated as much decentralization as was consistent with reasonable efficiency; the slogan was centralize information, decentralize power, so that central government could advise and assist, but not preempt local initiative. An application of Mill's approach is easily found in his own views on education. Parents had a duty to educate their children, and might be legally compelled to do so; it was obviously intolerable to make them pay for this education if they were already poor; it was dangerous for the state to take over education as a centralized activity. The remedy was to enforce the duty on parents, give grants to individuals to pay the charges of schools, leave most education in private hands, but set up some state schools as models of good practice.[13]

This statement of Mill's views on education illustrates effectively the development of the liberal view. Parents had a duty or moral obligation to educate their children. This social duty was so important, he believed, that it outweighed the rights of individual parents. Hence, the state was justified, in Mill's view, to use its coercive power to require the education of children. But Mill also acknowledged the problems created by the market's inherent inequality—some parents might not be able to educate their children as moral obligation and state regulations required—so he advocated government grants to make education of poor children possible. Too much state involvement in education was "dangerous," but some state action, the operation of "model schools," for example, was desirable.

Mill's views on education, as on other similar social issues, reflect the evolution of liberalism in his time. The guiding principle was still "laissez-faire"; when in doubt, state interference was to be avoided. But, within a political economy based on markets and individuals, some limited government actions were desirable. The questions, for Mill as for liberal thinkers since his time, are when, how, and how far? When is government's visible hand justified as an assistant to or replacement for the invisible hand of the market? How should the state act? How far can the state go before its interference with individual rights and liberties is abusive?

Many liberals today believe that the state has some role to play in equalizing income, although there is much disagreement about how much redistribution is desirable and how much is too much. Many liberals also see advantages in state actions to preserve the environment, to promote education and training, to improve transportation and communication, and to advance science and the arts. The *degree* of state action needed in each case remains controversial, however, even among liberals.

The War, the Depression, and Mr. Keynes

John Maynard Keynes[14] (pronounced "canes") stands out in the development of IPE and in the evolution of the liberal perspective. Keynes (1883–1946) developed an interesting and subtle strain of the liberal perspective that we call **Keynesian** economics or perhaps Keynesian political economy. The Keynesian version of liberalism (and there are many liberals who would not include Keynes in their ranks!) combines state and market influence in a way that, while still in the spirit of Adam Smith, relies on the "invisible hand" on a narrower range of issues and sees a larger, but still limited, sphere of constructive state action.

Keynes's political economy was shaped by his experiences with three of the defining events of the twentieth century: World War I, the rise of the Marxist-Leninist Soviet Union, and the worldwide Great Depression of the 1930s. From World War I, Keynes learned the dangers of undiluted mercantilism. The Great War and its unstable aftermath were, in his view, the result of nationalism, greed, and vengeance. Clearly states could go much too far in the name of national interest!

Keynes's experiences in and with the Soviet Union discouraged any thought he might have had of adopting a Marxist or communist point of view. Keynes viewed Leninism as a religion, with a strong emotional appeal that capitalism lacked, not a theory of political economy. He found the Soviet regime repressive, its disregard for individual freedom intolerable.

Having rejected mercantilism, like Adam Smith, and communism, like Václav Havel, it might appear that Maynard Keynes would necessarily be a liberal. But Keynes was critical, too, of the cult of the market that extreme liberalism represents. Here he was influenced by the Great Depression of the 1930s, which he interpreted as evidence that the invisible hand sometimes errs in catastrophic ways. As early as 1926, Keynes wrote:

> Let us clear from the ground the metaphysical or general principles upon which, from time to time, *laissez-faire* has been founded. It is *not* true that individuals possess a prescriptive "Natural liberty" in their economic activities. There is *no* "compact" conferring perpetual rights on those who Have or on those who Acquire. The world is *not* so governed from above that private and social interest always coincide. It is *not* so managed here below that in practice they coincide. It is *not* a correct deduction from the Principles of Economics that enlightened self-interest always operates in the public interest. Nor is it true that self-interest generally *is* enlightened; more often individuals

acting separately to promote their own ends are too ignorant or too weak to attain even these. Experience does *not* show that individuals, when they make up a social unit, are always less clear-sighted than when they act separately.[15]

In Keynes's view, individuals and markets tended to make decisions that were particularly unwise when faced with situations where the future is unknown and there is no effective way to share risks or coordinate otherwise chaotic actions. Here Keynes seems to foresee the Great Depression that came just a few years later.

> Many of the greatest economic evils of our time are the fruits of risk, uncertainty, and ignorance. . . . Yet the cure lies outside the operations of individuals; it may even be to the interest of individuals to aggravate the disease. . . . These measures would involve Society in exercising directive intelligence through some appropriate organ of action over many of the inner intricacies of private business, yet it would leave private initiative and enterprise unhindered.[16]

In other words, Keynes thought that the state could and should use its power to fortify and improve the market, but not along the aggressive, nationalistic lines of mercantilism, and not with the oppressive force of communism. Keynes was, at heart, still a liberal, who believed in the positive force of the market.

> These reflections have been directed towards possible improvements in the technique of modern Capitalism by the agency of collective action. There is nothing in them which is seriously incompatible with what seems to me to be the essential characteristic of Capitalism, namely the dependence upon the intense appeal to the money-making and money-loving instincts of individuals as the main motive force of the economic machine.[17]
>
> For my part, I think that Capitalism, wisely managed, can probably be made more efficient for attaining economic ends than any alternative system yet in sight, but that in itself is in many ways objectionable. Our problem is to work out a social organization which shall be as efficient as possible without offending our notions of a satisfactory way of life.[18]

Keynes's perspective on IPE finds strengths and weaknesses in both state and market. While he advocated free markets in a wide domain, including international trade and finance, for the most part, he still believed that positive government action was both useful and necessary to deal with problems that the invisible hand would not set right. These problems included especially the macroeconomic diseases of inflation and unemployment.

Keynes doubted that markets could fully coordinate the actions of individuals to achieve their best interests. During the Great Depression, for example, people were uncertain and afraid and tended to hold on to their money, neither spending it nor banking it. This might have been wise for them individually, but with millions of people behaving this way, the flow of spending that supports jobs and creates incomes diminished, creating unemployment, and generating more fear and uncertainty. The "paradox of saving" is that it is good for families but, taken to the extreme, it can be bad for the economy. The "invisible hand" loses its grip.

Keynes also doubted that people are invariably rational in their behavior. The stock market, he said, was influenced by the "animal spirits" of traders. The stock market crash of 1929 showed what can happen when investors are spooked and stampede.

Keynes developed a new and somewhat complex strain of IPE that was liberal on the international front but recognized a need for firm state action internally, to overcome the obstacles of risk, uncertainty, and ignorance. Keynes's ideas formed and shaped many modern institutions, ranging from the system of international trade and finance, on one hand, to the programs of unemployment insurance, social security, and bank deposit insurance on the other.

THE KEYNESIAN COMPROMISE

Keynes's complex view of political economy shaped the world's IPE for a generation when it became embedded in the post–World War II *Bretton Woods system* of international political and economic arrangements and institutions. Near the end of World War II, leaders of the Allied nations met at a hotel in Bretton Woods, New Hampshire, to forge global structures that would change the course of history from the war-depression-war pattern of the first half of the twentieth century. Keynes headed the British delegation to Bretton Woods, and the Bretton Woods system, while not Keynes's plan, certainly reflected many of his ideas.

The postwar **Bretton Woods** system has been called the *Keynesian compromise* or a system of "embedded liberalism." This system envisioned a liberal international system, with open markets and free trade. Within this system, however, individual nations would be able to undertake the sorts of domestic policies that Keynes advocated for moderating inflation, controlling unemployment, and encouraging economic growth. In other words, the state had a fairly important macroeconomic role *within* each nation, but free markets were intended to dominate relations *between* nations. Bretton Woods can thus be thought of as something of a compromise between a strong market and a strong state (hence "Keynesian compromise"), or as a strong state embedded in a strong market ("embedded liberalism").

The Bretton Woods system will be discussed in greater depth later in this book (especially in chapters 6 through 8). For now, however, it is important to note that Bretton Woods represented a fundamental change in liberalism. After Keynes and Bretton Woods, liberals no longer viewed IPE as state versus market. Rather, liberals sought the right degree and nature of state intervention within an overall system of open markets. The difference between liberalism and mercantilism, while still clear in general, became blurred in places.

THE LIBERAL VIEW OF HEGEMONY

The theory of *hegemonic stability* is another variation on the liberal theme, different from Keynes but clearly reflecting the Keynesian spirit.[19] This theory looks at the role of state and market in the global economy and observes that international markets work best when certain international **public goods** are present.[20] These public goods include such things as free trade, peace and security, or at least a balance of powers, and a sound system of international payments.

Each of these public goods is costly to provide, and each suffers from what economists call the *free-rider problem.* Individuals and nations who do not contribute to the cost of providing these public goods will still be able to benefit from them. Under these circumstances, it will often be the case that the world economy will suffer, since no nation will be willing to bear all the costs of enforcing free trade, sound money, and so on, while others derive benefits without paying. At certain times, however, there emerges one nation that dominates the world economy. That nation finds it in its own interest to provide international public goods, even taking free riders into account. The ***hegemon*** benefits so much from the growth and success of the world economy that it is willing to bear the costs of providing international public goods to smaller or weaker states, who find it in their interest to cooperate in order to preserve their "free ride."

The liberal theory of hegemonic stability asserts that, when a hegemon arises, the world economy tends to grow and prosper, as the benefits of free trade, peace and security, sound money, etc., stimulate markets everywhere. When the hegemon fails, however, these public goods disappear and the world economy stagnates or declines. Political economists generally recognize three instances of hegemonic stability in modern history: The United Provinces (Holland) was the hegemon in the eighteenth century, Great Britain was the hegemon in the nineteenth century, and the United States performed the hegemon's function for much of the postwar era.

The hegemonic stability theory has stimulated a great deal of discussion. Scholars ask, what happens when there is no hegemon? Is the U.S. still a hegemon? If the U.S. is a "hegemon in decline" (like Great Britain before World War I), then is some sort of group hegemon possible, involving the European Union or perhaps a U.S.–Japan "bigemony"?

Scholars also debate the motives and effects of hegemony. Is the hegemon unselfish, draining itself dry in the end as it tries to keep the international system running? Or is the hegemon selfish and imperialistic, draining the rest of the world to fill its coffers? (See box.)

Like the Keynesian viewpoint, the liberal theory of hegemonic stability is based on the strength and resiliency of the market as a form of social and economic organization. Whereas Keynes thought that the state needed to be active within nations, to assure economic growth and stability, hegemonic stability theory asserts that some state—the hegemon—needs to shoulder an international role if markets are to achieve their potential. Where Keynes called for domestic policy, then, hegemonic stability focuses on international policies.

THREE PERSPECTIVES ON HEGEMONY

Few ideas in IPE have generated so much discussion and debate as has hegemony. Who are the hegemons? What are their motives? How do they behave? What effect do they have on the IPE? This chapter introduced the idea of hegemony in the context of the liberal theory of hegemonic stability as developed in the postwar period. This brief box provides a glimpse of some alternative views of hegemony.

A hegemon is created when the richest and most powerful nation within some sphere of the international political economy assumes responsibility for organizing a system of international political and economic relations. Most IPE scholars identify three instances of hegemony in the modern period of history: the United Provinces (Holland) in the eighteenth century, the United Kingdom in the nineteenth century, and the United States since the end of World War II. In the years between hegemons, as during the period between World Wars I and II, no single nation-state dominates or organizes the international system.

Liberals, as noted in the text, generally view the hegemon as the key to a positive-sum game. The hegemon supplies the public goods, such as security and free trade, that make the international system function more efficiently. This increases the range and degree of mutually advantageous transactions that take place. The *benevolent hegemon* bears most of the costs of maintaining this system, but also reaps most of the gains, since its own success is so tightly bound to the success of its partner nations. The hegemon is guided by what we might call enlightened self-interest—its self-interest is best served by maintaining the security and prosperity of others. Liberal scholars thus view the behavior of the United States in the postwar IPE, including its role in the Bretton Woods monetary system (see chapter 6), and the NATO security system (see chapter 9) as examples of an enlightened hegemon at work. The problem with hegemony, in the liberal view, is that the costs of hegemony tend to rise and weaken the hegemon's base of wealth and power. If this condition persists, the security and prosperity of the IPE is threatened.

The notion of the benevolent hegemon, however, is challenged from two intellectual directions. Realists see hegemony as part of a mercantilist strategy of dominance. Proponents of the *modern world system* view (to be developed in chapter 4), see hegemony as part of a grand cycle of history. All three views of hegemony provide important insights into the nature of IPE relations.

Nation-states are guided by self-interest, according to the realists (see chapter 2). The realist analysis of hegemony, therefore, focuses on the *selfish hegemon*. As the richest and most powerful nation, the hegemon is able to call the tune, to set the rules of the game for international political and economic relations. It is only natural, realists argue, for the hegemon to establish rules and relationships that will favor it over its partners and competitors. The hegemon uses its dominant position to gain wealth and power from others in the international system, which is a logical extension of the mercantilist view of IPE.

The temptations of selfish hegemony are great, according to realists, and it is to be expected that the hegemon will eventually overreach, seeking more international influence than it can maintain. "Imperial overreach" weakens hegemony and leads to its decline.[21]

Political realists view the United States as a classic example of a selfish hegemon. The U.S. established the postwar "rules of the game" with a built-in bias in favor of U.S. interests. Through the GATT and the World Trade Organization, for example, the U.S. supported a system of free world trade. This might have benefited other countries, re-

Continued

THREE PERSPECTIVES ON HEGEMONY, *continued*

alists argue, but it benefited the U.S. most of all since, in the days following the end of World War II, the U.S. was the largest industrial producer and so got the lion's share of the gains from a free trade system.

In the same way, realists argue that the U.S. was the selfish hegemon on monetary fronts. The Bretton Woods monetary system put the U.S. dollar at the center of global finance. This arrangement burdened the U.S. with special obligations, but also gave it opportunities to abuse the system. For a time, the U.S. could run up international debts and pay for them by simply printing dollars—an advantage that other debtor nations, who had to pay with real resources—were not permitted.

Realists look at U.S. security policy in the same light. They focus on the extent to which the postwar security structure, the so-called **Pax Americana** that included NATO, served U.S. interests more than the interests of its allies. The pattern of the selfish hegemon can be found throughout the IPE. The decline of the United States in recent decades is seen as the result of its "imperial overreach" during the 1960s and 1970s.

A third perspective on hegemony is provided by the *modern world system* (MWS) theory (which will be explored in chapter 4). Briefly, MWS theory looks at the IPE as the interaction of an industrial *core* and an agricultural **periphery** taking place within the global system of capitalism. MWS theory focuses on the long-term nature of IPE relationships and thus views hegemony as part of a long-term cycle within the industrial core. Christopher Chase-Dunn notes

> a fluctuation of hegemony versus multicentricity in the distribution of military power and economic competitive advantage in production among core states. Hegemonic periods are those in which power and competitive advantage are relatively concentrated in a single hegemonic state. Multicentric periods are those in which there is a more equal distribution of power and competitive advantage among core states. In only a very rough sense is this a cycle because its periodicy is very uneven.[22]

An oversimplified MWS account of the hegemonic cycle might go like this: A rich and powerful nation gains control over the core following a world war. Eventually, however, the hegemon falls into decline, leading to a period where there may be several important core nation-states held in a **balance of power**. The balance eventually breaks down, war follows, and a new hegemon rises from the ashes. Hegemony in this view is neither benevolent nor selfish so much as it is part of the nature of capitalist international relations. The postwar hegemony of the United States is part of the larger pattern of capitalism in the MWS view.

An active scholarly controversy exists about the nature and consequences of hegemony. As is often the case, however, the three viewpoints presented here help illuminate different aspects of the situation, so we do not necessarily need to *choose* a single view of hegemony, but can gain insights from its many-sidedness. One scholar who has taken this position is David P. Calleo, who has described the benevolent hegemon and the selfish hegemon as two stages in a larger hegemonic cycle. Calleo notes that

> while the [liberal] hegemonic view served well enough to inspire the creation of the *Pax Americana*, it also carried troubling implications for its future, the future that now seems fast upon us. Hegemony has a tendency to break down because of the absolute or relative weakening of the hegemonic power itself. A hegemon in decay begins to exploit the system in order to compensate for its progressing debility.[23]

Continued

THREE PERSPECTIVES ON HEGEMONY, continued

Two important questions regarding hegemony will appear repeatedly in this book. The first is the question of decline—is the United States hegemon in decline (or decay, to use Calleo's term)? If so, what does this mean for the U.S. and for the world? The second question follows from the first: if the U.S. *is* a declining hegemon, then *what next?* Is this the end of hegemony and the start of a new multicentered system, as the MWS theorists would suggest? Or will some other hegemon rise up to take the place of the U.S.? If so, *who?*

CONSERVATISM: THE RESURGENCE OF CLASSICAL LIBERALISM

The Keynesian flavor of liberalism, markets swirled with a distinct state stripe, became the mainstream IPE view in the Western industrial democracies during the years from the 1930s to the 1970s. In some places, such as Hong Kong, the market was emphasized to a greater extent, creating a dynamic, free-wheeling, free-market system. In other places, such as Sweden, the role of the state was emphasized to a greater degree, creating a more socialist system.[24] Generally, however, the industrialized nations balanced state and market forces along the lines of the Keynesian compromise, using state power to supplement, strengthen, and stabilize the market economy, within the liberal Bretton Woods system of international institutions.[25]

During this period, the term *liberal* in political discourse came to mean something different from what it means historically in IPE. *Liberal* came to be associated with the stronger state role that the Keynesians and eventually the socialists advocated. In other words, *liberal,* a view that emphasizes the market, came to mean an emphasis on the state. The opposite of the new "liberalism" is the "old liberalism," which came to be called conservatism! In most respects, contemporary conservative views mirror those of the classical liberals, such as Adam Smith.

During the 1960s, for example, state policy in the United States became much more active than in previous decades. The federal government took strong steps at home and abroad in such varied areas as space exploration, the Vietnam War, civil rights, the "Great Society" antipoverty programs, Medicare medical insurance for the elderly, and regulation of business and the environment. Especially during this period, the term *liberal* became associated with advocates of a strong state.

The rising influence of the state in socialist countries and in "liberal" industrial nations stimulated a resurgence of "conservative" classical liberal views. Two influential leaders of this movement were the Austrian Friedrich von Hayek (1899–1992) and the American Milton Friedman (1912–   ), both economists and both Nobel prize winners in their field. Hayek and Friedman renewed Adam Smith's call for "laissez-faire" in a world where the goals of state intervention were much different than in Smith's day, but many of its methods (taxation, regulation, etc.) were the same.

Hayek's most influential work was perhaps *The Road to Serfdom* (1944), where he argued that socialism and growing state influence represented fundamental threats to individual liberty. *The Road to Serfdom* bases its condemnation of state action on arguments of moral philosophy. Friedman's *Capitalism and Freedom* (1962) argued forcefully for minimal state intervention in private affairs and pointed out the inherent inequities and inefficiencies of government controls. For Friedman, political freedom was inexorably linked to economic freedom, and both were best protected by free markets not state actions, however well-intentioned. Together with others, Hayek and Friedman laid out an intellectual framework and policy agenda that was distinctly in the spirit of Adam Smith, in direct opposition to the prevailing Keynesian ideas of the 1960s and 1970s.

As the Keynesian compromise broke down in the 1970s, classical liberal ideas like those of Hayek and Friedman became increasingly popular and powerful. These forces reached their zenith in the 1980s as classical liberalism became a dominant political ideology.

REAGAN, THATCHER, AND THE NEOCONSERVATIVES

In the 1980s, the classical liberal view of IPE asserted itself forcefully through a movement that is often called *neoconservatism* (which could just as well have been termed *neoliberalism!*). The chief practitioners of neoconservative IPE were Prime Minister Margaret Thatcher of Great Britain and U.S. President Ronald Reagan. These two strong leaders advocated free markets at home and on the international front, and minimal state interference in all spheres of activity except security, where a strong anti-Communist stand was advocated. This view of IPE owes far more to Adam Smith, Friedrich von Hayek, and Milton Friedman than to Maynard Keynes.

The neoconservative policies of Reagan and Thatcher were designed to reduce state control of private sector activities. In the United States, this took the form of tax cuts and deregulation of markets. The top income tax rate in the U.S. was cut in stages from 70 percent in 1980 to 33 percent in 1986. Telephone, commercial airline, and trucking industries were subject to dramatic deregulation, allowing greater competition and freedom to set prices.

Deregulation in Britain was accompanied by a dramatic reduction in state ownership of business and assets. Publicly owned firms and publicly held housing was "privatized," reducing the size of government and its influence on individual decisions.

The success of these classical liberal policies in the United States and Britain, combined with the collapse of communism in Eastern Europe, has led to a dramatic renewal of liberal policies around the world. Deregulation and privatization are widespread policies in the 1990s; the influence of Reagan and Thatcher can be seen today all over the world, from Africa to Europe, from South America to Asia. The neoconservative perspective on IPE remains influential. It calls for a reduced state role in the market through such actions as deregulation of industry, privatization of state-owned enterprises, and lower tax burdens on businesses and individuals. To an important extent, the "conservative revolution" of classical liberalism continues today, although the perennial problems of the balance between state and market remain everywhere controversial.

LIBERALISM TODAY

With the collapse of communism and the increasing influence of liberal views and market forces around the world, the 1990s would seem to be the dawn of the liberal era. Liberalism today, however, retains all the stripes and variations of its past, which makes it complex and interesting. There are many variations of the "liberal" perspective on IPE. The classical "liberal" views of Smith and Ricardo exist alongside the very similar "conservative" ideas of Reagan and Thatcher and the somewhat more "progressive" views of Keynes.

Václav Havel reflects a modern liberal's view of these matters. Writing about energy policy in Czechoslovakia, he calls for greater use of the market than in Communist times, but

> Even so, I think—and I am newly persuaded of this every day—that there are problems that the marketplace cannot and will not solve by itself. . . . One doesn't need to be an expert to understand that the marketplace alone cannot decide which direction Czechoslovakia should take. . . . Clearly the state will play a diminishing role in guiding the economy and deciding where, by whom, how, and how much. . . . Its role will be to come up with appropriate legislation and economic policies to encourage development in the desired direction, that direction being towards decentralization, plurality of sources, efficiency, ecological soundness, and diversification of foreign suppliers.[26]

In fact, as president of the Czech and Slovak republics, Havel worried that the emphasis on the market might go *too* far, with disastrous social results for both market and state. Moving from too strong a state (communism) to too weak a state might risk a backlash and a return to authoritarian rule. Here Havel warns against adopting liberal policies to an unwise extreme:

> The market economy is as natural and matter-of-fact to me as air. After all, it is a system of human economic activity that has been tried and found to work over centuries (centuries? millennia!). It is the system that best corresponds to human nature. But precisely because it is so down-to-earth, it is not, and cannot constitute, a world view, a philosophy, or an ideology. Even less does it contain the meaning of life. It seems both ridiculous and dangerous when . . . the market economy suddenly becomes a cult, a collection of dogmas, uncompromisingly defended and more important, even, than what the economic system is intended to serve—that is, life itself.[27]

So what can we conclude about liberalism today (other than that it is confusingly named?). Liberalism is a view of IPE that sees markets as more important than states. The role of the market is as a peaceful coordinating process, which brings together individuals in a mutually advantageous, positive-sum game. The role of state power is negligible (Smith), largely confined to security structures (Reagan and Thatcher), or stronger, but mainly used to strengthen and stabilize markets (Keynes). In any case, the market is seen as the driving force of IPE, and state power is generally suspect and must be justified by appeal to reason.

This liberal view of IPE contrasts sharply with the perspectives explored in the previous chapter and the next one. Mercantilists of all persuasions conceive of a more powerful state, and doubt the market's ability to pursue the national interest on its own. The next chapter looks at the viewpoint of Marx, Lenin, and structuralism, which see the market as being fundamentally flawed in several respects. By contrast, all the different liberals discussed here have far more faith in individuals and markets.

DISCUSSION QUESTIONS

1. Adam Smith and Václav Havel are both liberals in the sense this term is used in IPE. Explain what views Smith and Havel share regarding the market, the state, human nature, and power.
2. How do liberals such as David Ricardo view international trade? Why do they hold this opinion? Explain how the Corn Laws debate in nineteenth century Britain illustrates the conflict between mercantilist and liberal views of international trade.
3. John Stuart Mill and John Maynard Keynes thought that government could play a positive role in correcting problems in the market. Discuss the specific types of "market failures" that Mill and Keynes perceived and the types of government actions they advocated. If Mill and Keynes favored some state action in the market, how can we consider them liberals? Explain.
4. The term "liberal" in IPE means something different from what it means in everyday political discussions. Explain the difference and briefly explain how and why the term took on its current meaning.

SUGGESTED READINGS

Michael J. Boskin. *Reagan and the Economy.* San Francisco: ICS Press, 1987.

Milton Friedman. *Capitalism and Freedom.* Chicago: University of Chicago Press, 1962.

John Kenneth Galbraith. Especially "The New World of Adam Smith" and "John Maynard Keynes", in *Economics in Perspective.* Boston: Houghton-Mifflin, 1987.

Václav Havel. *Summer Meditations,* trans. Paul Wilson. New York: Knopf, 1992.

John Maynard Keynes. *Essays in Persuasion.* New York: W. W. Norton, 1963.

Charles P. Kindleberger. *Money and Power: The Economics of International Politics and the Politics of International Economics.* New York: Basic Books, 1970.

Kent Mathews and Patrick Minford. "Mrs Thatcher's economic policies. 1979–87." *Economic Policy* (October 1987): 57–102.

Thomas K. McCraw. "The Trouble with Adam Smith." *The American Scholar* (Summer 1992): 353–373.

David Ricardo. *The Principles of Political Economy and Taxation.* London: Dent, 1973.

Adam Smith. *The Wealth of Nations.* New York: Dutton, 1964.

NOTES

1. Václav Havel, "What I Believe," in *Summer Meditations,* trans. Paul Wilson (New York: Knopf, 1992), 62. Havel was president of the Czech and Slovak Federal Republic when these words were written, and they must be interpreted in the context of Czechoslovakia's overthrow of its communist government. In 1992, Czechoslovakia split into the separate Czech and Slovak republics.

2. Adam Smith, *The Wealth of Nations* (New York: Dutton, 1964), 398. *The Wealth of Nations* was first published in 1776, a noteworthy year in liberal IPE. Do not confuse Adam Smith, the classical liberal, with "Adam Smith," the contemporary business journalist who uses this famous pen name.
3. Ibid., 400.
4. Ralf Dahrendorf, "Liberalism," in John Eatwell, Murray Milgate, and Peter Newman, eds., *The New Palgrave: Invisible Hand* (New York: W. W. Norton, 1989), 183.
5. Smith, *The Wealth of Nations*, 400.
6. Ibid., 117.
7. To Smith, the "state" meant Britain's Parliament, which represented the interests of the landed gentry, *not* the entrepreneurs and citizens of the growing industrial centers. Not until the 1830s was Parliament reformed to distribute political power more widely. As a Scot without landed estates, Smith had some reason to question the power structure of his time.
8. Smith, *Wealth of Nations*, 401.
9. Ibid., 410.
10. David Ricardo, *The Principles of Political Economy and Taxation* (London: Dent, 1973), 81.
11. J. S. Mill's dates place him between the life spans of Adam Smith and J. M. Keynes, which is roughly where he falls, as well, in the development of liberal thought.
12. Alan Ryan, "John Stuart Mill," in *The New Palgrave: The Invisible Hand*, 201.
13. Ibid., 208.
14. He was known as Maynard Keynes, to distinguish him from his father, the economist John Neville Keynes.
15. John Maynard Keynes, "The End of Laissez-Faire," in *Essays in Persuasion* (New York: W. W. Norton, 1963), 312.
16. Ibid., 317–318.
17. Ibid., 319.
18. Ibid., 321.
19. The American economist Charles Kindleberger is generally credited as the originator of the hegemonic stability theory. See his *Money and Power: The Economics of International Politics and the Politics of International Economics* (New York: Basic Books, 1970).
20. A *public good* is a good or service which, once made available to someone, can be consumed or used by all without cost. The classic example of a public good is a lighthouse, which warns ships of a hazard.
21. See Paul Kennedy, *The Rise and Fall of the Great Powers* (New York: Random House, 1987) for an historical account of this viewpoint.
22. Christopher Chase-Dunn, *Global Formation* (Cambridge, MA: Blackwell, 1989), 50.
23. David P. Calleo, *Beyond American Hegemony* (New York: Basic Books, 1987), 149.
24. See the box in chapter 1 for a definition of socialism and the other important "isms."
25. This discussion refers to the nations of Western Europe and North America, for the most part. The communist nations and less developed countries were generally organized along different lines.
26. Havel, *Summer Meditations*, 72–73.
27. Ibid.

4

Marx, Lenin, and the Structuralist Perspective

OVERVIEW

Karl Marx is one of the most imposing figures in the history of political economy. With the collapse of communism in Russia and Eastern Europe, it is tempting to conclude that "Marx is dead" and to move on to other, easier pursuits. However, ideas that originated with Marx remain very much alive today. Theories that incorporate notions of class struggle, exploitation, imperialism, and technical change, to name just a few, remain important tools of IPE analysis.

This chapter explores a number of theories, ideas, and concepts whose roots are located in *Marxist* and *Leninist* thought. The general heading **structuralism** accounts for some of the more recent theories and concepts that incorporate a number of Marx's and Lenin's ideas.

Modern structuralists often ask questions that others tend to overlook or downplay. Indeed, there are many problems in IPE that cannot be understood or completely appreciated without considering Marx's viewpoint and the more recent structuralist perspectives he helped pioneer. The underlying notion uniting the ideas of what we will call *structuralism* is that structure conditions outcome. Since capitalism was primarily a national phenomenon in Marx's time, he focused most of his analysis on national economies and how the class structure resulted in exploitation, conflict, and crisis within nation-states.

V. I. Lenin expanded Marx's study to account explicitly for imperialism, manifest in the dominant and exploitative relationship of industrial countries with their colonial possessions.

More recently, a number of structuralists focus on a variety of issues associated with imperialism or, otherwise, with the relationship of developing to developed countries. Two concepts that are integral to these studies are the **dependency** of third and fourth world countries on industrialized first world countries, and the **modern world system** theory, which assigns nations a role in the international division of labor.

Those who hold structuralist views see the global political economy in ways fundamentally different from liberals and mercantilists. The keys for them are the national and international economic structures, which they consider to be the driving force behind IPE. "Economics determines politics," as the saying goes. Likewise, whereas liberals and mercantilists make individuals and the state their respective basic units of analysis, structuralists focus on class and the global political economy (often referred to as the *modern world system*).

The history of all hitherto existing society is the history of class struggles.[1]

Karl Marx and Friedrich Engels

Imperialism is capitalism in that stage of development in which the domination of monopolies and finance capital has established itself; in which the export of capital has acquired pronounced importance; in which the partition of all the territories of the globe among the great capitalist powers has been completed.[2]

V. I. Lenin

The Third World countries of today were drawn into the capitalist world market under regimes of formal and informal colonialism, as appendages of the metropolitan nations to supply raw materials and exotic commodities to the industrial center.[3]

Joan Robinson

On January 1, 1994, a small army of peasant guerrillas seized six towns in the poor Mexican state of Chiapas. The "Chiapas Awakening," as it was called by some, was a protest against a political and economic system that the peasants saw as fundamentally biased against them. The date of the revolt was carefully chosen for its symbolic value. New Year's Day, 1994, was the date when the North American Free Trade Agreement (NAFTA) came into force, uniting Mexico with Canada and the United States in a huge open market. NAFTA, the rebels believed, would serve to increase their exploitation by the capitalist system. In revolting against the Mexican system of political economy, they were revolting against the inherent inequality of certain kinds of economic development.

The Chiapas Awakening clearly was neither liberal nor mercantilist in nature. The rebels protested against both the force of the market and the collective power of the state. The intellectual forefather of the Chiapas rebellion was Karl Marx, not Adam Smith or Friedrich List. The Chiapas Awakening reflected the third perspective on IPE, which we term *structuralism.*

This chapter explores the intellectual family tree of structuralism from its historical roots in the industrial revolution to its several branches in the world today. The quotations that opened this chapter, by Karl Marx, V. I. Lenin, and Joan Robinson, hint at where the discussion in this chapter will take us. We will first explore the early roots of the structuralist perspective in the writings of Karl Marx. Marx thought that power was rooted in the ownership of production capital (the means of production), which shaped the relationship among different classes within a nation. Lenin saw imperialism—the domination of industrializing nations over dependent colonial possessions—as a necessary stage of capitalism. Later in the chapter, we will explore a number of contemporary structuralist viewpoints that incorporate variations on these themes.

Some people tend to look at all of IPE from the structuralist perspective, rejecting as hopelessly biased the other viewpoints we have discussed so far. In the same way, economic liberals and mercantilists usually reject the structuralist view as fatally flawed.

In this book, we take a firm stand on middle ground. The structuralist perspective forces us to analyze problems, issues, and events that might be overlooked if we limited ourselves to the liberal and mercantilist viewpoints alone. For example, issues of class, exploitation, the distribution of wealth and power, dependency, and global aspects of capitalism take center stage.

Moreover, this perspective is, at its roots, a critical one, raising challenges to the existing state of affairs. First, many see in structuralism not only the tools to conduct a scientific analysis of existing capitalist arrangements but also the grounds for a moral critique of the inequality and exploitation that capitalism produces within and between countries. Second, this framework of analysis is the only one that allows us to view IPE "from below," i.e., from the perspective of the oppressed classes and poor, developing third world nations. In contrast to mercantilism and liberalism, it gives a voice to the powerless. Finally, structuralism focuses on what is dynamic in IPE, seeing capitalism and other modes of production as driven by conflict and crisis and subject to change. What exists now is a system and set of structures that emerged at a particular time and will eventually be replaced by a new and different system of political economy.

We should make it clear at this point that a good many of the more recent structuralists do not subscribe to Marx's or Lenin's views in a prescriptive sense— that is, they do not ideologically agree with many of the political implications that flow from Marxist or Leninist ideas. However, these structuralists base a good deal of their analysis of IPE on many of Marx's and Lenin's more well-known perceptions and arguments.

MARX AND HISTORY

The first great scholar to pioneer a structural approach to political economy was Karl Marx (1818–1883). Born in Trier, Germany, Marx did his greatest work while living in England, spending hours in research at the British Museum in London. Many of his views reflect things he and his collaborator, Friedrich Engels, studied about English mills and factories at the height of the industrial revolution. Adults and children often labored under dreadful working conditions and lived in abject poverty and squalor. Marx's theory of history, his notion of class conflict, and his critique of capitalism must all be understood in the context of nineteenth century Europe's cultural, political, and economic climate.

A word of caution is in order concerning Marx and Marxism. Marx wrote millions of words; in so vast a body of work, he necessarily treated the main themes repeatedly, and not always consistently. What Marx "said" or "thought" about any interesting issue is, therefore, subject to some dispute. In the same way, Marxist scholars have interpreted Marx's writings in many ways. There is not, therefore, a definitive reading of Marx, any more than there is a definitive interpretation of the Bible or performance of a Beethoven sonata. Marxism is at once a theory of economics, politics, sociology, and ethics. For some, it is also a call to action.

Marx understood history to be a great, dynamic, evolving creature, determined fundamentally by economic and technological forces. Marx believed that through a process called *historical materialism*[4] these forces can be objectively explained and understood just like any other natural law.

Historical materialism takes as its starting point the notion that the *forces of production* of society (i.e., the sum total of knowledge and technology contained in society) set the parameters for the kind of system of political economy, or *mode of production,* that is possible. As Marx put it, "the hand mill gives you society with the feudal lord, the steam mill society with the industrial capitalist."[5] The economic structure (what Marx called the *relations of production,* or class relations) that emerge from such a mode of production in turn determines the social and ethical structures of society.

It is in the contradictions or conflicts between the forces of production and the relations of production in a society that Marx sees the mechanism for evolutionary and revolutionary change. Marx sees the course of history as steadily evolving. The process of change from one system of political economy (or mode of production, in Marx's words) to another is rooted in the growing contradiction between the forces of production (technological development) and the class or property relations in which they develop.

Since class relations change more slowly than technological development, social change is impeded, fostering conflict between the classes. An example today would be computers, which open up possibilities of different class relations and more free time for workers. But because capitalists control how technology is used, many of the computer's potential gains are not realized. When that conflict becomes so severe as to block the advance of human development, a social revolution sweeps away the existing legal and political arrangements and replaces them with ones more compatible with continued social progress.

In this way, history has evolved through distinct epochs or stages: primitive communism, slavery, feudalism, capitalism, socialism, and finally arrival at pure communism. In each of these modes of production, there is a dialectical process whereby inherently unstable and tortured opposing economic forces and counterforces lead to crisis, revolution, and to the next stage of history. And for Marx, the agents of that change are human beings organized in conflicting social classes.

MARX AND CLASS STRUGGLE

> For Marx, power was the inescapable fact of economic life; it proceeded from the possession of property and was thus the natural inevitable possession of the capitalist.[6]

Caught in history's capitalist era, Marx tried to understand the nature of the political economy and the forces pushing toward crisis and for change. Marx did not approach the questions of political economy from the perspectives of either the liberals or the mercantilists. He did not frame his questions in terms of the individual (market) versus society (state). Rather, influenced by the human relationships that he saw in his factory visits, where the capital-owning *bourgeoisie* seemingly exploited the laboring *proletariat*, Marx looked at social change from an angle that revealed deep class cleavages. For Marx, a *class* was a set of persons who stood in the same objective relationship to the means of production. According to Buchholz:

> Each system of production creates ruling and ruled classes. Each epoch is marked by a particular way of extracting income for the rulers. In Roman times, whoever owned a slave owned a claim on output. In feudal times, lords owned a claim on the output of serfs. Under capitalism, owners of factories and land owned a claim on the output of their wage laborers.[7]

Critical for Marx is the fundamental imbalance of power between the classes. To a liberal, the bourgeoisie and proletariat should be capable of forming a peaceful and mutually advantageous relationship. To Marx, however, the bourgeoisie and the proletariat are trapped in a decidedly one-sided relationship, with an "unemployed army" of workers frustrating the ability of the labor force to organize itself, and giving the capitalists the upper hand in all negotiations. The pressure of competition and profit-maximization drive the bourgeoisie to ruthlessly exploit the workers they employ. According to Marx and Engels,

> Modern industry has converted the little workshop of patriarchal master into the great factory of the industrial capitalist. Masses of laborers, crowded into the factory, are organized like soldiers. As privates of the industrial army they are placed under the command of a perfect hierarchy of officers and sergeants. Not only are they slaves of the bourgeois class, and of the bourgeois state; they are daily and hourly enslaved by the machine, by the overlooker, and above all, by the individual bourgeois manufacturer himself. The more openly this despotism proclaims gain to be its end and aim, the more petty, the more hateful and the more embittering it is.[8]

Marx argued that the concentration of wealth in the hands of fewer and fewer capitalists leads to the impoverishment of greater numbers of laborers. At the same time, new technology gradually replaces labor, driving up the reserve army of un-employed and driving down the pay workers receive. Ultimately, this process results in a mass of proletarian misery, setting the stage for revolution. A popular saying attributed to Marx and Engels was that capitalism produces its own "gravediggers."[9]

Marx is critical of the bourgeoisie for the callous manner in which the proletariat are treated. In *The Communist Manifesto*, he and Engels assert that the bourgeoisie

> has left no other bond between man and man than naked self-interest. . . . It has drowned the most heavenly ecstasies of religious fervor, of chivalrous enthusiasm, of Philistine sentimentalism, in the icy water of egotistical calculation. It has resolved personal worth into exchange value, and in place of the numberless indefeasible chartered freedoms, has set up that single, unconscionable freedom—Free Trade. In one word, for exploitation, veiled by religious and political illusions, it has substituted naked, shameless, direct brutal exploitation.[10]

MARX AND THE CRISIS OF CAPITALISM

Marx's attitude toward capitalism and exploitation can be frustrating, even if you believe that his views are fundamentally correct. Although he points out the abuses of capitalism, he also finds merit in its effects. Capitalism is, for Marx, more than an unhappy stop on the road to socialism, it is also a *necessary* stage, which builds wealth and raises material living standards. For Marx, it is the dynamic nature of market capitalism that lies at the heart of political economy. Rational men, driven by fierce competition, assault the status quo where they find it, transforming the world.

According to Marxian analysis, capitalism has an historic role, which is to transform the world. In so doing, capitalism accomplishes two goals at once. First, it breaks down slavery and feudalism, which are its historical (and dialectical) antecedents. Second, it creates the social and economic foundations for the eventual transition to a "higher" level of social development.

> The bourgeoisie has through its exploitation of the world market given a cosmopolitan character to production and consumption in every country. . . . The bourgeoisie, by the rapid improvement of all instruments of production, by the immensely facilitated means of communication, draws all nations, even the most barbarian, into civilization. The cheap prices of its commodities are the heavy artillery with which it batters down all Chinese walls, with which it forces the barbarians' intensely obstinate hatred of foreigners to capitulate. It compels all nations, on pain of extinction, to adopt the bourgeois mode of production; it compels them to introduce what it calls civilization into their midst, i.e., to become bourgeois themselves. In a word, it creates a world after its own image.[11]

It would seem, then, that the Marxian vision foresees the triumph of capitalism over other world orders.[12] In fact, Marx believes that capitalism is fundamentally flawed. As was discussed above, capitalism contains the seeds of its own destruction. The crisis of capitalism is inevitable. He identified three objective laws of this mode of production.

The law of the falling rate of profit holds that as capitalists try to gain a competitive advantage by investing in new labor-saving and productive technologies, unemployment increases and the rate of profit decreases. Surplus value (or profit) can only come from living labor and not machines, and since production is increasingly based on less labor, even with very high rates of exploitation of those still working, the rate of profit tends to fall.

The law of disproportionality (also called the *problem of underconsumption*)[13] argues that capitalism, because of its anarchic, unplanned nature, is prone to instability. For a variety of reasons, capitalism is subject to overproduction or, the obverse side of the same coin, underconsumption. That is, capitalists are not able to sell everything they produce at a profit and workers cannot afford to buy what they make. This disproportionality between supply and demand leads to wild fluctuations in the history of capitalism, with periodic booms and busts. This increases the likelihood of social unrest and the prospects for revolution and change. In response, capitalist governments have often stepped in to smooth out the development of the economy by, for example, creating a large military-industrial complex.

The law of concentration (or *accumulation of capital*) holds that capitalism tends to produce increasing inequality in the distribution of income and wealth. As the bourgeoisie continue to exploit the proletariat and weaker capitalists are swallowed by stronger, bigger ones, wealth and the ownership of capital becomes increasingly concentrated in fewer and fewer hands. This, then, makes more visible the inequality in the system and exacerbates the effects of the law of disproportionality, since the mass of impoverished consumers lack purchasing power.

The curse of capitalism, seen in this light, is its deceptive logic. Workers and business owners are indeed all rational individuals, as Adam Smith would have us believe, acting primarily in their own self-interest. In this case, however, the invisible hand does not benignly guide everyone so that all of society benefits. Rather, individual rationality adds up to collective irrationality. Increasing numbers of the proletariat are driven to cutthroat competition for jobs, driving wages and working conditions down to shocking levels, trading even their children's youthful vigor for a little more money. The bourgeoisie, equally driven by competitive forces, check their moral and ethical beliefs at the factory door and, for the sake of efficiency and productivity, thoroughly exploit their fellow citizens.

ORTHODOX MARXISTS AND REVISIONISTS

Despite the failure of the great proletarian revolution to occur as Marx had predicted it would in the mid-nineteenth century, his ideas remained popular for a number of thinkers and their followers well into the twentieth century. Eduard Bernstein, Karl Kautsky, and Rosa Luxemburg were active in the Social Democratic Party (SPD). The views of Bernstein, Kautsky, and Luxemburg span a wide spectrum on the issue of how socialism can be achieved: whether it would come about gradually under its own power or if it should be proactively encouraged by means of political organization and action.

Continued

ORTHODOX MARXISTS AND REVISIONISTS, *continued*

Eduard Bernstein championed the cause of evolutionary reform. He joined the SPD in 1872. He was exiled to Zurich and later to London where he spent time with Engels and formulated his critique of Marxism, *Evolutionary Socialism.* Bernstein returned to Germany in 1900 and became a leader of the revisionist school of Marxist thought.

Bernstein argued that English workers were not that bad off. Likewise, German workers benefited from reforms initiated by the civil service. He was pragmatic to the extent that he preferred parliamentary tactics to revolution. Bernstein believed that society could gradually evolve into socialism in a nonviolent fashion. He attacked Marx's notion of the inevitability of change. For Bernstein, men are ethical beings. Hence, the arrival of socialism is not predetermined, but is ethically desirable: a matter of human will. Bernstein also attacked Marx's economic theory of value and surplus value. Finally, he faulted Marx for overstating the argument about the monopolistic tendencies of capitalism. In fact, Bernstein nearly abandoned the class concept altogether as part of his own argument that capitalism was not producing a single proletariat but, instead, several distinct classes.

Karl Kautsky is known for his orthodox Marxist views, even if he and his followers revised Marx's and Engels's views. Kautsky argued that the timing of Marx's revolution was off and that Marx's theory remained a general tendency. The concentration of capital was slower than Marx had predicted it would be.

Would socialism develop out of methods that were reform oriented (Bernstein's position) or would it be revolution that produced the ultimate order? Kautsky remained a traditional Marxist in that he suggested that socialism would be the result of revolution. However, according to Kautsky, revolution did not imply violence. Also a pragmatist, Kautsky believed that standing armies were likely to defeat revolutionary movements. He therefore supported any kind of revolution that looked to government to support the proletariat. Peaceful methods such as parliamentarianism, strikes, and press propaganda stood more of a chance against oppression than revolutionary tactics.

In contrast to the more peaceful methods of transition to socialism supported by both Bernstein and Kautsky, their peer, Rosa Luxemburg, stands in stark contrast. Luxemburg established herself as the spokesperson for the left-wing membership of the SPD. Her ideals of Marxism were combined with fiery and heroic action.

Luxemburg helped found the Polish Workers League in 1889. She too was exiled to Zurich and later moved to Germany where she joined the leadership of the working class movement. She returned to Poland and organized the Polish Socialist party modeled after Lenin's Bolshevik party. She spent time in a Warsaw prison for revolutionary activity. Back in Germany her support for revolutionary tactics isolated her from the rest of the party.

The ideas presented here demonstrate the variety of perspectives Marx's theories gave birth to, even while he was still alive. Bernstein and Kautsky both significantly revised many of Marx's theories, including operating within the existing capitalist state structure. On the other hand, the revolutionary Rosa Luxemburg spent a good deal of time on the issue of imperialism and with capitalism's role in the international economy. Many of her views about imperialism and revolutionary tactics are reflected in the writings of Lenin, who just a short time later was to apply many of the principles of Marxism to the situation in Russia.

MARX AND STRUCTURALISM

So far, we have just scratched the surface of Marx and Marxism, and a deeper analysis of his work and its influence lies well beyond the scope of this text.[14] Let us pause, then, and briefly attempt to restate Marx in a way that will help us in later sections.

Marx's analysis finds a home under the general heading of *structuralism* (or perhaps *economic structuralism*) because he views the economic structure to be the strongest single influence on society.[15] Marx focused on the *production* structure inherent in capitalism, seeing in it a dynamic that produces classes, leads to class struggle, and generates crises that lead to revolution and the next stage in history. For Marx, it is the structure that dominates events, more so than ideas, nature, or military generals. Marx saw people trapped in a production structure that shaped them and that they could change only by acting collectively and heroically.

Marx, then, sees IPE in terms of class exploitation driven by market forces. Where is the state in Marx's view? Where the state is a powerful force to mercantilists, and a dangerous force to liberals, to Marx it is *not* an *independent* force. In Marx's view, the state and the bourgeoisie are intertwined to such an extent that two cannot be separated. The state exists to support and defend the interests of the dominant class of capitalist bourgeois owners.

LENIN AND IMPERIALISM

V. I. Lenin (1870–1924) is best known for his role in the Russian Revolution of 1917 and the founding of the Soviet Union. Lenin symbolized for many people the principles and ideas of the 1917 Revolution. In fact, in many ways, Lenin turned Marx on his head by placing politics over economics when he argued that Russia had gone through its capitalist stage of history and was ready for a second, socialist revolution.

Here we focus on Lenin's ideas about imperialism more than on his revolutionary strategies. Lenin developed a perspective on IPE that took Marx's class struggle, based on the mode of production, and used it to explain capitalism's international effects as transmitted through the production and finance structures of rich industrial countries to the poorer developing regions of the world. Lenin's famous summary of his views is *Imperialism: The Highest Stage of Capitalism* (1917).[16]

Marx said that capitalism, driven by its three laws, would come to revolutionary crisis and suffer internal class revolt, paving the way for the transition to socialism. Lenin observed that capitalist nations had avoided this crisis by *expanding* the pool of workers they exploited. Capitalism, he argued, "had escaped its three laws of motion through overseas imperialism. The acquisition of colonies had enabled the capitalist economies to dispose of their unconsumed goods, to acquire cheap resources, and to vent their surplus capital."[17]

In short, Lenin added to Marx what Robert Gilpin has called a "fourth law" of capitalism, which we might call the *law of capitalist imperialism*: "as capitalist economies mature, as capital accumulates, and as profit rates fall, the capitalist economies are compelled to seize colonies and create dependencies to serve as markets, investment outlets, and sources of food and raw materials. In competition with one another, they divide up the colonial world in accordance with their relative strengths."[18]

To Lenin, imperialism is another portion of the capitalist epoch of history (referred to as the highest stage of capitalism) that the world must endure on the road to communism. According to Lenin; "Monopoly is the transition from capitalism to a higher system."[19]

The critical element fueling imperialism, according to Lenin, was the decline of national economic competition and the growth of monopolies. Based on Marx's law of concentration, what emerged was an aggregation of market power into the hands of a few "cartels, syndicates and trusts, and merging with them, the capital of a dozen or so banks manipulating thousands of millions." Lenin goes on to argue that

> Monopoly is exactly the opposite of free competition; but we have seen the latter being transformed into monopoly before our very eyes, creating large-scale industry and eliminating small industry, replacing large-scale industry by still larger-scale industry, finally leading to such a concentration of production and capital that monopoly has been and is the result.[20]

The key for Lenin was that because monopolies concentrated capital, they could not find sufficient investment opportunities in industrial regions of the world. They therefore found it necessary to export capital around the globe to earn sufficient profits.

Lenin argued that imperialist expansion allowed capitalism to postpone its inevitable crisis and metamorphosis into socialism. It also created new, serious problems for the world. Lenin viewed World War I as an imperialist war, caused by tensions that arose from the simultaneous expansion of several European empires. As nations at the core of capitalism competed to expand their exploitative sphere, their interests intersected and conflicted with one another, producing the Great War.

Lenin's role in the Revolution of 1917 was to help defeat liberal political forces that sought to keep Russia within the European capitalist system. Under Lenin's leadership, Russia essentially withdrew from Europe and its imperialist conflicts, and resolved to move quickly and on its own toward a communist system free of class conflict and imperialist wars.

LENIN AND INTERNATIONAL CAPITALISM

Lenin's imperialist theory of capitalism has been very influential, so it is worthwhile briefly considering a few other aspects of his analysis. Lenin sought to explain how it was that capitalism shifted from internal to international exploitation, and how the inequality among classes had as its parallel the law of uneven development among nations.

For Lenin, profit-seeking capitalists could not be expected to use surplus capital to improve the living standards of the proletariat. Therefore, capitalist societies would remain unevenly developed ones, with some classes prospering as others were mired in poverty. The imperial phase of capitalism simply transferred this duality of wealth and poverty onto the world stage, as capitalists, seeking to maintain and even increase their profits, exported what contemporaries of Lenin called "backward" regions of the world. These poor peripheral countries were now integrated into the world economy as the new "proletariats" of the world. According to Lenin:

> Monopolist capitalist combines—cartels, syndicates, trusts—divide among themselves, first of all, the whole internal market of a country, and impose their control, more or less completely, upon the industry of that country. But under capitalism the home market is inevitably bound up with the foreign market. Capitalism long ago created a world market.[21]

The uneven development of society within a nation now took place on an international scale.

Lenin saw imperial capitalism spreading through two structures of the IPE: production and finance. Both of these structures were, under capitalism, so constituted as to create dependency and facilitate exploitation. Cutthroat competition among poorer nations made them easy targets for monopolies in the production structure in the capitalist core. The same forces were at work within the finance structure, where the superabundance of finance capital, controlled by monopolistic banks, was used to exploit less developed countries.

The bottom line of imperialism, for Lenin, was that the rich capitalist nations were able to delay their final crisis by keeping the poorer nations underdeveloped and deep in debt, and dependent on them for manufactured goods, jobs, and financial resources. It is not surprising, then, that Lenin's theory of imperialism has been very influential, especially among intellectuals in the less developed countries, where his views have shaped policy and attitudes toward international trade and finance generally.

We include Lenin's imperialism under the general heading of "structuralism," as we did with Marx's theories, because its analysis is based on the assumption that it is in capitalism's nature for the finance and production structures among nations to be biased in favor of the owners of capital. While, in theory, the relationship between capital-abundant nations and capital-scarce nations should be one of *interdependence*, since each needs the other for maximum growth, in practice the result is *dependence*, exploitation, and uneven development. The same forces that drive the bourgeoisie to exploit the proletariat ultimately drive the capitalist core nations to dominate and exploit less developed countries.

No attempt to consider the IPE of North-South relations is complete without taking imperialism's perspective into account. To some extent, Lenin's ideas are the basis of the theories of dependency and of the modern world system, to which we will shortly turn.

OTHER ASPECTS OF THE STRUCTURALIST PERSPECTIVE

The fundamental notion of structuralism is that economic structure heavily influences the distribution of wealth and power. According to this viewpoint, institutions associated with global capitalism are inherently biased in favor of the dominant

---

CASE STUDY: NAFTA AND THE MAQUILADORIZATION OF MEXICO

The political economy of U.S.-Mexico relations has long been controversial. These two countries share more than just a long border: they also have history, economic interests, and mutual suspicions in common. Closer political and economic relations between the U.S. and Mexico have been talked about for years, but it was only in the 1980s that any real progress was made in bringing the two nations closer together. The North American Free Trade Agreement (NAFTA) is, in this respect, a signal achievement. NAFTA, if fully implemented, will serve to unite in many ways the economies of Canada, the United States, and Mexico. In theory, goods and services will be free to move all around this massive market just as if there were no national borders.

Structuralists are concerned that closer links between the U.S. and Mexico will serve to systematically underdevelop the Mexican economy, making it even more dependent on the U.S. for trade, finance, knowledge, and security. One aspect of the NAFTA debate in Mexico, therefore, has concerned the possible *maquiladorization* of Mexico through NAFTA.

Maquiladoras are a distinct aspect of the U.S.-Mexican production structure. This term is used to refer to special manufacturing plants, generally located close to the U.S.-Mexico border. These factories can import duty-free parts, semi-finished goods, and other items from the U.S. These are then finished or assembled by lower-wage Mexican workers and freely re-exported to the U.S. market.

In the United States, maquiladoras are seen by some workers as a threat to their jobs. They worry that they will be unable to compete with low-wage Mexican assembly-line workers.

In Mexico, the worry is different. Those who fear the maquiladorization of Mexico see these factories as a tool of dependency. While these businesses use low-skilled Mexican labor, they do not provide much training or education. The higher-skilled jobs remain in the United States for the most part, they say. In addition, the maquiladora division of labor is structured so that most capital investment and the greatest technological resources are located in U.S. markets.

Mexican critics believe that NAFTA will produce a maquiladora economy throughout Mexico, with low wages, low technology, and little chance for advancement. Proponents of NAFTA, on the other hand, see the maquiladoras as the first steps toward modern industrialization, with the improved technologies and rising incomes this would bring. They see the past problems of the maquiladoras as the temporary costs associated with industrialization.

How will NAFTA affect the U.S. and Mexico? Structuralists tend to think that NAFTA will benefit the U.S. and increase Mexican dependency on its northern neighbor. This view contrasts sharply with the liberal view that NAFTA will benefit both nations through greater mutually advantageous interaction. A mercantilist, however, would be suspicious of both sides; free trade could weaken the U.S., but it could also weaken Mexico, depending on how NAFTA changes each nation's cycle of wealth and power.

For an interesting discussion of this issue, see *The Political Economy of North American Free Trade*, edited by Ricardo Grinspun and Maxwell A. Cameron (New York: St. Martin's Press, 1993). Special notice should be taken of "The Maquiladorisation of the Mexican Economy" by Kathryn Kopinak, pages 141–162.

---

powers, creating a web of dependency that mirrors, in some ways, the relationship of nineteenth century mother countries to their colonial possessions.

Marx focused on the biases inherent in the production structure under capitalism that caused the bourgeoisie to exploit the proletariat. Lenin expanded this point of view to take into account exploitation of the structure of international finance and ways in which exploitation is transmitted internationally through imperialism. Other structuralists have continued along this line of reasoning, exploring the biased character of the security structure and the knowledge structure.

Structuralists argue that security structures linking rich countries with poorer ones are another aspect of imperialism. The security links between the Soviet Union and its Warsaw Pact allies prior to 1989 are one example. The Communist governments of East Germany and Hungary were dependent on Moscow for security, a fact that Soviet leaders used to systematically exploit the citizens of these countries. Structuralists argue, as well, that LDC regimes that are dependent on the United States for security create a structure that fosters exploitation.

From the structuralist perspective, imperialist exploitation also works through the knowledge structure. Capitalist countries control access to technology, which they use to their own advantage. Less developed countries tend to acquire low-end technology, which limits their productivity and growth, while factories in the capitalist core states retain the most advanced technology, which gives them a monopoly in the most valuable products. Because LDCs rarely get advanced technology, they rarely acquire the resources they need to advance further. They remain dependent on others for technology and so are unable to break the ties that exploit them.

This perspective, then, sees systematic exploitation and imperialism in each of the four IPE structures: production, finance, security, and knowledge. A nation's place in the world thus depends on its access to production capital, finance capital, security resources, and technological advances. Given the biases in these structures, there is little that a nation can do to alter its global status.

MODERN WORLD SYSTEM THEORY

The structuralist perspective has many variants in the modern world. These different viewpoints share the basic idea that the structure of the global economy strongly influences the IPE. Beyond this, however, they differ in many important ways.

One fascinating contemporary variant of the structuralist perspective focuses on the way in which the global system has developed since the middle of the fifteenth century. This is the *modern world system* (MWS) theory[22] originated by Immanuel Wallerstein and developed by a number of scholars, including Christopher Chase-Dunn. Capitalist in nature, the world system largely determines political and social relations, both within and between nations and other international entities.

For Wallerstein, the world economy provides the sole means of organization in the international system. The modern world system exhibits the following characteristics: a single division of labor whereby nation-states are mutually dependent upon economic exchange; the sale of products and goods for the sake of profit; and, finally, the division of the world into three functional areas or socioeconomic units, which correspond to the role nations within these regions play in the international economy.

From the MWS perspective the capitalist *core* states of northwest Europe in the sixteenth century moved beyond agricultural specialization to higher-skilled industries and modes of production by penetrating and absorbing other regions into the capitalist world economy. Through this process, Eastern Europe became the agricultural *periphery* and exported grains, bullion, wood, cotton, and sugar to the core. Mediterranean Europe and its labor-intensive industries became the *semi-periphery* or intermediary between the core and periphery.

It would be easy to define the core, periphery, and semi-periphery in terms of the types of nations within each group (such as the U.S., China, and Korea, respectively), but the MWS is not based primarily on the nation-state. In this theory, the core represents a geographic region made up of nation-states that play a partial role in the modern world system. The force of bourgeoisie interests actually exists, in varying degrees, in every country. Every nation has elements of core, periphery, and semi-periphery, although not equally so. In common with Marx, then, the MWS theory looks at IPE in terms of class relations and patterns of exploitation.

According to Wallerstein, the core states dominate the peripheral states through unequal exchange for the purpose of extracting cheap raw materials instead of, as Lenin argued, merely using the periphery as a market for dumping surplus production. The core interacts with the semi-periphery and periphery through the global structure of capitalism, exploiting these regions but also transforming them. The semi-periphery serves more of a political than an economic role; it is both exploited and exploiter, diffusing opposition of the periphery to the core region.

Interestingly, on some issues, Wallerstein attempts to bridge mercantilism (and political realism) with Marxist views about the relationship of politics to economics. For instance, as a mercantilist would, he accepts the notion that the world is politically arranged in an anarchical manner, i.e., there is no *single* sovereign political authority to govern interstate relations. However, much like a Marxist-Leninist, he proposes that power politics and social differences are also conditioned by the capitalist structure of the world economy.

According to Wallerstein, capitalists within core nation-states use state authority as an instrument to maximize individual profit. Historically, the state served economic interests to the extent that "state machineries of the core states were strengthened to meet the needs of capitalist landowners and their merchant allies."[23] Also Wallerstein argues that "once created," state machineries, have a certain amount of autonomy.[24] On the other hand, politics is constrained by economic structure. He asserts, for instance, that strong (core) states dominate weak (peripheral) ones because placement of the nation-state in the world capitalist system affects its ability to influence its global role. As Wallerstein puts it; "The functioning then of a capitalist world-economy requires that groups pursue their economic interests within a single world market while seeking to distort this market for their benefit by organizing to exert influence on states, some of which are far more powerful than others but none of which controls the world-market in its entirety."[25]

Wallerstein's conception of the modern world system has gained a good deal of notoriety in the last twenty years. He offers us a recipe of ideas and concepts that are relatively easy to understand and that account for a large part of the relationship of Northern developed to Southern developing nations. "Semi-periphery" also seems to fit the status of the newly industrialized countries (NICs). Furthermore, the MWS approach to structuralism sees exploitation as an inherent element of the capitalist structures both within and among core, periphery, and semi-periphery.

One thing that is problematic about Wallerstein's views is precisely what makes them so attractive: his comprehensive yet almost simple way of characterizing IPE. Many criticize his theory for being too deterministic, both economically and in terms of the constraining effects of the *global* capitalist system. Nation-states are not free to choose courses of action or policies. Instead, they are relegated to playing economically determined roles. Finally, Wallerstein is faulted for viewing capitalism as the end-product of current history.

DEPENDENCY THEORY

Another contemporary variant of the structuralist perspective is called *dependency theory*. A wide range of views can be grouped together under this heading. Their differences, however, are less important to us here than what they have in common, which is the view that the structure of the global political economy essentially enslaves the less developed countries of the "South" by making them dependent on the nations of the capitalist core of the "North."[26] Theotonio Dos Santos has written:

> By dependence we mean a situation in which the economy of certain countries is conditioned by the development and expansion of another economy to which the former is subjected. The relation of interdependence between two or more economics, and between these and world trade, assumes the form of dependence when some countries (the dominant ones) can expand and can be self-sustaining, while others (the dependent ones) can do this only as a reflection of that expansion, which can have either a positive or a negative effect on their immediate development.[27]

Dos Santos sees three eras of dependence in modern history: colonial dependence (during the eighteenth and nineteenth centuries), financial-industrial dependence (during the nineteenth and early twentieth centuries), and a structure of dependence today based on the postwar multinational corporations.

One dependency theorist in particular has focused a good deal of attention on the effects of imperialism in Latin America. Andre Gunder Frank rejects the Marxist notion that societies go through different stages or modes of production as they develop. However, he supports the imperialism thesis that connections between developed and developing regions of the world resulted in exploitation of peripheral regions by metropolitan capitalist countries.

Frank is noted for his "development of underdevelopment" thesis. He argues that developing nations never were "underdeveloped" in the sense that one might think of them as "backward" or traditional societies. Instead, once great civilizations in their own right, the developing regions of the world *became* underdeveloped as a result of their colonization by the Western industrialized nations. Along with exploitation, imperialism produced underdevelopment: "historical research demonstrates that contemporary underdevelopment is in large part the historical product of past and continuing economic and other relations between the satellite underdeveloped and the now developed metropolitan countries."[28]

How are developing nations to develop if in fact they are exploited by the developed capitalist industrial powers? Dependency theorists have suggested a variety of responses to this trap. A number of researchers—for example, Andre Gunder Frank—have called for peripheral nations to withdraw from the global political economy. In the 1950s and 1960s, the leadership of many socialist movements in the third world favored revolutionary tactics and ideological mass movements to change not only the fundamental dynamic of both the political and economic order of their society, but also the world capitalist system.

More recently, dependency theorists have recommended a variety of other strategies and policies by which developing nations could industrialize and develop. Raul Prebisch, an Argentinean economist, was instrumental in founding, under the auspices of the United Nations, the United Nations Committee on Trade and Development (UNCTAD). The developing nations who have joined this body within the UN have made it their goal to monitor and recommend policies that would, in effect, help redistribute power and income between Northern developed and Southern developing countries. These and other dependency theorists, however, have been more aggressive about reforming the international economy and have supported the calls for a New International Economic Order (NIEO) which gained momentum shortly after the OPEC oil price hike in 1973.

The important point to make here is that dependency theories have served as part of a critique of the relationship of the metropolitan to satellite, or core to peripheral, nations. Whether or not that relationship can—or even should—be equalized is a matter developed elsewhere. These theories will be important to our discussion of "The Development Dilemma" in chapter 15.

STRUCTURALISM IN PERSPECTIVE

To an important extent, the twentieth century has been defined by the political, economic, and intellectual forces of economic nationalism, liberalism, and structuralism. Structuralism has had a profound influence on world events in this period.

In Russia, Joseph Stalin implemented the ruthless and rigid system of centralized political and economic control in an attempt to achieve a transition to communism without the necessary intermediate steps of capitalism, imperialism, and socialism. In China, Mao Zedong led a revolt and fashioned another communist state within a completely different cultural context. In Cuba, Fidel Castro has created a communist state that in most respects is cut off from the global economy, in an attempt to avoid the dependency dilemma. Structuralist views are influential in all regions of the world, perhaps especially in Latin America.

The fact that so much of the world's population has been governed by leaders who have been influenced by structuralism demonstrates the importance of this perspective. The tension between the forces of national interest, self-interest, and class-based dependency are fundamental to the world and to political economy.

This chapter began with Marx and ended with Dos Santos. What ties these writers together and links them with the many authors and ideas that came in between? The tie that binds here is the notion that the different structures of the IPE do not benefit everyone, as liberals believe, nor are they tools that enable, or tools that enhance state power, as mercantilists believe. Rather, the structuralist perspective holds that in the system of global capitalism that dominates the world today, these structures are systematically and inherently biased in favor of certain classes of individuals and nations; the Marx-Lenin laws of capitalism tend to hold on at a global level.

Some people ask if studying structuralism in the postcommunist era is worthwhile. The answer is yes, as the Chiapas Awakening of 1994 makes clear. The structuralist perspective encompasses far more than the Soviet model of communism. This perspective on IPE is revealing and represents a powerful intellectual and political influence.

DISCUSSION QUESTIONS

1. After reading the chapter compare and contrast structuralism with mercantilism and liberalism in the following areas:
   a. the dominant actors
   b. political versus economic motivation behind actor behavior
   c. the role of the state in the economy
2. How did Marx's and Lenin's views shape those of structuralism? Be specific and give examples from the reading.
3. Outline the essential characteristics/features of Marxism, dependency theory, and the modern world system approach.
4. Employing a structuralist approach, outline the significant changes that have occurred in the relationship of the Northern industrialized nations to the Southern developing countries since the late 1960s.

SUGGESTED READINGS

Anthony Brewer. *Marxist Theories of Imperialism: A Critical Survey*, 2nd ed. New York: Routledge, 1990.

Christopher Chase-Dunn. *Global Formation: Structures of the World Economy*. Cambridge MA: Basil Blackwell, 1989.

Benjamin J. Cohen. *The Question of Imperialism*. New York: Basic Books, 1973.

Theotonio Dos Santos. "The Structure of Dependency." In George T. Crane and Abla Amawi, eds., *The Theoretical Evolution of International Political Economy*. New York: Oxford University Press, 1990.

John Kenneth Galbraith. Especially chapter 11, in *Economics in Perspective*. Boston: Houghton-Mifflin, 1987.

Robert Gilpin. *The Political Economy of International Relations*. Princeton, NJ: Princeton University Press, 1987.

V. I. Lenin. *Imperialism: The Highest Stage of Capitalism*. New York: International Publishers, 1939.

Karl Marx. *Capital*, Friedrich Engels, ed. Chicago: Encyclopedia Britannica, 1952.

Karl Marx and Friedrich Engels. *The Communist Manifesto*. New York: Washington Square Press, 1965.

Joan Robinson. "Trade in Primary Commodities." In Jeffry A. Frieden and David A. Lake, eds. *International Political Economy: Perspectives on Global Power and Wealth*, 2nd ed. New York: St. Martin's Press, 1991.

NOTES

1. Karl Marx and Friedrich Engels, *The Communist Manifesto*, Samuel Beer, ed., (New York: Appleton-Century-Crofts, 1955), 9.
2. V. I. Lenin, *Imperialism: The Highest Stage of Capitalism* (New York: International Publishers Co., 1939).
3. Joan Robinson, "Trade in Primary Commodities," in Jeffrey A. Frieden and David A. Lake, eds., *International Political Economy*, 2nd ed. (New York: St Martin's Press, 1991), 376.
4. For a discussion of Marx's methodology, see Todd G. Buchholz, *New Ideas from Dead Economists* (New York: New American Library, 1989), 113–120.
5. Karl Marx, *The Poverty of Philosophy* (New York: International Publishers, 1963), 122.
6. John Kenneth Galbraith, *Economics in Perspective* (Boston: Houghton-Mifflin, 1987), 133.
7. Buchholz, *New Ideas from Dead Economists*, 115.
8. Marx and Engels, *The Communist Manifesto*, p. 17.
9. Ibid., 22.
10. Ibid., 12
11. Ibid., 13–14
12. See the comments by Václav Havel regarding the "cult of the market" in chapter 3 for an indication of this viewpoint.
13. A more analytical definition of disproportionality and its place in Marx's theory can be found in Paul M. Sweezy, *The Theory of Capitalist Development* (New York: Monthly Review Press, 1970), ch. 5.
14. See the suggested readings on Marx and Marxism at the end of this chapter.
15. We have used the term *structuralism* in a general sense here. At a more advanced level, "economic structuralism" is differentiated from "political structuralism." In economic structuralism, it is the structure of economic relations that most influences society. In political structuralism, it is the structure of political power that is most influential.
16. Lenin, *Imperialism*.
17. Robert Gilpin, *The Political Economy of International Relations* (Princeton, NJ: Princeton University Press, 1987), 38.
18. Ibid., 39.
19. Lenin argues that "this is a new stage of world concentration of capital and production, incomparably higher than the preceding stages." Lenin, *Imperialism*, 68.
20. Ibid., 88.
21. Ibid., 68.
22. Immanuel Wallerstein, "The Rise and Future Demise of the World Capitalist System: Concepts for Comparative Analysis," *Comparative Studies in Society and History*, 16 (September 1974): 387–415.
23. Ibid., 402.
24. Ibid.
25. Ibid., 406.
26. Dependency theory is thus seen as an interpretation of North-South IPE relations.
27. Theotonio Dos Santos, "The Structure of Dependence," *American Economic Review* 60 (1970): 231–236.
28. Andre Gunder Frank, *Capitalism and Underdevelopment in Latin America: Historical Studies of Chile and Brazil* (New York: Monthly Review Press, 1967), 9.

5

The Rational Choice Approach to IPE

Professor Elizabeth Nunn

OVERVIEW

This chapter introduces an analytical method that helps political economists understand problems, issues, and events in international political economy. This method is called the *rational choice* approach to IPE because it focuses on individual actors and the choices that they make. This approach was originally developed by economists, who sought to apply their analytical models to questions that had traditionally been considered only by political scientists. Now rational choice theory is used by many scholars throughout the social sciences.

Thus far, our discussion of IPE has characterized state actions as reflecting some national interest while markets embody the choices made by self-interested individuals. Governments choose policies to promote this "national interest." But how does a government enact policies? Governments are made up of people, and these people make the choices and are the acting agents for this government. Thus, individuals make decisions in markets and individuals make decisions in government for the state. This raises the question: what is the difference between individuals acting in their self-interest in markets and their actions in government?

Rational choice theory says there is no difference. Individuals make decisions in order to make themselves better off. In the economic realm of markets, "better off" is easily translated into more income or wealth (for individuals) and more profit (for firms). In the realm of government, "better off" is much more ambiguous. We begin by identifying the objectives of individuals acting for government and attempt to clarify what would make these individuals "better off." With this foundation, we can then explain the interaction between nations and the friction between states and markets from the perspective of individuals attempting to serve their own interests.

The rational choice perspective adds a unique dimension to IPE by focusing on individuals in the state and the genesis of government decision making. In economic lingo, rational choice provides the "micro" foundations for the more aggregate, "macro" IPE theories of mercantilism, liberalism, and structuralism.

The proprietors of land were anciently the legislators of every part of Europe. The laws relating to land, therefore, were all calculated for what they supposed the interest of the proprietor.[1]

Adam Smith

Adam Smith knew that economic interests affected political decisions. Over two hundred years ago, as this passage from *The Wealth of Nations* shows, he acknowledged the market's influence on the legislator's decisions. Smith's legislators might have been public-minded citizens, but when it came to laws relating to land, they voted their self-interest, not the public interest. The idea that we can understand public choices by looking at the self-interests of those who make public policy is thus an old idea, but an important one. This chapter introduces a method of analysis called *rational choice theory* that helps us understand many problems, issues, and events in IPE by focusing on the choices made by self-interested individuals, especially those involved in making government policies.

Rational choice theory provides a model of government that focuses on individuals and the factors influencing their decision making. Using methods traditionally associated with economics, the decision-making behavior of public officials is modeled as the problem of maximizing self-interest subject to a number of constraints. That is, public officials make choices regarding government policy, laws, and regulations in order to make themselves personally better off. Their choices are limited or constrained by the rules of government, their access to information, and their own uncertainty about the future.

RATIONAL CHOICE THEORY VS. PHILOSOPHICAL PERSPECTIVES

How does rational choice theory fit into the framework of IPE discussed in the first chapters of this book? The rational choice approach is a method of analysis, not a theoretical perspective. Mercantilism, liberalism, and structuralism, as developed in the last three chapters, provide three different perspectives on the interaction between state and market. Each perspective looks at state-market relations from a different point of view, focusing on different aspects and judging with a different set of values. The rational choice approach provides a method for examining the behavior of individuals under each perspective. It is then possible to identify the conditions under which mercantilist, liberal, or structuralist choices are made. Rational choice is not an alternative to the perspectives thus far presented. Rather, rational choice theory supports these three IPE perspectives with an analytical model of human behavior.

The three IPE perspectives we have studied represent *normative* theories, which means that they are based on values and lead to value judgments. Rational choice theory, on the other hand, attempts to be a *positive* theory, which observes the world and tries to develop an understanding between cause and effect. The IPE perspectives are thus more like philosophy in this regard, while rational choice theory is more like physics.[2]

THE STATE AND THE INDIVIDUAL

The rational choice model dissects the motives behind government behavior. Governments—the state—do not make decisions, people do. State actions are made by individual voters, elected representatives, or appointed bureaucrats. Hence, a better understanding of government decisions requires a better understanding of the individuals who make decisions for the state. Rational choice theory examines the behavior of these individuals using the standard tools of economic reasoning. That is, we assume that public officials are rational, self-interested persons who make choices to improve their personal well-being. These choices are constrained by the organizational structure of the government, national and international law, the limits of knowledge, and other factors. Given what they know and the limits on their choices, public officials make decisions that they perceive to be in their best interests—which may not always be in the best interests of the general population.

In this model, government laws, policies, and institutions are the result of the interaction of individuals and the political and economic environment in which they make choices. So, to understand the international political economy, we must understand not only the individuals in government and their behavior, but also the broader political market and culture that affect them. Political organization and culture most differentiates nations, leading to radically different policy choices. The institutional and organizational structure of governments and international relations is dynamic, and the differences between nations and cultures generate uncertainty and lead to different objectives for decisionmakers. Douglass C. North, 1993

Nobel laureate in economic science, describes the political economist's problem this way:

> All theorizing in the social sciences builds, implicitly or explicitly, upon conceptions of human behavior. . . . Individuals make choices based on subjectively derived models that diverge among individuals and the information the actors receive is so incomplete that in most cases these divergent subjective models show no tendency to converge. Only when we understand these modifications in the behavior of the actors can we make sense out of the existence and structure of institutions and explain the direction of institutional change.[3]

To understand human behavior in the international political economy requires an understanding not just of the people who make decisions, but also their political environment, their information and its sources, and their cultural perspective. The rational choice approach provides a method with which to begin this analysis.

We begin our description of rational choice theory with a brief discussion of individual rational behavior and its implications for trade and market equilibrium. We then apply these ideas to the political arena in general, and IPE specifically. Following the theory, we analyze the behavior of U.S. members of Congress during the North American Free Trade Agreement (NAFTA) debate using the rational choice method. In the remaining sections, we integrate rational choice theory with mercantilism, liberalism, and structuralism. By modeling the source of government choices—that is, the behavior of individuals in the public sector—we have a more complete understanding of government actions and government reactions to changes in the international arena.

RATIONAL CHOICE AND HUMAN BEHAVIOR

The primary tenet of the rational choice approach is that individuals make choices to make themselves better off—to further their self-interest. We all have to make choices because we live in a world of scarcity: we do not have endless time, energy, or income. Our options are also limited by our environment and endowments. There are rules of behavior, values, norms, laws, information, and prices that further limit our options and guide our decision making. Individuals, then, are constantly making constrained choices. What is the best way to get home, given my car, the traffic on the highways, and the 55 mile per hour speed limit? Shall I buy T-bone steaks for dinner or hamburger or fried chicken, given the ten-dollar balance in my checking account? Will upgrading our company computer system maximize our profits, now or in the future? In each of these situations, individuals must make a choice subject to the constraints they face.

Economics applies this theory to consumer and producer behavior in the marketplace. Buyers maximize their happiness by purchasing items that give them the most benefit subject to the constraints of the item's cost and the buyer's income. Sellers, on the other hand, choose the production method and set the price and quantity of production of products in such a way as to maximize profit (revenue minus costs of production) subject to the characteristics of their product and its market, their competitors, and their predictions about the future. Applying this behavioral method to market choices has generated a rich and robust economic theory.

Rational choice applies this behavioral method to a different group of individual decisionmakers: public officials. The state, like the market, is made up of individuals, each of whom is trying to make him or herself better off. Anthony Downs, in *An Economic Theory of Democracy*, assumes "that every agent acts in accordance with this view of human nature. Thus, whenever we speak of rational behavior, we always mean rational behavior directed primarily towards selfish ends."[4] To make themselves better off, individuals in the state make self-interested choices subject to the constraints of their position, the law, their electorate, and their information.

If we want to use rational choice methods to understand the international policy choices of a government, we need to understand the behavior of the decisionmakers. The first order of business, then, is to identify the individual public official's goals. It is reasonable to assume, in this context, that individuals acting in the state try to benefit themselves in some way by serving as a public official. There are a number of ways that public service may provide private benefits. Public officials may benefit from the power they enjoy in office, from the income they receive as public employees, from knowing that they make other people better off with their service, or from the various effects of the actual laws and rules they enact while in office. Rational choice theory tries to identify the interests of individuals in the state and understand how these interests condition their behavior and, thus, affect state policies.

RATIONAL CHOICE IN THE POLITICAL MARKETPLACE

In order to benefit from public office, one must first achieve that office and then retain it. It follows that politicians, including members of Congress, the president, a city mayor, a state legislator, and a schoolboard member, make choices that help them get elected or reelected, and bureaucrats make choices that help them get reappointed. Note that the decisionmaker cannot achieve her objectives independent of other people. Citizen-voters decide who is elected or reelected. Presidents, governors, and mayors decide who is appointed to positions in the bureaucracy. Thus, public officials need to please those people who are necessary to help them reach their goal. There are three groups of people who are crucial in helping the official achieve reelection or reappointment: constituents, campaign contributors, and political parties. In the political marketplace, to use the language of economics, public officials are the "supply" of state policy and these groups—constituents, contributors, and political parties—are the "demand."

Constituents

To be reelected or reappointed, politicians and bureaucrats must serve their *primary* constituents (those individuals directly responsible for election or appointment decisions). A politician's primary constituents are the citizen-voters in her district. A bureaucrat's primary constituent is the individual (president, governor, or congressperson) who appointed her. These constituents are directly affected by the laws and rules established by public officials. Consequently, we would expect politicians to support laws and bureaucrats to enact and enforce rules that make her constituents happy. Just as we expect Nabisco to produce cookies that consumers like to eat and purchase again and again, government representatives who want to be elected or appointed again and again produce laws and rules that their primary constituents support.

Constituents do not base their electoral choice only on the laws adopted by their representatives.[5] During their tenure in office, public officials vote on hundreds of proposed laws. Many have little effect on the representative's constituency, and those laws that do affect the constituents are often sufficiently complicated to make determining the costs and benefits of such laws difficult. It is quite costly for an individual citizen to gather all the information on an elected official's public career and then translate that information into personal benefits and costs. Thus, citizens vote based on the information they hear (on radio or TV) or read (in newspapers or direct mailings) and according to a representative's affiliation with a political party. Political parties offer a convenient "brand name" for politicians to associate with, thus providing information to voters. In these cases, candidates do not need to serve their constituents through their public decision making. Rather, they can generate reelection votes through advertising or by affiliating with a preferred political party.

Campaign Contributors

Politicians collect money for campaign expenses from contributing special interest groups. These special interest groups may be groups of firms in an industry (like the Semiconductor Industry Association), a group of individuals with similar economic interests (like the AFL-CIO labor union), or a group of individuals with similar ideological interests (like the Sierra Club). The money donated by these contributors can be used during the politician's election campaign for flyers, advertising, and public events. This money is particularly important in modern elections, where the costs to voters of gathering information on candidates and the costs to politicians of distributing information is quite high. Statistical analysis of voting has shown that the more money spent by a candidate, the more likely he or she is to win the election.[6] This suggests that politicians often support and enact laws lobbied for by these special interest groups.

Political Parties

Politicians also vote for the policy positions espoused by the political party with which they affiliate. In most situations, this support corresponds with the first motivation of representing and pleasing constituents. In addition, political parties provide campaign funds for members and help coordinate election campaigns. Once in office, a politician can rely on party bonds to provide political allies, improving chances to pass laws favorable to constituents.

BRITAIN'S CORN LAWS: RATIONAL CHOICES IN THE NINETEENTH CENTURY

The Corn Laws approved by Britain's lawmakers in 1815 extended protective tariffs on imported bread grains, thereby increasing the price of domestic grains and increasing the profits to Britain's landowners and farmers. British lawmakers themselves had much to gain from such protection. Landed interests were strongly represented in Parliament. The landed aristocracy made up the vast majority of the House of Lords. Landowners also influenced the composition of the House of Commons through "proprietary rights of nomination and virtually irresistable influence."[7] It was certainly in their best interest to increase the value of the product of their land by raising the price of imported competition.

In 1846, the Corn Laws were repealed. What prompted this change of heart? During the intervening thirty years, industrial interests in Parliament fought against the landed interests to reduce or repeal these tariffs and to gain political influence, but were unsuccessful. Industrialists were threatened by the preferential treatment given to agriculture and the negative impact of protectionism on the foreign and domestic markets they were trying to develop. A number of young Manchester industrialists formed the Anti-Corn Law League in 1839. They "mounted a strong and effective campaign to influence public opinion."[8] This battle between industrialists and landowners drew the attention of the minority political party, the Whigs. The Whig party used the popular sentiment against the Corn Laws in its 1842 election campaign against the Tory party, which continued to support landed interests and the Corn Laws.

When the Tories won the election, the Corn Laws seemed secure. But Tory Prime Minister Sir Robert Peel was from the class of young industrialists. In 1845, disaster struck the Empire with the Irish potato blight. With thousands starving, Peel ignored his party's position and introduced a bill to repeal the Corn Laws, which would increase the availability and decrease the price of bread. With the support of most Whig members of Parliament, the bill passed in January 1846. This vote shifted political power in Britain from the landowners to the industrialists.

Repealing the Corn Laws provided great political benefits to Whig—soon renamed Liberal—politicians. Acting as the party of free trade and manufacturers that represented the new middle class, the Liberals differentiated themselves from the unpopular, landed nobility, thus increasing their own political influence. By identifying and serving the emerging economic interests in Britain, the Liberals secured power for over thirty years.

PRIVATE INTERESTS AND THE NATIONAL INTEREST

We expect politicians to pass bills that serve their constituents, contributing special interest groups, and their political party. But remember, reelection is not the primary goal. Public officials desire reelection or reappointment so that they may enjoy the many benefits of public office. There are many ways that a public official can gain benefits from state actions. Politicians may enact laws that protect their own economic or political interests, like the legislators Adam Smith wrote about. Examples abound of politicians voting to raise their own salaries, increasing the perquisites of public office, and changing electoral boundaries to increase their chances of reelection. Bureaucrats increase the benefits from their position by expanding their budgets, staff, and personal authority. But not all attempts to increase the benefits from office contradict the interests of the electorate.

Public officials may also enact laws and rules that meet their personal ideological preferences. Personal ideology simply refers to the laws and rules the public official believes are best for society, not necessarily what is best personally or for her constituents. For instance, a legislator may not receive campaign contributions from the Sierra Club or represent constituents in favor of natural resource protection, yet she may support a natural resource protection bill because she, personally, believes in it. A politician or bureaucrat may have personal beliefs on human rights, defense, immigration law, nuclear power, abortion rights, states' rights, international trade, world peace, and a myriad of other issues that affects how she votes on bills or the rules she enforces.

In other words, the rational choice method acknowledges that public officials often act to further their vision of the "national interest." But what does it mean for a public official to make a decision in the "national interest"? National interest, like "nation" itself, is not a clearly defined concept. One person could define the national interest as increasing the wealth and efficiency of the economy overall. National interest in this context would involve stabilizing prices, lowering unemployment, a more equitable distribution of income, and increasing national production and growth. These benefits are distributed among the nation's population, raising the general standard of living.

In other international policy situations, the "national interest" might refer to political alliances or military protection. A public official may believe that the citizens of the nation benefit from maintaining a political alliance with another country. This may be in the national interest for strategic or national security reasons, even if economic goals are sacrificed in the process. In other situations, public officials may perceive the national interest as living up to some ideals or values.

The idea that political choices are motivated by an individual's personal interests and her perception of the national interest adds realistic complexity to the rational choice theory of government decision making. More individual and government choices can be understood when these motivations are combined with the reelection motivations discussed above. Yet this also requires more information about the individuals—a level of information that is often unavailable and is subject to a variety of interpretations.

The daily experiences, cultural environment, and intellectual development of the public official determines her personal beliefs, for instance, or her conception of the national interest, and the specific benefits she perceives from her public office. This suggests that the decision-making behavior of public officials is *path dependent*—that is, that "the process by which we arrive at today's institutions (or choices) is relevant and constrains future choices."[9] In other words, history matters. A complete understanding of political behavior, then, requires a complete understanding of the individual, the environment in which she makes a decision, and the events that have led to this decision.

To sum up, politicians and bureaucrats make choices to increase the benefits they receive from their office. Their policy decisions may yield personal economic benefits, personal political benefits, ideological benefits, national economic benefits, or national political benefits.[10] To garner these benefits, public officials serve constituents, contributing special interests, party, self, and the nation. The priority that an individual gives these objectives depends on the individual. As long as such choices are perceived by the individual as increasing her well-being, be it economic, spiritual, ideological, or emotional, then the individual chooses rationally. Applying this approach to those in charge of international relations across nations should help us understand the course of international events.

RENT-SEEKING

Firms influence international policy through their associations with politicians. Trade policy, in particular, can be used to benefit individual firms or industries by protecting their markets, reducing their costs of production, and reducing competition. Firms can "encourage" politicians to support market-protecting tariffs or cost-reducing subsidies, for instance, by contributing to political campaign funds. Firms are willing to contribute because the policies would increase their profits. This behavior is termed *rent-seeking*.

In the language of economics, a *rent* is a financial return that derives from the scarcity of a resource. Actors and athletes, for example, earn high incomes in part because their talents are scarce or unique. Some business executives earn rent because they occupy a unique position within the hierarchy of the firm. Rent-seeking behavior attempts to create an artificial scarcity through government action for the purpose of earning higher returns. Rent-seeking is often associated with firms lobbying for policies that would secure for them monopoly power in their market. It also describes any firm seeking an increase in its profits through government intervention.

The logic is simple. If the owners of a firm or leaders in an industry believe they can increase their profits with a change in their nation's trade policy, they would be willing to spend up to the amount they expect their profits to increase to ensure the change. Since politicians make decisions on policy to maximize their own benefits, and they benefit from more campaign funds, they may be willing to vote for a change in the nation's trade policy in return for campaign contributions. Quid pro quo agreements are illegal under U.S. lobbying laws, yet support on bills does seem to follow campaign contributions.[11] Consider, for example, the activities of the U.S. semiconductor industry.

In 1977, the U.S. semiconductor industry established its own lobbying group, the Semiconductor Industry Association, to encourage government policies that would increase the industry's competitiveness against Japanese producers. In the 1980s, U.S. firms lost profits and market share. From 1983 to 1988, U.S. semiconductor equipment market share declined 12 percent, with "parallel declines in semiconductor production."[12] Facing shortfalls in research and development (R&D) funding, semiconductor firms needed to convince public officials that their industry needed and deserved special treatment by the government.[13] Industry pressure on public officials resulted in a number of government policies designed to protect the semiconductor industry. The Cooperative Research Act of 1984 allows American companies to conduct joint research without risking antitrust charges. The federal government also provided $500 million over five years for Sematech, a semiconductor research consortium. The most important policy was the 1986 special trade agreement with Japan, which set a target for opening Japan's market to foreign chips. When this target was not met, the U.S. levied tariffs on Japanese products.

Continued

RENT-SEEKING, *continued*

Semiconductor materials and equipment firms have gained political influence, profits, and market share through their lobbying group. Clyde Prestowitz, Jr., former U.S. chief trade negotiator with Japan, said of the Semiconductor Industry Association, "I think they've been the most effective lobbying group that I've seen. They've made a substantial contribution to changes in U.S. trade policy."[14] The trade policies with Japan halted the decline in the U.S. industry. Between 1987 and 1990, "American companies reversed a steep slide," gaining around $1 billion in sales.[15] By 1991, industry executives said Sematech had helped individual companies improve products and had led to cooperation within the industry. According to Sam Harrell, president of SEMI/Sematech, the liaison group between Sematech and equipment suppliers, "We have probably saved twenty to thirty companies that were going to go out of business."[16]

Firms in the semiconductor industry encouraged politicians to change the rules of the game using their lobbying group. By supporting politicians with campaign contributions, the firms were able to gain market share and increase their own profits. The self-interested behavior of public officials made rent-seeking work. Politicians supported the corporations in order to increase their own chances of reelection and make themselves better off. As long as politicians need campaign funds, firms who can identify benefits from changes in laws or rules can influence policy.

DOMESTIC POLICY VS. INTERNATIONAL RELATIONS

Despite the influence of national interest on a public official's choices, a decision-maker's personal political interests—including her drive for reelection—dominate other influences. The vast majority of empirical evidence suggests that public officials serve their reelection interests first.[17] International policy, however, does not always have a clear impact on citizen-voters. Constituents often do not care about the intricacies of international monetary institutions or our regulation of foreign trade. And when they do care, they often know very little about the complex implications of alternative policies, which leads them to support policies that would not make them better off.

Seldom will an individual representative be able to make herself personally better off with international trade or relations policy. Thus, constituent and personal objectives are probably not strong causal forces in determining a representative's support or opposition toward a particular international policy. Contributing special interest groups, then, have an inordinately strong influence on international policy.[18] Multinational corporations, internationally competitive industries, and organized economic groups seek and receive beneficial international policies. Lobbyists representing foreign governments also seek to influence public officials and the policies that would affect their government.[19]

Short-term economic and political interests are likely to overwhelm long-term objectives when making international policy choices. This, of course, generates inefficient policy outcomes, possibly making all interested individuals worse off in the long run. This does not mean that public officials behave irrationally. Since international and national events are so unpredictable, the benefits associated with serving long-term economic interests are less certain. Since most political agents must seek reelection or reappointment sooner rather than later, they need to please their constituents with short-run rather than long-run results. This describes much of the congressional wrangling over NAFTA, which was approved by the U.S. House of Representatives in November, 1993, with a vote of 234 to 200.

A RATIONAL CHOICE ANALYSIS OF NAFTA

NAFTA eliminates virtually all tariff and nontariff barriers to trade between the U.S., Mexico, and Canada by 1999. With few exceptions, this trade agreement allows free movement of products among the three countries. The economic and political implications of NAFTA must be considered in order to understand the voting behavior of U.S. legislators.

The immediate impact of lower tariffs on markets is straightforward. Lower costs of trade increase the quantity of imported and exported products in each nation and also lower the prices of these products. For a specific market, the lower tariffs may also lead to relocation of firms within the free market zone. That is, we expect firms to move their production operations to the location within the U.S., Mexico, or Canada that provides the lowest costs of production. This means that U.S. jobs could be lost when firms move to low-wage Mexico, for example. These economic implications generated both support and opposition to the agreement.

The lower prices and increased quantity of production benefit the people who most obviously influence a legislator's decision. Citizen-voters as well as the legislator are better off when they pay lower prices for cars, oil, lumber, wheat, and other products traded among the three nations. The downside of lower prices is that they lower the profits of producers that compete with suppliers from the other two nations. One would expect, then, that a legislator from a district with citizens who produce products in direct competition with Mexican and Canadian producers would, in the interests of her constituents, oppose the agreement. American wheat producers, for instance, argued vehemently against NAFTA on the grounds that the low price of Canadian wheat will out-compete the American product, driving wheat producers to bankruptcy. Earl Pomeroy, a representative from North Dakota, opposed the agreement because of the potential negative effects on his wheat-farming constituents.

In response to the concerns of legislators from agricultural districts, President Clinton made side-agreements to the treaty that would limit the negative impact of NAFTA on producers of beef, peanut butter, wheat, sugar, frozen concentrated orange juice, cucumbers, tomatoes, and wine. Representatives in wheat-growing regions, like Representatives Glenn English and Bill Brewster, Democrats from Oklahoma, pledged to support NAFTA after the administration agreed to negotiate with Canada to eliminate Canadian subsidies for wheat transportation and marketing.[20] Clearly, the economic interests of constituents influenced these legislators' decisions.

Supporters, like Washington State Representative Norm Dicks, saw potential economic gains to their constituents from increased trade and lower taxes on imports. Border states in the north and south where a large number of firms produce trading services, like transportation and marketing services, gain from increased trade with both nations. These economic interests explain the support for NAFTA from representatives of states where foreign trade employs many citizens.

Many House members opposed NAFTA because of the imminent competition from low-wage Mexican laborers and the detrimental effects on American laborers. In many cases, these representatives' constituents work as manufacturing laborers. Representatives Dick Gephardt of Missouri and David Bonior of Michigan, for instance, both come from districts with a significant number of workers in automobile plants. President Clinton, however, countered this position and gained support from concerned legislators by arguing that the agreement would create jobs by increasing the demand for U.S. products by the citizens of Mexico and Canada:

> There is no way any wealthy country in this world can increase jobs and incomes without increasing the number of people who buy that nation's products and services.[21]

The political interests of special interest groups and political parties also influenced voting behavior. Organized labor spoke strongly against NAFTA for a variety of reasons (see chapter 12). In turn, representatives who received campaign contributions from organized labor joined their opposition. A *New York Times* editorial on November 16, 1993, noted the large number of New York, New Jersey, and Connecticut Democrats opposed to the free trade agreement.

> Most opponents profess anxiety about NAFTA's impact on the local economy. But in private, some admit that their opposition owes more to calculations of political survival than to judgments of economic merit. Local Democrats fear the wrath of organized labor.[22]

Looking at political party interests, one would have expected President Clinton to oppose NAFTA. It was, after all, arranged by Republican President George Bush. A number of Clinton's advisors warned him of the electoral consequences of supporting an originally Republican-sponsored treaty.[23] Clinton's strong, though delayed, support of the free trade agreement split the Democratic party. Labor leaders, a strong Democratic contingent, still hold President Clinton accountable for any harm to their members as a result of the free trade agreement. They have implicitly and explicitly threatened to financially support pro-labor opponents of NAFTA supporters in future elections. Richard Gephardt and David Bonior, the House majority leader and majority whip, respectively, openly contradicted the president's assertions regarding the economic effects of NAFTA. Other Democrats remained loyal to the president. Tom Foley, House speaker, and Dan Rostenkowski, chair of the House Ways and Means Committee, pledged to support the president and NAFTA.

National interest or personal ideology influenced some legislators in their choice to support or oppose NAFTA. Representative Robert Torricelli, a New Jersey Democrat, voted against the treaty "for foreign policy reasons."[24]

In the final tally of votes, economic and political interests in favor of the treaty outweighed the opposition. Given the discussions in previous chapters, one might argue that NAFTA was evidence that liberalism best explains United States international trade policy. While, for NAFTA, this is the case, the rational choice analysis provides a deeper understanding of the source of this liberalism. Legislators did not vote for or against NAFTA because of their free trade philosophy. Rather, legislators supported or opposed NAFTA because it was the choice that best served their electoral, political, personal, and ideological interests.

THE IPE OF TARIFF POLICY

During the congressional debates over NAFTA, President Clinton pledged his support for free trade. Days later, Clinton arranged tariffs on Mexican and Canadian imports in order to win precious votes for the free trade agreement. "The president faces scathing criticism over the special-interest deals the White House hatched to secure the votes of particular lawmakers."[25] What explains this contradiction? How can Clinton support free trade, arguing its economic merits, and simultaneously organize limits on imports of Canadian wheat and reimpose tariffs on Mexican orange juice and cucumbers? Political, not economic or ideological, interests cause this apparent paradox. Consider the interests of citizen-voters and campaign contributors.

As consumers, citizen-voters are hurt by increases in tariffs. Tariffs raise the price of products, reducing the purchasing power of a consumer's income. As laborers, citizen-voters benefit from increasing tariff protection, but only when the tariffs apply to the specific industry in which they work. Such protection can raise profits and wages. Thus, general tariff increases would hurt a politician's electorate, while specific industry tariff increases may help this same electorate.

The campaign contributors most likely to care about tariff policy are business firms. Domestic producers who compete directly with foreign firms often lobby for industry-specific tariff protection. Increases in the tariffs for their industry would reduce the number of suppliers, raising the price of the product they sell. This results in higher revenue and, with no changes in costs of production, higher profits. Firms are less likely to support general tariff increases that raise the prices of all products. With prices rising, a firm can sell its products at a higher price, thus increasing revenue. But at the same time, these rising prices increase the costs of production. Rising production costs eat away at the increases in revenue, reducing or eliminating the benefits from tariff protection. A firm is best served by tariff increases in their specific industry, but tariff decreases in all other industries. General tariff increases are potentially harmful.

It is not paradoxical, then, that President Clinton would support general tariff reduction under NAFTA on one hand and industry-protecting trade policy on the other. This position generates political support from constituents and campaign-contributing firms, with minimum alienation in either group.

A RATIONAL CHOICE ANALYSIS OF GATT

Rational choice theory helps us understand why nations enact policies such as tariffs. The benefits of a tariff are highly concentrated, while the costs are highly diffused. Businesses and workers in the protected industry get most of the benefits and can afford to allocate time and money to influencing public officials. The groups who bear the costs are domestic consumers and foreign businesses. These groups have little influence on tariff legislation. It is natural for public officials to give greater weight to the welfare of domestic businesses over their foreign rivals. Consumers, who are also voters, *are* important to policymakers, but their influence on legislation such as tariffs seldom matches their numbers. The costs of a tariff in higher prices and reduced selection are high in the aggregate, but small for any individual consumer. Individual consumers remain rationally ignorant of tariff legislation because the cost of influencing legislation is much higher than any benefit they might expect.

Following this logic, it seems that the legislative process is biased in favor of tariff legislation since such laws pit concentrated interests against weak ones, and foreign interests against domestic ones. How, then, can we explain the success of the General Agreement on Tariffs and Trade (GATT) in reducing worldwide tariffs on manufactured goods during the postwar period?[26]

GATT has been successful in reducing the overall level of tariffs on manufactured goods because it alters the environment within which legislative choices are made. GATT is a multilateral package of tariff reductions, so tariffs and tariff reduction are decided for many industries and many countries simultaneously rather than one at a time. The U.S. agrees to reduce tariffs on German wine, for example, and Germany cuts tariffs for U.S. computers. The U.S. wine industry might, under other circumstances, be able to lobby successfully to keep its protective barrier against German wine, but under the GATT system, this industry group would now face competition from the U.S. computer industry, which would lobby in favor of GATT in order to gain freer access to the German market. Import-competing interests are thus opposed by export interests. When export interests are stronger, as they frequently are, freer trade wins out over protectionism.

This analysis of GATT illustrates an important insight provided by rational choice theory. While public policy depends on individual and national interests, it is also affected by the institutional arrangements for making these decisions. Legislation that considers tariffs one at a time is likely to produce many tariffs, as noted earlier. But the institutional set-up of GATT, which considers a great many tariff reductions all at once, is likely to produce freer trade. What public policy is made is conditioned by *how* public choices are made. The process by which decisions are reached matters as much as the decisionmakers and the factors that influence them for the final policy choice.

Political scientists who study IPE often refer to a given combination of actors (nations, businesses, public officials), interests, and institutions as a ***regime***. The regime is the environment in which policy is made. The GATT is an example of a *trade regime* in this context. The Cold War was an example of a *security regime*. To combine insights drawn from two different areas of IPE (rational choice and regimes), it is necessary to understand the nature of a given IPE regime (its actors, interests, and institutions) if we want to understand the rational choices that derive from it. When regimes change or shift, as with the rise of OPEC in the oil regime (see chapter 17) or the collapse of communism in the security regime (see chapter 9), the policy environment also changes, and new outcomes are likely to appear.[27]

MERCANTILISM: RATIONAL CHOICE AND JAPANESE TRADE POLICY

Japan's international trade policies provide an example of how rational choices lead to mercantilist policies. Consider the trade negotiations between Prime Minister Morihiro Hosokawa of Japan and President Bill Clinton on February 11, 1994. Clinton proposed a plan for opening Japanese markets to U.S. products. Clinton's team insisted on market share targets to establish a U.S. presence in Japan in the markets for cars, car parts, public procurement, and medical devices. The U.S. proposal recommended a mix of government control and deregulation of these markets. A *Wall Street Journal* report described the plan for the auto industry:

> the U.S. wants Japanese car makers to buy 20% more auto parts annually from foreign vendors—a pledge that would require Japanese government oversight. But at the same time, the U.S. is pressing Tokyo to deregulate its inspection and certification system and to loosen the grip Japanese car makers have on auto dealers. Those moves would reduce the power of the Japanese bureaucracy.[28]

Prime Minister Hosokawa refused Clinton's proposal and offered no immediate compromise alternative, but did promise continued work to open Japan's markets. Hosokawa made the following comment: "Soon after returning home we will consider the problem. Our side must come up with some wisdom, and Japan will do what it can on its own."[29]

With negotiations collapsed, President Clinton threatened retaliatory sanctions against Japanese products. Many onlookers expected Clinton to revive the trade provision known as Super 301. This would allow the U.S. to target Japan as an unfair trader and retaliate with restrictive trade policy.[30]

The prime minister's refusal to accept U.S. market targets and the possible sanctions could hurt Japanese consumers by raising prices and reducing product choice. Why, then, would Hosokawa take this mercantilist position? Is he acting out of a philosophical position? Is this rational behavior?

In February of 1994, Prime Minister Hosokawa was in a fight for his political life. Hosokawa was elected in August 1993, deposing the ruling Liberal Democratic Party, after promising the voters electoral reform. He vowed to resign if bills designed to clean up Japanese politics were not passed before the end of the year. The deadline came and went, with no reform legislation. When the Upper House of Parliament defeated four reform bills on January 21, Hosokawa needed to assert his control over the government.

The summit with President Clinton provided Prime Minister Hosokawa with this opportunity. Politically, then, a tough stance with the Americans boosted Hosokawa's reputation. According to *The Economist*, "the Japanese agree they must do something about this [Japan's trade surplus], but dislike the American plan." But the electorate supports Hosokawa's position: "Nearly all Japanese support this defiance. Immediately after the summit, businessmen, bureaucrats and even opposition politicians reckoned the prime minister had done the right thing."[31]

Politically, then, refusing Clinton's market reform plan for Japan made Prime Minister Hosokawa most "happy." He could still open Japan's markets, but with Japan at the lead rather than the United States. At a time when Hosokawa looked like a weak leader, he was able to stand up to the Americans. This made him more popular with his governing coalition and the voters. From this perspective, refusing the American proposal and taking a mercantilist stance was a rational decision.

By examining the nations and the leaders of the nations who support mercantilist policies, we can develop an understanding of how and why mercantilism serves their interests. It may be that individual leaders value political power. Strong state intervention and protection of the economy may provide that power. In other cases, the industries protected by mercantilist policies may have special influence over public officials. Thus, public officials protecting these industries may be serving their own political interests by promoting mercantilism. In other cases, the public officials may believe that protectionism serves the national interest and they personally value and seek to serve the national interest.

RATIONAL CHOICE AND STRUCTURALIST IPE

The rational choice method also illuminates the decisions of public officials under the structuralist perspective of IPE. According to this theory, government is a tool of the dominant class of capitalist bourgeois owners:

> Each step in the development of the bourgeoisie was accompanied by a corresponding political advance of that class. . . . [T]he bourgeoisie has at last, since the establishment of modern industry and of the world market, conquered for itself, in the modern representative state, exclusive political sway. The executive of the modern state is but a committee for managing the common affairs of the whole bourgeoisie.[32]

Since public officials in a bourgeois state are beholden to capitalists, it is in the officials' best interest to enact laws and rules that favor capitalist owners. Such laws would protect owners and expand their profits. Marx's view is that these laws necessarily exploit the proletariat. Continuous exploitation leads inevitably to revolution by the masses, who overthrow the bourgeois government. By serving their short-term self-interest of maintaining their positions, public officials guarantee their eventual fall from power. Not serving the interests of capitalists, however, guarantees their immediate fall from power.

Lenin's imperialist theory of capitalism also makes sense under rational choice theory. Capitalists are able to maintain their exploitative profits only when they can find viable consumers and cheap production resources. Once the capitalists of a nation exploit their laborers to a point where profits are falling, they look for new consumers and cheaper labor resources in other states. Exploiting consumers and resources in other nations requires political and military power, best provided by governments. To please the capitalists who keep them in office, public officials orchestrate imperialist expansions into other nations. These other nations, once controlled by the imperialist government, are forced into a position of dependency that maximizes the wealth of the capitalist owners. Government officials maintain this dependency with trade policy and military intervention. By serving the capitalists, public officials retain their positions of power.

Consider the controversy in Mexico over NAFTA (see the case study in chapter 4). Structuralists believe NAFTA increases Mexico's dependency on the United States by creating a Mexican economy of low-wage, low-technology industry. American capitalists and laborers both benefit from stunting economic growth in Mexico this way. High-wage, high-skill jobs stay in the United States, keeping American incomes high. Low-cost inputs from Mexico reduce the costs of production in the United States, increasing profits for capitalists. With their political and military power, the public officials controlled by these American interest groups were able to force this treaty on Mexican officials. The economic powers in one nation (the United States) control public officials, inducing them to exploit the citizens of another state (Mexico) through international trade policy. This exploitative policy was in the best interests of public officials because it served the economic agents, contributing interest groups, and voters, who keep them in power.

RATIONAL CHOICE AND LIBERALISM

The rational choice method is most often associated with the liberal perspective, since they both use economic tools to explain political behavior. But the two should not be considered synonymous. Rational choice is a theory of individual behavior, while liberalism is a philosophy regarding the interaction between states and markets.

An examination of the behavior of public officials using rational choice methods helps us understand why liberalism doesn't often apply in the world today. Liberalism seeks to divorce the state and the market. As long as economic agents influence public officials, their interests influence government policy. The rent-seeking and specific industry tariff protection discussed in this chapter's boxes are examples of government interference in markets that is encouraged by the political system. Individual public officials react to citizen-voters, contributing special interest groups, and political parties. There are numerous opportunities within these three groups for people to seek government interference in the market and for them to influence a public official's decision.

Liberal policies do happen, however, and they are becoming more popular in the late twentieth century. When economic agents believe less government intervention is in their personal interests, we would expect politicians to deliver less interventionist policy. NAFTA is an example. The constituent groups in support of the treaty, who believed they were best served by less government interference in the market, outweighed the opposition. Remember, too, that personal ideology and a public official's view of national interest matter. In a world where communist regimes disintegrate and capitalist economies flourish, liberal policies may seem quite attractive. Public officials may enact liberal policies not because their constituents demand them, but because the politicians themselves believe in them. Václav Havel's pursuit of market reforms in Czechoslovakia and, later, the Czech Republic, reflect his personal beliefs in liberalism.

Boris Yeltsin's position in Russia reflects both of these pressures. After his election on a reform platform, Yeltsin responded to the demands of the public, the Western democracies, and economists by enacting market reforms. On January 2, 1992, Yeltsin ended the government's control over most prices, a major step toward market reform and one demanded by free market economists. But the economic consequences have been severe. Inflation followed, with some prices rising tenfold. Income differences between labor classes have been exaggerated, creating class tensions. The negative effects of adopting liberal policies forced Yeltsin to rethink his reform agenda. With politicians and citizens reacting negatively to the liberal policies, his program shifted its emphasis. To maintain his position of power, Yeltsin must respond to constituent pressures, even if their political philosophies seem fickle.

THE CONTROVERSY OVER RATIONAL CHOICE

While rational choice has become increasingly important as a method of analysis in the social sciences, it is by no means universally accepted. Rational choice practitioners and theorists note the widespread applications of this analytical method throughout the social sciences and its usefulness in understanding social decision making. Critics question the limited view of what motivates human behavior and the failure of rational choice to explain important aspects of political behavior.

Rational choice theories receive criticism in four distinct areas.[33] Cultural theorists argue that rational choice ignores the role culture plays in influencing and constraining individual choices. Chalmers Johnson believes that "rational choice theory is explicitly oriented toward eliminating the variable of culture."[34] New areas of research in rational choice are attempting to address this criticism. Nobel prize winning economist Douglass North and others are actively researching the influence of culture and norms of behavior on learning and what this means for rational behavior.[35] According to Norman Schofield, rational choice theorist from Washington University in St. Louis, "Rational choice theory is forcing us to think more deeply about what rationality means."[36]

Psychologists criticize the rational choice method for misrepresenting the way humans make decisions. Cognitive psychologists argue that individuals are more likely to seek a certain minimum level of satisfaction than to constantly maximize their happiness. This behavior is called satisficing. Individuals who satisfice do not have complete

Continued

THE CONTROVERSY OVER RATIONAL CHOICE, *continued*

information nor the ability to identify the "best" option. Predicting behavior when individuals satisfice is much more difficult than under a rational choice assumption and requires extensive information about an individual, what she knows, and how she makes decisions.

The third group of critics comes from the field of experimental psychology. They argue that "neither the existence of preferences, the process by which preferences are pursued, nor the evaluation of information in the basic decision-making process is as consistent or efficient as rational choice" theory suggests.[37] This criticism questions the basic method of individual decision making used by both rational choice and economics by challenging the view that individuals are rational. Milton Friedman, among others, respond to these criticisms by noting that it is not necessary for individuals to consciously make rational choices, but to choose "as if they were seeking rationally to maximize their expected" benefits.[38]

Finally, strict rational choice theory has trouble explaining two important political issues: collective action and altruistic behavior. Much of what political scientists study involves individuals agreeing to and participating in group decision making. According to the rational choice method, individuals should realize that they can reap the benefits of these group decisions without paying the costs of participation. Economics refers to this as *free-riding*. As an example, the cost of going to the polls and participating in elections clearly outweighs the influence of each individual's vote on the outcome. Why, then, would anyone choose to vote? With respect to altruistic behavior, if individuals are self-interested and perceive no personal benefits from helping others, then rational choice would not predict that a motorist might stop to help a stranded driver on the Santa Monica freeway. While a strict reading of rational behavior cannot explain individuals choosing to vote or help a stranger, a broader view of individual preferences, as developed in the text of this chapter, allows the rational choice method to explain a broader set of behaviors, including collective action and altruism.

The rational choice method for analyzing human behavior is both theoretically robust and empirically predictive. While critics identify important weaknesses in the theory, new work by rational choice theorists is expanding the applicability and depth of the method. As noted by Ken Shepsle, a respected rational choice theorist, no one has offered any other theory that explains things better.[39]

CONCLUSION

These applications show the usefulness of the rational choice model of decision making. When analyzing specific decisions, this method provides depth to explanations of IPE events. As such, the rational choice model supplements and enhances traditional IPE perspectives.

The rational choice approach to IPE provides a unique perspective on international decision making. By exploring the motivations behind individuals' choices, the rational choice model gives us a more detailed understanding of international events. Rather than attempting to categorize all international events or national actions, rational choice theory treats all decisions as uniquely determined by the individuals involved, their personal preferences and objectives, their relationship with other decisionmakers, and the context (that is, time, place, and history) of the particular choice.

When accepting rational choice theory, we need not discard mercantilism, liberalism, or structuralism. Rather, the rational choice method supports these IPE theoretical perspectives with a unifying theory of human behavior. By examining a nation's decisionmakers, we can understand the choices they make in the name of their nation. Such understanding provides a more detailed picture of IPE events. With rational choice, IPE theories are reconnected to the people within the nations. This humanizes the study of states and markets as it deepens our understanding.

DISCUSSION QUESTIONS

1. How does rational choice analysis relate to the IPE perspectives of mercantilism, liberalism, and structuralism? Is rational choice a fourth perspective, or is it a method of analysis that can be used better to understand all three perspectives? Explain.
2. What assumptions does rational choice analysis make concerning the motives for human behavior? Do these assumptions always hold in daily life? Are they generally sound assumptions to make regarding economic and political decisions? Explain.
3. Mercantilist and liberal perspectives often draw distinct lines between individual interest and national interest. How does rational choice analysis bridge this gap? That is, how does rational choice analysis explain how individual interests combine to form state policies? Explain, using the issue of NAFTA to illustrate your argument.
4. What is rent-seeking behavior? How do firms use state power to earn profits? Does rent-seeking behavior make markets more efficient? Explain.

SUGGESTED READINGS

James E. Alt and Kenneth A. Shepsle, eds. *Perspectives on Positive Political Economy.* Cambridge, England: Cambridge University Press, 1990.

Robert H. Bates. *Markets and States in Tropical Africa.* Berkeley, CA: University of California Press, 1981.

———. *Toward a Political Economy of Development: A Rational Choice Perspective.* Berkeley, CA: University of California Press, 1988.

James M. Buchanan and Gordon Tullock. *The Calculus of Consent.* Ann Arbor, MI: University of Michigan Press, 1962.

Anthony Downs. *An Economic Theory of Democracy.* New York: Harper & Row, 1957.

Bruno S. Frey. *International Political Economics.* New York: Basil Blackwell, 1984.

David B. Johnson. *Public Choice: An Introduction to the New Political Economy.* Mountain View, CA: Bristlecone Books, 1991.

Douglass C. North. *Institutions, Institutional Change and Economic Performance.* Cambridge, England: Cambridge University Press, 1990.

Mancur Olson. *The Logic of Collective Action.* Cambridge, MA: Harvard University Press, 1965.

NOTES

1. Adam Smith, *The Wealth of Nations* (New York: Dutton, 1964), 349.
2. In fact, the IPE perspectives are moral philosophy and rational choice theory is economic science.
3. Douglass C. North, *Institutions, Institutional Change and Economic Performance* (Cambridge, England: Cambridge University Press, 1990), 17.
4. Anthony Downs, *An Economic Theory of Democracy* (New York: Harper & Row, 1957) 27.
5. See Richard Fenno, *Home Style: House Members in Their Districts* (Boston: Little, Brown, 1978); David Mayhew, *Congress: The Electoral Connection* (New Haven, CT: Yale University Press, 1974); and William Dougan and Michael Munger, "The Rationality of Ideology," *Journal of Law and Economics* (April 1989): 119–142.
6. Robert Tollison et.al., "Information and Voting: An Empirical Note," *Public Choice* (1975) 18:43–49; W. P. Welch, "Money and Votes: A Simultaneous Equation Model," *Public Choice* 36 (1981): 209–234; Gary C. Jacobson, "Money and Votes Reconsidered: Congressional Elections, 1972–1982," *Public Choice* 47(1985): 7–62.
7. F. M. L. Thompson, *English Landed Society in the Nineteenth Century* (London: Routledge & Kegan Paul, 1963), 45.
8. Rondo Cameron, *A Concise Economic History of the World* (New York: Oxford University Press, 1993), 276.
9. North, *Institutions, Institutional Change and Economic Performance*, 93.
10. See Tollison, "Public Choice and Legislation" in Virginia Law Review Vol 74: 339–371, no. 2, March 1988, for an excellent summary.
11. Richard Fenno, *Congressmen in Committees* (Boston: Little, Brown 1973).
12. National Advisory Committee on Semiconductors, "Preserving the Vital Base: America's Semiconductor Materials and Equipment Industry," working paper, July 1990, 25.
13. Andrew Pollack, "Pillar U.S. Chip Industry Eroding," *The New York Times*, 3 March 1989, D5.
14. Andrew Pollack, "A Small Lobby's Large Voice," *The New York Times*, 7 September 1989, D1.
15. Jacob Schlesinger, "U.S. Chip Makers Find 'Quotas' Help Them Crack Japan's Market," *The Wall Street Journal*, 20 December 1990, A1.
16. Andrew Pollack, "Sematech Starts to Make Progress," *The New York Times*, 19 April 1991, D1.
17. See Dougan and Munger, "The Rationality of Ideology," 119–142.
18. See Joseph P. Kalt, "The Political Economy of Federal Petroleum Price Policy: An Analysis of Voting in the U.S. Senate," in *The Economics and Politics of Oil Price Regulation*, Cambridge, MA: MIT Press 1981, 237–316, as an example of a complete industry analysis.
19. Ross Perot claimed that lobbyists from the Mexican government were working hard to convince representatives and senators to support NAFTA. Ross Perot with Pat Choate, *Save Your Job, Save Our Country: why NAFTA must be stopped—now!* New York: Hyperion, 1993.
20. Keith Bradsher, "Clinton's Shopping List for Votes Has Ring of Grocery Buyer's List," *The New York Times*, 17 November 1993, A11.
21. Keith Bradsher, "Majority in House Backs Trade Pact," *The New York Times*, 16 November 1993, A1.
22. Anonymous, "Running Scared from NAFTA," *The New York Times*, 16 November 1993, A16.
23. Jeff Faux, "NAFTA: A Warning for the President," *Harper's* 287 (September 1993): 13–15.
24. Keith Bradsher, "Majority in House Backs Trade Pact."
25. Bob Davis and Jackie Calmes, "Trade Win: House Approves NAFTA Providing President with Crucial Victory," *The Wall Street Journal*, 18 November 1993, A1.
26. See chapter 7 for a discussion of GATT and its successor, the WTO.

27. The language of regimes will be used explictly only on occasion in the chapters that follow, but this basic notion is used frequently as a way of thinking about different IPE problems and structures. See Joseph S. Nye and Robert O. Keohane, *Power and Interdependence: World Power in Transition,* (Boston: Little Brown, 1977).

28. Bob Davis and Jacob M. Schlesinger, "U.S. Plans Sanctions Move as Talks with Japan Fail," *The Wall Street Journal,* 14 February 1994, A8.

29. Ibid., A3.

30. Ibid., A3.

31. "Saying No," *The Economist,* 19 February 1994, 36.

32. Karl Marx and Friedrich Engels, *The Communist Manifesto,* in George T. Crane and Abla Amawi, *The Theoretical Evolution of International Political Economy: A Reader* (New York: Oxford University Press, 1991), 87.

33. See Kristen Renwick Monroe, ed., *The Economic Approach to Politics: A Critical Reassessment of the Theory of Rational Action* (New York: HarperCollins, 1991), for a more complete discussion of these issues.

34. Ellen Coughlin, "How Rational Is Rational Choice?," *Chronicle of Higher Education,* 7 December 1994, A16.

35. Arthur T. Denzau and Douglass C. North, "Shared Mental Models: Ideologies and Institutions," *Kyklos,* 47 (1994): 3–31.

36. Ibid.

37. Monroe, *The Economic Approach to Politics,* 7.

38. Milton Friedman, *Essays in Positive Economics,* (Chicago: University of Chicago Press, 1953), 21.

39. Couglin, "How Rational Is Rational Choice?"

Part II

IPE Structures:
Production, Finance,
Security,
and Knowledge

The first five chapters of this book have acquainted you with the fundamental notion of international political economy, the three principal IPE perspectives, and the method of rational choice that is frequently used to analyze and interpret IPE interactions. These chapters provide an intellectual foundation on which to build a more sophisticated understanding of the international political economy.

The next five chapters look at the sets of relationships that tie together nation-states and other actors and that link national and global markets in the IPE. These five chapters probe international trade, the international monetary system, international debt and finance, security, and knowledge and technology. The structures of IPE are built upon the foundation established in the first chapters. Although in this chapter we use the language of "structures," our analysis is not necessarily that of a "structuralist" approach. IPE structures describe or define a set of international relationships. Structuralism analyzes these structures in particular ways, often in the context of dependency relationships build into the capitalist system that these structures define. Our analysis here defines its goals more broadly. We mean to be open to liberal, mercantilist, and also structuralist interpretations of these structures or arrangements.

This section's information is important in it own right, but it will be especially useful to us in the last three parts of the text, when we tackle international and global problems. In these later sections, we will build upon the foundation of the IPE perspectives and the framework of the IPE structures to construct a clear yet sophisticated understanding of some of the most important issues of yesterday, today, and tomorrow.

THE STRUCTURES OF IPE

We begin with the production structure, which encompasses the critical issues of international trade. The production structure encompasses what is produced, where, under what conditions, and how it is sold, to whom, and on what terms. Some scholars have characterized the production structure as the ***international division of labor***, but it is really much more than that. In IPE, the production structure appears most frequently in matters involving international trade. The question of trade, of course, clearly poses the question of whether goods are produced at home or abroad, who gains as a result of this production, and what terms of trade prevail. Questions of production and trade are among the oldest, most controversial, most timely, and most important in IPE. The production structure is one of four sets of relationships, linkages, or "structures" that together define the IPE. We next analyze the finance structure, which is most effectively divided into two parts: the analysis of the international monetary system (chapter 7) and international finance and debt (chapter 8).

Older than the production structure, however, is the international security structure (chapter 9). The security structure defines the sets of relationships, agreements, understandings, and rules of behavior that affect the safety and security of states, groups, and individuals within the IPE. The security structure is the network of war and peace; hardly anything is older or more important than this. Some parts of the security structure are easy to see, such as the formal security alliances that NATO (the North Atlantic Treaty Organization) comprises. Other aspects are less visible or certain, but important nonetheless.

Finally, states and markets are also linked by a set of relationships involving knowledge, ideas, and technology. The knowledge structure is therefore the subject of chapter 10. Who has access to knowledge and technology, and on what terms, is a question of growing importance in the study of IPE today. More and more, knowledge and technology represent the ability to "do things" that dramatically affect the balance of power in the finance, production, and security spheres of life. Knowledge is power, it is said, but who has this power and how will it be used?

CUI BONO? WHO BENEFITS?

Professor Susan Strange, one of the leading IPE thinkers, proposes that we think of IPE in terms of the production, finance, security, and knowledge structures, and then, in looking at each set of relationships, we should ask the simple question "*cui bono?*" (who benefits?). Asking this question forces us to go beyond description to analysis—to identify not only the structure and how it works, but its relationship to other structures and their role in the international political economy. This is an important step.

Perhaps the most interesting thing about IPE is the fact that states and markets are generally involved in a number of simultaneous structural relationships, often on different terms, and usually with different partners. Understanding IPE, therefore, becomes a matter of holding in your mind a set of complex relationships and considering their collective implications.

6

International Trade

OVERVIEW

International trade is one of the international political economy's oldest and most controversial subjects. International trade stems from the **production structure** of the international political economy. Together with the international financial, technological, and international security structures, trade links nation-states, furthering their interdependence—a condition that benefits but is also a source of tension between states and different groups within them. Controversies about international trade stem from nation-state compulsion to capture trade's benefits while limiting its negative political and economic effects on society.

Since World War II, the political and economic importance of international trade has increased dramatically, intensifying academic and public debate about its significance. In previous chapters, we have hinted at the central role trade plays in IPE. Liberals like Adam Smith and David Ricardo viewed it as a mutually beneficial bonanza to individuals and states. Mercantilists like Friedrich List and Alexander Hamilton viewed trade as a zero-sum game that makes some nation-states wealthier and more powerful than others. Structuralists such as Karl Marx and V. I. Lenin saw trade as a means of exploitation and redistributing income between developed and developing nations. These conflicting views about trade continue today, conditioning our understanding of this key IPE activity.

This chapter surveys the IPE of international trade, with emphasis on postwar trade institutions and problems. The economic analysis of trade is contrasted with the political compulsion for states to manage trade in ways that derive its benefits but also limit its costs. After a brief history of the role of trade in the international political economy, attention is given to a variety of important but in some cases contradictory trends. On the one hand, some trade officials desire to further liberalize international trade by updating the General Agreement on Tariffs and Trade (GATT) trade rules and even transforming it into a World Trade Organization (WTO). All the while, these same officials have felt compelled to respond to (neo)mercantilist demands for trade protection. Some experts believe that by trying to have it both ways—to keep open and closed—the international trade system will inevitably result in world regional trading blocs.

In this chapter, we also survey a number of trade problems within and between the industrialized nations and less developed countries (LDCs). We discuss the use of trade as an instrument of foreign policy as well as the strategic trade policies that some states use in conjunction with businesses to make themselves more competitive in the international political economy.

In the absence of a world government, cross border trade is always subject to rules that must be politically negotiated among nations that are sovereign in their own realm but not outside their borders.[1]

Robert Kuttner

The economic impact of international trade is generally accepted but, as Robert Kuttner notes above, trade is *always* political as well. No topic is more quintessentially IPE than trade, and it is no surprise that for hundreds of years the time and talents of IPE scholars and practitioners have focused on trade issues.

International trade is a result of the production structure of the international political economy.[2] The production structure is the set of relationships that determine what is produced, where, by whom, how, for whom, and at what price. Commercial trade is a global activity that is generally carried out by individual entrepreneurs and firms (although some firms may be quite large). When we say that states trade with one another, we are referring to the sum total of trade done by a nation's businesses registered as the nation's trade.[3] Economic liberals, mercantilists, and structuralists all recognize the extent to which trade redistributes the world's resources and, in so doing, generates wealth and power for nation-states.

Liberals stress the economic benefits of trade that stem from a more efficient division of labor and use of the world's resources. Production for exports has a multiplier effect on an economy and helps generate jobs. Imports usually mean more goods for consumers to choose from, often at cheaper prices and of better quality than locally produced goods. Because trade benefits the parties that engage in it, it helps further international economic integration and ultimately world peace through economic cooperation.

Mercantilists, on the other hand, stress the politics of trade. Nation-states fear becoming too dependent on others for certain goods. States also naturally desire to protect themselves and their businesses from the negative effects of trade. Imports often cost jobs. The protectionist trade policies one state adopts to help its industries can unintentionally disrupt another economy through trade, which is one of the reasons why the North American Free Trade Agreement (NAFTA) and the Uruguay round of the General Agreement on Tariffs and Trade (GATT) recently received so much press attention. As in the recent case of the United Nations' effort to cut off all trade with Iraq during the Persian Gulf War, mercantilists also recognize the extent to which nations will often turn to trade embargoes or boycotts to punish or otherwise hurt other nations.

Structuralists emphasize how trade is used by the industrialized nations to either exploit or subordinate developing nations. For some structuralists, trade induces underdevelopment in some cases. Other structuralists focus on how reform of the international trade system, in conjunction with other international economic reforms, can benefit LDCs.

In these and many other examples, it is clear that the economics of trade cannot be separated from its political aspects. International trade has played a major role in the commercial and political development of the international political economy, and it continues to generate a good deal of wealth in the world at large. Since World War II, the importance of trade has increased for almost all nations because of the income it generates and the volume of goods that are exchanged and moved throughout the world. Since 1948, world trade has grown more rapidly than world production. Between 1945 and the late 1970s, the value of world exports increased dramatically. In 1975, the value of world exports reached $876 billion, and by 1980, were valued at $1.9 trillion (expressed in current dollars). By 1990, the value of world exports had jumped to nearly $3.4 trillion.[4]

Trade ties countries together, and in so doing, it generates a good deal of both economic and political interdependence. Since World War II, the capacity of a government to generate wealth or solve any number of problems has become conditioned by international interdependencies that make managing its own economy difficult, let alone managing the international economy.[5] Because trade plays such an important, if not large, role in most economies, states are more than ever compelled to regulate it so as to capture its benefits and limit its costs to their economies.

An IPE of international trade addresses the tension between what local entrepreneurs and nation-states politically and economically gain and lose from trade. How are their interests reconciled? Most trade problems, such as whether or not and how to restrict trade, derive from this fundamental issue. This chapter addresses this issue and explores the way it has shaped developments in the institutions, rules, and procedures of the postwar international trade system. Efforts to liberalize international trade (i.e., to facilitate exchanges by reducing trade barriers) through the GATT have met with limited success. At the global level, the goal of trade liberalization is gradually being replaced by a tacit agreement between nations to recognize and accept agreed-to methods and levels of trade protectionism. In an international environment where most nations are increasingly dependent on trade, limited protectionism is a second-best solution, preferable to failure to resolve trade disputes, which could result in losses to all parties.

THE MOTIVATION TO TRADE: THE THEORY OF COMPARATIVE ADVANTAGE

Cloth was the first manufactured good to become an important commodity in international trade. Trade in cloth was not generally based purely on need, since some type of cloth can be made by most people in most places. Rather, trade in cloth was based on the idea of *comparative advantage*, which holds that a nation should buy cloth from abroad when the cost of the import is less than the cost of home production.[6] David Ricardo is credited with the theory of comparative advantage, although the general idea existed long before. The theory of comparative advantage is one of the most influential theories in economics.

Before Ricardo's day, and even today, many people believed that international trade was based on the principle of *absolute advantage*: the nation that can produce the most of any commodity with a given amount of resources will have the deciding advantage in international trade in that good. Ricardo argued, however, that a nation might have an absolute advantage in producing a good and still import it because its *comparative advantage* lay elsewhere. A simple example will make this distinction clearer.

This story is about U.S. Supreme Court Justice Oliver Wendell Holmes, who was active early in the twentieth century, in the days when typewriters were crude, difficult, mechanical things, requiring strength as much as skill to operate. A large, beefy man, Justice Holmes is said to have been one of the fastest typists of his day—he had a distinct *absolute advantage* in typing. Despite this, Justice Holmes hired another person to type his speeches and rulings because it was more efficient that way. Although Justice Holmes had an absolute advantage in typing, his *comparative advantage* was in judicial work. Each hour he spent typing was very productive in terms of the pages typed, but the *opportunity cost* was too high. (The opportunity cost is the value of what is given up when a person chooses one option or activity over another.) The opportunity cost of typing for Justice Holmes was the legal analysis he could do instead. His time was far more valuable when used for legal analysis and scholarship than for typing. This made it inefficient for him to do his own typing. His secretary (also male) could not type nearly as fast as Justice Holmes, but was even less proficient in legal matters, so he was better suited to be a typist. The secretary had a low opportunity cost in typing, giving him the comparative advantage in this task.

It is clear that it was more efficient for Justice Holmes to write the legal opinions and for his secretary to type them, than it was for them to divide their labor in any other way. This is comparative advantage at work. The key to international trade and comparative advantage is, therefore, efficiency. Scarce resources can be used more efficiently if an international division of labor is applied, with each nation specializing in production of the goods and services that it can produce at a lower relative cost than can its trading partners. An item should be produced where it has the lowest opportunity cost.

The fundamental principal of comparative advantage is almost deceptively simple: it is better to buy or import a good when importing it requires less sacrifice than producing it at home. Ricardo measured this sacrifice in terms of opportunity costs. Today, we use a dollar yardstick—buy imports when they are cheaper than domestic substitutes; but the idea is the same. When we sacrifice less to produce goods, and do not waste resources, we are being efficient.

Using the idea of comparative advantage, Saudi Arabia should import wheat from the U.S., since the opportunity cost of growing wheat in the desert is enormous, while the opportunity cost of growing wheat in parts of the United States is very small. In the same way, the U.S. should import oil from Saudi Arabia, and not try to produce all the oil it needs, because the opportunity cost of oil production is so much lower in Saudi Arabia.

If trade were only about comparative advantage, it would not be so controversial. However, the question "*cui bono?*" remains. According to economic liberals, the issue of who benefits the most from these efficiencies depends upon whether the **terms of trade**[7] favor the importer or the exporting nation. If the price of oil is high compared to wheat, then Saudi Arabia will reap more of the gains from trade. If oil is relatively cheap, then the U.S. will derive more gain. Trading partners, like the U.S. and Saudi Arabia in this example, both gain from trade, so they are encouraged to trade. Yet each struggles to get a little larger share of the efficiency gains that trade creates.

Mercantilists, on the other hand, challenges the assumption that comparative advantage unconditionally benefits both parties. The national production structure generates goods for trade. Yet this structure reflects a distribution of national resources such that people are employed in different sections of the economy. While comparative advantages are theoretically dynamic—that is, shifts in a nation's resources and capabilities generate new opportunity costs, people employed in those industries are likely to resist moving into other occupations. For example, one reason farmers seek trade protection for their agricultural commodities is because they like to farm, even if commodity surpluses drive down food prices and weaken demand for their products.

Farmers often get trade protection for a number of reasons. First, even though they are relatively small in number compared to the size of other industries, they are politically strong due to their overrepresentation in national legislatures such as the United States, Western Europe, and Japan. Second, related to security concerns, many nations fear dependence on other nations for basic commodities. Most nations prefer being relatively self-sufficient when it comes to food and natural resources and raw materials that sustain a nation's industries.

For mercantilists, then, liberal trade theories do not wash in the real political world. Any number of domestic groups and industries may appeal to the state for protection—and receive it. Trade protection takes many forms: policies designed to encourage exports, and policies designed to discourage imports.

THE VOCABULARY OF TRADE POLICY

Some of the more important and most often used protectionist measures include:

- *Tariffs*   A tax placed on imported goods to raise the price of those goods, making them less attractive to consumers. Tariffs are used at times to raise government revenue (particularly in LDCs). Tariffs are more commonly a means to protect domestic industry from foreign competition.
- *Import Quotas*   A limit on the quantity of an item that can be imported into a nation. By limiting the quantity of imports, the quota tends to drive up the price of a good at the same time it restricts competition.
- *Export Quotas*   These international agreements limit the quantity of an item that a nation can export. The effect is to limit the number of goods imported into a country. Examples include *orderly marketing arrangements* (OMAs), *voluntary export restraints* (VERs) or *voluntary restraint agreements* (VRAs). The *multi-fibre agreement* establishes a system of export quotas for less developed countries, for example.
- *Export Subsidies*   Any measure that effectively reduces the price of an exported product, making it more attractive to potential foreign buyers.
- *Currency Devaluations*   The effect of devaluing one's currency is to make exports cheaper to other countries while imports from abroad become more expensive. Currency depreciation thus tends to achieve the effects, temporarily at least, of both a tariff (raising import prices) and an export subsidy (lowering the costs of exports). Currency changes affect the prices of all traded goods, however, while tariffs and subsidies generally apply to one good at a time.
- *Nontariff Barriers (NTBs)*   Other ways of limiting imports include government health and safety standards, domestic content legislation, licensing requirements, and labeling requirements. Such measures make it difficult for imported goods to be marketed or significantly raise the price of imported goods.
- *Strategic Trade Practices*   Efforts on the part of the state to *create* comparative advantages in trade by methods such as subsidizing research and development of a product, or providing subsidies to help an industry increase production to the point where it can move down the "learning curve" to achieve greater production efficiency than foreign competitors. Strategic trade practices are often associated with state industrial policies, i.e., intervention in the economy to promote specific patterns of industrial development.
- *Dumping*   The practice of selling an item for less abroad than at home. Dumping is an unfair trade practice when it is used to drive out competitors from an export market with the goal of creating monopoly power.
- *Countervailing Trade Practices*   Defensive measures taken on the part of the state to counter the advantage gained by another state when it adopts protectionist measures. Such practices include antidumping measures and the imposition of countervailing tariffs or quotas.

A BRIEF HISTORY OF TRADE

Mercantilism, liberalism, and structuralism each view the pluses and minuses of international trade differently. In a way, the history of international trade over the last five hundred years is a distillation of the evolution and development of IPE theories.

During the mercantilist period from the sixteenth through eighteenth centuries (see chapter 2), for example, European states aggressively sought to generate trade surpluses as a source of wealth for the state. Local industries were just getting off the ground and imports of intermediate goods were discouraged if they meant people would buy imported goods instead of locally produced goods. The territories the Europeans colonized provided gold, silver, and other precious metals, which increased their wealth. The Europeans often used their wealth to help pay for the many wars they fought with one another on and around the continent. This dynamic relationship between wealth and power lies at the heart of the mercantilist theory of trade.

For mercantilists, trade is one among many instruments the state tries to use to enhance its wealth and thus add to its power and prestige in relation to the power and prestige of other states.

Reacting to what they viewed as mercantilist abuses, Adam Smith and David Ricardo proposed a distinctly liberal theory of trade that dominated British policy for over a hundred years. The law of comparative advantage showed that free trade increased efficiency and made everyone better off. It mattered little to liberals, who produced the goods, where, how, or under what circumstances. The world was a global workshop, where everyone benefited, guided by the "invisible hand" of the market. Smith wrote that what was good for the individual consumer was good for the community. Smith was also an advocate of laissez-passer, or free trade, an idea that almost became a political and economic dictum. Countries should be free to produce and export goods, and at the same time, be free to import the goods they desired or could afford, without state interference. Thus, Smith also advocated a laissez-faire (leave alone) role for the state in the economy. Furthermore, he held out the hope that efficiency and commerce might replace war and conflict as the natural order of the international political economy.

Smith's and Ricardo's ideas about trade began to dominate British ideas about trade in the 1840s when the English Parliament overturned the Corn Laws and adopted a free trade policy. When English manufacturing industries replaced agriculture as the economic base of the economy, England began to import cheaper food products from abroad. England then went on to champion free trade policies and made popular the liberal notion of limited state intervention in the economy.

The industrial revolution generated a good deal of trade between the Europeans and their colonies. As it did, liberal and mercantilist ideas about trade competed with one another in academic and official circles. Because British industries were more mature than those of their continental competitors, Britain naturally supported a free trade policy to complement its laissez-faire attitude about government. Free trade exposed competitors to cheaper British products. While England remained an economic hegemon, its liberal ideas spread through the world.

First Alexander Hamilton and then Friedrich List challenged what became accepted liberal doctrine about trade (see chapter 2). From their mercantilist perspective, liberalism and free trade policies were nothing more than an academic

justification for England to maintain its dominant advantage over its trading partners on the continent and in the New World. Hamilton argued that U.S. infant industries and national independence and security required the employment of trade
protectionist measures.[8] The German Friedrich List argued that liberalism manifested unequal power among nations. Free trade must be preceded by greater equality between states, or at least a willingness on their part to share the benefits and
costs associated with trade. Furthermore, List argued that in a climate of rising economic nationalism, protectionist trade policies such as import tariffs and export subsidies were necessary if Europe's infant industries were to compete on an equal
footing with England's industries.[9]

By the turn of the twentieth century, protectionist trade policies were on the
rise as the major powers once again raced to grow their industries. After World War
I, some states adopted two different types of trade protectionism.[10] In conjunction
with expansionist foreign policies, Italy, Germany, and Japan used trade protectionism in a malevolent or aggressive manner to dominate the colonial possessions
they acquired. The other European powers and the United States acted in a more
benign manner, by adopting protectionist trade policies to counter the protection-
sist policies others employed to insulate their economies.

THE GREAT DEPRESSION: TRADE PROTECTION
ABOUNDS

During the Great Depression of the 1930s, trade protectionism spiraled upward while
international trade significantly decreased. Between 1929 and 1933, worldwide trade
declined by an estimated 54 percent, strangled in part by the Smoot-Hawley tariffs
in the United States and similar onerous trade barriers enacted elsewhere.[11] Many
historians argue that the trade situation and the depressed international economy
associated with it, helped generate the bleak economic conditions ultranationalist
leaders such as Mussolini and Hitler reacted to.

Structuralists look at the mercantilist period quite differently than do mercantilists and liberals. First, they label the early mercantilist period as one of *classical imperialism*. Imperialism of the major European powers originated in their own
economies. Mercantilist policies that emphasized exports were necessary when industrial capitalist societies experienced economic depression. Manufacturers over-
produced industrial products and financiers had a surplus of capital to invest abroad.
Colonies served at least two purposes. They were a place to dump these goods, and
they were also a place where investment could be made in industries that profited
from cheap labor and access to plentiful (i.e., inexpensive) quantities of natural resources and mineral deposits. Trade helped colonial mother countries dominate
and subjugate the undeveloped colonial territories of the world. Lenin argued that
national trade policies benefited most the dominant class in society—the bourgeoisie. In the period of *modern imperialism* toward the end of the nineteenth century, according to Lenin, capitalist countries used trade to spread capitalism into
underdeveloped regions of the world. The "soft" power of finance as much as the

"hard" power of colonial conquest helped establish empires of dependency and exploitation.

During the early colonial period, developing regions of the world remained on the *periphery* of the international trade system. They provided their "mother" countries with primary goods and mineral resources along with markets for manufactured products. Structuralists argue that industrializing *core* nations converted these resources and minerals into finished and semi-finished products, many of which were sold to other major powers and back to their colonies. From the perspective of many structuralists, to this day trade continues to play a key role in helping the imperialist industrialized nations subjugate the masses of people in developing regions of the world.

Andre Gunder Frank and other theorists who apply structuralist ideas and arguments to analyze the internal effects of colonialism and imperialism on such countries as Brazil, argue that trade helped generate *dependency* of peripheral regions and nations on the industrialized core nations. While particular sectors (enclaves) of core economies have developed, political and economic conditions for the masses of people within peripheral nations and regions have become *underdeveloped.*[12]

Likewise, modern world system structuralists, such as Immanual Wallerstein, link capitalist core countries to *peripheral* and *semi-peripheral* regions of the world. Patterns of international trade are largely determined by an international division of labor that accompanies capitalism. Trade helped spread capitalism from core nations to the underdeveloped peripheral nations.[13] Operating between the core and the periphery, semi-peripheral nations have successfully used trade to generate economic growth in a manner similar to the core, while providing the core with primary resources and markets in much the same way peripheral nations do.

Within these different structuralist perspectives there are a number of different views as to how trade might help more fairly distribute or even redistribute income among the nations of the world. Solutions to trade problems between the rich and poor vary from policies of autarchy (i.e., no trade at all) to rather cautious opinions that, for the most part, nations should be able to solve their trade problems amicably with one another.

THE GATT AND THE POSTWAR TRADE STRUCTURE

The United States first adopted a liberal outlook about trade in 1934 when President Franklin Roosevelt pressed Congress to pass the Reciprocal Trade Agreements Act in an attempt to help the U.S. economy recover from the depression. But the United States did not assume the mantle of managing the international trade system until shortly after World War II. Secretary of State Cordell Hull championed free trade as a way of overcoming international conflict. States' cooperation to bring down tariff barriers would generate economic growth and replace warfare as a means of settling international disputes.

The postwar structure of the world's IPE was cast in 1944 at Bretton Woods, New Hampshire. There, allied leaders, led by the United States and Great Britain, tried to create a new monetary order (see chapter 7) that would prevent many of the interwar economic conditions that led to World War II. In conjunction with this effort, the United States also promoted the creation of an International Trade Organization (ITO) that would oversee new (open) trade rules applied to tariffs, subsidies, and other protectionist measures. The ITO never got off the ground because a coalition of protectionist interests in the U.S. Congress forced the United States to withdraw from the agreement, effectively killing it.

President Harry Truman advanced a temporary alternative structure for multilateral trade negotiations under the GATT. In 1948, GATT became the primary organization responsible for the liberalization of international trade. The GATT sought to liberalize trade through a series of multilateral negotiations, called GATT rounds, where the main trading nations of the world would each agree to reduce their own protectionist barriers in return for freer access to other markets. One of the most famous GATT rounds was the Kennedy round (1962–1967). In the Kennedy round, tariffs on nonagricultural goods continued to decrease—by about 35 percent—across the board for states who participated in the agreement. In an effort to increase its trade, the United States alone reduced its tariff rates on nonagricultural imports by about 65 percent.

GATT promoted the principle of reciprocity—the so-called most favored nation (MFN) trading status—whereby when one state gave another an advantage by lowering its tariffs on that nation's goods, it would give that advantage to all states. Yet some nations have not been willing to automatically grant this privilege to their trading partners. In mercantilist fashion they often selectively grant it to those they politically favor or want to assist while withholding it from other states for any number of reasons. MFN became a carrot and stick instrument used by many nations. The GATT also allowed *exemptions* from generalized trade rules for certain goods and services, including agricultural products and quotas for the purpose of resolving balance-of-payments shortages.

GATT's membership is theoretically open to any nation, but until the 1980s most communist countries refused to join it, viewing GATT as a tool of Western imperialism. There are currently about 130 members of GATT, including many republics of the former Soviet Union.

During the 1960s and early 1970s, international economic interdependence increased while growth in world trade was a disappointment. Many nations did reduce their tariff barriers, however at the same time they devised new and more sophisticated ways of protecting their exports and otherwise limiting imports. By the time the Tokyo round of GATT (1973–1979) got underway, the level of tariffs on industrial products had decreased to an average of 9 percent. The Tokyo GATT round dealt with a growing number of NTBs that many believed were stifling world trade. It produced a series of rules reflecting significant changes that had recently occurred in international trade practices. The Tokyo round produced rules or codes covering a range of discriminatory trade practices, including the use of export subsidies, countervailing duties, dumping, government purchasing practices, government imposed product standards, and custom valuation and licensing requirements on importers. Some new rules were also devised that covered trade with developing nations.

THE INDUSTRIALIZED NATIONS:
PROTECTIONISM ENTRENCHED

In the 1970s and 1980s, the industrialized nations encountered a number of trade problems. From 1963 to 1973, trade among the industrialized nations quadrupled, but increased only two and one-half times in the next decade. Meanwhile, trade accounted for increasingly higher percentages of GDP in the industrialized nations in the 1980s: around 20 percent for the United States, 20 percent for Japan, and an average of 50 percent for members of the European Union (EU). To put it mildly, trade policy continued to be a serious issue of disagreement among the industrialized nations, reflecting their increasing dependence on it to help generate and maintain economic growth.

In spite of the Tokyo round, the use and variety of trade protectionist policies increased, making international trade appear more (neo)mercantilist in nature than ever. At least three interrelated factors contributed to the entrenchment of trade protectionism in the 1970s and '80s. First, many argue that the United States was reluctant to assume the costs of hegemonic leadership associated with keeping the international trade system open. As the U.S. trade deficit grew in the late 1960s, it challenged the then European Community's protectionist trade barriers, when earlier it had been willing to accept those barriers as the price Western Europe demanded to achieve U.S. security objectives in that region. In 1971, in order to correct its trade deficit, the United States unilaterally imposed a 10 percent surcharge on Japanese imports coming into the United States. This measure combined with U.S. unilateral action to end the convertibility of the dollar to gold, formally ending the Bretton Woods monetary system. These actions and others signaled to its allies that the U.S. would put its interests and those of its producers before its obligations to manage international trade by accepting the costs of some amount of protection against its trade goods.

A closely related second argument about the source of increasing protectionism at this time is made by those who claim that in the 1970s, U.S. political and economic hegemony declined *in relation to* an increase in political and economic influence by its Western EC partners, Japan, and the newly industrialized countries (NICs).[14] By the mid-1970s, the West European nations were increasingly reluctant to accept free trade as a standard by which to conduct exchanges. In much the same way that List had argued almost a century before, free trade benefited the hegemon and made it difficult for others to compete with its products. The Western Europeans felt compelled to adopt protectionist trade policies in support of their growing economies.

A third factor that contributed to growing protectionism in the 1970s and 1980s was increased expectations by groups that either benefited or were hurt by trade, and by the state that came under pressure to manage trade in conjunction with other parts of the economy. Mercantilists stress that trade became another "macroeconomic" policy issue that required state management in an assertive, if not aggressive, manner, if economic growth was to be generated and sustained in an interdependent international economic environment. Sometimes the demand for products was influenced as much by currency value fluctuations as changing consumer taste for a product. A decrease in exports meant thousands of jobs and pressure on legislators and government officials to "get tough" on other nations for policies that limited imports or subsidized exports.

STRATEGIC TRADE

By the 1970s, Japan's export-led growth trade strategy began to bear fruit. In Japan, the Ministry of International Trade and Industry (MITI) helped pick corporate winners it and other government officials felt would prosper in the international economy from state assistance (see chapter 13). Most of these industries were high-employment, high-technology firms whose future looked bright. Working closely with their national firms, the Japanese and the NICs began assisting their firms in ways that would put their firms in a strong competitive position. ***Strategic trade policies*** came to be synonymous with state efforts to either make the international economy more receptive to certain businesses[15] or block the access of competitive firms to domestic markets.

The practice of strategic trade then included "the use of threats, promises, and other bargaining techniques in order to alter the trading regime in ways that improve the market position and increase the profits of national corporations."[16] In the United States, for instance, the Omnibus Trade and Competitiveness Act of 1988 produced "Super 301," legislation that required trade officials to list "priority" countries that unfairly threatened U.S. exports (see chapter 10). Aside from export subsidies and the use of a variety of import limiting measures, proactive strategic trade policy measures included extended support for "infant industries" complemented by import protection and export promotion measures. Some states went out of their way to form joint ventures with firms in the research and development of new technologies and products. Another recent example is U.S. government assistance to Microsoft Corporation in an effort to crack down on Chinese computer software pirates.[17]

The point is that in a more competitive environment, comparative advantages are no longer fixed but can be manufactured by states and firms. Under such conditions, free trade policies are increasingly viewed as naive—a thing of the past. Nations that overexpose themselves to imports from other nations can be accused by their citizens of throwing away domestic jobs and undercutting the standard of living.[18] To compound matters, a good deal of international trade is no longer controlled by states but by multinationals. One expert argues that corporations have developed the capacity to "minimize taxes, skirt trade barriers, and take advantage of global shifts in comparative advantage."[19] Increasingly, intrafirm trade captures a larger portion of international trade: as much as an estimated one fourth to one third of all trade (see chapter 16). Global firms have been able to integrate production across national borders. This has increased competition between firms as well as rivalry and competition between firms and states.[20]

By the mid-1980s, the United States, the EU, Japan, some NICs, and some developing nations were accusing one another of unfair trade practices. The expectation was that they would be able to do no more than "level the playing field"— essentially try to contain unfair trade advantages. Politically, in this environment *fair trade* replaced *free trade* as a foreign economic policy objective of many states. Bilateral and multilateral trade forums became more important to produce equal or politically acceptable levels of protection.

One bilateral dispute that has generated a great deal of attention but also serious concern is the continuing series of U.S.-Japan trade disputes (see chapter 13). Essentially, the United States accuses Japan of not playing fair when it comes to its trade practices, and intentionally avoiding reform of its economy. During the mid-1980s, the U.S. trade deficit reached an all-time high of $160 billion. Japan accounted for as much as 37 percent of that deficit. Meanwhile, in the first half of the 1980s, the United States became a major importer of industrial goods, agricultural exports failed to make up for these imports, and an estimated 3 million people lost their jobs to foreign competition.

To correct its trade deficit, the United States pressured Japan to spend more for imports. A series of *bilateral trade talks* has covered a variety of items including agricultural goods such as rice and beef. The latest dispute involves autos, telecommunication equipment and services, insurance, and medical equipment.[21] At times, the U.S. Congress has threatened to implement numerous trade retaliatory measures should the Japanese not seriously reform their economy. Typically, Japan eventually agrees to make some reform and to import more U.S. goods. However, as is usually the case, trade talks bog down and are settled at the eleventh hour after threats from the United States and mention of a possible trade war.

U.S.-EU relations have not been as emotionally charged and as contentious as U.S.-Japanese trade relations.[22] Nonetheless, in 1986, the United States pressed the Europeans to import more U.S. agricultural products and to reform some of their Common Market trade discrimination practices. In this case, the United States threatened the EU with a trade war and with retaliatory practices of its own. Once again, the issue was temporarily settled at the eleventh hour.

Multilateral trade talks are another forum that have been used to solve trade disputes among the industrialized nations. Outside the dispute settlement mechanism of the GATT, efforts have been made by the industrialized nations to deal with common trade problems in a number of other forums. One is the *Group of 7* (G-7)—composed of the United States, Japan, Great Britain, France, Germany, Italy, and Canada.[23] National leaders and finance ministers meet yearly in cities such as Williamsburg, Virginia, Houston, Texas, Venice, Italy, and Versailles, France, to deal with a range of mutual problems, quite often one of the most pressing of which is international trade.

THE GATT URUGUAY ROUND AND BIRTH OF THE WTO

Under these conditions, the United States and a number of other countries pushed for a new round of the GATT negotiations on trade. The eighth GATT round—the Uruguay round—got underway in 1986 in Punta del Este, Uruguay.[24] Meeting routinely in Geneva, Switzerland, but also occasionally in other cities, the Uruguay round seemed headed for failure, but was finally completed on December 15, 1993.

The Uruguay round became known for three things in particular. First, like the Tokyo round, it attempted to deal with a number of trade issues that reflected increasing economic interdependence, a wider variety of exchanged goods and services, and more sophisticated ways of protecting products and services. The Uruguay round sought to reduce trade barriers on items such as services (e.g., insurance), intellectual property rights (e.g., on computer software), and investments. The United States had a comparative advantage in these areas and sought to gain access for them throughout the world.

A second issue in the Uruguay round was trade protection for agricultural products. Exempt from GATT rules and regulations largely because of the political sensitivity of the issue, trade reform of agriculture was one of the Uruguay round's main objectives. Some farmers in the United States, the EU, Japan, and other major agriculture producing nations received substantial assistance from their governments. The EU is reported to have spent as much as two thirds of its annual budget on agricultural subsidies, while the United States spent more on subsidies than the net income of U.S. farms.

During the Uruguay round, the United States, the Cairns Group (fourteen nations led by Australia), and at times Japan, led an effort to phase out all agricultural subsidies. They were opposed by the EU (especially France), which criticized the proposal to significantly reduce agricultural subsidies. As the Uruguay round's proceeded, agricultural trade became one of the major sticking points that deadlocked the negotiations on several occasions. Final agreement on agricultural trade was reached at the eleventh hour in November of 1993.

Finally, the Uruguay round made a concerted effort to involve the developing nations in the international trade system and in the trade negotiation process. In return for access to their economies, the developing nations made demands for increased access in the industrialized nations of many of their raw materials, and semi-finished and finished products.

After nearly collapsing at least two times, the Uruguay GATT agreement was finally approved in late 1994 and came into effect in early 1995. Many of those officials who favored the treaty argued that the 22,000 page agreement would result in a one-third decrease in world tariffs over a six year period, which would inject about a half trillion U.S. dollars into the world economy by the year 2000. Many U.S. exporters expected big gains, namely 20,000 jobs for every $1 billion increase in exports, and access to overseas markets for U.S. semiconductors, computers, and a variety of U.S. agricultural commodities.[25] The final agreement included measures to protect trade-related intellectual property rights (or so-called TRIPs), covering such items as copyrights, patents, and trademarks. Many of the industrialized nations expect increased foreign investment in their economies as a result of trade-related investment measures (TRIMs).

A good deal of controversy surrounds another element of the new GATT agreement—the new World Trade Organization (WTO). Composed of a small secretariat in Geneva, Switzerland, the WTO's job is to act as a forum for negotiating new trade deals and to implement the new GATT agreement. The WTO was designed to have more teeth in its dispute-settlement procedures—including the possibility of trade sanctions if judgments are disobeyed—than the earlier GATT dispute-settlement mechanism. The WTO's mechanism to settle trade disputes consists of an impartial panel of experts chosen by the WTO's dispute-resolution board. Every WTO member country is to have one vote, and thus, the WTO is not expected to be held hostage by the veto power of the more wealthy and powerful nations, as has been the case in the United Nations' Security Council. Many supporters of the WTO view it as something more significant than just another multilateral trade organization that tries to limit state subsidies, dumping, and other protectionist trade practices. For many economic liberals the WTO signifies a multinational effort to promote free trade, if not manage international trade, without the necessity of a national hegemon to impose order on the international trade system.

Critics of the latest GATT agreement, representing a wide variety of ideological perspectives, focus on the WTO's rule making authority and many of the regulations it oversees. For some, the WTO represents a threat to the sovereignty of nations—some U.S. critics charge, for instance, that third world countries can gang up on the U.S. and undermine many of its environmental, human rights, and labor standards and laws. Others argue that the new GATT agreement does not go far enough to protect the environment in many nations, or to regulate child labor or unfair wage practices in many LDCs. Still others charge that many U.S. laws in these policy areas will eventually be attacked as "illegal trade barriers" in closed WTO proceedings. Finally, some criticize the failure of the latest GATT agreement to reach consensus on measures that deal with issues such as the movement of "cultural products," like movies, across borders; insurance company, security firm, and bank access to other nations; and "local content" legislation.

The extent to which the WTO gains credibility and becomes an effective organization depends on many factors. It is too early to predict whether nations will abide by WTO decisions or simply withdraw from the WTO when trade disputes are decided against them.

REGIONAL TRADING BLOCS

Some trade experts expect that geographic or regional trading blocs are likely to play a greater role in shaping trade future trade rules and regulations. Trade blocs usually feature a dominant political power whose interests and objectives influence the trade policies of other bloc members. Perhaps the most powerful recent advocate of this view is the American economist Lester Thurow, whose 1992 book, *Head to Head: The Coming Economic Battle Among Japan, Europe, and the United States*, was a best-seller. Thurow writes:

> In the past half century the world has shifted from being a single polar economic world revolving around the United States to a tripolar world built upon Japan, the European Community, and the United States. . . . As a result the system that governed the world economy in the last half of the twentieth century will not be the system governing the world economy in the first half of the twenty-first century. A new system of quasi-trading blocks employing managed trade will emerge.[26]

Continued

REGIONAL TRADING BLOCS, *continued*

Bloc members enter formal or informal arrangements that create a division of labor, which enhances production efficiency through product specialization. Trade is promoted by liberalizing exchange practices, while local producers are assisted by a common set of trade protection measures that limit imports into the bloc. The currency of the local hegemon quite often serves as the key currency of the trade zone.

Most of the blocs that are in the early stage of development reflect both liberal and mercantilist trade policy objectives and practices. The EU was founded on the liberal principle of enhancing production specialization and efficiency and liberalizing trade between Union members (see chapter 11). Internal trade barriers between member states have gradually been reduced. Competitors from outside the EU have found it difficult to penetrate its markets. Other trade blocs either have emerged, or are in the process of emerging, to compete with the EU. In 1987, the United States and Canada formed a Free Trade Area (see chapter 12) and in 1993 extended it to include Mexico in a North American Free Trade Agreement (NAFTA). NAFTA members are not as integrated as are the members of the EU, but there is every reason to believe that increased trade and other financial transactions among the United States, Canada, and Mexico will enhance political economic cooperation and even integration.

Some trade experts speculate that in the next ten to fifteen years, NAFTA could be expanded to include more South American countries such as Chile, Colombia, Venezuela, Peru, Ecuador, and Bolivia.[27] Some of the regional trade associations that already exist are the Latin American Free Trade Association, the Central American Common Market, the Andean Group, the Association of Southeast Asian Nations, the Arab Cooperation Council, the Economic Community of West African States, and Asian Pacific Economic Cooperation (APEC) forum. APEC attempts to integrate eighteen Pacific and Asian nations into a nonbinding arrangement that would gradually remove trade barriers among members by 2020. As promoter of the agreement, the United States hopes to further liberalize trade among the members while accelerating economic growth in the Pacific-Asia region.[28]

Still others speculate about the development of a regional trade zone in East Asia dominated by Japan and its yen—the yen bloc. Given Japan's great dependency on external sources of raw materials, other Asian nations may be willing to form some sort of trade arrangement with Japan that would, in effect, increase Japan's ability to benefit from liberalizing trade with other nations around it while simultaneously protecting the industries of its bloc members.

Several things bother economic liberals about regional trading blocs. First is the extent to which they employ a variety of otherwise protectionist measures to assist local producers. These measures could generate more trade protectionism and neomercantilist practices on the national, regional-bloc, and global levels. President Clinton suggested that one of the main reasons the United States should support NAFTA was to lock up Mexico before the Japanese did.[29] The Clinton administration worried that if the United States did not quickly bring Mexico into its trade orbit, Japan would invest heavily in Mexico, possibly negating U.S. influence over Mexico's future trade policies.

What bothers liberals the most about bloc arrangements is their possible contribution to international conflict and even violence. Trade blocs quite often reflect political tensions that are played out in the economic arena. Liberals fear that these trade tensions may produce hostile relations that may even result in war. But liberal fears are not mercantilist fears. For mercantilists, trade blocs merely reflect the distribution of the world's wealth and power. Trade has become a structural feature of the international political economy, but the institutions and processes that structure comprises are primarily national in origin.

LDCs AND INTERNATIONAL TRADE

The successes of the Uruguay round make it *appear* that the forces of trade liberalism are currently winning out over the forces of mercantilism. Reality usually finds states continuing to adopt trade policies that reflect a mix of liberal and protectionist trade measures. Another important example of this trend is third world trade policies. The wealth generated by trade plays an important—if not the most important—role in economic development (see chapter 15). Trade accounts for as much as 75 percent of LDCs foreign exchange earnings. Yet LDCs complain that they account for only 28 percent of the world export market, and 40 percent of those exports come from the NICs. Many LDCs suffer chronic trade deficits. Benefiting from trade while limiting costs associated with it is as much a concern to third world leaders as it is to officials in developed parts of the world.

Trade played a large role in the development models LDCs were to choose from in the 1950s and 1960s.[30] As will be discussed in chapter 15, the liberal or Western-industrialized development model argued for employing trade as an "engine to growth." The industrialized nations presumed that LDCs would be able to specialize in the production and export of one or a few major products. Earnings from trade, supplemented by foreign aid and investment, would provide them with the income they needed to invest in industry as they transformed their economy from an agricultural base to an industrial base.

This strategy was severely criticized by those who feared dependency on the West and whose economies lacked the goods or products in demand on international markets. An alternative socialist development strategy recommended that nations become self-sufficient by developing local industries first and cutting themselves off from international trade because the price of primary commodities and other less sophisticated products often fluctuated greatly. LDCs should practice ***import substituting industrialization*** (producing goods at home instead of importing them) until such time that the nation was strong enough to trade on a more equal footing with the industrialized nations. Supporters of this strategy often made structuralist arguments about the use of trade by industrialized nations to exploit and dominate LDCs. Promoters of the socialist development model challenged the belief that the structure of international trade could ever benefit developing nations without some kind of fundamental transformation or reform of that system along socialist lines that addressed the inequality of nations.

Structuralists would argue that many third world development problems can be directly attributed to the international structure of trade, which they maintain is rigged against LDCs. Structuralists based their arguments about trade on the third world complaint that the *terms of trade* work to the advantage of the developed nations and against the developing nations. The prices LDCs received for their exports—foodstuffs, minerals such as tin, copper, and other metals, fibers and raw materials—have for the most part since World War II been gradually deteriorating, while the prices LDCs were required to pay for manufactured imports continued to rise.[31] Developing nations argue that they lack the capital, technology, and production facilities and knowledge to compete with the industrialized nations. LDCs have been forced to export more of their raw materials at cheaper prices, driving down local wages, to pay for more expensive capital goods produced in the developed nations.

Starting from an economically disadvantaged position, LDCs often face tariffs and other barriers imposed on their agricultural goods, semiprocessed metal and wood products, and labor-intensive consumer goods. Many LDCs accuse the developed nations of hypocrisy when it comes to living up to the principles of the liberal international trade system. Developed nations had an extensive history of using protectionist trade measures to promote the growth of their own economies. The GATT is an organization whose liberal trade policy objectives, regulations, and procedures usually reflect the interests of its richest and most powerful Northern industrialized nations. The industrialized nations use the GATT and other organizations, along with direct pressure, to bring down LDC tariff barriers, exposing LDC infant industries to competition with the more mature industries of the industrialized nations. Many LDCs believe that one of the main reasons the United States and other developed nations supported the GATT Uruguay round was their fear of losing third world export markets and access to their resources and raw materials.

Because of their growing numerical advantage in international organizations and multilateral agencies, LDCs have looked to these institutions as a setting where they could act as a bloc of nations in efforts to improve the terms of trade and reform of the rules and regulations of the international trade system. The issue of trade and developing nations has been the focus of the United Nations Committee on Trade and Development (UNCTAD), the Group of 77 (G-77), and demands for a new international economic order (NIEO) in the United Nations in the early 1970s (see chapter 15). Several NIEO proposals dealt specifically with demands for more cooperation between the North and South over trade issues and the access of Southern goods to Northern markets. Since then, many LDCs have called for preferential, nonreciprocal, and nondiscriminating treatment for their products.

Liberals would argue that by the late-1980s LDCs had become so well integrated into the international trade system that the industrialized nations had found it necessary to bargain with them for the purposes of producing a new and more comprehensive GATT agreement. Yet mercantilists argue that LDCs cannot expect any major redistribution of international wealth and power, or genuine reform of the international trade system, until they have more power or until the industrialized nations find it in their interest to pursue such an objective.

TRADE AS A FOREIGN POLICY TOOL

Yet another mercantilist compulsion of states is the use of trade as an instrument of foreign policy. If wealth is power, then trade is both—a fact as old as history. Athens may have sparked the Peloponnesian wars when it tried to restrict imports from one of Sparta's allies, Megara.[32] Threats of trade discrimination can be used to coerce a competitor or punish an enemy.

Trade sanctions take many forms, including boycotts, import restrictions, and embargoes that prohibit exports to another country. A nation may try to help an ally when other nations embargo exports to that nation. During the U.S. Civil War, for instance, Great Britain helped the Confederacy with war supplies and continued to purchase its cotton when the north tried to limit southern trade with England. In 1949 and 1951, the U.S. Congress passed the Export Control and Battle Acts that outlawed trade between U.S. businesses and the Soviet Union and Communist bloc countries. In 1963, the United States gradually increased its trade sanctions on Cuba to the level of a total embargo, dealing Cuba a crippling blow to its trade and economy.

In the 1980s, the Reagan administration applied a series of economic sanctions that included trade restrictions on a variety of third world nations it felt were either supporters of communist revolutionary movements (e.g., Nicaragua), sponsors of terrorism (e.g., Libya, Iran, Cuba, Syria, and the People's Democratic Republic of Yemen), or nations that were reluctant to give up the practice of apartheid (e.g., South Africa).[33] At the same time, the U.S. Department of Commerce handed out generalized systems of preferences (GSPs)—reductions of trade restrictions on certain goods—to Caribbean countries that supported U.S. anti-Communist foreign policy objectives in the region. The commerce department also kept a "black list" of those nations that for any political reason were not to receive GSPs. The objective in these cases was to impose an intolerable hardship on a society and to break the will of its people and leaders to carry on some type of unacceptable behavior.

A good deal of debate surrounds the question of the effectiveness of trade boycotts and embargoes. Generally, the conclusion is that they have a limited effect on the behavior of the intended target.[34] Some problems associated with establishing the effectiveness of trade sanctions are establishing what precisely the aims were of the sanctions and what would have happened had the sanctions not been employed in the first place. Experts have argued that a number of conditions must be present if nations are going to successfully use trade restrictions to punish a nation. Governments must be able to control its businesses or prevent certain goods from being shipped to another country. Businesses and governments can get around trade sanctions because goods produced in one country are hard to distinguish from those produced in another. Sometimes third party nations will provide a country with the goods that another country has boycotted. Thus, the more countries involved in a trade embargo, the more successful the embargo is likely to be. Still, it is difficult to determine how the target state will adjust to an embargo or boycott. When the United States imposed its grain embargo on the Soviet Union in 1980, not only did the Soviet Union turn to other suppliers for grain, but it also cut back on meat and feed grain rations for its own people. In the case of Nicaragua, U.S. economic sanctions increased popular resistance and support for the government to oppose imperial aggressors.

These and many other cases that employ trade as a mechanism to change the behavior of states or other actors demonstrate that, despite the few cases in which it has worked, nations will continue to be tempted to employ trade as a weapon. We can expect states to continue to use trade in this manner given the increasing economic interdependence of nations, which makes it easier for them to disrupt the economies of other nations and their preference not to use military force.

LIFTING THE BAN ON VIETNAM

In 1975, the United States banned trade with Vietnam in response to the defeat of South Vietnam by North Vietnam. Washington used a trade embargo to pressure Hanoi into releasing information about more than 2,200 U.S. military personnel listed as "missing in action" (MIAs) during the Vietnam War. In the late 1980s, the very poor country of Vietnam gradually abandoned Marxist economic theories and employed more market principles so as to stimulate economic growth and investment in the nation. Asian and European businesses began investing in an economy that had exhibited high growth rates. Following this lead, a number of U.S. businesses lobbied the administration and Congress to rescind the 1975 legislation that disallowed trade with Vietnam.

In the summer of 1993, the Clinton administration decided not to veto loans and aid the IMF and World Bank proposed to offer Vietnam.[35] It became increasingly clear that more and more U.S. goods were getting into Vietnam via third parties and middlemen who profited a great deal from the sales. Slowly the U.S. Senate began to show signs of a willingness to rescind the trade embargo. However, some MIA families and veteran groups actively lobbied the administration not to drop the embargo until Vietnam was more forthcoming about the MIAs.

In retrospect it seems clear that the president and some of his administrators were in favor of lifting the embargo all along but were nervous about the president potentially being embarrassed by his antiwar record.[36]

In early February of 1994, the president announced that the ban on trade with Vietnam would be rescinded and that he hoped that Vietnam would continue to provide the United States with information about the MIAs. U.S. companies immediately began making arrangements to set up shop in Vietnam.

Clearly the United States increasingly found itself caught in a bind—between the objective of not trading with a former enemy that was still being uncooperative and forsaking the economic benefits of trade with a fast-growing third world economy. One could argue that the benefits of trade won out over political considerations. However, it might also be argued that the United States reconciled its interest in trade with a desire to continue trying to shape the behavior of Vietnam by trading with it. In dropping the embargo, the United States merely gave up using trade as a stick and employed it as a carrot.

CONCLUSION: THE FUTURE OF INTERNATIONAL TRADE

What can we expect by way of future trade rules and regulations? First, many of the recent trends in trade are likely to continue. Despite the limited success of the GATT and bilateral efforts to liberalize trade practices, management of international trade requires that free trade give way to fair trade. A managed trade system best describes and accounts for the mixture of liberal and mercantilist trade practices that have become the objectives and trade policies of most states. Yet management of the international trade system will not be easy. In the United Nations and a number of other multilateral agencies connected to it, third world leaders are likely to continue voicing their concern over the terms of trade between developed and developing nations and to make proposals to reform the international trade system and other international finance mechanisms. Those voices will probably be paid attention to more often as LDCs become more competitive with the industrialized nations.

Trade disputes among the industrialized nations are an equally serious problem, with the potential to unravel many parts of the international trade system. Protectionism continues to take on new forms and to be a problem as states become even more dependent on trade to generate income. States will always be tempted to regulate trade, either for domestic political and economic reasons, or to use as an instrument of foreign policy in their relations with other nations. Tension between liberal and mercantilist motives are likely to be exacerbated by the lack of hegemonic authority to promote a relatively more open trade system. At this time, it is clear that the United States would rather promote the liberalization of trade through GATT and other multilateral bodies such as NAFTA and APEC. At the same time, Congress is more than willing to pressure the president to use any number of policy instruments to compel other nations to cooperate with the United States.

In the future, trade is likely to help integrate the former Soviet republics and East European states, along with other third world states, into the international economy. These nations and regions are likely to become of greater interest to the industrialized nations and NICs that seek more markets in these areas of the world.

Finally, in the future, international trade will become even more connected to issues that have until now seemed unrelated to trade. This has clearly been the case in monetary, technology, and national-security issues, and will increasingly become the case for environment and ecological problems (see chapter 19). Production and trade activities impact the environment in ways states and businesses never anticipated. As international trade increases, so does the demand for the consumption of more energy resources. Many would go so far as to calculate the cost of damage done to the environment in the exchange process.

The trade policies of the industrialized nations promise to continue to be of a mixed liberal and mercantilist variety. Many sing the praises of the new WTO and the GATT agreement reached in the Uruguay round of negotiations, while others remark that trade protectionism is at its highest peak since World War II. For many of the industrialized nations, the international trade system is in a state of liberal-mercantilist limbo. The United States lacks the hegemony, and quite possibly even the desire, to push for a greater amount of trade liberalization. Currently, as in the case of monetary policy, the international trade system is left dependent on cooperation by these nations to settle disputes in peaceful ways.

DISCUSSION QUESTIONS

1. Discuss and explain the role of trade in the international production structure. Why is the issue of trade so controversial?
2. Outline the basic ways that mercantilists, economic liberals, and structuralists view trade. (Note: Think about the tension between the politics and economics of trade.)
3. Which of the three IPE approaches best accounts for the relationship of the Northern industrialized nations to the Southern developing nations when it comes to trade? Explain and discuss.

4. Outline the reasons for what many would argue was increased trade protection during the 1970s and 1980s. Do you expect this trend to continue? Why? Why not?

5. How has the U.S. used trade as a tool to achieve its foreign policy objectives since World War II? Be specific and give examples.

6. Outline and discuss the most important issues of the GATT Uruguay round.

SUGGESTED READINGS

Jagdish Bhagwati. *Protectionism.* Cambridge, MA: MIT Press, 1991.

John M. Culbertson. *The Dangers of "Free Trade".* Madison, WI: 21st Century Press, 1985.

Arghiri Emmanuel. *Unequal Exchange: A Study of the Imperialism of Trade.* New York: Monthly Review Press, 1972.

Robert Kuttner. *The End of Laissez Faire.* New York: Knopf, 1991.

Stefanie Ann Lenway. *The Politics of U.S. International Trade: Protection, Expansion and Escape.* Marshfield, MA: Pittman Publishing, 1985.

Lester Thurow. *Head to Head: The Coming Economic Battle Among Japan, Europe, and America.* New York: William Morrow, 1992.

Trade: U.S. Policy Since 1945. Washington, DC: Congressional Quarterly Inc., 1984.

NOTES

1. Robert Kuttner, *The End of Laissez Faire* (New York: Knopf), 157.

2. For a more detailed discussion of the international production structure see Susan Strange, *States and Markets: An Introduction to International Political Economy* (New York: Basil Blackwell, 1988).

3. In some cases, state-owned industries engage in trade. This is referred to as *state trading.*

4. *International Trade Statistics Yearbook*, vol. 1 (New York: United Nations, 1990), Special Table A, s3.

5. A classic book on the subject of interdependence is Richard Cooper, *The Economics of Interdependence: Economic Policy in the Atlantic Community* (New York: McGraw-Hill, 1968).

6. To be more precise, comparative advantage is based on the notion of *opportunity cost* (one of the critical ideas of economics). Opportunity cost is defined as the value of the best alternative use of a scarce resource, such as labor or wool. The theory of comparative advantage holds that a nation should import cloth if the opportunity cost of the imported item (what must be given up to buy it) is less than the opportunity cost of domestic production (what must be given up to produce the item at home). The idea here is to give up as little as possible in acquiring the goods involved.

7. The *terms of trade* are the relative prices of goods in international trade. In the U.S.-Saudi Arabia example, the terms of trade would be the amount of wheat paid for each barrel of oil (or the quantity of oil paid for wheat). The terms of trade are generally measured in items of commodities (as opposed to ordinary money prices) to overcome the difficulties posed by exchange rates.

8. See Jacob E. Cooke, ed., *The Reports of Alexander Hamilton* (New York: Harper & Row, 1964).

9. See Friedrich List, "Political and Cosmopolitical Economy," in *The National System of Political Economy* (New York: Augustus M. Kelley, Reprints of Economic Classics, 1966).

10. Robert Gilpin, *The Political Economy of International Relations* (Princeton, NJ: Princeton University Press, 1987), 31–33.

11. Cited in Stefanie Ann Lenway, *The Politics of U.S. International Trade: Protection, Expansion and Escape* (Marshfield, MA: Pitman Publishing, 1985), 65.

12. Andre Gunder Frank, *Latin America: Underdevelopment or Revolution* (New York: Monthly Review Press, 1970).
13. See, for example, Immanuel Wallerstein, "The Rise and Future Demise of the World Capitalist System: Concepts for Comparative Analysis," *Comparative Studies in Society and History* 16: 387–415 (September, 1974).
14. This argument is made by Gilpin, *The Political Economy of International Relations.*
15. For a sophisticated account of strategic trade policy, see Paul Krugman, *Strategic Trade Policy and the New International Economics* (Cambridge, MA: MIT Press, 1986).
16. Gilpin, *The Political Economy of International Relations,* 215.
17. "U.S. Aids Microsoft in War on Software Piracy by Chinese," *The News Tribune,* 22 November 1994, E-5.
18. For a more detailed discussion of this argument, see John M. Culbertson, *The Dangers of "Free Trade"* (Madison, WI: 21st Century Press, 1985).
19. Gilpin, *The Political Economy of International Relations,* 218.
20. This is the theme of Strange, *States and Markets.*
21. "U.S. Taking Action Against Japanese in One Trade Case," *The New York Times,* 15 February 1994.
22. See Lester Thurow, *Head to Head: The Coming Economic Battle Among Japan, Europe, and America* (New York: William Morrow, 1992).
23. At this writing, Russia is to be added in the near future.
24. For a detailed description of the Uruguay round of GATT negotiations, see Sidney Golt, *The GATT Negotiations 1986–90: Origins, Issues & Prospects* (London: British–North American Committee, 1988).
25. "U.S. GATT Flap Reverberates around the World," *The Christian Science Monitor,* 23 November 1994, 1.
26. Thurow, *Head to Head,* 15–16.
27. "U.S. Plans Expanded Trade Zone," *The New York Times,* 4 February 1994, D1.
28. "Asia-Pacific Countries Near Agreement on Trade," *The New York Times,* 15 November 1994, A1.
29. "Will Treaty Give U.S. Global Edge?" *The Christian Science Monitor* 17 November 1993, 3.
30. For a more detailed discussion of these two development models, see James Weaver and Kenneth Jameson, *Economic Development: Competing Paradigms-Competing Parables* (Washington, D.C.: Agency for International Development, 1978).
31. According to the law of price elasticity, the price of primary exports gradually decreased because people everywhere spent more of their income on manufactured goods than they did on primary goods. Substitutes were also developed for many primary goods, contributing to a lack of demand for them.
32. David Baldwin, *Economic Statecraft* (Princeton, NJ: Princeton University Press, 1985).
33. "U.S. Export Controls," GIST (Washington, DC: The Department of State, March 1985).
34. Gary Hufbauer, Jeffrey Schott, and Kimberly Elliott, *Economic Sanctions Reconsidered* (Washington, DC: Institute for International Economics, 1990).
35. "Vietnam and U.S. Businesses Eager to Trade," *The New York Times,* 3 February 1994, A4.
36. "Clinton Continues to Tiptoe Through Vietnam Minefield," *The New York Times,* 3 February 1994, A1.

7

The International
Monetary System

OVERVIEW

The international political economy comprises nation-states and markets that are connected by a framework of simultaneous relationships or *structures* that condition their behavior and interaction. The finance structure describes the set of monetary or financial relationships in which states and markets exist. These financial relationships affect all the other types of interactions of states and markets to some degree.

The financial structure exists within what is called the international monetary system, one of the most abstract and enigmatic parts of IPE. The international monetary system can best be thought of as a set of rules and practices that govern how debts are honored and paid between and among nations. As always, there is the question *cui bono?*—who benefits from the way that world finances are organized? This chapter focuses on the international monetary system, which is an important element of the financial framework of the IPE. (Chapter 8, which looks at international debt, will continue this analysis of the finance structure.)

The other commonly discussed structures of IPE are relationships based on security, production (and trade), and access to knowledge and technology. These sets of relationships will also be discussed in upcoming chapters. At any given time, a set of relationships or structures exist that link states and markets in the spheres of finance, production, security, and knowledge.

This chapter will examine the IPE of exchange rates and the international monetary system, focusing on its post–World War II history and the problems and issues that dominate the contemporary world of international finance. Along the way we will stop for boxed sections that survey the most important international financial institutions (the IMF and World Bank) and consider the special case of the CFA franc, an example of the problems of soft currency countries in "French Africa."

. . . in exact proportion to the power of this system is its delicacy—I should hardly say too much if I said its danger. Only our familiarity blinds us to the marvelous nature of the system.[1]

I am by no means an alarmist. I believe our system, though curious and peculiar, may be worked safely; but if we wish to work it, we must study it. We must not think we have an easy task when we have a difficult task, or that we are living in a natural state when we are really living in an artificial one. Money will not manage itself, and Lombard Street has a great deal of money to manage.[2]

Walter Bagehot (1873)

Lombard Street is a short stretch of road in the City of London, the original square mile closest to Tower Bridge. Lombard Street is lined with banks and finance houses that still today display the colorful banners of the Italian traders who pioneered banking in medieval and renaissance England, giving it something of the feeling of the busy small-scale market street it once was. In the nineteenth century, Lombard Street was the center of the financial world. International monetary transactions involving states and markets throughout the globe were tied to or influenced somehow by the activities of the people and institutions on Lombard Street.

When Walter Bagehot[3] wrote about Lombard Street in the nineteenth century, he was really writing about the world's finance system and the framework or structure that conditioned the many relationships among states and markets. In the passages above, he stresses the power and also the delicacy of the financial structure, and the need for it to be managed effectively. Lombard Street is still a significant center of international finance, even though it is no longer the center of the monetary universe.

The biggest difference between the finance structure in Bagehot's time, more than a hundred years ago, and the finance structure today is that in Bagehot's day it was possible to go to a place like Lombard Street and meet the people who were a part of the tangible structure of world finance. By spending a day in a bank office or stock market trading floor in London, one could see what the world of financial IPE was all about. Today this world is far more decentralized and increasingly global, with computer networks and telecommunications replacing the person-to-person relationships of Bagehot's time. It is harder, therefore, to actually observe the financial network, or to see the framework of the international monetary system. It exists just the same, however. This chapter will help you perceive its outlines and understand how it has evolved. In chapter 8, we will examine another aspect of the financial structure—international debt—which operates within the financial environment created by the international monetary system.

This chapter has two main parts. The first section looks at the sometimes confusing world of foreign exchange and explores the causes and consequences of changing exchange rates. The second part of the chapter focuses on the international monetary system, the system that governs financial relations among nations. Here we will focus on the problem of creating an international monetary system that can satisfy the needs of states and markets in a dynamic and changing world. The goal of this chapter is to enable the student to understand what the international monetary system is and how foreign exchange works so that we can understand today's most important monetary problems and issues and appreciate how they affect us today, as individual citizens, nation-states, or business firms.

A STUDENT'S GUIDE TO FOREIGN EXCHANGE

Just as people in different nations often speak different languages (requiring translation to understand one another), they also tend to transact business in different currencies, requiring conversion from one type of money to another. To understand the international monetary system and how it affects the various structures of IPE, we must first understand a little about the exchange rate and become familiar with some of the special vocabulary of international finance.

Most people are first exposed to the vagaries of foreign exchange (FX) and the exchange rate when they travel abroad and face a purely practical problem: how many of my dollars will it cost to buy the pesos, pounds, marks, or yen that I need for my travels? People quickly become accustomed to FX math—using the exchange rate to convert from foreign currency into dollars and back again. Thus, if the **exchange rate** is $1.50 per British pound sterling, it follows that a £10 cheap theater ticket in London really costs $15 in U.S. currency (£10 × $1.50 per £ equals $15). In the same way, that ¥1,000 caffè latte at the airport in Tokyo really costs $10 if the yen–dollar exchange rate is ¥100 per US$ (¥1000 ÷ ¥100 per $ equals $10). Before long, tourists find themselves able to perform complex mental gymnastics to convert from one money to another using the FX rate.

Table 7–1 shows the exchange rates of selected currencies relative to the dollar on January 3, 1995. Exchange rates are determined by market forces for the most part and thus change every day as trends and events in IPE alter the supply and demand for one currency relative to another.

TABLE 7–1   Selected Exchange Rates for January 3, 1995

NATION AND CURRENCY UNIT	$ PER CURRENCY UNIT	FOREIGN CURRENCY UNITS PER $
Japan (¥ – yen)	$0.009945	¥100.55
Germany (DM – Deutschemark)	$0.6431	DM1.550
United Kingdom (£ – pound)	$1.5635	£0.6396
France (Ffr – French franc)	$0.1865	Ffr5.3620
Italy (£ – lira)	$0.000617	£1621.80
Mexico (N$ – new peso)	$0.1912	N$5.230
Canada—(C$ – Canadian dollar)	$0.7114	C$1.4057

Source: Washington Post, 4 January 1995, C8.

As Table 7–1 indicates, each exchange rate can be stated in two mathematically equivalent ways. The exchange rate between the U.S. dollar and the French franc, for example, can be thought of as about $0.20 or 20 cents per Ffr; or about 5 francs per dollar. For some currencies, such as the British pound, many people find it easier to keep track of the exchange rate in dollar terms (about $1.50 per pound) while other currencies, such as the Japanese yen, can be easier to understand using the other view—about 100 yen per U.S. dollar. For some currencies, such as the French franc or the Mexican peso, both ways are about equally easy to understand.

Although many people find it interesting that some currency units are seemingly worth so much more than others (a pound is more than a dollar, while a yen is about a penny), this is really not an important aspect of exchange rates. The exchange rate is just a way of converting values from one country's unit of measurement to another. It doesn't really matter what units are used. What *does* matter, however, is whether the measurement is valid and how it changes over time.

THE FX TICKET: A CURRENCY'S VALUE DEPENDS ON WHAT IT CAN BUY

It is useful to think of a nation's money as a ticket that can be exchanged for goods and services in the country that issues it. There are two types of tickets. **Hard currency** tickets are issued by large countries with reliable and predictable economic systems and stable internal and external political relations. They are traded widely and have well-known values. You can exchange a hard currency ticket in most other countries for the local currency. Countries that issue the "hardest" currencies today are the United States, Germany, Japan, Switzerland, and the United Kingdom.[4]

Soft currency tickets are not as widely accepted; a soft currency tends to be used in its home country, but not elsewhere because its value may be too uncertain or the volume of possible transactions insufficient to support an international trading network. Less developed countries and former eastern bloc states generally have soft currencies because their political relations are less stable than some other countries; in addition, their economies are small relative to the world market and face an uncertain future. A soft currency country usually must acquire hard currency (through exports or by borrowing) in order to purchase goods or services from other nations. A hard currency country, on the other hand, can generally exchange its own currency directly for other hard currencies, and therefore for foreign goods and services, a distinct advantage. Because only hard currencies get much international use, we'll focus on hard currencies in this chapter.

One important feature of the FX "ticket," unlike other types of tickets, is that it can be exchanged for so many different things. A ticket to *Phantom of the Opera*, for example, can only be exchanged for a chance to see a particular performance of this show. But a £ ticket can be exchanged for a £'s worth of British goods, services, or investments. You could even treat a £ ticket as a lottery ticket, buying it on speculation, hoping it will go up in value and earn a profit.

The value of a £ ticket or a $ ticket (to people in other countries) depends on what it can be traded for in terms of goods, services, investments, and potential lottery winnings. A currency generally rises and falls in value, therefore, with the value of the goods, services, and investments that it can buy on its home market. The powerful forces of supply and demand translate the $ ticket's worth into an exchange rate in worldwide foreign exchange markets.

While many economic forces affect exchange rates, two of the most important are inflation rate and interest rate changes. All else being equal, a nation's currency tends to depreciate when that nation experiences higher inflation rates. Inflation, a rise in overall prices, means that currency has less real purchasing power within its home country. This makes the currency less attractive to foreign buyers. The currency therefore tends to depreciate on foreign exchange markets to reflect its reduced real value at home. In the same way, if nation A has a lower inflation rate than nation B, its currency tends to appreciate, reflecting the relatively higher purchasing power of its money.

Interest rates also affect exchange rates because they influence the value and desirability of the investments that a particular currency can purchase. If interest rates rise in the United States, for example, then the demand for dollars to purchase U.S. government bonds and other interest-earning investments also increases, pushing the dollar's FX value higher. In the same way, lower interest rates can lead to a lower demand for the dollar, as dollar denominated investments become less attractive to foreigners.

While this simple relationship between interest rates and exchange rates generally holds true, there are important exceptions that should be considered, as when several related forces all act at once on the FX market. Sometimes, for example, accelerating inflation rates within a country drive up interest rates there; the force of inflation pushing the dollar down would then typically surmount the ability of interest rates to push it up. Economists say that what matters with respect to exchange rates is the *real interest rate* (adjusted for inflation's affects), not the *nominal* (unadjusted) interest rate. Only higher real interest rates can reliably increase a currency's value.

Nations can influence the FX rate through policies that affect their currency's value relative to other currencies. Interest rate changes, tax laws, domestic inflation rates, and a variety of regulations, therefore, affect the FX rate. Since a dollar is really a $ ticket, a ticket that can be exchanged for goods, services, or investments in the United States, the $ ticket's price (the FX rate) depends on the value of what the $ ticket buys. In other words, the FX rate of the dollar depends on the dollar's ability to buy U.S. goods, services, and investments and the worth of these resources to foreigners.

In today's world, with a global financial marketplace, a hard currency nation can most effectively vary the FX rate of its currency through manipulation of interest rates. If interest rates rise (or fall) in the U.S., interest-earning investments in the U.S. become worth more (or less) to foreigners. All else being equal, this increased (or decreased) value will be reflected in the FX rate. In 1993, for example, long-term interest rates fell in the United States. This made the $ ticket for investment less attractive for foreigners, since interest-earning assets in the U.S. were then less lucrative. It follows that the dollar depreciated or fell in value in 1993 relative to many other currencies.[5]

THE EFFECTS OF FX CHANGES

There is a special vocabulary that is used in discussing changes in the FX rate. When a currency becomes more valuable relative to other currencies, we say that it *appreciates*. When it becomes less valuable relative to other currencies, we say it *depreciates*. Suppose, for example, that the British pound currently trades at $1.50 per £. If the pound appreciates (becomes more valuable), then it takes more dollars to buy a pound, so the exchange rate might change to $1.60 per £. The pound has appreciated and the dollar depreciated (is less valuable relative to the pound).[6] These exchange rate changes are a little confusing until you get used to them. What would you say about the yen and the dollar if the FX rate changed from ¥120 per $ to ¥130 per $? (See the footnote for the answer.)[7] What would you say about the mark and the dollar if the exchange rate changed from 60 cents per DM to 65 cents per DM?[8]

Tourists quickly learn the rules of the foreign exchange game. As a tourist, interested in maximizing purchasing power and minimizing cost, you want whatever currency you hold the most of to appreciate! If you were visiting Tokyo, for example, you would want the dollar to appreciate from ¥100 to ¥120, since you would get more yen and therefore more value for each dollar you have. A Japanese student visiting the United States, however, would hope that the dollar would depreciate, so that the yen's purchasing power in terms of dollars would rise.

A change in the exchange rate, then, has a relatively simple and predictable effect on foreign visitors. Life is more complex for nation-states and international businesses, because a change in the FX rate has many different effects on them. To see this, and to see how nations may try to use the FX rate to their advantage, let's work through an example.

For a simple example, consider two countries, the U.S. and France, with two currencies ($ and Ffr), and focus on just one traded good, fine cotton dress shirts, which are meant to represent generally the goods traded between these countries. Suppose that the price is $50 for shirts made in the U.S. and Ffr 250 for shirts made in France (see Table 7–2). (It is natural that shirt manufacturers would price their goods in terms of their home-country currencies.) What does a U.S.-made shirt cost in France? What would a French shirt cost in the U.S.? The answer to these questions depends critically on the exchange rate between the two currencies.

Suppose, for simplicity, the current exchange rate is Ffr 5 per dollar, or 20 cents per franc. At this exchange rate (see Table 7–3), the shirts manufactured in France and the U.S. are priced very competitively. Indeed, adjusting for the exchange rates, they are equally priced in both countries. The Ffr 250 French shirts should sell for $50 in the United States, the same as U.S.-made shirts.[9] The $50 U.S.-made shirts should sell for Ffr 250 in France. The shirts of the two nations are equal values, if there are no style or quality differences to cause buyers to favor one over the other.

This starting point is an example of ***purchasing power parity*** (PPP), where money has the same purchasing power outside a nation as within it. At the PPP exchange rates, equally efficient producers in different countries tend to be equally competitive in international markets.[10] Put more simply, a person with $50 could buy one shirt, either U.S.-made or French, whether in the United States or France. At the PPP exchange rate, the significance of the FX rate effectively disappears. Purchases are made for reasons other than the FX value.

A change in the exchange rate tends to alter the competitive balance between nations, making one country's goods a better value than another. Suppose, for example, that the dollar *depreciated* relative to the franc, from Ffr 5 per dollar to Ffr 4 per dollar. (This is equivalent to the Ffr *appreciating* from 20 cents to 25 cents per franc.) This seemingly minor change in the FX rate will have, in fact, rather large impacts on shoppers and consumers in *both* France and the United States. Table 7–4 shows the initial impacts.

While the domestic prices of the two shirts stay the same ($50 for the U.S. shirt, Ffr 250 for the French shirt), their prices abroad are altered. The $50 U.S. shirt now costs just Ffr 200 in France. Since the dollar is cheaper to people with francs, the

TABLE 7–2   Price Comparisons of Two Shirts

Price of U.S.-made Shirt	$50
Price of French-made Shirt	Ffr 250

TABLE 7–3   Comparison Shopping—FX rate $1 = Ffr 5

	U.S. SHOPPER PRICES	*FRENCH SHOPPER PRICES*
U.S.-made Shirt	$50	$50 = Ffr 250
French-made Shirt	Ffr 250 = $50	Ffr 250

TABLE 7–4   Comparison Shopping—FX Rate $1 = Ffr 4

	U.S. SHOPPER PRICES	*FRENCH SHOPPER PRICES*
U.S.-made Shirt	$50	$50 = Ffr 200
French-made Shirt	Ffr 250 = $62.50	Ffr 250

U.S. product is cheaper, too. Assuming equal style and quality, we can expect French shoppers to switch to the cheaper U.S. goods.

A similar situation will prevail in the U.S. The French shirt still costs Ffr 250, but each franc now costs 25 cents, compared to 20 cents at the previous exchange rate. The French shirt therefore costs $62.50 in the United States (Ffr 250 ÷ 4 francs per dollar = $62.50). Buyers in the U.S. will also switch their purchases in favor of the U.S. products.

The depreciation of the dollar and equivalent appreciation of the franc alters the relative prices of goods in both countries. Buyers switch in favor of the relatively cheaper currency. As purchases of U.S. goods increase, production, jobs, and incomes rise in the U.S. As the demand for French goods falls, production, jobs, and incomes fall in France. The FX rate affects shirts, as the example here indicates, but it also affects *everything else* that a nation buys or sells on international markets. The FX rate is thus the one price that affects virtually all other prices. The impact of the FX rate on a nation's wealth and power can, therefore, be significant.[11]

When a currency's FX value is less than the PPP value that equalizes international prices, we say that it is *undervalued*. This would be the situation for the dollar in this example, since the PPP exchange rate is Ffr 5 per dollar, but the currency's value has fallen to Ffr 4. As you can see, there is considerable temptation for a mercantilist nation (or a political leader facing an important election) to attempt to achieve an undervalued currency by manipulating FX markets in some way. The undervalued currency would shift production and international trade in its favor. Having an undervalued currency is clearly good for domestic industries, since imports are discouraged and exports increase. There is a dark side to currency depreciation, however. Goods that *must* be imported will cost more when your currency is undervalued. If a nation imports many vital items, such as food or oil, this currency effect can tend to reduce living standards and retard economic growth, as well as cause inflation. In most cases, it is wrong to conclude either that a cheaper currency is good for a nation or that it is bad. Rather, changes in exchange rates tend to unleash a series of changes in external economic relations, some positive and some negative. The net effect is often hard to calculate.

Sometimes less developed nations try to gain some advantage from the FX rate by *overvaluing* their currency to get access to cheaper imported goods, shifting the terms of trade in their favor. The cost of imported products, including perhaps food, arms, and manufactured goods, is artificially low if a currency is overvalued. A less developed nation might try this overvaluation strategy if it was having trouble paying for imported technology, for example, or a vital resource such as oil. Although its own goods would become less competitive abroad, it could at least enjoy some imported items at lower cost.

In practice, it is very hard for LDCs to reap the gains of overvaluation in any meaningful way because their currencies are usually quite soft, which means that they are not much used in international business and finance. This does not stop them from trying, however, and many LDC currencies end up being systematically overvalued in an attempt, like as not, to buy imported military hardware for a little less. This almost invariably winds up choking domestic production, leaving the LDC dependent for help on foreign sellers and lenders.

CRISIS IN THE CFA FRANC ZONE

Fourteen African nations (Benin, Burkina Faso, Côte d'Ivoire, Mali, Niger, Senegal, Togo, Cameroon, the Central African Republic, Congo, Equatorial Guinea, the Islamic Republic of Cormoros, and Gabon) form a unique international financial structure called the African Franc Zone or the CFA zone. The currencies of these third world nations are pegged to the French franc, providing a stable foreign exchange relationship between France and nations that were once within its colonial sphere.

Membership in the CFA is a mixed blessing for these African nations. On one hand, they benefit from a much more stable exchange rate and hence more stable external economic relations than if their currency were allowed to "float" against other currencies. In essence, the members of the CFA zone, soft-currency countries in every objective respect, gain some aspect of "hard" currency by formally linking their money to the French franc. There are costs to this strategy, too, however. One important cost is that the value of their currency relative to, say, the U.S. dollar is determined by the relationship between the U.S. and French economies, not by factors relating to their own economies, which may be especially relevant in particular situations.

Over time in the 1980s and early 1990s, the CFA franc became overvalued. While the value of the franc, and therefore the CFA franc, might well have reflected the value of a French franc "ticket" in international trade, it did not reflect the corresponding value of a ticket to purchase the goods or services from these African nations' economies.

The fact that the CFA franc became overvalued created winners and losers within the CFA nations. The agricultural sector of the economy, for example, suffered from the currency imbalance. The fact that the CFA franc was overvalued made agricultural exports from these nations uncompetitive on international markets (since the CFA franc was relatively costly, their produce was costly to foreign buyers). At the same time, however, agricultural imports into the CFA zone were relatively cheap, since other currencies were undervalued relative to the CFA franc, putting pressure on African farmers to cut prices in order to compete. Important sectors—like agriculture—of the CFA nations were therefore disadvantaged by the CFA franc's high value.

Luxury goods, military weapons, oil, medicines, and other imported goods were made artificially cheap due to the CFA franc's condition, benefiting the minority of the population in the CFA zone who purchased large quantities of these items.

On January 12, 1994, the CFA franc was devalued by 50 percent relative to the French franc—a traumatic event indeed, since the FX rate is the one price that affects all other prices within a nation. The price of imported French goods doubled overnight for these African nations, and the cost of their own goods halved for for-

Continued

CRISIS IN THE CFA FRANC ZONE, *continued*

eign buyers, in terms of the French franc. Franc-denominated debts doubled in local currency terms. Although this financial action was intended to make the overvalued CFA nations competitive with other countries, in fact a wide net of winners and losers was created. In general, persons who exported goods and services outside the CFA zone found themselves more competitive, as did persons who produced goods that competed with imports. The cheaper CFA franc gave their products an advantage in the marketplace over more expensive foreign goods. Persons who purchased large quantities of imports, however, were worse off, as were those who owed foreign debts denominated in a hard currency such as the French franc, which was now much more expensive.

The impact on the African countries was sudden and dramatic as the cost, in terms of local currency, of imports from France (and other hard currency nations) shot up. The alternative to this devaluation, however, was also dismal. The *Financial Times* of London reported that "the alternative to devaluation was not rosy. French aid would have been entirely swallowed in helping CFA states to service their foreign debt because without devaluation these states would not have got fresh credit from the International Monetary Fund, the World Bank, and other donors. The relationship between the CFA members and France would have been increasingly like 'that of Cuba and the old Soviet Union. . . .' "[12]

The New York Times report also saw the CFA regime as a remnant of nineteenth century imperialism. "The nub of the French post-colonial relationship is economic. The Ivory Coast, for example, buys about 40 percent of its imports from France and the French own a third of the country's manufacturing industries. Elsewhere, more than half of French foreign aid goes to Africa, making France the continent's foremost patron."[13]

The sudden devaluation left many in France and in Africa "fuming," according to the *Financial Times*. "Politically, they accuse the French government of betraying its old colonies and friends in Africa. Economically, they see an end to a market in which African ability to purchase French goods was kept artificially high by a parity unchanged since 1948. Financially, they are reeling from the implications of having their African assets halved and cash flow severely disrupted."[14]

The New York Times reported that "people are trying to adapt to increases for nearly everything they eat and drink. Prices for pharmaceutical products, nearly all of which are imported, have soared. The cost of drugs for malaria, the continent's biggest killer, have nearly doubled in some places, putting them out of the reach of many Africans."[15]

The case of the CFA franc illustrates several important points about the financial structure as it relates to less developed countries such as these French-speaking African nations. Clearly, the foreign exchange rate matters; it affects the cost of precious imports, the price competitiveness of their exports, the value that foreigners assign to their assets, their ability to gain international support (IMF and World Bank backing) for their debts, and all manner of other issues. Exchange rates "count" for LDCs. A second point is that soft-currency LDCs are at a disadvantage in international finance. The CFA nations benefited from their fixed rate against the franc for over forty-five years, but at the critical moment in 1994 this was no protection from financial chaos.

"The measures that have been taken after the devaluation—IMF and World Bank decisions, the French forgiveness of debt—are all quite encouraging," according to Citibank official Robert Thornton, as quoted in the *New York Times* article. But considerable short-term pain must be endured in the form of falling material living standards before long-term gains due to expanding exports and rising levels of economic growth can be realized.

INTRODUCTION TO THE INTERNATIONAL MONETARY SYSTEM

The international monetary system is the set of relationships that determine how international payments are made and how international debts are settled.[16] Since international payments generally involve foreign exchange transactions—converting dollars, for example, into yen in order to pay for goods imported from Japan—it is convenient to think of the international monetary system as the system that organizes foreign exchange (FX, in international finance jargon).

The FX system organizes the terms and conditions for international payments and sets the method for determining the exchange rate between different countries' currencies (the FX rate). The three main types of systems that are important to us are:

- *Fixed* or **"pegged" exchange rates**, where the FX rate is most heavily influenced by state actions;
- *Flexible* or **"floating" exchange** rates, where international FX markets are the principle determinants of exchange rates; and
- *Managed* or **"coordinated" FX rates**, where states and markets are both important determinants of the FX rates.

In the twentieth century, we have experienced each of these different systems.

Each of these exchange rate systems attempts to achieve simultaneously two different and often conflicting goals. The first goal is stability. Stable FX rates and a stable FX system is a necessary condition for international trade and investment. Instability discourages individuals and nations from establishing close linkages and encourages nations to act in their own narrow self-interest. The "correct" FX value of one currency relative to another, however, tends to change over time as the economies of nations move in different directions at different speeds.

The FX system, therefore, also must be flexible enough to value different currencies effectively over time, which means that no currency can be allowed to be persistently overvalued (priced too high) or undervalued (priced too low) relative to other currencies. A currency that is consistently misvalued creates a distortion in international economic relations, which often leads to distorted political relations. During the period 1981–1985, for example, the U.S. dollar was persistently overvalued, which made U.S. goods less competitive in international marketplaces (an economic distortion). Congress threatened trade barriers and other measures against our political allies (political distortion) in an attempt to deal politically with an economic disequilibrium.

The FX system must also be flexible enough to deal with the inevitable unexpected events in the IPE. Changing international economic and political structures tend to distort financial flows from their historical patterns, and the FX systems need to be able to accommodate these changes, whether they are long term or transitory. In the 1970s, for example, the rise of OPEC and the corresponding surge in oil prices dramatically changed the pattern of international payments, shifting billions of dollars toward oil-exporting nations. In the 1990s, adjustment problems involve integrating countries such as Russia and China, which for political reasons previously had little involvement in international financial markets, into the global monetary system with a minimum of unnecessary distortions elsewhere.

The exchange rate system, therefore, must be both stable and flexible. It should be stable enough to encourage long-term commitments among and between nations, but it must be flexible enough to change smoothly with the times. You probably won't be surprised to discover that we have not yet found the perfect system to achieve these dual objectives, although several different approaches have been tried including fixed exchange rates, market-based exchange rates, and managed exchange rates.

FIXED FX: THE CLASSICAL GOLD STANDARD

A fixed exchange rate system attempts to tackle these problems through agreements by states to set exchange rates at "correct" levels, backed up by state actions to keep them there. The state therefore has a very significant role in managing a system of fixed exchange rates. The two most famous fixed exchange rate systems are the gold standard, which operated in the last decades of the nineteenth century, and the Bretton Woods gold–dollar standard, which worked more or less from about 1946 to about 1973.

Many people misunderstand the nature of the gold standard, viewing it as a sort of universal monetary cure. They think that simply tying (pegging) a currency to a given quantity of gold will assure stability and automatic adjustment to any imbalance. Their idea is at heart a liberal one—that if currencies are defined in terms of gold and gold is freely traded in international markets, then the "invisible hand" of the market will set the correct equilibrium price for gold and simultaneously balance international payments among nations. The fact that the world economy experienced tremendous growth during gold's rein in the nineteenth century is commonly cited as proof of the market's efficiency and the gold standard's wisdom.

It would be convenient if the world's international monetary problems could be solved by simply returning to the gold standard. Unfortunately, a closer look at financial history refutes this notion. Economic historians believe that the key to world economic growth during the period of the gold standard was not pure Adam Smith liberalism, but rather the effectiveness of Great Britain as an international financial hegemon.

The gold standard worked because Great Britain (and the Bank of England) were willing to play financial hegemon and bear the costs of keeping the world monetary system stable.[17] As the world's financial and trading leader, Britain had the most to gain from a stable and flexible world monetary system. But supporting such a system was costly, since at times it was necessary to sacrifice domestic concerns in order to preserve international order.[18] Sometimes, for example, it was necessary to raise British interest rates, depressing loan-financed economic activity at home and creating losses for holders of fixed-rate bonds, to preserve the pound's gold value. The cost of monetary hegemony for Britain was real.

Walter Bagehot's Lombard Street was the center of this hegemonic structure. The Bank of England controlled international flows of gold and currency so as to keep currencies stable and keep the FX system flexible. The cost of maintaining this role eventually weakened Britain's financial system, but it contributed to a period of tremendous world economic growth. When Britain could no longer afford these costs, the gold standard collapsed. Not since Keynes helped cut Britain's rigid "golden tethers" have serious economists believed that gold and laissez-faire are the simple prescription for monetary stability.

FIXED FX AGAIN: THE BRETTON WOODS SYSTEM

Post–World War II IPE was born in Bretton Woods, New Hampshire, and students of IPE necessarily become familiar with what is often called the Bretton Woods system. The Mount Washington Hotel in Bretton Woods was the site of an economic conference in 1944 that brought together the economic leaders of all the Allied nations. Their task, which they took very seriously, was to create a postwar economic order that would be stable and flexible, promote economic growth and development, and avoid the nationalistic pressures that led to two world wars in a single generation. It was a big job.

What came out of Bretton Woods was a set of international institutions and a particular form of international monetary system. The World Bank, the International Monetary Fund, and the General Agreement on Tariffs and Trade[19] were the institutions that evolved from these critical meetings, along with the Bretton Woods FX system, which characterized world monetary affairs from 1946 to about 1973.

The Bretton Woods system was an attempt to construct a set of IPE structures built on pluralistic international institutions, not solely the strength of a hegemonic power. The United States wanted an orderly system of international relations, but it was unwilling to assume the role that Great Britain had played in the nineteenth century, with its many burdens. Thus, whereas London's Lombard Street had been the center of the gold standard FX system, the multilateral international monetary system was meant to be the center of the Bretton Woods monetary system.

The Bretton Woods FX system can be thought of as a fixed exchange rate system built on a gold–dollar standard. Formally, each nation established a fixed value of its currency in terms of gold. The U.S. also established a gold value for its currency at the rate of $35 per ounce. In practice, however, this established a fixed FX rate between the dollar and other currencies, and the dollar became the medium for international transactions. It is convenient to think of the Bretton Woods FX system as a wheel with the dollar at its hub. It was thus the task of the United States, despite its reluctance to do so, to bear the hegemon's burden, regulating the dollar so as to provide financial stability and also the necessary degree of flexibility.[20]

This system worked well in the 1950s and the early 1960s, when the United States was clearly the world's strongest economic power. The United States supplied dollars to the world system, which stimulated economic growth in Europe and Japan, creating new and larger markets for U.S. goods and services. The period of Bretton

Wood's greatest success was, like the zenith of the gold standard, a time of unusually vigorous worldwide prosperity and growth.

Eventually, however, the United States became uncomfortable in the role of hegemon. As Europe and Japan expanded and achieved self-sustaining growth, they no longer required the large inflows of dollars. But the United States found it difficult to stem this flow, since sending dollars abroad (to purchase foreign goods or investments) was an effective way to manage an increasingly complex domestic situation. As David P. Calleo has argued, the United States changed from a "benevolent hegemon" to a "selfish hegemon," using its place at the center of things to preserve wealth and power, as the costs of hegemony weakened it.[21]

By the late 1960s, the United States was faced with a domestic war on poverty, an international war on communism (in Vietnam), and the burden of Bretton Woods hegemony, which called for greater financial discipline. Eventually, U.S. leaders were forced to choose between national interest and international responsibility, which is a fundamental tension in IPE. The key decision was made in 1971, when President Richard Nixon formally broke the link between the dollar and gold. The world slowly shook off its system of fixed exchange rates. By the oil shocks of 1973–1974, a system of flexible exchange rates had been established.

THE LESSONS OF BRETTON WOODS

What are the lessons of the Bretton Woods FX system? This is a controversial question in IPE. For pure Adam Smith liberals, the history of Bretton Woods illustrates the futility of trying to set exchange rates through state action rather than market forces. The state-based system was doomed from the start, according to liberals, because no government can know as much as well as the market can.

Others view Bretton Woods as an example of the important role of a benevolent hegemon in IPE. The world thrived so long as the United States was effective in its role as monetary hegemon, it seems. Since the collapse of the Bretton Woods system, world growth has been much slower and uneven. Scholars who take this point of view talk of the need for a new Bretton Woods agreement and a renewed hegemonic structure to manage the international monetary system.

Another lesson taken from Bretton Woods illustrates the temptations of hegemony. All hegemons, this realist argument goes, eventually become overextended and exploit their position for national gain or to preserve wealth and power.

Finally, there are those who see in results of Bretton Woods an example of selfish nationalistic action by the United States or even ruthless capitalist exploitation. The United States was the principal beneficiary of Bretton Woods, they argue, gaining economically at the expense of other countries. For them, Bretton Woods is an example of how power can be abused in IPE.

Neither the gold standard nor the Bretton Woods system achieved the dual goals of an exchange rate system. The gold standard was not flexible enough to adjust to a world where Britain was in decline and the United States and Germany were rising in economic and political importance. Gold was too rigid in this regard. The

Bretton Woods system, on the other hand, was not stable enough but also too rigid. Hard currency countries frequently changed their "fixed" rates against the dollar, to adjust to rapidly changing events and conditions. Many of the advantages of fixed rates were therefore lost. At the same time, the United States found it impossible to adjust the dollar's value (it was overvalued during much of the 1960s). So the Bretton Woods system was both too flexible on the edges and too rigid at the center.

Perhaps the most important lesson of Bretton Woods (and the gold standard) is that there is a fundamental tension between domestic needs and international responsibilities built into any structure of IPE. The stability of the IPE structure requires nations at times to sacrifice domestic political and economic interests in favor of international cooperation. Fixed exchange rates rely on states taking necessary internal and external actions to keep FX rates fixed. This is sometimes called the "discipline" of fixed FX rates. We now know that, faced with high unemployment or high defense bills, states are more likely to sacrifice FX stability and deal with these problems than ignore these problems in defense of their currencies.

But IPE needs both a strong international system and nations with strong domestic political and economic foundations, which creates a tension when a choice must be made between them. Great Britain minded its international responsibilities with great care, which caused it at times to take actions that weakened its domestic economy and eventually made it too weak to remain a hegemon. The United States, on the other hand, chose at critical moments to favor its domestic political and economic interests and to sacrifice its obligation to keep the Bretton Woods system running smoothly. This weakened the international economy, which ultimately also weakened the United States.

THE IMF AND THE WORLD BANK

The international monetary system is made up of a number of important institutions that students of IPE need to understand in basic terms. Here is a brief introduction to *central banks*, the *World Bank*, and the *International Monetary Fund*.

Central banks are the national monetary authorities that represent nation-states in the international arena. The Federal Reserve System, for example, is the U.S. central bank. If you look at U.S. currency, you will see that dollars are actually Federal Reserve notes, issued by the Federal Reserve. The Federal Reserve regulates the availability of money and credit within the United States, plays a role in regulating the banking system, and works with other countries' central banks. The Bank of England, the Bank of Japan, and the Bundesbank are the central banks of Great Britain, Japan, and Germany.

The **International Monetary Fund** is the central bankers' central bank. The IMF is an international organization that tries to create stable and responsive international financial relations among nations, just as central banks seek to create a favorable financial climate within each country's borders. The IMF has, since its creation at Bretton Woods, played an important role in the international monetary system.

The IMF's most controversial function is to serve as a "lender of last resort" in international finance. That is, the IMF stands ready to make loans to keep debtor nations

Continued

THE IMF AND THE WORLD BANK, *continued*

from collapsing under the weight of their obligations, possibly causing panic and chaos throughout the international financial system. The IMF's help, however, is "conditional." Countries that seek the IMF's help must be willing to accept the sorts of austere policies that it generally recommends—higher taxes, reduced government spending, cuts in subsidies, and the like. These policies tend to reduce living standards in a nation in the short run, but they are often effective in restoring fiscal stability. The IMF-sponsored reforms in Mexico, begun in the mid-1980s, achieved some success in providing a more stable foundation for Mexican economic growth, although Mexico's 1995 fiscal problems and currency crisis suggest that the mid-80s reforms did not achieve all their goals. Mercantilists, however, often see the IMF as acting in the interests of the U.S., its largest shareholder, and structuralists see the IMF as part of the capitalist core's systematic exploitation of the periphery.

The **World Bank** is another creation of Bretton Woods. The official name of the World Bank is the International Bank for Reconstruction and Development (IBRD), which is a bit more descriptive. In the period immediately after World War II, the World Bank funded efforts to reconstruct the economies of war-torn Europe. Since the 1950s, the World Bank has concentrated on the problems of less developed countries, making loans to LDCs at terms that are generally far better than they could get directly from international capital markets.

Like the IMF, the World Bank is controversial and its motives have been questioned. The bank makes loans for economic development purposes; it can make loans to improve railways or irrigation systems, for example, since such projects stimulate economic growth, but it cannot makes loans to improve social justice or reduce income inequality unless a financial return is likely. In recent years, the World Bank has been criticized for funding projects with undesirable environmental impacts—economic growth is often hard on nature—but it has recently begun "green" initiatives to promote environmentally friendly economic development in LDCs.

MARKETS AT WORK: FLOATING EXCHANGE RATES

Flexible or "floating" exchange rates are set by pure market forces, with a minimum of direct state influence. The hard currency FX system moved from fixed to flexible in the early 1970s, which was a time of enormous structural change in the world. Under a system of flexible FX rates, a nation's FX rate depends on the expected value of its FX ticket (to goods, services, and investments) relative to the tickets of other nations. The FX rate changes daily as economic and political conditions change. The dollar has mostly floated since 1973.

The flexible FX rate was intended to resolve the tension between domestic needs and international responsibilities by putting the market in charge of the international system, leaving states to look after their domestic political and economic priorities. Flexible exchange rates were also intended to replace the unwise or erratic state action of a hegemon with the smooth, logical, efficient action of the market. This, however, has not turned out to be the case. For one thing, it is impossible to isolate markets from states, since state actions necessarily influence the value of an FX ticket. Neither stability nor appropriate flexibility has been achieved to the extent that the architects of the flexible FX system envisioned.

Economic liberals, who tend to favor flexible FX rates, argue that the problem lies in unwise states and that flexible rates would work just fine if governments would behave. Realists today recognize that states cannot be relied on to follow laissez-faire policies when vital domestic or international interests are at stake. A truly laissez-faire floating exchange rate system is therefore only a theorist's vision, not a practical reality. There is a more important reason for the failure of floating exchange rates to achieve their goal of stability and flexibility. Put simply, the FX market is an instrument that has too many functions under a floating FX system. It cannot reliably perform them all at once.

The FX ticket is a claim on a number of different items. The dollar FX ticket buys U.S. manufactured goods, natural resources, physical assets (such as hotels or office buildings), business assets (such as RCA stock), and it is also a lottery ticket for speculators who bet for or against currencies on the international markets. It is probably too much to ask the FX rate to set the "right price" for the dollar so as to balance all these markets. Almost necessarily, some imbalance will occur.

In the mid-1980s, for example, the U.S. dollar was in high demand on currency markets as a ticket to purchase U.S. investments, such as government bonds and corporate shares. The dollar's FX price reflected this demand, rising to an FX rate of more than ¥250 during one period. This investment FX equilibrium threw international trade all out of balance, a problem from which the United States has not yet fully recovered. The high price of the dollar made U.S. goods and services very costly abroad, and foreign goods were artificially cheap for U.S. consumers. Imports increased and exports began to dry up. The U.S. trade imbalance soared.

In the 1990s, the dollar-yen exchange rate is under a different sort of pressure. Financial problems within Japan in the early 1990s caused Japanese firms to bring some of their investment funds back home, to stabilize the domestic economy. As Japanese investors converted dollars into yen, they caused the dollar to depreciate and the yen to appreciate. At one point in 1995, the dollar fell to nearly ¥80 per dollar. This makes U.S. goods inexpensive in Japan, but Japanese products more costly abroad. Japan's exports fell, making their domestic economic problems even worse.

It should be clear from this one example that whatever its advantages in theory, *in practice* floating exchange rates have proved to be so flexible in so many ways as to be unstable. The case of the dollar's swing from an overvalued ¥250 to an undervalued ¥80 is an extreme example, but a relevant one nonetheless, since U.S.-Japanese relations are so important in IPE today. The short-run political and economic decisions that are made based on FX fluctuations are unlikely to be in the long-run interest of the states and markets involved. In other words, if states consider *only* their domestic economic and political needs, there is no one to look after the international system, which becomes a "nonsystem."

This problem can be seen by again drawing from the recent history of U.S.-Japanese IPE relations. As the soaring dollar helped create a large and persistent U.S.-Japan trade imbalance in the 1980s, many business and political leaders called for mercantilist policies, such as domestic subsidies and trade restrictions, to restore U.S. economic power. The "liberal" FX structure created pressures for "mercantilist" policies with respect to the production and trade structures of IPE.

In summary, neither fixed nor floating exchange rates in the post–World War II period have succeeded in achieving the goals of stability and flexibility in the long run. The tension between domestic needs and international responsibilities remains unresolved. The state-based system of fixed exchange rates seems to depend too much on the strength and commitment of a hegemon. The market-based system of floating exchange rates seems to ask the invisible hand to do too many things at once, sacrificing stability in order to gain extreme flexibility. Neither system has provided the right balance between domestic interests and a stable international system.

STATES AND MARKETS TOGETHER: MANAGED EXCHANGE RATES

A third FX system that is often considered is called *managed exchange rates*. This system attempts to combine the best of both state and market actions, while trying to avoid their failings. The European Monetary System (EMS) is the most important recent example of managed exchange rates. Under the EMS, the currencies of many (but not all) members of the European Union are linked in a system designed to minimize instability through state action. The basic idea is that the market provides short-run flexibility, but that states will intervene to provide long-run stability. Currencies in the EMS stay relatively fixed against each other, varying by no more that about 5 percent on average in the short run.

The key to managed exchange rates is *policy coordination*. States, through their central banks, must agree to cooperate with each other, to avoid taking domestic actions that might provoke international instability. The idea is that if two national economies are going in the same direction at about the same speed, then their FX rates should remain fairly constant because the value of one FX ticket relative to the other should not change dramatically. This system works so long as both nations keep their pace and avoid temptations to speed up or slow down or change course, even if there are strong domestic interests in favor of changing speed or direction.

In other words, the practical problem with managed exchange rates is that policy coordination requires the state, at some point, to be willing to sacrifice what seems to be their nation interest in order to preserve a stable international financial structure. The classic tension between individual (nation) and group (nations) appears. Self-interest and national interest are powerful forces, so policy coordination in the long run is not guaranteed. While the EMS might need the central banks of France and Germany to coordinate their interest rate actions, for example, the sphere of cooperation is limited by the political strength of forces within these two nations that call for lower interest rates (to spur growth) or higher interest rates (to combat inflation). If the domestic interests of the two nations differ, international cooperation must almost inevitably be sacrificed.

It would be nice to say that managed exchange rates have been successful in Europe. In fact, the EMS has been very unstable and erratic in the 1990s. States have cooperated at times (sometimes at great cost), but also behaved selfishly and unpredictably at other times. We are still searching for an ideal FX system. In today's world, all three FX systems can be found somewhere. The dollar floats for the most part. Within the European Union, many of the currencies use the EMS managed system. Finally, most LDCs try to peg their soft currencies against the hard currency of their biggest trading partner. For example, Mexico's peso is pegged to the dollar.

THE PROBLEMS OF A WORLD MONETARY ORDER

> The Western financial system is rapidly coming to resemble nothing so much as a vast casino. Every day games are played in this casino that involve sums of money so large that they cannot be imagined. . . . This cannot help but have grave consequences.[22]

Perhaps the FX system requires a hegemon—a manager, to stimulate cooperation and keep the right balance of flexibility and stability, and keep finance from becoming a casino. But *not* a selfish hegemon. The problem, as Susan Strange and David Calleo have noted, is

> to have a manager without having a tyrant. In other words, the balance of power must be such that the country exercising the managerial hegemonic role is held to its task of defending the system rather than permitted to exploit it.[23]

This chapter does not end on a comforting note. The finance structure is of critical importance to the IPE, but we have seen that there are many unresolved issues and unsolved problems. The world clearly needs a stable FX system that is able to adapt effectively to changing structural conditions. Postwar history, however, provides few insights into how such a system can be designed and implemented. This is important since, as we have seen, problems in the financial structure can create or exacerbate problems elsewhere in the IPE.

The international monetary system interacts with other structures of IPE. The recent instability of this aspect of IPE has created both economic and political tensions, straining the trade, security, and technology structures that, together with the finance structure, link the nations and peoples of the world.

The problems of a world monetary order thus remain. We cannot take for granted the stability and adaptability of our financial structure, an important consideration as we turn to face the additional challenges of the future. In this sense, there is great stability in the international monetary system. Recall Walter Bagehot's comment on the financial structure of his day:

> I am by no means an alarmist. I believe our system, though curious and peculiar, may be worked safely; but if we wish to work it, we must study it. We must not think we have an easy task when we have a difficult task, or that we are living in a natural state when we are really living in an artificial one. Money will not manage itself, and Lombard Street has a great deal of money to manage.[24]

DISCUSSION QUESTIONS

1. Explain the difference between a hard currency and a soft currency. What disadvantages does a soft currency nation have when engaging in international trade? Explain.
2. What does it mean for a nation's currency to be overvalued? How does an overvalued currency affect that nation? Use the example of the CFA franc zone to explain the costs and benefits of an overvalued currency and the difficulties that arise when an overvalued currency is devalued.
3. The U.S. dollar depreciated dramatically relative to the Japanese yen in 1995. What impact would this event likely have on consumers and businesses in each country? Is a falling dollar good or bad for the United States? Explain.
4. What are the characteristics of a good international monetary system? Which system of exchange rates has met these goals—fixed FX, flexible FX, or managed FX? Explain.

SUGGESTED READINGS

David P. Calleo. *The Imperious Economy.* Cambridge, MA: Harvard University Press, 1982.

Kenneth W. Dam. *The Rules of the Game.* Chicago: University of Chicago Press, 1982.

Paul De Grauwe. *International Money: Post-war Trends and Theories.* New York: Oxford University Press, 1989.

———. *The Economics of Monetary Integration.* New York: Oxford University Press, 1992.

Barry Eichengreen, ed. *The Gold Standard in Theory and History.* New York: Methuen, 1985.

Yoichi Funabashi. *Managing the Dollar: From the Plaza to the Louvre.* Washington, DC: Institute for International Economics, 1988.

Charles P. Kindleberger. *International Capital Movements.* New York: Cambridge University Press, 1987.

———. *A Financial History of Western Europe*, 2nd ed. New York: Oxford University Press, 1993.

Michael Mandelbaum. Especially chapter 6 in *The Fate of Nations.* New York: Cambridge University Press, 1988.

Ronald I. McKinnon. *Money in International Exchange.* New York: Oxford University Press, 1979.

Paul Volcker and Toyoo Gyohten. *Changing Fortunes.* New York: Times Books, 1992.

Andrew Walter. *World Power and World Money.* New York: St. Martin's Press, 1991.

NOTES

1. Bagehot, Walter, *Lombard Street: A Description of the Money Market* (Philadelphia: Orion Editions, 1991), 8.
2. Ibid., 10.
3. Walter Bagehot (1826–1877) was editor of *The Economist* from 1860 to 1877 and one of the most influential writers on political economy of his day.
4. All the member nations of the European Union have relatively hard currencies because they are linked, or "pegged," in one way or another, to each other and therefore to the very hard German mark.
5. What really matters is inflation-adjusted interest rates in one country compared with similar inflation-adjusted interest rates in another country. If U.S. interest rates fall, for example, and interest rates fall equally in Great Britain, then the FX rate between the two nations is unlikely to change significantly.

6. Exchange rates always change inversely because we are comparing one against the other. If the exchange rate fell to $1.30 per £, we would say that the pound had depreciated (become less valuable), so the dollar has appreciated (become more valuable relative to the pound).

7. The yen depreciated, since it takes more yen to buy a dollar. The dollar has appreciated or gained in relative value.

8. The mark appreciated and the dollar depreciated.

9. These calculations ignore additional costs associated with foreign sales, such as transportation, tariffs, etc.

10. This is part of the "level playing field" that people in business and economics believe is necessary in international trade and finance. For the most part, however, the "level playing field" refers to nondiscriminatory trade barriers, such as tariffs, quotas, and subsidies.

11. All countries are not equally affected by FX changes at all times. Very "open" nations, like Great Britain, experience much greater FX effects than more "closed" economies, such as the U.S. The impact of an FX change also depends on the cause, direction, and magnitude of the change, and the coincident actions, if any, of other countries.

12. *Financial Times*, "Disquiet Over CFA Franc Fall," 28 January 1994, 6.

13. *The New York Times*, "French Currency Move Provokes Unrest in Africa," 23 February 1994, 6.

14. *Financial Times*, 28 January 1994, 6.

15. *The New York Times*, 23 February 1994, 1.

16. The international monetary system is in fact a "structure" of IPE in the sense used in this text. Since it is most commonly referred to as a "system," however, we use this terminology here.

17. See chapter 3 for a discussion of hegemony and the IPE controversies that surround this topic.

18. This point is easiest to see in the security structure. Britain's navy was used to preserve world peace during this period, but that navy was very costly to support. The domestic costs of the navy was the price Britain paid to gain the benefits of the hegemon.

19. The Bretton Woods agreements did not actually include the GATT. Proposals that emerged from Bretton Woods included a much stronger institution, the International Trade Organization (ITO), which was never implemented. The ITO would have had considerable authority to implement free trade policies. Its powers were probably greater than nations were willing to grant in the early postwar period. The weaker but still successful GATT emerged a few years later to fill the gap left by the ITO as an institution promoting open markets and free trade.

20. The International Monetary Fund lacks adequate resources to allow it to be the multilateral "lender of last resort" that was envisioned by the Bretton Woods architects.

21. See David P. Calleo, *The Imperious Economy* (Cambridge, MA: Harvard University Press, 1982) and *Beyond American Hegemony* (New York: Basic Books, 1987).

22. Susan Strange, *Casino Capitalism* (London: Basil Blackwell, 1986), 1–2.

23. David Calleo and Susan Strange, "Money and World Politics," in *Paths to International Political Economy*, Susan Strange, ed. (London: George Allen & Unwin, 1984), 115.

24. Bagehot, *Lombard Street*, 10.

8

Debt: The Political Economy of International Finance

OVERVIEW

It was not an accident that, when Charles Dickens wanted to write a story about how much people depend upon each other and how tightly our lives are linked together, he made his main character a money-lender named Scrooge. The story, of course, was *A Christmas Carol*, and it was based on the paradox that a creditor needs the people who are his debtors as much (more!) than they need him.

Debt creates a bond of unusual strength and complexity. Financial connections can be mutually advantageous avenues of economic intercourse, clever levers that raise wealth and power for all. It can also be a forceful weapon or even a snare that entraps borrower, lender, or both.

Financial connections have always been both local and global, involving both states and markets. In the past twenty years, however, technological change and liberal market reforms have essentially globalized the international debt structure, placing debt dynamics increasingly outside the jurisdiction of nation-states. These factors have changed both the nature of international debt and the state's role in the international financial structure.

This chapter has four purposes. The first is to introduce the vocabulary of international finance and survey the world of the balance of payments and the basic institutions that deal with debt on the international level. The second purpose is to outline three perspectives on international finance. We will briefly examine the international finance structure as seen from the liberal, mercantilist, and structuralist viewpoints.

A third section focuses on the changing nature of international finance in a world of instantaneous global telecommunications. We will examine the ways that the finance structure has changed and explain why. The LDC debt crisis of the 1980s is discussed as an example of the development of the global financial structure.

A theme that emerges from this discussion is the importance of cooperation among nation-states on issues involving international debt. This chapter ends, therefore, with an analysis of the "prisoners' dilemma" and the problem of achieving cooperation in a world beset by self-interest.

Twenty years from now economists will think of the 1980s not as the decade of the international debt crisis, nor of the dollar's boom and bust, still less of Reaganomics and "monetarism." All these mattered, but none of them marked a decisive change in the forces that drive the world economy. Yet the 1980s did witness such a change. During those years many of the boundaries between national financial markets dissolved and a truly global capital market began to emerge. It is for this that the past decade will be remembered. And, in all likelihood, the next one will be remembered for the world's struggles to cope with it.

The Economist (19 September 1992)[1]

Debt is one aspect of the international finance structure that demands special attention. Debt creates a set of important relationships that affect all aspects of IPE. Where a nation stands in the web of international finance affects its behavior. In this chapter, we will become acquainted with the peculiar language of international finance, examine the nature of international debt relationships, and begin to understand how this important part of the IPE is changing and what the consequences of change might be.

In simple terms, the finance structure comprises the set of relationships, institutions, and practices that bind together creditors and debtors, borrowers and lenders. These relationships exist within the framework provided by the international monetary system, which was discussed in chapter 7. The finance structure creates a pattern of rights and obligations that conditions the behavior of nations, businesses, and individuals. To a very important extent, what happens to trade, security, and technology in the IPE today depends on finance.

The finance structure deals in debt—the formal or informal obligations that link creditor and debtor. For most people, debt is largely a local concern, involving family, friends, or the bank up the street. The finance structure, however, has been international in its scope for hundreds of years. As early as the fourteenth century, for example, the Florentine banking firms of the Bardi and the Peruzzi were engaged in complex financial transactions throughout Europe.[2] The modern era of international finance can be dated to 1817, when London's Baring Brothers created an international financial structure to accommodate the massive indemnity payments imposed on France by the Treaty of Paris.[3]

Today, the international financial system is undergoing rapid and dramatic change. Finance is increasingly a *global* structure, where nation-states are less important and global markets a more powerful force. The *globalization* of finance is the single most important trend in finance today.

This globalization of finance both magnifies the tensions within the financial structure and causes these stresses to spread, like earthquake tremors, to the other structures of international political economy: trade, security, and knowledge. The fact that finance is increasingly global, for example, has accelerated the growth of global business firms, which produce and sell everywhere. Global finance makes global business possible. The changes we will discuss in this chapter are accelerating the pace of change throughout the international political economy.

THE NATURE AND SIGNIFICANCE OF FINANCE

Finance is sometimes perceived as a sterile enterprise. Plato, for example, condemned income earned through money-lending as unjust, since he could not see any goods or services being produced through financial paper-shuffling. To see finance this way, however, is to look only at shadows and to miss the real action. Financial transactions involve both shadow and substance. Real resources—the stuff of wealth and power, the difference between subsistence and luxury—form the substance. The paper trail that these resources leave behind as they move from one use to another—the checks, forms, certificates, and receipts—are the shadows of resources on the move.

Here is a paradox of finance. We tend to think of finance as sterile because we see the shadows and miss the movements of real resources, which take place far away from the paper involved. But the real substance here depends on the existence of its shadow (not the other way around, as in everyday life). Real resources are not easily moved from person to person or place to place under ordinary circumstances, so the development of efficient forms of finance (clever shadows!) is a necessary condition for the sorts of relationships that lie at the heart of international political economy.

The sets of relationships that form the financial structure bind together those who pay and those who receive. As with other IPE structures, the nature of these ties is complex and controversial—the question "*cui bono?*" must always be asked. The answer to this question is not always as one would expect. This is another paradox of finance. John Maynard Keynes once noted that if he owed the bank a hundred pounds sterling and couldn't pay it, he was in trouble. But if he owed a hundred thousand pounds and couldn't pay, the *bank* was in trouble. The character of a financial relationship thus depends on the quantities involved as well as the nature of the connections it creates.

THE VOCABULARY OF INTERNATIONAL FINANCE

Like most other fields, international finance has a specialized vocabulary that it uses to describe the world. The traditional view of international finance uses the nation-state as its frame of reference, and its lexicon reflects this fact. At this level, the ideas of international finance are built around the concept of the *balance of payments*.

Balance of Payments

The balance of payments is a statistical record of all the international transactions undertaken by the residents of one nation with those of other nations in a given year, measured in current dollars. In simple terms, the balance of payments measures the inflows and outflows of money from one nation to other nations. Each international transaction involves both substance and shadow, which gives the balance of payments a dual importance. The substance—the goods, services, and ownership claims that move from country to country—are what really count, but they are too hard to quantify in themselves and pretty much impossible to add up and analyze in their natural state (this is a "mixing apples and oranges" problem). So the balance of payments records the shadows—the equal and opposite money movements—that accompany the real resource transfers. When a car is imported from Japan, for example, money moves from the U.S. to Japan (the shadow) and the automobile resource moves from Japan to the U.S. (substance). The money outflow from the U.S. is therefore the shadow of the inflow of a real resource.

The balance of payments is divided into two parts, which reflect the impact of international transactions on current income and on national wealth. The *current account* measures the way international transactions affect current national income. The *capital account* measures the impact of international transactions on a nation's wealth. Each balance of payments account can take one of three possible forms:

- A *surplus*, where money inflows exceed money outflows;
- A *deficit*, where money outflows exceed money inflows; or
- An *equilibrium*, where money inflows and outflows just balance.

The Current Account

The current account is an indicator of the impact of international transactions on a nation's income. Much of the language of international finance is British, and in Britain a "current account" is what we in the United States call a "checking account." Thinking of the current account as a nation's checking account is helpful in seeing its real meaning. Like a checking account, the current account records "deposits" or money inflows that derive from sales of currently produced goods and services, receipts of profits and interest from foreign investments, plus unilateral transfers from other nations.[4] These deposits are offset by money outflows due to purchases of goods and services from other countries and payments of profits and interest to foreign investors (plus unilateral transfers to other nations).[5] Examples of these transactions are given in Table 8–1.

If a nation has a *current account surplus*, it means that the "deposits" or earnings are greater than the "withdrawals" or expenditures, so that on net these international transactions have increased national income, measured in dollar terms. If a nation has a *current account deficit*, on the other hand, it means that outflows or withdrawals are greater than inflows or deposits in a particular year, and that the net effect of these international transactions is to reduce the national income of the deficit country.

The Capital Account

The capital account is an indicator of the impact of international transactions on a nation's wealth. The capital account measures international transactions involving the existing resources that make up a nation's wealth—the ownership of its physical, intellectual, and natural resources. Examples of capital account transactions are given in Table 8–1. When a nation has a *capital account surplus*, therefore, it means that the flow of funds into a country, purchasing these assets, is greater than the flow of funds out of the country buying foreign assets. When a nation has a capital account surplus, it ends up with more money, but fewer assets and less wealth measured in these terms. Put another way, a nation with a capital account surplus is a *borrower* nation, or has experienced a net increase in foreign ownership of its wealth. In this situation, the money shadows accumulate, while the substance is transferred abroad!

A nation with a *capital account deficit*, on the other hand, experiences money outflows (to purchase foreign assets) that exceed money inflows (to buy domestic

TABLE 8–1   Balance of Payments Transactions

	EXAMPLES OF MONEY INFLOWS	EXAMPLES OF MONEY OUTFLOWS
Current Account	Money received for exports of goods and services to foreign buyers, profit and interest received from U.S.-owned foreign assets, and unilateral transfers from other nations	Money paid for imports of goods, services, profit and interest paid to the foreign owners of U.S. assets, and unilateral transfers to foreign persons
Capital Account	Money received from foreign buyers for sale of U.S. bonds, stocks, real estate, patents, or other assets	Money paid to foreign sellers for purchase of foreign bonds, stocks, real estate, patents, or other assets

assets). It has a net outflow of money but a net increase in its wealth, measured in these terms. Put another way, a nation with a capital account deficit is a net creditor nation, or experiences a net increase in its ownership of foreign wealth. The interpretation of the current account and capital account conditions are summarized in Table 8–2.

The current account and the capital account are the key concepts in understanding a nation's standing in the international finance structure. Since these terms are fairly technical, however, it isn't unusual for speakers and writers to substitute more common but less exact terms. Sometimes, for example, a person will say that a nation has a "balance of payments" deficit, which is impossible in fact, since the balance of payments by definition, balances. Usually, this person means that there is a current account deficit, with payments for goods, services, and transfers exceeding the corresponding receipts.

The Balance of Trade

It is common to find reference to the *trade deficit* in discussions of international finance. This refers to the balance of trade, which is included in the current account. The *balance of trade* measures the dollar value of payments and receipts for goods and services. Information about the balance of trade is important and gets plenty of attention in the press, usually as an indication of the nature of international competition. The balance of trade is an incomplete measure of the impact of international transactions on the economy, however, since it does not take into account payments and receipts of investment income and unilateral transfers. The current account, which includes these items in addition to those in the balance of trade, is therefore a better indicator of how international economic relations impact a nation. Sometimes people will discuss the *trade balance* when they really mean the *current account balance*. It is important not to confuse the two different but related concepts.

Table 8–3 presents data on the balance of payments of the United States for 1992. These figures indicate that the United States imported $96 billion of goods more than it exported, but sold $56 billion more services than it bought. Its balance of trade was thus a deficit of $40 billion. The United States received a net $6 billion of investment income, but paid a net $32 billion of unilateral transfers. Summing the figures for merchandise trade, trade in services, investment income, and uni-

TABLE 8–2   Interpretation of Balance of Payments Accounts

	SURPLUS	*DEFICIT*
Current Account	Net increase in national income due to international transactions	Net decrease in national income due to international transactions
Capital Account	Increase in foreign ownership of domestic assets; "net debtor" nation	Increase in domestic ownership of foreign assets; "net creditor" nation

TABLE 8–3   Balance of Payments Position of the United States, 1992

ITEM	BALANCE	INFLOWS	OUTFLOWS
Merchandise Trade	–$96 billion	+$440 billion	–$536 billion
Trade in Services	+$56 billion		
Balance of Trade	–$40 billion		
Investment Income	+$ 6 billion	+$110 billion	–$104 billion
Unilateral Transfers	–$32 billion		
Current Account	–$66 billion		
Capital Account	+$78 billion	+$129 billion	–$ 51 billion
Statistical Discrepancy	+$12 billion		

Source: *Economic Report of the President*, 1994 (Table B-103). Figures may not sum due to rounding.

lateral transfers results in a current account deficit of $66 billion. On net, international transactions reduced U.S. national income by $66 billion in 1991.

A capital account surplus of $78 billion offset the current account deficit. Foreigners purchased U.S. assets by $78 billion more than U.S. residents gained ownership of foreign assets. On net, then, U.S. ownership of wealth decreased by $78 billion in 1994. In theory, the capital account surplus should exactly offset the current account deficit. In practice, however, it is impossible actually to monitor all transactions involving the nations of the world. The $12 billion statistical discrepancy seen here is not uncommon in balance of payments records.

HOW INTERNATIONAL PAYMENTS BALANCE

Under normal circumstances, a surplus in one account must be offset by a deficit in the other.[6] This is the "balance" in the balance of payments. A nation that has a current account deficit, for example, must either borrow funds from abroad or sell off assets to foreign buyers to pay its international bills and thus achieve an overall payments balance. A current account deficit therefore requires a capital account surplus. In the same way, a nation with a current account surplus has excess funds to purchase foreign assets, creating a capital account deficit.

Why does the balance of payments balance? The technical reason is that double-entry account books must always balance. The practical reason is that each international transaction involves foreign exchange, and for the foreign exchange markets to balance (make supply and demand equal), it is necessary for inflows and outflows of a currency to balance.[7] When a dollar leaves the United States, to pay for a foreign good or service (creating a current account deficit), for example, it must normally return in some offsetting transaction. Either it will return as a current account transaction (balancing the current account) or it will return as a capital account transaction, balancing the current account outflow with a capital account inflow.

For most of the past twenty years, Japan and the United States have had mirror-image balance of payments positions.[8] The United States has experienced persistent deficits in the current account, which have been offset by borrowing and sales of assets, which provide a surplus in the capital account. Japan, on the other hand, has experienced persistent capital account deficits, due to its high savings rates, which produce funds for foreign investment. This capital account deficit for Japan is offset by a current account surplus.

ANATOMY OF A BALANCE OF PAYMENTS CRISIS

What limits a nation's ability to run a current account deficit? Essentially a nation can continue to experience a deficit in the current account so long as it can obtain the necessary funds through a capital account surplus—that is, so long as it is able to borrow funds from abroad or to find foreign buyers for its assets. When these assets are exhausted or—more realistically—when foreign lenders are unwilling to extend additional credit, a predictable but unfortunate chain of events is set in motion.

The initial effects of a balance of payments crisis can be quite dramatic. The lack of foreign lending can create a crisis in the country's banking system, sending interest rates shooting up and inducing "capital flight," a condition where many people try to transfer their bank accounts out of the country, to "safe harbor" nations. Together, these factors create an extreme shortage of funds in the debtor nation. These financial problems are compounded by reactions in the international trade sector of the economy. Because of the iron logic of the balance of payments, a nation that is unable to borrow (capital account) cannot afford to import (current account). International trade is disrupted and needed imports are often impossible to obtain.

A balance of payments crisis is a bad thing, both for the nation that experiences it and for the other nations of the world, since trade and international finance relationships are distorted by such a crisis. It is conceivable that crisis in one nation, along with that nation's attempts to deal with its problems, could spawn additional crises elsewhere. Economic peril can spread from nation to nation, much as it did during the Great Depression of the 1930s.

Although a balance of payments crisis is, fundamentally, an *economic* problem, it quickly translates into a *political* problem, since it usually falls to the state and its political leadership to propose and implement the frequently harsh policies that may be necessary to bring international payments back into balance. International economics thus affects domestic politics, and vice versa.

To prevent international debt calamities, the architects of the postwar Bretton Woods system of international finance provided a "lender of last resort," a term that refers to a hegemonic state or international institution that continues to lend after all others cease in order to provide the international financial structure with additional stability in times of crisis. In today's international monetary system, the International Monetary Fund (IMF) is the world's lender of last resort for balance of payments purposes.[9]

The IMF enters the picture when it is clear that a balance of payments debt crisis is looming, either when a nation experiences increasing difficulties financing its current account deficit or, as in the case of Mexico in 1982, when outright default on existing

Continued

ANATOMY OF A BALANCE OF PAYMENTS CRISIS, *continued*

debt seemed imminent. The IMF provides credit or *liquidity* to get the debtor nation through a period of adjustment, so that it can eventually achieve sustained growth. IMF loans are subject to stringent conditions.[10] IMF conditionality is controversial. A typical IMF debt plan involves a number of politically unpopular policies designed to restore economic balance, including

- *Currency Devaluation*   The value of the nation's currency is reduced relative to other major currencies. This makes imports more expensive, but reduces the cost of exports to foreign buyers, thus reducing the current account deficit.[11]
- *Price Stability*   Restrictive policies are enacted in an attempt to bring the inflation rate down. Since high or unpredictable inflation can scare off foreign investors or lenders, lower and more stable inflation rates improve the investment climate.
- *Fiscal Austerity*   The government is typically required to cut spending and subsidies, raise taxes, and "privatize" publicly owned enterprises. These policies reduce government borrowing, which is often an important cause of the nation's capital account problems.
- *Tariff Liberalization*   Restrictive trade policies are reduced or eliminated, encouraging both imports (especially of raw materials and unfinished goods) and exports.
- *Social Safety Net*   Because many of the policies already discussed reduce living standards and can be especially hard on the poor, it is generally necessary to construct sound social programs to reduce the negative impacts of such things as higher import prices, reduced subsidies, and higher taxes.

The logic of the IMF's "lender of last resort" policies is to reduce the current account deficit in the short run by increasing exports and reducing imports and simultaneously to help finance the capital account needs by stemming capital flight and limiting new borrowing needs. In the long run, these policies are also intended to encourage economic growth, making the nation better able to pay its old debts and less dependent on credit in the future.

Especially in the short run, "austerity" policies create tremendous political pressures because the debtor-nation government must enact policies that lower living standards and impose hardship. In essence, the government must sacrifice domestic autonomy for the sake of its international financial stability. The "austerity" measures that are required are never popular and generally fall harder on some groups than on others. These problems often weaken the state's ability to achieve its policies, which can lead to a further escalation of international financial problems. In short, international financial crisis thus leads to domestic political crisis, which can exacerbate and deepen the economic crisis. A debt crisis can therefore be a political and economic nightmare, which makes the "lender of last resort"—the IMF—an even more important international institution.

Although the IMF and the debtor-nation government work together to deal with the debt crisis in theory, in practice the relationship can be conflictual, with the IMF responsible for international financial stability and the debtor-nation government responding to domestic political forces. The negotiations between them require some diplomacy, since a strong state is needed if IMF-approved austerity policies are to be implemented, but some programs tend to create political turmoil and weaken the existing government. Resolving a debt crisis is thus a delicate matter, with international economic stability balanced against domestic political realities.

Continued

ANATOMY OF A BALANCE OF PAYMENTS CRISIS, *continued*

The IMF is frequently criticized for ignoring political priorities, putting too much emphasis on economic balance relative to social justice and the needs of the poor. "Austerity programs" often hit the poor far harder than the rich. The alternative to IMF conditional aid, however, is that a nation must withdraw essentially from international economic relationships, a fate generally worse than whatever policies are necessary to receive IMF adjustment assistance.

THREE PERSPECTIVES ON THE INTERNATIONAL FINANCE STRUCTURE

The sets of relationships that form the international finance structure are complex. At the broadest level, this structure connects nations with current account surpluses (creditor nations) with those with current account deficits (debtor nations). In the 1980s, for example, this structure connected Japan (a creditor) with the United States (a debtor) and the nations of the industrial North (creditor) with those in Latin America and Africa, the less developed South (debtor). In the 1990s, a new set of connections has been added as formerly communist debtor nations have entered the international financial structure.

What are we to make of the connections that the finance structure forms? What is the relationship between debtor and creditor? Who benefits from the structure of international debt? The answers to these questions are different depending upon the viewpoint we assume.

Liberals, mercantilists, and structuralists take differing views of the nature of international financial structures, based in part on their differing interpretations of IPE history. In particular, they take different positions on the nature of Britain's role in international finance in the second half of the nineteenth century. These competing interpretations of history provide the foundation for different views of current financial relationships, such as the creditor-debtor structure that has linked Japan and the United States since the early 1980s.

The Liberal Perspective

The liberal perspective favored by mainstream economists tends to view international financial transactions as mutually advantageous free market events. North-South loans, for example, are seen as benefiting both borrower and lender. Such loans are possible, in theory, because the rate of return on investment in less developed economies is often considerably higher than in older industrialized markets, where many high-profit opportunities have long since been exploited. A loan from the North to the South under these circumstances provides the lender with a higher return than was possible at home and yet provides the borrower with the capital that is needed to take advantage of local conditions. Without this North-South flow of funds and resources, both borrower and lender would be worse off.

Some events of the early 1990s, for example, fit the liberal view to a T. Investment returns in the "newly emerging" markets in East Asia, such as Malaysia, China, and Hong Kong, were much higher than those in the United States and Europe, attracting funds from these nations. The "debtor" nations experienced rapid economic growth while providing profits for foreign investors.

The liberal perspective on international finance has deep roots. This point of view conditioned British foreign investment policy in the nineteenth and early twentieth centuries, when relatively large capital flows from Britain financed economic development in the Commonwealth countries and Latin America. Liberals in Britain saw these international capital movements as fostering economic development in the debtor nations and providing British capitalists with higher returns than could be achieved at home. Essentially, this same point of view guided the foreign financial policy of the United States until the 1980s. The large volume U.S. foreign loans and investments during the 1950s and 1960s were seen as mutually beneficial voluntary transactions. Since 1980, however, the U.S. has experienced a period of persistent current account deficits. Many people in the U.S. have become concerned with the U.S. "dependence" on foreign investment.

The Mercantilist Perspective

The mercantilist perspective on international finance also has a long history that is rooted in Britain's policies of the nineteenth century. The mercantilist view of IPE holds that there is a dynamic interrelationship between wealth and power and that it is the responsibility of the state to use its power to produce wealth, which in turn creates more power. The liberal policies of Great Britain, both with respect to its colonies and with other countries, were viewed as quintessentially mercantilist by List and others. The funds that Britain loaned or invested in less developed countries were generally used to purchase industrial goods, such as iron, steel, and railroad equipment from British firms. Britain's capital account outflows, therefore, produced industrial exports, which strengthened the British economy, in mercantilist terms, and increased its current account surplus. This is the classic mercantilist cycle of international trade and finance. Foreign loans finance exports, which create additional funds for even more foreign loans. The "productive power" of the creditor nation grows as its current account surplus surges.[12]

In recent years, Japan has been accused by some academics and policymakers of adopting mercantilist financial policies, building industrial power by using international finance along the same lines as Britain in the nineteenth century. Many of Japan's actions have a mercantilist color to them, so it is perhaps natural that Japan's capital account surplus and current account deficit would be seen as two sides of a classic mercantilist wealth-power cycle.

Not everyone believes that Japanese capital exports are part of a mercantilist strategy, however. One opposing school holds that Japan's foreign investments are a natural result of that nation's traditionally high savings rate. The mathematics of the balance of payments, then, dictates that Japan experience a current account surplus to balance the capital account deficit that overseas investment flows create. From this point of view, Japan's actions are not calculated strategy so much as simply the economic consequences of its high propensity to save.[13]

Another interesting view of Japan's international financial policies holds that Japan trades wealth for power—that during the era of the Cold War, Japan's capital flows to the United States were exchanged for U.S. military protection of Japanese interests and Japan itself. This "special relationship" has been called the ***nichibei economy***, a term referring to the increased integration of the Japanese and U.S. economies, accomplished in part through clcse financial relationships.[14] Forbidden by its postwar constitution from raising a military force, it is argued, Japan took the savings and traded them for international security, gaining increased control over U.S. assets in the process. Japan thus helped finance U.S. military hegemony and created an interdependence that assured U.S. interest in Japanese security problems.

The Structuralist Perspective

V. I. Lenin's structuralist analysis of international finance provides a third view of this subject. In his book *Imperialism: The Highest Stage of Capitalism,* Lenin argued that capitalism was able to delay its inevitable collapse through international expansion (see chapter 4). Although Lenin was obviously concerned with European-centered colonial empires of the nineteenth century, he singled out international finance as a particular tool of capitalist imperialism.

Lenin asserted that the foreign lending practices of the British and the Germans created an exploitative web that snared countries in the periphery. These less developed nations became dependent on core nations for capital in the first place, then soon became dependent on them as markets for exports of primary products, which they depended upon for income. Earnings from these exports paid profit and interest to core nations, providing resources for another round of loans. A vicious cycle is thus created, with debtor LDCs growing increasingly dependent upon core creditor nations, and remaining trapped in the production of basic commodities while the core continues to industrialize.

It is not hard to find data that support the structuralist view of international debt. For a variety of reasons, we might expect to find that resources generally would be transferred from the rich North to the poorer South. Such a pattern would make sense both from the liberal view of international investment opportunities and from a common-sense view of rich helping poor. For many years, however, the finance structure has systematically transferred resources from poor South to rich North, as the principal and interest on international debts have been paid. This shocking pattern, which has many causes, is seemingly consistent with the exploitation and dependency hypotheses of the structuralists.

THE GLOBAL FINANCIAL STRUCTURE

One of the most profound changes in the IPE is the increasingly *global* nature of the financial structure. That is, finance is less and less a structure that links nations, and is more and more a concern of the global market, where national borders and regulations are relatively unimportant. Richard O'Brien writes:

> The end of geography, as a concept applied to international financial relationships, refers to a state of economic development where geographic location no longer matters in finance, or matters much less that hitherto. . . . The end of geography is a challenge to all participants in the world economy, to developing as well as developed economies, to public and private policymakers, to producers and consumers of financial services. It involves the debate over the role of the nation-state, integration of nations, and the disintegration of existing federations.[15]

The key idea here is that finance is a way of moving resources from person to person and from place to place—the "clever shadows" mentioned at the start of this chapter. Once these shadows are able to move freely everywhere and anywhere, it means that resources are equally free to move, since shadow and substance are linked. To the extent that "national interest" is identified with control over these resources, it follows that global finance reduces the state's ability to locate and protect its interests.

The movement from *international* finance to *global* finance may seem a bit obscure, but it is significant. To simplify, we can think of international finance as a system of financial markets, each centered in a nation-state and regulated by that state. International transactions are between and among these centers. Global finance, on the other hand, refers to a system of financial relationships with no real center in any state. Global financial markets, which transcend national borders, are the form and substance of the global financial structure. Global finance goes on twenty-four hours a day. Individual nations can influence the pattern of global finance, but have little ability to control it, since global markets, like flooding rivers, find ways over and around any obstruction.

What caused the rise of the global financial structure? At least three forces can be identified with the emergence of global markets: structural economic change, a shift in IPE philosophy, and technological change. Together, these three sets of forces changed the pattern of international financial relationships.

Several changes in the international economic structure created the conditions for the emergence of global finance: the rise of Japan and Europe, the growth of the NICs, and the advent of the Organization of Petroleum Exporting Countries (OPEC). Beginning in the 1970s, Japan began to experience rising living standards and high rates of economic growth that dramatically changed its status in the world economy. Along with the increasingly prosperous nations of the European Community,[16] Japan became a major economic player. The rise of Japan and Europe created new centers of international finance, reducing somewhat the importance of New York and London in this regard. At the same time, the newly industrialized countries (NICs) began to emerge, creating additional patterns of international financial activity.

The largest single event, however, was undoubtedly the rise of OPEC and the tremendous shifts in the pattern of international financial flows that followed the oil price increases of the 1970s. Almost overnight, the pattern of postwar finance changed, with billions of dollars being transferred along previously nonexistent financial channels. Just as the Baring loan of 1817, which financed France's indemnity to England and its allies after Napoleon's defeat, led to the modern system of *international* finance, the OPEC oil crisis of 1973–1974 can be viewed as the event that ultimately created the *global* financial network. Responding to the demands of recycling OPEC "petrodollars" and accommodating the financial needs of a world economy where Japan, Europe, and the NICs were increasingly important, the financial markets developed the basic tools of global finance.

These tools would not have been sufficient to create global finance, however, if government regulations had not also changed. As noted earlier, the postwar system of international finance was based on the ability of a nation-state to regulate economic activities within its geographic area. In some nations, these regulations were mercantilistic in their intent, or even based on the notion that finance could cause dependency. In the United States and Europe, however, postwar financial policies were heavily influenced by the experience of financial collapse during the Great Depression of the 1930s. These policies therefore reflected a Keynesian view—that strong state influences were used to protect financial markets, limiting potentially destructive competition, and especially regulating international financial movements. During the Great Depression, financial panic and collapse was transmitted by markets from one nation to others. It was thought that by isolating each nation's financial system and then regulating it, global financial crisis and collapse could be avoided.

This pattern of financial regulation, already strained by the structural economic changes mentioned earlier, gave way to a change in political philosophy in the early 1980s. In Britain and the United States, national leaders emerged who swept aside the prevailing Keynesian orthodoxy in favor of a return to the classical liberal "laissez-faire" ideas of Adam Smith. Margaret Thatcher and Ronald Reagan championed the deregulation of financial markets, both within their nations and in the international arena. The result of the rise of liberal policies was a growth of the market as the driving force in international finance.

The final step in the creation of the global financial system was technological: the electronic communications revolution that has produced super-fast computers, instantaneous worldwide communications, and the ability to link people and machines in communications networks of awesome power and efficiency. Equipped with a notebook computer and a modem, an individual can access financial markets around the world. This technological revolution spelled the "end of geography" so far as finance was concerned. By the 1990s, with the end of the Cold War removing some of the last important barriers to international transactions, it mattered relatively little "where" a transaction was made. What mattered were the what, how, and why—information to be digitized and transmitted anywhere in the world.

The financial structure did not "go global" all at once. Indeed, national policies and state actions still carry some weight, so geography does matter, after all. But the globalization of finance has changed the nature of finance, making it far less state-based and more market oriented.[17]

THE IMPACT OF GLOBAL FINANCE ON IPE

It may be too soon to tell the ultimate impact of the globalization of finance on the international political economy. It is clear, however, that this change in the financial structure will transform, to some degree, each of the other IPE structures discussed in this book. Global finance, for example, has accelerated the tendency toward global production. The logic of international trade changes when resources can be moved more easily from place to place, creating new factories, stores, and communications networks. What is produced, where, for whom, and how—the key issues of the production structure—must all be reevaluated in this new light.

In the same way, the set of relationships that make up the knowledge structure are influenced by the globalization of finance. Knowledge and technology are becoming increasingly diffused, by the communications revolution and the globalization of production that is taking place. The financial revolution is at once a product of this trend and is accelerated by it.

Even the security structure is changing under the influence of global finance. Global investment opportunities are channeling resources to China and Vietnam, for example, countries that were until recently isolated from the United States because of security concerns. Increasing financial interconnectedness seems to be eroding the factors that divide nations.

It would seem that the emergence of the global financial structure marks the triumph of the market over the state. With resources free to move anywhere in the world, and government regulations nearly powerless to influence them, it would seem that the state is increasingly an irrelevant actor in the financial structure. This appearance is deceptive, however. Paradoxically, just when markets seem to dominate financial relationships, the role of the state has also increased in importance. But that role has changed. No longer is the state's role to isolate financial markets and regulate their stability. The new role of the state in global finance—to foster cooperation and coordination—can be seen through an examination of the LDC debt crisis of the 1980s and the role of the state in its successful resolution.

THE LDC DEBT CRISIS

By most counts, the LDC debt crisis began in 1982, when Mexico announced that it would default on its bank debt, and lasted until 1994, when Brazil, the largest LDC debtor, successfully resolved its financial problems. The news was reported in matter-of-fact style:

BRAZIL CLOSES CHAPTER RE DEBTS

NEW YORK (April 16, 1994)—Brazil Friday completed its external debt financing package covering approximately $49 billion in commercial bank debt, Citibank's vice-chairman and Brazil's Minister of Finance said in a joint statement.

"Brazil today achieved an important milestone in its continuing programme of economic reform," said Ruben Ricupero, Brazil's Minister of Finance in the statement.

"Today's closing is an historic day for Brazil in allowing it to normalize relations with its external creditors and giving further momentum to its programme of economic opening and reform," said William Rhodes, vice-chairman at Citibank. "Brazil should now have easier and less expensive access to the international capital markets," Rhodes said.

Rhodes said the closing of the Brazil debt deal marks the end of the international debt crisis among Latin America's major economies, which began in 1982 when Mexico announced that it was no longer able to service its external debt.[18]

The history of the LDC debt crisis illustrates several important points about the international finance structure and raises important questions about the stability of this key part of the international political economy.

The LDC debt crisis was a consequence, in part, of the early stages of the globalization of finance. As financial flows became increasingly global in the late 1970s, powered by changing economic structures, market deregulation, and technological change, financial centers in the industrial North increasingly sought high returns wherever they could be found. Banks and other financial institutions turned their attention to the less developed South, which had previously received financial resources more through official and government sources rather than through the markets. LDCs thought that conditions were advantageous to take on new debt, especially since inflation rates were running ahead of interest rates on loans, creating negative *real* interest rates, which traditionally favor borrowers.[19] In theory, these loans should have achieved the success that the liberal perspective predicts: economic growth and higher returns for both borrower and lender. In practice, however, the uncoordinated actions of the market created a trap for both debtor nations and their creditors. In retrospect, it appears that too much was loaned by too many.

As many countries tried to expand their exports at once (to gain income to repay the loans), commodity prices collapsed, leaving the nations worse off than before the loans, in many cases. This problem was exacerbated in the early 1980s by a recession that slowed down economic activity throughout the industrialized North, shrinking the market for LDC exports. The banks continued to make additional loans, to provide even more resources for economic development and also to pay interest on the earlier loans. The debt grew exponentially, both in terms of the burden on the LDC nations and as a risk to the solvency of the financial institution involved. Soon Keynes's paradox of finance was clear: with so much debt outstanding, it was the banks who were in as much trouble as the debtor nations. The debtor nations owed more than they could reasonably be expected to repay, yet then continued to borrow more and more in order to meet their short-run obligations. The banks had lent so much to the LDCs that they faced disaster if the debtors declared default, so they made even more loans to keep the old loans from being declared worthless. A vicious cycle of debt and more debt had been created.

How serious was the LDC debt crisis at its worst point? Looking back over modern history, the nearest parallel is probably the condition of Germany after World War I. The German economy was in shambles, its political system in chaos, yet the Treaty of Versailles imposed an enormous debt in the form of war reparations owed to the Allied victors. The cause of the debt was different in these two cases, but the potential impact was much the same.

Table 8–4 shows that external debt was still a very serious burden for many LDCs in 1991. Brazil's total foreign debt was 36.9 percent of its national income, for example, and the annual interest burden amounted to over 17 percent of its export earnings. While Brazil and Mexico had the largest debts, this table indicates that Argentina, Nigeria, Chile, and Nicaragua faced perhaps the greatest debt burdens.

The creditor nations in the 1980s feared for the economic consequences of a default on the loans—which would have removed the LDC debtors from access to

TABLE 8–4   Financial Indicators of Selected Debtor Nations, 1991

NATION	TOTAL EXTERNAL DEBT	DEBT AS PERCENT OF GNP	DEBT SERVICE AS PERCENT OF EXPORTS
Brazil	$116 billion	36.9%	17.3%
Mexico	$101 billion	28.8%	15.4%
Indonesia	$ 73 billion	66.4%	13.2%
India	$ 71 billion	29.3%	13.6%
Argentina	$ 63 billion	49.2%	25.1%
China	$ 60 billion	16.4%	5.3%
Poland	$ 52 billion	68.5%	3.3%
Turkey	$ 50 billion	48.1%	12.8%
Nigeria	$ 34 billion	108.8%	16.8%
Chile	$ 17 billion	60.7%	24.3%
Nicaragua	$ 10 billion	153.5%	62.4%

Source: World Bank, *World Development Report 1993*.

world credit markets and caused a crisis in the banking systems of Japan, Europe, and the United States. But they feared, too, the consequences to the international political economy if the LDCs were to do what was necessary to repay the loans in full. To honor such huge debt and interest burdens would have required harsh mercantilist policies to restrict imports and expand exports, which would create problems in the industrialized nations that rely on LDCs as markets for their manufactured goods. The political consequences of repayment were perhaps even more frightening. The discipline and sacrifice that would have been necessary for the LDCs to service their debt would have created great social and political unrest: riots, revolt, revolution. Adolf Hitler's National Socialist (Nazi) party emerged in post–World War I Germany under conditions like these. The market's invisible hand clearly failed in the deregulated global financial markets of the 1980s.

Given the situation just described, it seems obvious that everyone—borrowers and lenders, too—would benefit from debt relief. Debt relief takes many forms, but the basic idea is for the creditors to reduce the burden of debt on the debtors, to adjust that burden down to levels that can reasonably be paid. Interest rates can be reduced, repayment schedules stretched out farther into the future, and some debt can be forgiven, written off by the creditor as a uncollectable debt.

Debt relief would obviously help the debtor nations, by reducing their international obligations, but it would also help the creditor banks, by clearing their books of bad loans and reducing the risks they faced from default. The banks, however, found themselves unable to grant debt relief because they were caught in a situation that is called the *prisoners' dilemma* (see box that follows). The problem was that debt relief, which was in their collective interest, was not in the individual self-interest of each bank. Every bank wanted the others to forgive debt, but they were unwilling to do so themselves. This is because the banks that *cooperate* and grant relief would bear a cost, but the gains would be shared by all the banks, even those that gave up nothing. Under these circumstances, each bank had the incentive to be a **"free rider"** and let someone else bear the burden of debt relief. It is unsurprising, given the high stakes and the intensely competitive nature of international finance, that no one was willing to forgive LDC debts, and the vicious cycle of LDC debt continued.

CREATING COOPERATION: THE BRADY PLAN

Many attempts were made to solve the LDC debt problem, but the prisoners' dilemma of LDC debt was finally broken in the late 1980s by the **Brady Plan**, named for Nicholas Brady, U.S. Secretary of the Treasury in the Bush administration. The Brady Plan is complex in details, but simple in concept. The United States government stepped into the negotiations and offered to refinance the external debt of Mexico provided that *all* lenders accepted specific measures of debt relief, including interest rate cuts, payments rescheduling, and some measure of forgiveness. Under the Brady Plan, private banks exchanged their Mexican debt for a lesser amount of U.S. government securities—"Brady Bonds"—that are backed by corresponding Mexican obligations. Mexico pays the U.S., which pays the creditors. Under this scheme, Mexico benefits from debt relief, the banks reduce the risk of default, and the United States government avoids the possibility of financial instability.

The U.S. government used the power of the state to break the destructive standoff that the prisoners' dilemma created. The government was able to change the

---

THE PRISONERS' DILEMMA

Two burglars are captured by the police near the scene of a theft. The police are certain that they worked as a team to commit the robbery, but the only evidence they have is some of the loot, which the crooks did not have time to sell or hide.

The criminals are put into separate cells. Each is told the following. "We have enough evidence to charge you with possession of stolen merchandise. It is certain that you will go to jail for six months. But we'd like to make you a deal. If you will give evidence against your partner so that he can be convicted of the more serious crime of burglary, and if no other evidence against you appears, we will recommend that you be released on probation, a very minor punishment. Your guilty partner, however, will spend three years in jail. Which do you choose: six months in jail, or probation?"

Most people would rather go free than go to jail, and a short jail term is preferable to a long one. This is a situation, therefore, where it is in the individual interest of each prisoner to give evidence and take the lighter sentence. It is clearly better to be free on probation than to spend six months in prison. When *both* prisoners give evidence, however, *both* receive the heavier punishment of three years in prison. But while it is in their collective interests to *cooperate* and keep quiet, it is in their individual interests to *defect* and take action that benefits one and harms the other. Because of the nature of the incentives that the prisoners face, it is likely that they will choose the actions (defect/defect) that leave them both the worst possible outcome.

Continued

THE PRISONERS' DILEMMA, *continued*

Though the plight of the prisoners is sad, it is not one that is likely to make honest citizens lose much sleep. The conflict of collective and individual interests that it illustrates, however, is not limited to crooks. Rather, the prisoners' dilemma is part and parcel of everyday life and, therefore part of the international political economy.

The nuclear standoff of the Cold War, for example, is a case of the prisoners' dilemma where mutual interests were well served. Cooperation, in this case, meant not using nuclear weapons. To "defect" in this context was to launch a preemptive nuclear strike against the other power. For a number of reasons, including the high stakes involved and the uncertainty of survival—neither the United States nor the Soviet Union ever chose to defect from their deadly equilibrium.

In other IPE situations, however, the dismal logic of self-interest seems to rule. Many less developed countries have experienced dramatic deforestation in recent decades. Trees are cut and forests destroyed for fuel to heat and cook and sometimes to sell as hardwood lumber. As the forests are destroyed, the resource base shrinks, land erodes, farming productivity falls, and wood for heat and cooking becomes even harder to find. It would clearly be in the collective interest of the population to limit tree-cutting and stop the loss of the forest. But to each individual, cutting another tree is beneficial personally, since the loss, which is shared with the rest of society, is more than offset by the private gain.

Can cooperation be assured, or at least encouraged? Or is defection and disaster the general fate of people and nations? Political economists have studied the prisoners' dilemma in some detail because of its important role in many aspects of life.[20] Several lessons have been learned. The first is that cooperation is more likely when the persons involved are part of long-term relationships, where they will face the consequences of their actions again and again. Defection is more likely when the situation is a "one-shot" relationship, unlikely to be repeated. Cooperation is also more likely when the number of individuals is small and the impact of any defection correspondingly high on all involved. In large groups, with costs and benefits widely diffused, free-riding and defection are far more likely. Finally, cooperation can be encouraged by "side payments," where potential gainers bribe likely defectors to go along. Such side payments are most likely to succeed if one participant is so large (and its share of the gains from cooperation so great) that it is always in its interest to promote cooperation. This "player" becomes, in essence, a hegemon, willing to bear the costs of organizing a cooperative effort because its share of the resulting gains are so great.

---

game, by threatening those who failed to cooperate with a total loss. Suddenly it was in everyone's interest to support debt forgiveness. Only the state, acting in the collective interests of the banks and the debtor nations, could have achieved this result.[21]

The Brady Plan was successful in resolving the prisoners' dilemma in Mexico (although it could not prevent Mexico's subsequent balance of payment problems), and has been applied to many other LDC debtor nations. With their impossible debt burdens reduced, many of these nations have achieved greater economic success and political stability. By the time Brazil's debt problem was addressed in 1994, the pattern of cooperation was so firmly established that no Brady Bond intervention was necessary. The creditors and debtors were able to work out a scheme for debt relief without intervention by the U.S. government.

STATES AND MARKETS IN GLOBAL FINANCE

It may be years before the effects of the LDC debt crisis are forgotten, but we can hope that even then the lessons of this situation will remain. The debt crisis shows that market competition can sometimes backfire when competition is caught up in a prisoners' dilemma like this one.

The globalization of financial markets has created increased interdependence among nations, since all are linked to the global market. These strong market forces seem to require equally strong—and coordinated—state actions to balance them. The global markets already exist, but a system of coordinated state actions is still at an early stage of development. Economic and political dilemmas, like the LDC debt crisis, remain distinctly possible in this IPE environment.

The fundamental tension of political economy therefore remains. The global structure of finance is clearly market driven and market based, and it seems beyond the power of any single nation or group of nations to alter this fact. The old role of the state in international finance—to isolate financial markets and regulate them in the interests of stability—is clearly less important now. It seems, however, that the early predictions of a state-free global finance structure are premature. The role of the state in international finance is different, as the debt crisis shows, and still evolving. The fundamental tension between and dynamic interaction of states and markets in international finance continues.

DISCUSSION QUESTIONS

1. The U.S. has recently experienced the condition of a current account deficit and a capital account surplus. Explain the meaning and significance of this condition for the U.S. In this combination of current account and capital account balances an expected or unexpected event (i.e., is it more likely to have deficits or surpluses in *both* accounts simultaneously, rather than a surplus in one account and a deficit in another)? Explain.
2. What is the International Monetary Fund (IMF)? The IMF recommends what specific policies to nations that experience persistent current account deficits? How would these policies affect the U.S. if they were implemented in that country? Explain.
3. The financial structure has become increasingly globalized in recent years. Compare and contrast the mercantilist, liberal, and structuralist viewpoints of the finance structure. Which of these perspectives do you find most persuasive? Explain.
4. The Prisoners' Dilemma illustrates an important conflict between individual and group interests. Discuss the meaning and significance of the Prisoners' Dilemma and explain how it applies to the LDC debt crisis of the 1980s.

SUGGESTED READINGS

Robert Z. Aliber. "The Debt Cycle in Latin America." In Jeffry A. Frieden and David A. Lake. *International Political Economy.* New York: St. Martin's Press, 1991.
Robert M. Axelrod. *The Evolution of Cooperation.* New York: Basic Books, 1984.

"Fear of Finance: Survey of International Finance." *The Economist*, 19 September 1992.

Paul Kennedy. Especially chapter 3 in *Preparing for the Twenty-first Century*. New York: Random House, 1993.

Charles P. Kindleberger. *International Financial Movements.* Cambridge, England: Cambridge University Press, 1987.

———. *The International Economic Order.* Cambridge, MA: MIT Press, 1988.

———. *A Financial History of Western Europe*, 2nd ed. New York: Oxford University Press, 1993.

Paul Krugman. *The Age of Diminished Expectations*, 2nd ed. Cambridge, MA: MIT Press, 1994.

V. I. Lenin. *Imperialism: The Highest Stage of Capitalism.* New York: International Publishers, 1939.

Richard O'Brien. *Global Financial Integration.* New York: Council on Foreign Relations, 1992.

"Sisters in the Wood: A Survey of the IMF and the World Bank." *The Economist*, 12 October 1991.

Sweder Van Wijnbergen. "Mexico and the Brady Plan." *Economic Policy* 12 (April 1991): 13–56.

Michael Veseth. *Mountains of Debt.* New York: Oxford University Press, 1990.

NOTES

1. "Fear of Finance" supplement, *The Economist*, 19 September 1992, 1.
2. Michael Veseth, *Mountains of Debt*, (New York: Oxford University Press, 1990), p. 31. Both these firms collapsed in 1343 when England defaulted on a series of war loans, an event that shows that international financial crisis is at least as old as international finance itself.
3. Ibid., 126–127.
4. Unilateral transfers include governmental foreign aid and private gifts from persons and organizations in one country to those in another country.
5. Although unilateral transfers appear last on the list of current account transactions, they are sometimes very important items. Earlier in this century, for example, the U.S. experienced huge transfer outflows as immigrants from abroad sent funds back home to their families, many of whom also eventually emigrated to the United States. The Marshall Plan transfers of the early postwar period were also an important international transfer, which aided in rebuilding Europe. More recently, the United States received large transfers from its allies in the Persian Gulf War, to help defray U.S. military costs.
6. The money inflows and money outflows correspond to the demand and supply of the foreign exchange for a currency. Since these two must balance under normal circumstances, the payments that they represent must also balance.
7. The intuitive reason is this: Imagine a dollar going out of the country to purchase imported coffee (current account outflow). Logically, that dollar must return to the U.S., to be "redeemed" for a good or service, or asset. If the dollar does not return to buy a good or service, which would balance the current account, it must return to purchase an asset, creating an offsetting transaction on the capital account.
8. Although the U.S. and Japan are compared here, it is important to understand that the balance of payments measures a nation's economic transactions with the *rest of the world*, not with any single foreign country.
9. See discussion of the IMF and the World Bank in chapter 7.
10. The IMF can provide credit in a number of ways, including the issuance of *special drawing rights* (so-called "paper gold"), which are special reserves used in international transactions between central banks.
11. See discussion of depreciation of a currency in chapter 7.
12. Although it is clear that British foreign investments in LDCs did in fact result in increased industrial exports, the impact may not have been as beneficial to Britain as most mercantilists thought. Some economic historians believe that the close links between British capital exports and its industrial exports had the effect of discouraging

innovation in British industry. Britain stuck with its iron, steel, and cloth industries in the late nineteenth century when other nations—Germany, Sweden, the United States—were moving into more profitable science-intensive industries such as chemicals and electrical goods. It has been argued that the British stuck by their old industries in part because of the reliable foreign markets their international investments created. It is also asserted by some that Britain's capital exports systematically deprived domestic firms of the resources they would have needed to participate fully in the scientific industrial revolution of the late nineteenth century. This controversial issue is unresolved among economic historians, however.

13. Paul Krugman is one proponent of this viewpoint. See his *The Age of Diminished Expectations*, 2nd ed. (Cambridge, MA: MIT Press, 1994).

14. See Robert Gilpin, *The Political Economy of International Relations* (Princeton, NJ: Princeton University Press, 1987), 328–340 for a discussion of the *nichibei economy*.

15. Richard O'Brien, *Global Financial Integration: The End of Geography*, (New York: Council on Foreign Relations Press, 1992), 1.

16. Now the European Union (EU).

17. How have these market-driven financial systems performed? This is a controversial question, as are so many in IPE. Certainly, global financial markets have grown quickly, exhibiting the dynamic nature of markets, but they have also experienced a number of crises, leading some to believe that these markets may not be as stable as the system of regulated financial markets they replace.

18. "Brazil Closes Chapter re Debt," from Reuters, 16 April 1994, copied from the Prodigy ® service.

19. Negative real interest rates exist when inflation rates exceed the interest rate over the term of a loan. In simple terms, this benefits the borrower because loan repayments have less purchasing power (*lower real value*) than the amount borrowed. The borrower gains purchasing power under these circumstances, even accounting for interest payments made.

20. See, for example, Robert M. Axelrod, *The Evolution of Cooperation* (New York: Basic Books, 1984).

21. See discussion in Krugman, *The Age of Diminished Expectations*.

9

The International Security Structure

OVERVIEW

National security concerns have been the foundation and influenced the international political economy since the seventeenth century, when the nation-state became the major political actor in the international system. When nation-states protect and defend themselves, they produce a configuration of military and economic power referred to as the *international security structure*. War and peace, as well as wealth and power, are outcomes of the international security structure. This structure is the foundation upon which the international production (see chapter 6), finance (see chapters 7 and 8), and knowledge (see chapter 10) structures operate. The international security structure also provides a framework within which to study the role of national security in the international political economy.

In this chapter, we examine a number of developments during the Cold War (1947–1989) that led to significant changes in the international security structure and to a transformation in the way officials and academics now think about the problem of national security. During the Cold War, the connection between economics and national security tightened, resulting in a broader definition of the term *national security*. Many public officials increasingly felt more threatened by the effects of international economic interdependence and other economic challenges to their nation than they did physical, military threats. *Economic warfare* has become a regular phrase in the IPE lexicon.

In this chapter, we use different elements of the three IPE approaches (mercantilism, liberalism, and structuralism) to account for some ways in which the international production, finance, and knowledge structures, in particular, influenced developments in the international security structure during the Cold War. Five features of the Cold War international security structure interest us the most: (1) the configuration of political and economic (hegemonic) power; (2) the impact the Cold War international security structure had on the "rules of the game," i.e., the ways nations interacted with one another in the areas of military and economic relations; (3) shifts in the underlying elements of power within the international security structure, many of which were generated by developments in the international production, finance, and knowledge structures; (4) the changing role of less developed countries (LDCs); and finally, (5) changes in the ways industrialized nations and LDCs came to perceive as threatening the effects of international economic interdependence.

In the conclusion of the chapter, we argue that changes in the number and intensity of military, economic, and environmental threats to nation-states do not constitute the development of an entirely new international security structure.

Since ancient Athens taxed its empire to raise a fleet against Sparta, there has always been a strong connection between wealth and military power and, therefore, in the most simple and direct way, between economics and national security.[1]

Aaron Friedberg

National security matters as much today as it did in ancient Greece. Just ask the Chechen fighters battling Russian troops in Grozny, Russia. However, things are much more complicated today than it was for the Greeks. The international security structure shapes the way nations interact with one another politically and economically, more so than it did for the Greeks. During the Cold War, the United States resorted to use of its economy to help contain the Soviet Union and further other political and economic interests. And, unlike for the Greeks, the international economy today—broadly defined to include environmental problems (see chapter 19)—has become both a source of insecurity and a threat to many nation-states.

In recent years the international security structure has changed in many ways, but two changes stand out the most. National security has come to mean more than just military security—a broader definition of the term is required. And this definition seems to be different for nations of the industrial North than for the (LDCs) of the South.

THE COLD WAR AND THE CHANGING DEFINITION
OF NATIONAL SECURITY

The Cold War refers to the protracted confrontation between the United States and the Soviet Union that dominated the international security structure from 1947 to 1989. Tension and hostility between these two nations shaped developments in the international security structure and IPE more than anything else in the second half of this century. During the Cold War, the two principles never directly engaged each other for fear that the "cold" war of words would become a "hot" shooting war. Yet countless numbers of people died in smaller regional conflicts in third world countries where the superpowers and their allies did fight it out with one another. The Cold War also absorbed billions of dollars, disrupted millions of lives, and left an entire generation fearful of a nuclear holocaust.

The definition of national security underwent a transformation in the industrialized nations during this period. Before World War II, national security issues centered mainly around defense of the "homeland." John Herz argues that the nation-state was imagined to have a "hard shell" around it.[2] States often used their economy as they would any other weapon to achieve a variety of foreign policy objectives. Economic warfare often played a strategic role in the form of trade embargoes and other economic sanctions, as in the case of the allied defeat of Nazi Germany and Japan.

Also during the Cold War, a number of changes in international security structure occurred related especially to developments in the international knowledge structure that helped change decisionmakers' views about national security. The weapons of mass destruction the two superpowers produced to defend themselves also generated a good deal of political tension and insecurity, both nationally and internationally. Increasingly, the United States and other industrialized nations found nuclear power to be of limited value in changing the behavior of other states. After the Vietnam War, many officials and academics argued that conventional military power had limited utility in an international political economy where other major powers had as much if not more political and economic influence than the United States and the Soviet Union. National security had become inseparable from such economic problems and threats to nation-states.

The OPEC oil crises of 1973 and 1979 helped intensify international economic interdependence throughout the 1970s and 1980s. New sources of economic power became nonmilitary threats to many nations and their leaders. New technologies and methods of global communication, propaganda, environmental problems, and economic interdependence generated by international trade, finance, and multinational corporate business activity increasingly penetrated the hard shell around most nation-states. These economic developments, together with increasingly limited financial resources at home, also constrained the state's ability to pursue simultaneously national security and other political and economic objectives. The connection between the economy and national security tightened to the point that officials realized that too much money spent on defense could weaken an economy, and thus could jeopardize a nation's economy along with its military capacity and effectiveness.

A SELECTED CHRONOLOGY OF COLD WAR POLITICAL AND ECONOMIC DEVELOPMENTS

1945	The U.S., U.S.S.R., and Great Britain meet at Yalta and divide up Central and Eastern Europe.
	The United Nations charter is signed in San Francisco. The U.S. drops atomic bombs on Hiroshima and Nagasaki; Japan surrenders.
1946	Churchill makes "iron curtain" speech in Missouri, warns U.S. of Soviet aggression.
1948	The Truman Doctrine and Marshall Plan employed to "contain" the U.S.S.R.
1949	The U.S.S.R. detonates first A-bomb. NATO created. Communist forces take over China. Bipolarity hardens.
1950–53	The Korean war: the U.S. leads UN effort to contain communism. U.S. nuclear weapons don't deter communist aggression in the third world.
1955	The Warsaw Pact created; the Soviet Union mirrors Western allies.
1956	The Hungarian Revolution, the Soviet Union crushes Hungarian dissent.
1962	The Cuban Missile Crisis: the U.S. and U.S.S.R. go to the brink and back off.
1964	The U.S. deploys regular military forces in Vietnam to contain communism in Southeast Asia.
1968	The U.S.S.R. suppresses the coup and dissidents in Czechoslovakia.
	The Tet offensive occurs in Vietnam: The U.S. suffers a political defeat. The war turns downward. Bipolarity diffuses.
1972	The U.S. and U.S.S.R. enter into a détente. (peaceful co-existence). SALT I arms control agreement ushers in bipolycentric international security structure.
	Nixon goes to the Peoples' Republic of China. The PRC takes UN Security Council seat.
1973	OPEC raises the price of oil after the Israeli-Egyptian war; the third world takes on new importance. Resource scarcity becomes major issue.
1979	The U.S.S.R. invades Afghanistan. Détente derailed. The Soviets have their Vietnam?
1983	The U.S. invades Grenada: Reagan tries to contain communism again.
1989	The U.S. invades Panama; new security threats from the third world including drugs.
	The Berlin Wall is penetrated; symbolic end to the Cold War.
1990	Iraq invades Kuwait: the third world and oil remain security issues.
1991	The Persian Gulf War: the U.S. heads UN force to save the oil.

THE NORTH AND SOUTH: THE BURDEN OF INTERDEPENDENCE

With the end of the Cold War, nuclear war does not appear to be as great a threat as it once was. The intense ideological rivalry that marked much of the period seems to have been replaced by less contentious military relations among the Northern industrialized nations. These nations now appear to be less concerned about traditional military-type national security issues and more concerned about a variety of economic and environmental threats to their societies. The extreme of this argument today is that economic threats to nations have virtually replaced physical, military threats. For instance, the United States, Japan, and the European Union have all threatened each other with a trade war at one time or another. In other cases, much is made of the United States' dependency on Japan and other industrialized nations for semiconductors and other sophisticated technologies Japan could withhold from the United States during a real war.

The situation for Southern LDCs, however, has been quite different, yet similar in some ways to the case of the industrialized nations. Many LDCs still think of their nation-state as having a hard shell around it and national security in a narrow manner, similar to the way the industrialized nations thought about the problem until the early 1970s. War is as yet a routine feature of the relationship of many third (middle and low income) and fourth (the poorest) world countries to one another. In parts of Africa, Latin America, the Middle East, and the rest of Asia, ethnic, religious, and cultural differences generate a good deal of tension that often leads to conflict and even war. Increasingly many LDCs face a variety of problems such as low income growth or abject poverty, overpopulation, and an array of other economic and environmentally threatening issues that deter them from realizing their development goals and that are viewed as potential if not real threats to national security.

Structuralists would also be quick to point out that a good deal of war in LDCs is a product of the industrialized nations' practices of neoimperialism and neocolonialism (see chapter 4). In nearly all parts of the world, these practices have incited ethnic and nationalist movements as nations or groups of people struggle to form their own nation-state. Russia (Chechnya), Bosnia, Somalia, Palestine, and Rwanda come to mind.

Compared to their industrialized nation counterparts, the weapons of war many LDCs have today are for the most part profoundly more sophisticated and destructive than were the weapons the industrial powers used up until the twentieth century. LDCs are also greater in number than were the industrialized nations. For many of them, the stakes associated with economic development and national security appear to be much greater than they were for the industrialized nations earlier.

Despite what seems to be a reluctance on the part of many industrialized nations to either spend the money or fight wars, war remains a threatening if not recurring feature of the international political economy, in part because nations as yet feel quite insecure. Economics, including developments in the international production, finance, and knowledge structures, have come to gradually play a greater role in shaping developments in the international security structure. And it remains true that the international security structure acts as the floor under much of international economic activity.

THE THREE IPE APPROACHES TO NATIONAL SECURITY

How do we account for these trends whereby academics and officials in developed regions of the world have broadened the definition of national security while officials in LDCs still think of national security in primarily political-military ways? Each IPE approach captures a distinct part of the economic–national security connection but is limited in its coverage of changes that occurred in the international security structure during the Cold War.

Mercantilists and their realist cousins (see chapter 2) argue that nations seek to increase their wealth as a way of enhancing their power and ultimately their national security. In a self-help international system where the security of each nation cannot be guaranteed,[3] each nation must individually, or in cooperation with other states, provide for its own defense. For mercantilists, the economy is a secondary matter to state security concerns. Wealth buys weapons and feeds soldiers and the civilians who support the war effort. The economy becomes another weapon in the state's arsenal of instruments to enhance security. LDCs are less secure because they are generally militarily and economically weaker than the industrialized nations.

Mercantilists tend to overlook the role of the market and economic activity in shaping the security concerns of states. Some mercantilists have become more aware of the effect the economy has on security interests as of late, but many of them continue to hold that when pushed to the wall, national security concerns are and should be more important than economic concerns.[4]

As we outlined in chapter 3, economic liberals believe that national security objectives tend to get in the way of cooperative relationships that result from market activity. Overemphasis on defense leads to unnecessary defense spending and disrupts both the national and international economies. Although liberals are correct to point out that waste and inefficiency can weaken a state, they must separate politics from economics to make their points. Yet markets do not operate in a political vacuum. Rather, it could be argued that all economic activity rests upon some sort of political order, or "rules of the game," that manifest an understanding between a variety of actors, whether they be consumers, nation-states, or international businesses. Markets alone fail to provide the state security; the state must provide it much as it does any other collective good. The same holds true for states in many LDCs that tend to be weak or lack the capacity to ensure the defense of the nation.

Although war often shatters or distorts the normal political and economic patterns of human social relations, it does not preclude all economic activity from taking place. Nor does peace guarantee that economic activity will always be most productive or efficient. Within those parameters, policymakers must design and implement some policies or some sort of strategy that balances economic with national security objectives.

Structuralists (see chapter 4) view national security primarily in the context of how, in the eighteenth and nineteenth centuries, the industrializing capitalist states used national security as an excuse for their practices of imperialism and colonialism. Today, neoimperialism generates a good deal of LDC dependency on the industrialized nations but also a good deal of national insecurity in the third and fourth worlds. Furthermore, the state in industrial economies and LDCs still protects and defends the interests of a bourgeoisie class of corporate and military interests that are prone to waste and squander national resources against a variety of imagined external threats.

Still another structuralist argument is that poorer states have been the most warlike, while the industrialized nations have been less interested in war because of the great expense it generates. War and other forms of aggression stem from frustration and relative deprivation. However, studies show that the poorest countries cannot afford to make war. Thus, as nations develop they are better able to afford the weapons of war.[5]

The problem with this perspective is that while many government officials, especially in LDCs, continue to employ the structuralist critique to explain the origin of many of their national security problems, the approach itself offers little in the way of concrete strategies the state might employ to solve those problems. Short of revolution or a complete reordering of the distribution of wealth and power in the international political economy, state leaders must also balance a variety of national security concerns with their economic capacity to solve these problems.

Employing the separate IPE approaches to explain the IPE of national security leaves one with the feeling that each approach distorts the relationship of economics to national security. Nor can the complexity of the situation today be captured by simply combining these approaches, for each contains elements that are exclusive of one another. In the last of this chapter, we examine closely different aspects of the international security structure that transcend the three IPE perspectives in the ways that effect war and peace, as well as with the creation and distribution of wealth and power in the world.

THE BALANCE OF POWER AND THE INTERNATIONAL SECURITY STRUCTURE

Many mercantilists subscribe to the realist idea that war and peace are principally by-products of the *balance of power* among the major powers in the international system.[6] Politically and economically stronger states are more likely than weaker states to be able to secure themselves. A number of factors and conditions are likely to make some states more powerful than others: a relatively large land mass and population; a favorable geographic position; an abundance of, or access to, natural resources and raw materials acquired through trade, all of which contribute to a strong economy and industrial base; and the wisdom of certain military and civilian leaders. The ingredients of power are continually being distributed and redistributed around the world as states interact with one another.

The key for mercantilists and realists is the built-in tendency in the international security structure for states to balance power among one another. In a rational realpolitik manner, states and their leaders choose to remain at peace rather than fight for what they want when faced with power that is at least as great as theirs. Many realists argue that when power is distributed roughly equally among the major powers, peace is the likely by-product. Yet when one power attempts to assert itself over others (as Nazi Germany did during World War II), or when nations perceive that they have fallen behind more powerful states (as President Reagan argued the United States had done in the early 1980s), states may feel threatened and may use war to try to reestablish the balance of power. Yet the United States and Soviet Union were precluded from using nuclear weapons on each other due to the risk that nuclear weapons would create more damage than either society would be able to politically and economically tolerate (discussed in more detail below).

An important feature of the international security structure is the formation of alliances or coalitions of states into polar configurations. A pole is either formally or informally dominated by a political or economic hegemonic power. By 1947, the United States and the Soviet Union emerged as the two dominant powers of a **bipolar** international security structure: the U.S.S.R., based on its military power and control over Eastern Europe, and the United States, based on its military power but also its economic wealth and growing economic influence in the world. Conflicting political and economic ideologies and differences over who would control Central and Eastern Europe shaped the hostile outlooks of these two blocs, and precipitated the Cold War.[7] In zero-sum fashion, the two "superpowers" (so designated because of their potential to make and deploy nuclear weapons) began organizing two distinct political, economic, and military camps.[8] In 1949, for example, the United States formed an alliance—the North Atlantic Treaty Organization (NATO)—with its Western European allies to protect them from the Soviet Union. In return for this protection, many NATO members made available to the United States military bases in Western Europe. As part of a division of labor, the fifteen other NATO members were also supposed to provide NATO with conventional forces and equipment to defend Western Europe from a Soviet attack. The Soviet Union responded by organizing the Warsaw Pact military alliance with its Eastern European allies.

During the Cold War, the United States and the Soviet Union continued to mirror each other in ways that entrenched an international security structure primarily bipolar in character until the early 1970s. For example, in 1947, the Truman administration adopted the objective of "containment"[9] of the Soviet Union and announced the Truman Doctrine: "to support free peoples who are resisting attempted subjugation by armed minorities or by outside pressures," meaning communism. Likewise, the Soviet Union soon responded with a strategy of "wars of national liberation" to free those LDCs it perceived to be held captive by either the United States or other capitalist states.

THE EVOLUTION OF MULTIPOLARITY

Some mercantilists and realists argue that in the 1970s the bipolar international security structure gradually gave way to a "bipolycentric"[10] configuration of power, while others argue that either multipolarity or tripolarity replaced bipolarity. Essentially, the bipolar international security structure was loosened and transformed, in part, by a shift in the underlying factors and conditions that make states powerful. *Bipolycentrism* refers to the continued superpower status of the United States and Soviet Union, paralleled by the growing political and economic strength of members of the European Community (now referred to as the European Union), Japan, the PRC, and the newly industrialized countries (NICs). Many of these states had become powerful not necessarily because of their military strength but, as in the case of Japan, because of their growing global economic influence, or in the case of the PRC, because of its growing political influence in global affairs. After the Vietnam War, the national security advisor to President Nixon, Dr. Henry Kissinger, promoted the idea of a purposefully managed multipolar balance of power among the U.S., U.S.S.R., EU, Japan, and PRC. Kissinger argued that a pentagonal balance of power better reflected the actual distribution of power in the international system after the Vietnam War and was an alternative to a potentially dangerous bipolar system. Still other realists believe that during the late 1970s the United States, Soviet Union, and PRC made up a tripolar balance of power. On occasions, President Carter tried to play the "China card" to condition Soviet and Chinese behavior related to such issues as human rights, trade, and arms control agreements.

There are a good many problems associated with the realist concept of the balance of power.[11] For one, it is quite ambiguous and has meant many different things to officials and academics over the years. States and their leaders are assumed to know when and if power is equally distributed among nations or alliances. Even if they could actually measure the amount of power states have and perceive the weight of its distribution, it remains questionable whether or not a balance of power between states really produces peace. Some critics charge that a balance of power may in fact compel one state to attack another should it feel insecure about having the same amount of power its enemy has. National security, then, clearly involves a subjective judgment on the part of national leaders as to the acceptability of any distribution of power.

HEGEMONIC POWER AND INTERNATIONAL SECURITY

Hegemonic stability theorists argue that at any given time since the sixteenth century there has been only one hegemon (dominant power) dominating the international security structure and the political economic institutions and processes within it.[12] England never *balanced* power with another state. Rather its naval power helped it control the seas and manage the international security structure in ways that other nations found either beneficial or too costly to politically or economically change.

Most hegemonic stability theorists posit that security is a collective good hegemons provide weaker states. Hegemons stabilize the international security structure to the extent that, as providers of security, they "acquire a certain kind of power which lets them determine, and perhaps limit, the range of choices, or options available to others."[13] One version of hegemonic stability theory argues that states rationally choose to go along with the hierarchical order of the distribution of power in the international system until such time that the hegemon, its partners, or both, decide to change their roles.[14] War results from military challenges to the hegemon, ultimately producing a new hegemon that accepts the responsibility for and attempts to reorder the major political and economic institutions and principles of the international security structure. For instance, Hitler wanted to change the security structure so that Germany would gain more power and control more territory.

Germany's aggression resulted in unified countermeasures by those opposed to a fundamental reordering of the international security structure. The defeat of Nazi Germany and its allies, however, eventually produced a new hegemon—the United States—to fill the vacuum left by Great Britain's decline.

Another version of hegemonic stability theory marries features of mercantilism with liberalism. Charles Kindleberger, for instance, argues that U.S. military and economic power at the end of World War II helped create, institutionalize, and enforce liberal international economic institutions and principles in the international political economy after World War II.[15] Liberal economic ideals and values survive as long as the United States finds it in its interest to promote free trade and other liberal economic practices. By the late 1960s, however, the political and economic costs associated with providing security and maintaining an open international economy became prohibitive, and the United States found it necessary to respond to mercantilist trade policies with protectionist trade policies of its own (see chapter 6).

Other hegemonic stability theorists argue that the United States merely faced a situation where its allies and other states had increased their political and economic power and influence relative to the United States', forcing it to coordinate with, rather than impose military and economic policies on, its allies and other industrial powers.[16] Still others of the "declinist" school of thought emphasize the extent to which a weakened U.S. economy beginning in the 1970s resulted in a decline of U.S. power and unwillingness to perform hegemonic responsibilities.[17]

Still another variation of the hegemonic stability theory is George Modelski's long-cycle theory.[18] Modelski posits that political and economic decline is a built-in feature of a cycle of hegemonic ascension and decline that lasts for approximately one hundred years. Hegemons rise and fall depending on their control over the most important elements of power in the world. U.S. hegemony was predicated on nuclear power and a viable capitalist economy. On the other hand, many modern world system theorists (see chapter 4) argue, as many structuralists do, that both the international security structure and political hegemony are conditioned by the underlying capitalist structure of the international economy.[19] Internationally, states are ordered into three tiers of core, semi-peripheral, and peripheral nations. The world economy is an international division of labor whereby advanced capitalist core states extract resources and wealth from peripheral states. In the process, capitalism is entrenched throughout much of the world. Capitalism in the form of the international finance and trade structures is responsible for a good deal of war in peripheral states, due to the backwardness and underdevelopment it generates. Shifts in the international distribution of wealth and power also generate wars in the core states.

Today, the configuration of power the international security structure exhibits is a controversial issue we will touch on in the conclusion. Before then, we turn to the ways in which the international security structure conditioned international economic relations. Likewise, we will discuss a number of developments in the international economy that generated changes in the international security structure and gradually precipitated a broader and more complex definition of national security.

COLD WAR MILITARY STRATEGIES: THE RULES
OF THE GAME

The tight bipolar security structure of the early Cold War period conditioned national leaders to play by certain military and economic rules in a manner that reflected great concern over the physical defense of the nation-state. Ironically, it was these rules that helped change the way leaders of the industrialized nations in particular gradually thought about national security in more economic terms. These changes reflect a number of developments in the international production, finance, and knowledge structures.

When the United States dropped atomic bombs on Hiroshima and Nagasaki, it ushered in revolutionary changes in views about national security. Technology had always played a role in improving the capacity of weapons to inflict more damage on combatants and later on civilians. Yet the impact of nuclear technology went beyond the comprehension of even some of those military personnel and scientists who built it. For instance, Robert Oppenheimer, probably the most famous of scientists to work on the bomb, said he thought of the words of a Bhagavad Gita poem when he witnessed the first test of an atomic bomb: "I have become death, the destroyer of worlds."[20]

The role of the atomic bomb in the U.S. and Soviet arsenals added to the hostile relations between the two superpowers and helped create a rather unique security dilemma. Paradoxically, as the United States and Soviet Union each produced and deployed more nuclear, chemical, and other weapons of mass destruction to protect their allies and themselves, they also frightened each other, compelling each to increase the size of its arsenal. Early on in the Cold War, when the United States had a monopoly on nuclear weapons, its immediate military objective shifted from formal defense—protecting oneself after an attack occurs—to threats of massive retaliation if the Soviet Union attacked it or one of its allies. U.S. planes based in Western Europe could easily reach Soviet cities and industrial targets. After the Soviet Union tested its first atomic device in 1949 and gradually built up its nuclear arsenal in the 1950s, U.S. military strategy gradually shifted to deterrence: preventing the Soviet Union from initiating an attack on the United States or its allies.

Throughout the 1950s and 60s, the superpowers gradually became in thrall to a nuclear conundrum from which neither could escape by building bigger or more effective nuclear weapons. Nuclear strategy and the sophisticated technology it employed produced a psychology and logic—many label absurd[21]—whereby in order to deter the Soviet Union from attacking it, the United States would have to consider destroying the U.S.S.R., which could result in the destruction of the United States, and quite possibly ending the existence of all humanity.[22]

Many realists argue that the bipolar international security structure that incorporated a role for nuclear weapons constrained the choices of U.S. and Soviet officials and established new rules of the game when it came to fighting wars. When North Korea attacked South Korea in 1950, President Truman did not retaliate with nuclear weapons for fear of starting World War III. He responded by organizing a

United Nations effort to meet communist aggression in South Korea. After driving the North Koreans deep into North Korea, the Chinese entered the war to defend themselves against UN forces. The Korean war produced at least three lessons in the minds of many U.S. officials. First, direct engagement with Soviet or Chinese troops could widen any war and raise the stakes for the major powers beyond the intentions of officials. Second, conventional warfare or "police action" was judged most appropriate to meet Soviet aggression in contested areas outside U.S. and communist spheres of influence—even if it resulted in the death of some 34,000 U.S. and allied soldiers, in this case. Finally, nuclear weapons were judged inappropriate for anything but deterring other nuclear weapons.

Throughout the rest of the 1950s and into the 1960s, U.S. defense officials and academics debated how best to deter the U.S.S.R. when it would eventually have as many nuclear weapons as the United States. Supporters of an *active deterrent* military posture argued that the president should have more options rather than be forced to make an "all or nothing" decision about using nuclear weapons. Nuclear weapons were judged to be just like any other battlefield weapon that had a lot of military utility. The key was to have more military power than the enemy and to compel him to contemplate unacceptable levels of destruction that would result from retaliation. After Korea, the Eisenhower administration proposed a "New Look" to U.S. nuclear strategy that would enhance U.S. deterrence by deploying tactical (short- to mid-range) nuclear weapons along the Iron Curtain between Western and Eastern Europe. Nuclear weapons were cheaper than a large standing army and helped the administration cut the Pentagon's budget. Critics charge that there was nothing new about this strategy at all. Secretary of State John Foster Dulles simply made louder and more frequent threats of nuclear retaliation on the Soviet Union. In reality, the United States was not about to roll back the Soviet Union from Eastern Europe or do anything that might trigger another world war. Despite its shortcomings, supporters of an active deterrence strategy successfully lobbied for development of the hydrogen bomb based on the argument that the United States should rely primarily on its technological advantage to stay ahead of the Soviet Union.

The Soviets learned to play by many of the same national security rules during the Cuban missile crisis in 1962 when they placed medium-range ballistic missiles in Cuba. President Kennedy declared the action unacceptable because it upset the strategic balance of power. The U.S.S.R. withdrew its missiles after thirteen tense days.[23] Just how close the United States and Soviet Union came to nuclear war is a matter of some debate. Secretary of State Dean Rusk said that "we looked into the mouth of the cannon; the Russians flinched."[24] It is clear, though, that neither the U.S. or U.S.S.R. desired a nuclear war and that leaders went out of their way to prevent one.

Strategically it also became clear to U.S. officials that the Soviet Union would soon be able to attack the United States with intercontinental ballistic missiles launched from Soviet soil. The U.S. strategy of massive retaliation proved to be seriously flawed. After the Cuban missile crisis, many officials came to believe that neither the U.S. nor the U.S.S.R. would gain by initiating a first-strike attack on the other. Supporters of a *passive deterrence* strategy argued that the United States should pursue a policy of *mutually assured destruction* (MAD), reflecting the insanity of either side initiating a nuclear war it could not win. Nuclear war had become unthinkable; it was not just another type of war. Increasingly more sophisticated and destructive technology required the superpowers to accept and institutionalize a relationship of relative equality.

Supporters of MAD argued that the United States and Soviet Union should also pursue arms control agreements to improve communication and manage the content of their arsenals. Passive deterrence types were also critical of antiballistic missile (ABM) systems because they interjected an element of instability between the superpowers, sending the arms race into a search for newer and ever more sophisticated weapons. Self-defense measures were to be avoided because they compelled each side to launch a preemptive strike before a defensive system could be put into place.

Throughout most of the Cold War, the superpowers continued to mirror each other when it came to the compulsion to spend for weapon R&D, production, deployment, and stockpiling. By the late 1960s, a "balance of terror" had replaced a balance of power relationship between the two superpowers and their allies. In the 1970s, nuclear weapons gradually became even more technologically sophisticated in terms of damage and accuracy. Some critics feared that the superpowers could no longer make clear distinctions between offensive and defensive weapons.[25] Crisis situations became especially dangerous. Some strategic experts feared that a crisis could escalate to all-out war if officials felt compelled to launch their weapons before the enemy destroyed them.

In the late 1970s and early 1980s, the Carter and Reagan administrations shifted U.S. strategic doctrine back to an active deterrence posture as continued improvement in Soviet weapons technology contributed to another round of hostile U.S.-Soviet relations. President Reagan introduced a new generation of strategic weapons into the U.S. arsenal. The old idea of using smaller nuclear weapons for warfighting purposes regained support within the administration and Pentagon. President Reagan's proposal to build a "Star Wars" program also pushed U.S. strategic doctrine back into a threatening (defensive) active deterrent posture. Meanwhile, occasional computer glitches led to false alarms, nearly precipitating unintentional launches of U.S. nuclear weapons. Clearly, technology was outrunning the ability of politicians to control the weapons that were supposed to enhance U.S. national security.

At the height of the Cold War, national security issues preoccupied the United States and Soviet Union and their allies. Yet politicians did not appear to be compelled to use nuclear weapons by a bipolar international security structure and developments in the international technology structure. Paradoxically, while the superpowers prepared for nuclear war, the possibility of war did compel them to negotiate a series of arms control treaties, agreements, and confidence-building measures to limit the chances of using nuclear and other weapons of mass destruction. Meanwhile, the relationship between the superpowers and LDCs was not as positive as it was between the U.S. and U.S.S.R.

THE VIETNAM WAR

Many realists argue that the bipolar international security structure compelled the United States and Soviet Union to establish and adhere to certain rules when it came to LDCs. With their alliances relatively fixed, the U.S. and U.S.S.R. contested each other for political, military, and economic influence in the third world. After the Korean War, French Indochina (Vietnam, Laos, and Cambodia) became test cases of U.S. resolve to fight international communism. When U.S. troops entered South Vietnam in 1964 many LDCs were viewed as outside the formal bloc or *sphere of influence* of the superpowers. To contain international communism in LDCs, the United States used a variety of means including covert activity to topple pro-communist regimes. When necessary, the U.S. military engaged nationalist communist forces. The Soviet Union tended to mirror U.S. behavior in its support of pro-communist revolutions in Central and Latin America, the Middle East, Africa, and parts of Asia.

The longer U.S. servicemen fought in South Vietnam (1964–1973), the more vehemently U.S. officialdom debated the issue of an appropriate military strategy to win the war. U.S. conventional weapons seemed inappropriate for the kind of low-intensity warfare North Vietnam forced the United States to engage in. As in Korea, politics prevented the U.S. from using nuclear weapons (which it did consider) because of the war's proximate closeness to the U.S.S.R. and PRC. During the Tet (New Year) celebration of 1968, the North Vietnamese launched a military offensive all over South Vietnam. While U.S. military forces eventually prevailed, a groundswell of U.S. public criticism arose against the war. It gradually became clear that military weapons, along with the U.S. economy and technological-industrial capacity, could not gain political victory in South Vietnam. The United States could deter the Soviet Union from initiating a nuclear attack on the U.S., but it could not stop, nor was it willing to pay the political (in the number of dead) and economic costs associated with containing communism in Southeast Asia.

The United States had underestimated the political and economic strength and capabilities of the North Vietnamese and Viet Cong, who would stop at nothing to win the war, including incurring high casualty rates. Nationalism and an anti-imperialism campaign drove the North Vietnamese as much as their communist ideology. The defeat of the United States in Vietnam undermined ideas about the appropriateness of military force in LDCs and the idea that they were merely dominos waiting to fall to communism. The role of LDCs in the international security structure was complicated; LDCs were more than just ex-colonies that aspired to democratic values and capitalism. It would take more than superior conventional weapons and sophisticated technology to win the hearts and minds of people in developing nations.

Despite the rhetoric, North Vietnam no longer seemed to be a real security threat to the United States. The Nixon Doctrine announced to the world that U.S. troops would no longer be used to contain communism in third world nations. Some realists worried that the Vietnam War undermined the United States' global political reputation. Others questioned U.S. resolve and the effectiveness of its military to defend U.S. allies in other areas of the world. Some hegemonic stability theorists feared that the United States had grown weary of its hegemonic and strategic responsibilities.

After the Vietnam War, U.S. officials began to retreat inward and focus more on economic problems. The Congress and public resisted using U.S. military personnel to assist other anticommunist movements for fear of getting bogged down in another military-political no-win situation. The term *Vietnam syndrome* came to connote the reluctance of the United States to intervene in another country unless it was sure it could do so successfully, in a short period of time, and could withdraw quickly from the fray at small political (the number of soldiers killed) and economic costs.

The Vietnam syndrome clearly influenced the rationale behind, and method and duration of, U.S. interventions in Grenada, Panama, Somalia, and other countries. Presidents Reagan and Bush made sure there was public support for these incursions and that U.S. operations would be of a short duration and with clear objectives. Even if operations in the Persian Gulf lasted six months, the Vietnam syndrome clearly played a role in the outlook of U.S. officials in the Gulf War. Recently, President Clinton obviously was under the influence of the Vietnam syndrome when considering U.S. policy relating to Somalia, Bosnia, Haiti, and North Korea, among any number of situations where U.S. forces might be used for any length of time.

During the Cold War, bipolarity and hegemonic roles clearly shaped U.S. and Soviet military rules of the game pertaining to their allies and LDCs during the Cold War. Restrained superpower behavior marked the conduct of warfare in Korea, the Cuban missile crisis, and Vietnam. The Vietnam War was a watershed event that also contributed to loosening the bipolar international security structure. It weakened the resolve of the United States and other industrialized nations to fight unconventional wars in third world regions, and opened the way for economic issues and threats to play a greater role in the IPE.[26]

Ironically, the Vietnam War and other strategic features of a bipolar international security structure helped gradually weaken bipolarity and pushed the economy higher up the agenda of most nations. At the height of the Cold War in the late 1960s, national security issues of a physical (military) nature preoccupied the United States and Soviet Union, and their allies. Yet politicians did not let bipolarity compel them to use nuclear weapons. Paradoxically, in the 1970s, while the superpowers continued to prepare for nuclear war, the very possibility of war compelled them to negotiate a series of arms control treaties and agreements along with confidence-building measures to limit the use of nuclear and other weapons of mass destruction. New and more sophisticated weapon technologies became not only more costly, but also increasingly more unpopular with the public in industrialized nations.

Meanwhile, a number of developments in the international economy also helped loosen bipolarity and weaken U.S. hegemony, gradually becoming new sources of insecurity for nation-states. Developments in the production and finance structures would contribute to the emergence of more centers of power—many of them in the third world.

ECONOMIC STATECRAFT

During the Cold War, bipolarity and the limited utility of nuclear weapons compelled the United States to use its economy to contain the Soviet Union. A bipolar international security structure was also conducive to the entrenchment of capitalism and to the globalization of the international economy.

Mercantilists and realists argue that in 1947 and 1948, many U.S. officials believed that an economically weakened Western Europe would be easy prey to communism. Marshall Plan aid provided Western Europe with about $13 billion in financial aid and trade concessions.[27] Other U.S. allies in developing regions of the world were also given financial aid, along with technological and military assistance, in an effort to check Soviet influence. This aid benefited U.S. industries that produced more weapons but also goods for trade.

Mercantilists and realists also argue that the International Monetary Fund (IMF), World Bank, and General Agreement on Tariffs and Trade (GATT), among other multilateral financial and trade institutions, served as instruments of economic statecraft in an attempt by the United States to construct an international economic order favoring U.S. economic and security interests, as well as containing communism. Through these institutions and accompanying policies, the United States successfully tied together the Western industrialized capitalist economies and separated them from the communist economies. On many occasions, the United States also used trade embargoes, boycotts, and other economic sanctions to contain the Soviet Union. Mercantilists and realists also credit multinational corporations (MNCs) with helping to tie together the Western industrialized capitalist nations.

Structuralists and other radical revisionists agree with mercantilists that the United States used foreign direct investment to construct an international economy favorable to its political and economic interests.[28] However, structuralists also give a great deal of attention to MNC activity in LDCs, and to the extent to which U.S. Cold War objectives were driven primarily by U.S. corporate interests in developing regions of the world.[29] The United States attempted to overthrow what it perceived to be pro-socialist governments in Iran, Guatemala, the Dominican Republic, and later Chile. In these and other countries, CIA activities complemented U.S. corporate interests.[30] A popular structuralist argument in the late 1960s was that the United States and other industrialized nations helped generate a good deal of poverty and underdevelopment in many LDCs via their neoimperial and neocolonial investment practices in LDCs.[31] MNCs fomented much political instability and discontent, adding to the political and economic insecurity of LDCs.

Economic liberals and some hegemonic stability theorists argue that at the end of World War II, military power helped the United States liberalize (open up) and stabilize the international economy by promoting the creation and funding of the international IMF, the World Bank, and the GATT. This strategy worked until the early 1970s. Until then, U.S. nuclear power provided a security umbrella over most of the industrialized nations. The United States and its allies also benefited from increasing international trade and foreign direct investment that helped integrate the international economy.

By the mid 1970s, the international economic environment for the industrialized nations had become more hostile related in great part to increasing international economic interdependence.[32] The allies increasingly disagreed with one another about action regarding the Soviet Union in a weakening bipolar international security structure. Meanwhile, the industrialized nations had also become more dependent on trade and foreign direct investment to generate and sustain national economic growth. Two consequences were that U.S. corporations had to compete with each other and with the corporations of other industrialized nations. In what soon became a bipolycentric, if not a multipolar international security structure, corporations could not afford to be as political as they might have been earlier. Many of them supported détente with the Soviet Union and lobbied their governments to allow them to invest in Eastern Europe and in other socialist bloc nations. By the early 1980s, the Reagan administration had difficulty preventing U.S. and Western European corporations from working on the Soviet natural gas pipeline into Western Europe.

As the international economy pulled nations closer together, they also felt compelled to maintain more control over their economies. National leaders also felt that defending their national security required them to overcome national dependencies and vulnerabilities to other nations, all the while trying to either sustain or enhance economic growth. Despite liberal international economic objectives, many U.S. and other leaders of industrialized nations came under pressure to protect domestic groups from the harmful effects of the international economy by adopting any number of protectionist trade or investment measures. Demands for trade protection increasingly challenged the value and utility of free trade.

Interestingly, it was in the 1970s that Japan's economically successful but also mercantilist trading practices (see chapter 13) became of greater significance to the U.S. and Western Europe in particular. Japan's threat to the United States did not constitute a physical threat so much as its trade and investment policies forced national leaders to make undesirable adjustments in domestic political and economic institutions and policies. Quite often these adjustments translated into politically and socially undesirable lifestyle changes, such as importing large numbers of Japanese goods or selling huge national industries to the Japanese, Dutch, or other foreigners. Policymakers found it increasingly difficult to counteract what they interpreted as economic threats to their national security in other than benign (unintentional) mercantilist ways.[33]

The 1980s witnessed increasing "head to head"[34] economic competition among the industrialized nations, and among the industrialized nations and LDCs (see chapter 15). The gradual dissemination of wealth and power by means of international trade and investment throughout much of the industrialized and developing worlds, including the NICs, helped even more to strengthen the multipolar character of the international security structure and to weaken U.S. hegemony. Whereas earlier economic statecraft proved to have some utility in achieving political objectives, in an increasingly competitive international economic environment, its effectiveness was called into question. Paradoxically, in an international security structure where nuclear and even some conventional weapons seemed to have less political utility, states were increasingly compelled to practice economic statecraft to achieve a variety of political and economic objectives.

This situation paralleled the situation in the 1980s and now in the 1990s where many state leaders find themselves caught in a bind between pursuit of mercantilist and liberal trade, investment, and other economic policy objectives and strategies. On the one hand, they desire the benefits of growing international economic integration and interdependence that are to be gained by practicing liberal economic policies. On the other hand, international economic interdependence has had a down side. Many officials feel compelled to adopt protectionist policies and to use a variety of economic weapons to counter the benign mercantilist policies of other nations and to insulate themselves from the dislocating effects of the international political economy (see chapter 2).

THE OPEC OIL CRISIS: MORE SHIFTS
IN THE UNDERLYING ELEMENTS OF POWER

Part of the explanation for why focus gradually shifted away from military to economic security threats during the Cold War lies in still another shift in the factors that make states powerful. During the first and second OPEC oil crises many nations became dependent on energy—especially oil—and other energy resources.[35] The scarcity of natural resources and raw materials soon became a major security issue for almost all nations, raising issues about the environment (see chapter 19).

When OPEC significantly raised the price of oil, it touched off an international economic recession. Many nations became vulnerable to oil-producing nations and their political objectives. The economics of oil blended with OPEC's efforts to use the commodity as a political weapon to change the distribution of wealth and power in the international political economy. The OPEC oil crises also foreshadowed the entrenchment of North-South struggle between the developed and developing nations (see chapter 15), as well as a multipolar international security structure. The oil crises also made it difficult to undo political and economic interdependencies in the international political economy. If industrial development and economic growth was to continue, most states needed energy and other resources. Earlier in the Cold War, many LDCs had been important to the United States primarily as allies in its battle to contain international communism. Now the United States and other industrialized nations were dependent on oil-producing and other LDCs for access to natural resources and other "strategic" raw materials to feed the industrial base of their economies.

THE POLITICAL ECONOMY OF NATIONAL SECURITY

The tension that results from trying to balance mercantilist with liberal ideas and policies also shows up in the case of defense spending. Defense has always been one of government's biggest budget items. Defense is a collective good society must support through taxation and deficit spending.

Early in the Cold War, the intensity of threats associated with bipolarity and the development and deployment of weapons of mass destruction forced many states to shift major parts of their economy to maintaining a permanent state of military readiness. Mercantilists believe that one justification of state intervention in the economy was that a certain amount of labor had to be shifted out of agriculture, manufacturing, and service industries into the military- and defense-related industries. Large numbers of soldiers had to be trained, fed, paid, and their families cared for. Money had to be spent on the research and development of new weapons and technology used in different national defense systems.

In the 1960s and early 1970s, defense spending became a primary policy issue for many of the major powers that came under scrutiny from their societies to increase economic growth and standards of living. In the United States, the cost of the Vietnam War generated a great deal of criticism and anger. As international economic interdependence grew in the 1970s and 1980s, $600 toilet seats and many other examples of waste and inefficiency in the military establishment stole newspaper headlines. A common theme of many mercantilist and liberal experts was that excessive defense spending contributed to inflation and economic inefficiency and waste. David Calleo argued that multipolarity and a declining emphasis on military security threats necessitated that the United States' allies spend more for their own defense.[36] Excess defense spending drove up the U.S. national debt, which had to be paid for with foreign purchases of securities, government borrowed money, or with foreign investments in the United States.

Seymour Melman and other structuralist and Marxist-radical scholars argued that a "permanent war economy" benefited primarily state and military officials.[37] Excessive government spending distorted the production of military weapons at the expense of civilian goods, and compelled the United States and other industrial nations to fight unnecessary wars. A number of critics charge that in a post–Cold War atmosphere, a political "iron triangle" still exists among defense contractors, Pentagon officials, and congresspersons whose mutual interests are served by an inflated defense budget. Much like former Soviet industries in a socialist setting, the military services and defense-related industries are like pigs at a government trough.

Meanwhile, mercantilist supporters of defense spending usually argue that it economically benefits society in a number of ways. Defense spending and war tends to heat up an economy and create jobs that might not otherwise exist. Some industries benefit more than others, given the goods they produce. Defense monies trickle out and down to other parts of the economy. New technologies developed by defense-related industries create goods and products that can be used in other sectors of the economy. For example, the development of new jet engines for fighter aircraft helped promote the development of jet engines for commercial aircraft.

Recently, some economic liberals argued that in many cases defense spending could benefit from a healthy dose of market forces interjected into the weapons design, manufacturing, and trade processes.[38] In some cases, states can save costs by using "off-the-shelf" items instead of investing in the development of new weapons. In a more cooperative international environment, there is much to gain should NATO partners decide to share the costs of codesigning and coproducing technology with one another. In some cases, states and international businesses could coproduce certain products. And in a more competitive international economy, defense items may be procured more cheaply from other nations. Yet mercantilists point out that these benefits presuppose political cooperation on the part of what are essentially former allies. Tolchin and Tolchin would go so far as to caution that some states may become too dependent on other states.[39] A popular example is U.S. dependency on Japan for microchips, semiconductors, and other sophisticated equipment used in many U.S. weapon systems.

Many claim that economic problems associated with the defense costs created severe headaches for the Soviet Union, and may in fact have caused its breakup. It is also interesting to note that the Western European nations dealt with their defense cost problems differently than the United States. In their path to a common market and now to an even more integrated European Union (see chapter 11), many of them made a conscious attempt to restrain defense spending in accordance with more limited security objectives. Following this less militaristic course may ultimately help the EU members win the economic "head-to-head" competition among the United States, Japan, and the European Union.

THE POST–COLD WAR INTERNATIONAL SECURITY STRUCTURE: THE PERSIAN GULF WAR

Changes in the international security structure continue to occur at an unexpected and fast pace. Even if the Cold War appears to finally be ended, peace is not breaking out all over. Few people paint a rosy picture of current global security issues. Many political and economic conditions continue to threaten nation-states, though war in the Balkans and in many developing regions of the world remains localized and doesn't disrupt the entire international political economy.

By the end of the Cold War, in many industrialized nations it seemed as though the issue of national security shifted attention from hard military threats to softer threats on nation-states stemming from the economy and the environment.[40] Meanwhile, in many developing nations a good deal of conventional, guerrilla, and other types of nonnuclear warfare demonstrates that war and military threats remain a regular feature of the international security structure. Debt, low standards of living, failed development strategies, hunger, overpopulation, the spread of diseases, the proliferation of all types of weapons, ethnic and religious conflict, along with unfulfilled expectations, are just some of the conditions that shape the security policies of many LDCs.[41]

By one estimate, forty states—most of them in the third world—possess the technological capacity to produce nuclear weapons.[42] Structuralists would also remind us that the United States and Russia have been the largest dealers of arms to LDCs. During the 1994 debacle in Rwanda, twelve nations tried to sell arms to both sides in the bloody civil war.[43] Recession in the West and the collapse of the U.S.S.R. have compelled both state and industry officials to sell more fighters, bombers, and even submarines to almost anyone who will buy them.[44]

Like the OPEC oil crises, the recent Persian Gulf War broadened national security perspectives to account for a number of newer political and economic developments in the international security structure. The Middle East remains of critical importance to the industrialized nations because of their continuing dependency on oil. On August 2, 1990, Iraq surprised Kuwait when it invaded and took control of the whole nation in a few short hours. Saddam Hussein wanted Kuwait's oil and decided to take it by force. The invasion of Kuwait destabilized the entire region and threatened the United States and its allies' influence over Kuwaiti oil and political influence in the region. The United States' attack on Iraq provided it with an opportunity to once again use force to maintain its influence over oil production in the Middle East.

In many ways, the Persian Gulf War was a media spectacle.[45] It went beyond the "dinner hour" reporting of the Vietnam War in that from the time Iraq invaded Kuwait through both desert operations, press coverage was immediate and globally transmitted and received. Some CNN reporters became celebrities for their courage, but also for their hairstyles and for the bush jackets they wore. The commander of U.S. and allied forces, General Norman Schwarzkopf, became a television celebrity. In other ways, the war resembled an arcade video game. Cameras were loaded onto planes, and the U.S. military fed reporters lots of footage of these "smart bombs" destroying their targets.

In Vietnam, the United States was frustrated by its inability to use many of its more sophisticated weapons. The Persian Gulf War, however, presented the U.S. military with an opportunity to test its ability to defeat a third world nation with appropriately trained forces and an assortment of technologically advanced weapons. Aside from the use of many of its latest fighters, helicopters, tanks, personnel carriers, and guided missiles, the weapon that received the most attention was the Patriot missile, which targeted the old Soviet short-range Scud missiles that Iraq used to strike and provoke Saudi Arabia and Israel.

Since the end of the war, a number of critics have argued that the United States and its allies may have been more lucky than able when it came to defeating Iraq. First, had Saddam attacked Saudi Arabia, allied forces may have faced a more difficult task. According to Robert Lieber, "At best, this might have triggered a longer, less successful, and far more costly war."[46] Second, Saudi Arabia made up much of the difference in oil that was not produced during the war. The International Energy Agency released stored oil from supply stocks, helping to keep oil prices in line. Yet prices were not kept low enough to prevent inflation and a new round of economic recession in the West. In other words, the industrialized nations were lucky not to have found themselves facing yet a third oil crisis. Third, other critics charge that the terrain and topography of Kuwait were appropriate for the kinds of weapons the U.S. used in the war. Wars in other regions of the third world might not always prove to be so easy to win. Fourth, the United States became dependent on new technologies and weapons to destroy much of Iraq's industrial base. Ironically, the United States has become dependent on Japan and other countries for much of the technology used in these weapons.[47]

At least one critic charges that the Persian Gulf War encouraged for the first time the use of another new instrument of death and destruction, namely the ecological damage to the environment Saddam Hussein inflicted on the region when he torched over five hundred Kuwaiti oil fields in a last-minute act of desperation.[48] Oil fires burned countless millions of barrels of oil per day and contributed to high levels of air pollution and lower daytime temperatures in affected areas. Other effects of the war were oil spilled into the Gulf waters, destroying marine ecosystems and harming fish and other wildlife. Clearly, the Persian Gulf War was not the clean victory CNN portrayed.

THE FUTURE OF THE INTERNATIONAL SECURITY STRUCTURE

The Persian Gulf War demonstrates that war is still a response to national insecurities in the international security structure. It also raises the question of what type of international security structure we will have in the twenty-first century and what role the economy will play in that structure. One thing that is clear is that during the Cold War the relationship of the economy to national security tightened. Beyond that, only a few other trends seem clear.

More than a few people have made the argument that in the near future, economic issues will dominate state agendas. People will desire the economic benefits of peace and will be less willing to pay the costs associated with war-related national defense. John Mueller goes so far as to suggest that among the industrialized nations, major war has become obsolete.[49] In the near future, however, all nations will face a combination of new and old security issues that can be expected to generate more conflict and warfare. Let us not forget that this century has been one of the bloodiest in human history, and that security threats are a reason prima facie for the existence of the nation-state. As national security threats have become multifaceted and more complex, so have they also become too difficult to prioritize and solve.

For the time being, the many changes we have discussed—a number of which have their origin in the international production, finance, and knowledge structures—constitute a change within the international security structure, but not in the nature of that structure itself because it remains dominated by the nation-state, as yet the ultimate source of political sovereignty in the world.[50] At this time, the jury is still out as to whether the international security structure of the "new world order" will be primarily multipolar or unipolar. Hegemonic theorists also disagree as to whether or not the U.S. is actually in decline or remains top dog among a number of potential future hegemons.

Meanwhile, we should continue to focus on the international security structure because it conditions developments in the other three structures. Future political and economic changes that are bound to occur in that structure could eventually produce an entirely different security structure. At one extreme, the necessity of states to limit the harmful effects of war—to stay away from the abyss of mass destruction—compels them to view global security as an integral part of their own security. This could mandate a configuration of power dominated by larger political units such as the United Nations. The increasingly tight relationship among wealth and power and threats stemming from international economic interdependence add to the argument that the global community needs to get "beyond the nation-state" and stress cooperation over narrow self-interests.

At the same time, however, there is ample evidence to suggest that political and economic trends appear to be working in the opposite direction. The end of the Cold War provides certain ethnic groups or even tribes that are cosmopolitan in outlook with an opportunity to succeed where nation-states cannot.[51] Others suggest that the nation-state will break down and that city-states such as Stuttgart, Milan, Barcelona, Lyon, Osaka, and San Francisco will mark the political economic landscape based on their ability to preserve local identity and work with MNCs.[52]

The bottom line for this subject is therefore a chilling one, a climax suitable perhaps for a Tom Clancy thriller. We know that the international security structure matters a lot. Indeed, in the lives of the persons who read this book, probably nothing matters more, since not only the fate of the international political economy but quite possibly the earth and human race rest on it.

DISCUSSION QUESTIONS

1. Outline and discuss the ways in which each of the three major IPE approaches would view major changes in the national security during the Cold War.
2. Discuss the ways in which technology shaped the bipolar security structure and rules, particularly developments in nuclear strategy.
3. Outline and discuss some of the ways in which economic developments in trade and multinational corporate activity shaped the international security structure after the Vietnam War.
4. Outline and discuss what you think the international security structure will look like in the early twentieth century in terms of:
   a. polarity (the number of hegemons)
   b. the prevalence of military, economic, political, or other issues
   c. the factors that will make nations wealthy or powerful

SUGGESTED READINGS

Edgar Bottome. *The Balance of Terror: Nuclear Weapons and the Illusion of Security 1945–1985.* Boston: Beacon Press, 1986.

Aaron L. Friedberg. "The Changing Relationship Between Economics and National Security." *Political Science Quarterly* 106 (Summer 1991): 265–276.

Ethan B. Kapstein. *The Political Economy of National Security: A Global Perspective.* New York: McGraw-Hill, 1992.

Joel Kotkin. *Tribes: How Race, Religion and Identity Determine Success in the New Global Economy.* New York: Random House, 1992.

Robert J. Lieber. "Oil and Power after the Gulf War." In Theodore Rueter, ed., *The United States in the World Economy.* New York: McGraw-Hill, 1994.

Joseph S. Nye, Jr. "The Changing Nature of World Power." *Political Science Quarterly* 105 (Summer 1990): 177–192.

James S. Olson and Randy Roberts. *Where the Domino Fell: America and Vietnam, 1945–1990.* New York: St. Martin's Press, 1992.

Martin and Susan J. Tolchin. *Selling Our Security: The Erosion of America's Assets.* New York: Penguin Books, 1992.

Daniel Yergin. *The Prize: The Epic Quest for Oil, Money and Power.* New York: Simon & Schuster, 1991.

NOTES

1. Aaron L. Friedberg, "The Changing Relationship Between Economics and National Security," *Political Science Quarterly* 106 (Summer 1991): 195–212.
2. This is the theme of John H. Herz, "Rise and Demise of the Territorial State," in John H. Herz, ed., *The Nation-State and the Crisis of World Politics* (New York: McKay, 1976).
3. This is the assumption many realists and neorealists make about the international security structure. Realists tend to view the source of state behavior originating in individual leaders or within society. Neorealists emphasize the international state system as a source of state behavior. See Kenneth Waltz, *Man, the State and War* (New York: Columbia University Press, 1959) and also his *Theory of International Politics* (Reading, MA: Addison-Wesley, 1979).
4. The classic mercantilist-realist statement about the relationship of wealth to power was made by Jacob Viner, "Power Versus Plenty," *World Politics* (1948): 1–29.
5. Nazli Chouchi and Robert C. North, *Nations in Conflict* (San Francisco: Freeman, 1975).
6. The classic realist statement about power and its configuration into the balance of power is made by Hans Morgenthau, *Politics Among Nations: The Struggle for Power and Peace* (New York: Knopf, 1961), 101–166.
7. A good account of the Cold War from a mainly U.S. perspective is Stephen E. Ambrose, *Rise to Globalism: American Foreign Policy Since 1938*, 5th ed. (New York: Penguin Books, 1989). See also Walter LaFeber, *America, Russia, and the Cold War, 1945–1975* (New York: Wiley, 1976). An excellent piece of research on the conditions in Europe leading to U.S.-Soviet differences is Daniel Yergin, *Shattered Peace: The Origins of the Cold War and the National Security State* (Boston: Houghton-Mifflin, 1977).
8. For a review of developments in this period viewed from a U.S. perspective, see Zbigniew Brzezinski, "How the Cold War Was Played," *Foreign Affairs* 51 (October 1972): 181–204.
9. The objective of containment is attributed to George Kennan, a U.S. Foreign Service officer at the time. Kennan majestically outlines the containment objective in "X," "The Sources of Soviet Conduction" *Foreign Affairs* 25 (1947): 566–582.
10. For a more detailed discussion of this concept, see John Spanier, *The Games Nations Play*, 2nd ed. (New York: Praeger, 1975).
11. For a more detailed discussion of some of these problems, see Inis Claude, *Power and International Relations* (New York: Random House, 1962), and A. F. K. Organski, *World Politics* (New York: Knopf, 1968).
12. Some historians and theorists view Portugal, Spain, France, and the Netherlands as hegemons. For a summary of arguments related to this issue, see Joseph Nye, "The Changing Nature of World Power," *Political Science Quarterly* 105 (Summer 1990): 177–192.
13. Susan Strange, *States and Markets: An Introduction to International Political Economy* (New York: Basil Blackwell, 1988), 45.
14. Robert Gilpin, *War and Change in World Politics* (New York: Cambridge University Press, 1981).
15. Charles Kindleberger, *The International Economic Order: Essays on Financial Crises and International Public Goods* (Cambridge, MA: MIT Press, 1988).
16. This is the theme of much of David Calleo's work. See his *The Imperious Economy* (Cambridge, MA: Harvard University Press, 1982). See also Benjamin J. Cohen, (ed)

"The Revolution in Atlantic Economic Relations: A Bargain Comes Unstuck," in Wolfram Hanrieder, ed., *The United States and Western Europe: Political, Economic, and Strategic Perspectives* (Cambridge, MA: Winthrop, 1974), 106–133.

17. See, for example, Joshua Goldstein, *Long Cycles: Prosperity and War in the Modern Age* (New Haven, CT: Yale University Press, 1988).

18. George Modelski, "The Long Cycle of Global Politics and the Nation-State," *Comparative Studies in Society and History* 20 (1978): 214–238.

19. This is the theme of Immanuel Wallerstein, "The Rise and Future Demise of the World Capitalist System," *Comparative Studies in Society and History* 16 (September 1974): 387–415.

20. These are the words Oppenheimer says in the film footage of this account. The poem he was referring to actually says "I am time grown old, creating world destruction, set in motion to anihilate the worlds; even without you, all these warriors arrayed in hostile ranks will cease to exist." See *Bhagavad-Gita*, translated by Barbara Miller (New York: Bantam Books, 1986) 11: 32: 103. Our thanks to our colleague Stuart Smithers for securing this poem for us.

21. There are many well-known critics of the arms race. See, for example, Solly Zuckerman, *Nuclear Illusion and Reality* (New York: Vintage Books, 1982); Nigel Calder, *Nuclear Nightmares: An Investigation into Possible Wars* (New York: Penguin, 1982); and Helen Caldicott, *Missile Envy: The Arms Race and Nuclear War* (New York: Bantam Books, 1986).

22. For a discussion of the effects of nuclear war, see Paul Ehrlich, Carl Sagan, Donald Kennedy, and W. O. Roberts, *The Cold and the Dark* (New York: W. W. Norton, 1984).

23. For an interesting account of the Cuban missile crisis from an insider's view, see Robert F. Kennedy, *Thirteen Days: A Memoir of the Cuban Missile Crisis* (New York: W. W. Norton, 1969).

24. Ibid., 18.

25. Morton Halperin, "Strategic Nuclear Forces," in Joseph Kruzel, ed., *American Defense Arsenal* (MA: D. C. Health, 1988), 67–88.

26. One of the most comprehensive and well-written books on the Vietnam War is James S. Olson and Randy Roberts, *Where the Domino Fell: America and Vietnam 1945–1990* (New York: St. Martin's Press, 1991).

27. Estimates vary as to precisely how much the United States gave Western Europe under the Marshall Plan.

28. For a more detailed discussion of this argument, see Gabriel Kolko, *The Roots of American Foreign Policy* (Boston: Beacon Press, 1969), especially pp. 48–87, and Harry Magdoff, *The Age of Imperialism: The Economics of U.S. Foreign Policy* (New York: Monthly Review Press, 1969).

29. A representative piece of literature on the subject is Carl Oglesby, "The Free World's Corporate Empire," in Michael Parenti, ed., *Trends and Tragedies in American Foreign Policy* (Boston: Little, Brown, 1971), 75–90.

30. There is good deal of literature on the subject of multinational corporations and their connection to U.S. business interests. For a broad overview of the subject, see Richard J. Barnet and Ronald E. Muller, *Global Reach: The Power of the Multinational Corporations* (New York: Touchstone, 1974).

31. In chapter 4, we outlined the dependency argument made popular by Andre Gunder Frank, *Latin America: Underdevelopment or Revolution* (New York: Monthly Review Press, 1970).

32. One of the earliest studies of interdepenendence was Richard N. Cooper, *The Economics of Interdependence: Economic Policy in the Atlantic Community* (New York: McGraw-Hill, 1968).

33. For a more detailed discussion of this idea, see Robert Gilpin, *The Political Economy of International Relations* (Princeton, NJ: Princeton University Press, 1987), 404–405.

34. This phenomena became the focus of Lester Thurow's book, *Head to Head: The Coming Economic Battle Among Japan, Europe, and America* (New York: William Morrow, 1992).

35. For a detailed account of the history of the oil issue and OPEC's role in it, see Daniel Yergin, *The Prize: The Epic Quest for Oil, Money and Power* (New York: Simon & Schuster, 1991).

36. This theme is discussed at great length in David P. Calleo, *Beyond American Hegemony: The Future of the Western Alliance* (New York: Basic Books, 1987).

37. See, for example, Seymour Melman, *The Permanent War Economy: American Capitalism in Decline* (New York: Simon & Schuster, 1974).

38. This is the thesis of Ethan Kapstein, *The Political Economy of National Security: A Global Perspective* (New York: McGraw-Hill, 1992).

39. See Martin and Susan Tolchin, *Selling Our Security: The Erosion of America's Assets* (New York: Penguin, 1992), especially pp. 71–137.

40. The distinction between hard and soft elements of power is made by Nye, "The Changing Nature of World Power."

41. For a discussion of many of the bleak problems facing LDCs, see Robert D. Kaplan, "The Coming Anarchy," *The Atlantic Monthly* 273 (February 1994): 44–76.

42. John Simpson and Darryl Howlett, "The NPT Conference: Stumbling Toward 1995," *International Security* 19 (1994): 41–71.

43. These numbers come from Stephen D. Goose and Frank Smyth, "Arming Genocide in Rwanda," *Foreign Affairs* 73 (Sept/Oct 1994): 86–96. Our thanks to our students David Feinberg and Jason Mangone for bringing this article to our attention.

44. For a good discussion of the arms trade issue, see Richard Bitzinger "The Globalization of the Arms Industry: The Next Proliferation Challenge," *International Security* 19 (Fall 1994): 170–198.

45. For a detailed discussion of the role of the media in the war, see Marie Gottschalk, "Operation Desert Cloud: The Media and the Gulf War," *World Policy Journal* 9 (Summer 1992): 449–486.

46. See Robert J. Lieber, "Oil and Power after the Gulf War," in Theodore Rueter, ed., *The United States in the World Political Economy* (New York: McGraw-Hill, 1994), 193–194.

47. Tolchin and Tolchin, *Selling Our Security*.

48. For a more detailed discussion of the ecological damage done to the region, see Michael G. Renner, "Military Victory, Ecological Defeat," *World Watch* (July/August 1991): 27–33.

49. John Mueller, "The Obsolescence of Major War," *Bulletin of Peace Proposals* 21 (1990).

50. This point is made by Robert Gilpin, in his *War and Change in World Politics*.

51. See Joel Kotkin, *Tribes: How Race, Religion and Identity Determine Success in the New Global Economy* (New York: Random House, 1992).

52. See "Five Centuries later, 'City-States' Are Back," *The Seattle Times*, 5 June 1994, A3.

10

Knowledge and Technology: The Basis of Wealth and Power

Professor Ross Singleton

OVERVIEW

Throughout history, but particularly in today's world, wealth and power flow from access to and control of knowledge and technology. In this chapter we examine the creation and diffusion of knowledge and technology. Who controls this process and how?

We begin by defining terms. What is technology? What is the nature of technological innovation? We then consider the notion of dynamic comparative advantage—the idea that countries can *create* comparative advantage given sufficient access to knowledge and technology.

The role of intellectual property rights, which control access to knowledge and the diffusion of technology, will be considered from the liberal, mercantilist, and structuralist perspectives. Do these rights further the development of the world market, thereby enhancing the benefits of specialization and trade? Do these rights provide a basis for national advantage in a struggle for wealth and power among nations? Or do these rights limit the transfer of technology to developing countries, thereby deepening their dependency?

The efforts of the United States to control the flow of technology beyond its borders using trade laws and the GATT process are examined in detail. These efforts include enhancing the international protection of intellectual property rights (patents, trademarks, and copyrights).

Efforts to harmonize the treatment of intellectual property rights across national boundaries and conflicts among developed countries (particularly between the United States and Japan) regarding this process will also be considered. Finally, we will analyze the important process of the transfer of technology from developed to developing countries.

The power of machinery, combined with the perfection of transport facilities in modern times, affords to the manufacturing State an immense superiority over the mere agricultural State. . . . in a manufacturing State there is not a path which leads more rapidly to wealth and position than that of invention and discovery.[1]

Friedrich List

Economic change and technological development, like wars or sporting tournaments, are usually not beneficial to all. Progress, welcomed by optimistic voices from the Enlightenment to our present age, benefits those groups or nations that are able to take advantage of the newer methods and science, just as it damages others that are less prepared technologically, culturally, and politically to respond to change.[2]

Paul Kennedy

Students of IPE today find themselves in the midst of a technological-information revolution that will have political, economic, and social impacts, many believe, as profound as the industrial revolution of the nineteenth century. Scientists and engineers have made it possible for us to do things that were not just impossible a few years ago, they were absolutely unimaginable. Science fiction barely keeps ahead of science fact.

The industrial revolution had enormous impact on the international political economy because it altered global patterns of wealth and power. Looking closely, we can see the industrial revolution's influence on many momentous events and trends: World War I, the Russian Revolution, the rise and decline of colonial empires, and much more. This makes the current revolution in science and technology an even more important factor in IPE because, compared to the industrial revolution, the changes in science and technology today are broader—affecting more aspects of life, faster, and more globally. What happens to IPE in the future increasingly depends on how the world's states and markets accommodate scientific and technical changes today.

The common notion that "knowledge is power" has therefore taken on profound significance. Individuals, business firms, and nations that control access to knowledge in the form of scientific understanding and technological innovation can often enjoy a clear competitive advantage in the world market, allowing them to dominate political and economic processes.

Three important trends have become apparent over the last twenty years. First, knowledge and technology have become increasingly important as determinants of wealth and power. Economic success and political influence increasingly require technological prowess more than just natural resources. Second, the pace of technological change has quickened. Computers and machines have long physical lifetimes, but very short economic lives, given the speed with which more powerful and useful replacements are produced. Finally, knowledge and technology are increasingly dispersed. The computer and communications revolutions make it possible for complex data and ideas to move instantaneously from desk to desk within a business and from country to country around the world.

These three trends essentially mean that knowledge is wealth and it is power—for those who have access to it and can control it. Those individuals, firms, and nations that are unable to acquire advanced technology, or cannot innovate at a competitive rate, will necessarily fall behind. In his book *The Work of Nations*, Robert Reich imagines a world where knowledge and technology create an international class system.[3] Persons and nations are "haves" or "have-nots" based on how they "plug in" to the "global web" of the future. One needn't go so far as Mr. Reich in order to understand the importance of knowledge and technology in the future.

THE INTERNATIONAL KNOWLEDGE STRUCTURE

The *international knowledge structure* is the set of relationships that governs access to knowledge and technology around the world. It is a web of rules, practices, institutions, and bargains that determines who owns and can make use of knowledge and technology, where, how, and on what terms. This structure is rapidly growing and changing, which adds an exciting dynamic element to its nature.

The knowledge structure establishes a set of linkages between and among states and markets in just the same general way as the production, finance and debt, and security structures that have been discussed in this part of the textbook. To an important extent, a nation's position within the international political economy is determined by where it falls in the overlapping web that these four structures create.

What makes the international knowledge structure especially important today is the extent to which it interacts with the other IPE structures and thus conditions all the IPE relationships. Indeed, it would be hard to overstate the importance of knowledge and technology today. The role of knowledge and technology in the security structure was seen clearly in chapter 9. To an important extent, the IPE of the Cold War was driven by technology. The strategy of nuclear deterrence was chosen by the United States in the early postwar years in part because technology made nuclear weapons appear to be a less costly strategy than conventional weapons. The high costs of the arms race, which was also a technology race, contributed to the pressures that brought the Cold War to an end in the 1980s. It seems likely that knowledge and technology will continue to influence the security structure in the years to come.

Knowledge and technology have had a tremendous impact on the international financial structures discussed in chapters 7 and 8. Advances in computer and communications technology have resulted in a global financial system by making national borders and regulations almost irrelevant. As technology continues to advance, it will no doubt influence the financial structure in new ways. Today, for example, financial markets increasingly trade complex instruments called *derivatives* (because their value is derived from movements of other financial items, such as interest rates and exchange rates). Derivatives can be so complex that supercomputers, such as those used to track missiles, must be used merely to calculate their value. Technological change has made markets in these financial instruments possible; further advances are sure to shape financial relationships in future years.

The impact of knowledge and technology on international trade and the production structure (see chapter 6) is especially significant and will, therefore, be the focus of most of the rest of this chapter. The production structure is the set of relationships that determines what is produced, where, how, for whom, and on what terms. Each and every aspect of the production function is now affected in important ways by technology and technological change. Advances in science and technology mean that new goods and services are being produced, in new and unexpected places, in ways different from the past, and distributed in new ways to new patterns of consumers. The knowledge structure and the production structure are now so intertwined that it is almost impossible to separate them in practice as we do here for analytical purposes.

Consider some of the consequences of rapid technological change within the production structure. Individuals who have the educational background and ability to understand and use sophisticated technologies, those whom Robert Reich has christened the "symbolic analysts," are in great demand wherever they are located.[4] Motorola, Digital Equipment, and other U.S. corporations have recently located software development subsidiaries in India to take advantage of the plethora of software engineers that country's universities produce.

Because of their global reach and their control of knowledge and technology, business firms now rival states and markets for command of scarce resources and for control of wealth and power. Firms in today's competitive world market find themselves on an innovation treadmill. Success requires the constant development of new product and process technologies. The ability to protect technological innovations from immediate imitation is therefore critical. Without patent, trademark, and copyright protection (*intellectual property rights*), firms would find it difficult to recoup investment in new technologies.[5] Firms that are able to develop and control technology can produce and market their products and services throughout the world. Revolutions in data processing, transportation, and communications have made global reach a reality. Firms have become paramount actors in the international political economy arena.

Nations also struggle to become or remain competitive in the new world economy. Countries as diverse as El Salvador, China, Hungary, Russia, and the United

States share the common desire to grow and prosper by competing in the world market. Power in international relations now depends in large measure on a nation's ability to generate technological innovation and wealth.[6] The name of the economic and political game for governments of states and for the managers of firms is winning and maintaining a large market share of high value-added goods and services.[7] Clearly, winning or even holding their own in this game will require nations to develop or have access to the newest and best technology.

THE NATURE AND IMPACT OF TECHNOLOGICAL INNOVATION

Technology is the knowledge of how to combine resources to produce goods and services. Technological innovation comes in two varieties—product and process innovation. *Product innovation* is the development of new or better products. Product innovation can create entirely new markets and enormous benefits to consumers. The personal computer, ATM (cash) machines, and a whole range of pharmaceutical products come readily to mind as recent examples of product innovation. *Process innovation* is the development of more efficient, lower-cost production techniques. The robotics revolution led by Japanese producers, and managerial innovations (also by Japanese producers) are perhaps the most dramatic recent examples of process innovation.

Technological innovation is largely the product of investment in research and development by individual firms. But governments clearly can also play an important role in the process. Governments recognize that technological growth has historically been a key determinant of economic growth. For example, "advances in knowledge" accounted for an estimated 68 percent of increase in labor productivity and 28 percent of the growth in U.S. income between 1929 and 1982.[8] Governments also recognize the significance of technological innovation in the creation of comparative advantage. Therefore, governments have attempted to encourage technological growth in a variety of ways. Governments often subsidize basic science research within universities or research institutes. Governments sometimes subsidize research and development by firms or encourage the formation of research consortia among firms. And governments provide protection for intellectual property in the form of patents, trademarks, and copyrights.

Rapid technological change has many important effects on the world around us. Two that are worth special mention here are: the *product life cycle*, which illustrates how technological change leads to globalization of production; and the ability of a nation to *create comparative advantage* through strategic investment in knowledge and technology.

The Product Life Cycle

The product life cycle was described in the 1970s by political economist Raymond Vernon (see chapter 16 for further discussion of this topic). Vernon observed that some products that the United States once produced and even exported were eventually produced abroad and became imports. This life cycle (from export to import) is in part based on the interaction of product and process innovation. The United States, with its individualistic liberal IPE perspective, has for years been especially strong in *product innovation*. U.S. firms invent new products, develop them for the home market, and eventually export some of their production to other countries with similar needs.

Other nations, however, such as Japan, have shown greater success in *process innovation*. They find better ways to make existing products, often improving the basic goods in the process. As process innovation is applied, production is shifted abroad from U.S. factories. The new producer may be an especially innovative firm in Japan, or it could be a low-cost producer in a newly industrialized country (NIC) or less developed country (LDC), especially if innovation has standardized the product and simplified its construction. The United States then imports at low cost the item it once exported.

One of the most famous examples of the product life cycle is the videocassette recorder (VCR). VCR technology was invented by a U.S. firm to provide recording facilities for television stations. European and Japanese firms took this product, designed for a limited market, and used process innovation skills to create the mass market electronic device we know today.

Once upon a time, it was probably enough to be successful in product innovation—new products could be produced, supplying profits and jobs for years and years. Today, however, with the rapid pace of technological change and the speed with which new ideas are diffused around the globe, process innovation has become perhaps the more important technological advantage.

Creating Comparative Advantage

The post–World War II Japanese experience and the more recent experience of the Asian "Tigers"—Hong Kong, South Korea, Taiwan, and Singapore—demonstrate the ability of nations to create comparative advantage in the production of high value-added goods. Unwilling to accept their "natural" role in the world economy as producers of unskilled, labor-intensive goods, these nations have, through partnerships between government and business, developed their technology base sufficiently to become producers and exporters of high-technology goods and services. These countries have all invested in the educational infrastructure necessary to support high-tech production. They have also acquired technology from foreign sources and have developed their own capability to create new process and, to a lesser extent, product innovation. Firms in these countries now compete head to head for world market share in high value-added goods with U.S. and European firms.[9]

The transfer of technology from developed-country firms played a key role in the success of Japan and the Asian Tigers. Many developing countries are eager to follow this same path to development. Whether or not this model will succeed in Latin America, Africa, and Eastern Europe remains to be seen, but the transfer of technology will be a dominant issue in international political economy for some time to come. Clearly, firms within the developed countries own and control most of the technology that is so vital to international competition and the future of less developed countries. A technological leader among developed nations, the United States has, understandably, taken the lead in defining the terms and conditions under which the transfer of technology will occur.

THE IPE OF TECHNOLOGY AND INTELLECTUAL PROPERTY RIGHTS (IPRs)

If we stop for a moment and look back over the last few pages, an interesting dilemma appears. Knowledge and technology have become increasingly important in the IPE in many ways. With the rapid pace of technological change, new products and new processes are especially valuable to individuals, business firms, and nations because of the wealth and power that derives from them. To gain the maximum advantage, however, one needs to *control access* to new knowledge and technology—to keep others from using the products of research and innovation without paying in full for the right. At the same time, however, the computer and communications revolutions are making it easier and more efficient to move information around, making the control of access harder and harder. In short, precisely when the control of technology is of greatest value, it has become much more difficult and cumbersome.

It is unsurprising, given all the potential wealth and power that is at stake here, that the control of information has become a very important issue in international political economy. The vocabulary of this part of IPE is somewhat technical, but the issues are important enough to make learning the new terms worthwhile. What is at stake, after all, is the technological future.

The key concept in the IPE of the knowledge structure today is *intellectual property rights* (IPR). A *property right* (generic term) is the right to control use of some *thing*, such as a house, or car, or a book. It is possible to make markets in these things because their property rights are well defined and well enforced. That is, it is possible to determine who owns a house and who doesn't, and a person who uses a house that belongs to someone else without first concluding a bargain will be punished. We can feel secure in our ownership of everyday goods because this system of property rights works relatively well.

Intellectual property rights are the rights to control use of *intellectual property*— an invention, or creative work such as a novel or poem. Patents, copyrights, trademarks, and other systems of intellectual property rights are the mechanisms normally used to control access to new ideas. Intellectual property rights are most effective when the state defines and enforces them strictly. This creates a problem, however, since there are many different states, which may have many different rules regarding intellectual property rights. The inventor of a new process may be unable to stop a firm in another country from using his or her ideas if that country has less strict rules regarding patents, for example.

Intellectual property rights have thus become a critical issue for both those nations that own patents, copyrights, etc., and those nations that seek to use them to produce goods and earn incomes. One goal of the Uruguay round of the GATT negotiations was to reach some agreement regarding intellectual property rights, but there is still much progress to be made on this front.

THREE PERSPECTIVES ON INTELLECTUAL PROPERTY RIGHTS

In the liberal view, property rights are fundamental to the functioning of a market system. Property rights create a powerful incentive to use resources efficiently. Property rights establish a direct link between effort and reward. A privately owned farm, for example, is efficiently operated because the owner of the farm is legally entitled to all of the income that farm generates. The farmer strives to maximize the productivity of his land in order to maximize his own income. Similarly, individuals and firms have a powerful incentive to innovate and invent when they are legally entitled to the income associated with that process. Intellectual property rights—patents, trademarks, and copyrights—create the link between effort and reward.

Invention and innovation (commercialization of an invention) involve the creation of knowledge. And knowledge, by its nature, is nonrival. That is, the knowledge one firm uses can also be used by other firms. (By contrast, the ton of steel that one firm uses cannot also be used by other firms. Steel is a rival good.) The knowledge that one firm develops in the form of product and process innovation can also be used by other firms. Consequently, unless firms can legally deny the use of newly created knowledge to other firms, rapid imitation will eliminate the profits from innovation necessary to recoup the original investment in research and development (R & D) that created the new knowledge. The efforts necessary to develop new technology would not be rewarded. Without intellectual property rights, insufficient resources would be devoted to R & D, and far fewer new and lower-cost products would be available to consumers.

From the liberal perspective, then, international protection of IPRs is essential if the world market economy is to enjoy the extraordinary benefits of rapid technological growth. International IPR conventions should be strengthened to guarantee the effective protection of technological innovation. The winners in this process will ultimately be consumers the world over who will enjoy the availability of an astonishing variety of new products—from genetically engineered foodstuffs and medicines to educational and entertainment multimedia software. The only real losers will be those firms and individuals who will no longer profit from copying the creative, innovative efforts of others.

Mercantilists see the process of technological innovation in a much different light. Knowledge is a source of national wealth and power. Recall, according to this school of thought discussed in chapter 2, that production, not consumption, is critical to the national interest. The ability to produce is the true measure of a nation's wealth and power. Technology, then, the knowledge of production, largely determines a nation's place in the world. Nations must develop and then closely guard their own technology, and technology controlled by other nations must be acquired. Technological dependence must be avoided.

The protection of IPRs for *domestic* firms is clearly appropriate in order to foster domestic technological innovation. Equal protection for technology owned by foreign firms, however, is unlikely to be in the national interest. Rather, government policy in this area should facilitate the acquisition of foreign-owned technology at the lowest cost possible. Increased international protection of IPRs is, then, not necessarily in the national interest. Protecting intellectual property of national firms in domestic and foreign markets is appropriate, but reciprocal protection for foreign firms in domestic markets should be resisted—recall that trade is, according to this view, a zero-sum game. One nation's gains in international market share come at the expense of some other nation's losses. The battle for markets will be won by the nation that can best exploit its technological advantages.

An additional insight provided by mercantilist thought regards imbalances in stages of national development. List and Hamilton, early mercantilists, argued that free trade benefits the most developed manufacturing nation(s) at the expense of lesser developed nations (see chapter 2). Similarly, international conventions that protect intellectual property rights will benefit those nations with the most advanced technological capabilities at the expense of less technologically developed nations. In this regard, mercantilist and structuralist thought is similar.

Structuralists contend that IPRs increase the dependency of the periphery on the core. IPRs are tools of dependency. The developed nations use IPRs to maintain their technological advantage over third world countries. Patents, trademarks, and copyrights are used to monopolize third world markets, to extract and repatriate excessive profits from third world countries, and to deepen and legitimate dependency.

From the point of view of dependency theorists, then, the winners from more stringent international enforcement of IPRs are clearly the developed countries and their firms. The losers are the people of third world countries who pay monopoly prices for many goods and services and who receive the benefits of technological transfer only on terms dictated by firms of the developed world. We will consider further the North-South aspects of IPRs in a later section of this chapter. First, it is appropriate to review the efforts of the United States to protect IPRs and then consider the degree of cooperation and conflict among developed countries regarding IPRs.

U.S. EFFORTS TO PROTECT INTELLECTUAL PROPERTY RIGHTS

> The increased significance of technological diffusion and the increasingly arbitrary nature of comparative advantage as well as military security concerns are causing the United States to make the protection of its high technology industries an important priority. In addition to its own effort to slow down the outflow of industrial know-how, the U.S. has placed the international protection of intellectual property rights on the agenda of trade negotiations.[10]
>
> *Robert Gilpin*

U.S. firms have played a major role in elevating the protection of intellectual property rights (IPRs) to the status of a major U.S. foreign policy issue. The Intellectual

Property Committee, an ad hoc coalition of twelve major U.S. corporations representing the entire spectrum of industries, was established in 1986 with the goal of increasing the international protection of IPRs.[11]

The Intellectual Property Committee contends there is a direct link between the protection of IPRs and U.S. international competitiveness. Without adequate protection of IPRs, U.S. firms find it difficult to profit from product and process innovation. Foreign firms that infringe on IPRs have lower development costs, since they are merely copying original technological innovations. Consequently, these infringing firms can underprice the U.S. firms that incurred the original development costs. A new generation of semiconductors can cost $100 million or more to develop, and yet these same chips can be copied for less than $1 million. A popular software package that sells for $500 in the United States has been copied and sold for as little as $7.50 in foreign countries.[12] Piracy of U.S. entertainment media, including tape recordings and video tapes, has become epidemic in many parts of the world. The U.S. International Trade Commission has estimated that the overall loss to U.S. business from foreign infringement of IPRs in 1986 alone was between $43 billion and $61 billion.[13] Responding to pressure from U.S. businesses, the U.S. government has attempted to increase the international protection of IPRs through unilateral, bilateral, and multilateral means.

Under U.S. trade law, the government can impose unilateral retaliatory trade sanctions against countries that fail to adequately protect IPRs. Special Section 301 of the 1988 Omnibus Trade and Competition Act, generally called *Super 301*, requires the United States Trade Representative (USTR) to retaliate against countries that "deny adequate and effective protection of intellectual property rights" or "deny fair and equitable market access to United States persons that rely upon intellectual property protection."[14] Super 301 requires the USTR to create a list every year of *priority foreign countries* that have failed to adequately protect IPRs. After investigating the acts, practices, and policies of the offending country, the USTR may institute immediate trade sanctions, including the elimination of trade concessions and the imposition of import restrictions or duties. Or the USTR may choose to negotiate a bilateral agreement with the offending country to eliminate the cause of the action.

In 1989, the USTR identified no *priority countries*. Instead, a *watch list* was created, of twenty-five countries "whose practices deserve special attention." Eight countries—Brazil, India, Republic of Korea, Mexico, People's Republic of China, Saudi Arabia, Taiwan, and Thailand—were placed on a priority watch list as countries that formally met the criteria of priority foreign countries, but who were making satisfactory progress in bilateral and multilateral negotiations to address shortcomings in the protection of IPRs.[15]

Section 337 of the Tariff Act of 1930 as amended by the Omnibus Trade and Competitiveness Act is designed to eliminate the importation into the U.S. of goods that infringe on IPRs. Under the amended Section 337, the complainant must merely demonstrate that an infringement of an IPR occurred rather than *substantial injury*, as the original law required. The International Trade Commission can issue an exclusion order or a cease and desist order in response to complaints.[16]

The unilateral trade sanctions made possible by U.S. trade laws have been criticized by its trading partners as violations of GATT provisions. In fact, Section 337 has been challenged before a GATT tribunal.[17] U.S. efforts to negotiate bilateral agreements to improve the protection of IPRs are much less controversial.

With the stick of unilateral trade sanctions firmly in hand, the United States has been quite successful in negotiating bilateral agreements with many countries to improve the protection of IPRs. Negotiated changes in the treatment of IPRs have occurred in several countries, including Singapore, Malaysia, Thailand, the People's Republic of China, Taiwan, and South Korea. Bilateral disputes and negotiations continue between the United States and Brazil, India, Thailand, Japan, and the European Union.

In 1991, while negotiating the North American Free Trade Agreement (NAFTA) with the United States, Mexico enacted comprehensive patent and copyright laws. The final NAFTA agreement "locks in" these Mexican reforms. As a result of the NAFTA negotiations, Mexico will now give copyright protection to software programs, satellite transmissions, and audio and video recordings. Better patent protection and protection of trade secrets and proprietary information in Mexico and Canada are also major accomplishments of NAFTA.[18]

The twelve U.S. firms that constitute the Intellectual Property Committee urged U.S. trade negotiators to place the protection of IPRs on the agenda for the Uruguay round of the GATT negotiations. The multilateral approach (described below) to the international enforcement of IPRs had, in the opinion of these U.S. firms, largely failed to provide adequate protection. More effective enforcement of IPRs, it was hoped, could be negotiated by linking the protection of IPRs to multilateral trade negotiation.

Multilateral agreements to protect IPRs include the Berne Convention, concluded in 1886 to define copyright protection, and the Paris Convention signed by the U.S. in 1887, which ostensibly provides protection for patents, trademarks, and industrial designs. In 1967, the World Intellectual Property Organization (WIPO), a United Nations agency, was created to monitor adherence to the Berne and Paris conventions. WIPO has been roundly criticized by firms in developed nations because its defined minimum standards of protection are inadequate and because it lacks effective enforcement and dispute resolution mechanisms. Developed country firms are pessimistic that WIPO will ever provide meaningful IPR protection because the policy and agenda of this United Nations agency are controlled by developing countries who, arguably, generally oppose IPR reforms.[19] We will explore developing country attitudes toward IPR protection later in this chapter.

The GATT agreement concluded in 1993 did include, at the insistence of the U.S. and other developed nations, provisions regarding trade-related intellectual property rights (TRIPs). TRIP negotiations centered on effective enforcement of IPRs, on the definition of multilateral dispute resolution mechanisms, and on acceptable minimum standards of national protection.[20] Special concessions were also negotiated for developing countries that need time to create or amend IPR laws in order to conform to the minimum standards that will be required as a condition for their continued participation in GATT.[21]

COOPERATION AND CONFLICT AMONG INDUSTRIALIZED COUNTRIES

The developed nations of the world have, not surprisingly, supported the efforts spearheaded by the United States to enhance the international protection of IPRs, including the inclusion of TRIPs in the Uruguay round of GATT negotiations. Current discussions are underway within WIPO to enhance protection of performers, producers of sound recordings, and broadcasters. Enhanced trademark protection in the form of the Madrid Protocol is also under discussion.[22] There has also been a concerted effort among these nations to reach agreements to "harmonize" IPR laws across national boundaries.

One example of the need for harmonization involves the issue of "first to file" versus "first to invent" with respect to the awarding of patent rights. The United States finds itself at odds with most other countries by granting patents on a "first to invent" basis. In Japan, Sankyo, a Japanese firm, was granted the patent on a new anticholesterol drug, whereas in the United States, Merck, a U.S. firm, was granted a patent on the same drug. Merck was able to verify prior invention even though Sankyo had been the first to file in both countries.[23] This kind of conflict will be avoided when developed countries succeed in "harmonizing" IPR laws.

Although developed countries are cooperating in important ways, conflict between and among them over IPRs still exists to a significant degree. The basis of competitive advantage among developed countries in high-technology industries is knowledge.[24] Patterns of trade reflect the success national firms have had in developing new products and processes. And the success of national firms depends in large measure on the national organization of competition and policy toward knowledge creation.[25] Disputes among developed nations involving the treatment of intellectual property are to be expected given the centrality of knowledge and technology to competitive advantage. Conflict over the treatment of IPRs between Japan and the United States has been particularly serious in the past and continues to be a major foreign policy concern for both countries.

In the mid-1980s, the U.S. government, in response to its trade deficit with Japan, instituted bilateral trade talks with the Japanese called the *market-oriented, sector-specific* (MOSS) talks, designed to increase U.S. access to Japanese markets. The MOSS talks in electronics focused on the protection of U.S. technology, particularly semiconductor chip design and software created in the United States. As a result of these talks, the Japanese did adopt legislation extending fifty-year copyright protection for software and ten-year protection for original chip design, thereby harmonizing Japanese practices with U.S. standards.[26]

In the mid-1990s, however, the U.S. continues to blame its ongoing huge trade deficit with Japan largely on Japan's discriminatory treatment of IPRs. Whereas the U.S. grants exclusivity to Japanese innovators thereby allowing them to develop strong brand names and market niches in the U.S., according to Assistant Secretary of Commerce and Commissioner of Patents and Trademarks Bruce Lehman, U.S. firms are denied true exclusivity in Japan. According to Lehman, "If U.S. companies are fortunate enough to survive the gauntlet and the years of delay of the Japanese Patent Office, the most they can hope for—given the Japanese system of dependent patents—is royalty revenue from their Japanese competitors, rather than the true exclusivity which is necessary to open that market to competition."[27] Japan's discrimination against U.S. firms is certainly a clear example of the mercantilist approach to IPRs. Japan has recently been placed on the Super 301 watch list (discussed earlier in this chapter) because it is suspected of not adequately enforcing IPRs.

One would expect that Japan will at some point adopt a more liberal attitude toward IPR protection, either in response to U.S. and European pressure or in the realization that a more liberal approach both befits and benefits a major, technologically advanced trading nation. (See chapter 13 for a discussion of U.S.-Japanese economic and political relations.)

CASE STUDY: PATENTING LIFE—THE INTERNATIONAL HARMONIZATION OF BIOTECHNOLOGY PROTECTION

In April of 1988, a white mouse made history by becoming the first animal ever to be patented in the United States The "Harvard mouse," as it is known, was developed by Philip Leder of Harvard University and his colleague Timothy Stewart, now at Genentech, Inc., using genetic engineering. They "invented" the extraordinary mouse by inserting a human cancer gene into mouse egg cells. The mouse satisfied the requirements for protection as an invention under U.S. patent law because of its novelty and its usefulness in cancer research.

Microbes, plants, and, lately, other animals have also received patent protection from the U.S. Patent Office. In response to pressure from the United States and from its own biotechnology industry, the European Union is currently considering proposals to create comparable biotechnology protection. Developing countries are also being pressured by the United States to extend IPR protection to biotechnology via bilateral negotiations and multilateral negotiations under the GATT agreement.[28]

Many countries offer very limited protection, if any, for biotechnology because the agricultural, pharmaceutical, and medical products and processes that result from biotechnological innovation are considered fundamental rights and needs of the people. About thirty-five countries offer no patent protection for food products, among them Denmark, Brazil, China, Finland, Colombia, Egypt, New Zealand, and Venezuela. Animal and plant varieties are excluded from patent protection in forty-five countries, including the EU member countries, Brazil, Canada, Ghana, Colombia, Cuba, Israel, Kenya, Malaysia, Nigeria, South Africa, Switzerland, and Thailand.[29] Many countries offer only process patents for pharmaceutical products, intending to create a powerful incentive for rival firms to develop different processes to produce the new and unpatented product. The reduced level of patent protection for biotechnology in many countries also reflects to some degree their greater reliance on government-sponsored, university biotechnology research, which does not require patent incentives.

Continued

CASE STUDY: PATENTING LIFE—THE INTERNATIONAL HARMONIZATION OF BIOTECHNOLOGY PROTECTION, *continued*

The efforts of the U.S. government to increase the international protection of biotechnology arises from political pressure brought to bear by U.S. biotechnology firms that want to protect their competitive advantage in international markets. Many other developed and developing country governments are also beginning to feel the same pressures from their own budding biotechnology industries. But there are many thorny issues associated with the protection of biotechnology that must be resolved before international harmonization can occur.

The primary controversial issue has been whether or not living organisms are patentable. In the 1980s, the U.S. Supreme Court handed down several key decisions (in 1980 for an engineered microorganism; in 1985 for a maize plant and its components; and in 1988 for the aforementioned mouse) that set new precedents in this regard. The issue, according to the Court in the 1980 case, is not living versus nonliving but rather products of nature, living or not, versus human interventions.[30] Presumably, products of nature are not patentable, whereas products of human intervention may be. Although this legal issue appears to be resolved in the United States, many other controversial legal, technical, economic, and ethical issues remain.

If the international harmonization of biotechnology protection can be accomplished, great benefits might be forthcoming. A farmer anywhere in the world might buy a seed that has a U.S. company's disease resistance gene, an Egyptian company's drought resistance gene, and a Brazilian company's nutritional enhancement gene. Of course, the consequences of harmonization will likely be very different when viewed from a mercantilist or structuralist perspective.

NORTH-SOUTH CONFLICTS OVER INTELLECTUAL PROPERTY RIGHTS

Many developing nations oppose the TRIPs provisions in the new GATT agreement. They argue that WIPO is the appropriate forum for discussing the norms and standards of IPRs. And, more fundamentally, they argue that the efforts by the United States and other developed countries to strengthen the international protection of IPRs has focused on the enhancement of the proprietary aspects of IPRs, thereby reinforcing monopoly privileges, while weakening the aspects of IPRs that promote the prompt and widespread diffusion of new technology.[31] For example, the TRIPs provisions broaden the scope and duration of patent protection and therefore of monopoly privilege, while enervating working requirements that foster technological diffusion.

The basic premise of developing nations in granting a patent is that the firm granted the patent will produce the patented product or use the patented process *in the country granting the patent.*[32] When the patent is "worked" locally, technological spillovers are generated. Scientists, technicians, and engineers in the patent-granting country become familiar with the technology. And, domestic firms may be called on to supply inputs into the production process thereby upgrading their technological sophistication. As the technology is diffused throughout the domestic economy, it may become the basis for *domestic* technological innovation.

This premise is certainly consistent with the fundamental rationale for patents in any context. Patents represent a trade-off. The innovator is granted an exclusive right to produce the new product or use the new process. In exchange, the new knowledge the innovator has created is disclosed and made public in the patent application process so that others have access to this knowledge and can thereby create additional new knowledge. If patent rights were not available, innovators would attempt to keep new knowledge secret to avoid imitation. Patents and the working of patents facilitate the diffusion and creation of new knowledge.

The Paris Convention states that failure to work a patent is an abuse of patent rights. A compulsory license can be issued to another firm to guarantee local production. Firms from developed countries have argued that imports of the patented product or the product made with the patented process constitute working the patent. Developing countries have long opposed this notion. From their point of view, imports do not generate the same spillover benefits that domestic production would. Imports do not result in the transfer of technology—only local production accomplishes that.[33] Some analysts have gone so far as to oppose the creation of patent systems in developing countries on this basis. The granting of patents by developing countries, they argue, is akin to granting exclusive import rights to certain foreign firms allowing them to monopolize the local market and eliminate other (especially local) firms.[34]

The United States and other developed nations, against the protests of developing nations, included provisions in the GATT negotiations that will permit imports to constitute the working of a patent. The South Commission argued forcefully that the inclusion of IPRs under the GATT will have "significant adverse effects on the pace of generation, absorption, adaptation and assimilation of technical change in the developing countries."[35]

C. Niranjan Rao summarizes the sentiment of many critics of the TRIPs provisions of the GATT agreement as follows:

> By asking for a GATT based agreement on IPRs, the developed countries are seeking to bring in a system which fits into their trade strategies and preserves their technological superiority. These proposals are much tougher and pro-patentee than the Paris Convention. Such an agreement, given the concentration of ownership of patents in large multinational corporations from highly developed countries, will make the third world free playground for the trade and investment decisions of these MNCs.[36]

An additional area of contention between developed and developing countries concerns copyright protection. The developed countries, led by the United States, have recently been demanding stronger international copyright protection. The mind-set of developing countries in this regard can be best understood by considering the historical role of the United States in international copyright protection. Early on, the United States was more of a consumer of works produced by foreign authors than a producer for foreign markets. Consequently, the United States refused to sign the Berne Copyright Agreement or even respect foreign copyrights until forced to do so by the growth of its own artistic and literary community. In fact, the United States did not sign the Berne Agreement until 1989. The United States, then, is a "Johnny-come-lately" when it comes to the international enforcement of copyright protection.[37]

Even though most developing countries are also consumers of works by foreign authors and artists and generally are not producing works for other countries, they are being pressured by the United States and other developed countries to respect foreign copyrights.

There are no guarantees that developing countries will benefit from strengthening their systems of IPR protection. However, for those countries attempting to follow outward-oriented development strategies, the risk of trade retaliation and the need to attract foreign direct investment provide strong incentives to comply with developed country demands for stronger IPR protection.[38]

CASE STUDY: ASIAN DEVELOPING COUNTRIES—TIGERS OR COPYCATS?

"Ralph Lauren" polo shirts sell for $4 in Bangkok and "Rolex" watches (that have a wrist-life of six months) cost $8 each. Pirated video and audio tapes, sometimes with misspelled names, are available by the truckload at very low prices. Walt Disney released the film *Aladdin* in the United States in November 1992, and pirated copies were on sale in Bangkok within two weeks. In May 1993, Microsoft found pirated versions of MS-DOS 6 on sale in Singapore before the product's official release in the United States.[39] The worldwide sales of pirated compact discs doubled to 73 million from 1992 to 1993 primarily because of unauthorized production in China.[40]

The International Intellectual Property Alliance, noted in the text, estimates that U.S. companies lost $2 billion in potential sales in 1992 to the ten worst-offending Asian countries. This figure may well underestimate the loss because some imitations are very hard to distinguish from the real thing. Microsoft's own managers could not identify pirated copies of their Windows and MS-DOS products sold in Taiwan. Even the hologram placed on the software to prohibit copying had been counterfeited by a university in China.[41]

Inadequate protection of trademarks probably is the most important violation of intellectual property.[42] A trademark is a sign or symbol (including logos and names) registered by a manufacturer or merchant to identify goods and services. Protection is usually granted for ten years and is renewable as long as the trademark is effectively used.

In a broader sense, trademarks are essential to the efficient functioning of the market. Trademarks convey information and protect investments in the production of quality goods and services. Trademarks help consumers select products of high quality and reliability. Consumers come to rely on trademarked products. Consequently, search costs are reduced. Trademarks also motivate producers to maintain quality standards. Producers who do so know they will be rewarded with repeat purchases by consumers who have come to trust their trademark. Without adequate trademark protection, then, consumers will necessarily spend more hours attempting to discern quality differences, and producers will be discouraged from investing in the production of quality goods and services.

Copyrights protect the expression of an idea, not the idea itself. Copyright protection is provided to authors of original works, including literary, artistic, and scientific works. Software and databases are also afforded copyright protection in a growing num-

Continued

CASE STUDY: ASIAN DEVELOPING COUNTRIES—TIGERS OR COPYCATS?,
continued

ber of developed and developing countries. Copyrights generally allow the owner to prevent the unauthorized reproduction, distribution (including rental), sale, and adaptation of original work. Protection lasts for the life of the author plus fifty years.[43] Copyrights, like patents, are necessary to encourage innovation. Without this protection, rapid reproduction by rivals would diminish the return on investment in the creation of new computer software, computerized databases, literary, artistic, or scientific work.

Intense pressure is being brought to bear by the United States on Asian countries to increase their protection of trademarks and copyrights. Thailand, for example, was listed as a "priority foreign country" by the United States Trade Representative in 1992 (under Super 301 provisions as described in the text) and therefore is subject to retaliatory trade sanctions. Thailand fired the official in charge of the enforcement of intellectual property rights on April 20, 1993, and launched a series of raids on counterfeiters resulting in public burnings of pirated materials as the April 30 deadline approached for the USTR's new watch lists.[44]

China made a substantial formal commitment to copyright protection in October 1992 by issuing regulations to protect foreign works consistent with the requirements of the Berne Copyright Convention. But China's commitment to actually enforce copyright protection remains questionable, as noted in the first paragraph of this case.[45]

CONCLUSION

The issues surrounding the development and control of knowledge and technology clearly play a central role in international political economy. Whether viewed from a liberal, mercantilist, or structuralist perspective, knowledge and technology form an increasingly critical basis of wealth and power. In this era of global competition, individuals, firms, and nations understand that knowledge and technology confer competitive advantage. That the protection of intellectual property rights has risen to the status of a major foreign policy concern for the United States and many other countries is not surprising. The knowledge structure, like the production structure, the finance structure, and the security structure clearly constrains the options and conditions the behavior of individuals, firms, and nations, and therefore affects the wealth and power they enjoy.

DISCUSSION QUESTIONS

1. What are intellectual property rights (IPRs) and why are they important in today's global markets? Briefly compare and contrast the mercantilist, liberal, and structuralist views of IPRs.
2. What three trends have become apparent over the last 20 years regarding the role of knowledge and technology in IPE? Explain.
3. Trade-related intellectual property rights (TRIPs) were a controversial issue raised in the GATT's Uruguay round. Explain what TRIPs are and discuss briefly the issues raised in these GATT negotiations.

4. Discuss the Product Life Cycle phenomenon, with emphasis on the role of technology and knowledge in this process. What issues regarding IPRs are raised by the Product Life Cycle business pattern? Explain.

SUGGESTED READINGS

Paolo Bifani. "The International Stakes of Biotechnology and the Patent War: Considerations after the Uruguay Round." *Agriculture and Human Values* (Spring 1993).

Carol J. Bilzi, esq. "Towards an Intellectual Property Agreement in the GATT: View from the Private Sector." *Georgia Journal of International and Comparative Law* 19: 2(1989).

Michael Porter. *The Competitive Advantage of Nations.* New York: The Free Press, 1990.

C. Niranjan Rao. "Trade Related Aspects of Intellectual Property Rights: Question of Patents." *Economic and Political Weekly*, 13 May 1989.

Brent W. Sadler. "Intellectual Property Protection through International Trade." *Houston Journal of International Law*, 14: 393(1992).

W. E. Siebeck, ed. *Strengthening Protection of IP in Developing Countries: A Survey of the Literature.* World Bank Discussion Paper no. 112, Washington, DC, 1990.

Susan Strange. *States and Markets: An Introduction to International Political Economy.* New York: Basil Blackwell, 1988.

Laura D'Andrea Tyson. *Who's Bashing Whom?: Trade Conflict in High-Technology Industries.* Washington, DC: The Institute for International Economics, 1992.

NOTES

1. Friedrich List, *The National System of Political Economy* (New York: August M. Kelley, 1966), 201–202.
2. Paul Kennedy, *Preparing for the Twenty-first Century* (New York: Random House, 1993), 15.
3. Robert Reich, *The Work of Nations* (New York: Knopf, 1991).
4. Ibid., 177–180.
5. Patents are issued by a government conferring the exclusive right to make, use, or sell an invention for a period generally ranging from fifteen to twenty years (counted from date of filing). Trademarks are signs or symbols (including logos and names) registered by a manufacturer or merchant to identify goods and services. Protection is usually granted for ten years and is renewable. Copyrights protect the expression of an idea, not the idea itself. Copyright protection is provided to authors of original works of authorship, including literary, artistic, and scientific works. Copyrights are also issued for software and databases in a growing number of countries. Copyrights prohibit unauthorized reproduction, distribution (including rental), sale, and adaptation of original work. Protection lasts for the life of the author, plus fifty years. For more detailed descriptions of these and other intellectual property rights, see Carlo M. Correa, *Intellectual Property Rights and Foreign Direct Investment* (New York: United Nations, Publication ST/CTC/SER.A/24, 1993), 8–9.
6. Thomas D. Lairson and David Skidmore, *International Political Economy* (Orlando, FL: Harcourt Brace Jovanovich College Publishers, 1993).
7. Susan Strange, "An Eclectic Approach," in Craig Murphy and Roger Tooze, eds, *The New International Political Economy* (Boulder, CO: Lynne Rienner Publishers, 1991).
8. Edward F. Denison, *Trends in American Economic Growth, 1929–1982* (Washington, DC: Brookings, 1985), 30.
9. This is one theme of Lester Thurow's best-selling book, *Head to Head: The Coming Economic Battle Among Japan, Europe, and America* (New York: William & Morrow, 1991).

10. Robert Gilpin, *The Political Economy of Intenational Relations* (Princeton, NJ: Princeton University Press, 1987).

11. Carol J. Bilzi, esq., "Towards an Intellectual Property Agreement in the GATT: View from the Private Sector," *Georgia Journal of International and Comparative Law* 19:2(1989):343.

12. Bilzi, "Towards an Intellectual Property Agreement in the GATT," 345.

13. Richard A. Morford, "Intellectual Property Protection: A US Priority," *Georgia Journal of International and Comparative Law* 19:2(1989):336.

14. Omnibus Trade and Competitiveness Act of 1988, tit. I, subtit. C, pt. 1, § 1303, Pub. L. No. 100–418, 102 Stat. 1179–81 (codified at 19 S.S.C. § 2242 [1992]).

15. Brent W. Sadler, "International Property Protection Through International Trade," *Houston Journal of International Law* 14:393(1992):416.

16. Ibid., 408.

17. Ibid.

18. Gary Clyde Hufbauer and Jeffrey J. Schott, *NAFTA: An Assessment* (Washington, DC: Institute for International Economics, 1993), 85.

19. Sadler, "Intellectual Property Protection Through International Trade," 401.

20. Critics of the TRIPs proposal argue that the effort to impose new international uniform standards at higher levels for IPR protection contradicts the GATT's traditional commitment to the principle of national treatment. By requiring reciprocity, the TRIPs proposal would violate existing GATT provisions that refer to the non-reciprocity of trade relationships between developed and developing countries. See Paolo Bifani, "The International Stakes of Biotechnology and the Patent War: Considerations after the Uruguay Round," *Agriculture and Human Values* (Spring 1993): 56.

21. Bilzi, "Toward an Intellectual Property Agreement in the GATT," 346.

22. Bruce Lehman, Assistant Secretary of Commerce and Commissioner of Patents and Trademarks, remarks before the Section of Patent, Trademark and Copyright Law, American Bar Association, New York, 10 August 1993, 6.

23. Dennis W. Carlton and Jeffrey M. Perloff, *Modern Industrial Organization* (Glenview, IL: Scott, Foresman, 1990), 661.

24. Laura D'Andrea Tyson, *Who's Bashing Whom?: Trade Conflict in High Technology Industries* (Washington, DC: Institute for International Economics, 1992), 18.

25. See Michael E. Porter, *The Competitive Advantage of Nations* (New York: The Free Press, 1990), for a discussion of how differences in national organization of competition and policies toward knowledge creation affect competitive position in international trade and investment.

26. Tyson, *Who's Bashing Whom*, 59.

27. Bruce A. Lehman, remarks before the American Bar Association, 5.

28. John A. Barton, "Patenting Life," *Scientific American* 264 (March 1991): 41.

29. Paolo Bifani, "The International Stakes of Biotechnology and the Patent War: Considerations after the Uruguay Round," *Agriculture and Human Values* (Spring, 1993): 48.

30. Ibid., 50.

31. Ibid., 55–56.

32. C. Niranjan Rao, "Trade Related Aspects of Intellectual Property Rights; Question of Patents," *Economic and Political Weekly*, 13 May 1989, 1053.

33. Ibid., 1055.

34. See R. Vayrynen, "International Patenting as a Means of Technological Dominance," *International Social Science Journal* 30 (1978): 315–337

35. Rao, "Trade Related Aspects of Intellectual Property Rights," 1056.

36. Ibid.

37. Lewis Shapiro, "The Role of Intellectual Property Protection and International Competitiveness," *Antitrust Law Journal* 58 (1989): 577.

38. C. A. Primo Braza, "The Developing Country Case for and against IPP," in W. E. Siebeck, ed., *Strengthening Protection of IP in Developing Countries: A Survey of the Literature*, World Bank Discussion Paper no. 112, Washington, DC, 1990, 232.
39. "Caveat Vendor," *The Economist* 1 May 1993, 33.
40. "Worldwide Pirate Disc Sales Double to 75m," *Financial Times* 2 June 1994, 4.
41. "Caveat Vendor," 33.
42. Carlos M. Correa, *Intellectual Property Rights and Foreign Direct Investment,* (New York: United Nations Publication ST/CTC/ERS.A/24, 1993), 14.
43. Ibid., 8.
44. "Caveat Vendor," 33.
45. East Asian Executuve Reports, February 1993, 5.

Part III

State-Market Tensions Today

Part III presents four case studies of IPE analysis: the European Union, NAFTA, Japan, and nations in transition from communism to capitalism. While these studies are informative about four important sets of nations, they are intended to have broader application. Each study poses a particular question that applies around the globe. Students are challenged, therefore, to master the specific applications and at the same time appreciate the more general themes that derive from them.

Chapter 11 examines the specific case of economic and political integration in Europe, which has been one of the most important IPE events of the twentieth century. This study raises a larger question: which force is stronger—the political forces that divide nations or the global market forces that unite them? The tension between economics and politics is critical to Europe's development, but it conditions international behavior in all parts of the world.

The North American Free Trade Agreement (NAFTA) is the topic of chapter 12. On the surface, one might expect a good deal of overlap between this chapter and the previous one. NAFTA is a program of economic and political integration, similar in nature but weaker in degree. The tensions between integrating economies and disintegrating politics exists here, too. But this chapter develops a different theme. Global markets diminish the state's sovereignty and pose something of a challenge to democracy. This tension between market processes and democratic processes is particularly clear in NAFTA, but once again has nearly universal application. It is a fundamental tension of IPE.

Readers will learn a lot about Japan and the global IPE in chapter 13. This chapter's discussion of the capitalist developmental state, however, raises broader questions about the roles of states and markets in national development strategies. The discussion of Japan's changing role in the global political economy raises questions about the role of hegemons in international political and economic relations. These questions apply especially to Japan, but have broad implications elsewhere in the IPE.

Finally, chapter 14's analysis of "States and Markets in Transition" focuses specifically on Russia, Poland, and China—three nations that are moving from systems of classical socialism to more market oriented and, in the case of Russia and Poland, more democratic systems of political economy. How do such fundamental changes in states and markets interact? Do political reforms encourage economic change or hinder it? How do economic reforms affect political decisions? These questions are critical in Russia, Poland, and China, but equally so to a long list of other nations around the world.

11

The European Union: The Economics and Politics of Integration

OVERVIEW

This chapter examines the political economy of economic integration, which is one of the most powerful dynamics of this era in world history. Increasingly, nations are driven to unite their economies for greater efficiency and growth. Integrated markets do not necessarily mean integrated states, however. The fundamental tension between economics and politics is revealed in heightened relief in the process of integration. This chapter examines the IPE of economic integration by looking at its most important example, the integration of Europe.

The European Union formally began life in 1957 as the European Economic Community (EEC), often called the *Common Market*. In the 1980s, the economic element in the group's name was eliminated, creating the *European Community* (EC) or often just "the Community," not so much because the economic function was diminished, but because the political and social functions were growing. In 1993, the name changed again to the *European Union* (EU), further evidence that integration was spreading from the economic sphere to the political and social spheres of European life.

The European Union is the product of nearly forty years of political and economic activity aimed at creating a cooperative and growing environment for Europe. It is, on one hand, arguably the largest and richest unified market in the world—a postwar success story. It is, on the other hand, arguably the weakest of political alliances imaginable, ever on the verge of collapse. The fundamental question that the European Union seeks to answer in our day is whether economics is more important than politics. That is, whether the dynamic, individualistic motives of the market matter more than the unifying social values of the nation or state. Significantly, this is still an unanswered question at the end of the twentieth century.

This chapter presents an interpretive history of economic integration in Europe (chapter 12 examines NAFTA and economic integration in North America). Monetary integration, a complex but important topic, is treated as a boxed case study. The chapter ends in speculation about how the forces of economics and politics will shape Europe's future.

The European Community, if it were to become politically cohesive, would have the population, resources, economic wealth, technological, and actual and potential military strength to be the preeminent power of the twenty-first century.[1]
Samuel P. Huntington

The international political economy at the end of the twentieth century seems to be pulled in two opposite directions. One force, *nationalism*, is seemingly tearing asunder nations and groups of nations that, for much of the twentieth century, have been stable political entities. The list of nations and regions that are feeling the force of nationalistic pressures is long; an incomplete list includes Canada, the former Yugoslavia and former Czechoslovakia, the former Soviet Union, Great Britain, Germany, South Africa, and India.

At the same time, however, another force is seemingly binding different nations together, creating suprastate alliances. The unifying pull of *integration*, creating one out of many, is causing nations to give up some autonomy in return for the potential benefits of membership in a cooperative alliance. The list of these multinational alliances and cooperative agreements is nearly as long as the previous list, including the European Union (EU), the North American Free Trade Agreement (NAFTA), the Asian-Pacific Economic Cooperation group (APEC), and the

Mercosur, Andean Group, and Central American Common Market in Central and South America.

The motivations for these alliances and cooperatives are many. The driving force behind many of these groups is economic, so this trend is often referred to as *economic integration* (unifying the economic structures of a group of nations). In political economy, we study the dynamic interactions between states and markets, so we may expect that the integration of markets has important consequences for states. Economic integration makes possible (or perhaps makes necessary) a greater degree of political integration. The tension between the forces of economics and politics here makes the trend toward greater cooperation a controversial one.

THE LOGIC OF ECONOMIC INTEGRATION

Economic integration is the process by which a group of nation-states agree to ignore their national boundaries for at least some economic purposes, creating a larger and more tightly connected system of markets. Economists view economic integration as an example of the *theory of the second best*. If it is impossible to gain global free trade (the "first best" option for liberal economists), then open regional free trade groups represent an attractive "second best" solution. Realists, who do not necessarily agree that free trade is best, nonetheless find integration an interesting phenomenon because economic integration sometimes leads to political and social cooperation or integration.

There are several degrees of economic integration that nations can attain. A *free trade area* (FTA) involves a relatively minimal degree of integration. Nations in a FTA agree to eliminate tariff barriers to trade for goods and services they produce themselves. Each nation, however, retains the right to set its own tariff barriers with respect to products from outside the FTA. The fact that some goods are tariff-free in FTA transactions, but other goods are still subject to differential trade barriers complicates intra-FTA trade and therefore limits the effective degree of integration.

The North American Free Trade Agreement (NAFTA) is an example of a FTA. When NAFTA is fully implemented, goods from the United States, Canada, and Mexico will be traded freely within the NAFTA borders. Goods from other countries, however, will be subject to the differential tariff barriers of these three countries. If, for example, Canada has a lower tariff on French wine than does the United States, then any shipments of French wine that happen to flow through Canada to the United States will be subject to an additional tariff upon entering the United States To be sure that proper tariffs are collected, all goods will be accompanied by some sort of certificate of origin.

The next level of economic integration is called a *customs union*. (*Customs* is another word for a tariff.) Under a custom union, a group of nations agree both to tariff-free trade within their collective borders and to a common set of external trade barriers. If NAFTA were to evolve into a customs union, for example, the United States, Canada, and Mexico would need to agree to a unified set of tariff barriers that would apply to products from other countries. The Treaty of Rome, which created the original European Economic Community, was based upon the idea of a custom union.

The movement to a customs union is an important step in terms of economic and political integration. The nations involved give up some degree of their sovereignty or national political autonomy, since they can no longer set their own trade barriers without consulting their economic partners. What they gain from this is a far greater degree of economic integration. Products flow more easily within a customs union, with no need for border inspections or customs fees because of the unified trade structure. In practice, of course, the elimination of trade barriers is not as complete as theory would suggest, since member nations retain the right to impose some non-tariff trade barriers, such as health and safety standards, for example. Still, a customs union is an effective means of increasing market size and stimulating growth and efficiency.

An *economic union* is the final stage of economic and political integration. In an economic union, non-tariff barriers are eliminated along with tariff barriers, creating an even more fully integrated market. The degree of integration in an economic union goes further than this, however. Member nations in an economic union agree to four "freedoms" of movement: of goods, services, people, and capital. These four freedoms represent significant limitations on national sovereignty, but they can also have significant effects on economic activity. The European Union, when its current plans are fully implemented, will become an economic union.

The free movement of goods is more complicated than it may seem, for it goes beyond the elimination of tariff barriers. Free goods movement requires a variety of governmental health, safety, and other standards and regulations to be "harmonized" so that, at least in theory, a product that can be sold somewhere in the economic union can, in fact, be sold everywhere in it (aside from obvious technical barriers that can prevent sale, such as differences in electrical systems among nations, or the difference between left-hand drive and right-hand drive automobile systems).

Free movement of services is also more complex than it may seem. The service sector of international trade includes many industries, such as banking and finance, traditionally subject to heavy regulation that varies considerably among nations. Free movement of people requires a unified immigration policy, since a person free to enter and work in one member of the economic union would, in theory, be able to live and work anywhere in the area. Finally, free movement of capital means that individual nations give up their ability to regulate investment in-flows and out-flows. Many nations have traditionally imposed capital controls to encourage domestic investment, promote financial stability, or reduce foreign exchange variations. These controls are not eliminated in an economic union, but they must be "harmonized" so that national regulations are similar enough that they do not become a barrier to economic activity.

The most successful economic union in the world is the United States, if we consider it an alliance of the separate states. Consider how freely goods, services, people, and capital move from one state to another. This gigantic single market has been remarkably flexible and dynamic, making it a model for other developed nations. Consider, however, the degree of political complexity that is inherent in such a system as the United States. The elaborate system of economic and political federalism that characterizes the U.S. political economy is much different from relations that typically exist among and between autonomous nation-states. Economic integration is thus as significant politically as it is economically.

GROWTH AND EFFICIENCY: THE ECONOMICS OF INTEGRATION

Economic integration is appealing because it is one way for nations to achieve greater efficiency in their use of scarce resources and higher rates of economic growth. In the lingo of economics, integration produces static efficiency gains and dynamic efficiency gains.

Economic integration promotes greater efficiency in resource use (economists call this *static efficiency*) for two main reasons. First, with completely free trade within the area, each member nation is able to specialize in producing the goods and services in which it is most efficient. Protective barriers that preserve inefficient industries and promote redundancy are eliminated. Economists believe that these gains from efficient specialization are significant. Second, the creation of a larger, integrated market promotes efficiency in certain industries where large-scale production or long production runs are possible. These gains from "economies of scale" make products cheaper and more competitive.

These static gains are important, but they tend to reach their potential fairly soon after economic integration occurs. The more important economic benefit of integration occurs in the long run, as *dynamic efficiency* promotes economic growth. The logic here is that a larger and more competitive market is likely to be more innovative. As internal trade barriers are removed, previously protected firms are forced to compete with one another. Firms become more efficient and "nimble."

If economic integration is successful, economic growth rates tend to increase, which raises living standards. Even a small rise in growth can be significant. If, for example, economic integration causes the long-term rate of economic growth to rise by one or two percentage points, the long-run impact would be that at the end of a single generation, the living standard could be about double what would have occurred without integration! Thus, economic integration need produce only a little extra growth to have a considerable long-term effect on people's lives.

SOVEREIGNTY AT RISK: THE POLITICS OF INTEGRATION

It is not simply for economic reasons that great attention ought to be paid to Europe's future. It is engaged in a political experiment of the highest importance concerning how human societies think about themselves and relationships with others.[2]

Paul Kennedy

Most of the discussion of economic integration tends to focus on the benefits of a larger market. There are, however, many political impacts that must be considered.

There is, to some degree, a trade-off between economic benefits and political costs. The closer the economic ties among nations, the closer their political ties. When nations agree to cooperate closely in the economic sphere, they commit themselves to closer political cooperation, too. Thus, for example, the economic efficiency and growth promised by an economic union requires that a nation negotiate a new immigration policy, safety standards, methods of financial regulation, and adopt a harmonized system of investment controls. These important political choices are no longer influenced mainly by the preferences and interests of domestic voters and groups—now the wishes of groups in other member countries must also be considered. Some observers have complained that economic integration creates a "democracy deficit" by breaking the link between political choices and the electorate.

The fundamental political problem posed by economic integration is the loss of sovereignty that occurs when nations form regional trade blocs. These pluralistic organizations necessarily place constraints on the actions of sovereign nation-states. At some point, each member state risks being forced to ignore national interests—political, economic, social, or cultural—as a consequence of maintaining its international obligations. This tension between national interest and international obligations is fundamental to multinational institutions, and poses a severe dilemma for states, which tend to value security and autonomy above all else. Given the importance of this political tension, the extent of integration we observe in the world today should perhaps surprise us more than it does.

Economic integration creates political tensions in another way. As markets merge, the location and intensity of economic activity changes. Some industries in a particular nation expand, while others contract. Some unions gain members and power, others lose them. The changing geography of wealth and power within each member nation necessarily changes the political landscape.

The view that economic integration weakens political power is not shared by all. Another school of thought holds that integration weakens the hold of national interest groups on political decisions. Broad multinational policies are less likely to benefit specific interest groups in each country, in their view, since their ability to influence legislation is watered down in international negotiations. The resulting policies may better reflect the public interest and be less influenced by special interests. It has been argued, for example, that labor unions in France have undue influence on public policy, which is leavened in a useful way when policies are made at the European Union level, rather than at the national level. This concern, of course, assumes that the "public interest" of the different members of the integrated group are not dissimilar.

There is also the view that individual nations may gain political power, especially in relations with other nations, by being members of a powerful economic alliance. This is the argument that Belgium, for example, is a more potent political presence as a leading nation of the European Union than if it were simply a small but autonomous European nation making its own way in international politics. It is also argued that smaller countries are far more powerful as members of a larger group than they would be as separate, unaffiliated individual nations.

THE POLITICAL CONSEQUENCES OF MONETARY UNION

There is no better example of the tension created by political and economic integration than the issue of *monetary union* in Europe. For many years, economists and business people have suggested that the next logical step in creation of a single European market is the creation of a single currency for Europe—or the next best thing, which is a system of firmly linked exchange rates.

The logic of a single European currency, which eventually would replace the separate national currencies of EU members, is that it would create additional static and dynamic efficiency gains. The current system of many individual currencies adds cost and risk to international transactions. Costs are created each time a currency must be converted from, say, British pounds to French francs. Risks exist due to the variable nature of exchange rates; each time an exchange rate changes, the value of revenues, costs, and inventories changes for firms doing business across national borders. For a pan-European multinational enterprise, these costs and risks can be substantial. Europe's big single market would be more efficient if national currencies were replaced by a *European Currency Unit*.

Students in the United States can appreciate this logic. Imagine how much more difficult economic life would be if each state in the United States had its own currency, which fluctuated daily relative to the currencies of other states. Travel, shopping, and business would be much more complicated in such a system, which is just what Europeans face today.

Why doesn't the EU adopt a single currency? Part of the answer is tradition. Money is deeply rooted in any culture, and giving up a national currency, with its history and patriotic symbolism, would be hard to do. But the problem goes deeper than emotion.

Having a single currency, or a system of rigidly fixed exchange rates, which amounts to the same thing, would require great unity of purpose for the European nations. As discussed in chapter 7, the value of a nation's currency depends upon what it can buy. This in turn is affected by the nature of its economic and political policies. A single currency would require that the same economic and political policies apply to all of Europe on a wide range of issues. Individual nations would give up the option of taking independent action on matters such as inflation, unemployment, taxes, interest rates, or debt. This is a lot of sovereignty to give up.

Creating a single currency would likely alter the balance of power among EU members. Where would the European Central Bank be located? Whose interests would dominate it? Many believe that Germany would be the favorite to dominate a unified EU monetary system. This unsettles other nations whose economies are perhaps poorer or less vital than Germany's or whose economic and political interests lie elsewhere.

The issue of German leadership of a European Monetary System is a complex one. Some EU members would object to a German-led system, fearing that Germany's interests would dominate the continent at the expense of smaller nations. Others might find German leadership appealing. The German central bank, the Bundesbank, has a history of resisting the temptation to inflate its currency. It might prove useful to have anti-inflation Germany in charge of monetary policy, this argument goes, so that other countries are not faced with the political temptation of buying votes with higher wages, for example, which would later lead to higher prices.

Many people within Germany are uncomfortable with the prospect of German leadership, too, fearing that Germany might at some point be forced to sacrifice its domestic interests in order to maintain its leadership function. The tension between domestic needs and international obligations is fundamental to situations like this one.

Monetary union, with the possibility of a single currency, remains on the EU's agenda. It remains to be seen, however, if the logic of economic efficiency will prove stronger than patriotic emotions or concerns over the balance of political power.

THE BIRTH OF THE EUROPEAN ECONOMIC COMMUNITY

The idea of the economic integration of Europe is not a new one, but Europe's postwar leaders had good reason for putting integration at the top of their agenda. The history of Europe in the twentieth century had been dominated by war, depression, and revolution. Although each of these events was complex in itself, each demonstrated the cost of failure to achieve cooperation on economic and political matters (and the danger of aggressive mercantilist behavior by big nations on a small continent).

Economic integration, it was thought, might provide the liberal antidote to the threats of mercantilist recidivism, on the one hand, and communist expansion on the other. Ricardo had thought that

> Under a system of perfectly free commerce, each country naturally devotes its capital and labour to such employments as are most beneficial to each. The pursuit of individual advantage is admirably connected with the universal good of the whole. By stimulating industry, by rewarding ingenuity, and by using most efficaciously the peculiar powers bestowed by nature, it distributes labour most effectively and most economically: while, by increasing the general mass of productions, it diffuses general benefit, and binds together, by one common tie of interest and intercourse, the universal society of nations throughout the civilized world.[3]

Thus, in theory, economic cooperation and the gains therefrom would strengthen the cooperative ties that bind European nations together. More than this was desired. Postwar Western leaders sought to create strong, democratic, capitalist nations to provide a firm wall of resistance to the spread of communism.

The Marshall Plan (1948) was perhaps the first postwar step toward building an integrated European economy. General George Marshall (President Truman's secretary of state) called upon the nations of Europe to form a continent-wide economic market—like the mass market of the United States. Marshall Plan aid was designed to hasten economic recovery by providing a resource base on which to build a European economy. This U.S. aid may have discouraged European nations from adopting the "beggar thy neighbor" policies that limited cooperation after World War I and so contributed to the global conflict that followed. An integrated Europe could never succeed as a US initiative, however; European leadership was necessary.

Many visions of a more united Europe were expressed in the early postwar period. Churchill's vision of a United States of Europe was discussed alongside De Gaulle's less ambitious "Europe of States." It was Jean Monnet, a French political economist who held many positions during a long and distinguished career, who provided the key intellectual guidance.[4] Although Monnet talked of a grand vision of a United States of Europe, he proposed a much narrower alliance along functional lines: a zone of free trade uniting the heavy-industry regions that spanned the French-German border. This plan, for the *European Coal and Steel Community* (ECSC), was implemented by Robert Schuman, a French statesman, in 1950. The ECSC was the critical test case for economic and political cooperation between France and Germany. It was, by all accounts, a great success and thereby provided a model for further efforts at integration in Western Europe.

A fuller measure of economic integration was achieved in 1957: the Treaty of Rome created the *European Economic Community* (EEC, or the Common Market), a customs union that brought together the markets of Italy, France, Belgium, Luxembourg, the Netherlands, and West Germany. This union of "the Six" was a great success because these nations were natural trading partners who could, therefore, benefit from the static and dynamic benefits of economic integration. Indeed, it would be hard to find a set of nations that might be more suited, economically, to open markets.[5] Their limited but still very important economic union also benefited, however, from global trends of the time. Postwar recovery soon gave way to a global economic boom, which only served to strengthen the ties of prosperity that united Europe against the political and social forces that always act to drive nations apart.

Great Britain participated in the negotiations for the Treaty of Rome, but decided in the end to stand apart from the EEC. There were many reasons for this decision, which was eventually reversed at some cost to Britain. The British were concerned, first of all, about the loss of political and economic autonomy that necessarily accompanies economic integration. British politicians (and probably most British citizens) were hesitant to cede decision-making power to others or to share it with the French and the Germans. Britain was forced to weigh the trade-off among self-determination, domestic democracy, and the economic growth, which presented a constant tension in economic integration. Britain was also unwilling to give up either its "imperial preferences"—preferential trading relations with the Commonwealth nations—or its "special relationship" with the United States that it so highly valued.

Britain balked, therefore, at its first opportunity to enter the EEC, but it dared not be isolated from free trade in Europe. It organized, therefore, a weaker alliance of trading nations called the European Free Trade Area (EFTA). The EFTA brought together Denmark, Sweden, Austria, Switzerland, Portugal, and the United Kingdom. A free trade area, as noted earlier in this chapter, imposes fewer restrictions on national policy than does a customs union like the EEC. But it can also provide fewer opportunities for economic gain. In fact, the nations of the EFTA offered only limited opportunities for the static and dynamic gains that the EEC experienced. Geographical separation, deep cultural divisions, huge economic gaps between rich nations (Switzerland, Great Britain) and poor (Portugal) all combined to limit trade and growth. The EFTA never was and never would be the engine of economic growth that the EEC offered. It was inevitable, then, that EFTA members would eventually seek EEC membership.[6]

Despite its remarkable success in gaining cooperation from nations that had engaged in two world wars, it would be wrong to paint an overly rosy picture of the EEC. Trade among member nations was never entirely free. Nontariff barriers to trade abounded, and sometimes nations would simply refuse to accept imports of any items from another member, in open violation of the Treaty of Rome, because of domestic political or economic concerns. It was also necessary to create an elaborate system of agricultural subsidies across the EEC to defuse political opposition from powerful farm groups. The *Common Agricultural Policy* (CAP) provided for a complex pattern of payments to farmers in all EEC nations (although not equally in each). A far cry from free trade and laissez-faire liberalism, the CAP was seen as a necessary evil: subsidies to farmers were one price of achieving greater liberalism and cooperation in other spheres of economic life. Besides, a unified system of farm payments was an improvement over the pattern of destructive competition in subsidies that might otherwise result. The CAP may have been necessary to the creation of the EEC, but it became a ticking time bomb, with ever growing costs, that eventually exploded in the 1980s, creating a budget crisis.

The EEC changed names in 1967, becoming the European Community (EC). The EEC formally joined with the ECSC and Euratom, another pan-Europe organization, to create an institution with broader responsibilities. The change in name signaled an intention to move beyond purely economic issues, although economic concerns continued to dominate EC discussion.

THE COMMON AGRICULTURAL POLICY

The Common Agricultural Policy (CAP) is one of the most controversial and divisive elements of economic and political integration in Europe. The CAP is an EU-wide system of agricultural subsidies, financed through value-added taxes imposed by EU member nations. The CAP is far and away the largest item of expenditure of the European Union and has been a point of contention both within the EU and in its relations with other nations.

Almost every nation subsidizes or protects its farm interests to some extent, a fact that reveals the economic significance and political clout of agriculture, even in this "postindustrial" era. The CAP provided Europe's farmers with high prices through a system of price supports. The EU purchases excess farm produce to keep prices from falling and farm incomes from declining—a system that benefits farmers at the expense of the taxpaying public. Over the years, the CAP's guarantees have encouraged European farmers to expand production to a vast degree, creating "mountains" of dairy products and "lakes" of wine and olive oil, for example. These mountains and lakes owe their existence entirely to the CAP, since without it, prices would decline and surplus production would be eliminated.

The CAP divided EU members because the distribution of tax costs and the distribution of farm subsidies is far from even. Great Britain, for example, frequently has complained that the CAP benefits others at its expense. The rising CAP cost, and its unequal impact, became an especially severe internal political problem in the 1980s, when Britain threatened to withhold tax payments unless major CAP reforms were undertaken.

The CAP also created tension between the EU and its international trading partners, particularly the United States, during the Uruguay round of GATT negotiations. One of the Uruguay round's principal goals was to reduce worldwide agricultural subsidies, which distort trade patterns and encourage protectionism. The vast CAP subsi-

Continued

THE COMMON AGRICULTURAL POLICY, *continued*

dies were clearly opposite to the goals of these GATT discussions, forcing the EU to consider ways to reduce or eliminate them. The United States was especially interested in reducing CAP subsidies; lower CAP subsidies would benefit U.S. agricultural exports and also permit the United States to reduce the levels of its own farm subsidies.

Eventually, both the internal and external pressures just described caused the EU to implement plans to reduce CAP subsidies, but the proposed cutbacks are relatively modest and came only after France, leader of the EU farm lobby, threatened to bring the entire GATT round to a halt.

The CAP thus remains a divisive issue, especially with EU expansion continuing and world trade liberalization proceeding. The issue of farm subsidies in Europe is likely to remain controversial, both as an internal budget matter and as a matter of international economic diplomacy.

BROADER AND DEEPER: THE EC, 1973–1993

The second stage in the development of the European Union lasted from 1973 to 1993 and had two distinct stages. The EC broadened in all respects—geographically, economically, socially, and politically—from 1973 to 1986. Then it engaged in a dramatic experiment in deepening from 1985 to 1993. At the end of this period, the EC was transformed into a much more complex and potentially more influential creature.

The EC broadened its geographic vision in several stages from 1973 to 1986. Great Britain finally entered the EC on January 1, 1973, along with Ireland and fellow EFTA member Denmark. Britain took the leap only after two controversial referenda and a series of painful negotiations. By all accounts, Britain entered in 1973 on terms that were distinctly inferior to those offered in 1957. Britain's status as a European nation was determined, but its ambivalence about its relationship to Europe remained.

Greece entered the EC in 1981, followed by Spain and Portugal in 1986. In all three cases, EC membership was in part a reward for the triumph of democratic institutions over authoritarian governments. Free trade and closer economic ties were intended to solidify democracy and protect it from communist influences.

The broader market was not in all respects a stronger market, however. The entry of the poorer nations of Ireland, Greece, Spain, and Portugal magnified a variety of tensions within the EC. These less developed nations were less clearly a part of the pan-European market. Lower living standards limited the extent of their trade with richer member states. Lower wage structures threatened some jobs in EC industries. Finally, the entry of four largely agricultural nations to EC institutions, including the CAP, put severe fiscal strains on the other nations. The broader market was surely in the long-run interest of the EC, but it imposed great stress on cooperative relationships in the short run.

These economic and political stresses reached a peak in the mid-1980s. Higher and higher EC program costs, imposing a disproportionate burden on Great Britain, precipitated a split in the EC. Jacques Delors, the newly appointed president of the

European Commission, traveled from capitol to capitol seeking ways to reunite the governments and peoples of the EC in some common enterprise. What could restore a measure of unity and cooperation? A common defense and foreign policy? A common monetary system? In the end, Delors concluded that international trade, which had brought the EC together in the first place, was the force most likely to reenergize Europe. In 1985, Delors produced a white paper proposing the creation of a single integrated market by 1992. The *Single Market Act* formalized this grand experiment in market deepening.

It might seem that the EC was already a single market—in theory no tariff barriers separated EC markets, and in practice goods flowed fairly freely across national borders. If, however, a single market is defined according to the principles observed in the United States (the world's single largest market and often its most dynamic one, too), then Europe was still a long way from its goal. Under Delors's leadership, the EC identified two hundred general areas where agreement on "directives" was needed to achieve the goal of a unified market. The 1992 Single Market plan was off and running.

The goals of Europe 1992 might be characterized as "four freedoms": free movement of goods, of services, of capital, and of people. Each of these freedoms is much harder to achieve in practice than to imagine in theory. Free movement of goods, for example, requires much more than the absence of tariff and quota barriers if the freedom is to mean very much. There exist hundreds of nontariff barriers to the free production and sale of goods that must be addressed. Health, safety, and technical standards, each of which plays a constructive role, all can discourage imports from other countries (by raising the cost of selling) and encourage the purchase of domestically produced goods. These standards must be leveled (or *harmonized*, in the jargon of the trade) to allow, to the maximum possible extent, a good that can be sold anywhere in the group to be sold everywhere. (Some standards are difficult to harmonize because, for example, of the inevitable differences in such established factors as electrical voltage and automobile and road setups.) In many industries, the cost of satisfying these standards and proving regulatory compliance far exceeded in height any imaginable tariff barrier to trade.

Services represent an increasing proportion of world trade. Achieving free movement of services, such as financial and insurance services, is a tricky task, given the complex systems of financial regulations that each nation has in place. Free movement of money or capital requires the dismantling of capital controls and investment regulations, which affect flows of funds into and out of a nation. Finally, free movement of people requires agreement on many points, most especially the adoption of a common immigration policy. Once a person has entered one EU nation, he or she is free to enter any other.

Delors's Single Market initiative posed a real challenge to the EC member states. The year 1992 promised the creation of a larger, more dynamic market, with the wealth and political power that would flow therefrom. To achieve this big goal, however, required each nation to sacrifice its interests on hundreds of smaller issues, many of which had important domestic political impact, before the four freedoms could be achieved.

National sovereignty and economic growth were often in conflict. Germany, for example, desired to see its own high environmental standards applied to all EC vehicles. Environmentalism is an important social value in Germany and the Green party is a potent political force on some issues. These environmental regulations are costly, however, and were opposed on economic grounds by countries such as Greece and Portugal. To a certain extent, at least, the four freedoms for the EC as a whole actually required sacrifice of some domestic freedoms, such as the right to self-determination of environmental and safety standards.[7]

Although not all the goals of the Single Market were achieved by January 1, 1993, the basic thrust of the 1992 program succeeded. Europe, however, did not immediately experience the spurt of growth and efficiency that had been expected. Instead, 1993 and 1994 found Europe caught in a deep slump, with unemployment rates as high as 20 percent in Spain, for example. Europe's mid-1990s recession had many causes, including the burdens created by the collapse of communism in Eastern Europe and the stresses of rapid structural economic changes combined with long-term social and demographic changes.

Because the Single Market plan proved to be no panacea for Europe's economic problems, some writers have asked "so what?" Were the gains from 1992 worth the painful costs? The answer to this question is that it is too early to tell. It is especially too early to dismiss the Single Market as a failure. When economic integration works, it works by increasing somewhat the rate of economic growth over a long period of time. It takes time, for example, for new investments made in anticipation of the bigger market to come on-line and contribute to prosperity. Even then, however, the effects in any single year may be small. A 1.5 percent increase in the average rate of growth (an increase from, say, 2.0 to 3.5 percent), ends up doubling living standards over the course of a fifty-year period, compared with the standard of living without this growth boost. If the Single Market were to be even half this effective in raising living standards in the next half century, it would be judged a clear success.

THE DEVELOPMENT OF POLITICAL INSTITUTIONS

The Treaty of Rome did more than commit six nations to economic integration; it also began the process of developing a set of political institutions to make policy, settle disputes, and provide leadership for Europe. The most important political institutions in the EU today are the European Commission (and its president), the Council of Ministers, the European Council, the European Parliament, and the European Court of Justice. Each of these institutions plays a specific role in setting the delicate balance between the national interests of member nations and the collective interest of the EU itself.

The European Commission acts as the EU's executive cabinet. Commissioners are nominated by member states (two each from the larger countries, one each from the smaller ones). Each commissioner has a special "portfolio" of responsibilities, such as competition or agriculture, making her or his responsibilities equivalent to

TABLE 11–1   Expansion of the European Union

YEAR	NATION	ORGANIZATION
1957	Belgium	EEC
1957	France	EEC
1957	Germany	EEC
1957	Italy	EEC
1957	Luxembourg	EEC
1957	Netherlands	EEC
1973	Denmark	EEC
1973	Ireland	EEC
1973	Great Britain	EEC
1981	Greece	EEC
1986	Portugal	European Community
1986	Spain	European Community
1995	Austria	European Union
1995	Finland	European Union
1995	Sweden	European Union

cabinet ministers or secretaries in a typical nation-state. The president of the European Commission is the EU's chief executive officer, leading policy initiatives and representing the EU to international organizations such as the Group of Seven (G-7).[8] Jacques Santer, the former prime minister of Luxembourg, began his term as president of the European Commission in January 1995, replacing Jacques Delors of France.

While the European Commission is designed to advance wide European interests, the Council of Ministers, the EU's main legislative body, is intended to provide a balancing forum for more narrow national interests. The Council of Ministers comprises one member from each member state, usually the foreign minister. The Commission provides a forum for discussion and enactment of high-level policies. The voting rules of the EU allow a minority of member states to block action in the European Commission when they believe their national interests are threatened.

The European Parliament is a much larger body, with 567 members as of 1994, chosen through direct elections in each member state (thus voters in EU member nations elect both national and EU representatives). Germany had ninety-nine "Euro-MPs" in 1994—the largest number of any EU member. The Parliament is organized along political party lines, not according to national citizenship. Socialists from all EU nations act together, for example, as do conservatives and other party groups. The Parliament thus provides a forum for debate and discussion from the perspective of political ideology, not national interest (Council of Ministers) or European interest (European Commission). Interestingly, the Parliament is the only institution chosen directly by the citizens of the EU, not its constituent governments. The European Parliament is not a legislative body, but can have important influence over EU policies.

The heads of government of EU members meet regularly as the European Council to consider high-level concerns. Leadership of the council rotates from nation to nation every six months, allowing each nation in turn a chance to shape in important ways the agenda of the body.

The European Court of Justice is made up of one representative from each of the EU member nations. The Court of Justice adjudicates conflicts between and among the EU and its member nations. The Court provides an independent agency to interpret and enforce EU agreements.

These EU institutions provide a comprehensive if somewhat unwieldy organization for setting policy and making decisions that affect the entire EU. In the early days of the EU, this political superstructure had more form than substance—its political powers were relatively limited and symbolic. As political and economic integration progressed, however, these political institutions have grown in importance. In a way, the broader and deeper EU has "grown into" its political clothing in the decades since the Treaty of Rome.

The broadening and deepening of the EU over the past twenty-five years has created real political problems, which daily test the strength of the Union's political institutions. Deepening necessarily forced each member state to cede some economic and political powers to EU institutions, as more and more policies and regulations became EU-wide, not national, in scope. Widening has also posed political problems, because any increase in the size of the Union necessarily reduced the clout of existing members, who find their votes reduced in relative importance. These threats to nation-state sovereignty pose threats to EU unity. In 1994, Spain briefly threatened to try to block negotiations to admit Sweden to the EU, for example, because Spanish leaders feared their nation would lose political power and economic benefits from EU widening.[9]

THE EUROPEAN UNION TODAY

The European Community officially became the European Union (EU) in 1993 with the adoption of the Maastricht Treaty for economic and political union. The EU expanded in 1995 to include Finland, Sweden, and Austria.[10] The EU also took action to create a political and economic integration process that could include countries such as Hungary, the Czech Republic, Poland, and perhaps even Turkey, either as full members of the EU or perhaps as part of a looser group called the *European Economic Space.* Deepening (Maastricht) and broadening (EES) thus remain at the top of the EC agenda.

Although the goal of a single market was adopted in 1985 in part because European leaders were unwilling to consider more ambitious challenges, such as political and monetary integration or a united foreign policy, the fact is that increased cooperation in some spheres of IPE necessarily creates the need for greater cooperation elsewhere. Consider, for example, what the United States would look like if it were organized along the lines of EC 1992. There would be one big market, with free movement of people, money, goods and services, but there would also be fifty different cur-

TABLE 11–2   Political Institutions of the European Union

POLITICAL INSTITUTION	FUNCTION
President of the European Commission	Head of state of the European Union. Leads the European Commission and represents the EU to other nations.
European Commission	The executive branch of the EU, serving much the same function as the cabinet in the United States or the UK. Makes policy recommendations to the Council of Ministers. Represents the EU in economic relations with other countries or international organizations.
Council of Ministers	The legislative body of the EU. Composed of cabinet ministers from the member governments.
European Council	Summit meetings among the top leaders of the member states are called at least once every six months by the country holding the presidency of the Council of Ministers. This meeting of heads of state and government is called the European Council.
European Parliament	The only body of the EU whose members are directly elected by the citizens of its member states. Formerly only a consultative body, the Parliament gained new influence under the Treaty on European Union. Although the European Parliament formally meets in Strasbourg, France, most of its work is done in Brussels. European Parliament committees review legislation proposed by the European Commission and may propose amendments to the legislation before submitting it to the Council of Ministers. The Parliament may veto a proposal after it reaches the Council of Ministers if it disagrees with the council's position.
European Court of Justice	The "Supreme Court" of EU law. Composed of 13 judges who are appointed to 6-year terms. The court deals with disputes between member governments and EU institutions and among EU institutions, and with appeals against EC rulings or decisions.

rencies and monetary standards, fifty different fiscal and foreign policies, and a great deal of conflict and confusion as some states moved in opposite directions from the others. It is unlikely, of course, that Europe will soon adopt a federal structure with so strong a central government as the United States (although such a system was not entirely outside Jean Monnet's vision). It is still true, however, that the lack of a unified political and economic structure limits the benefits from economic integration.

The Maastricht Treaty was an attempt to further deepen the EU by establishing a timetable for closer cooperation on several fronts.[11] Most importantly,

Maastricht called for the creation of a single European currency, along with a European central bank.[12] The plan, as conceived at Maastricht, was for the nations of the EC to progressively coordinate their national economic policies, establish a fixed exchange rate among their currencies, then move to a single currency for all Europe. In nontechnical terms, this plan requires that the national economies all begin to move in the same direction at the same speed, then eventually link themselves together permanently by adopting a common currency, and turning control of both speed and direction over to central authority.

There are many problems associated with the Maastricht plan. Perhaps the most critical, in the short run, is the difficulty of getting agreement on speed and direction of economic policy, given that different European nations face different economic and social problems or have different priorities in making policies. Even before Maastricht was ratified, for example, the European monetary system was rocked by financial crisis when a number of countries (France, Great Britain, Ireland, and Italy) found themselves determined to proceed in a different direction from Germany, the EU's monetary powerhouse. Germany, faced with the high costs of unification between its eastern and western parts, sought to slow down its economy, to forestall an increase in the inflation rate. France and the other nations, however, wanted to speed up so as to fight high unemployment. The lack of coordination did not contribute constructively to either economic or political union, and called into question the cooperative assumptions on which Maastricht was based. The future of deepening in the European Union, in short, is in doubt.

THE FUTURE OF ECONOMIC AND POLITICAL INTEGRATION IN EUROPE

Where does the European Union go from here? This question is an important one for several reasons. First, of course, is the fact that the EU is so large in so many ways—people, market size, and military power. What happens to the EU happens to all of us, in some fashion, given the interconnected nature of IPE. Another reason, however, is the importance of the European Union as a grand experiment in integration. If these diverse nations can successfully integrate, then there are important implications for the other nations of the world. If they *cannot* succeed in integration, this will provide a lesson, too.

One way to think about the future of the European Union is to consider four nonmutually exclusive scenarios. In the future, the EU could choose the strategy of a broader union, a deeper economic union, a deeper political union, or a better union.[13]

A Broader Union

This scenario is fairly straightforward and, some say, almost inevitable. With the end of the Cold War, the definition of Europe has changed. The artificial division between East and West is gone. The EU, invented in part to unite the West against the East, now faces the problem of expansion. Three new nations, Sweden, Finland, and

Austria, became members of the European Union at the start of 1995, and there is a long line of nations waiting to apply for membership. In economic terms, these countries range from Hungary and the Czech Republic at the relatively rich end (but still a good deal poorer than either Greece or Portugal, the poorest of current EU members) to Poland in the middle, to Turkey at the end of the spectrum closest to poverty. Some see a broader Union reaching from the Atlantic to the Urals, including many states of the former Soviet Union. Others look south and see a Mediterranean union that includes Morocco, Algeria, and perhaps other North African states with historic ties to Europe. Many think that the EU will broaden in both directions, pushed and pulled by the forces of history and culture more than the calculated logic of economics and politics.

Perhaps it is Europe's fate to become a Grand Alliance, but what character would a union of such clearly different state-market units have? Unlike the original six of the Treaty of Rome, a much broader union must include nations with far different living standards, forms of government, and experience with free markets and democratic institutions. What sort of union would these disparate nations achieve?

One popular notion is that a broader European Union would be a "three-speed" enterprise. One group of nations would be a "high-speed" Europe, which would be highly integrated in both economic and political terms. This group might include all the current members, or perhaps just the wealthiest and most stable nations. A second, slower-speed group, the European Economic Area, would be less fully integrated. These nations would share in the single market created in 1992, but would participate less completely in political and other matters. Finally, the "low-gear" group would belong to the European Economic Space, which would have the lowest level of integration. You can imagine Ukraine, for example, moving up from "space" to "area" to "union" as its economic and political institutions are solidified and match more closely those of the "core" nations of the EU.

Broadening the EU is not without problems, however, as the 1994 negotiations to add Sweden, Finland, and Austria made clear. Economic and political problems both were apparent. Spain, for example, held up entrance talks until it was sure that its economic interests were not threatened by the expanded group. Spain and the UK both objected to the fact that, in a larger union, their votes would carry relatively less weight in the making of EU policy. They say their political autonomy, already attenuated by EU membership itself, was made even weaker as the EU grew.

The lesson of the 1994–1995 broadening of the EU is that any significant enlargement of the EU will require some measure of economic and political deepening. That is, the economic and political spheres of European life must become even more thoroughly integrated if they are to withstand the pressures that enlargement is sure to exert.

A Deeper Economic Union

A second direction for the European Union would be to strengthen its economic links. Given the progress made by the 1992 Single Market initiative in reducing barriers to intra-union trade, a further economic deepening would necessarily take the form of coordination of monetary and fiscal policy. A deeper economic union would require common taxes, common subsidies, common social programs, and a common system of money and credit. In short, the way to deepen the economy of Europe would be to remove those remaining economic differences that still limit market integration.

A deeper economic union would increase economic efficiency and stimulate further growth—important factors for Europe. The trade-off, of course, would be a further attenuation of national rights. Common fiscal and monetary policies make business more efficient, but limit state power to pursue national interest. This is a serious matter given the great differences that still exist in the economic conditions of European nations—especially since these differences are likely to increase, not diminish, if the Union broadens, as planned, to include many other states.

How can national interests still be served with more and more economic policy under common control? A more effective system of political decision-making would be necessary to accommodate effective but responsive policy decisions. Economic deepening, therefore, seems to require political deepening.

A Deeper Political Union

A third scenario focuses on the internal politics of the European Union, whatever its geographic breadth or economic depth. A deeper political union would mean that Union members would strengthen the institutions of collective decision-making, so that the Union could take more unified actions, take them on more important matters, and make them more decisively.

The political structure of the European Union reflects its history. While the benefits of economic integration have always been appreciated, few have been willing to pay the price, which is a loss of political autonomy. From De Gaulle to Thatcher to today, there have always been important European leaders who were unwilling to trade collective economic benefits if that meant a loss in their ability to pursue and protect national interests.[14] It may be inevitable for national interests to clash, just as the regional interests of states are often at odds in the United States. Political deepening would require, however, that Europe find a way to resolve these conflicts so that they would not prevent unified action on important matters.

At the heart of political deepening is the creation of a stronger *federal* system of government for Europe, where a central government exercises power and makes political decisions based on some system of representation. A federal system is a middle road between the extremes of total *pluralism*, where each nation goes its own way, and an *autocracy*, where one nation (or a coalition) dominates. Federalism comes in many different shades and hues. The federal system in the United States, for example, has evolved to the current state where the central government has broad powers. Germany's federal system, on the other hand, gives the central government a limited range of responsibilities (economic and foreign policy), and retains much more power in the regional *länder* or "state" governments.

The EU *is* a federal system, some have argued, where collective interests and national interests are carefully balanced. But it has taken a pluralistic approach to politics. Individual nations or small groups have been able to block policies that were counter to their interests. On many important matters, individual nations could "opt out" or choose not to be bound by EU policy. This highly pluralist approach was offered as a practical way to allow EU nations to agree on those matters where there was a high degree of consensus without the concern that they might have other, more contentious, policies forced upon them by a voting bloc.

The problem of political deepening is a serious one. In the early 1990s, the EU sometimes found itself an economic giant but a political midget. In the Iraq-Kuwait war and again in the conflict in Bosnia, European nations found themselves unwilling to make strong policy as a group because of differences in perceived national interest, and unable to take strong action individually because of limited national resources.

With the end of the Cold War, it seems likely that Europe will play a larger role in foreign policy and global security matters. Europe's economic strength lies in its union. Political deepening would develop a corresponding strength in its federal system of government.

A Better Union

The final scenario is not so much that the EU becomes broader or deeper or both, but that it simply becomes a *better* union. In this scenario, the European Union would return to its roots and then reconsider what *union* really means. *The Economist* proposed that

> What the European Union has most conspicuously lost is a sense of purpose. What is Europe for? That simple question is a vital one for an entity so liable to disunity among the states that compose it. . . . To such as Jean Monnet and Robert Schuman, Europe's primary aim was to end the continent's ancient rivalries by replacing them with a sense of mutual interest.[15]

A better Union would be one that forges a stronger sense of "general will," to use Jean Jacques Rousseau's term, and reflects an emphasis on the common interests of Europeans more than the special interests of European nations. If there is a "general will" to be tapped, as *The Economist* seems to think, then broadening and deepening should be possible. Indeed, broadening and deepening are exercises in strengthening common interests. Without such a "general will," however, a broader and deeper union seems unrealistic.

The notion of a "better union" suggests that these four scenarios for Europe's future may not be separate after all. Perhaps a meaningful Europe, given today's political and economic realities, must be broader, to reflect the end of the Cold War, deeper in both politics and economics to accommodate its geographic expansion, and better so that there is a true social foundation to political and economic structures. Perhaps Europe needs to become a broader, deeper, and better union. But is this possible, given the inevitable tension between states and markets, between collective interest and national interest, particularly given Europe's history of conflict?

INTEGRATION AND DISINTEGRATION

In 1992 Europe was caught in the clash between two opposing forces: The logic of economics and interdependence that spells community, and the logic of ethnicity and nationality that demands separation. . . . With [the Cold War's] demise Europe's nations and nationalities were liberated from past constraints and dependency. They are now freer to follow their own needs than at any time since 1945. Hence it is not a safe bet that the logic of unity and interdependence will prevail.[16]

Josef Joffe

The nineteenth century was a time of nation building in Europe. Europe achieved its modern form, a collection of unified nation-states, late in the 1800s. Germany and Italy, old nations, became unified states about a hundred years after the upstart United States.

What are the consequences of the modern nation-state? The twentieth century has been defined, to a considerable extent, by the process of answering this question, which began in World War I and is perhaps only now coming to an end. (Some commentators, cleverly, have framed this as the journey from Sarajevo/1914 to Sarajevo/1993.) The twenty-first century will, perhaps, be defined by the search for whatever replaces the nation-state. (Some might call this the search for postmodern IPE.)

The modern nation-state is being pulled by two opposing forces. In the nineteenth and twentieth centuries, the nation-state proved a stable and strong institution because of the existence of a national political interest that coincided, generally, with a national economic interest. The political interest was shaped by external threats that were best met by policies of national defense. The threat of the Cold War, for example, helped create a German national interest in security, and a French national interest in security, and a reason for these two groups to put aside other factors to unite for their common defense. At the same time, the growth of economic activities created distinct national economies capable, to some degree, of macroeconomic management. In short, the nation-state had a valid political economy identity and purpose, even though it was seldom a unified body in other terms, such as culture, language, or history.

These two important defining forces of the nation-state—security and economics—have both changed dramatically in the last quarter of the twentieth century. The end of the Cold War's bipolar confrontation has not reduced security concerns around the world, but it has changed them. Organizations of nation-states such as NATO or the Warsaw Pact had a clear purpose in the Cold War, but are less obviously relevant when the threat of nuclear arms is based in India or North Korea, not the Soviet Union.

Technological revolutions have also changed the way that economies operate. Markets are increasingly either global or very local. Fewer and fewer products and jobs are tied to markets that fall principally within the nation-state. The ability of any nation to manage its own economy has been greatly weakened. The economic rationale for the nation-state still exists, but it is different now than before.

The nation-state is now simultaneously pulled in two directions. One force pulls toward international or global systems of organization of economics and politics. Many problems are now too large to be considered meaningfully by individual nations. At the same time, however, nations are also torn by increasingly local issues where subnational differences and concerns dominate.

It is easy to see both these trends in the world today. The North American Free Trade Agreement (NAFTA), for example, illustrates the way that global markets are creating supranational systems of political and economic organization. At the same time, how-

Continued

INTEGRATION AND DISINTEGRATION, *continued*

ever, NAFTA-member Canada is being pulled apart internally by forces of culture (English versus French ethnicity), history, and economics (west versus east).

Europe is also experiencing these forces. The growth of the European Union is an example of supranational forces at work, which the disintegration into multiple units of former nation-states such as Yugoslavia, Czechoslovakia, and the Soviet Union illustrates for local and regional differences. The nation-state is clearly caught in the middle in this squeeze, with its power and relevance weakened but still generally an important force.

These trends raise many questions in international political economy. Some observers foresee the deterioration of the nation-state, replaced for all intents and purposes by regional trading blocks (Lester Thurow). Others take this one step further, predicting a complete globalization of economics and politics, with the nation-state replaced by the multinational corporation (Paul Kennedy) or by a global class system (Robert Reich) as the organizing force of the IPE. Finally, others have a dual vision: global economics and local politics, bypassing the nation-state entirely.

These issues, which affect the entire IPE, are especially important in the European Union. Will the EU become a strong supranational structure, its politics mirroring its economics; will it remain a body of autonomous nation-states; or will it evolve into a geographic structure that encompasses various regions and localities?

One possibility is that none of these structures will dominate the EU, but rather they will all play a part in a federal system. Federalism is a system of overlapping layers of government, with different layers responding to different types of economic and social problems. Germany and the United States have two strong systems of federal-type governments as compared to the United Kingdom, whose government is far more unitary.

Nation-states would still have a role in a federal EU, but it would be one different from the present. Issues of pan-European importance or effect would be determined at one level, those of purely local or regional impact at another. The "little *s*" nation-states of Europe would become more like the "big S" states of the United States, completing, perhaps, Jean Monnet's vision of a United States of Europe.

If the twentieth century has been a puzzle about the consequences of the nation-state, the twenty-first century may be the answer to the question "what happens next?"

EURO-OPTIMISTS AND EURO-PESSIMISTS

There are optimists and pessimists about the future of the European Union. The so-called Euro-pessimists tend to focus on the deep historical divisions that separate the nations of Europe and keep them from cooperating. When faced with the problem of determining a unified policy regarding the violence within the former Yugoslavia, for example, the EU was paralyzed by ties of national interest dating from the nineteenth century and before.[17]

The point some Euro-pessimists make is that the universal pursuit of wealth is not strong enough to serve as a foundation for a true community of nations. The Italian journalist Luigi Barzini, in his 1983 book, *The Europeans,* put it like this:

> The reason why economic union is a dead-end street is that it is based on a limited, over-simplified, and inadequate philosophy that became predominant in Europe after the Second World War. It was believed to be the final solution of all problems. It holds these

truths to be self-evident: one, that the economy is the principal motor of history; two, that an increasingly bigger GNP was the only and sufficient condition for progress. . . . There would be nothing wrong in this philosophy if man (single or en masse) were always a rational human being who knew what was best for him and his progeny and was always moved by the right economic choices. He is not. . . . The motivations of sudden and violent tempest in public opinion, revolts, revolutions, and wars have notoriously been many and irrational, religious, ideological, social, dynastic, patriotic, psychological, the hatred of a tyrant or neighbor, and the defense of national honor.[18]

Euro-optimists, on the other hand, see today's Union as far more than the economic enterprise formed by the Treaty of Rome. They genuinely believe in a general European will that can nurture a broader, deeper, better union. The optimistic *Economist*, for example, sees in the EU flag (a circle of stars on a blue field) a strong symbol of real unity of purpose. They see this flag and the Union it represents as an achievable political goal, not a pragmatic economic alliance of convenience.

Lift your eyes from the gutter to Europe's stars. . . . Above all, the great political aim of the European Union must mean that the admission, in some form, of East European countries is made the top priority, together with the achievement of a more or less stable relationship with Russia. Enlargement will bust the EU's budget, and force all sorts of institutional change. But these problems can be solved. . . . After all, it was awkward to establish the Community in the first place. But with an eye on the stars, it was done.[19]

DISCUSSION QUESTIONS

1. What is the European Union (EU)? How has it evolved over the last fifty years? Discuss both its broadening and its deepening. What is its importance today?
2. The theme of this chapter is the tension between the uniting force of markets versus the dividing force of the state. Discuss the ways that markets bring the citizens of different countries together and the economic benefits that integration creates. Discuss the political, cultural, and historical forces that bear on the state, keeping nations apart.
3. Explain the difference between static efficiency and dynamic efficiency. How is each important to the integration process? Explain.
4. The widening and deepening of the European Union has increased economic gains, but intensified political pressures. Discuss the political problems, citing specific examples where possible.
5. What is the Common Agricultural Policy (CAP)? Explain how and why the CAP creates tensions both among EU members and between the EU and its international trading partners.

SUGGESTED READINGS

Nicholas Colchester and David Buchan. *Europower*. London: The Economist Books, 1990.
Paul De Grauwe. *The Economics of Monetary Integration*. New York: Oxford University Press, 1992.

Michael Emerson et al. *The Economics of 1992.* New York: Oxford University Press, 1988.

Clifford Hackett. *Cautious Revolution: The European Community Arrives.* New York: Praeger, 1990.

Gary Clyde Hufbauer, (ed). *Europe 1992: An American Perspective.* Washington, DC: Brookings Institution, 1990.

Paul Kennedy. *Preparing for the Twenty-first Century.* New York: Random House, 1993.

Charles P. Kindleberger. *A Financial History of Western Europe,* 2nd ed. New York: Oxford University Press, 1993.

John Pinder. *European Community: The Building of a Union.* New York: Oxford University Press, 1991.

Lester Thurow. *Head to Head: The Coming Economic Battle Among Japan, Europe, and America.* New York: William Morrow, 1992.

NOTES

1. Samuel Huntington, "The US—Decline or Renewal?," *Foreign Affairs* 67 (Winter 1989–90): 93–94.
2. Paul Kennedy, *Preparing for the Twenty-First Century* (New York: Random House, 1993), 286.
3. David Ricardo, *The Principles of Political Economy* (London: Dent, 1973), 81.
4. Monnet served as deputy director of the League of Nations in the 1920s, a position that no doubt taught him both the need for cooperation among European nations and the tremendous difficulty of achieving that cooperation.
5. They were not, of course, natural political allies, which has created many difficulties. But one of the aims of economic integration has been to overcome political divisions.
6. Not all could enter the EEC, however. Recall that one goal of economic integration was to create a capitalist democratic barrier to communism. EEC members were required, therefore, to be democratic members of the Western alliance. This kept neutral nations (Switzerland) or nations with authoritative government (Austria at this time) from achieving membership.
7. Some have termed this loss the *democracy deficit* of economic integration.
8. The Group of Seven nations are the United States, Japan, Germany, Canada, France, Italy, and the United Kingdom.
9. Spain feared that the expansion of the EU to include Sweden, Finland, and Austria would dilute its voting power in EU political institutions, thereby reducing its ability to veto policies that threatened its national interests. Spain was also concerned that Sweden's entry would harm its fisheries industries.
10. Norway declined to join the EU after the issue was narrowly defeated in a national referendum in 1994.
11. Maastricht is the town in the Netherlands where the treaty was first signed in 1992.
12. The single currency, when and if it appears, is likely to be called the ecu. *Ecu* stands for *european currency unit*, although it is also the name of a French coin dating from the tenth century.
13. This list assumes, of course, that any change at all is possible or even likely.
14. This should not be a surprise, given the long history of conflict in Europe.
15. "Europe Is in the Gutter," *The Economist,* 21, May 1994, 14.
16. Josef Joffe, "The New Europe: Yesterday's Ghosts," *Foreign Affairs* 72 (1992/93): 43.
17. France has a long association with Serbia, while Germany's ties to the Austro-Hungarian empire tie it to Croatian interests.
18. Luigi Barzini, *The Europeans* (New York: Simon & Schuster, 1983), 260–261.
19. "Europe Is in the Gutter," 14.

12

Democracy
and Markets:
The IPE of NAFTA

Professor David J. Sousa

OVERVIEW

This chapter focuses on the effort at the economic integration of the United States, Canada, and Mexico through the North American Free Trade Agreement (NAFTA), focusing especially on U.S.-Mexico relations. It reviews the reasons that Mexican and U.S. leaders entered into the agreement, and sketches NAFTA's basic goals and provisions. The chapter then turns to a discussion of the reasons that some groups in the United States resisted integration with Mexico despite the clear economic benefits of free trade.

The controversy over NAFTA illustrates a key issue in political economy: the tension between the "logics" of democracy and the market. NAFTA stoked U.S. citizens' fears about the impact of the emerging world economy on their jobs and communities, and heightened their frustration at their inability to influence the international economic forces that increasingly shape their lives. The pressures of international economic competition and the global mobility of capital (which are increased by free trade agreements like NAFTA) may threaten the health, safety, labor, and environmental standards enjoyed by citizens in the advanced industrial democracies. Critics of free trade agreements like NAFTA see growing tensions between citizens' democratic claims to rights of clean air and water, safe working environments, healthy food, and decent wages and the prerogatives of business leaders seeking to maximize economic efficiency.

The chapter shows that democratic claims can violate the logic of the free market, and argues that the clash of democratic and market values is becoming increasingly important in debates over free trade.

The issue of free trade with Mexico stirred passions rarely seen in United States politics. For some, the North American Free Trade Agreement (NAFTA) symbolized the United States' acceptance of the globalization of the world economy, and marked the beginning of an effort at hemispheric integration to meet the European and Asian challenges of the twenty-first century. Free trade with Mexico would be a boon for the United States, guaranteeing access to Mexican markets and creating thousands of export-based jobs. For others, however, NAFTA was a lightning rod for concerns about a lingering recession, and for deeper fears of a long-term erosion in the strength of the U.S. economy. Critics of NAFTA feared that Mexico's low wages and weak environmental, health, and safety regulations would lead U.S. companies to divert investment and production south of the border; these concerns resonated with pessimistic workers who had experienced declining incomes and seen mass layoffs, and were deeply apprehensive about their economic futures. After a furious public debate, and in the face of sharply divided public opinion, NAFTA narrowly passed in Congress. The agreement now governs trade relations among the United States, Mexico, and Canada.

The public row over free trade with Mexico was in sharp contrast to the consensus among economists that the agreement was desirable, and that all parties would benefit from a lowering of barriers to trade. During the NAFTA debate, some three hundred economists, liberal and conservative alike, signed a letter to President Bill Clinton stating their support for the agreement. They argued that free trade with Mexico would have minimal but ultimately positive effects on incomes and employment in the United States.[1] U.S. trade barriers against Mexican products were low before NAFTA, and U.S. workers were much more productive than their Mexican counterparts; few economists believed that even completely eliminating barriers to trade would produce huge shifts in investment and employment from the United States to Mexico. NAFTA's advocates, steeped in a theoretical tradition that holds that free trade yields maximum efficiency and welfare for all parties, saw the deal's benefits as self-evident, and dismissed their opponents as narrow-minded protectionists foolishly trying to hold back the tide of global economic change. MIT economist Paul Krugman called NAFTA "economically trivial" for the United States, and denounced the "simplistic rhetoric" marshaled by its critics. He wrote,

> The hard core opposition . . . is rooted in a modern populism that desperately wants to defend industrial America against the forces that are transforming us into a service economy. . . . [C]linging to the four percent average tariff the United States currently

levies on imports from Mexico might save a few low-wage industrial jobs for a while, but it would do almost nothing to stop or even slow the long-run trends that are the real concern of NAFTA's opponents.[2]

This chapter explores the contrast between the intense public struggle over NAFTA and the overwhelming agreement among economists and other members of the North American elite that free trade is desirable. The public debate over NAFTA was often superficial, but this chapter shows that it grew out of a fundamental tension in political economy. Robert Gilpin took a long step toward understanding this tension with his analysis of the conflict between the "logic of the state," which is to locate economic activity where it will best serve state interests, and the "logic of the market," which is to locate economic activities where they can be carried on most efficiently.[3] Gilpin's discussion is a good beginning point, but it is not as useful as it might be because it treats all states similarly and fails to account for conflict *within* states, especially democratic ones, over exactly what "the logic of the state" should be. This chapter argues that the key to understanding the NAFTA fight lies in understanding the clash between the logic of the market and the expanding logic of democracy. Citizens' groups influenced the agreement in some ways, but the struggle over NAFTA grew out of the reality that, at a fundamental level, these logics could not be reconciled.

This chapter offers an overview of NAFTA, and circles back to discuss the clash of values generated by the push for free trade. It will argue that while economists and others may be right to dismiss some protectionists as selfish and short-sighted, this is all too simple. The globalization of capital has thrown up powerful new challenges to democratic institutions, and in some areas the fight for protection is less about saving inefficient industries than about protecting democracy: guarding past gains made in the political arena, and expanding the spheres of life in which citizens exercise some control over forces that shape their lives. Free trade may maximize economic efficiency, but efficiency is not everywhere and always the highest value. Some opponents of NAFTA asserted alternative values—rights to clean air and water, healthy food, viable communities, decent wages and working conditions—and it is an injustice to treat them as selfish, simple-minded protectionists. NAFTA was perhaps the first concrete target available to U.S. citizens concerned about the effects of the ongoing shift of employment and investment to the third world on the domestic economy and on environmental, health, safety, and labor standards. These citizens feared that hard-won standards—these new rights—would be undermined by rules that facilitated the movement of capital to a country with weaker regulations and much lower wages. In this light, it is not surprising that there was a bitter public debate over free trade with Mexico.

WHAT IS NAFTA?

NAFTA was the culmination of a process set in motion by two Mexican presidents, Miguel de la Madrid Hurtado and Carlos Salinas de Gortari, in response to the Mexican economic crisis of the 1980s. The collapse of world oil prices and the failure of Mexico's long-standing efforts at import substitution had left the country facing a crushing foreign debt, staggering federal deficits, soaring inflation, high unemployment, and collapsing standards of living. Mexico was effectively bankrupt, and in 1982 announced that it could not pay its foreign debt. In response to this crisis, de la Madrid and his successor, Salinas, strove to liberalize the Mexican economy. The Mexicans lowered tariff barriers on many products, sold off numerous government-owned enterprises, and signed the General Agreement on Tariffs and Trade, an international accord aimed at opening world markets. Salinas negotiated debt relief with the United States, cut public expenditures, relaxed laws that had inhibited foreign investment, and reprivatized the largest Mexican banks. He fervently embraced economic liberalism, attacking what he called the "outmoded view that confuses being progressive with being statist."[4]

The Salinas policies aimed at attracting foreign investment and promoting exports were quite successful. Foreign direct investment in Mexico nearly doubled, from $17.1 billion in 1986 to $34 billion in 1991. Mexico's manufacturing sector grew rapidly, and manufactures quickly displaced oil as the country's most important exports. Trade with the U.S. increased dramatically, doubling between 1987 and 1990 and growing another 50 percent between 1990 and 1991. Salinas was desperate to attract new foreign investment, and because 85 percent of Mexico's manufactured exports are shipped to the United States, stable access to the U.S. market became increasingly important to the Mexicans.[5]

In June 1990, President Salinas requested a free trade agreement with the United States. His decision to seek economic integration was controversial in a country with a long tradition of suspicion and hostility toward its powerful northern neighbor, but Salinas stressed his determination to push his country into the first world, and advanced an image of a "new Mexico" with its economic house largely in order, capable of meeting the challenges of global competition. NAFTA would be an instrument of economic change and a powerful symbol of the commitment to liberalism that is Salinas's most important legacy. Mexican writer Carlos Monsivais observed, "Salinas is NAFTA; his whole administration is NAFTA. He has bet so loudly, so heavily. It's like political theology; we will all go to heaven or we will all go to hell."[6]

If Salinas's "new Mexico" would be heaven, opponents of NAFTA in the United States had a very different vision of his country. NAFTA's critics saw Mexico as "Latin America's most authoritarian state except for Cuba and Peru," attempting to attract foreign investment by maintaining low wages, weak regulations, and a powerful apparatus for containing dissent and labor agitation.[7] Salinas's election victory in 1988 is widely reported to have been stolen from a candidate who left Salinas's party, the PRI, to oppose the liberal turn in economic policy; wages had long been held below the rate of inflation by agreement between the government and state-controlled unions, despite steady gains in productivity; dissident union leaders have been jailed; Mexico's labor and environmental regulations are at best weakly enforced. The "new Mexico" is still an undemocratic country riven by poverty and extreme inequality, as the January 1994 peasant rebellion in the impoverished southern state of Chiapas (staged on the day that NAFTA took effect) reminded the world. NAFTA's critics worried deeply about the impact of economic integration on U.S. employment, wages, and labor and environmental standards.

How did U.S. officials view the call for a free trade agreement? The Bush ad-

ministration was at first hesitant about free trade with Mexico, but a number of political and economic factors ultimately led it to pursue NAFTA. Bush was frustrated
with the slow pace of GATT negotiations, wished to do something to address the growing problem of illegal immigration, and had an interest in buttressing liberalizing
forces and a friendly president in Mexico. The health of the Mexican economy is extremely important to the United States. The countries are increasingly interdependent, as was evidenced in 1982 when Mexico's announcement that it could not repay
its international debts put seven of the nine largest U.S. banks (which had loaned billions to Mexico) on the brink of bankruptcy. Bush hoped that the Salinas policy would
strengthen the Mexican economy in ways that would avert future crises, and that economic vitality would buttress political order there. Finally, NAFTA offered substantial benefits to U.S. firms, which could team their capital and technological expertise
with low-wage Mexican labor in joint production efforts, much like Japanese companies operating beyond Japan's borders in Asia—the United States could reap some
of the advantages of participation in a trading bloc.[8] Mexico offered a young, literate
pool of low-wage labor and a growing market for U.S. products (in an average year,
approximately 70 percent of Mexico's merchandise imports come from the United
States). U.S. firms have a substantial interest in the growth of the Mexican economy—
a $1 increase in Mexican GDP yields a 15¢ increase in U.S. exports.[9]

In September 1990, President George Bush announced that he would begin
talks with the Mexicans. The administration first won "fast-track authority" from
Congress, which meant that legislators would have to vote yes or no on the deal as
negotiated by the Bush administration and representatives of the Mexican and
Canadian governments—members of Congress would not be allowed to offer amend-
ments protecting constituency interests. The Bush administration claimed that without "fast track," it would have been impossible to negotiate NAFTA, because the
Mexicans and Canadians would have feared that the deal would unravel in the legislative process in Washington. The three nations finalized the agreement in August
of 1992, laying the foundation for a trading bloc of 358 million citizens and
economies with GDPs totalling $6.2 trillion.

"FROM THE YUKON TO THE YUCATAN": THE CORE OF THE DEAL

The North American Free Trade Agreement comes in five volumes and weighs nearly
fifteen pounds, and is supplemented by accords on labor, the environment, and procedures for dealing with the problems of industries adversely affected by free trade.
Despite its length and complexity, NAFTA's goal is very simple: to eliminate or lower
barriers to trade in goods and many services, and create a limited common market
"from the Yukon to the Yucatan."

The agreement has two major elements: it reduces or eliminates U.S., Mexican,
and Canadian tariffs on many goods produced in North America, and facilitates investment across borders on the continent. But it is important to note that NAFTA
does not eliminate all trade barriers—the agreement contains provisions protecting
economic interests in all three countries against free trade.[10]

First, NAFTA will eliminate tariffs on approximately nine thousand categories of goods sold in North America by the year 2008. On January 1, 1994, the volume of U.S. exports entering Mexico duty free jumped from 20 percent to 50 percent, and two thirds of Mexican products entered the U.S. free of tariffs. The remaining tariffs will disappear over five-, ten-, or fifteen-year periods mandated by the accord; these delays were negotiated to give some firms and economic sectors time to prepare for free trade. Before NAFTA, Mexico had much higher tariff and nontariff barriers in place than the U.S., so the Mexicans have made far more significant tariff reductions.

Only goods adhering to NAFTA's "rules of origin" move across North American borders duty free: goods must be produced in North America to qualify for duty-free treatment. Goods assembled in North America from components imported from elsewhere are eligible if the final product is substantially different from the imported materials—for example, timber imported by Mexico from Brazil could not then be shipped into the United States or Canada duty free, but paper made in Mexico from Brazilian wood pulp would qualify. NAFTA also requires that some products have substantial "North American content" to receive duty-free treatment: for example, automobiles, footwear, and chemicals must contain at least 50 percent North American components. The nationality of a factory's owners is irrelevant under the agreement—Nissan may ship automobiles from its modern Mexican facility to the United States duty free, as long as those cars meet NAFTA's requirements for North American content.

Second, NAFTA protects the property rights of those who invest across borders in North America, and eliminates practices that had long discouraged foreign investment in Mexico. NAFTA requires each signatory country to treat foreign investors no differently than domestic investors, and prohibits governments from imposing any special "performance requirements" on foreign investors. For example, before NAFTA, Mexico often required foreign-owned firms to buy certain inputs locally, or to export a specified percentage of their goods. Such requirements, which act as "nontariff barriers" to trade, violate the free trade agreement; businesses confronting them may appeal to a three-nation panel for damages. Further, in another provision aimed directly at Mexico, NAFTA discourages the nationalization (or government seizure) of private enterprises by requiring governments to pay immediate and fair compensation to the nationalized firm's owners. Mexico is hungry for foreign investment, and the protections offered to investors by these provisions will undoubtedly increase investment there by "extending U.S. style property rights continent-wide. Investors can move as freely from the U.S. to Mexico as from Ohio to Kentucky."[11]

Again, while NAFTA lowers many trade barriers, it offers protectionist safeguards for certain domestic producers in all three countries. First, there are the so-called "snap-back" provisions, which allow governments to reimpose tariffs temporarily to protect specific economic sectors suffering substantial losses due to import surges. For example, if Mexican tomatoes flood the U.S. market and drive down prices, Washington can throw up tariff barriers against imported tomatoes while U.S. growers adjust to the new competitive environment. Second, each country insisted on protecting certain domestic industries, and the agreement contains many such arrangements. For example, Mexico protected its oil and gas drilling enterprises, and the United States its shipping industry. Third, many protectionist provisions emerged from the political process in the United States. President Clinton made many concessions to individual members of Congress, especially those representing agricultural interests, and the Mexicans agreed to reinterpret some of the original language of NAFTA to allow these concessions. One such agreement empowered the U.S. to impose steep tariffs on orange concentrate if Mexican exports rise and the price drops to a specified level for a period of five days.[12] These provisions violate the spirit of free trade, but they were necessary to complete the free trade agreement—legislators withheld support for NAFTA until these arrangements were made.

While these are NAFTA's major elements, the deal has many other crucial components. There are provisions (aimed at Mexico) requiring each country to protect rights in "intellectual property" like copyrights and trademarks, and rules that will allow U.S. and Canadian banks to penetrate the Mexican market for financial services. Perhaps more significantly, the original text of NAFTA, later supplemented by "side agreements" negotiated by the Clinton administration (see below) contained important provisions on health and the environment. NAFTA does *not* require the three countries to adopt the same regulations protecting the food supply or the environment. The three countries made a nonbinding pledge to seek the "highest standard" of protection, but there is no way to force any country to raise its standards. The agreement requires each party to use international standards, set by a variety of international bodies, as the basis for their own regulations. Countries may set higher standards if they deem them necessary, but if those standards lack a "scientific basis"[13] they may be challenged as unfair barriers to trade. For example, the United States may insist on standards governing pesticide residues on produce that are stricter than the international standard, but if the scientific basis is in doubt, Mexico could challenge the U.S. law.

NAFTA supporters argued that U.S. regulations would not be threatened by free trade, but its critics were skeptical. They pointed out that under GATT, Mexico had challenged a U.S. law restricting the importation of tuna caught in ways that kill dolphins as an unreasonable barrier to trade. The fact that the GATT tribunal had sided with Mexico suggested that U.S. standards might well be in jeopardy.[14]

SUPPLEMENTAL AGREEMENTS ON THE ENVIRONMENT AND LABOR

As noted earlier, concerns about the effects of free trade on U.S. labor and environmental standards clouded NAFTA's prospects for acceptance by the Congress. Like all poor countries, Mexico is an environmental laggard, with weak enforcement of its laws and virtually no infrastructure for dealing with environmental problems. NAFTA critics feared that (1) Mexico's weak environmental regulations would be a magnet for firms seeking to escape tougher laws in the United States and Canada;

(2) the pressure of competition would force the United States to lower its own environmental standards; and (3) substantial, unregulated economic growth in Mexico would be environmentally disastrous. Tim Golden of *The New York Times* wrote:

> As officials evoke images of a vast consumer market with boundless opportunities for investment, Mexico's basic lack of environmental services is glaring: in the Valley of Mexico, home to the capital and some 16 million people, almost nine tenths of the waste water goes untreated, according to government figures. For some 60,000 industrial companies there is a single toxic waste landfill. There are no commercial incinerators for toxic wastes.[15]

A crucial source of concern for environmentalists was the condition of the border region, which had become an environmental disaster area as a result of the success of the so-called "maquiladora" program. This program, begun in the mid-1960s, offered companies operating on the Mexican side of the border tariff advantages to the extent that their material inputs came from the United States. The success of the maquiladoras led to a proliferation of virtually unregulated, labor-intensive factory operations in the border area, new concentrations of population, and a massive pollution problem.[16] Visitors to Big Bend National Park in southeast Texas can see the brown haze that is a product of the maquiladoras; in San Elizario, Texas, which draws water from an aquifer that extends under the border, 35 percent of children contract hepatitis by age eight, and 90 percent of adults have it by age 35.[17] The border mess was a substantial problem in and of itself, with estimated cleanup costs ranging from $5 billion to $15 billion. But more, it became a symbol of the possible environmental consequences of economic growth in Mexico, and the irresponsibility of firms operating south of the border.

There were also substantial fears about NAFTA's impact on U.S. employment. In 1992, average hourly compensation for Mexican manufacturing workers was $2.35 per hour, while average compensation for U.S. factory workers was $16.17.[18] NAFTA critics believed that Mexico's low-wage strategy for attracting investment and employment would eviscerate important parts of the U.S. industrial base, causing massive job losses in high-wage, blue-collar sectors in the United States. Some economists explained that the productivity advantages of U.S. workers made them competitive with Mexican labor, even at a much higher wage; others argued that U.S. workers had already lost that advantage to some Mexican plants, and that in the long run it would disappear.[19] In any event, at a time of growing unemployment and slowing wage gains, many U.S. workers perceived a direct threat from NAFTA. They worried that they could not maintain their standards of living in the face of competition from workers being paid third world wages just south of the border.

During the 1992 presidential election campaign, Bill Clinton endorsed NAFTA in general terms, but argued that it would have to be supplemented by "side agreements" protecting the environment and U.S. labor before he could give it his full support. The "side agreements" eventually negotiated by the Clinton administration did not create any new labor or environmental regulations, and required no harmonization of the three countries' labor or environmental standards.[20] Instead, they set up mechanisms to encourage the three countries to enforce existing environmental and labor laws, and to sanction those that try to use lax enforcement to attract investment and create competitive advantage for their firms. Further, the U.S. and Mexico created a *North American Development Bank* to help finance the costs of cleanup in the border area and the construction of sewage and water treatment facilities. The "side agreements" received mixed reviews from environmental groups, and were dismissed as completely inadequate by organized labor in the United States.

NAFTA did not "take environmental standards out of competition" by forcing Mexico to conform to U.S. or Canadian laws, but some environmental groups (including the National Wildlife Federation and the Audubon Society) were pleased with the deal. Others were not so sanguine. In a full page ad in *The New York Times*, the Sierra Club ripped NAFTA as an "environmental catastrophe," complaining that it would undermine U.S. environmental laws and conservation efforts, and that companies moving to Mexico to evade the Environmental Protection Agency would create a "toxic hell" south of the border.[21] Union leaders were united in bitter opposition to NAFTA, arguing that they had gained even less from the side agreements than the environmentalists.[22] AFL-CIO President Lane Kirkland called NAFTA a "poison pill" and cried,

> Our people aren't sheltered in economic think tanks and they don't draw Laffer curves on cocktail napkins, but they didn't just fall off the back of a watermelon truck either. They know from bitter experience what will happen when a super-sunbelt opens for business south of the border. They are not interested in seeing Mexico turned into an economy for gringo bankers and flagless empire-building corporations, nor their brothers and sisters there indentured to their service.[23]

Obviously, the agreement was and remains quite controversial in some circles.

"A GREAT SUCKING SOUND"?

Texas billionaire and 1992 independent presidential candidate Ross Perot was one of the most visible leaders of the fight against NAFTA. He constantly repeated his claim that once the Congress adopted NAFTA, U.S. citizens would hear a "great sucking sound" as low wages and weak regulations drew U.S. companies and millions of U.S. workers' jobs to Mexico.

Why would U.S. policymakers strike such a bad deal? For Perot, NAFTA reflected a corrupt political culture in Washington, where influence is for sale. The combined political clout of U.S. businesses that would benefit from free trade and the Mexican government (working through U.S. citizens acting as paid foreign lobbyists) made it possible to enact an agreement that, in Perot's eyes, would cripple the U.S. economy and cost millions of jobs. Perot made anti-NAFTA speeches all over the country and published *Save Your Job, Save Our Country: Why NAFTA Must Be Stopped—Now*, an entertaining if sometimes exaggerated attack on NAFTA and the political forces pushing for free trade.[24]

One of the high points of the long debate over NAFTA was Perot's nationally televised debate with Vice President Al Gore on the *Larry King Live* show. Public opinion

Continued

"A GREAT SUCKING SOUND"?, *continued*

was sharply split, and NAFTA's fate in Congress was hardly clear when the two met for what turned out to be a highly contentious exchange. While both the vice president and Perot engaged in pointed personal attacks and significantly exaggerated their points, most media observers concluded that Gore was more persuasive than Perot, and that the Gore–Perot debate turned the national tide in favor of NAFTA.

In some ways, democratic critics of NAFTA valued Perot's high-profile opposition to the agreement, but in the end the billionaire's political weaknesses and the sometimes flawed arguments he made against the agreement overshadowed some of the serious concerns being advanced by labor, environmental, and citizens' groups with democratic concerns about NAFTA.

MARKETS, DEMOCRACY, AND PROTECTIONISM

The theory underlying NAFTA is well established. Most economic liberals insist that free trade yields the most efficient allocation of resources, greater incomes, and higher productivity for all partners. Obviously NAFTA will hurt some sectors in all three economies; it will hit hard at some U.S. agricultural interests, and will cost some U.S. industrial workers their present jobs. But in theory, free trade should raise all three countries' incomes, generating growth in relatively more efficient sectors. While protectionism may serve the interests of some industries, from a national perspective it is simply foolish—nations pursuing protectionist policies are in effect choosing to be less efficient and, ultimately, poorer.

In this view, protectionist policies emerge when inefficient domestic industries lobby government for protection from foreign competition. Politicians are willing to grant protectionist policies because doing so may serve their short-term electoral interests—industries and unions lobbying for protection provide campaign contributions and other forms of political support. Consumers in the protectionist country pay higher prices for goods; protected industries lose the spur of foreign competition and grow ever more inefficient. The mainstream economists' most charitable view of protectionists is that they are short-sighted, irrationally opposing the best long-run policy. Less charitably, those demanding trade barriers are dismissed as selfish special interests, using government power to enrich themselves at a high cost to consumers and the society at large. Protectionism is a subsidy to the inefficient, and anathema to market values. It is seen as a blatant *political* interference with the natural workings of the market.

But in the NAFTA debate, different kinds of arguments—some that might be called democratic—were raised in opposition to those of the economic liberals. Democratic critics of NAFTA attacked the secrecy of the trade negotiations, and argued that citizens' groups and workers should have been directly represented in the process. They questioned the "fast-track" procedure that was followed in Congress, and complained about the power of the unaccountable international commissions that set the health and environmental standards by which the validity of U.S. regulations would be judged. In part these critics scored the process of negotiation and ratification for being insufficiently open to input from citizens' groups. But their arguments sometimes went deeper than this, pointing to a conflict between the very logics of the market and democracy.

DEMOCRACY AND MARKETS

Political scientist Charles Lindblom provides insights into the nature of this conflict. He argues that the free market constrains democratic decision-making processes, and that at a fundamental level, democracy and the market are at odds.[25] Market economies are marked by private control of decisions about investment and production. Business leaders decide, on the basis of rational calculations of self-interest, whether to invest, and where, when, and how much to produce. These are *private* decisions, and business leaders have a right and a responsibility to maximize the return on their (and their stockholders') investments. As they do so, society sees the most efficient use of its productive resources.

Lindblom observes that business leaders' *private* decisions have enormous *public* consequences. That is, if the leaders of a local manufacturing enterprise decide that it will be profitable to invest in new production facilities and to expand output, local employment will rise and with it the economic health of the community. What is good for Boeing is, in important respects, good for the citizens of Seattle, Washington; when 3M Corporation thrives, the people of Saint Paul, Minnesota, reap substantial benefits in jobs and tax revenues. Conversely, if business leaders determine that it is economically rational to slow production or, worse, move their facilities to another state or country, unemployment will likely rise and the community may suffer. In extreme cases, like those in some of the old steel-producing areas of Ohio and Indiana, citizens may see a rapid deterioration in their communities, with fewer jobs, collapsing property values, deteriorating infrastructure, failing schools, and rising crime.

What is the relationship between capitalism and democracy? Lindblom contends that business leaders' control of investment and production decisions give them a "privileged position" in democratic political systems. Politicians considering raising taxes or increasing the regulatory burden on business, even for broadly popular purposes, must take into account the impact of their actions on the calculations of business leaders. When elected officials enact reforms that increase the cost of production and reduce profitability, society is "punished" as rational business managers reduce output and employment. In the worst case, managers will move their operations to a state or country with a "better business climate"—that is, a place with less intrusive regulations, a smaller public sector, and lower wages. Lindblom argues that in many cases the mere threat of disinvestment is enough to prevent citizens and their elected officials from attempting to build on existing reforms, and may even cause them to back away from established reforms. The political and social consequences of disinvestment give business leaders substantial leverage over the policy-making process, and a kind of trump against political decisions that impinge upon their interests.

It is important to remember that Lindblom does not argue that business leaders are villains with evil motives. He sees them as rational actors seeking to maximize the return on their investments, who respond to public policies that increase profitability (for example, tax incentives) by expanding output, and to public policies that reduce profitability (for example, higher taxes or stringent workplace safety rules) by cutting back. This points to the conflict between the *logics* of the market and democracy. The democratic impulse is to bring decisions on issues affecting the society at large under popular, or *public*, control. But in free market systems, a whole range of decisions with important public consequences are *private*, held in the hands of rational, profit-seeking busine..s leaders. Citizens may prefer more government spending for universal health care, or tighter environmental and workplace safety regulations. They may organize to win higher wages and better working conditions. But these popular impulses may undermine profitability in ways that are unacceptable to business managers—democratic claims often violate the logic of the market.

DEMOCRACY, MARKETS, AND NAFTA

What does this have to do with NAFTA? Lindblom characterizes the market as a "prison," suggesting that while there is room for policymakers to increase taxes, redistribute wealth, or impose regulations, there are basic limits (the bars on the prison cell) set by the privileged position of business. Some argue that the globalization of the economy and the increasing mobility of capital have tightened the constraints that the market places on democratic decision-making processes by making the threat of disinvestment much more real; trade agreements like NAFTA facilitate disinvestment from countries with higher wages and stricter regulations to places like Mexico, where goods can be produced at lower cost. The social, political, and economic gains made by citizens and workers in the industrial democracies are increasingly difficult to sustain in the emerging world economy because they increase the cost of doing business for firms that can more and more easily move their operations to lower-cost environments. In Lindblom's terms, trade deals like NAFTA make the punishment that society suffers for efforts to reform the market swifter and surer in coming.

Obviously, production jobs have been moving from the industrialized nations to the third world for decades, and many U.S. firms and low-skill jobs moved to Mexico long before NAFTA. Most economists think that NAFTA will barely accelerate this process; as noted earlier, Krugman argued that NAFTA will have negligible effects on the U.S. economy, and that the trade agreement should be understood as a "foreign policy" aimed at stabilizing Mexico and strengthening its economy.[26] While some criticisms of NAFTA may have been misplaced, the political attack on the agreement represented something much larger. How can U.S. citizens begin to assert themselves against the enormous, virtually uncontrollable changes in the world economy that are increasingly shaping their life prospects? NAFTA's critics made the agreement a symbol of the global economic changes whose consequences trouble many citizens. As was noted earlier, the agreement with Mexico was the first tangible target for citizens increasingly frustrated about the impact of the globalization of capital on the scope of democracy and the simple quality of life in the United States.

Journalist William Greider has characterized the global marketplace as a "closet dictator," pressuring not only firms but political leaders to do whatever is necessary to make their economies more competitive. He quoted German social critic Wolfgang Sachs, who observed, "The fear of falling behind in international competition has become the predominant organizing principle of politics. Both enterprises and states see themselves as trapped in a situation of relentless competition, where each participant is dependent on the decisions of all other players. What falls by the wayside in this hurly-burly is the possibility for self-determination."[27] The pressures of global competition are forcing companies to streamline their operations (resulting in radical "downsizing," or mass layoffs) and the U.S. government to consider massive new investments in education and infrastructure to increase competitiveness. They are also bringing pressures on domestic labor, environmental, and health and safety standards, giving strength to arguments that we must "get government off the backs of business" to compete in the global economy. While it is easy to understand these arguments as aimed at inefficient and unnecessary government regulation of business, they also reflect the power of the market's logic—given the international economic pressures we confront, we may not be able to afford the environmental, labor, and health and safety laws that citizens have demanded and won through the democratic process over the last half century.

Dissatisfaction with free trade is likely to grow more intense with time, in part because new kinds of rights claimed by citizens increasingly bring them into conflict with the prerogatives of business leaders. Through history, rights claims have evolved from the purely *political* (rights to vote and speak), to claims to rights to basic *economic security* (unemployment compensation, welfare, old-age pensions), to what might be termed *social and political-economic* rights (a healthy environment, decent wages and safe working conditions, viable communities, consumer protections, health care). The language of rights is powerful in the West—it has torn down monarchies, established universal suffrage, and shattered legal segregation and apartheid.[28] In recent years, it has even made government benefits like Social Security nearly inviolable ("We have a *right* to that money!"). Citizen and labor groups opposing NAFTA made expansive claims to rights in jobs, good wages, viable communities, safe food, and clean air and water that, they maintained, should be respected by policymakers and even corporate interests. They raised bold, even radical, questions: why should property rights and the mobility of capital supersede other social and political-economic rights claimed by citizens? When democratic claims and the logic of the market collide, how should the conflict be resolved? Why do we so often accord market values a higher priority than democratic ones?

It would be simplistic to characterize the NAFTA fight as a struggle between democratic forces and antidemocratic business groups, economists, and politicians. But the power of economic arguments for free trade should not distract us from the fact that NAFTA and other international trade agreements are part of a process— the emergence of a global economy marked by tremendous capital mobility—that challenges citizens' capacities to exercise any measure of control over fundamental decisions shaping their life prospects and the future of their communities. Free trade may maximize economic efficiency and wealth, but it also restricts the scope of democratic decision making.

CONCLUSION: DEMOCRACY, NAFTA, AND THE FUTURE OF U.S. TRADE POLICY

From the perspective of groups interested in protecting U.S. environmental, labor, and health standards from the effects of globalization, NAFTA appears as at best a mixed bag and at worst a stunning defeat. For these groups, perhaps the most positive thing to come out of NAFTA was the battle itself. Environmental, labor, and citizens' organizations managed tu mobilize their members and to focus media attention on an international trade issue, and to increase public awareness of their concerns about free trade. Citizens could grasp the issue of free trade with Mexico, and the fight crystallized many citizens' concerns that the globalization of production was working against their interests. The opposition to NAFTA brought labor and environmental concerns with free trade principles into focus, and at least for a moment pushed one of the great questions of our time onto the public agenda: How should the U.S. deal with the globalization of the economy, and the resulting pressures on labor, health and safety standards, and democracy itself?

NAFTA's defenders argue that the United States must embrace change in the global economy, and protect democracy by finding ways to prosper in the new global order. The most familiar and powerful approach in this vein is the "investment" strategy championed by Clinton Labor Secretary Robert Reich.[29] Reich argues that the United States must accept the global nature of the market system and the incredible mobility of physical and financial capital—capital is *going* to move to Mexico and elsewhere—and adapt to these new facts of life. His prescription is simple: we must invest in *human capital*, training our people to perform skilled jobs that add high value to products, and our *physical infrastructure* (roads, railroads, ports, communications and computer networks) to attract investment and the kinds of jobs that Americans want and expect, paying the kinds of wages to which they are accustomed. The United States cannot stop the forces that are moving low-skill production jobs to the third world. Instead, it must prepare its labor force to perform the "brain work" that is ever more in demand in increasingly sophisticated global production processes. In Reich's vision, Mexicans and Thais and Malaysians will sew and rivet and hammer; U.S. workers will be "symbolic analysts," conceiving and designing new products and performing the complex, creative functions that bring the best wages in the new world economy.

The Reich model is attractive to Democratic party politicians, as well as to a good number of economists on the left and (many fewer) right. But it will be difficult to implement the program. U.S. budget deficits are so large that the huge investments required are virtually inconceivable to many citizens, interest groups, and members of Congress. Bill Clinton proposed a large investment package in his first year as president, but the program was cut to ribbons for budgetary and political reasons. While the United States does not lack the resources to pursue the "investment strategy" for dealing with the deleterious effects of globalization, it may lack the will to marshal those resources by severely cutting expenditures for current consumption.

Beyond this, even if it were vigorously pursued, the investment strategy would not address the problems of millions of U.S. workers still unable to compete in the

global economy, and would not mitigate the growing social and economic polarization that Reich sees as a product of the globalization of production. Even while the
"symbolic analysts" prosper, many Americans will remain in competition with low-
wage workers abroad, suffering the inevitable consequences of declining incomes
and lowered living standards. The result is a sharp polarization in the income distribution. Reich fears a dark future marked by what he calls the "secession" of the
symbolic analysts from the rest of the society. The better-off will be increasingly isolated from their fellow citizens economically, demographically, even psychologically.
They will retreat into gated communities for themselves and private schools for their
children, and increasingly see that they have little in common with other Americans.
Our normal political discourse will be as polarized as the NAFTA debate, with elites
fervently embracing free trade and dismissing their opponents as simple-minded
populists manipulated by demagogues, and apprehensive citizens and workers fearful that they are being sold down the river by their leaders. Reich hopes that massive investments in people and infrastructure will energize the American economy,
mitigating these divisive trends and maintaining at least some threads of community and social comity in a polarizing political-economic order.

Democratic critics of NAFTA have argued for a different response to the challenge of globalization, one that would use one of the most significant inducements
the United States has—access to its huge consumer market—to ratchet up labor and
environmental standards abroad. Terry Collingsworth and colleagues argue that citizens and policymakers must take a stand against agreements like NAFTA, which encourage firms to shift production to make "use of highly productive workers kept
cheap by the labor policies of a government more interested in keeping investors
happy than in ensuring a decent wage for its citizens."[30] The mechanism, they argue,
should be the imposition of global labor standards that would help to put an *absolute
floor* under wages and working conditions worldwide. They point to the 1937 U.S.
Fair Labor Standards Act, which outlawed child labor, and to Franklin Roosevelt's
supporting declaration that "Goods produced under conditions which do not meet
rudimentary standards of decency should be regarded as contraband and ought not
to pollute the channels of interstate commerce." Collingsworth and his colleagues
argue that global standards would slow the movement of capital to ever cheaper
labor markets worldwide, and that higher wages for impoverished third world workers would increase global demand for goods, raising global economic prosperity.
Further, it would be a beginning toward protecting domestic labor standards. Greider
wrote,

> For ordinary Americans, traditionally independent and insular, the challenge requires
> them to think anew their place in the world. The only plausible way that citizens can
> defend themselves and their nation against the forces of globalization is to link their
> own interests cooperatively with the interests of other peoples in other nations—that
> is, with foreigners who are competitors for the jobs and production but who are also
> victimized by the system. Americans will have to create new democratic alliances across
> national borders with the less prosperous people caught in the same dilemma. Together
> they have to impose new political standards on the multinational enterprises and on
> their own governments.[31]

The United States has pursued a limited version of this strategy under a number of laws, the most prominent of which is the General System of Preferences Act (GSP). The GSP offers duty-free trade in some goods to some developing countries that meet certain labor and human rights standards: recognition of the rights of workers to unionize and bargain collectively, the prohibition of child labor and compulsory labor, reasonable standards for worker health and safety, and a mechanism for implementing a minimum wage. Presumably, the GSP encourages those countries to maintain at least these minimal standards; Collingsworth et alia would like to see the GSP standards significantly strengthened and extended to NAFTA and GATT.[32] Advocates of this approach argue that labor, environmental, and citizens' organizations should play a meaningful role in international trade negotiations, and that trade agreements must explicitly recognize and protect the fundamental rights of workers and citizens against the effects of globalization. This is asking for a great deal—for democratic values and human rights standards to play as powerful a role as the logic of the market in shaping the future of world economy.

This chapter began with the observation that much of the public debate over NAFTA was overheated, with both proponents and critics of the deal exaggerating its likely effects. Most economists argued that the United States would see marginal benefits from the deal, and that Mexico would enjoy significant economic growth as a result of NAFTA and its broader embrace of liberalism. There was little reason, they thought, for the deafening sound and fury. But behind the inflated rhetoric, the sound that they heard was the clash of great value systems, of the logic of the market with its incessant drive for lower costs and higher efficiency, and the logic of democracy, with citizens' claims to rights to control crucial decisions shaping their lives and the future of their communities. With NAFTA, we saw the language of rights enter the trade debate. Trade politics will never be the same.

DISCUSSION QUESTIONS

1. What is the North American Free Trade Agreement (NAFTA)? What nations are parties to this agreement? What have they agreed to do? What is the significance of NAFTA today?
2. The theme of this chapter is that markets can sometimes constrain the choices of the state, limiting the realm of democratic decision-making. The market can be a "prison." How does this theme apply to NAFTA? How do the supplemental agreements of NAFTA illustrate this theme? Explain.
3. Charles Lindblom contends that business leaders have a "privileged position" in democratic political systems, giving their interests undue weight in political decisions. Where does this power or influence come from? How can it be used?
4. Suppose that the voters of a nation decided to put domestic environmental concerns ahead of all other factors in making public policy. How would this affect the nature of their economic and political relations with other countries and with the global markets? How does this illustrate Lindblom's point? What, then, should citizens do if they value the environment? Explain.

SUGGESTED READINGS

Mario Bognanno and Kathryn Ready. *The North American Free Trade Agreement: Labor, Industry, and Government Perspectives.* Westport, CT: Quantum Books, 1993.

Samuel Bowles and Herbert Gintis. *Democracy and Capitalism.* New York: Basic Books, 1982.

William Greider. "The Global Marketplace: A Closet Dictator." In *The Case Against Free Trade.* San Francisco: Earth Island Press, 1993.

Paul Krugman. "The Uncomfortable Truth about NAFTA: It's Foreign Policy, Stupid." *Foreign Affairs* 72 (1993).

Charles Lindblom. "The Market as Prison," *Journal of Politics* 44 (1982).

Peter A. Morici. "Free Trade with Mexico." *Foreign Policy* 87 (1992).

Robert A. Pastor. *Integration with Mexico.* New York: Twentieth Century Fund Press, 1993.

Sidney Weintraub. "US-Mexico Free Trade: Implications for the United States." *Journal of Interamerican Studies and World Affairs* 34 (1992).

NOTES

1. Before NAFTA, the average U.S. tariff on Mexican goods was only 3.4 percent. Sidney Weintraub, "US-Mexico Free Trade: Implications for the United States," *Journal of Interamerican Studies and World Affairs* 34 (1992): 34.

2. Paul Krugman, "The Uncomfortable Truth About NAFTA: It's Foreign Policy, Stupid," *Foreign Affairs* 72 (1993): 13–14. For a critical view of NAFTA, see Jeff Faux, "The Crumbling Case for NAFTA," *Dissent* 40 (Summer 1993): 309–315.

3. Robert Gilpin, *The Political Economy of International Relations* (Princeton, NJ: Princeton University Press, 1987), 11.

4. Robert A. Pastor, *Integration with Mexico* (New York: Twentieth Century Fund Press, 1993), 17–20.

5. M. Delal Baer, "North American Free Trade," *Foreign Affairs* (Fall 1991): 132–133.

6. Tim Golden, "U.S. Vote Crucial for Mexico's Chief and His Party," *The New York Times*, 17 November 1993, A20.

7. Douglas Payne, "Mexico, Bound," *The New York Times*, 20 November 1994, A21.

8. Pastor, *Integration with Mexico*, 14–15; Peter Morici, "Free Trade With Mexico," *Foreign Policy* 87 (Summer 1992): 88.

9. Weintraub, "US-Mexico Free Trade," 32–33.

10. This section draws on David S. Cloud, "The Nuts and Bolts of NAFTA," *Congressional Quarterly Weekly Report* 51 (November 20, 1993): 3174–3183; "What's in the Trade Pact?" *The New York Times*, 14 November 1993, A14; and Anne M. Driscoll, "Embracing Change, Enhancing Competitiveness: NAFTA's Key Provisions," *Business America*, 18 October 1993, 14–25. See also *The NAFTA*, Vol. 1 (Washington, DC: U.S. Government Printing Office, 1993).

11. Jonathan Schlefer, "History Counsels 'No' on Nafta ..." *The New York Times*, 14 November 1993, C11.

12. David E. Rosenbaum, "Administration Sweetens Trade Agreement," *The New York Times*, 4 November 1993, A19; Keith E. Bradsher, "Clinton's Shopping List for Votes Has Ring of Grocery Buyer's List," *The New York Times*, 17 November 1993, A21.

13. *The NAFTA*, vol. 1, 7-30–7-31.

14. Lori Wallach, "Hidden Dangers of NAFTA and GATT," in *The Case Against Free Trade: GATT, NAFTA, and the Globalization of Corporate Power* (San Francisco: Earth Island Books, 1991), 23–64. See also Marian Burros, "Eating Well," *The New York Times*, 28 April 1993, C4. On the dolphin issue, see David Phillips, "Dolphins and GATT," in *The Case Against Free Trade*, 133–138.

15. Tim Golden, "A History of Pollution in Mexico Casts Clouds over Trade Accord," *The New York Times*, 16 August 1993, A1.

16. By 1994, the maquiladora program included 2,155 factories employing 544,500 workers; approximately 20 percent of Mexico's manufacturing workers are employed in the maquiladoras. NAFTA will probably end the maquiladoras' growth by eliminating the special trade advantages they enjoyed. Joshua Cohen, *Business Mexico*, 4 (1994): 52–55; see also Pastor, *Integration with Mexico*, 13–14.

17. Pastor, *Integration with Mexico*, 55.

18. Sheldon Friedman, "NAFTA as Social Dumping," *Challenge* (September/October 1992): 28–29.

19. Harley Shaiken, "Two Myths About Mexico," *The New York Times*, 22 August 1993, D15.

20. For example, the accord on the environment recognizes "the right of each Party to establish its own levels of domestic environmental protection . . . and to adopt or modify accordingly its environmental laws and regulations." See *NAFTA Supplemental Agreements* (Washington, DC: Government Printing Office, 1993), 3.

21. *The New York Times*, 15 November 1993, A5. See also David S. Cloud, "Environmental Groups Look for Ways to Ensure a 'Green' Trade Agreement," *Congressional Quarterly Weekly Report*, 28 November 1992, 3712–3713.

22. Anthony DePalma, "Law Protects Mexico's Workers, But Its Enforcement Is Often Lax," *The New York Times*, 15 August 1993, A1; Keith Bradsher, "Side Agreements to Accord Vary in Ambition," *The New York Times*, 19 September 1993, A1.

23. Lane Kirkland, "Labor Unions and Change," *Vital Speeches* 60 (15 November 1993): 81–84. See also Mark Anderson, "NAFTA's Impact on Labor," in Mario Bognanno and Kathryn Ready, *The North American Free Trade Agreement: Labor, Industry, and Government Perspectives* (Westport, CT: Quantum Books, 1993), 55–60.

24. Ross Perot with Pat Choate, *Save Your Job, Save Our Country: Why NAFTA Must Be Stopped—Now!* (New York: Hyperion, 1993).

25. Charles E. Lindblom, "The Market as Prison," *Journal of Politics* 44 (1982): 324–336.

26. Krugman, "It's Foreign Policy, Stupid."

27. William Greider, "The Global Marketplace: A Closet Dictator," in *The Case Against Free Trade*, 204.

28. Samuel Bowles and Herbert Gintis, *Democracy and Capitalism* (New York: Basic Books, 1982).

29. Robert B. Reich, *The Work of Nations* (New York: Vintage, 1991).

30. Terry Collingsworth, J. William Goold, and Pharis J. Harvey, "Time for a Global New Deal," *Foreign Affairs* (January/February 1994): 8–13.

31. Greider, "The Global Marketplace," 196.

32. Collingsworth et al., "Global New Deal," 12–13.

13

Japan
and the International
Political Economy

Professor Karl J. Fields
Professor Elizabeth Norville

OVERVIEW

This chapter examines Japan's evolving and expanding role in the international political economy. In so doing, it applies a number of the key concepts with which you are already familiar to a specific context or case study. Japan is a useful and noteworthy case not only because of its rapid and remarkable economic development, but also because of the way in which this economic development was achieved and its consequences for the international political economy.

Japan's situational imperatives—its extreme resource dependency, feudal history, and particular introduction to the international political economy—have predisposed it to adopt and maintain a mercantilist strategy of national development. Defeated in World War II, Japan resisted early attempts by the United States to remake it as a liberal capitalist economy and willingly pursued a single-minded strategy of state-sponsored economic development as a Cold War client of the United States. The United States fostered this development and tolerated its illiberal excesses as long as Cold War logic prevailed. But the collapse of this logic, the continued expansion of Japan's global economic influence, and the relative decline of the United States are forcing a reconfiguration of both Japan's bilateral relationship with the United States and its position and role in the international political economy.

In this chapter we examine the historical and institutional factors shaping Japan's particular version of economic nationalism and its stunning success in "catching up" economically with the West. We then explore Japan's efforts to adjust to its new-found position of equal, having caught up with and in some cases surpassed its erstwhile mentors.

This expanded influence and potential status as hegemon have presented Japan with both problems and opportunities. We highlight these prospects by examining recent developments in Japan's bilateral trading relationship with the United States and discussing the extent of Japan's capacity and willingness to assume global responsibilities in the financial arena. We note three possible future scenarios—Pax Americana, Pax Nipponica, and joint hegemony—and offer evidence from Japan's role as the world's dominant creditor nation to support each of them.

Assessing the importance of the historical trends and events that have converged in these final years of the twentieth century, one scholar concluded simply: "The Cold War is over, and Japan has won."[1] Like a phoenix from the ashes, within a single generation, Japan has risen from military defeat and economic devastation to become a world-class producer, exporter, and financier.

How Japan achieved this economic "miracle" and how it manages its new status in the global political economy are the focus of this chapter. Understanding what makes Japan "tick" is important both for Japan's trading partners, who must compete with Japan in the global political economy, and for developing countries who hope to learn from Japan's developmental experience. This chapter argues that while capitalist markets have been an important part of this explanation, Japan has employed a version of "developmental capitalism" that allows for a much greater government role in promoting Japan's international competitiveness than is typical in Anglo-American liberal capitalism. This different mixture of state intervention and market forces is not necessarily better or worse, but it comes with different trade-offs and creates different winners and losers.

Japan's historical willingness to learn from abroad and tribelike inferiority complex inspired a catchup conviction with enough force to propel it to the top ranks of the international hierarchy. Japan's postwar economic success has brought it enormous wealth and has posed both opportunities and obligations that go along with becoming a dominant power in the international political economy. However, this newfound wealth and power have also made its neighbors nervous and have forced Japan itself to do a great deal of soul searching about its global responsibilities. Japan excelled as a follower, but now must think about how to lead, a role that neither Japan nor the rest of the world are either completely comfortable with or can long avoid.

HISTORY: FROM ISOLATIONIST TO IMPERIALIST

George Ball, former U.S. undersecretary of state once remarked that Japan's history

> has never been charted by the same kind of wavering curve that has marked the progress of other countries; instead it resembles more a succession of straight lines, broken periodically by sharp angles as the whole nation, moving full speed, has suddenly wheeled like a well-drilled army corps to follow a new course. There is nothing in all human history to match it.[2]

These abrupt pivots took Japan from centuries of xenophobic isolation to open-armed emulation of the West in the last decades of the nineteenth century, from militarist imperialism to pacifist commercialism in the first half of this century, and from a position of economic straggler to reluctant leader in the global political economy in the postwar era.

Despite these remarkable about-faces, Japan's association with the world has also been marked by several continuities. The first of these is Japan as emulator. Throughout history, Japan has borrowed liberally from the ideas, institutions, and technologies of those cultures and societies seen as having something superior to Japan's own. The Japanese, however, have in no way felt compelled to maintain the purity of these borrowings from abroad, adapting them to fit their own needs and, in the course of this process, often improving or enhancing the original.

While we may be aware that VCRs and corporate "quality control circles" were both adopted from the United States and then adapted to Japan (and subsequently reintroduced to the United States), the same can also be said for Zen Buddhism and chopsticks, which were borrowed from China. Japan was introduced to Confucianism via Korea, and Western science and technology via the Dutch. It copied its first national constitution from the Prussians (Americans literally wrote Japan's current constitution) and also adopted the German school system. When a local Japanese militia was soundly defeated by British gunships in the 1860s, the militia leaders surrendered and immediately requested to come on board the British man-of-war to see (and learn from) what had defeated them.

Second, the Japanese have always viewed the world in terms of hierarchy. International entities (countries, empires, races) like internal entities (family members, classes, companies) are seen and ranked in stair-step fashion. For most of Japan's history, Japanese have viewed their nation as inferior to its powerful neighbors—China, Russia, Britain, and the United States. But as Japan has risen in stature and these neighboring countries have declined either relatively or absolutely, Japan has frequently shifted from idolizing to disdaining these countries.

A final continuity is Japan's national corporatism. Japan's island status and the relative homogeneity of the Japanese people have given them a very strong and sharply delineated sense of nationalism. This sense of tribe has often led the Japanese to adopt a mercantilist view of the world, with zero-sum gains and losses accruing either to Japan or its competitors. It has also inspired the Japanese to great sacrifice on behalf of their nation, often acting as Ball described—a "well-drilled army corps"—in both former military exploits and more recent economic campaigns. While there have been important voices of opposition to national marching orders of both the imperial and commercial variety, the Japanese have strong social and cultural incentives to comply and cooperate. We need to keep these continuities in mind as we trace the "sharp angles" of Japan's modern history.

Pre-Meiji: Looking Inward

When European traders and missionaries first began arriving on Japan's shores in the midsixteenth century, they found a Japan that, for all its cultural differences, had a social and political economy strikingly similar to that of feudal Europe some three hundred years earlier. At the end of the sixteenth century, one family emerged as the most powerful among these feudal lords and was able to name its successive patriarchs as the shogun, or dominant overlords, of Japan.

Over the next two and a half centuries, this dynasty led Japan from decentralized martial anarchy to increasing national unification under the guidance of a highly capable bureaucracy, staffed by members of the former warrior or samurai class. This legacy of a skilled, disciplined, and highly respected bureaucracy intensely loyal to its political leaders gave Japan a very valuable asset in its modernization drive during the last century and a resilient capacity for enduring rapid change.

This shogunal government also severed Japan's ties with the rest of the world through a "closed country" policy of almost total seclusion. During the first half of the seventeenth century, the government expelled all foreign missionaries, virtually cut off foreign trade, and made travel abroad punishable by death.

Meiji Mercantilism: Rich Country, Strong Army

Two and a half centuries of seclusion were brought to an abrupt end with the arrival of U.S. Commodore Matthew Perry and his squadron of four American warships in 1853 with a presidential mandate to open trade negotiations with Japan. Well aware of China's failed efforts to resist Western gunboat diplomacy a decade earlier, the Japanese government acquiesced to a series of unequal treaties over the next few years, which opened certain Japanese ports to foreign trade.

This forced opening threw Japan into a quandary about how to react to this Western threat and the superior technology behind it. Although there was general consensus about the need to strengthen Japan's national defense, the role of foreigners and foreign learning was much debated. In the short run, xenophobic samurai terrorists succeeded in both angering the foreigners and weakening the government. In the long run, a group of forward-looking moderate reformer samurai prevailed, crushing the terrorists, ousting the crumbling feudal government in a near-bloodless coup, and establishing a new revolutionary government in 1868 in the name of the youthful Meiji emperor.

This group of young samurai-turned-bureaucrats presided over a revolutionary overhaul of the Japanese political economy and its foreign policy. These leaders were witnessing the literal carving up of neighboring China at the hands of Western colonial powers and realized quick action would be necessary to avoid a similar fate. As good mercantilists, Japan's leaders were convinced of the intimate relationship between economic development and industrialization on one hand, and military and political power in the international arena on the other. They promoted a mercantilist national policy of simultaneously building a "rich country and a strong army" (*fukoku kyoohei*).

Japan's "well-drilled army corps" of public bureaucrats, militarists, and private industrialists succeeded remarkably well on both counts of this national policy, establishing in the same broad stroke Japan as the first non-Western industrial capitalist economy and the first non-Western imperialist power. The state bureaucracy, staffed by able former samurai, played a crucial role in this Meiji industrialization working hand in hand with huge private conglomerates known as *zaibatsu*.

In less than fifty years, Japan went from a position of backwater isolation to that of the first non-Western world power in the international political economy. Over the next several decades, Japan industrialized at a frenetic pace, defeated both China and Russia in decisive military victories, and began a systematic imperial expansion throughout Asia. Inspired by both a perceived destiny to unite its Asian neighbors under its influence in a "Greater East Asian co-prosperity sphere" and the growing demands of a ravenous military-industrial complex, Japan saw its relations with both its Asian neighbors and the Western powers spiral downward during the 1930s as the Japanese empire expanded. Budding democracy within Japan during the 1920s gave way to rising militarism and ultranationalism, propelling Japan into war first with China and then the United States and its Western allies.

American Occupation: The Remaking of Japan

Like its nineteenth century policy of seclusion, Japan's twentieth century imperial expansion ended abruptly as the result of foreign pressure. In this case, it took the form of military defeat and U.S. military occupation of Japan for seven years. And like Commodore Perry before him, U.S. General Douglas MacArthur forced processes of change in Japan that ultimately proved beneficial but that Japan would have likely been unable to make for itself. General MacArthur and his reform-minded administrators remained in Japan from the time of its surrender in 1945 until 1952, launching sweeping changes in the country's political, social, and economic institutions.

Initially planning to remake Japan as the Switzerland of Asia, MacArthur and his staff purged the military, ultranationalist societies, and most wartime political leaders and *zaibatsu* business leaders. This purge destroyed the military class, replaced entrenched politicians with technocrats, replaced *zaibatsu* families with professional managers, and most significantly, left the bureaucracy intact and in a position of overwhelming power relative to the other groups. MacArthur also presided over the rewriting of the Japanese constitution (including a clause renouncing forever the use of war or offensive military force), the breaking-up of the *zaibatsu*, extending the vote to all men and women, and guaranteeing to Japanese citizens civil rights similar to those in America.

But with the "loss of China" and the onset of the Cold War, MacArthur and the U.S. government began to fear that Japan too could fall to communism.

This led to an about-face in occupation policy in 1947. The earlier emphasis on Japan as a Switzerland gave way to one of Japan as a full, albeit still unarmed, ally of the West with the full support and protection of the United States as patron. Conservative politicians supporting the alliance (many of whom had been previously purged) were rehabilitated and came to dominate Japanese politics. The broken-up *zaibatsu* reemerged as more loosely organized *keiretsu* and quickly regained their dominance of the Japanese economy. With the elite bureaucracy at the helm and as a favored client of the United States, Japan was ready for its remarkable postwar catchup.

POST–WORLD WAR II: PLAYING CATCH UP

Japan's extraordinary economic achievements during the post–World War II period have inspired awe, and some trepidation, throughout the world. In the course of three decades, Japan transformed itself from a war-devastated country, whose industrial recovery centered on the production of "cheap gadgets" and light consumer goods, into an affluent and technologically sophisticated global industrial leader. In trade, Japanese export successes have contributed to expanding surpluses in the country's international accounts since the 1970s. These huge surpluses have been invested abroad, creating a huge stock of foreign assets for Japan. Indeed, by the mid-1980s, Japan had risen to prominence as the world's largest net creditor nation. Japanese economic growth following the American occupation was remarkable for its magnitude, speed, and downright relentlessness. Between 1957 and 1984, Japan's gross national product increased from $30.8 billion to $1.261 trillion, a 42-fold jump.[3] Moreover, Japan's economy grew at an annual rate of 9 percent per year during the high-growth years of the 1960s.[4]

Multiple Explanations of Japan's Economic Success

Within a single generation, Japan rose from the ashes to become a world-class producer, exporter, and financier. How was this economic "miracle" achieved? This question has been the subject of a great deal of scholarly debate. Understanding what makes Japan "tick" is particularly important for Japan's trading partners, who must compete with Japan in the international political economy.

Analysts have identified a wide range of reasons for Japan's economic success. The popular notion of "Japan, Inc." reflects the belief that the Japanese people are simply a more cooperative bunch than the rest of us. Unlike prototypical "individualistic" Americans who thrive amid dissent, the Japanese tend to favor group solidarity and consensus. As the argument runs, the government, corporate management, and workers in Japan all agree on the primacy of economic development as a societal goal, and have worked together to achieve this end. In this, as well as in more specific ways, Japanese cultural traits have translated into high economic growth.

Others have discovered the roots of Japan's success in unique features of its domestic economy, notably the "three sacred treasures" of semi-lifetime employment, seniority wage scales, and company (as opposed to industrywide) unions. These institutions are said to contribute to employee loyalty, and to a high degree of harmony between workers and management.

Economists as a rule have focused on the primacy of market forces in Japan.[5] They highlight the role of individual and corporate initiative in a mostly open marketplace as the central drive behind economic development in Japan. According to this line of reasoning, there is nothing exceptional about Japanese-style capitalism, and noneconomic factors have played a negligible part in Japan's economic development. To the extent that the government has positively influenced economic growth, it has been through wise macroeconomic policies. For example, Japan's tax system has been historically conducive to high investment rates. The country's lack of antitrust regulations has also been a boon to business. Japanese companies are allowed to pool their resources in the pursuit of joint research and development.

Those that emphasize the role of private initiative in Japan's development are particularly critical of the view that "industrial policy" is very relevant to understanding Japan's remarkable economic performance. They are skeptical about the ability of economic bureaucrats to devise a coherent national economic plan that anticipates the "winner" and "loser" industries of the future.

A final argument about the roots of Japanese economic success after World War II focuses on the role of the government or state in fostering Japan's economic development. Advocates of this "developmental state" argument take issue with both the cultural perspective (that Japanese behavior can be reduced to the society's "Japaneseness") and the economics perspective (that Japan operates according to free market principles). According to this perspective, the various "unique institutions" found in Japan are not isolated phenomena, but rather they are best understood as parts of a larger political and economic system. The state stands at the helm of this "GNP machine." During the postwar period, the Japanese government set its sights on catching up with the West industrially, and pursued this goal with single-mindedness.

Because it challenges conventional "liberal" understandings of how capitalism functions, and because the view has become increasingly prominent in U.S. policy-making circles, some care will be taken to delineate the "developmental state" argument. The following discussion elaborates on the nature of the Japanese state, and its methods of intervening in the Japanese economy to promote industrial development.[6]

Mercantilism Meets Capitalism: The Developmental State

Those subscribing to this developmental-state explanation depict Japan as possessing a distinct variant of capitalism,[7] one that contrasts dramatically with the Anglo-American model. Three major factors distinguish *laissez-faire* capitalism from *developmental* capitalism. The role of the state, the general code of economic conduct, and underlying philosophical assumptions will be discussed in turn.

The Role of the State   The factor that perhaps most distinguishes the two forms of capitalism is the function of the state in the economy. Where laissez-faire capitalism is practiced, such as in the United States, the state functions as a referee in the marketplace, making sure participants in the free enterprise system observe the rules of the game.

The government's major regulatory functions include maintaining an open and competitive market and protecting consumers. By contrast, in developmental capitalist systems such as Japan, the state exchanges referee garb for a player's jersey. An actual market player itself, the government does not obsess on rules and procedures, but rather preoccupies itself with substantive social goals, most especially with promoting the international competitiveness of industry. The state's industrial policy is geared toward this end.

Codes of Economic Conduct   Beyond the central role of the state in the economy, a general code of economic conduct throughout the entire political and economic system characterizes developmental capitalism. Lester Thurow's concepts of "consumer economics" and "producer economics" capture key differences in the guiding principles of laissez-faire and development capitalism, respectively.[8] Where principles of consumer economics reign, market participants are driven by the desire to maximize profits. Here, the overall measure of economic performance for the society is consumer welfare.

On the other hand, in producer-oriented countries, profit maximization is certainly desirable for capitalists, but hardly an end in itself. In countries such as Japan, managers aim rather for market share as an avenue to "strategic conquest" for their firms. The measures of performance in a production-oriented system are high savings and high investment, not increased consumption and leisure.

A frequently noted feature of the Japanese economy is the substantial size of its national savings. Japan's gross national savings (as a percent of gross national product) at its zenith, reached nearly 40 percent in the postwar period.[9] Japanese households account for a substantial share of the national savings. Between 1960 and 1980, the Japanese on average saved around 20 percent of their disposable personal income, which was at least three times the amount the average American saved during the same period.[10] Countries geared toward producer economics are organized to suppress consumption and encourage investment. During the latter half of the 1980s, Japan invested 35.6 percent of its gross national product, compared to a 17 percent investment ratio in the United States.[11]

Underlying Philosophical Assumptions   Finally, distinct assumptions about the essential nature of economic activity undergird laissez-faire and developmental capitalism. From your knowledge of liberalism and mercantilism, you have probably already been able to identify the intellectual forebears of each of these strands of capitalism. While capitalism as we have come to know it in the West clearly possesses liberal roots, capitalism in Japan was built on mercantilist assumptions about the nature of economic production and exchange.

In an article in *The Atlantic Monthly*, James Fallows examines the different premises operating behind "Anglo-American" and Japanese thinking about economics.[12] Here, he notes the great extent to which John Locke and Adam Smith have influenced British and American understanding of how society should function.

From Locke, we have learned the supreme importance of individuals. From Smith, we have learned that free markets will maximize prosperity. Articles of faith in the West, these beliefs are not universally accepted in other parts of the world. In Japan, the welfare of the group takes precedence over individual rights. And in Japan, the ideas of German philosopher Friedrich List carry much more weight than do those of Adam Smith. As Fallows notes: "In Japan economics has in effect been considered a branch of geopolitics—that is, as the key to the nation's strength on vulnerability in dealing with other powers."[13]

The two economic visions divide dramatically over their perception of the degree of harmony and conflict in the international political economy. In outlining the two clashing worldviews of Adam Smith and Friedrich List, Fallows comments on the tremendous optimism among Americans and British that everyone can prosper at once from international economic exchange. World trade is viewed as a *positive-sum game*. But mercantilists in general, and the Japanese in particular, view business rather as war. Superior economic powers will inevitably vanquish those nations that fall behind. Trade is a *zero-sum game*. "Therefore nations must think about it strategically, not just as a matter of where they can buy the cheapest shirt this week."[14]

JAPANESE INDUSTRIAL POLICY

Japan's developmental state employs *industrial policy* to coordinate the nation's industrial adjustment in order to sustain long-run growth and global competitiveness. The concept of *dynamic comparative advantage* lies at the heart of industrial policy. This means that a government can actually work to create an enduring competitive advantage in industries where a country may have at one time had a comparative disadvantage. Industrial policies are used to influence the industrial structure of the entire economy, as well as to fashion developments within specific sectors and firms. The government's kit of policy tools will vary depending on the needs of the economy and the capacity of the government.

The Ministry of International Trade and Industry (MITI) and the other economic bureaucracies that carry out industrial policy in Japan do not seek to repress market forces when they intervene in the economy. Rather, the state aims to preserve competition and private enterprise so as to avoid some of the well-known problems associated with centrally planned economies, such as endless bureaucratic red tape. On the other hand, under developmental capitalism, market forces are not allowed full reign in determining how resources are allocated. The market mechanism is considered inadequate for assuring a smooth and timely adjustment of the nation's industrial structure.

An important prerequisite for effective industrial policy is a "strong" state. That is, the government must not be captive to interest group pressures within society, but rather must be invested with broad authority to formulate and implement economic policy. According to much empirical research on Japan, the economic bureaucracy has historically enjoyed a tremendous degree of latitude in policy making, especially given that Japan is supposed to be a "democratic" nation.

The period from 1949 to 1973 marks the heyday of Japanese industrial policy. After 1973, Japan's highly orchestrated "growth system" loosened somewhat in the face of heightened trade friction and internationalization of the Japanese economy. Since the 1970s, Japanese industrial policy has been specifically designed to target and promote new strategic "sunrise" industries, and to ease the transition of declining "sunset" industries.

Rich Uncle Sam: A Necessary Condition
for Japan's Success?

The cultural explanation, the "free markets" explanation, and the "developmental state" explanation of Japanese economic development all share one common feature—they focus on the domestic determinants of Japanese economic success. An argument that we have not yet considered draws attention rather to the importance of the international context in which Japan's phenomenal economic growth occurred. Arguably, Japan's economic success can be explained largely by the Cold War, and the relationship between the United States and Japan that it produced.

Kenneth Pyle and Don Hellman are among those who have underscored the extent to which Japan benefited from the post–World War II international order. Pyle details the ways in which the Cold War rivalry between the United States and the Soviet Union led the United States to shelter Japan from the vagaries of international politics, permitting the Japanese to focus their attention and resources on achieving economic growth.[15] Likewise, Hellman refers to the "international greenhouse effect" of U.S. patronage, which permitted Japan to flourish "free from the costs and uncertainties of full participation in international political and security affairs."[16]

U.S. policy toward Japan in the post–World War II period logically followed from its preoccupation with the Soviet Union. In order to "contain" the Soviet spread of communism, the United States saw fit to establish allies around the world. As noted in the first section of this chapter, the mission of the U.S. occupation thus shifted from promoting democratic reforms to rehabilitating Japan as America's chief Asian ally against the Soviet foe at the outset of the Cold War.

Advocates of the so-called "free rider" thesis have pointed to at least three specific ways in which the U.S.-Japanese relationship during the Cold War supported Japanese economic growth. First, the United States footed the bill for Japanese defense, thus freeing up Japanese resources for industrial production. By the terms of the U.S.-Japanese security treaty signed in 1951, the U.S. guaranteed Japan's security in exchange for extensive military prerogatives in Japan. Japan had essentially allowed itself to become a military satellite of the United States in order to focus single-mindedly on a mercantilist program of catching up with the West economically.

Second, the United States provided cheap technology transfers to Japan following World War II. The importation of technology from the more industrially advanced United States allowed Japanese producers to accelerate the development process. Japan was especially dependent on technology imports in the high-growth industries that were targeted for development.

Finally, the United States promoted the Japanese economic buildup through its international trade policy. Following the war, the United States worked to maintain a free trading order in the capitalist world. The United States opened wide its markets to Japanese exports and did not require the favor to be returned in kind during much of the Cold War period. However, the increasing global competitiveness of Japanese industry, and Japan's accompanying trade surplus with the United States, gave rise to expanding political friction between the trading partners. Since the late 1960s, trade tensions between the United States and Japan have gradually heightened in intensity and broadened in scope. But as long as Cold War security concerns prevailed in U.S. policy-making circles, the United States did not require Japan to maintain reciprocity in bilateral relations. Over time, however, growing U.S. protectionist sentiment has increasingly impinged on Japan's ability to take a "free ride" in the international trading arena.

JAPAN AT THE CROSSROADS: ALL CAUGHT UP

By the end of the Cold War, Japan had achieved its ambition of catching up with the West industrially. As Japan has reached the top tier of global powers, the country's passivity in international political affairs has become increasingly inappropriate. Steering clear of international involvements in the political-strategic arena, Japan has behaved more like an international trading company than a nation-state. The phrase "economic giant, political pygmy" has often been used to describe Japan's skewed international profile.

Dramatically altered international circumstances have especially created strains in the traditional patron-client relationship between the United States and Japan. Is it reasonable to expect the world's biggest debtor nation, the United States, to cover much of the expense for the defense of the world's biggest creditor nation? Fundamental changes in the international power structure are forcing Japan to re-assess its behavior in the international system. The concept of *burdensharing* has entered into the Japanese vocabulary, as the Japanese elite ponder Japan's future role in the world. The nation has excelled as a "follower." Now Japan must think about how to "lead." This section examines Japan's efforts to adjust its behavior to fit with new international political realities.

First, we examine current developments in Japan's bilateral relationship with the U.S. in the trading arena, specifically focusing on the *framework talks* in the early 1990s. These talks provide good commentary on adjustments in the U.S.-Japanese relationship resulting from the two countries' more nearly equal economic status. Second, we consider how Japan is responding to its position as the world's largest creditor nation. How Japan disposes of its excess capital gives a good indication of its willingness to assume more global leadership. Discussion here focuses on foreign aid and foreign debt financing.

The U.S.-Japanese Framework Talks: A New Game?

By the 1990s, the United States had endured over two decades of trade deficits with Japan. Unsuccessful efforts over an extended period to correct the bilateral trade deficit, which by now reached the $50 billion range, had intensified politi-cal friction. During the summer of 1993, a frustrated Clinton administration ini-tiated the U.S.-Japan framework talks. The "framework" was a comprehensive program of trade negotiations encompassing five baskets of issues that the U.S. considered to be at the heart of its trade deficit with Japan: (1) sector-specific trade in autos and auto parts; (2) Japanese compliance with existing agreements; (3) government procurement of foreign goods and services; (4) the removal of regulatory barriers that impeded imports; and (5) technology and foreign direct investment related issues.

Much of the program reflected an old familiar agenda for dealing with chronic trade problems. For several years, the U.S. had sought better market access by focusing on specific industrial sectors in which globally competitive U.S. producers hadn't been able to make inroads into the Japanese market. And demands for implementation of existing agreements to remove structural barriers to trade incorporated the goals of the so-called *structural impediments initiative* (SII) proposed by President George Bush in 1989. This initiative marked an effort to go beyond the more standard solutions of market access measures and macroeconomic policy coordination, to the correction of deep-seated government and business practices that allegedly contributed to the trade imbalance. For example, U.S. negotiators identified the Japanese *keiretsu*, or business families, as a "structural" barrier to free trade.

What was considered to be novel about the framework talks was the explicit focus on *results*. Instead of pursuing the usual negotiating goal of securing changes in Japanese procedures (e.g., tariff reductions or reform of the customs process), the U.S. would gauge progress on the trade front in terms of actual improvements in the trade imbalance. A lack of progress would result in retaliatory trade sanctions against Japan. *Objective criteria* would measure compliance with the agreements. The United States was now demanding "tangible progress" in correcting the trade imbalance. The United States wanted to see concrete results in terms of increased Japanese imports, greater market share, and a reduced Japanese trade surplus. The Japanese balked at the idea of "numerical targets," and this issue became the most contentious one in the talks.

Two features of the framework talks serve to illustrate how the equalization of economic power between the two countries has altered the traditional patron-client relationship. First, Japan has become more defiant toward its former benefactor. After one day of discussion in Washington, D.C., in February of 1994, President Bill Clinton and Prime Minister Morihiro Hosokawa sharply broke off trade negotiations. Contrary to the usual pattern of succumbing to U.S. demands at the very last moment, Japan rejected out of hand any provisions that would require it to meet numerical targets. Expecting Japan to follow its customary diplomatic priorities, the U.S. trade team had no fallback position. The impasse took the two countries to the brink of a trade war. For several years, the Japanese had been ruminating about the need to take a less servile stance toward the Americans. Here, the Japanese acted on the impulse to "say no."[17]

A second striking feature of the framework negotiations was that they underscored an interesting reversal in the rhetoric of U.S. and Japanese leaders toward trade. In these talks, the United States challenged the underpinnings of the open trading system, while Japan came across as an arch defender of free trade.

The Japanese complained that the U.S. "results-oriented" trade strategy in the framework talks smacked of "managed trade," which was anathema to the free trading order that the United States had worked so diligently to uphold after World War II. And in fact, U.S. insistence on setting targets for market shares and import volumes did spell political management of trade flows. The policy of managed trade has become increasingly attractive to U.S. leaders as the best way to deal with Japan. Says Clyde Prestowitz, "Rather than call them crooks and cheats for not buying our supercomputers, why not sit down and talk with them about how many they are going to buy?"[18] The framework talks took the advice to heart.

To suggest that the United States has abandoned the norms and principles of free trade would not be accurate. But one can detect an accelerating erosion of U.S. commitment to free trade in recent years. On the other hand, as Japan has become a more prominent global economic power, the country has increasingly identified its interests with the maintenance of a free trading system. The "free riding" arrangement that Japan enjoyed during much of the Cold War period, whereby Japan protects its home markets and takes advantage of more open foreign markets, is no longer tenable. Japan's trading partners are demanding fairness and reciprocity in trade. Under these circumstances, promoting all-around market openness is a much more attractive option for Japan than the opposite alternative of the reciprocal closure of markets.

Japan and the Hegemonic Stability Theory

Besides its bilateral U.S. relationship, Japan is experiencing tremendous growing pains in dealing with the world at large. We next consider Japan's willingness to assume hegemonic responsibilities for the management of the international political economy. *Hegemonic stability theory* (HST), as introduced in chapter 3, contends the international political economy functions most peacefully and predictably when certain public goods are present. A *public good*, you recall, is any good or service that can be consumed or used by all without cost once it is provided. Valued public goods in the international political economy include such things as peace, a relatively open trade system, standards of weights and measures (including currency), stable exchange rates, environmental safeguards, foreign aid, and last-resort lending.

Within a nation-state, public goods such as defense, free trade, and currency are provided by the national or federal government. But in the absence of world government, both liberal and neorealist theorists argue these goods and services will be made available in the IPE only if there is an overwhelmingly powerful nation or hegemonic power both capable and willing to provide them. Such a hegemon, the theory contends, has both the domestic resources (capacity) and global interests (motivation) to shoulder these burdens, even in the face of inevitable free riders.

All goes smoothly until the costs of carrying these free riders and the hubris of "imperial overstretch" weaken the hegemon and erode its ability and willingness to maintain its global commitments. Unfortunately, while a peaceful and prosperous IPE may continue to demand public goods, the international system does not automatically create a new hegemon to supply them in the wake of hegemonic decline. Japan's economic rise in recent years, combined with the continued relative decline of American hegemony, has therefore thrust Japan into a spotlight of controversy concerning its future role as a potential hegemon.

What, then, is Japan's future role? Scholars of Japanese foreign policy have put forward three broad options available to Japan, which may be labeled *Pax Nipponica, Pax Americana,* and *joint hegemony.*[19]

For increasing numbers of Japanese, the notion of some form of Pax Nipponica, or Japanese hegemony, is becoming more appealing. And there is evidence, at least in some areas, that Japan has developed the capacity (if not always the will) to assume a measure of these hegemonic responsibilities. Japan, as the largest creditor nation and the largest donor of overseas development assistance, now has global economic impact equal to that of the United States. Japanese GNP per capita exceeds that of America, the Japanese yen is now the currency of choice in many Asian financial transactions, and the world is adopting Japanese practices as international standards in areas from banking to labor relations.

Alternatively, Pax Americana, or American hegemony, would entail the continuation of the status quo in which the United States remains the dominant power in the IPE with Japan as its junior partner. During the Cold War, this policy made great sense to the United States as it nurtured Japan as an economic giant free from the costs and potential dangers of political and military power. Many are still comfortable with this arrangement, including Japanese pacifists and industrialists, as well as Asian and Western nations fearful of a militarily and even politically resurgent Japan.

A potential intermediate scenario proposed by many is some sort of shared or joint hegemony between the United States and Japan, labeled also *bigemony, nichibei hegemony,* or *Pax Consortis.* Convincing arguments about the virtues of sharing responsibilities based on the strengths of each nation—American global experience and overwhelming military superiority combined with Japanese wealth and unmatched economic and technological prowess—are supported by the extent to which this division of labor and growing interdependence has already occurred. Neither nation can act independently of the other for long in today's global economy without threatening damage to the other, and to the IPE in general. Together, it is argued, these two nations could provide the public goods necessary to maintain peace and prosperity in the global economy.

Japan's Prospects as Global Hegemon: Three Case Studies

Where, then, does Japan stand? Which of these scenarios is most likely? An analysis of Japanese capital recycling practices provides perhaps the best gauge of the country's inclinations toward hegemonic leadership. As the world's largest net creditor nation, Japan certainly possesses already the ability to provide a number of important stabilizing functions in the international political economy. Does the pattern of Japanese capital recycling reflect a continuation of Japan's "old" narrow-minded pursuit of wealth? Or can we find evidence of a more broad-minded, public-spirited Japan that assumes some responsibility for the global welfare, and not just for national well-being?

Here, we examine three important instances in which Japan possesses at least the capability for assuming the role of global leader: overseas development assistance (ODA); management of the third world debt crisis; and U.S. debt financing. As will become clear, Japan's track record in the provision of public goods in these issue-areas is mixed. Japan's ODA program and response to the third world debt crisis both suggest that Japan is still far from achieving its potential as a hegemonic leader. However, Japan's dollar diplomacy during the 1980s provides evidence that Japan on occasion has been willing to assume hegemonic burdens.

Japan and Foreign Aid

In 1989, Japan's US$8.9 billion in ODA or foreign aid surpassed that of the United States, making Japan for the first time the world's largest donor. In 1990, its nearly US$10 billion in foreign assistance still represented less than one third of 1 percent of Japan's total GNP, signaling much room for expansion.[20] In 1993, ODA expenditures exceeded US$11.25 billion, making Japan the top aid donor for three consecutive years.[21] Observers both inside and outside of Japan have noted that this kind of nonmilitary development assistance could provide Japan with an important and perhaps more acceptable means of influence in the global political economy. But just as the United States has been chided for promoting its Cold War security interests under the guise of humanitarian foreign aid, the Japanese have also been criticized for harboring less-than-pure motives—using development assistance to support not military but economic interests.

Japan's foreign aid program began in the 1950s as primarily a vehicle for war reparations, but by the 1960s had become a growing means of promoting exports to and raw material imports from developing countries in Asia. As Japan's global economic interests expanded in the 1970s, so did its development assistance—to African countries running large trade deficits with Japan and, more importantly, to the Middle East where the Japanese government exchanged economic aid projects for oil contracts. And as Japan's massive financial clout grew during the 1980s, so did the scope and scale of its ODA. As the world's largest creditor nation, Japan funds a wide variety of development projects in numerous countries, not just Asia, Africa, and the Near East, but also Central and Eastern Europe, Latin America, and the Caribbean.[22]

However, even as Japan's ODA becomes more generous and perhaps less directly tied to Japan's economic interests, it remains mired in controversy. Despite promises of change, critics point out Japan's aid program is still largely a closed-loop system in which most contracts are awarded to Japanese companies at the expense of local businesses or foreign bidders. Moreover, critics argue, these infrastructural projects—roads, bridges, dams, power plants, and industrial parks—are built to facilitate the commercial interests of Japanese foreign investors (often after bribing local politicians), not local capital. Japanese ODA is also blamed for financing the relocation of many of Japan's polluting industries to developing countries and the deforestation of tropical jungles in Southeast Asia and Latin America.[23]

Others, however, note the outstanding economic performance of virtually all the Asian recipients of Japanese assistance as evidence that in fact Japan's Asian development strategy has been mutually beneficial. In spite of its potential problems or shortcomings, proponents argue, overall, Japanese development assistance has been an essential factor in the successful economic growth of a number of developing countries, particularly those of Southeast Asia.

On balance, despite pledges from the Japanese government to increase the portion of its aid for purely humanitarian and environmental concerns,[24] Japan remains motivated more by self-interest than altruism, and is much more concerned with its own economic prosperity than the broader needs of the international political economy. But as its global influence expands, it will become increasingly difficult for Japan to resist hegemonic responsibilities in its foreign aid policy precisely because it will be increasingly difficult to discern between Japan's own economic interests and those of the IPE, however they might be defined.

Japan's Role in Managing the Third World Debt Crisis

The third world debt crisis created a tremendous opportunity for Japan to assume global leadership in the international political economy. As the world's largest creditor nation, Japan has been better equipped than any other country to function as a "lender of last resort" for developing countries besieged by balance of payments difficulties. Since the early 1980s, the question has been whether or not Japan would be willing to use its vast financial resources to help ease the third world debt crisis. And given that it has been in the best interests of creditors and debtors alike to work out a joint solution to the problem, to what extent would Japan take the lead in organizing the cooperative effort—cajoling and bribing others to share in the costs of third world debt management? In short, would Japan carry out its hegemonic duties in the international monetary system?

The historical record shows that on the whole, Japan has not played a leadership role in managing the third world debt problem that is commensurate with its creditor nation status. At most, Japan played a supporting role in the early phases of debt management. However, over the course of time, Japan unquestionably has shifted its ground from a passive player to an increasingly assertive global player.

Staggering amounts of third world debt pointed to a highly volatile situation in the international financial system in the early 1980s. Japan's large presence in the international financial system gave it a substantial stake in the overall stability of the system. Moreover, the exposure of Japanese banks, which held a substantial share of the outstanding debt, created an especially big incentive for Japan to get involved in efforts to defuse the debt bomb.

In the tense atmosphere of late 1982, when the debt crisis surfaced, the U.S. and the International Monetary Fund took the lead both in developing an overall strategy and in working out the practical mechanics for coping with the "liquidity" crisis in the third world. The U.S. emphasis on debt *restructuring* (somewhat modified by the Baker Initiative of October 1985) would continue through most of the 1980s. The Japanese banks and government completely complied with the U.S. strategy.[25] Contrary to Japan's international reputation as a "free rider" in the international political economy, Japanese banks were among the most cooperative in debt restructuring.

While Japan mostly tagged along behind the United States in its response to the debt crisis, the Japanese did at times try to assume a more prominent role in managing the problem. Japan's capital recycling plan and debt-reduction initiatives both illustrate the general awkwardness associated with Japanese forays onto the global political stage.

During a 1987 visit to the United States, Prime Minister Yasuhiro Nakasone announced with great fanfare Japan's new plan to channel $30 billion to major third world debtor countries through international lending agencies. It was underscored that money from the so-called "recycling facility" would be "untied" (unlike much of Japanese ODA), and that much of the funds would be reserved for Latin America, a region outside of Japan's traditional sphere of influence.

Was this bold initiative the act of a budding hegemon providing public goods to stabilize the international monetary system? In reality, the capital recycling plan was perhaps more a response to U.S. pressure on Japan to use its trade surplus to help out third world debtors than a truly independent hegemonic act. And the "public good" quality of the package became more questionable as details about the plan surfaced. For example, it turned out that only a small portion of the money was earmarked for Latin America, the epicenter of the debt disaster.

The development of Japan's international management skills appears to have been limited as much by U.S. ambivalence as by Japan's own reticence. The United States has constantly urged Japan to take on more global responsibilities. But at the same time, the United States has had difficulty in relinquishing its own authority in the international monetary system. The U.S. response to Japan's initiative to change the overall debt strategy of the creditor countries underscores U.S. uneasiness with an independent and assertive Japan. Throughout the 1980s, the United States pushed Japan to shoulder more of the burden in managing the third world debt crisis. But when Japanese officials proposed to shift the focus of international debt management from debt restructuring to debt reduction in 1988, the United States squashed the proposal, as the following box will illustrate.

THE JAPANESE PROPOSAL FOR DEBT REDUCTION

During the latter half of the 1980s, it was apparent that the U.S.-designed debt "restructuring" strategy had worked to mitigate the banking crisis, but had not at all eased the problem for debtor countries. Developing countries were collapsing economically under the weight of their huge debt burdens and, as a result, were becoming increasingly politically unstable. Worsening conditions in the third world led a number of interested parties to the conclusion that what these countries needed was not more money and time to repay their debt, but actual debt reduction. In June 1986, Senator Bill Bradley had unsuccessfully lobbied for a third world debt plan that would cut interest rates and forgive principal on loans. Some big commercial banks themselves had been quietly shedding their loans to the third world since 1987.[26] Japan sought to give more momentum to this trend.

Continued

THE JAPANESE PROPOSAL FOR DEBT REDUCTION, *continued*

At the Toronto economic summit meeting of advanced industrial countries in June 1988, Japanese leaders formally proposed that the creditor countries switch the emphasis of international debt management toward debt reduction. The United States immediately shot the proposal down, viewing the debt reduction plan as an unwelcome rival to the United States own Baker plan. In a more forceful bid to lead the way in international debt management, Japanese officials pledged new loans and reintroduced the *Miyazawa Plan* (named for Japan's finance minister) at the meeting of the World Bank and the IMF in Berlin during the fall of 1988. The Japanese failed to elaborate any details of the plan, so that the proposal seemed half-baked. Nevertheless, the general thrust of the plan toward debt relief was clear. Again, the United States roundly criticized the Japanese plan for a number of reasons, including its lack of details and failure to comply with the conservative, gradualist principles of the Baker Plan.[27] Then in April 1989, U.S. Treasury Secretary Nicholas Brady reversed course and announced a debt-reduction program, dubbed the *Brady Plan.* Since the U.S. plan adopted major portions of the Miyazawa Plan, Japanese officials wondered, half-jokingly, if it shouldn't be called the "Bra-zawa" plan. Said one Japanese official of the new debt reduction scheme: "Actually, we're happy to call it the Brady plan . . . but perhaps with an asterisk that it's backed by Japanese money."[28] Japan was the first and only nation to put up a substantial sum of money to support the Brady Plan. The Bush administration confessed that it couldn't approach Japan's $4.5 billion contribution, due to its huge budget and trade deficits.

Japanese Dollar Diplomacy

Economist and Japan watcher David Hale contends that future historians will note with some ironic delight that financial bureaucrats in Japan, the industrial world's least deregulated economy, "helped to rescue the Reagan administration and the international economic system from currency misalignments, trade imbalances, and financial crises." For these achievements, Hale commends Japan as "the great stabilizing force in the world financial system during the 1980s."[29]

Where is the evidence of Japan's impressive contribution to international economic stability? It is not in Japanese actions in the developing world, but rather in Japan's shoring up of a fellow advanced industrial country that had gotten itself into a financial pickle. During much of the 1980s, experts believed that the global trading and monetary systems had entered a period of crisis. Huge and expanding global balance-of-payments imbalances were at the heart of the concerns about an imminent "systemic crisis." In particular, the international accounts of the United States and Japan were completely out of whack.[30]

The global balance of payments in the advanced industrial world was extremely problematic. Beyond the obvious political friction between the United States and Japan caused by the bilateral trade imbalance, experts doubted whether or not the United States could continue to depend on foreign capital to finance its burgeoning current account deficit. There was fear that foreign investors would shy away from U.S. assets because of concerns that America's steady accumulation of debt would lead to a collapse of the dollar, which spelled capital losses for them. Economist

Stephen Marris warned of the potential for a "hard landing" of the U.S. economy, which would sink into recession and bring the rest of the world down with it.

The "hard landing" scenario never came to pass, largely because Japanese investors proved to be reliable financiers of the U.S. current account deficit throughout the decade. These institutional investors stayed with U.S. dollar assets through thick and through thin. During the early 1980s, the bilateral financial arrangement was mutually attractive. Japanese institutional investors earned a nice return on their investment, and the Reagan administration was provided with the funds to pursue an expansionary fiscal policy.

It was after the dollar began its steep decline in late 1985 that Japan's commitment to the U.S. and to the stability of international financial markets was truly tested. It is a well-known rule of thumb that investors should pull out of a falling currency. While the declining dollar led most European investors to abandon their portfolio investment in the U.S., Japanese investors held the line. Even as the dollar plummeted, they continued to buy U.S. dollar securities. In doing so, they prevented a sharp rise in U.S. interest rates, which could easily have precipitated Marris's "hard landing." As a result of dollar depreciation, Japanese institutional investors incurred huge losses. From 1985 to 1987, Japanese life insurers reported losing about $30 billion in the value of their U.S. portfolio holdings.[31] Clearly, broader concerns superseded the narrow commercial interests of Japan's private financiers.

In order to understand the Japanese sacrifices made in the interest of stabilizing the international financial system, we need to recognize the efforts of Japanese government officials. In a more laissez-faire economy, it would have been difficult for the government to convince private investors to act in a way that was so directly in opposition to their own interests. In Japan's "developmental" state, the leverage available to government officials for influencing private investment decisions is substantial. Thus, the Japanese finance ministry was able to employ "administrative guidance" to prevent Japanese investors from dumping their dollar securities. Through such strong-arm tactics to keep private Japanese capital flowing and through the direct intervention by Japan's central bank to buy dollars, Japanese government officials steadied the dollar and stabilized the international financial system.

The Verdict on Japanese Hegemony

Based on Japan's track record as a creditor nation, it is difficult to predict Japan's future prospects as a hegemonic leader in the international political economy. Japan's willingness to provide public goods varies among the three cases examined.

The case of ODA best represents a continuation of Japan's old mercantilist habits. The overwhelming bulk of Japan's development assistance has targeted recipients strategic to Japan's economic development, either because of their geographic proximity or their possession of vital resources. Moreover, most aid continues to be contributed in the form of infrastructural contracts constructed by and for the benefit of Japanese commercial interests. There is relatively little cooperation between the United States and Japan in overseas development assistance, and much suspicion and accusation about the other's intentions.

Japan's involvement in international debt management suggests the potential for "bigemony" in the global political economy. However, the case points to a number of snags that remain to be worked out for Japan's participation in joint burdensharing. For the top brass in the international monetary system, each manager's political authority continues to lag behind the actual ability to contribute to the public good. The United States is less able, but more than willing, to take charge strategically. Japan has the resources, but continues to leave global political leadership primarily to the United States.

The final case of U.S. debt financing provides the most promising evidence that Japan may yet serve as the lead manager of the global political economy. And here the international news is good.

In the instance of dollar diplomacy, David Hale argues that "Because Japan still retains more of the features of a command economy than the Anglo-Saxon nations, the Ministry of Finance and Bank of Japan have been able to pursue economic stabilization policies which lessened the danger of America's large external deficits producing skyrocketing interest rates and a recession."[32] In short, Japanese-style capitalism may help to assure that the government's public-minded pursuit of global stability will prevail over the more narrow concerns of private market-players.

CONCLUSION

The concern of this chapter has been Japan and the international political economy. Historically secluded from much of the world before this century, Japan has assumed, with a mixture of justifiable pride and reluctance, a position at center stage. Its credentials include a version of state-guided, producer-oriented capitalism contrary to the liberal tradition, and a decades-long patronage under the auspices of the United States, liberalism's chief postwar proponent. But the success of the client and the declining motivation of the patron have combined with a global shift that has altered both the script and the relevant actors.

Simply put, the collapse of the Cold War structure of international politics has rendered the old U.S.-Japanese relationship completely out of date. After World War II, the United States saw in Japan a country vital to U.S. security, but whose economic activities had little bearing on U.S. well-being. Changed global circumstances have turned this perception on its head. Now, Japan is strategically less important to the United States, and in the economic realm the United States now views Japan as a major threat to U.S. welfare. From Japan's vantage, the end of the Cold War and economic maturity have translated into a new sense of independence. The U.S. security guarantee is less important to Japan and Japan is less dependent on U.S. technology transfers for further economic development. Japan and the United States are like an old married couple being pressured to reconstitute their relationship. The old division of labor won't work, and each must adapt to the new reality of the other partner's capabilities and interests.

Under these changed circumstances, can we expect a continuation of Pax Americana? The major problem with this option is, of course, the inability and unwillingness of the United States, as the world's largest debtor nation, to provide the markets and bankroll the security of the world's largest creditor nation. It is equally irksome to Japanese nationals who see Japan as having the right and obligation to shake off its image as "political pygmy" and assume a more prominent role of leadership in global political, if not military, affairs.

Pax Nipponica, too, is unlikely, at least in the short run, for both domestic and international reasons. First and foremost, although Japan's defense budget is among the world's largest and its self-defense force among the most technologically advanced, Japan has neither the capacity nor the will to provide international peace. Buttressed by constitutional restrictions and strong (though not universal) pacifist sentiment within Japan and bitter memories of Japanese imperialism among its Asian neighbors, Japan is not likely to soon become an independent military power.

Security aside, Japan has also been reluctant to assume either the economic burdens or political consequences of economic hegemony, as the case studies in this chapter have shown. Without fundamental change, Japan's political economy will not be prepared to absorb either foreign exports and investments or the waves of foreign laborers, students, and immigrants in the fashion typically associated with a global hegemon.

And while much good could come of a harmonious bigemony, there are significant obstacles to this course as well. Efforts of integration and the collective burden-sharing of public goods among the culturally similar nations of Europe have been extremely difficult. These same efforts between two nations separated by an ocean and with very divergent cultures and historical backgrounds must pose an even greater challenge. Distrust and suspicion of the other's actions and intent are inevitable.

For example, was U.S.-Japanese cooperation in the Gulf War (American military might funded by the Japanese) an instance of harmonious bigemony, a case of American arm-twisting of a reticent ally, or simply an example of the wealthy Japanese bankrolling American mercenaries to preserve Japan's oil interests? Familiarity may breed not greater harmony, but contempt. Remember the point made earlier, just because a stable IPE may demand public goods, neither the international system nor its constituent parts guarantee to supply them.

This, however, raises a final option—that of an IPE with no global hegemon. Does the IPE necessarily and always demand a hegemon to provide essential public goods? Put differently, in the absence of a dominant global power and in our particular historical situation at the end of the Cold War if not the "end of history,"[33] can public goods be generated differently? There is much discussion now of the emergence of three "quasi-trading blocs" in Europe, North American, and Asia, with a regional hegemon providing public goods in each zone.[34] More fundamentally, has peace, traditionally the most costly and precious of these public goods, become now a "free good" that no longer requires production? If true, does the world still require a hegemon, at least of the traditional variety? Or are we now living in a "post-hegemonic world," a world that is being peacefully integrated by global market forces?[35]

Whatever the case, Japan's economic prowess and colossal financial strength assure it a spot in the limelight for many years to come—though it may take Japan, and the rest of the world, some time to become accustomed to it.

DISCUSSION QUESTIONS

1. Are Japan's mercantilist proclivities a product of its culture (and thus unlikely to change), or is Japan simply going through an economic nationalist stage common to many countries during their "catch-up" phase of development?
2. Is the United States' growing balance of trade deficit with Japan an American problem, a Japanese problem, or not even a problem? Who is to blame? What is the solution?
3. Does Japan have the capacity and the will to be the next global hegemon? What other alternatives, if any, do you see as more likely?
4. Outline the impact of an increasingly dominant Japan on the webs of relationships that link together the international political economy. How would Japanese hegemony impact the finance, production, security, and knowledge structures that make up the IPE?

SUGGESTED READINGS

James Fallows. *Looking at the Sun.* New York: Pantheon, 1994.

Takashi Inoguchi. "Four Japanese Scenarios for the Future." *International Affairs* 65 (Winter 1988/89):15–28.

Chalmers Johnson. "The End of American Hegemony and the Future of US-Japan Relations." *Harvard International Review* (Anniversary Issue 1990):126–131.

Kenneth Pyle. *The Japanese Question: Power and Purpose in a New Era.* Washington, DC: American Enterprise Institute Press, 1992.

Lester Thurow. *Head to Head: The Coming Economic Battle Among Japan, Europe, and the United States.* New York: William Morrow, 1992.

Kozo Yamamura and Daniel Okimoto, eds. *The Political Economy of Japan: The Changing International Context*, vol. 2. Stanford, CA: Stanford University Press, 1987.

NOTES

1. Chalmers Johnson, quoted from video, *Losing the War with Japan*, Front Line Series, 1991.
2. As cited by Kenneth Pyle, *The Japanese Question: Power and Purpose in a New Era* (Washington, DC: AEI Press, 1992), 12.
3. Kozo Yamamura and Daniel Okimoto, eds., *The Political Economy of Japan: The Changing International Context*, vol. 2 (Stanford, CA: Stanford University Press, 1987), 175.
4. Kozo Yamamura and Yasukichi Yasuba, eds., *The Political Economy of Japan: The Domestic Transformation*, vol. 1 (Stanford, CA: Stanford University Press, 1987), 95.
5. Some representative works include: Gary Saxonhouse, "Industrial Restructuring in Japan," *The Journal of Japanese Studies* (Summer 1979); Charles Schultze, "Industrial Policy: A Dissent," *The Brookings Review* (Fall 1983): 3–12; Philip H. Trezise, "Industrial Policy in Japan," in Margaret Dewar, ed., *Industrial Vitalization: Toward a National Industrial Policy* (New York: Pergamon Press, 1982); and Hugh Patrick, "The Future of the Japanese Economy," *The Journal of Japanese Studies* (Summer 1977).
6. For an overview of alternative explanations of the Japanese miracle, see Chalmers Johnson, "The End of American Hegemony and the Future of U.S.-Japan Relations," *Harvard International Review* (Anniversary Issue 1990): 126–131.
7. Adherents to this position have been labeled *revisionists* because they reject the orthodox view that capitalist democracies all look and act alike. Revisionists do not argue that

Japan is evil or wrong, but rather that Japan is *different* from other advanced industrial democracies. See *Business Week*, 7 August 1989, 444–451.

8. See Lester Thurow, *Head to Head: The Coming Economic Battle Among Japan, Europe, and America* (New York: William Morrow, 1992), 113–151.

9. Yamamura and Yasuba, *The Political Economy of Japan*, vol. 1, 138.

10. Ibid., 100.

11. Thurow, *Head to Head*, 127.

12. See James Fallows, "How the World Works," *The Atlantic Monthly* (December 1993).

13. Ibid., 64.

14. Ibid., 71.

15. Pyle, *The Japanese Question*, 43.

16. Donald Hellman, "Japanese Politics and Foreign Policy: Elitist Democracy within an American Greenhouse," in Yamamura and Okimoto, eds., *The Political Economy of Japan: The Changing International Context*, vol. 2 (Stanford, CA: Stanford University Press, 1988), 345.

17. In 1987, Sony President Akio Morita and politician Shintaro Ishihara published a book called *The Japan That Can Say No*, which satisfied the yearnings of many Japanese and caused a sensation on both sides of the Paciific.

18. "Rewriting the Book on How to Deal with Japan," *Business Week*, 7 August 1989, 49.

19. For discussions of these future scenarios, see Takashi Inoguchi, "Four Japanese Scenarios for the Future," *International Affairs* 65 (Winter 1988/89):15–28; and Johnson, "The End of American Hegemony and the Future of U.S.-Japan Relations."

20. Phillip J. Meeks, "Hegemons in History," in Tsuneo Akaha and Frank Langdon, eds., *Japan in the Post-Hegemonic World* (Boulder, CO: Lynne Reiner, 1993), 63.

21. "Japan Is Top Aid Donor for Third Consecutive Year," *Japan Times*, 25 June 1994.

22. Meeks, "Hegemons in History," 63; Tsuneo Akaha and Frank Langdon, "Japan and the Post-Hegemonic World," in Akaha and Langdon, *Japan in the Post-Hegemonic World*, 8.

23. "Profits and Power: Japan's Foreign-Aid Machine." *San Jose Mercury News*, 19–21 April 1992; Koji Taira, "Japan as Number Two: New Thoughts on the Hegemonic Theory of World Governance," in Akaha and Langdon, *Japan in the Post-Hegemonic World*, 155.

24. *San Jose Mercury News*, 19–21 April 1992.

25. Barbara Stallings, "The Reluctant Giant: Japan and the Latin American Debt Crisis," in Susan J. Pharr, ed., *Japan and the Third World* (forthcoming).

26. "Big Banks Shift From 3d World," *The New York times*, 27 July 1988, D1.

27. "U.S. Critical of Japanese Debt Relief Plan," *Asian Wall Street Journal*, 27 September 1988, A1.

28. "Japan Takes a Leading Role in the Third-World Debt Crisis," *The New York Times*, 17 April 1989, A1.

29. David Hale, "The Japanese Ministry of Finance and Dollar Diplomacy During the Late 1980s; or How the University of Tokyo Law School Saved America from the University of Chicago Economics Department," *Kemper Financial Services, Inc.* (July 1989): 1–2.

30. Through the decade, the current accounts of the U.S. and Japan moved in opposite directions, and with unprecedented rapidity. For years, the current accounts of both the U.S. and Japan had fluctuated within 1 percent of GNP. After 1983, the U.S. current account deficit increased to levels exceeding 4 percent of GNP, and the Japanese current account surplus increased to a similar range. Capital account imbalances mirrored these current account imbalances. Japan recycled its surplus abroad, while the U.S. financed its current account deficit by importing foreign capital. The U.S. borrowed so much from abroad that by the end of 1987, the U.S. net debt of $368 billion approximated the gross debt of all of Latin America. Meanwhile, the surge of Japanese capital flows during the 1980s raised Japan's net worth from $11.5 billion to $400 billion worth of net foreign assets by the end of the decade. Sources for above statistics: Ryutaro Komiya, "The Global Payments Imbalance, the 'Systemic Crisis' and the Japan-U.S. Economic Relations," conference paper for MITI symposium, June 1988, 10; and

Martin Feldstein, "Correcting the Trade Deficit," *Foreign Affairs* 65 (Spring 1987): 795–796.

31. "Japanese Shift Investment Flows and Bring Cash Home" *The New York Times*, 22 March 1992, A12.
32. Hale, "The Japanese Ministry of Finance and Dollar Diplomacy During the Late 1980s," (1989):1.
33. Frances Fukuyama, "The End of History," *National Interest* (Summer 1989):3–35.
34. Thurow, *Head to Head*.
35. Taira, "Japan As Number Two," 261.

14

States and Markets in Transition

OVERVIEW

One of the greatest challenges that a nation can face is to change the entire nature of its political and economic system. Making such a dramatic change essentially redefines the ways that individuals relate to each other and to the state. The fundamental tension between states and markets is magnified as social institutions and individual responsibilities are altered.

This chapter examines the problems of states and markets in transition from one system of IPE to another. The goal of this chapter is to explore the nature of the transitions from communism to capitalism and the changing tensions these transitions produce.

This chapter begins with a general overview of the problems of states and markets in transition, and the global context within which their changes occur. We then focus first on what might be called the *classical socialist system*, commonly referred to as the *communist system*, and explore the economic, political, and social changes that formerly communist nations are experiencing. Russia, Poland, and China are singled out for special attention in this discussion because they represent three different approaches to the problems of economic and political transition.

Finally, we reflect on the problems and opportunities of the transition states and speculate about the future that awaits these nations. While each instance of transition has its unique properties, the role of the state in fostering economic transformation is critical. Economic reforms are most effective when they have strong political backing.

Mankind always sets itself only such tasks as it can solve; since, looking at the matter more closely, we will always find that the task itself arises only when the material conditions necessary for its solution already exist or are at least in the process of formation.[1]

Karl Marx (1859)

If someone had told Karl Marx that by the end of the twentieth century much of the world would be caught up in a grand task—a transition from one system of political economy to another—chances are he would have shown no surprise. Marx believed in an undeniable force of history that transforms the world, as capitalism replaces feudalism, socialism replaces capitalism, and communism finally replaces socialism. Marx would have assumed that by the 1990s the masses would be moving again—Workers of the World, Unite!—on the one-way road from capitalism to communism. On this Marx was clear and sure.

Consider how surprised Marx would be, then, to discover the world of the 1990s evolving, in part, from a "communist" system of state-market relations based on the ideas of Marx and Lenin to free-market democracy—the "capitalism" whose doom Marx foretold!

This fundamental change in the structure of the IPE has profound impact on all aspects of international relations. With the fall of Soviet communism has come the end of the Cold War, the breakdown of the bipolar international security structure, and the creation of many new channels of social, political, and economic interaction. The final consequences of these changes can only be imagined, but their nature must be understood. This chapter focuses on the crucial issues of states and markets in transition from one system of state-market relations to another.

STATES AND MARKETS IN TRANSITION

Change is stressful. Change in something as complex and important as a nation's system of political economy causes stresses and strains at all levels: individual, market, class, nation, region, globe. It is significant, therefore, that perhaps half of the world's population will experience the stress of a change in their system of political economy during the 1990s. These are stressful times for the IPE, with so many states and markets in transition. The nature of the strain, however, is different in each case.

One group of nations is engulfed in the problems of the dramatic transition from communism, or classical socialism, to some form of democratic capitalism—these are the "formers" as Czech leader Václav Havel has called them: the former members of the Warsaw Pact, including Hungary and Poland, and the former states of the Soviet Union, such as Russia and Ukraine.[2] These nations are trying to develop liberal economic institutions and democratic political institutions at the same time—a daunting task that requires a wholesale shift from a focus on collective interests to an emphasis on individual rights. Other nations, like China and Vietnam, are engaged in a somewhat less extreme but perhaps even more difficult transition, from communism (classical socialism) to *market socialism*, a hybrid system that retains central power in the state, but encourages private economic activities.[3]

This chapter cannot predict what will happen to these states and markets in transition. We can, however, explore the nature of the changes under way and examine briefly the recent history of economic and political reform. This survey will help us better understand the problems and stresses of today's world, and the prospects for tomorrow.

Every transition has three stages: the old order; the transition process itself, often characterized as *reform* of the old order or *revolt* against it; and the new order that finally emerges. We begin our discussion with an examination of the "old order" of communism. This is what the Hungarian political economist János Kornai calls *classical socialism*, which is the set of fundamental political economy relationships implemented by Joseph Stalin (1879–1953) in the Soviet Union and Mao Zedong (1893–1976) in China. This is the system of political economy that we commonly call *communism*.[4]

COMMUNISM AND THE CLASSICAL SOCIALIST SYSTEM

Socialism is a political economy system of communal ownership of production resources, with a strong emphasis on economic equality. There are various degrees of socialism, ranging from limited public ownership of resources in the United States, for example, to the opposite extreme, the classical socialist system, that we associate with communism in the Soviet Union and elsewhere. It is common to call these nations "communist" because of the importance of the Communist party in their political structures, and so it is tempting to label their form of political economy "communism." For Marx, however, and for the Communist parties in these countries, the term *communism* is reserved for the final stage in Marx's historical progression, when the state "withers away" and communal ownership becomes the natural order. Communism in this sense was never achieved and the state was always a dominant force in the communist nations.

To preserve this distinction, we generally will use the term *classical socialism* to refer to the social and political economy structure and use *communism* the way Marx did, in reference to the social goal and final stage of the historical progression. Hopefully this will not be too confusing. Table 14–1 shows the fourteen countries that adopted "communist" or classical socialist systems, with the dates of transition.[5] With the exception of North Korea and Cuba, each of these countries had begun the transition from the "old order" of classical socialism to some "new order" by the early 1990s.

It is instructive to consider the general characteristics of the classical socialist system. Here are highly stylized and oversimplified descriptions of the principal political and economic aspects of classical socialism, which are useful background for us in considering the problems of transition.[6]

The politics and economics of the classical socialist system are completely intertwined—the state *is* the market, for all practical purposes. It is a mistake, therefore, to discuss political and economic aspects of the system separately. Having made this point, it is still true that we must begin somewhere, and so we start with a discussion of the fundamental nature of politics in classical socialism, so that we can see more clearly, in the next section, the strong impact of politics on the economy.

THE POLITICS OF CLASSICAL SOCIALISM

It is convenient to break this analysis into four parts: power, ideology, government, and external political relations. Together, these elements define the political and economic basis of classical socialism.

Power

Power is rooted in one party, the Communist party, which uses a powerful bureaucracy to carry out its policies. Membership in the Communist party generally is limited to about 5 to 10 percent of the population, although a much larger percentage may participate in party-led programs and movements. Power in this system is thus *political* power; wealth plays but a small part in the power structure because of the emphasis on collective ownership and economic equality. In theory, this creates a classless society. In practice, this centralization of power produces a class system reminiscent of Marx's bourgeoisie and proletariat, but based on the access to political power and bureaucratic influence, not the ownership of the means of production. The irony of class divisions within a theoretically classless society are the source of a well-known Soviet joke: "Under capitalism, man exploits man. Under communism,

TABLE 14–1   The Classical Socialist Countries

COUNTRY	YEAR	COUNTRY	YEAR
Soviet Union	1917	Poland	1948
Mongolia	1921	Romania	1948
Albania	1944	North Korea	1948
Yugoslavia	1945	China	1949
Bulgaria	1947	East Germany	1949
Czechoslovakia	1948	Vietnam	1954
Hungary	1948	Cuba	1959

it is the other way around." In his classic 1976 report, *The Russians*, Hedrick Smith described some of the privileges of the *Nomenklatura*, or party elite:

> Officially, there are only two classes, the workers and peasants, and a "stratum" of employees—white collar workers and intelligentsia. It is only the upper portion of this intelligentsia which constitutes the real privileged class. Its core is the apex of the Communist Party and the Government, the political bureaucracy that runs the country, joined by the senior economic managers, most influential scientific administrators, the princes of the Party and propaganda network.[7]

This concentration of power in the Communist party is perhaps the most important distinguishing characteristic of "communism." In the United States, for example, power comes in two types—political and economic—and in many shapes and flavors. Power is not equally dispersed in the United States, but it is more equally distributed than in any of the classical socialist systems.

The critical importance of power and party in classical socialism means that virtually all important issues are ultimately *political* issues. Economic reforms, which occupy much of the discussion of this chapter, are also political in their nature. Any effort to change any aspect of the classical socialist system necessarily shifts political power within the Communist party. It would be an error to begin to try to understand any aspect of classical socialism without first considering the political causes and effects.

Ideology

The exercise of power in the classical socialist system is guided by a set of official beliefs, "the party line," concerning social, economic, and political relationships. Based fundamentally on Marx and Lenin, this ideology emphasizes the importance of power, both as a tool to achieve various ends and as an end in itself. Communist party dogma places high value on revolution as a social and political process and stresses the superiority of a socialist form of social and economic organization. Because the means of production are collectively owned, this argument holds, resources can be allocated to those industries that best serve the collective interest and achieve the highest levels of economic growth (compared to a capitalist system of private ownership, where resources go where the private benefits are highest). Living standards do not typically rise quickly, however, because investment is directed toward heavy industries, not consumer goods. "Personality cults," which use leaders and heroes to personify these official beliefs, are a common way to communicate ideology to the masses. Stalin and Mao were important both as real leaders and as ideological symbols, reminding citizens of the important beliefs that guided their country.

Government

Government in classical socialist states is based on the Communist party, which is the only political party. In fact, there is no functional difference between state and party. The system of one-party governance that prevailed in the Soviet Union provides a useful example of how this system worked.

Governance in the Soviet Union was based on the Communist party of the Soviet Union, which had a peak membership of less than 20 million out of a total population of nearly 300 million. Political power was limited to party members, and distributed in a very hierarchical manner.

About 400,000 primary party organizations formed the "grassroots" of the system, but power was heavily concentrated at the top, with rural, city, district, regional, and republic committees filling in the gaps. The most powerful institutions were the All-Union Congress, the party's supreme policy-making body; the Central Committee, elected by the Congress; the Political Bureau (Politburo), chosen by the Central Committee; and the Secretariat. The General Secretary of the Communist party was the effective head of government as well as party. Governmental administration took place through a huge bureaucracy that effectively encompassed the entire nation, given the dominant role of the state in all aspects of life.

Government under classical socialism lacked the defining elements of Western democracy: political parties, contested elections, interest groups. In effect, government reflected the interests of the ruling elites, heavily conditioned by party ideology.

External Political Relations

External political relations also reflect ideological concerns. The first external political organization, for example, was Comintern (for Communist International), which was founded in 1919 by V. I. Lenin to assert Communist leadership of the world socialist movement. Non-Communist countries were excluded from membership. Comintern disbanded in 1935, but political relations since then have tended to be closest with other classical socialist states. For many years, the *Warsaw Pact* essentially defined a sphere of political alliances, for example. The Warsaw Pact was a military alliance formed by the Soviet Union to counterbalance the North Atlantic Treaty Organization (NATO). Political relations with other classical socialist states were fundamentally different from those with capitalist countries and with non-aligned less developed countries. In general, ideology guided and determined foreign policy in all areas.

THE ECONOMICS OF CLASSICAL SOCIALISM

The economy of a classical socialist state was heavily conditioned by politics and ideology. It is convenient to examine the economy in terms of the role of property, the nature of economic coordinating mechanisms, the role of prices, and external economic relations.

Property

Communal ownership of the means of production is the hallmark of any form of socialism and this is especially true in classical socialism, its extreme form. This is not to say that there is no private property. Private ownership of personal possessions unrelated to economic production is generally the same as under capitalism. What is important is that the means of production are publicly owned. In agriculture, for example, farming tends to be *communal*, with many families working in common fields, using shared tools and equipment, and sharing their production, both with one another and with the state. In industry and commerce, communal ownership translates into state ownership of the physical plant, and state planning of business strategy. Actual production decisions are made through the bureaucracy or, in some cases, by worker organizations or cooperatives. The goal of common ownership is to eliminate the social waste and class inequality that are associated with private ownership. The reality is frequently that resources are not efficiently used because of the lack of individual incentives to do so. Workers who will receive the same share of a farm's output whether they toil faithfully or just lean on a shovel can be expected to shirk to some extent. It is unsurprising, therefore, that when private plots of land, farmed for one's individual benefit, were allowed, they proved to be several times more productive than the much bigger communal agricultural operations.

Economic Coordination Mechanisms

There are many ways that human behavior can be coordinated or regulated so that the actions of many individuals combine to produce a desirable society. Most of us are familiar with two main coordination mechanisms that might be called the *market* and the *bureaucracy*. In the United States, we rely on the market's invisible hand, for the most part, to coordinate the production and distribution of goods and services such as food, clothing, and shelter. We rely on the bureaucracy or the government, however, to coordinate the production and distribution of other items, such as public schooling, public parks, and public safety. Under classical socialism, the market is not entirely eliminated as a coordinating mechanism ("black markets,"[8] for example, typically exist along with legal "white" markets), but the emphasis is definitely put on bureaucratic coordination. This distribution of authority mirrors the distribution of power.

Coordinating the activities of entire industries or even whole nations is a complex and difficult task. Wise decisions require enormous amounts of information and a detailed understanding of the interrelationships among firms, regions, and industries. It was common, therefore, for mistakes to be made in planning and production decisions. Specific items were subject to spot shortages and surpluses, sometimes of enormous size. An error in planning annual steel production levels, for example, might make it impossible to produce enough rail cars to get an unusually large wheat crop to market. The resulting food shortages could affect other areas of the economy.

Another problem is that planning is necessarily a quantitative exercise, and numerical goals or targets are not always effective in communicating priorities. The story is told, for example, of a Soviet nail factory built to satisfy the needs of the construction industry. Under capitalism, the factory would try to make profits by producing at low cost the types and sizes of nails that were most in demand. If the factory produced too many nails, or nails of the wrong size, or made them at inefficiently high cost, they would lose profits and have to face the consequences of their bad decisions. Under classical socialism, however, the factory would be given a production target and would try to meet that target. Meeting the target was the sole criterion of efficiency. Legend has it that one year the nail factory was given a target of ten tons of nails and found that the easiest way to achieve the planners' wishes was to produce one huge ten-ton nail. It satisfied the plan, but the nail was useless to anyone. To remedy this, the story goes, the planners specified their target differently the next year, using quantity of output instead of weight as the quantitative measure. The factory was ordered to produce a million nails. They satisfied the plan the easiest possible way, making a million teeny-tiny nails. Again the factory's output was worthless, although the planners' targets were met.[9] The moral of the story is that planning targets are often less efficient than market discipline in encouraging efficient resource use.

High rates of growth are the standard of success to planners in classical socialist systems, and their technique is often called *forced growth*. The idea of forced growth is to try to get twenty years of growth into five or ten calendar years by pushing investment into those areas that will have the largest long-term impact on the nation's economy. This is possible, of course, due to the centralized bureaucratic system of economic coordination. Whereas in a system of market coordination, investment decisions are driven by profit expectations, investment in a planned economy was generally guided by principles like these: build large factories rather than small ones, support heavy industry rather than consumer goods, encourage domestic production rather than imports, support manufacturing rather than services. Production of military and defense goods also received high priority.

Living standards under the classical socialist system were relatively low compared to those in Western industrialized economies, but the distribution of money income was somewhat more equal, and there was greater economic security. Low material living standards are the natural consequence of the system of bureaucratic coordination that systematically favored industrial investment over consumer goods. The wages, also set by bureaucratic action, were remarkably "flat," with skilled physicians receiving little more per month than an untrained orderly. This pay scale reflected Marxian ideology. Actual living standards, as noted before, were less equal than wage payments, because access to power was more important than access to money in acquiring desirable and scarce goods and services.

Employment was also a centrally planned activity, with relatively little discretion given to individual managers. It was hard for a "boss" to fire a worker, but it was also hard for a worker to change jobs. Job security and rigidity went hand in hand, and neither worker nor manager had much incentive to increase productivity. This fact, combined with low wages and living standards, gave rise to a popular Russian saying, "We pretend to work and they pretend to pay us."

Coordination is a complex task; the invisible hand of the market may not always perform this function very well, but the programs of bureaucratic control found in most classical socialist systems were seldom an improvement.

The Role of Prices

Prices are key elements of any system based on market coordination. Prices are the signal lights that tell individual consumers and producers about the cost and benefits of different actions and thus coordinates their independent actions in the market. Prices also serve to ration scarce items. Scarcity drives prices up, which limits the quantities purchased in the market. In a capitalist system, therefore, prices rise and fall all the time. The role of prices under a system of bureaucratic coordination is much different. Prices in a classical socialist economy tend to be far more rigid and unchanging than under capitalism. In the Soviet Union, for example, the price of bread remained absolutely unchanged from 1917 to 1989. Prices seldom reflect the value of items to consumers, the value of resources used in production, or the relative abundance or scarcity of a good in the market. Rather, prices were often set to further a political or ideological goal. Housing, basic foodstuffs, and public transportation usually had very low prices compared to nonsocialist countries. The low prices, however, were often misleading, since items such as shoes or fresh meat were often unavailable or of very low quality. Long lines and quality debasement were the flip side of low price. Imported goods and consumer durables such as automobiles and refrigerators, on the other hand, were overpriced by comparison. The high prices were intended to discourage consumption of these items, so that scarce resources could be used instead for production of items that ranked higher in the planners' priorities.

These nonmarket prices created a paradox: workers in the Soviet Union received low pay, but there were so few consumer goods for workers to buy that they unintentionally accumulated large sums of unspent rubles. This "ruble overhang" created long lines even for the overpriced big-ticket goods. Stories of other inefficiencies are common. In Poland, for example, the price of wheat was set high, to encourage production, and the price of bread was set low, to help accommodate the low living standards of industry workers. It is said that Polish pig farmers, who could not afford to feed their livestock wheat or corn, fed them bread instead, because its price was so artificially low.

External Economic Relations

Ideology and geopolitics also condition the nature of external relations for classical socialist nations. The Cold War's security structure was the strongest single factor defining the nature of external relations. Trade, finance, and technology issues all were of secondary importance compared with security concerns.

Classical socialist economies mostly engaged in external economic relations with other similar nations, extending the domestic system on a regional scale. What little trade with market economies that took place was often in the form of *barter* or *countertrade*, where goods are swapped for other goods, with no money changing hands. What we think of as "normal" international economic relations were difficult, of course, because of the two completely different systems of coordination in use. Prices, in particular, had different purposes and different meanings in the systems. Since trade was also a planned activity, international transactions had to serve some definite national need, such as compensate for crop failures, acquire new technology, or gain political influence and power.

Taken together, these characteristics of classical socialism create a political economy where each of the important economic and political structures is centered in the state, where all important choices can be molded according to a single national ideological agenda. Power is centered in the state, and through the state in the Communist party. All issues are therefore ultimately political issues that affect the distribution of power within the Communist party. This structure allows classical socialism to achieve certain "macro" goals, such as rapid expansion of heavy industry and the large-scale production of military and defense goods. Certain "micro" objectives must be foregone, however, such as the efficient production and distribution of consumer goods, and high levels of worker productivity and personal initiative. The classical socialist system was effective, therefore, when the "macro" goals of growth and defense dominated national agendas, as in the Soviet Union during the 1930s through the 1950s, China after 1949, and Eastern Europe after 1945. When the agenda shifted, for many reasons, to matters of individual living standards, rising productivity, international competitiveness, and political and economic freedom, the classical socialist system proved ineffective.

THE PROBLEMS OF TRANSITION

The transition from one system of political economy to another is a complex and stressful exercise because, in part, it requires the redefinition of the "givens" or rules by which many aspects of life are governed. This situation is illustrated by the story of Mikhail Gorbachev and the Canadian farmer. In 1983, when Gorbachev was the minister of agriculture in the Soviet Union, he traveled to Canada to see how their farmers worked.

> At one stop, he tested one farmer: "Who makes you get up in the morning?" The farmer, nonplussed, said he got going on his own. At home, Gorbachev knew it would take the hounding of state farm supervisors and the threat of disciplinary action to get many farm workers on the job. In another encounter, he asked to see a farm's labor force, expecting the typical Soviet collective, and was taken aback when the farmer replied that he farmed several hundred acres with just his family and a few hired hands. Sharing his secret, the farmer showed Gorbachev his tractors and other modern farm machinery, close to $100,000 worth. "Do they trust you with all this?" Gorbachev asked, assuming that the equipment belonged to some government agency because he could not imagine a single farmer's owning such an expensive array of equipment. By the accounts of Canadian officials, Gorbachev walked away muttering, "We'll never have this for fifty years."[10]

The transition from the political economy of classical socialism necessarily requires a complete recasting of political and economic relationships, both within an economy and with respect to external relations. Abel Aganbegyan, the Russian political economist who was an architect of perestroika, captured in undramatic terms the essential nature of transition.

> The most important lesson to be drawn from an analysis of the past concerns the *need for democratisation of society* as the indispensable element in a successful *perestroika*. Only through democratisation can the majority of working people be brought into the management process. The way forward lies in self-management.[11]

Aganbegyan is saying that political reform (democratization) is necessary for economic reform (self-management), and that economic reform is the "way forward." But economic and political reforms are hard to separate. Adam Przeworski has written:

> The durability of the new democracies will depend, however, not only on their institutional structure and the ideology of the major political forces, but to a large extent on their economic performance. Profound economic reforms must be undertaken if there is to be any hope that the deterioration in living conditions experienced by many nascent democratic countries will ever cease. . . . Yet structural transformations of economic systems are a plunge into the unknown; they are driven by desperation and hope, not by reliable blueprints.[12]

The next two sections try to sketch the outlines of the political and economic problems facing classical socialist nations, as prelude to our survey of three case studies of nations taking steps into this unknown territory.

THE POLITICS OF TRANSITION

Any change in the system of classical socialism necessarily requires radical change in all elements of the political structure: power, ideology, government, and external political relations.

Power

The transition away from the classical socialist system requires a radical redistribution of power. First, the move to freer markets requires that economic and political power be separated, at least to some extent. The power to set wages and prices and the power to set foreign policy, for example, cannot both be held by the Communist party. Second, both economic and political power must be decentralized. Politically, this means the creation of a multiparty system of government and democratically made decisions. Economically, this means a movement to some form of private ownership, free markets, a system of flexible wages and prices, and individual "self-management" in buying and selling decisions.

Under *market socialism*, the ownership of key resources is retained by the state in the interest of equality, while the responsibility for choices about the production and distribution of goods and services is given over to individuals acting through markets. Under *capitalism*, the role of the state is further reduced, and many publicly owned resources are *privatized*—either sold to private buyers or converted into privately held corporations.[13]

These political and economic changes require an essential reorientation of the vectors of power. Under classical socialism, power often flows down from the top (the party and state), and with it goes the authority for decision making. Individuals have little direct power and little authority over economic and political matters. The "transition" to another system of political economy may require a "revolution" of power, with power essentially located in individuals and interest groups and flowing *up*.

Ideology

Marxist ideology necessarily plays a smaller role, or at least a different role, as a guide to social and economic policy during "transition." This fact can have important consequences. John Maynard Keynes argued that communism's greatest appeal was not so much as a system of social organization but as a religion, or set of dogmatic beliefs. These beliefs could bind people together, Keynes wrote, much better than the tenets of self-interest that are the basis of the market.[14] The question is, what values and beliefs, if any, will replace communist ideology during and after the transition period? Extreme individualism, extreme nationalism, or even fascism are all options as a guide to individual and collective behavior for nations in transition. Having given up Marx and Lenin as guides, whom will they be guided by now?

Government

The change from classical socialism to a democratic form of government requires a fundamental transformation of society. Consider the vast number of changes that are necessary in individual behavior and collective institutions. Democratic systems typically operate based on multiparty systems, with competing beliefs or ideologies, active interest groups, and contested elections. This is as far as it is possible to get from the single-party system that characterized classical socialism. In a democratic system, power resides with individual voters, at least in theory, who are free to elect representatives or throw them out.

The transition to democracy necessarily requires the formation of political parties, the organization of interest groups, and the education of voters. But before these actions can be taken effectively, constitutional decisions must be made. That is, a system of government and rules of political action must be agreed to, to serve as the basis for the transition to democracy. Here we encounter a Catch-22: constitutional decisions must be made before legitimate governments can be formed, but how can a constitution be agreed to without first having a legitimate government to write it? This conundrum accounts, perhaps, for the instability of many postcommunist governments. Constitutions produce elections, which soon end in calls for a new constitution.[15]

Democratic constitution-writing is a delicate business. The problems of balancing competing interests, regions, and ethnic groups, which were all previously resolved behind closed party doors, now must be addressed in the open. Failure to resolve these problems are highly visible: ethnic and regional conflict in the Russian Federation and the breakup of Yugoslavia and Czechoslovakia into autonomous states are potent examples of the political conflicts that have occurred in recent years.

External Political Relations

Freed from ideological constraints, the state can engage in a far wider range of external political relations. Foreign policy must essentially be reinvented. This causes inevitable strains in both bilateral and multilateral political relations. Russia, for example, has pursued foreign relations initiatives that would have been impossible for the Soviet Union. Russia now meets (as a nonmember) with the Group of Seven (G-7), the leaders of the world's industrial democracies. Many former Warsaw Pact nations have applied for membership in NATO! These changing external relations both reflect internal political changes and at the same time impose stresses on them. There are also considerable adjustments to be made by the other nations engaged in these relations.

THE ECONOMICS OF TRANSITION

Economic transition also requires new institutions and ways of thinking, as well as a radical dismantling of the system of state ownership.

Property

The transition from communism to capitalism or a socialist market system requires a redefinition of property. Under the classical socialist system, the means of production are communal—owned by all of society and therefore not owned by any individual. Private ownership is typical under capitalism. Public ownership combined with private use is common under market socialism (the means of production are rented to private users by the state). The transition to some degree of private ownership is a critical but awkward one, because it requires rules of law and practice that determine who owns what and on what terms. Decisive laws and rules necessarily create winners and losers and thus create political instability. Ambiguous rules and laws, which may be politically tempting, are bad economics because they can keep market mechanisms from working efficiently. It is difficult to buy, sell, and make contracts if it is unclear who owns what. The problem of defining and enforcing property rights is often complicated by a variety of claimants to a given farm or factory. Who *should* own a Ukrainian farm—the peasants who work it today, the family that owned it before its seizure by the Communist state, or the entrepreneur who is willing to bid the most for the farm's title on the open market?

Economic Coordination Mechanisms

Prices replace the bureaucracy as coordinating mechanisms during the transition from classical socialism to another system. Although government coordination is still necessary in some parts of the political economy, the rise of markets necessitates the increased use of prices to allocate and distribute scarce resources. The logic of the market is that prices are critical bits of information that individual consumers, workers, and producers use in their decision making. Market prices contain information about the relative cost of producing goods and services, the relative value that buyers place on them, and the point at which the market clears without shortage or surplus. Prices generally perform these functions in the United States, for example.

The fundamental difficulty in moving to a decentralized system of coordination is the problem of responsibility. Under a decentralized system, individuals are responsible for gathering information, making decisions, and taking actions. This is totally different from the system of orders and reports that characterize classical socialism. For individuals, this "transition" is, again, more of a revolution.

The Role of Prices

For economies in transition, the problem is that the role of prices in a market economy, as stated above, are fundamentally at odds with their role in classical socialism, as stated earlier in this chapter. Under classical socialism, the bureaucratic apparatus sets prices to influence individual actions so as to further a social goal. It did not matter very much if the prices failed to reflect cost, or consumer valuation, or even the balance of demand and supply. With a market economy, the prices are set by the "invisible hand" of the market—by everyone or no one, as you please—and aim to achieve no social goal other than efficiency.

The transition from one way of using prices to another is necessarily stressful. This is so in part because the move from administered prices to efficient market prices dramatically affects the world of a typical consumer. Items, like bread in Russia, that were once scarce but cheap soon become costly but widely available. Goods that were artificially low-priced rise in cost while other items, such as cars and refrigerators, might come down in price. The impact on a family's standard of living can be quite significant until prices and wages adjust to an equilibrium.

A related problem is the fact that it is uncommon for all prices to adjust simultaneously to a new market or social market system. A retired family, for example, might see the prices they pay for food, rent, and transportation all rise while their government-paid pension remains fixed in money terms. Or some prices may be "set free" to fly with the market while others are held prisoner to state regulation. Such situations inevitably lead to some inefficiency where state and market forces intersect.

Political coordinating mechanisms must also change. Competing political parties are as unfamiliar to people in former communist states as is market competition. A difficult transition to multiparty government is perhaps to be expected.

External Economic Relations

The collapse of communism as a widespread system of political economy brought with it the end of the Cold War and its deep security divisions. With the end of the Cold War came a complete redefinition of external relations in all four structural areas: security, trade, finance, and knowledge and technology. Essentially, the former classical socialist states entered into the broader sphere of the international political economy. It is not a simple matter for a group of nations to enter into the mainstream of Western IPE after such a long period of isolation from it. Each nation, for example, must find a way to establish itself within a new security structure: Several Eastern Europe nations have proposed themselves for membership in the North Atlantic Treaty Organization (NATO), which was originally formed to present a unified opposition to communism in Europe. China must establish itself within its own Asian security structure. These adjustments to new security relationships are awkward and difficult for all nations and people involved.

Integration into the non-Communist trade, finance, and knowledge structures are only a little less awkward, however, in part because they are all based on markets, which are still unfamiliar institutions to those raised in the classical socialist institution. There is also the difficult adjustment to a new set of institutions—such as the IMF, World Bank, GATT, and the WTO, for example—and a new set of "rules of the game." Several Eastern European nations have applied for membership in the European Union. And fundamental problems remain, such as the transition from inconvertible "soft" currencies to international monetary forms. Essentially, then, everything about the external relations of these nations changes, while internal relationships are also being redefined. The transition to the market thus requires a radical reorientation of foreign and domestic priorities.

CASE STUDY: ECONOMIC AND POLITICAL REFORM IN RUSSIA

> Political reform cannot be put on hold while economic reform is carried out, nor can economic change be frozen to allow political reform. Rather, economic changes affect political transformation and political changes shape economic transformation. Missing this point has handicapped both analysis of Russia and reform.[16]

Any examination of the states and markets that are in transition today must begin with Russia, and any discussion of Russia must begin with history, for the tides of time pull hard on Russia.[17] Russia has undergone at least *six* major attempts at economic and political liberalization during modern history, and the problems of the 1990s can only be understood in this historical context.

Russia (and the Soviet Union) existed as a classical socialist state from 1917 to 1989, but the issues of political and market reforms go back much further, at least to the freeing of the serfs by Czar Alexander II in 1861–1864. Prime Minister Pyotr Stolypin's land reforms (1906 to 1911) tried to establish private land holdings. V. I. Lenin's "New Economic Policy" (1921 to 1928) attempted to introduce market forces into some areas of Soviet economic life. None of these three reform programs was successful in creating a more dynamic system of political economy, perhaps because each focused on the economic more than the political. This was necessary, however, because economic reform upset the balance of political power. Those who favored economic reform had something to gain within the Communist hierarchy. Those who had something to lose in the party obviously had to oppose reform, or find a way to put it to their use. Economic reform was an end in itself, but it was also a means to gain political power.

Writing about these early reform efforts, *The Economist* noted, "all collapsed when the autocrat of the day abruptly withdrew support for the reforms might threaten his (unreformed) powers. . . . The failure to implement political reform means economic policies have not had enough political support."[18] Stalin's thorough and forceful implementation of the classical socialist system in the 1930s put a nearly indelible stamp on Russia and the Soviet Union that remained essentially untouched so long as he lived and ruled. Centralized power, bureaucratic control, giant factories, and collective farms became the definitive system of classical socialism.

Stalin's death in 1953 left a temporary power vacuum, making both political and economic reform possible, especially after party leader Nikita Khrushchev denounced Stalin in 1956, revealing openly the abuses of Stalin's era. Prime Minister Alexei Kosygin championed the first post–Stalin reform attempt in 1965, a year after Khrushchev's fall from power. Like previous attempts, the Kosygin reforms focused on economic liberalization instead of political reform. Price reforms, greater freedom for factory managers, and reorganization of the planning bureaucracy were the main features of this plan. Kosygin's reforms failed because they went too far and not far enough at the same time. They went too far in the sense that they threatened the structure of political power, which was still centered in the party, the state, and the bureaucracy. The political backlash against the reforms quickly brought them to an end. The Kosygin reforms failed to go far enough, on the other hand, because they tiptoed into the sea of markets without getting wet enough to feel any benefits. Kosygin's plan tried to have things both ways—market prices, but no markets, manager authority but not control. And it didn't address agriculture, which has always been a critical sector of the Russian economy. As a result, no surge of economic benefits was felt that might have withstood the political counteroffensive that soon killed the Kosygin plan.[19]

The fifth set of reform movements is associated with Mikhail Gorbachev, who came to power in 1985. Gorbachev inherited a stagnant economy at a time when the costs of the Cold War were being keenly felt in the Soviet Union and Eastern Europe. Gorbachev had personal experience of both the failures of classical socialism and the successes of free markets, as he saw during his visit to Canadian farmers cited above. He proposed a set of widespread, comprehensive economic reforms, backed by the power he held as Communist party head. The key terms of the Gorbachev reforms were *glasnost* and *perestroika*. **Glasnost** means *openness*, the idea that the reforms would be carried out openly and discussed openly. Glasnost represented a small crack in the walls of power, providing a bit of political reform. Even this threatened the existing power structure, however. **Perestroika** means *restructuring* or *reformation*, referring to the attempt to implement widespread market reforms in the economy.

The perestroika reforms of the economy were clearly more ambitious than the glasnost reforms of the political sphere of Soviet life. But even perestroika was a half-measure—an attempt at transition more than revolution. Factory managers were, in theory, given greater authority to make production decisions, but the state planning bureaucracy was still in place and maintained its power, too. It was unclear just where the balance of power stood. Private ownership and private enterprise were encouraged, but prices remained regulated. It was unclear how markets could work without market prices.

As important as these structural and institutional problems, however, was the difficulty in effecting change in a system with such a long history of failed reforms. It was difficult to get people to adapt to a new system that they believed would not last. Why give up secure old ways for risky new ones? It is also difficult to change habits and attitudes that were shaped by long experience under classical socialism. The shift from classical socialism to markets is, for the people involved, more revolution than evolution. The lack of credible political change, which would alter the structure of power and authority, gave people little hope for substantive economic reform.

The most recent reform movement—as of this writing, the "sixth wave" of reform—is associated with Russian President Boris Yeltsin. The Yeltsin reforms are different in several respects from the earlier programs described previously. First, and most significant, is the fact that they occur after the collapse of communism, the end of the Cold War's bipolar security structure, and the breakup, in fact, of the Soviet Union into a collection of smaller nation-states. The Russia that Yeltsin inherited upon his 1990 election as president is different in fundamental ways from those of any previous twentieth century Russian leader. It was necessarily the case that economic reform be accompanied by political reform, since the structures of party control and civil governance had been transformed.

These more democratic political changes created an environment favorable to new external political and economic relationships, which could strengthen or reinforce the domestic reforms, as through aid or foreign investment. Yeltsin and his advisors could conceive of a "virtuous cycle" or reform. Political changes, weakening the party and the planning bureaucracy, would support market economic reforms. The economic changes, in turn, could raise living standards and thus validate the political reform. Under a "best case scenario," economic and political reforms would reinforce one another and move Russia smoothly if not quickly into the ranks of industrial democracies.

But the specter of a vicious cycle of policy reform lurked in the shadows. If the political reforms were weak or poorly supported, they might produce the sort of half-hearted and unsuccessful economic changes common in Russian and Soviet history. If these reforms failed to produce an economic dividend, or instead caused the economy to decline sharply, the result could be a political backlash against the reforms, perhaps a revolution back to hard-line Stalinist policies, or perhaps the rise of strongly nationalist policies.

Yegor Gaidar, the architect of Yeltsin's economic reforms, moved forcefully to implement economic reforms along a wide front. Price liberalization, privatization, and other reform schemes were adopted broadly and with little residual dependence on central planning. In general, the economy was opened up to market forces and the first steps to integrate it into the global economy were taken.

What will be the fate of the Yeltsin political and economic reforms or similar reform attempts that may follow? The early indicators of success were not promising. An attempt by Communist hard-liners to overthrow the Yeltsin government in 1993 ended in violence, with military units loyal to Yeltsin shelling the Parliament building in October 1993 to force out leaders of the political revolt. Political reform and political stability have not gone hand in hand, and there are some indications of the emergence of support for neofascist parties and candidates.

Early experience with economic reforms has been unfavorable as well. High inflation, rapid depreciation of the ruble, and falling production has resulted in a dramatic reduction in average living standards for many Russians. The economic growth that reformers promise may appear eventually, but in the short run the pain of reform is real.

Significantly, it may be the problems of political reform that limit attempts at economic reform. Modern democratic governments respond to organized interests above all, and in postcommunist states, perhaps the most powerful and best organized political interests are those who oppose change. The ability of these interest groups to oppose and ultimately to block change—both economic and political— cannot be overstated. The fundamental constitutional questions of how to balance competing interests and resolve conflict are yet to be answered.

At first glance, then, the vital signs of the Yeltsin reforms look weak. Economic success is not supporting the political reforms, and political crises have weakened the backing for the new economic policies. But Yeltsin's program may not be doomed. Economic and political assistance from foreign governments and international agencies could help support the changes now under way. In addition, the slow task of opening Russia to the structures of the global economy should eventually bear fruit. Perhaps the new international environment will help these domestic reforms succeed where past attempts failed. Russia's fate is of critical importance. "Will Russia's reforms succeed?" is one of the half-dozen most important questions in IPE today. Russia is, however, only the largest of the many states that became sovereign when the Soviet Union broke up. Russian reforms, therefore, do not happen in a vacuum. The success or failure of other "formers" will have consequences for economic and political reform in Russia.

CASE STUDY: "SHOCK THERAPY" IN POLAND

Poland's experience of economic and political reform is much different from the history of reform in Russia and the Soviet Union, and perhaps offers some hint of the prospects for successful change in other countries. As of this writing, Poland's reforms are widely seen as a success. Although Poland's political stability is still somewhat uncertain following the success of some former Communists in recent elections, its economy has expanded dramatically. Indeed, Poland was the fastest growing economy in Europe in 1993–1994. Poland's application for membership in the European Union will be given serious consideration.

Poland and Russia differ in so many important ways that it is difficult to present a valid comparison of their transition experience. Poland is much smaller, of course, and its experience of classical socialism is a good deal shorter than Russia's. The most importance difference for our purposes, however, is that in Poland political reform preceded economic reform and was the driving force for it. The real history of transition in Poland probably begins with the founding of the Solidarity trade union in 1980. Although many of the goals of Solidarity were really economic, the thrust was purely political. Led by shipyard worker Lech Wałesa, Solidarity used strikes and political activism to make political gains in the Soviet-backed Communist regime that held power.

By 1989, when a Solidarity-led government was elected, conditions were right for transition to a market system. The Polish economy was, by this point, in a thoroughly miserable condition because of the breakdown of planning authority during the final months of the Communist regime. Inflation was high, international debts at crisis level, and production in a deep slump. Finance Minister Leszek Balcerowicz reacted with a *shock therapy* program, designed to make the transition from planned economy to market economy in one giant step. There were several reasons for the choice of shock therapy rather than a gradual liberalization, as we have seen in Russia. The first was that political reform was already in progress and economic reform was part of Solidarity's platform. The second reason was that even relatively unpleasant economic reforms, if they contained a glimmer of hope for the future, would be well received, after the struggle against the recent trend of dismal planned economic performance with little hope for improvement. The third reason was the simplest: necessity. By 1990, the Polish economy was in such terrible shape that *something* had to be done.

The Solidarity economic reforms aimed to make the transition to a market economy in a "big bang" instead of a slow leak. Balcerowicz eliminated most price controls, lowered barriers to foreign trade and investment, moved to make the currency, the zloty, convertible, and engaged in widespread privatization of state-owned firms. All these internal policies were supported effectively by international agencies such as the IMF and the World Bank.

By 1993, Poland finally saw the benefits of economic reform. Industrial production, which fell by more than 40 percent, finally advanced above its pre-reform level, fueled now by private firms, not state enterprise. Inflation was lower and other key indicators of the economy's condition were stabilized. The tangible benefits of economic restructuring—more jobs, stable wages, and well-stocked store shelves—could now be glimpsed.

Just one year later, Poland's prospects looked downright rosy. Poland successfully renegotiated its international debts in 1994, laying the groundwork for a surge in foreign investment. Although unemployment was still uncomfortably high, living standards still far below those of European Union nations, and the political equilibrium still uncertain (ex-Communists did well in Polish elections), economic growth was strong and there was great optimism about the nation's future.

Poland learned that "shock therapy" is painful, but that market liberalizations can work—if they are backed by a strong state commitment. Poland also learned, however, that market gains are seldom universal. Some citizens gained tremendously from the opportunities presented by free markets and more open borders. Others, however, suffered great losses and saw their living standard plummet. Poland took seriously the challenge of creating a "social safety net" of government programs to help those left behind by the market changes. Poland's programs were limited, however, because of the nation's inherent resource limitations and the many other problems the government also faced.

There is a political riddle hidden in Poland's apparent economic success. Poland moved quickly to a democratic system of government, but does the elected government make policy? The painful "shock therapy" reforms have prevailed, while the elected government has changed. "Shock therapy" continued even when political leaders seemed to oppose it. Economic policy, it seems, is more potent at this point than political leadership. While Poland's economy appears on the road to good health, therefore, the same cannot be said with confidence about its institutions of democratic government.

Poland's reforms started sooner than Russia's, were broader and deeper in their ambitions, and had firmer political support. While it took three or four years for the first real gains to be realized, when they came they were significant and helped solidify backing for further reforms. Economic reforms in Hungary and the Czech Republic, adopted after Poland's "big bang," appear headed toward the same relative success.

CASE STUDY: CHINA'S TRANSITION TO MARKET SOCIALISM

The transition from planned economy to market economy has gone on the longest in the People's Republic of China and has achieved the greatest success. In 1992, *The Economist* reported that

> A visitor to China this autumn—provided he can secure a seat on the vastly overbooked flights going from Hong Kong or Tokyo—is greeted on arrival by the world's biggest economic boom. Shops are clogged with people buying consumer goods, often costly ones like western designed clothes. Factories, offices and homes are being built as fast as round-the-clock construction crews can put them up.[20]

China's economic success may inspire other nations engaged in political and economic reform, but China's case is unique and any attempt to distill lessons from China's experience must take into account its special features. The first and perhaps most important factor is that, unlike Russia and Poland, China's goal has been to introduce market forces to stimulate the economy but without giving up Communist party power.[21] China's, then, is a transition from classical socialism to market socialism or, put another way, from communism to what some have called "market Leninism."[22] China intends economic reform without political change, which reduces some state-market tensions but magnifies others.

After the Communist revolution in 1949, Chinese leader Mao Zedong introduced a classical socialist system based on the Stalinist model, with state ownership of the means of production, collective farms, and other features described earlier in this chapter. Under Mao, China tried many different programs to generate economic growth while preserving state control. The Great Leap Forward, for example, was a vigorous attempt to push industrial development. During the Cultural Revolution, however, Western influences were discouraged and attention returned to traditional communist values. Some early efforts at market-based reform were attempted.

After Mao's death, Deng Xiaoping assumed leadership and introduced a plan for economic reform, which was adopted by the Central Committee of the Communist party of China in December 1978. Deng's program was called "the bird in the cage," the free bird of the market growing and flying, but held within the sturdy cage of central planning control. The metaphor of the caged bird is useful in understanding the tensions of economic reform in China. The free bird and its cage are antithetical— at some point they cannot both exist. Either the bird is uncaged, or it is not free—or some new order emerges.

Deng's reforms, implemented in 1979, aimed to reform the economy by planting the seeds of individual enterprise deep in China's culture while simultaneously opening China to the global economic environment. Internal reform focused on agriculture and the hundreds of millions of Chinese workers tied to the land. Deng broke up the communal forms, expanding the size of private farm plots. Collective farms were replaced with traditional family units, which were allowed to sell excess produce through free markets. Agricultural production increased dramatically as these reforms took root. The increasingly prosperous family farms stimulated growth of private rural enterprises as well. At the same time, Deng's plan created "the open door." Barriers to international trade and finance were lowered, opening China to global markets and foreign investment.

Taken together, these two reforms created an environment highly favorable to economic development. The agricultural reforms, which created a free market in food, brought immediate gains to the population. Food producers were more efficient and their efforts better rewarded, while food consumers benefited from increased production. These short run gains were then followed by long-term improvements in China's economic health due to its increased involvement in international trade and the resources it gained through foreign investment.[23]

Deng's 1979 reforms introduced market forces in two important sectors of China's economy (the birds), but retained central planning in industry and elsewhere (the cage). China is so large, however, that it was possible to experiment with even more radical reform plans, and four "special economic zones" were created to attract additional foreign investment and gain experience with a market-based system. These four zones were strategically located to take advantage of commerce with Hong Kong, and their dramatic success in industrialization eventually led to the creation of additional "special zones" in other regions.

So successful was Deng's 1979 program that it was followed by market-oriented reforms in the industrial sectors in 1984 and then again in 1987. Taken together

> These developments have created an economy that looks less socialist all the time. China's industrial structure resembles that of its East Asian neighbors far more than that of its former ideological friends in Russia and Eastern Europe. Chinese industrial output is dominated by a huge number of small firms rather than vice versa. . . . Mr. Deng said he was aiming to build "socialism with Chinese characteristics." It is now obvious that he has been building capitalism with Chinese characteristics.[24]

The increasingly ambitious flights of the market bird have put more and more strain on the central planner cage. The freedom movement of the late 1980s, which reached its zenith in the Tiananmen confrontation and massacre of 1989, was a clear sign of the conflict between individual rights and state control. At many points throughout China, the logic of the market and the rule of the state have crossed paths, creating conflict and tension. This is especially true in the many areas where market forces put new demands on the state—for example, for greater infrastructure investment freer trade, and control of inflation. Such rapid changes in the market inevitably affect the state. How will the Communist party react, especially in the coming years as its leadership changes to the next generation?

While some inside and outside argue that China needs a "big bang" of political reform, Chinese leaders argue for a careful, pragmatic approach, stressing regions and experimental zones, and avoiding extremes. They have called this careful process "crossing the river by feeling the stones underfoot" (as opposed, presumably, to crossing the river by throwing yourself into it). This careful pragmatic approach may be the right one for China, given its massive size and recent history. The economic benefits the Chinese have experienced in the last fifteen years may have strengthened the foundation of the state as much as it has created tension in the planning bureaucracy. The market river, however, rushes faster and faster, and there may not be time to feel each stone on the riverbed.

In many respects, however, all the real questions about China are political. What will happen when Deng dies, as he will? Will the state remain unified with the party? Or will the competition we see in markets be transferred to the political arena? Will China remain a strong state, or will it fragment, as other postcommunist nations have?

In the years since 1979, China has had great success in introducing free markets while retaining a considerable measure of power in the Communist party and the bureaucracy. How the increasing state-market tensions and interactions will be resolved in the end is still uncertain.

STATES AND MARKETS IN TRANSITION: TENSIONS, ISSUES, AND LESSONS

The following story is told of the Mao-era Chinese leader Zhou Enlai who visited Paris and toured the site of the Bastille and other monuments to the 1789 French Revolution. As a famous revolutionary himself, Zhou was asked to give his opinion of the outcome of the French Revolution—was it a success? It was, he said, *too soon to tell.*[25]

Zhou was really making two points with this comment. The first is that great changes take a long time to work themselves out. The birth of communism in 1917 is still having important effects. Who knows how long it will take for the effects of the collapse of communism to be fully felt? But Zhou also meant to say that change is a constant in IPE. Like rocks and pebbles tossed into a pond, the direct and indirect effects spread and mix, forming many patterns on the water's surface.

This is the problem we have today when considering the transition from communism to market socialism or capitalism. Such great changes, happening at such speed, taking place in a dynamic international environment, are hard for us to fully digest. Who knows how long it will take for the results to become apparent?

In the meantime, we search for clues, and there are some to be found. IPE provides the first clue: political economy today is distinctly *international* in character. China and Poland have experienced relative success in their efforts at transition because they have intentionally opened themselves to international influences. International aid has played an important part in Poland's adjustment to a new political economy system, while international trade and investment have been critical elements in China's success. Russia, in contrast, has had difficulty integrating itself into the international system, having been so long shut off from the international structures of production, finance, security, and knowledge. Perhaps as Russia gains experience and success in these areas, it will develop a set of external relations that better support its internal efforts at change.

A second lesson is that perhaps reform is an all-or-nothing proposition. Gradual reform in Russia has a long history of failure. "Shock therapy" in Poland, and roughly equivalent wholesale regional economic liberalizations in China, appear to be relatively successful. There may be both political and economic reasons for these differences. Politically, it may be that a sudden and dramatic shift in political economy weakens interest groups that oppose change, especially the old communist elites. Gradual reform may give these groups the time and resources to block reforms. From an economic standpoint, it may be that the economy is too interdependent to be changed one sector or market at a time. The lack of reform in any one important part of the economy may doom reform elsewhere. A "big bang" of reform, with domestic policy and sound external support, may be the only real choice.

Here, tentatively, is a third lesson. Market forces are more alike than they are different because, perhaps, people in different countries at different times face such fundamentally similar economic problems. What differs—and therefore creates the difference in the transition away from communism—are history, culture, and especially the nature of the state. When states strongly support market changes, as in Poland and China, these transformations bear fruit. Weaker states, or states with weak commitments to change, have a history of failure. Effective political change may therefore be a necessary, but not sufficient, condition for economic change. It is necessary to create a credible state to engage in the new range of state-market interactions. This observation allows for cautious optimism regarding Russia and the other states and markets in transition. As *The Economist* has noted,

> Much of the current wave of reform is not just about giving Russia better economic policies or a more representative political system. It is also about creating a state within which better government and a more efficient economy are possible. Many of the reversals have been caused not by faults in policy design but by the difficulty of implementing any policy in a country that lacks some of the essential features of statehood. The sixth wave of reform can make Russia a modern state. Given time, it will. But it has not done so yet.[26]

DISCUSSION QUESTIONS

1. What is the "classical socialist system" and how does it differ from "communism"? What nations have adopted the classical socialist system at different times during the twentieth century? Which nations currently employ this system? Explain.

2. What are the essential characteristics of the classical socialist system? How does this system differ from market socialism and from capitalism? How do the roles of state and market differ among these three systems of political economy? Explain.

3. Compare and contrast the economic and political reforms in Russia and in Poland. Suggest factors that have made Poland's reforms more successful, at this point, than those in Russia. Are there any general lessons to be derived from this experience? Explain.

4. How are China's reform experiences different from those of Russia and Poland? Focus on differences in both means and ends. China aims to reform its market without a radical alteration in its political system. Is it possible to so dramatically change the market without changing the state? Explain.

SUGGESTED READINGS

Abel Aganbegyan. *The Economic Challenge of Perestroika*. Bloomington, IN: Indiana University Press, 1988.

"Don't Give Up Now: A Survey of Business in Eastern Europe." *The Economist*, 21 September 1991.

John King Fairbank. especially chs. 20–21 in *China: A New History*. Cambridge, MA: The Belknap Press, 1992.

Václav Havel. "A Call for Sacrifice." *Foreign Affairs* 73 (March/April 1994).

Shafiqul Islam. "Moscow's Rough Road to Capitalism." *Foreign Affairs* 72 (Spring 1993).

Paul Kennedy. *Preparing for the Twenty-first Century*. New York: Random House, 1993.

David Kennett and Marc Lieberman, (eds). *The Road to Capitalism*. Fort Worth, TX: The Dryden Press, 1992.

János Kornai. *The Socialist System: The Political Economy of Communism*. Princeton, NJ: Princeton University Press, 1992.

David Lipton and Jeffrey Sachs. "Creating a Market Economy in Eastern Europe: The Case of Poland." *Brookings Papers on Economic Activity* 1 (1990).

———. "Prospects for Russia's Economic Reforms." *Brookings Papers on Economic Activity* 2 (1992).

Dwight Perkins. "Completing China's Move the Market." *Journal of Economic Perspectives* 8 (Spring 1994).

Adam Przeworski. *Democracy and the Market*. Cambridge, England: Cambridge University Press, 1991.

"Rejoined: A Survey of Eastern Europe." *The Economist*, 13 March 1993.

Jeffrey Sachs and Wing T. Woo. "Structural Factors in the Economic Reforms of China, Eastern Europe, and the Former Soviet Union." *Economic Policy* 18 (April 1994).

Andrei Shleiffer and Robert W. Vishny. "The Politics of Market Socialism." *Journal of Economic Perspectives* 8 (Spring 1994).

Hedrick Smith. *The Russians*. New York: Times Books, 1976.

———. *The New Russians*. New York: Random House, 1990.

John Williamson, (ed). *The Political Economy of Policy Reform*. Washington, DC: Institute for International Economics, 1994.

David K. Willis. *Klass: How Russians Really Live*. New York: Avon Books, 1985.

NOTES

1. Karl Marx, *A Contribution to the Critique of Political Economy*, Preface, repr. in *Selected Works*, vol. 1 (New York: International Publishers 1942).

2. Václav Havel, "A Call for Sacrifice," *Foreign Affairs* 73 (March/April 1994): 2–7.

3. Classical socialism is sometimes called *state socialism* to make clear its difference from *market socialism*.

4. See János Kornai, *The Socialist System: The Political Economy of Communism* (Princeton, NJ: Princeton University Press, 1992).

5. Excerpted from Table 1–1, of Kornai, *The Socialist System*, 6–7. The reference date for this list is 1987, before the collapse of communist governments in Eastern Europe.

6. János Kornai's book *The Socialist System* is the main reference for the material in this section, especially as it concerns economic structure.

7. Hedrick Smith, *The Russians* (New York: Times Books, 1976), 28–29.

8. See Smith, *The Russians*, 81–101 for a discussion of black markets in the Soviet Union.

9. This story is repeated often enough that it might be true. If so, there is no record of what happened to the nail factory in the third year.

10. Hedrick Smith, *The New Russians* (New York: Random House, 1990), 74.

11. Abel Aganbegyan, *The Economic Challenge of Perestroika* (Bloomington, IN: Indiana University Press, 1988) 65.

12. Adam Przeworski, *Democracy and the Market* (Cambridge, England: Cambridge University Press, 1991), 189.

13. This can be done, for example, by giving each citizen a share in each "privatized" industry, with some shares perhaps retained in state ownership. Shares can then be bought and sold and a corporate board elected. Communal ownership is thus replaced by widespread private ownership of key industries.

14. See John Maynard Keynes, "A Short View of Russia," in his *Essays in Persuasion* (New York: Norton, 1963), 297–311.

15. This is not a new pattern. Students of U.S. history will remember that the U.S. Constitution replaced the previous Articles of Confederation.

16. Michael McFaul, "Why Russia's Politics Matter," *Foreign Affairs* 74 (January/February 1995): 89.

17. When our colleague Professor Ted Taranovski hears someone discussing the "Russian revolution," for example, he is compelled to ask, "Which one?" The many revolutions of Russia are notable for their *compound* impacts as much if not more than their separate effects.

18. "Russia: The Sixth Wave," *The Economist*, 5 December 1992, 17.

19. For an excellent short discussion of the Kosygin and Gorbachev reforms, see "Russia's Last Chance," *The Economist*, 11 March 1989, 85–86.

20. "When China Wakes: A Survey of China," *The Economist*, 28 November 1992, 4.

21. This makes China's reforms much like the Kosygin reforms in the Soviet Union.

22. Nicholas D. Kristof, "China Sees 'Market-Leninism' as a Way to Future," *The New York Times*, 6 September 1993, 1.

23. In the spirit of the caged bird, however, these foreign investments were tightly regulated and often took the form of partnerships with state enterprises.

24. "When China Wakes: A Survey of China," 8.

25. Quoted in Simon Shama's book on the French revolution, *Citizens* (New York: Knopf, 1989), xiii.

26. "Russia: The Sixth Wave," 26.

Part IV

IPE North and South

Many of the most interesting and important IPE problems revolve around what are termed "North-South" relations. The "North" is made up of the industrialized nations that were first to develop and have grown to be relatively rich. The "South" consists of the poorer, less industrialized nations of the world, many of which are former colonies of "North" states. North-South is therefore IPE shorthand for rich-poor, with differences in wealth creating further differences in power, status, and influence.

The three chapters in part IV look at three different aspects of North-South IPE that are especially relevant today. Chapter 15 examines the "development dilemma:" the particular problems of "South" countries that have conditioned their economic development or lack thereof. This chapter examines the differences between the newly industrialized countries (the NICs), which have achieved industrialization and development success, versus the plight of the many less developed countries (LDCs).

Chapter 16 tackles a particularly controversial aspect of North-South IPE—that of multinational corporations (MNCs). MNCs are seen by some as engines of growth for LDCs, and by others as tools of exploitation. Chapter 16 lays out the arguments clearly and without bias, inviting you to make up your own mind.

Finally, chapter 17 looks at the political economy of oil and energy. Oil is a commodity that for a hundred years has linked the industrialized nations of the North with the resource-rich regions of the South. The IPE of oil provides a particularly important case study of North-South relations and their political and economic implications.

15

The Development Dilemma: NICs and LDCs

Professor Sunil Kukreja

OVERVIEW

A pervasive problem of the international political economy is the tension that exists between the industrialized countries of the North and the less developed countries of the South. A major source of that tension is a series of issues related to what is commonly referred to as the *development dilemma*. For much of the twentieth century, the overwhelming majority of the world's population who live in developing nations have not experienced the kind of economic prosperity and affluence the vast majority of people in developed countries have. An obvious question is: given the great amount of wealth produced in the world each year, why have so many less developed countries (LDCs) remained impoverished, "underdeveloped," or "undeveloped"? The issue of development has confronted most of the LDCs since the middle of this century, when many of them formally became independent nations. For the most part, economic development is an objective many LDCs are unlikely to achieve well into the next century.

There are many theories about the causes of underdevelopment and what to do about it. This chapter examines some of those theories and explores other aspects of the development dilemma. It provides a brief overview of the broad economic but also political and social disparities that distinguish the developed and the newly developing from the less developed LDCs. Discussion turns to the origin of these gaps—the historical context and circumstances that resulted in depressed circumstances that many LDCs find themselves in. Also examined is LDC use of international organizations as a mechanism for change in some of the institutions and processes of the international political economy.

While economic development does not appear to be forthcoming for many developing nations for a variety of reasons, the newly industrialized countries are the success stories of development in the postwar era. This chapter also explores the factors that account for the success of many of the NICs and some key obstacles for the LDCs in Africa, where development remains most elusive.

What the countries of the South have in common transcends their differences; it gives them a shared identity and a reason to work together for common objectives. . . . The primary bond that links the countries and peoples of the South is their desire to escape from poverty and underdevelopment.[1]

The South Commission (1990)

Development (or the lack thereof) is a global problem, not confined only to poor nations. Parts of industrialized-developed nations remain underdeveloped. One need only travel through the old industrial sections or decaying regions of almost any industrialized nation to realize they have more in common with some of the developing nations than they do with their own. However, as this century comes to a close, the great majority of the world's population is located in less developed regions of the world where the standard of living pales in comparison to that in the industrialized nations. The international political economy is marked by two significant income gaps. One is the widely recognized gap between the rich and poor nations, and the other is the growing differences between groups of LDCs.

The industrialized nations have, for the most part, achieved a certain level of development—a term generally associated with economic growth and that connotes a modern nation. *Development* is defined as the ability of a nation to produce economic wealth, which in turn transforms society from a subsistence- or agricultural-based economy to one where most of society's wealth is derived from the production of manufactured goods and services. In developed-industrialized societies, the majority of the population usually lives in urban-industrial areas, are quite literate, and are well fed and housed. Per capita incomes in industrialized nations generally range from about $12,000 to more than $21,000 per year.[2]

The characteristics of LDCs usually contrast sharply with those of the developed nations.[3] Most LDCs exhibit very low income levels. Average yearly income varies from roughly $500 to $1,000, although several nations have per capita income of only about $300. Starvation caused by war or drought may be present in some nations, while in many others, as many as one third of the population is seriously malnourished (they lack certain food nutrients; see chapter 18). One half of all people in LDCs do not have adequate drinking water, lack basic shelter, and are illiterate. These conditions are all directly attributable to poverty, or the lack of income to demand products in the market. An estimated 80 percent of the world's wealth is possessed by a minority of the world's population, most of whom live in the industrialized nations, while the vast majority of humanity living in LDCs must share the other 20 percent of the world's wealth.

The growing gap between rich and poor nations raises questions about equity and fairness related to the distribution of the world's resources.[4] Increasingly, though, another gap between nations is getting more attention, and that is the vast differences in levels of development between LDCs. Development efforts and other circumstances have produced gradations of success. In the 1950s and 1960s, LDCs had a great deal in common, especially their colonial history and potential for growth. More recently, a few have begun to realize some economic success. By 1990, the leading East and Southeast Asian economies such as Singapore, Taiwan, South Korea, Malaysia, and Hong Kong were some of the fastest growing economies in the world. Yet many low-income developing countries (especially in sub-Saharan Africa) continue to struggle with widespread poverty and a lower overall standard of living. Within the developing regions of the world, there appear to be at least four categories of nations: the richer oil-exporting nations; the economically dynamic NICs; the poorest countries, which include the sub-Saharan African nations; and the majority of other LDCs who are still thought of as third world nations.

A few economic indicators demonstrate this trend. Between 1965 and 1989, for example, Niger's average per capita GNP growth rate was –2.4 percent, while oil-rich Oman experienced an annual average of 6.4 percent. Even more vivid has been the performance of economies like Singapore and Taiwan—both averaging a per capita GNP growth of approximately 7 percent between 1965 and 1989. Disparities between LDCs is also reflected in regional growth trends. Over this same period, sub-Saharan Africa lagged furthest behind in its economic performance, with an annual average GNP (per capita) growth rate of 0.3 percent, as East Asia led the way with an average of 5.2 percent.[5]

These basic variations among regions are further complicated by severe disparities within regions and even within nations as well. In the fast growing regions of East and Southeast Asia, Singaporeans enjoy a per capita GNP of over $11,000, but nearby Indonesians less than $600. Similarly, Algeria enjoys a per capita GNP comparable to that of Argentina in South America and Malaysia in Southeast Asia, while its Egyptian neighbors have a GNP comparable to that of Indonesia. Another noteworthy contrast among LDCs is presented in Table 15–1. The low rate of economic growth in sub-Saharan countries is associated with a low adult literacy and life expectancy. By contrast, these indicators in East Asia and Latin America are approaching those of the developed regions.

The distribution of income within LDCs is difficult to measure. In most cases income distribution is heavily skewed in favor of a wealthy minority or powerful elite.

Income distribution remains one of the most controversial and urgent development problems. It drives to the heart of the matter—overcoming poverty and generating economic growth.

THE THIRD WORLD AND THE PARADOX OF ECONOMIC DEVELOPMENT

To understand the development dilemma, we must understand some of the history of the LDCs—how they came to be in the position they are in and what problems must be overcome by those less successful in their efforts. By the 1950s, many of the former European colonial empires and territories began to disintegrate and new nation-states emerged in their place. The dismantling of the colonial empires unfolded differently in Asia, Africa, and Latin America. By the end of the 1950s, many of the former colonies became independent and many more were on the threshold of a new international order shaped by the Cold War between the United States and the (former) Soviet Union. As these new nation-states began to shape their respective national identities, it appeared that the long-standing colonial domination of the West had come to a close. Politically, the third world had been born. Yet many of the newly formed nations of Asia, Latin America, and Africa confronted pressing and complex economic, political, and social problems that made it difficult to create truly sovereign national institutional structures.

Foremost on the agenda of many of the newcomers was the economic development dilemma—the lack of economic development and prosperity. The stark economic differences and disparities between the developed and less developed countries became the defining feature of what later became referred to as the *North-South dilemma*, the North consisting of the developed, industrialized countries of Western Europe and North America and the South being the LDCs of the world. The North-South distinction was more than a label; in fact, as we shall see in the next section, it also came to symbolize the often tense political and economic climate between the developed and less developed worlds. This inequality in wealth

TABLE 15–1   Selected Basic Indicators

REGION	LIFE EXPECTANCY (YEARS)		ADULT LITERACY (%)		GDP PER CAPITA ($)	
	1960	1990	1960	1990	1970	1990
Sub-Saharan Africa	40	51	28	47	N/A	N/A
East Asia	47	70	N/A	74	730	2,220
Southeast Asia	45	63	67	84	1,000	2,590
South Asia	44	58	33	42	700	1,250
Latin America and Caribbean	56	67	76	85	2,140	4,490
Arab States	46	62	30	51	1,310	3,380

Source: Human Development Report (1993) p. 213.

and prosperity became the centerpiece of the new problems and issues in the post-war international economic order.

For the LDCs, economic development was crucial not just as an end in itself, but also as a means for ensuring sustained political development, independence, and a cultural identity. Much of the success of the newly independent states in the postwar international climate as well as in domestic politics depended on the ability of leaders to deliver on the promises that helped propel nationalist and independence movements. As such, economic development—characterized by a growing and prosperous economy—was crucial in order to establish a national identity and also ensure political stability domestically.

In this postwar climate, with decolonization underway, at least four major forces shaped the development dilemma for LDCs. First, colonial wounds were in many ways still fresh and deep. In this regard, political leaders often viewed former colonial powers with some suspicion. The social and economic impact and exploits of colonialism and capitalism were surely responsible for the economic "backwardness" of their new nation-states. Second, the way many LDCs dealt with their development problem was not merely a response to politically and economically exploitative colonial conditions but a resistance to cultural domination by the West as well.[6] In some parts of the developing world, these sentiments helped shape a cautious approach to adopting Western influence and methods of economic development. As we shall see, this view of the developed countries by third world leaders remained quite strong and influential and became a central notion behind the solidarity of developing countries in the 1970s.

The third force to shape the economic development dilemma for many LDCs was the Cold War. Proximity to the United States or its allies or historical connections to former mother countries often shaped the kind of political and economic strategies LDCs chose when it came to economic development. Likewise, support for the Eastern bloc of nations by some LDCs blended with a preference for non-Western development strategies.

Finally, and paradoxically, the economic success of the developed countries also provided a strong rationale for some LDCs to follow in their footsteps, or at least adopt market-oriented prescriptions for economic development. The emergence of new international institutions like the IMF, the World Bank, and the General Agreement on Tariffs and Trade (GATT), whose role was to coordinate international trade, symbolized the expanding significance of the market in the world economy. To many observers (especially in less developed regions), these institutions were largely controlled by the developed countries. The political significance of pursuing a Western economic development strategy would also signal a tacit association with the West in the Cold War. Yet, in many cases, association with Western institutions offered real opportunities LDCs had to consider in their formula for pursuing a partnership with the industrialized nations and economic development. Hence, the participation of the LDCs in the postwar international economy with the developed countries remained as a debatable option.

These forces combined to set the stage for the dynamics of the development process and North-South relations in the later stages of the Cold War. In the next section, we turn directly to the substance of the North-South dialogue that represented much of the framework for addressing development issues and problems.

THE NORTH-SOUTH DEBATE

Recognizing that, individually, LDCs were unable to exert significant influence on the international system and its institutions, a number of countries, mainly from the Southern developing region of the world, attempted to promote a collective identity. The 1955 Afro-Asian Bandung Conference in Indonesia is widely regarded as the first major step to forging that identity and is the genesis of what came to be viewed as a Southern perspective. Lead by Jawaharlal Nehru of India, Marshal Tito of Yugoslavia, Achmed Sukarno of Indonesia, and Gamal Abdel Nasser of Egypt, heads of state from the developing countries initiated a dialogue among themselves that subsequently led to the formation of the Non-Aligned Movement in 1961. As a political banner of many newly independent LDCs, the Non-Aligned Movement expanded to include a number of countries from Latin America. This movement served three purposes. First, it was to be the LDCs' political arm for addressing initiatives against the remaining remnants of colonialism (especially in Africa). Second, it was to be their vehicle for positioning themselves outside the sphere of the Cold War scenario, and lastly, it was to promote the interests of the LDCs.

One of the main priorities of what came to be referred to as the *Southern nations* was the issue of neocolonialism, or the continued economic domination of LDCs by the industrialized countries. A number of political leaders and intellectuals[7] argued that while the era of colonialism was largely over, former colonies were basically trapped in a capitalist international economic system dominated by institutions and mechanisms tilted in favor of the developed countries. In a "neocolonial" environment, multinational corporations and their subsidiaries, for instance, owned and controlled a substantial part of LDC economic resources. Often backed by their home-based governments, the wealth and political influence of multinationals gave them and the industrialized nations the ability to control international markets of commodities from LDCs.

One such scenario frequently noted was the case of oil companies. For much of the twentieth century, seven major (Western) oil companies controlled the exploration, processing, and supply of oil in a number of oil-rich regions. These "seven sisters," as they were known, often worked to divide the market share, regulate supply, and preserve their control over resources in developing countries. In varying degrees, these companies were seen to be supported by their respective home governments. With such political support, the major oil companies negotiated terms (involving some royalty for the host country) that ensured the companies control of oil exploration and distribution in the international market.[8]

Advocates of the neocolonial argument claimed that complementing the domination of multinational corporations was a restrictive system of trade, financial, and technological transfer that compounded the economic vulnerability of LDCs and weakened development prospects. In chapter 6, we discussed the LDC claim that the international terms of trade committed them to be producers of raw materials and primary goods. LDCs were disadvantaged by the head start the industrialized nations got in the production of value-added products and their extensive use of protectionist trade measures. Technological innovations and gains in productivity largely occurred in the developed countries, and the LDCs found themselves lagging and unable to compete in the areas of new product development or production. Tight legal controls, copyrights, and licensing often curbed LDCs' access to such technology. The financial power of large multinationals, coupled with the developed countries' influence on the international financial system, also meant that developed countries and multinationals could influence the LDCs' access to funds for economic development.

UNCTAD AND THE NIEO

Frustrated by their efforts to develop, increasing numbers of LDCs turned to their membership in international organizations to foster third world solidarity and momentum for change in the international political economy. In 1964, the United Nations Conference on Trade and Development (UNCTAD) was established largely through the efforts of seventy-seven LDCs that became known as the Group of 77 (G-77). UNCTAD meets roughly every four years in the capital city of an LDC. While its membership has increased over the years, G-77 has been the LDCs' representative organization at UNCTAD sessions. The G-77 sought to make UNCTAD a mechanism for dialogue and negotiation between the LDCs and the developed countries on trade, finance, and other development issues. At UNCTAD I, the G-77 proposed a new international trade organization to replace GATT. For the most part, the developed countries resisted UNCTAD initiatives when it came to trade and other economic activities. Nevertheless, through UNCTAD, LDCs were gradually able to secure some concessions and preferential treatment—a Generalized System of Preferences (GSPs)—on tariffs for their exports to developed nations.

The Organization of Petroleum Exporting Countries (OPEC)[9] helped generate attention to Southern concerns in 1973 when this cartel made up of oil-producing LDCs embargoed oil shipments to some of the industrialized nations and significantly raised the price of oil (see chapter 17). A 400 percent increase in the price of oil jolted the developed economies and temporarily altered the global balance of political and economic power. By extension it also complicated the development dilemma.

Following World War II, the industrialized countries (in spite of the postwar reconstruction, or perhaps largely fueled by it) had experienced considerable economic growth. Western oil companies dominated the petroleum industry from exploration to marketing, and had historically provided cheap and abundant access to the energy needs of the industrialized world. The cartel's pricing actions helped dampen economic growth and spurred an inflationary trend in the developed countries. From the standpoint of relations between the developed and less developed nations, the latter was to gain considerable leverage for the time being. The developed countries—being highly dependent on oil-exporting countries for their energy—could no longer ignore the considerable impact oil-producing countries from the South had on the economic well-being of the industrialized world.

OPEC political and economic leverage resulted in the 6th Special Session of the UN General Assembly in 1974, which called for the establishment of a *New International Economic Order* (NIEO). This program for action was designed largely to facilitate the pace of development among LDCs and change the unequal economic balance between the LDCs and the industrialized nations. The development prospects of the LDCs were believed to be intimately tied to the larger functioning of the world economic order. Unlike previous efforts, the NIEO was seen by LDCs not so much as an attempt to fine-tune the existing international economic order but an effort to elevate the issue of economic development to the top of the international agenda, changing respective institutional structures and making them more conducive to LDC development concerns. The NIEO included calls for:

1. Creation of an integrated program for commodities (IPC), to stockpile and control the price of commodities during periods of oversupply and scarcity
2. Extension and liberalization of GSPs
3. Development of a debt-relief program
4. Increasing official development assistance from the rich, developed nations of the North to the less developed South
5. Changing the decision-making process in major international institutions such as the United Nations, IMF, and the World Bank to give more voice to Southern nations and reduce developed nations' control of these institutions
6. Increasing the economic sovereignty of LDCs. Several initiatives were stipulated under this umbrella. Key among them were: ensuring LDCs' greater control over their natural resources; increased access to Western technology; the ability to regulate multinationals; and preferential trade policies that would stabilize prices for commodities from LDCs and ensure these countries greater access to developed countries' markets.

Despite the United Nations' adoption of these objectives, its implementation in the years that followed remained incomplete. A number of factors contributed to the lack of the NIEO's success. Foremost among these was the general opposition of the industrialized countries to the NIEO initiatives, making its implementation difficult. These countries, led by the United States, did not consider the initiatives as central to the development concerns and dilemma of LDCs. Furthermore, many officials argued that the initiatives promoted an atmosphere of "micromanaging" the global economy, a task that, on the one hand, would be impractical, and on the other, restrictive of the free market. Finally, many officials of the industrialized nations interpreted Southern demands for a NIEO as a political threat related to an effort by radical LDCs to redistribute global wealth and power.

Further, while the OPEC oil crisis created momentum for cooperation among LDCs to seek substantive institutional reforms through the NIEO initiatives, the LDCs were plagued by competing and conflicting national interests, which often un-

dermined their attempts at cooperation and unity. OPE
the prosperity of its member states added to the disp
among the LDCs. Although OPEC made small loans ar
members were more inclined to pursue their own na
interests rather than use their collective strength to pr
the NIEO initiatives.

Added to this, the international oil crisis also
problems for the non-oil producing LDCs. For many poor LD
cost of energy simply compounded already acute economic problems.
many of the poorer LDCs became increasingly dependent on the private banks
the developed countries and other multilateral institutions for financing their balance of payment deficits. The cumulative effect of the oil crisis was a global recession, which may well have hit the non-oil-producing LDCs harder than the more stable developed economies. This merely served to deflect attention from the NIEO and undermined the position of the LDCs.[10]

It is important to recognize that the unfolding of the North-South dialogue was shaped by fundamental theoretical debates, each presenting a different interpretation about the political economy of development and proposing different paths for development. In the following section, we survey three different perspectives on development.

THE LIBERAL MODEL AND ECONOMIC DEVELOPMENT

Much of the North's resistance to the efforts of the South to restructure the international political economy reflects the North's conviction about the functioning of the international market and the performance of the liberal model of economic development. Two general and interrelated points characterize the North's position on the economic development question in the South.

Advocating the liberal or Western model of development, the United States and other developed countries have insisted that with active participation and integration into the global market, LDCs would, in due course, experience economic growth. Trade is the primary stimulus—the "engine to growth" as it were—for increasing productivity and raising income levels in an LDC. Integration in the international economy through trade is supposed to stimulate growth, diffuse new technologies, generate investments, and transform traditional social-cultural practices that are incompatible with the market ethos. As "latecomers," LDCs undertaking efforts to use the market to develop and industrialize have a distinct opportunity and hindsight to benefit from the pitfalls and policy mistakes of the now developed North. Such hindsight translates into less waste of resources and inefficiency, but also accelerates the development process for LDCs.

One of the critical features of the liberal model is that a major obstacle to economic development in LDCs stems from the anemic capital, productivity, and technological base of the economy. Added to these constraints are other institutional structures in many LDCs, such as a weak infrastructure and educational sysem, along with traditional cultural value systems that hinder the prospects for development. Following this line of reasoning, the liberal model largely deemphasizes the importance of international political and economic structural conditions in explaining the process of economic development (or lack thereof). Instead, it focuses on the internal conditions in LDCs that promote or stifle economic development.[11]

One of the most influential liberal assessments of the development dilemma to emerge was the work of W. W. Rostow.[12] According to Rostow, like the developed nations of the North, the less developed South must undergo a series of changes in their socioeconomic system in order to develop and industrialize. This "evolutionary" change is represented by a series of stages of economic growth that society passes through on its way to development. Traditional society experiences low levels of economic productivity due to the lack of technological development and a traditional social system of fatalistic values where individuals are constrained by rigid social goals. Increases in education and literacy, entrepreneurship, and investments in raw material and infrastructure expand the level of commercial activity. The seeds of economic growth are planted, even if new ideas that create a good deal of disharmony, even conflict, in society bring about changes that are compatible with the process of economic development.

In the critical "take-off" stage, the pace of change accelerates. New industries increase rapidly as the entrepreneurial spirit becomes more dominant. The emergence of a capitalist class accelerates the change by initiating new economic activity, industrialization, and adopting new production processes. Conversely, the influence of traditional social values and goals diminishes. Existing economic activities such as extraction of raw materials and agriculture are also modernized. Later stages are characterized by the use of advanced technology and a relatively high level of savings and investment (approximately 15 to 20 percent of GNP) that sustains the drive to economic maturity. Countries with a higher level of savings and investments are, according to Rostow, more likely to grow and develop at a much faster rate than those with a lower savings rate. The final stage of mass consumption and self-sustaining growth follows when the major sectors of the economy are able to meet the consumer demands for goods and services for a large cross section of the population, which helps sustain the high level of economic activity.

Rostow's theory of economic development was largely based on the historical experience of Western nations, especially Britain and the United States. He perceived the stages of development as universal, arguing that in the long run, the North can model the development process for the South. The historical development and diffusion of technology will inevitably lead to changes that are necessary in the early stages of the economic development process.

Multilateral development and financial institutions like the World Bank and the IMF have consistently been promoters of the liberal model. During the 1980s, for example, a number of LDCs (especially in Africa and Latin America) were entangled with an excessive debt burden, declining revenues from primary commodity exports, declining agriculture output, and overall economic stagnation. Desperately in need of external help, many were prescribed the *structural adjustment programs* (SAPs) by these international lending institutions. What is important to recognize is, like previous efforts, the SAPs reflected a strong endorsement of the liberal assumptions for development. These measures generally consisted of the same themes for the recipient government. Foremost among these were stabilizing the latter's financial situation, encouraging privatization in place of direct government involvement in operating industries, and opening the economy to international trade and competition.

While these policies were seen as draconian by many governments in Africa and Latin America, the IMF and World Bank saw them as essential measures in releasing these economies from the bureaucratic and inefficient tentacles of state control and artificial manipulation of the economy.

DEPENDENCY: DEVELOPMENT OR UNDERDEVELOPMENT?

By the 1960s, liberal assumptions about the development prospects for many LDCs came under intense criticism from a number of scholars, especially in Latin America. These critics of the liberal model of development were primarily from the United Nations' Economic Commission for Latin America (ECLA). Among the earlier critiques was the work of Raul Prebisch,[13] which provided a significant momentum for the dependency perspective and its interpretation of the development dilemma among LDCs.

A promoter of UNCTAD, Prebisch argued that the development dilemma in Latin America was inextricably linked to factors outside of the region. Prebisch was especially critical of the existing international division of labor and free trade system. He and others argued that international trade system reinforced the LDCs' role as producers of primary products and raw materials, while the developed countries continued to prosper as producers of industrial products. This international division of labor reinforced the dependence of the LDCs on the developed nations to be outlets for LDC primary products. In addition, production specialization also perpetuated LDC dependence on the developed countries for capital and technology, each of which were seen as essential for LDCs to generate economic development.

Dependence was considered particularly significant, as it contributed to the underdevelopment of the LDCs.[14] Early dependency theorists made a distinction between *under*development and *un*development. The latter was characterized by lack of development, the former by the outcome of a process that further regressed and undermined LDC economies while simultaneously contributing to the development of their counterparts in the industrial world. As such, underdevelopment in the LDCs was viewed as a product of the development process in industrialized regions. Underdevelopment and development were two facets of a singular global structure, much like the two sides of a coin.[15] Osvaldo Sunkel and Pedro Paz have noted that "both underdevelopment and development are aspects of the same phenomenon, both are historically simultaneous, both are linked functionally and, therefore, interact and condition each other mutually."[16]

This basic thesis represented the embryo of much of the analyses of dependency theorists during the 1960s and 1970s, and was most forcefully articulated by Andre Gunder Frank in *Capitalism and Underdevelopment in Latin America*. According to this perspective, underdevelopment has its origins in the colonial order and European expansion prior to the twentieth century. Through political domination, the colonial powers successfully extracted raw materials and resources necessary for their development while impoverishing their colonies. While the decolonization process removed the political dominance of the European powers, the basic economic linkage and division of labor between the two remained largely intact, resulting in neocolonialism. Frank argued that the international capitalist economic order was organized along the lines of a metropolis-satellite system (regions) in which the metropolis state exploited and controlled the satellite by extracting economic surplus and wealth from the latter.

There are a number of mechanisms that reproduce this relationship and deepen the underdevelopment process in LDCs. Through multinational corporations, profits generated in LDCs are transferred out of LDCs. Investments in technology and other innovations are often dated or inappropriate and do not enhance the competitive edge of LDCs. The extensive resources of the multinationals also enable them to circumvent restrictive and regulatory measures in LDCs. Another widely cited mechanism is the unequal exchange relationship. The LDCs' "comparative advantage" in primary products and raw material is highly vulnerable to international market prices, which are generally well below those of manufactured goods that LDCs have to import from the developed countries. Over time, this creates a massive net outflow of revenue.

According to some dependency theorists, another avenue of exploitation is the international financial system and foreign aid. Foreign banks of the wealthier nations gain a stronghold on private lending. Critics charge that these banks are less interested in the development of a country than they are in acquiring lucrative terms for loans to LDCs. This results in a form of extended financial dependence for the indebted country and generous interest receipts for foreign banks. These theorists are also skeptical about foreign aid. They argue that the political and economic strings attached to such assistance reinforces a dominant-subordinate relationship between the developed and less developed nations.[17]

Within this framework, a number of differing interpretations about the approach to change emerged. For Andre Gunder Frank, the capitalist world economy posed the biggest obstacle for LDCs. Development for the poorer countries was inconsistent with their continued integration into the world economy. Instead, a socialist path was the only solution to this dilemma. In cases such as China from the early 1960s until 1972, through state ownership and control, a nation's economy is restructured primarily by severing economic ties with the developed capitalist world. In place of this, mutually beneficial ties with other socialist countries are supposed to eliminate the exploitative relations that govern the capitalist world economy and reverse the underdevelopment process.

Other approaches to the dependency dilemma have been less radical. The import substitution path to development has been one such alternative. This strategy, highly mercantilist and nationalistic (although not anticapitalist) in character, advocates constraints on adverse external influences (such as foreign manufactured goods and multinational corporations) in order to promote self-sufficiency and internal development. In place of importing manufactured goods, local manufacturing is prescribed. Promoting these enterprises requires strict controls on imported goods to reduce competition from abroad. The state plays a direct role in controlling strategic industries like utilities and energy, which are fundamental to the resource base of a manufacturing economy. As we see in the next section, the import substitution path was indeed a popular one, especially among some major Latin American economies.

Finally, after a good deal of dissatisfaction with these different models, many LDCs have adopted what essentially amounts to a combination of all of them. The "self-reliance" model emphasizes mixing economic growth with efforts to redistribute income over the largest number of people so as to establish a firm economic base in a nation with unique conditions. Basic human needs are targets of public policy and poverty eradication efforts. Linkages with external sources of income through trade, aid, and foreign direct investment are conditioned upon control over them and their impact on the national economy. As with all of these models, the state plays a major role in controlling investment in rural and industrial sectors of the economy, and making political, social, and economic adjustments when necessary. And finally, as in other models, the goal of development is an industrial society with sufficient production to meet the needs of society. Very few development experts have attempted to devise a model of development that did not seek to achieve this outcome.

UJAMAA: AN EXPERIMENT IN SELF-SUFFICIENCY

Following independence in 1961, Tanzania—like other LDCs—sought development by promoting economic growth via the liberal development strategy. However, this effort was short-lived, as Tanzania was unable to address its acute economic problems. Declining revenues from cash crop exports—something that Tanzania relied on heavily—worsened its financial stability.[18] Added to this, Tanzania had an anemic industrial base, and together, these circumstances created unemployment problems for an already impoverished nation. In 1967, the charismatic President Julius Nyerere ushered in an alternative approach to development based on self-sufficiency.

Under his leadership, Tanzania implemented an elaborate system of populist socialism. The centerpiece of this model took advantage of the country's highly rural and agrarian socioeconomic structure. Through governmental action, thousands of agricultural collectives, known as Ujamaa villages, were established throughout the Tanzanian countryside. Contrary to the liberal development model, Nyerere's experiment emphasized that the traditional, rural community-based African culture provided a "natural" basis for instituting Ujamaa villages. These agrarian villages would be the vehicle for building a prosperous and equitable society.

In the process, millions of peasants were uprooted and relocated to these villages. Each village had about two hundred households, each with its own small plot of land,

Continued

UJAMAA: AN EXPERIMENT IN SELF-SUFFICIENCY, *continued*

and a communal farm with a central distribution location linking the households together. The agricultural production of each village was sold to the government and production was monitored and managed by a local coordinator.[19]

By the end of the 1970s, much of rural life in Tanzania had been transformed. Over a third of the villages had medical clinics available, and almost half had a clean water supply. Locally run schools in villages helped raise the literacy rate as well. However, Tanzania also incurred some heavy debts. High oil prices during the 1970s were a tremendous drain on its revenue, while Tanzania's export earnings declined over the same period. The impact of the international market, coupled with low productivity due to governmental inefficiencies and natural disasters, created severe shortages in food supply and resources.

By the end of the 1980s, Julius Nyerere's vision of development through populist socialism had lost most of its steam. As a result, Tanzania has had to restructure its restrictive trade policies and increasingly has looked to the major international donors and lending institutions for assistance. Ironically, it had to turn back to the very international organizations and market it had sought to distance itself from through this experiment in self-sufficiency.

THE NEWLY INDUSTRIALIZING COUNTRIES

Over the past three decades there have been significant changes in the economic development patterns for a number of countries, especially in Asia and Latin America. By the 1980s, South Korea, Taiwan, Hong Kong, and Singapore were widely being recognized as the new economic "tigers" in East Asia. The tremendous growth in these countries led many observers to increasingly group them as "newcomers" on the path to industrialization and development. Given recent growth rates in Malaysia and Thailand, these two countries are also being regarded as potential NICs. Ironically, high expectations since the 1950s for the third world to catch up with the industrial countries rested with the anticipated success of major Latin American countries like Argentina, Brazil, and Mexico. Instead, it has been the success of the East Asian NICs that has amazed, puzzled, and intrigued many. As one source puts it:

> The Asian NICs—Hong Kong, Singapore, South Korea, and Taiwan—have achieved growth rates virtually without historical precedent. . . . The speed with which the NICs have industrialized is astonishing. Nineteenth-century development in Europe and North America . . . pale in comparison with the record of the NICs.[20]

One illustrative comparison between the East Asian and Latin American NICs is presented in Table 15–2. By the end of the 1960s, the four East Asian NICs were outperforming the major Latin American economies in growth rate. This pattern continued through the 1970s, although Brazil's growth rate in the 1970s was comparable to that of South Korea and Hong Kong.

Although some sharp economic and historical differences distinguish each of the NICs from one another, an understanding of the contrasting success of the East

Asian and Latin American NICs can be found in the fundamentally different paths taken by these two groups of countries. South Korea and Taiwan, for example, have pursued a strategy known as *export-oriented growth*; in Latin America, Mexico and Brazil are two cases that began with the *import-substitution strategy*.

Export-oriented approach is based on a combination of liberal and mercantilist prescriptions for economic growth and development. For one, it calls for the state to strongly emphasize a country's comparative advantage in selected sectors of the economy and to promote exports from these sectors. However, instead of depending on a noninterventionist state and free-trade policies, the East Asian NICs aggressively pursued specific national and international policies that changed the basic structure and functioning of their economies. While there are specific differences between the East Asian NICs, certain common trends can be identified.

First, the export-oriented policies of East Asian NICs involved changing the fundamental composition of their production. Prior to the 1960s, like other developing countries, South Korea and Taiwan began promoting manufacturing with a particular emphasis on labor-intensive consumer goods. To accomplish this, the respective governments set up mercantilist-style restrictions to protect "infant" consumer manufacturing industries from foreign competition. This initial strategy had the added benefit of raising the level of employment, which theoretically also helped stabilize the political situation. The governments provided strong financial backing and incentives to promote manufacturing. (More on this point later.) The strategy used in this initial push to generate a viable manufacturing sector was not unlike that pursued by Japan in the earlier part of this century and later after World War II (see chapter 13).

By the late 1960s, South Korea and Taiwan began to ease into the next phase of restructuring. Specifically, these countries increased their international market share by promoting the export of domestically manufactured durable goods. State intervention again played a strategic role in launching this initial export promotion effort. Selective barriers on imported goods remained in place, although raw ma-

TABLE 15–2   Growth of Real GDP: Selected East Asian and Latin American NICs (Compounded Annual Percentage Change)

COUNTRY	1960–70	1970–80	1980–86
S. Korea	9.5	8.2	8.3
Taiwan	9.6	9.7	6.8
Hong Kong	9.3	8.7	6.2
Singapore	9.2	9.1	5.3
Argentina	3.0	2.5	–0.9
Brazil	N/A	8.6	2.8*
Mexico	7.0	6.6	0.7
Venezuela	6.1	4.1	–0.2

*(1980–85)

Source: Seiji Naya et al., eds., *Lessons in Development* (San Francisco: International Center for Economic Growth, 1989), 282–283.

terial imports necessary for manufacturing were not suppressed, and selected domestic manufacturing industries were targeted with fiscal incentives to stimulate the level of exports. Another policy was to devalue the national currency, making exports from these East Asian countries more competitive in the international marketplace and imports less attractive to consumers domestically.[21] In a sense, through these measures the NICs created comparative advantages for their manufactured products.

During the 1970s, South Korea's manufacturing sector expanded into heavy (technologically intensive) industries including steel, petrochemicals, and automobiles. By 1980, these efforts in restructuring the economy were bearing fruit. Manufacturing's share of GDP in South Korea climbed from 14 percent in 1960 to 30 percent in 1980 as agriculture's share decreased from 37 percent to 15 percent over the same period. In Taiwan, manufacturing's share of GDP increased from 22 percent (1960) to 42 percent (1980) and this shift corresponded with agriculture's decline from 29 percent to 8 percent.[22]

A second major component of this export-led growth strategy—one that is also seen by advocates of the liberal model as a crucial ingredient—involved promoting a high level of savings and investment (including intense efforts in research and development). The liberal perspective suggests that without the necessary capital, basic investments in infrastructure, resource development, and equipment, growth would be quite impossible. Hence, capital formation is central to development. Generally, the East Asian NICs have been very successful at structuring specific institutional and policy measures to achieve this goal. As Table 15–3 shows, in 1960, the four major East Asian NICs all had a savings rate well below the three major Latin American economies, and by 1970, the picture had changed considerably as the East Asian economies essentially matched the savings rate in the major Latin American economies.

A combination of factors (in varying degrees) contributed to this process. In South Korea, for example, an increase in personal household savings was a major source of savings, largely stimulated by raising interest rates on bank deposits. The government also helped establish private banks and financial institutions, which began to overshadow traditional and informal money markets widely used by small private customers. This financial policy allowed the government to increase its oversight of financial stability and savings in the economy.[23] The growth of financial institutions in Singapore and Hong Kong was also crucial to the capital formation process in these countries. Interestingly, the former developed an approach where government maintained a tight control and oversight over financial institutions while the latter leaned in the opposite direction of minimal regulation of the financial sector.[24]

This high savings rate among the East Asian NICs was also generated by maintaining strict controls on both public and private consumption. Strict fiscal policies have helped keep budget deficits well under control. One result of this deliberate fiscal approach was budget deficits that were among the lowest in the developing world and a persistently low inflation rate in the East Asian economies compared to their Latin American counterparts. In Hong Kong and Singapore (historically free-

TABLE 15–3   Gross Domestic Savings (Expressed as Percentage of GDP)

	1960	1970	1979	1986	1991
South Korea	1	15	28	35	37
Taiwan	13	26	N/A	36	N/A
Hong Kong	6	25	28	27	33†
Singapore	–3	21	26	40	45†
Brazil	21	20	21	24	23†
Mexico	18	21	26	27*	20
Argentina	21	22	35	11	15

*1985

†1990

Source: The World Bank, *World Development Report 1981* (New York: Oxford University Press, 1981); Seiji Naya et al., eds., *Lessons in Development* (San Francisco: International Center for International Growth, 1989), 289–290; Anis Chowdhury and Iyanatul Islam, *The Newly Industrializing Economies of East Asia* (New York: Routledge, 1993), 128; The United Nations, *Human Development Report, 1994*, (New York: Oxford University Press, 1994).

market-based economies), public sector consumption in 1960 was relatively low to begin with—7 percent and 8 percent of GDP, respectively. In South Korea, it dropped from 15 to 11 percent by 1979.[25] This situation lent itself well to promoting investment in the productive sectors of the economy—which is precisely what the East Asian NICs have accomplished since the 1960s.

The influx of foreign capital and aid in East Asia is another crucial aspect of the capital formation process there. Cold War tensions and the Korean War both had a strong influence on the flow of Western aid into South Korea and Taiwan. South Korea's dependence on foreign aid was especially crucial following the Korean War in the 1950s. According to one estimate, approximately 70 percent of South Korea's domestic capital formation came from foreign aid during much of the 1950s.[26] Taiwan's domestic capital formation also depended heavily on foreign capital during the same period—about 40 percent was externally financed. Recall that this was also the period when South Korea and Taiwan underwent structural transformation in production, using protective measures to insulate its newly emerging light manufacturing industries from foreign competition.

Throughout the literature on economic development, education and human resource development are recurrent features. It is no surprise that the success of the East Asian NICs have called even more attention to these issues. The combined impact of investment strategies in education and job training in the NICs have resulted in a quality labor force creating increased economic efficiency, industrial flexibility, and greater economic equality. Government initiatives in reducing the illiteracy rate and providing adequate access to job training is evident in comparatively high enrollment rates and government expenditure directed toward creating an educated and skilled workforce. For example, by 1972, government spending on education was almost 16 percent of the government's public expenditures in South Korea and

Singapore. Others like Malaysia and Thailand were also investing heavily in education, with 23 percent and 20 percent of government spending, respectively.[27] The important point here is not that government expenditures in education have resulted in economic development. Rather, in a number of NICs, the emphasis on education has led to the growth of a literate and skilled workforce, which has been essential to the success of the industrial and investment policies and has promoted growth in productivity.

Finally, as we have seen, the state in these countries has been instrumental in setting and shaping development policies. South Korea presents a typical case in point. In 1961, the military came to power following a coup and established the Economic Planning Board, which, among other things, acquired powers to control the nation's investment strategy. With the guidance of the military government, which dictated economic policy, the board became a coordinating body among the various governmental agencies. This centralization of power was reflected in the weakening of political parties and electoral politics in South Korea. Another significant development was the systematic weakening of labor unions, which allowed the government greater control over implementing and enforcing its economic agenda.

This emphasis on a strong state to direct economic restructuring and export promotion is not exclusive to South Korea. Recall from the discussion in chapter 13 that Japan's phenomenal rise as a major global economic power is often attributed to its peculiar brand of capitalism. Of special importance has been the active role of the Japanese state in leading and guiding economic policy and the global competitiveness of its major industries. Some analysts see the East Asian economies as following closely along the path of a mercantilist style "developmental capitalism" paved by Japan. Others go further and point out that the East Asian economies have also been stimulated by Japanese investment, expertise, technology, and closer economic integration with the Japanese economy.[28]

Like South Korea, other East Asian NICs (such as Malaysia and Taiwan) have also developed strong central governments to manage their growth process. Having a strong state that supports capitalist development is often seen by some politicians and academics in the region as necessary. The state's role is considered especially crucial in the early and intermediary stages of the process (i.e., during the initial import-substitution stage and then during the transition to an export-led growth stage). As one prominent Malaysian politician noted:

> In most East Asian countries, politics is a means to an end. Leaders behave in a political manner they think will best achieve one objective: Filling the stomachs of their people. . . . The Western model has politics as an end in itself. The objective . . . is not about filling stomachs but about an ideal system. . . . The Asian countries that are doing well are those which, from the Western viewpoint, are not quite fully democratic. . . . There is a consensus in this region that economic development must precede political development. It is popularly felt that restrictions on politics are necessary, albeit temporary.[29]

The East Asia economies make no apologies for the suppression of Western-style democracy. In each of the above cases, the state has played a central role in guiding the transition of these economies from being exporters of primary products to being exporters of manufactured goods to the rest of the world.

The experience among the major Latin American economies has been quite different. But, as in the case of East Asia, the situation has been influenced by a complex set of forces. Recall that during the 1950s, Latin American scholars were increasingly skeptical of the "comparative advantage" road to development, and the dependency critique became an influential framework for development in that region. This critique fostered opposition to dependence on foreign capital and trade to promote development, which resulted in restrictive trade policies and stringent regulation and control of foreign investment. Instead, the inward-looking and nationalistic import substitution approach was implemented. This approach was supposed to reduce dependence on foreign capital, technology, and markets by promoting "home-grown" industries.

Government leaders and scholars alike were convinced that specializing in primary commodity products was an inherent disadvantage for developing countries in the region. The adverse terms of trade made manufactured imports a major foreign exchange drain that did not add to any tangible development. For this to change, countries like Brazil and Mexico, which had a relatively fragile industrial base, had to undertake significant steps to build a viable and sustaining manufacturing sector. After all, given the large internal consumer market in Brazil and Mexico, a shift in emphasis from importing manufactured consumer products to producing them locally would translate into new jobs across the economy, improve the adverse balance of payment situation, and promote economic development.

The import substitution path taken by countries like Brazil and Mexico can best be described as a series of stages during which these countries moved from being exporters of primary commodities to developing an indigenous industrial base. The first stage of the import substitution strategy was not unlike that followed by the East Asian NICs. By the 1950s, Brazil and Mexico were well into the process of promoting local manufacture of consumer goods (such as processed foods, textiles, and footwear) and curtailing foreign imports with protectionist measures. However, there were some significant differences affecting the import substitution strategies between the East Asian and Latin American cases. Historically, the resource- and agriculture-rich Latin American economies have been significantly more dependent on primary exports than their East Asian counterparts like Taiwan and South Korea.[30] Moving away from this deeply entrenched primary product economy was easier said than done.

Furthermore, protectionist policies were used more heavily in countries like Brazil to displace the foreign share of its consumer market, while in East Asia the focus of these measures was to enhance the international competitiveness of locally produced goods. Hence, by the late 1960s, as South Korea was moving into promoting its exports while maintaining some barriers, Brazil and Mexico were moving into the next stage of intensifying their import substitution strategy. Ironically, instead of reducing its dependence on foreign capital, borrowing from abroad to finance the deepening of its import substitution was necessary. This second stage of import substitution involved expanding the manufacture of labor-intensive consumer goods along with diversifying into capital-intensive goods as well.[31] In this stage, the role of the government also expanded; state-owned enterprises expanded. This increasing presence of the state was associated with increased concentration of production in the hands of a few firms (often state-owned) that were not as productive as privately owned enterprises.[32]

Through this strategy, however, Brazil, Mexico, and others were able to generate sustained economic growth. Brazil had a 9 percent annual average growth in GDP between 1965 and 1980. Mexico and Venezuela lagged behind but still averaged a growth rate of 6.5 percent and 3.7 percent, respectively. The manufacturing sector in these countries also had a higher growth rate in relation to agriculture.[33] However, the performance of these economies was not as strong as the export-oriented East Asian NICs. Brazil and Mexico had largely managed this growth by heavily depending on the domestic consumer market instead of the international market. In order to sustain growth, production reflected the consumption patterns of those with purchasing power. Ironically, this further aggravated income inequality as the gap between the "haves" and "have-nots" increased. By contrast, the income inequality gap among the East Asian NICs narrowed.[34]

Many highly protected industries remained uncompetitive and Latin NICs remained heavily dependent on the export of volatile primary goods. Conspicuous state-run enterprises and imprudent government spending were heavily financed through foreign borrowing (see Table 15–4), fueling an unprecedented fiscal crisis in these countries. By 1980, a number of Latin American economies were buried in debt. Excessive, and more important, inefficient government spending to implement import substitution policies was catching up with these countries. As their growth rates withered, the inflation rate in countries like Brazil hovered over 2,000 percent.

Under domestic and international pressure from lending institutions, Brazil has been stripping away at the layers of import substitution policies. Privatization of the economy was a primary part of the prescribed solution, accompanied by reductions in tariffs. Meanwhile, Brazil's exports are growing. In the early 1990s, foreign investment has also increased. However, controlling inflation has perhaps become the country's biggest challenge. The government's inability to curb spending and put its fiscal house in order continues to put pressure on the inflation spiral. To control inflation, Brazil has gone through five currency changes over the past decade,

TABLE 15–4   External Public Debt (US$ billions) (Numbers in parentheses are percentage of GNP)

	1970	1979	1988	1991
Argentina	1.8 (7.6)	8.7 (8.6)	48.1 (57.0)	63.7 (49.0)
Brazil	3.2 (7.2)	35.0 (17.7)	89.8 (26.3)	34.4 (65.0)
Mexico	3.2 (9.7)	28.8 (24.5)	81.2 (48.0)	101.7 (37.0)
Venezuela	0.7 (6.6)	9.8 (20.0)	25.4 (41.1)	116.5 (29.0)

Source: The World Bank, *World Development Report*, 1981 and 1990; United Nations, *Human Development Report*, 1994 (New York: Oxford University Press, 1994).

most recently in 1994. As one of the world's largest economies attempts to change course and move away from an inward-looking strategy to development, the process continues to be slow and costly.

MALAYSIA: ADJUSTING TO SUCCESS

Malaysia's economy, one of the fastest growing in Southeast Asia, has transformed a little-known developing country into a new league of emerging NICs. For the past forty years, as experts and pundits of development paid close attention to the Brazils, South Koreas, and Taiwans of the world, Malaysia paved its own road to growth with little notoriety.

The influx of Chinese and Indian immigrants during the nineteenth and first half of the twentieth century created an ethnically mixed social order as these groups co-existed with the *Bumiputras* (Malays). Following independence from Britain in 1957, Malaysia underwent some pressing times marred by political instability. Traditionally an exporter of primary products, Malaysia was heavily dependent on tin and rubber for export earnings. In 1969, racial tensions (especially among the Chinese and Malays) erupted into riots, and the nation seemed destined to undergo some turbulent years of economic stagnation and even civil war.

Instead, the ruling government, made up of a coalition of the three major ethnic parties, mapped out an economic program to lead Malaysia through the coming decades. It was widely believed that if not addressed, the economic inequality among the major groups would continue to be a major cause of instability. Aside from foreign ownership of large mining and agricultural businesses, the Malaysian economy during the 1960s was largely dominated by an entrepreneurial class that was disproportionally Chinese. The Malays, who made up the majority of the population, were largely marginalized. Under Malay leadership, however, the ethnically mixed ruling party put in place a national program for development that directly confronted the existing economic disparity between ethnic groups.

In the early 1970s, the New Economic Policy (NEP) was launched, and Malaysia has not looked back since. This policy was designed to gradually increase the Malays' share of ownership of capital and participation in the capitalist economy, while reorganizing the economic structure of production itself. Part of this redistribution process would occur by providing Malays with special incentives to invest, reserving ownership rights to economically disenfranchised Malays, and instituting for Malaysia a quota system in the government bureaucracies and public universities.

This redistribution occurred simultaneously with an intensive effort to attract foreign investment into new industrial and manufacturing ventures where joint involvement with local capital would be a desired part of the effort. Wages were tightly controlled and inflation was also kept in check. In the early 1970s, per capita income was less than $400 and by 1993 it was nearly $3,000. This improved standard of living has helped cushion ethnic tensions, while the redistribution of wealth continues.

Malaysia's development has created its own peculiar economic problems. One of the more pressing economic concerns it confronts is the shortage of highly skilled and specialized labor. As the country has become an attractive site for assembly and electronics manufacturing multinationals, its cheap labor pool is being quickly absorbed. Malaysia's efforts to sustain the current momentum of growth and development by diversifying its manufacturing base has created demands for local technological "know-how." This dilemma was quite evident when in the 1980s, Malaysia began producing automobiles.

Continued

MALAYSIA ADJUSTING TO SUCCESS, *continued*

Lacking a sufficient technological base, Malaysia's auto producing venture had to be launched with the cooperation of Mitsubishi of Japan. Malaysia's concerns about the shortage of technically skilled labor and competition from neighboring countries (with cheaper labor supply for labor-intensive foreign multinational ventures) can be expected to continue as it drives toward increased industrialization. Pressed to keep rising labor costs from discouraging foreign investment, the government has been soft on illegal immigration (especially from neighboring Indonesia and the Philippines).

As ethnic tensions from the late 1960s continue to be eased by prosperity and a growing manufacturing base (which accounts for over 60 percent of export earnings), economic concerns appear on the horizon. Renewed efforts to privatize certain state-owned utility enterprises and continued political stability, however, will be important for Malaysia's efforts to sustain its current pace of economic development.

LOSING GROUND: THE AFRICAN PREDICAMENT

The development problem is unquestionably most acute in Africa. Not surprisingly, Africa is also where we find the majority and the most dire of the LDCs. Directly related to the extent of the problem among these LDCs has been the sluggish performance of these economies. While each case is certainly unique, there are some clear threads running through the situations of many of these LDCs. In this section, we shall briefly outline some general but fundamental points that highlight the problem.

Like the NICs, there has been no shortage of desire for development among the LDCs in Africa.[35] Yet one expert notes: "It is quite hazardous to talk of development strategies in Africa . . . because it is not in the least clear that many African countries have a strategy which is identifiable."[36]

Although this may be an extreme characterization, the absence of consistency or an "identifiable" strategy can be traced to the absence of established and legitimate political institutions in many of these LDCs capable of promoting sustained policies. "Although the most pressing problems in Africa today are economic in nature, governments on the continent are more concerned about their political survival."[37] One basic indicator of this is the massive resources that have been diverted to arms expenditures and other repressive state efforts.[38] Hence, political survival has consistently competed with economic development priorities. In a region hard pressed to provide the basic amenities for its citizens, this diversion of resources indeed comes at a very high price.

The historical link that many African countries have had with the international economy continues to influence the fate of these LDCs. Since the early days of the colonial era, the African economies have been deeply entrenched in agriculture and primary commodity production (essentially directed for external consumption). Although this "comparative advantage" is not inherently detrimental, the almost exclusive reliance on primary commodity exports has left the LDCs consistently vulnerable to price volitility and unfavorable terms of trade for these commodities in the international market.

Most of the LDCs have been unable to markedly diversify their economies. On aggregate, agriculture in Africa made up 47 percent of GDP in 1965 and had dropped to 38 percent by 1984. Industry's share of GDP during the same period increased from 15 to 16 percent. In Asia, agriculture declined from 42 to 36 percent of GDP as industry's share grew from 28 to 36 percent over the same period.[39] As a result, diversification remains a major priority to the development agenda for most African LDCs. Compounding this reliance on agriculture is the excessive dependence on limited products as the "bread and butter" of these economies. This phenomenon, known as commodity concentration, has been a conspicuous feature of most African LDCs. As a case in point, the level of commodity concentration in Zambia and Burundi has been over 90 percent during the 1970s and 1980s. Nigeria, which has been one of the few exceptions to move away from agriculture (and be classified as a middle-income country), has instead become excessively dependent on oil, which accounts for 90 percent of exports.[40]

Further, the economic crunch has been exacerbated by a systemic financial crisis. Since the oil crisis in the 1970s, the LDCs in Africa have seen their debt burden steadily and sharply increase from 25 percent in 1975 to 76 percent in 1987.[41] Of course, the debt crisis is not exclusive to Africa's LDCs. But the burden has been especially crippling, since many LDCs were experiencing reductions in export revenue. The IMF has attempted to steer these economies out of this situation by insisting that excessive government spending, agriculture subsidies, and artificial currency controls be eliminated. While there is some movement in this direction, skeptics insist that unless primary commodities prices in the international market rebound, the financial situation for these economies will not improve appreciably.

We also cannot ignore the complex ecological and physical impediments and conflicts that shape the history of the region. Obviously, development prospects in the region have been shaped by these factors. The Sudan is a typical case in point. With over 130 tribes, Sudan has historically been marred with ethnic, religious, and tribal tensions.[42] The Sudanese have also struggled to maintain a delicate balance between their largely subsistence agriculture system and the delicate ecology of the region. However, the inappropriate use of imported technology and intensification of commodity production for export (advocated by IMF) has damaged the subsistence economy and the productive capacity of arable land. The devastation from ethnic conflicts for political control or survival has further compounded the ecological and productivity problem. In 1984, over 4 million people were displaced from their homes and the food shortage intensified. While the economic costs have been severe, the human costs remain immeasurable. The experience of LDCs in Africa provides a poignant illustration of the collective interplay between IPE, local politics, economic survival strategies, and the environment.

CONCLUSION

Over the past fifty years, the development process for third world countries has been their foremost challenge. A complex mix of conditions both internal and external to these countries will continue to affect the outcome of development efforts. The

East-West conflict was an influential international constraint that shaped the political economy of development. Along with this, the developed world's domination of capital, technology, and the institutional structures of the global economy helped generate strong political momentum among LDCs to change the rules of the game and address the imbalance in global political and economic power and wealth.

As the world economy continues to undergo restructuring, we can certainly expect changes in development prospects for LDCs. Although the implications are far from being clear, the propensity toward trading blocs in Europe, North America, and a more integrated Pacific Rim–East Asia will most certainly shift national and international priorities. Over the past five decades, most of the LDCs have forged alliances like the G-77 and UNCTAD to help mobilize support for their economic agenda. The capacity of developing countries to sustain such collective measures (to tilt the dominance of the developed countries) will certainly be affected as regional ties or blocs become reinforced. One highly likely consequence is that LDCs will be differentially affected by such changes in the world economy. Arguably, third world interests may not be as easily definable as they have been until now.

Disparate development trends in recent decades also add to the potential weakening of a third world alliance. Already, the East Asian NICs are increasingly coming to resemble the developed countries economically, and have less in common with the LDCs of Latin America or Africa. This trend where some developing countries grow and develop faster than others will most certainly continue. In fact, the gap between the NICs and other LDCs is growing wider as desperately poor countries like Chad, Haiti, Bangladesh, Zaire, and many others are trapped in economic paralysis.

Alongside the external contingencies, conditions within each country are also crucial to the prospects for development. Any assessment of development must consider a number of critical issues about the state of affairs within a developing country and how these issues impact on development prospects. Chief among these considerations must be an assessment of the role of the state and the private sector in promoting and guiding the development process. As we have seen, for example, liberal policies that would ideally tilt the scale strongly in favor of a free-trade approach also stress the importance of a stable but noninterventionist state. The state can, however, accelerate the performance of the free market through prudent and stable fiscal and monetary policies. The export-led growth of East Asian NICs has partly vindicated proponents of the liberal model. However, mercantilist trade policies in South Korea, Taiwan, and other Asian countries also drive home the strategic role of an aggressive state in the development process.

It is equally important to recognize that unique sociohistorical circumstances within each developing nation will continue to strongly influence not only the character of the state but also its relationship to the market and the larger international order. Recognizing the role of ethnic conflicts, class divisions, and other societal-specific conditions can provide much needed insight into the nature and role of the state in developing countries, and the development path taken. Countries like Iraq, The Sudan, Haiti, Somalia, Rwanda, Algeria, and others are entangled in national and regional tensions and conflicts. These internal and regional conditions will certainly affect the character of the state and its role in the larger economy.

DISCUSSION QUESTIONS

1. The development dilemma has two distinct elements: the growing gap between rich and poor nations (North and South) and the increasing differences among less developed countries themselves (LDCs). Discuss these trends, citing evidence from this chapter.
2. What four forces have shaped the development process for LDCs? How do these forces create tensions within LDCs and between LDCs and industrial nations? Explain.
3. Compare and contrast the liberal ideas regarding economic development and export-led growth with the dependency perspective and the policy of import-substituting growth. How do market forces stimulate economic development? How do these same forces create dependency and underdevelopment? Explain.
4. What nations are included in the ranks of the newly industrialized countries (NICs)? What specific factors seem to differentiate the NICs from the LDCs? What role does the state play in NIC development? Explain.

SUGGESTED READINGS

Berch Berberoglu. *The Political Economy of Development: Development Theory and the Prospects for Change in the Third World.* Albany, NY: State University of New York, 1992.

Stephan Haggard. *Pathways from the Periphery: The Politics of Growth in the Newly Industrializing Countries.* Ithaca, NY: Cornell University Press, 1990.

Nigel Harris. *The End of the Third World.* New York: The Meredith Press, 1986.

B. Hughes, ed. *Achieving Industrialization in East Asia.* Sydney, Australia: Cambridge University Press, 1988.

William James, Seiji Naya, and Gerald Meier. *Asian Development: Economic Success and Policy Lessons.* Madison, WI: University of Wisconsin Press, 1989.

World Bank Policy Research Reports. *The East Asian Miracle: Economic Growth and Public Policy.* New York: Oxford University Press, 1993.

NOTES

1. The South Commission, *The Challenge to the South* (New York: Oxford University Press, 1990), 1.
2. Figures from The World Bank, *World Development Report 1991* (New York: Oxford University Press, 1991).
3. There are numerous sources of comparison of the developed with the developing nations. These figures and trends are drawn from Josuhua Goldstein, *International Relations* (New York: HarperCollins, 1994), 467–469.
4. For a sophisticated discussion of the political economy of development, see Charles K. Wilber, *The Political Economy of Development and Under-Development* (New York: Random House, 1988). See also Kenneth P. Jameson and James H. Weaver, *Economic Development* (Washington, DC: University Press of America, 1981).
5. The World Bank, *World Development Report 1991*, 204–205.
6. See Daniel Chirot, *Social Change in the Twentieth Century* (New York: Harcourt Brace, 1977), 173.

7. One of the leading voices of the antineocolonial movement was the former president of Ghana, K. Nkrumah, who articulated this thesis in his book, *Neo-colonialism: The Last Stage of Imperialism* (London: Nelson, 1965).

8. Joan Edelman Spero, *The Politics of International Economic Relations* (New York: St. Martin's Press, 1981), 246–247.

9. OPEC was formed in 1960 and its membership includes Iran, Iraq, Algeria, Nigeria, Gabon, Libya, Kuwait, Qatar, Saudi Arabia, United Arab Emirates, Ecuador, and Venezuela.

10. Robert Gilpin, *The Political Economy of International Relations* (Princeton, NJ: Princeton University Press, 1987), 300.

11. See Thomas Sowell, "Second Thoughts about the Third World," *Harper's* (November, 1983).

12. Walt W. Rostow, *The Stages of Economic Growth: A Non-Communist Manifesto* (London: Cambridge University Press, 1960).

13. Raul Prebisch, *The Economic Development of Latin America and Its Principal Problems* (New York: United Nations, 1950).

14. It is worth noting that much of the analyses of these early dependency theorists were based on the experiences of countries in Latin America.

15. Andre Gunder Frank, *Capitalism and Underdevelopment in Latin America* (New York: Monthly Review Press, 1967).

16. Osvaldo Sunkel and Pedro Paz, *El subdesarrollo latinoamericano y la teoría del desarrollo* (Mexico: Siglo Veintiuno de Espana 1970), 6, as quoted in J. Samuel Valenzuela and Arturo Valenzuela, "Modernization and Dependency," *Comparative Politics* 10 (1978) 543–557.

17. For a good discussion of this position, see Teresa Hayter, *Aid as Imperialism* (Middlesex, Eng. Penguin, 1971).

18. Andrew Webster, *Introduction to the Sociology of Development* (Atlantic Highlands, NJ: Humanities Press, 1990), 177.

19. Ibid., 178.

20. William E. James, Seiji Naya, and Gerald M. Meier, *Asian Development: Economic Success and Policy Lessons* (Madison, WI: University of Wisconsin Press, 1989), 10.

21. For example, see Wontack Hong, *Trade, Distortions, and Employment Growth in Korea* (Seoul: Korea Development Institute, 1979).

22. Seiji Naya et al., eds., *Lessons in Development* (San Francisco: International Center for International Growth, 1989), 287.

23. James, Naya, and Meier, *Asian Development*, 69–74.

24. Ibid., 81.

25. The World Bank, *World Development Report 1981* (New York: Oxford University Press, 1981).

26. Stephan Haggard, *Pathways from the Periphery: The Politics of Growth in the Newly Industrializing Countries.* (Ithaca, NY: Cornell University Press, 1990), 196.

27. The World Bank, *World Development Report 1984* (New York: Oxford University Press, 1984).

28. See James Fallows, *Looking at the Sun* (New York: Pantheon, 1994).

29. Musa Hitam, "How Politics Makes Asia Successful," *Asian Business* (December 1993): 39.

30. Jorge Ospina Sardi, "Trade Policy in Latin America," in Seiji Naya et al., eds., *Lessons in Development*, 81.

31. Haggard, *Pathways from the Periphery*, 26.

32. Youngil Lim, "Comparing Brazil and Korea," in Seiji Naya et al., eds., *Lessons in Development*, 102–103.

33. The World Bank, *World Development Report*, 1991.

34. Nigel Harris, *The End of the Third World* (New York: The Meredith Press, 1986), 90–91.

35. See Claude Ake, *A Political Economy of Africa* (New York: Longman, 1981), 141.

36. Ibid., 143–144.

37. Julius E. Nyang'oro, *The State and Capitalist Development in Africa* (New York: Praeger, 1989), 147.
38. See Sunil Kukreja, "Militarization Among Peripheral Nations," *Sociological Viewpoints* 8 (Fall 1992).
39. Adedotun O. Phillips, "Structural Change and Transformation of African Economies," in Adebayo Adedeji et al., eds., *The Challenge of African Economic Recovery and Development* (Portland, OR: Frank Cass, 1991), 458.
40. Nyang'oro, *The State and Capitalist Development in Africa*, 40.
41. Figures from the World Bank, *World Development Report, 1988* (New York: Oxford University Press, 1988), 31.
42. This discussion of the Sudan is based on Mohamed Suliman, "Civil War in the Sudan: From Ethnic to Ecological Conflict," *The Ecologist* 23 (May 1993).

16

The IPE
of Multinational
Corporations

Professor Leon Grunberg

OVERVIEW

Multinational corporations are key agents transforming the international political and economic landscape. Because they are highly visible organizations, with great power and mobility, they inspire both awe and fear. It is the purpose of this chapter to lay out, dispassionately, what these organizations are, where they come from, and where they go, and to assess the impact they have on countries and workers around the globe.

Multinational corporations are firms engaged in productive activities in several countries. The vast majority originate in rich, developed countries and much of their foreign investment goes to other rich nations.

Typically, they go overseas because they possess some special advantage they want to exploit fully and because there are benefits to locating their activities overseas. These benefits may result from avoiding barriers to imports to employing cheaper, foreign labor.

While most political economists will agree with the above summary, there is far more debate as to the kinds of effects they have. Economic liberals see them as forces for positive change, spreading good things like technology and efficiency around the world. Economic nationalists see them as threatening the sovereignty of nation-states. Marxists and structuralists worry that they are creating a world marked by inequality and dependency.

This chapter does not take sides. Rather, it presents each side's case so that the reader can reach his or her own conclusion.

Although the multinational corporation spreads production over the world, it concentrates coordination and planning in key cities, and preserves power and income for the privileged.[1]

Stephen Hymer (1972)

I have long dreamed of buying an island owned by no nation and of establishing the World Headquarters of the Dow company on the truly neutral ground of such an island, beholden to no nation or society.[2]

Carl A. Gerstacker, chairman of Dow Chemical Company

As these comments indicate, perhaps no other aspect of IPE has generated more controversy and grandiose claims than multinational corporations (MNCs). There is, after all, something awe-inspiring and intimidating about huge, powerful economic organizations that span the globe. In the 1960s and 1970s, as the sudden explosion in their numbers and the expansion of their reach hit the public's and academic communities' consciousness, there was a flood of critical commentaries sounding alarm bells and warning of the dangers they posed to national sovereignty and to the security and stability of workers' lives around the globe.[3] Today, several decades later, as they have become an integral and established part of the international economic landscape, the criticisms have been muted. Multinational corporations have now become, in the words of *The Economist* magazine, "everybody's favorite monsters."[4] Rich, poor, former communist and still communist nations all compete to attract MNCs to their shores. With the collapse of the Soviet economic model and with growing MNC control of a huge portion of the world's crucial economic resources (e.g., capital, technology, and management skills), it now appears as if there are few viable alternatives to a capitalist development strategy. For many countries, especially developing ones, attracting MNCs as part of that strategy becomes the only game around. Still, the underlying fears and criticisms have not disappeared. For even as they have become "everybody's favorites," they are still "monsters" bestriding the globe.

This chapter will try to cut through both the awe and the fear these economic organizations produce. It will be our purpose to examine MNCs dispassionately, and to answer a series of basic questions: What are MNCs? Where do they come from and where do they go? Why do they exist at all? How do they operate? And how are the various groups and governments affected by MNC activities? Only then can we assess the nature of their role in the IPE of today and tomorrow.

THE NATURE OF MULTINATIONAL CORPORATIONS

Multinational corporations (MNCs) are economic organizations engaged in productive activities in two or more countries. Typically, they have their headquarters in their country of origin (their home country) and expand overseas by building or acquiring affiliates or subsidiaries in other countries (the host). This kind of expansion is referred to as *foreign direct investment* (FDI) because it involves engagement in directly productive activities overseas, such as Ford establishing a plant in Mexico to build cars, or Citibank setting up a branch office in London to provide financial services. Foreign direct investment has expanded at phenomenal rates since World War II. In the 1980s, for example, FDI grew at 28.9 percent per year, three times the rate of world trade, and has been a key force integrating the world economy.[5] But FDI is not the only factor transforming economic relations around the globe. Trade and portfolio investments also connect national economies and have also grown rapidly. Indeed, portfolio investment flows, which refer to the international movement of money in search of high rates of return in currency and financial markets, dwarf the dollar value of the two other kinds of activities. We will not discuss portfolio investment in this chapter but restrict ourselves to FDI—or what amounts to the same thing, the productive activities of MNCs.

Although there are 37,000 MNCs with some 170,000 foreign affiliates worldwide, ownership and control of such assets is heavily concentrated. For example, just 1 percent of MNCs own half the total of all existing foreign assets.[6] The story of FDI is still primarily the story of large MNCs. Before World War II, many of the major multinational corporations were in extractive and natural resource sectors (for example, the oil producers Shell, Exxon, and BP). After World War II, manufacturing corporations like GM, Ford, Siemens, Sony, and Phillips Electronics dominated FDI. Increasingly, the newest and fastest growing wave of MNCs are in services, with companies like Citibank and Nomura Securities providing financial services around the globe. Some of these companies have sales revenues that exceed the gross domestic product of many countries in the world; and increasingly, the majority of these large MNCs have affiliates in many countries rather than just a handful. It is precisely such characteristics that gives them such clout and attracts labels like "leviathan" and "monster."

WHERE DO THEY COME FROM AND WHERE DO THEY GO?

One of the common yet understandable misconceptions about FDI is that most of it flows from rich, developed nations to poor, developing ones. Nothing could be further from the truth. FDI is in fact an activity conducted primarily between rich countries. The United Nations Center for Transnational Corporations, the leading monitor of MNC activity, estimates that developed economies were not only the home (source) of over 95 percent of recent foreign direct investment flows, but also the host (recipient) of over 80 percent of such flows. Indeed, in the period since 1985, just five rich nations (the U.S., the UK, Germany, Japan, and France) were the home of almost 70 percent and the host of 57 percent of all FDI flows.[7] These facts should modify the popular notion that MNCs are solely or even mainly concerned with finding locations with the cheapest labor. While this might be true for some MNCs engaged in particularly simple and labor-intensive processes, for many others the more important concerns seem to be access and proximity to rich consumer markets and matching the locational moves of large rival MNCs.

However, we do not wish to imply by this that the activities of MNCs are unimportant to the development process in poor countries. A few large, powerful MNCs can significantly influence and possibly distort the political economy of a small, poor country. Rather, it reminds us that focusing all of our attention on MNCs in the developing world will create a narrow and misleading picture of the role of MNCs in the international political economy.

Looking more closely at the changes in the geographic origins and destinations of FDI reveals some dramatic trends that in a sense mirror the change in relative economic power of the leading economies in the world. For much of the century, the powerful U.S. economy accounted for the lion's share of all outward FDI in the world. As late as the 1970s, the U.S. still accounted for more than 40 percent of total outward FDI. By the early 1990s, however, that figure had dropped to below 14 percent.[8] Although U.S. MNCs still dominate international economic activity because they have accumulated a large stock of foreign assets over many decades of FDI, it is Germany and, in particular, Japan that have recently experienced the most rapid growth in outward FDI. Japan's share of outward FDI jumped from less than 1 percent in 1960 to almost 12 percent in 1985, and by the late 1980s, Japan ranked first in terms of the annual flow of outward FDI.[9]

Much of that outflow from Japan, Germany, and other rich European countries went to the United States, which by the mid-1980s became the most popular destination for MNCs, receiving some 40 to 50 percent of all FDI flows. In the early 1970s, only 7.2 percent of such flows went to the United States. This sudden surge in MNC activity in the U.S. created quite an ironic public reaction. Ironic because some Americans were voicing the very same fears and painting similar images that Europeans and Canadians had used decades earlier in response to the entry of U.S. MNCs into their countries.

At that time, the Europeans worried about the U.S. takeover of Europe, and Canada felt that it was becoming a dependent outpost of the U.S. economy.[10] In the 1990s, the tables were reversed and it was Americans who fretted about the Japanese invasion of the United States as famous institutions, like Rockefeller Center and Columbia Pictures, came under Japanese ownership. Even such a quintessentially American cultural pastime as baseball was penetrated by foreigners, as the Japanese video game producer, Nintendo, bought a majority share in the Seattle Mariners team.

But while these concerns are understandable, are they justified? The most forceful argument that such fears are exaggerated and misplaced has been made by the political economist Robert Reich. In a provocative book, *The Work of Nations*, he argues that the nationality of corporations is becoming irrelevant. Japanese companies investing in the United States may do more to advance the standard of living of Americans than do American MNCs investing in Latin America or Asia. In one case, the factories, offices, machinery, and jobs are in the United States, and in the other they are located in foreign countries. The policy conclusion for Reich seems inescapable: "Nations can no longer substantially enhance the wealth of their citizens by subsidizing, protecting, or otherwise increasing the profitability of 'their corporations.' "[11]

If Reich is right, then the case of Japan seems to present a puzzle. Despite becoming a major source of outward FDI, Japan has virtually no inward FDI. Unlike the United States, Britain, France, and Germany, where between 10 to 20 percent of total sales are accounted for by foreign-owned MNCs, in Japan it is less than 1 percent.[12] Indeed, to give you an idea of how little FDI there is in Japan, just two Japanese acquisitions of U.S. companies (Matsushita's of MCA and Sony's of Columbia Pictures) equal the entire value of the stock of inward FDI in Japan.[13] The primary reason for this minimal FDI has been the Japanese government's decades-long policy of setting up bureaucratic delays and barriers to frustrate inward FDI. Why Japan pursued such policies is a matter of debate but probably has a lot to do with its history of economic nationalism and a desire to protect its growing companies. When Japanese companies became world-class competitors and went global in the 1970s and 1980s, other nations pressured Japan to open its borders to foreign MNCs. The government responded by removing most of the legal and bureaucratic barriers in 1980. But inward FDI still remains low, most probably because of the existence of *keiretsus* (corporations that are linked into a group by extensive cross-shareholdings) that make it extremely difficult for a foreign MNC to merge or acquire a Japanese corporation that is part of such a group.[14] This imbalance in the relationship between Japan and other countries—that Japan can buy foreign firms, but outsiders find it almost impossible to acquire major Japanese firms—is bound to be an additional source of tension in the IPE of the next few years.

Finally, before we leave this section, we need to note a couple of trends about FDI in the developing world. As we have pointed out, very little of FDI originates from or goes to developing countries. Of the small amount that goes to developing countries, about two thirds goes to just ten countries in Latin America and Asia (primarily Brazil, Mexico, Singapore, Malaysia, Hong Kong, and China).[15] These countries either have very large internal markets or have developed quite a sophisticated infrastructure (e.g., ports, banking, education).

It is also from among these countries that we see the development of a small but growing number of MNCs. These fast-growing industrializing economies are increasingly the home of FDI that flows to other developing countries. In particular, FDI flows from East Asia's newly industrialized countries (for example, Hong Kong, South Korea, and Singapore) have recently become larger sources of investment in countries like China, Indonesia, and Malaysia than those from Japan and the United States.[16]

REASONS FOR FOREIGN DIRECT INVESTMENT, OR WHY DO FIRMS INVEST OVERSEAS?

There exists no single elegant theory to account for foreign direct investment, as there is for international trade. Indeed, the existence and growth of international networks of subsidiaries controlled by the headquarters of large MNCs doesn't fit very comfortably into the perfectly competitive world of neoclassical economics, the dominant intellectual paradigm in economics. In this textbook world, firms would not grow beyond the size of a single efficient plant. Such plants would purchase necessary supplies from other independent firms (not from sister subsidiaries within the MNC) and would sell via exports what they produced at their single locations (rather than produce and sell their products in various locations around the globe). If they possessed a particularly unique technology, they might, for a fee, allow a foreign company to use that technology (often called a *licensing arrangement*). In such a world, multinational corporations would not exist. But as we have seen, such firms are pervasive and are beginning to dominate international economic activity. An understanding of this development, therefore, requires a less idealized and a more concrete *examination of the actual behavior of firms*. If we want to understand why MNCs exist, we have to look at what kinds of firms are multinational, and at their motives for investing overseas.

A comprehensive explanation of MNC decisions to invest overseas comprises several elements.[17] Perhaps the most important element is that the firm possess some *firm-specific competitive advantage*. This is important because the firm must be able to overcome the disadvantage of doing business a long way from home against foreign firms that will be more familiar with the local environment. There are several kinds of advantages that enable firms to go overseas and compete successfully against foreign producers. An important one is size. MNCs are usually large and have market power. They can, therefore, obtain finance capital relatively easily and at favorable terms. Furthermore, they are often technological or marketing leaders in their industry. They may, like Xerox corporation, have pioneered a particular product, or like Toyota, developed an efficient system of production. Or they may have tremendous marketing power because of a brand name, like Coca-Cola, McDonald's, or Hilton Hotels. These advantages enable such firms to compete successfully in foreign countries.

Such firms could, of course, sell or license their technological or marketing advantages to foreign firms, thereby benefiting indirectly from their advantages. Some in fact do so via licensing agreements and partnerships or alliances. But many do not, insisting on complete ownership and control of their advantages. The primary reasons for this are twofold. First, when control of the advantage remains within the MNC, the MNC captures all the benefits that flow from the advantage. Since marketing and technological advantages often enable MNCs to earn high rates of return, they have a financial reason not to want to share these gains with others, especially firms that may be potential rivals. Secondly, supply or licensing agreements involve some degree of uncertainty. Will the licensee do as good a job as the licensing firm would at producing or marketing the product? For many firms, the uncertainties are sufficiently large to make full control attractive. Keeping the advantages in-house, as it were, is the second element in the explanation and is often referred to as *internalizing the firm-specific advantages.*

These two elements still do not satisfactorily answer why firms don't supply foreign markets by exports. A firm could maintain full control of its particular competitive advantage and export the product from its home country. Coca-Cola or Xerox copiers can obviously be shipped from the United States all over the world. One answer to the question has to do with what are sometimes called *location-specific advantages.* That is, there are advantages to producing at the foreign location itself, which the firm can only enjoy by being there. When the MNC locates overseas, it can obtain much better information about changes in customer tastes and can also respond more quickly to such changes. It avoids the transport costs involved with exporting across long distances and can enjoy the same labor costs as its rivals in that foreign market. Some governments, in an effort to assist domestic producers, raise barriers to imports. Getting under trade barriers becomes an additional, and often very important, reason for firms to locate inside the foreign country, thereby eliminating that particular disadvantage. One example among many is Nissan and Honda opening production facilities in Britain so they could get around Italian and French quotas placed on Japanese car imports. By producing in Britain, a member country of the European Union, these companies could circumvent the restrictions.

Raymond Vernon has married these location-specific advantages with the evolutionary life cycle of products to account for the timing and sequence of FDI by U.S. manufacturers.[18] The *product life-cycle theory,* as it is called, argues that at the birth of a new product, the firm faces few competitors and will tend to locate all its production close to its customers and research and development center. In this way it can more easily adapt the product to conditions in its primary market. Foreign markets are served by exports. As the product matures and the production process becomes routine and more easily imitated, foreign competitors begin to challenge the export markets of the pioneering firm. As we have seen, such foreign firms may be able to undercut the prices or services offered by the pioneering firm because they enjoy location-specific advantages. In order to preserve its market share, the pioneering firm may set up production facilities in the foreign country. As the product approaches old age, and price competition becomes more severe, with perhaps the entry of low-cost rivals from developing countries, MNCs are again compelled to shift some of their production in search of even cheaper locations.

Another important element of the explanation for FDI concerns the strategies these large firms employ to remain competitive with their main rivals. Researchers have noticed that much U.S. FDI in the 1960s and 1970s occurred in "bunches," with several MNCs in an industry all locating in a foreign country or area at roughly the same time. Did all these companies have similar firm-specific advantages and did they all happen to discover the location-specific advantages by chance at the same time? This seems unlikely. More plausible is that many of the MNCs were matching the actions of their competitors lest one of them gain an edge by being the only one going overseas. By "following the leader" and acting in packs, these firms try to minimize their risks and maintain a certain market stability or competitive equilibrium in the industry.[19] This behavior pattern has continued. A current example of such packlike behavior can be seen in the European chemical industry. European MNCs like Ciba, BASF, Bayer, and ICI are all, at about the same time, in the process of shifting the production of bulk chemicals out of the stagnant markets of Europe and to the faster growing Asian markets.[20]

In sum, we can say that FDI is typically carried out by large firms possessing some particular competitive advantage that they do not want to share with rivals. These firms tend to become multinational so they can enjoy the advantages of locating in a foreign site. Such locational advantages include getting under trade barriers, operating close to large markets, and gaining access to inexpensive labor.

In the future, as the revolutions in communications and transportation shrink the globe and facilitate continued international economic activity, and as more and more firms become multinational, explanations of FDI will shift from a focus on why firms becomes multinational (many of them already are), to *how they behave as multinationals*. Also, as MNCs from different developed countries increasingly succeed in cross-penetrating each other's markets, the main competitive battles may revolve less on access to markets and more on who has the best technological innovations and the lowest production costs.

THE IMPACT OF MULTINATIONAL CORPORATIONS

We have now reached the heart of the controversy that swirls around MNCs. Should they be welcomed as forces for positive and progressive change in the international political economy, or do they help create a highly unequal and destructive global economy? Do they help the development of poor countries, or do they exploit and distort their economies? There are no simple or conclusive answers to these questions. How we assess the impact of MNCs depends on a variety of conditioning factors: on whether the host country is rich or poor; on whether the MNC investment is deep-rooted and long-term, or shallow and short-term; on the alternatives available to the host country; and on a variety of other factors we shall presently examine. A final assessment also depends on one's perspective and values. If one believes that economic growth overrides all other considerations, then one is likely to see MNCs as sources of progress in the world. However, if one believes that the pursuit of equitable and balanced (perhaps even slow) development is preferable, then MNCs may represent forces exacerbating inequality and exploitation. Rather than pick sides, we will provide you with a balanced account of the impact of MNCs by presenting the arguments made by each side in the controversy. It will be for you, the reader, to weigh the strengths of the contending positions, test them against actual cases and situations, and reach your own conclusions.

THE POSITIVE VIEW

Host Country Effects

Arguments in support of MNCs are usually made by liberal political economists and by the business community.[21] Since MNCs tend to be successful companies that possess a variety of competitive advantages, much of the positive case for them rests on the things they bring into host countries. MNCs, it is argued, transfer technology, products, finance capital, and sophisticated management techniques to countries that lack these. This infusion of resources into host nations would, for example, tend to create jobs and to raise the skill level of the workforce as it learns to utilize the modern technology that MNCs transfer into the country. These positive additions to a country's economy are greater if the MNC investment is in a new or "greenfield" site than if the MNC simply acquires an existing local company.[22] In the first case, there is, presumably, a pure addition to the productive capacity of the nation, for without the foreign investment, that factory and its associated jobs would not have existed. While acquisitions may be less attractive to host countries, there is still some benefit, since the MNCs are likely to manage the operations more efficiently than the previous owners. As Robert Reich puts it, MNCs invest overseas because "they think they can utilize the other nation's assets and its workers better than that nation's investors and managers can [thus] rendering the assets and workers more productive than before."[23] A telling example is the case of Toyota, which took over the management of a General Motors plant in California and managed to raise productivity by 50 percent and to reduce absenteeism substantially.

In addition to the direct positive effects of MNCs, there may also be spillover effects onto other companies and sectors in the economy of the host nation. For example, if Ford builds a car factory in Brazil, this *could* lead to the expansion of domestic supplier firms in the steel or rubber industries and to an increase in work for dealers and advertising agencies, *provided*, of course, that Ford buys its supplies in the host market and sells much of its production locally. In other words, the degree to which MNCs are linked with domestic firms is an important factor conditioning the extent of the spillover effects into the host economy. That is why many host governments insist that MNCs include a certain proportion of domestically produced materials and supplies in their final products. Other indirect benefits include the increased competition MNCs provide local firms, which may prod them to respond to the more efficient foreign rival by adopting the best practices of these MNCs. There can be little doubt that the U.S. "big three" automakers were shaken out of their complacency by the success of Japanese autos, both imported and manufactured in the U.S. by Japanese transplants.

Multinational corporations are also credited with helping to improve a nation's balance of payments (see chapter 8). On the capital side of the account, there is a flow of capital into the economy when the MNC builds a new subsidiary or acquires an existing one. Of course, the key question is the capital balance after one subtracts the subsequent outflow of capital in the form of repatriated profits, license fees, and royalties that the subsidiary sends home to its parent. While one may ex-

pect the capital balance to be negative over time, since MNCs expect not only to recoup their outlay but also to make a profit, it is the positive effect on trade that supporters of MNCs point to. MNCs can be expected to reduce a country's imports by
substituting domestically produced products for those that were previously imported, and to increase a country's exports. MNCs, because of their international
scope, have far better marketing and distribution systems than domestic firms, and
are, therefore, very successful exporters. Indeed, some MNC subsidiaries in developing countries serve primarily as export platforms, producing goods almost ex-
clusively for sale in other countries. Again, however, one has to examine *the net effect*
on trade, since many of these MNCs import much of their supplies from other subsidiaries of the MNC.

Home Country Effects

So far, we have focused on the positive effects on host countries. But do these gains
for the host country come at the expense of home countries? Do capital, technology, and management skill that go overseas mean fewer jobs in, and less exports
from, the home country? This is a very hard question to answer definitively because
we cannot be sure what would have happened to the resources of the MNC if they
had not gone overseas. Would, for example, the plant that was closed in the home
country, so that the MNC could transfer its production to a cheaper labor site, have
survived anyway? There is no way to be sure. Proponents of MNCs, however, argue
that these companies make economically rational decisions. They transfer production overseas or open new factories in foreign countries as a defensive measure in
response to competitive pressures. If they did not, they would jeopardize their access to foreign markets and perhaps the survival of the entire company—and with
it the jobs of their workforce. Moreover, proponents argue that foreign direct investment can actually stimulate economic activity in the home country. U.S. MNCs,
for example, export a great deal of their domestic output to their subsidiaries abroad.
If these subsidiaries did not exist, there would be no guarantee that foreign markets
for these exports would exist at all.

   Finally, and at a more general, systemic level, proponents of MNCs make a series of political and cultural claims about the benefits of MNCs. At the systemic level,
MNCs are viewed as forces integrating the world's economies, thereby reducing nationalism and international tensions. By increasing trade between nations, by connecting workers from different countries into one MNC network, and by spreading
similar consumer products to all corners of the world, they undermine national differences and help create a world citizen with modern tastes and habits. Furthermore,
by developing global rather than national horizons and by helping revolutionize the
international flows of capital and communications, MNCs compel governments to
collaborate politically so that they can regulate and control these new international
forces. In a similar vein, supporters of MNCs and of a more borderless economic
world also claim that the economic growth that results from a more open world economy will foster a more liberal and democratic political order in countries that previously endured authoritarian regimes.

THE NEGATIVE VIEW

The case against MNCs has been spearheaded by radical-structuralists. At the most general level, they argue that MNCs integrate poor nations into an unequally structured world system, with poor countries languishing on the periphery, heavily dependent for their development on the decisions and actions of capitalists ensconced in MNC headquarters in rich core nations. The policy implications of the most radical of the dependency school arguments is for poor countries to cut their dependence by closing their doors to MNCs.[24] Whatever the merits of such a view, this is not a policy many countries are currently pursuing. Even communist countries like China and Cuba seek to attract MNCs to their shores. We shall, therefore, examine, at a lower level of analysis, some of the possible specific negative effects of MNC investment on, first, the host, and then the home countries.

Host Country Effects

Many of the less ideological arguments against MNCs rest on the particular conditions surrounding their investment. Take the issue of the supposed transfer of capital when FDI occurs. In several cases, MNCs may borrow the money for foreign investment in the local host market rather than transfer it from its home base. Since lenders believe it is safer to advance loans to large organizations, the MNCs may squeeze out young, potentially viable local firms from the local market and retard the *independent* development of indigenous businesses. Similarly, further capital investment may come from the profits of the subsidiary rather than from the parent company. When one adds the outflow of capital in the form of repatriated profits, the net infusion of capital into host nations may be much smaller than MNC supporters claim.

Doubts have also been raised about the benefits of the transferred technology, especially for poorer developing countries. First, the vast bulk of the research and development capability of MNCs remains at home in the parent company. Very little is carried out in developing countries.[25] Therefore, MNCs, it is argued, do not help develop an *independent* capacity to generate new technology in the host countries. Since locals receive little training and experience developing new products and processes, when the MNCs leave, little that was of lasting benefit remains. This would be particularly true for MNCs producing for export in low-labor-cost locations, for they are likely to be short-term residents in these countries.

Second, there is the question of the appropriateness or suitability of the transferred technology for the host nation. Is a product or process developed in a rich country like the U.S., to meet its particular circumstances, appropriate for poor countries? For example, is a manufacturing process that is highly automated best suited for a country like India, with a huge labor force, or would a labor-intensive technology be more appropriate for its needs? Similarly, is it appropriate for MNCs to introduce products primarily produced for sale in developed nations into poor countries that have massive unmet basic needs? Was Nestlé misguided or worse in marketing its infant powdered formula to African and Latin American women who had no access to safe water and who were breast-feeding their babies? Anyone who has visited developing countries will be struck by the ubiquity of American soft drinks and cigarettes. Should nutritionally empty drinks and cancer-causing products be so heavily promoted by MNCs? Questions such as these have no easy answers. How one responds depends on one's values and on an assessment of the alternatives developing countries face. For example, defenders of the MNCs might argue that the transfer of capital-intensive technology is better than no such technology if that is the alternative, and that providing consumers in poor countries with the same choices as those in rich nations assumes they are equally capable of making sensible choices.

Perhaps most important from the host countries' perspective is the *degree of linkage* between the MNCs subsidiaries and the local economy. The more the MNC employs local workers and managers and the more it contracts with local firms for supplies and services, the greater will be the beneficial spillover effects. MNCs that set up subsidiaries in host countries primarily to service the local market, as is often the case with FDI in developed nations, are likely to develop contractual linkages with local firms. Those primarily interested in *outsourcing*—that is, producing in overseas locations for export, usually back to the home market—tend not to develop extensive linkages with local firms. Indeed, several countries in Asia and Central and Latin America have set up special "export processing zones" explicitly to attract MNC investment.

The U.S.-Mexican border, with its two thousand or so maquiladoras, is perhaps the best-known example of such a zone. This zone provides U.S. MNCs with comparatively cheap, nonunion labor, in sites close to the large U.S. market. Taxes and tariffs are virtually eliminated, and environmental and labor laws are weakly enforced. U.S. MNCs in the garment, electronic, and auto industries have flocked to the zone, importing parts from the United States for assembly in Mexico and then shipping the finished products back to the United States. Similarly, in the field of semiconductors, U.S. MNCs pioneered the strategy of manufacturing wafers in the United States, air-freighting them to Asia for assembly into circuits, and then air-freighting them back to the United States for sale. The problem for some host countries is that such MNCs sink few deep roots into the economy, transferring little research and development and developing few linkages with local firms. This is particularly true of the maquiladoras in Mexico, which purchased only 2 percent of their total inputs in Mexico.[26]

There are several other specific criticisms that can be leveled at MNCs, and most of these focus on their impact on developing countries. Critics charge that MNCs tend to exploit workers in developing countries by paying them low wages and by providing them with inadequate benefits and unsafe working conditions. Some MNCs have also been accused of transferring environmentally unsafe production processes to poorer countries to escape strict U.S. or European environmental regulations. All these issues are highly controversial, and making a fair assessment depends to a considerable extent on one's frame of reference. If the actions of MNCs (whether it be on working conditions or environmental matters) are compared to those they pursue in developed countries like the United States, then there is no doubt that MNCs can be seen to be taking advantage of developing nations. However, if one compares MNC behavior to that of local firms in developing countries, then they are certainly no worse (and often are better) economic citizens.[27]

Finally, we need to consider briefly the effects of MNCs on the political conditions in host countries. MNCs are primarily concerned with a stable business climate wherein they can make uninterrupted profits. They certainly are not in the business of promoting democracy or any other human rights. MNCs have operated quite happily in countries ruled by left-wing and right-wing authoritarian regimes. Perhaps the most flagrant example of economic interests overriding political differences was the case of the Gulf Oil Company in the socialist African country of Angola. Here was a case of Communist Cuban troops protecting the oil refineries of a U.S. MNC, Gulf Oil Company, from guerrilla fighters supported by the United States and South African governments.[28]

Sometimes, when their interests were threatened, some MNCs have pressed their home governments to intervene in the internal political affairs of other nations. Most blatant was United Fruit's successful campaign to undermine the elected government of Guatemala in the 1950s. Angered by the expropriation of idle land it owned and what it considered inadequate compensation, even though the dollar amount was based on its own tax records, the company lobbied the Eisenhower administration to orchestrate a military coup. The coup ushered in several decades of repressive rule in Guatemala.[29] Perhaps somewhat less blatantly, U.S. MNCs like ITT were also implicated in the overthrow of the elected Allende government in Chile in 1973.[30] While these are extreme cases, they do show how the political independence of developing countries may be severely constrained by the presence of large MNCs from powerful rich nations.

It is only fair to point out that MNCs also are subject to political pressures. Government pressure or well-organized public campaigns can effect change in MNC behavior. A recent example is the success of a grassroots campaign to force many U.S. MNCs to disinvest from their operations in South Africa. Similarly, a consumer boycott of Nestlé and the subsequent involvement of the World Health Organization forced Nestlé and other infant formula manufacturers to change their marketing practices.[31]

Negative Effects on Home Countries

The central question raised by outward FDI for a home country is what such an outflow of capital, technology, and other goods does for that nation's standard of living. The claim made by trade unions and their academic supporters is that outward foreign direct investment means a loss of jobs in the home country and the gradual "deindustrialization" of the nation's economy.[32] There is little disagreement that jobs do disappear when MNCs locate productive activities overseas. Job losses have been especially heavy for routine production workers as MNCs find it relatively easy to transfer such routine work as assembly operations, keypunching, data processing, and even simple coding of computer software to cheaper overseas locations. The critical questions are, first, whether such job losses are balanced by the creation of new jobs stimulated by FDI, and, second, what would have happened to the lost jobs if no foreign investment had been made. Would foreign competition have eliminated these jobs anyway, albeit more slowly? While it is difficult to give definitive answers to questions subject to a host of varying assumptions, critics of MNCs nevertheless point out that even if there is a net positive effect on employment from FDI, those who lose their jobs are rarely the same people who get the newly created jobs. As several commentators have pointed out, many of the lost jobs are in routine production activities, while those created are in professional, clerical, and service fields.[33] It is these routine production workers, already reeling from the effects of technological change, who represent the greatest source of opposition to outward FDI and to free trade pacts like the North American Free Trade Agreement.

Governments of both home and host countries are also interested in the tax revenues MNCs generate. An MNC operating in several countries typically should pay taxes to each government on the profits it earns doing business in that country. Problems arise, however, because a sizeable portion of the business MNCs conduct is between their own subsidiaries or affiliates. A fairly typical case might involve a U.S. electronics manufacturer sending various parts to its subsidiary in Mexico for assembly and shipment back to the company in the United States. Similarly, management from the U.S. parent may be sent to the Mexican subsidiary to help local managers iron out production problems. The prices charged for these exchanges of goods and services are known as *transfer prices* because they don't occur between independent firms in the market. They are determined by the staff at parent headquarters.

Given that many countries have different tax rates, one can see why MNCs might be tempted to manipulate transfer prices so as to minimize their total tax burden. If Mexico had a higher tax rate than the United States, then MNCs can overprice the goods and services sent to Mexico and underprice the finished goods shipped back to the United States. In this way, little or no profit will be "earned" in Mexico and tax payments to the Mexican government will be minimized. The manipulation of transfer prices can get even more complex when MNCs use countries with very low taxes (known as tax havens) as invoicing offices. In these cases, the invoices (but not the actual goods and services) for all transactions between subsidiaries are routed through the tax havens and profits are "earned" there, thereby avoiding taxes in both the host and the home countries.[34] No one is sure how large the transfer pricing problem is, since it is very difficult for outsiders, including tax authorities, to prove that the transfer prices are different from market prices. What we can say is that the opportunity for such manipulation is vast—intracompany trade by some estimates, now accounts for one third of total world trade.[35]

THE IMPACT OF MNCs: SUMMING UP

As we have seen, both the proponents and the critics of MNCs make good arguments in support of their positions. Proponents of MNCs have the advantage of being able to point to the successes of developing nations like Singapore, Taiwan, Mexico, and Brazil that have welcomed FDI. The recent success story of Malaysia seems to reinforce their case. Malaysia has seen its per capita income and GNP grow by over 6 percent a year, in part due to the large role foreign direct investment played in developing its manufacturing sector (since 1967, 60 percent of manufacturing investment has been based on foreign capital).[36] China seems to be rapidly following suit with a similar strategy. These are powerful real-life examples that bolster the position of advocates of open borders and foreign direct investment. Critics of MNCs have a harder time making their case because there are so few examples of countries succeeding in their economic development using alternative strategies. Japan is one country that comes to mind, but there may be unique conditions attached to its development that make it hard for poor developing countries to grow while emulating Japan's closed door policies toward inward FDI.

Lacking viable alternative development strategies, most governments and workers around the world have to be players in the global economy. Their best strategy, therefore, is to bargain with MNCs over the terms of FDI, seeking as best they can to get the most favorable terms they can. As we will see, while some countries and workforces are not completely helpless in their bargaining with MNCs, on the whole the relations tend to be asymmetric with much of the advantage in the hands of MNCs. This view is not shared by all political economists. Stephen Krasner argues, from an economic nationalist perspective, that nations have substantial bargaining power because they can deny MNCs access to their territory.[37] However, we believe that unless nations possess large quantities of resources, like raw materials, capital, technology, and the like, the tactic of closing off your territory to FDI, in today's world, is a little like shooting yourself in the foot.

BARGAINING RELATIONS BETWEEN MNCs AND GOVERNMENTS AND WORKERS

The MNCs' bargaining advantage is based on two factors. One is their control of scarce and crucial economic resources. The second flows from their mobility, allowing them to transfer resources around the globe. This global mobility means that MNCs often have the luxury of being able to choose where they will locate their resources and activities from a wide range of alternatives. Workers and governments, rooted as they are to certain locations, are thrown into competition with each other to attract MNCs. The business press is full of examples of MNCs being able to extract special benefits from governments, or concessions from workforces, because of their ability to play them off one against the other. Workers are particularly vulnerable to the actual or potential ability of MNCs to move around the globe. Low-skilled workers engaged in low-technology production have very little bargaining power because of the availability of a vast global pool of such workers. They are easily substituted. In the battle for FDI in these economic sectors, we can expect fairly frequent locational moves as MNCs move down the ladder of countries seeking lower-cost labor forces. Even some high-skill workforces in developed countries are vulnerable to locational shifts as more countries develop large pools of educated and well-trained workforces (e.g., India, South Korea, Singapore). In the future, pressure on workers' wages and working conditions from lower-cost locations can be expected to intensify as more productive activities become international. In these circumstances, workers' bargaining power will continue to erode, local and national unions will lose more power, and more workers from around the globe will be forced to compete with each other.

A recent, fairly typical example of such MNC-inspired worker competition involves Hoover, a European appliance maker owned by the U.S. MNC, Maytag. In 1992, Hoover decided to run down its plant in Dijon, France, and to transfer production to a plant in Scotland. The transfer will mean the loss of six hundred jobs in France and the gain of four hundred jobs in Scotland. To win the jobs, the Scottish workforce agreed to accept new working practices and limits on strike action. These concessions, coupled with the lower labor costs in Scotland, tipped the balance in favor of the Glasgow plant. The French government protested the decision and accused the British of "social dumping"—that is, of eroding workers' rights so as to attract foreign investment.[38]

Governments are also compelled to compete in "bidding wars" to attract MNCs. While it is clear that the primary factors determining where MNCs invest have to do with location-specific advantages of the country or the overall strategic plan of the MNC, it is also true that once an MNC has narrowed its choice of sites to two or three locations, then incentives do affect the final decision.[39] (See the following case study for an example of the "bidding war" between state governments in the U.S. to attract a Mercedes-Benz plant.)

Only international cooperation between national workforces and governments can reduce the bargaining advantages of MNCs. For example, in Europe, union representatives from several different subsidiaries of MNCs like Ford, GM, and Phillips have established company councils to facilitate the sharing of information and to coordinate bargaining with the parent company. Workers in Europe have also pushed hard for the adoption of a "social charter" by the European Union that would harmonize labor laws across the member states (so far Britain refuses to sign on to this charter). Similarly, some small developing countries have sought to harmonize the rules and conditions governing FDI in their countries so as to strengthen their bargaining position. The Andean Pact, comprising Columbia, Chile, Peru, and Venezuela, established a common set of regulations to govern FDI in the 1970s so as to minimize competitive bidding among themselves. Among the regulations were limits on profit repatriation and controls on technology transfers and increased requirements for local participation in the ownership of the subsidiary.[40]

These efforts rarely turn out to be very successful at redressing the balance of bargaining power. Take the attempt at international union cooperation. MNCs can often break union bonds of solidarity by making subsidiary workforces compete for investment resources. With large-scale unemployment in many European countries, it becomes hard for each workforce not to try and save its own skin when the issue boils down to "their jobs or ours," especially when "they" are of a different nationality.[41]

Still, the picture is not completely gloomy. Developed countries, with their large domestic markets, modern and well-developed infrastructures (roads, ports, and the like), large pools of educated workers, and stable political climates are attractive to MNCs and thus have considerable bargaining power. Ironically, these governments rarely seek to impose restrictions on the activities of MNCs. As both home and host of MNCs, such governments are liable to retaliation against their home-based MNCs should they act too harshly against other countries' MNCs.

Some developing countries are also gaining leverage in their bargaining relations with MNCs. Singapore, for example, because of its superb transportation and communication infrastructure, and its excellent science and technology research centers, is beginning to attract regional headquarters of MNCs, thereby winning for itself considerably more of the high-income-producing functions carried out by MNCs. Similarly, India, with its abundant supply of relatively inexpensive English-speaking engineers and scientists has attracted nearly every major computer and software producer in the U.S. to set up operations there. The companies include Texas Instruments, Motorola, Hewlett Packard, Apple Computers, Sun Microsystems, Intel, Dell, and IBM.[42] Developing countries with such locational advantages will find several MNCs competing to locate there and can negotiate more favorable terms for inward foreign direct investment. It should be noted, of course, that other than the advantage of possessing scarce natural resources and cheap labor (which is really no advantage, since it is so widely available), most of the critical competitive advantages countries possess are man-made. They are, in fact, the result of the development efforts of the host country itself. While MNCs can assist the process of development, it is domestic factors that overwhelmingly determine the quality of the infrastructure, the level of education and training of the population, and the political situation.

CONCLUSION

We now come to the final and most speculative question about MNCs: What will be their impact on the IPE of tomorrow? Looking into the future is always a hazardous business. And in the case of MNCs and the international political economy, the prognostications are especially difficult since political and economic forces pull in opposite directions.

If we follow a strictly *economic logic*, we can foresee that international economic activity will continue to grow at a rapid pace. Technological advances in transportation and telecommunications will shrink the world, and the mobility of MNCs and the fierce competitive battles among them will prompt them to spread their reach to all corners of the globe. This intensified economic competition will also entice many MNCs to seek shelter and respite from the rigors of these fierce economic battles by forming alliances and partnership across borders. This is already happening in several industries. In aircraft manufacturing, Boeing and its main rival, the European Airbus consortium, talk of collaborating on a new supersonic airplane. Airlines from around the world are teaming up in cross-border partnerships to provide customers with truly international service. British Airways, for example, owns 22 percent of USAir and 25 percent of Australia's Quantas Airways. KLM Royal Dutch Airlines owns 20 percent of Northwest, and Delta has cross-shareholdings with Swissair and Singapore Airlines.[43] In electronics, IBM (U.S.), Siemens (Germany), and Toshiba (Japan) have joined together to develop a new computer chip. Not only are they collaborating in the research and development of the chip, but they also plan to produce the chip jointly.[44]

These trends have prompted Robert Reich to see a future where corporations do indeed lose their national identities, becoming global organizations that integrate the world according to their purposes. The big winners in this newly integrated world will not be particular nations and their citizens but highly skilled individuals ("symbolic analysts," Reich calls them) who can operate effectively in the high-tech world of the future. These individuals will form an international elite separated by income and lifestyle from their fellow citizens in each of their countries of origin. This scenario, if taken to its logical extreme, suggests a highly stratified world, with an international class of symbolic analysts and capitalists having significant power in the world and perhaps a weakening of the power of national governments.

Of course, neither Reich nor any other thoughtful political economist goes so far as to suggest that the power of national governments will erode to the point that nation-states become irrelevant. While many agree that the task of governing and regulating national economies will be made more difficult by the presence of MNCs, few believe national governments will surrender their large numbers of prerogatives easily. As Raymond Vernon puts it: "With jobs, taxes, payment balances, and technological achievement seemingly at stake, governments are bound to act in an effort to defend national interests and respond to national pressures."[45]

In other words, there is also a countervailing and equally powerful *political logic* at work. Individuals remain deeply wedded to their national identities, and it is nation-states, not corporations, that enforce laws, levy taxes, and organize armies. Indeed, as peoples' economic lives become increasingly governed by large, distant international forces, one might expect ordinary citizens to demand greater political influence over their national governments. It is for these reasons that the historian Paul Kennedy concludes: "Even if the autonomy and functions of the state have been eroded by transnational trends, no adequate substitute has emerged to replace it as the key unit in responding to global change."[46] We are left, therefore, contemplating a future marked by continuing tension between political and economic forces.

CASE STUDY: WOOING MULTINATIONAL CORPORATIONS—THE CASE OF MERCEDES-BENZ

Multinational corporations are in great demand around the globe. Whenever a large, well-known company announces that it is planning to establish a manufacturing facility, several countries engage in a fierce bidding war to attract the investment to their shores. The following example gives a fairly typical picture of the lengths to which governments (national and regional) will go to capture MNC investment. It also indicates the advantage in bargaining power MNCs possess relative to governments.

Mercedes-Benz is a quintessentially German manufacturer, well known for its excellent engineering and high-quality cars and trucks. In 1993, it made the decision to internationalize its production. Several factors combined to prompt the decision: labor

Continued

CASE STUDY: WOOING MULTINATIONAL CORPORATIONS—THE CASE OF MERCEDES-BENZ, *continued*

costs in Germany were extremely high; the German currency, the Deutschemark, was highly valued against the dollar, raising the price of its cars in its main export market, the United States; and Japanese MNCs began challenging Mercedes' domination of the luxury car market with the Lexus, Infinity, and Acura models. Mercedes' decision to build a new Jeep-like sports-utility vehicle in a foreign location was part of its strategy to overcome these difficulties.

A team of Mercedes executives began a worldwide selection process in January 1993 and quickly narrowed the search to North America. Not only is the United States the main market for sports-utility vehicles, but the combined costs of labor, parts, and transportation would be lowest there. Transportation would be a substantial portion of the costs, since Mercedes planned to import engines and other components from Germany and to export over half of the finished vehicles to non-U.S. markets.

The Mercedes team, with the help of a consultant, then examined a hundred sites in thirty-five states of the United States. The team visited six final sites, and quickly narrowed the choice to South and North Carolina and Alabama. Each is a state with right-to-work laws and low unionization rates. North Carolina's package of incentives added up to $108 million. South Carolina offered about $130 million worth of incentives, in a package similar to one that had recently enticed BMW to locate its first U.S. plant there. But it was Alabama, with its $253 million incentive package that had snared the $300 million plant.

Alabama, a state with a reputation as a backward place holding few attractions for MNCs, went all out to win the investment. The incentive package included: $92 million to purchase and develop the site; $77 million for improvements to highways, utilities, and other infrastructure; tax abatement on machinery and equipment; and $60 million on education and training. The University of Alabama even agreed to run a special "Saturday School" to help the children of German Mercedes managers keep up with the higher standards in science and math back home in Germany. All this would be paid for by the taxpayers of Alabama. The governor of North Carolina was particularly upset by a tax break the Alabama legislature passed (labeled by some the "Benz Bill"), which allowed Mercedes to withhold 5 percent of employees' wages to pay off Mercedes debts.

The wooing of Mercedes went beyond financial incentives. It included an offer to name a section of an interstate highway "the Mercedes-Benz autobahn," airplane and helicopter tours, visits by the governor of Alabama and other state officials to Mercedes headquarters in Germany, a billboard in German near the site welcoming Mercedes, and the governor driving a Mercedes as the official state car. It is not surprising to read that a Mercedes executive claimed it was "Alabama's zeal" that was the deciding factor.

In return, fifteen hundred workers would get good-paying jobs, and several more thousand jobs would be created in supplier firms, restaurants, and the like.

Sources: "Why Mercedes Is Alabama Bound," *Business Week,* 11 October 1993; "The Invaders Are Welcome," *The Economist,* 8 January 1994; "Alabama Steers Mercedes South," *ENR,* 11 October 1993.

DISCUSSION QUESTIONS

1. "Most multinational corporations are headquartered in the United States and take advantage of cheap labor in less developed countries to manufacture goods that are then sold in the United States." What is right and what is wrong with this statement as a general description of MNCs? Explain.

2. What is meant by "firm-specific competitive advantage"? How and why is this factor important in our understanding of the logic of foreign direct investment of MNCs? Explain.
3. What impacts do MNCs have on their home countries? On their host countries? Compare and contrast the different points of view on this question. What is your own opinion?
4. How does the growing importance of global markets and MNCs alter the role of the state in home and host countries? Explain.

SUGGESTED READINGS

Richard J. Barnet and Ronald E. Müller. *Global Reach: The Power of the Multinational Corporations.* New York: Touchstone, 1974.

R. E. Caves. *Multinational Enterprise and Economic Analysis.* Cambridge, England: Cambridge University Press, 1982.

Peter Dicken. *Global Shift: The Internationalization of Economic Activity.* London: Paul Chapman Publishing, 1992.

John H. Dunning. *Explaining International Production.* London: Unwin Hyman, 1988.

Kenneth A. Froot, (ed.) *Foreign Direct Investment.* Chicago: The University of Chicago Press, 1993.

Stephen H. Hymer. *The International Operations of National Firms: A Study of Direct Foreign Investment.* Cambridge, MA: MIT Press, 1976.

Robert B. Reich. *The Work of Nations: Preparing Ourselves for 21st Century Capitalism.* New York: Vintage Books, 1992.

United Nations Conference on Trade and Development (UNCTAD), *World Investment Report 1993: Transnational Corporations and Integrated International Production.* New York: United Nations, 1993. (Also see previous reports.)

Raymond Vernon. *Sovereignty at Bay: The Multinational Spread of U.S. Enterprises.* New York: Basic Books, 1971.

NOTES

1. Stephen Hymer, "The Internationalization of Capital," *Journal of Economic Issues* 6 (March 1972):104.
2. Cited in Richard J. Barnet and Ronald Müller, *Global Reach: The Power of the Multinational Corporations* (New York: Touchstone, 1994), 16.
3. One of the most prominent critical works was Barnet and Müller's *Global Reach.*
4. *The Economist,* 27 March 1993.
5. Cited in Edward M. Graham and Paul R. Krugman, "The Surge in Foreign Direct Investment in the 1980s," in Kenneth A. Froot, ed., *Foreign Direct Investment* (Chicago: University of Chicago Press, 1993), 13.
6. United Nations Conference on Trade and Development (UNCTAD) Programme on Transnational Corporations, *World Investment Report 1993: Transnational Corporations and Integrated International Production* (New York: United Nations, 1993), 22. These United Nations reports are excellent sources of data on MNCs.
7. Cited in Graham and Krugman, *Foreign Direct Investment,* 14.
8. Robert E. Lipsey, "Foreign Direct Investment in the United States: Changes Over Three Decades," in Froot, *Foreign Direct Investment,* 115.
9. Peter Dicken, *Global Shift: The Internationalization of Economic Activity,* 2nd ed. (London: Paul Chapman Publishing, 1992), 52–53.

10. See Jean-Jacques Servan Schreiber, *The American Challenge* (London: Hamish Hamilton, 1968) for a discussion of the perceived U.S. threat to Europe.

11. Robert B. Reich, *The Work of Nations: Preparing Ourselves for 21st Century Capitalism* (New York: Vintage, 1991), 153.

12. Cited in Froot, *Foreign Direct Investment*, 108.

13. Robert Lawrence, "Japan's Low Levels of Inward Investment," in Froot, *Foreign Direct Investment*, 86.

14. It should be noted that well over 50 percent of FDI involves acquisitions of existing corporations or assets. Because members of *keiretsus* own a sizeable portion of each other's shares, they can collectively block any takeover attempt by a foreign competitor. For a fuller discussion of FDI in Japan, see Mark Mason, *American Multinationals and Japan: The Political Economy of Capital Controls, 1899–1980* (Cambridge, MA: Harvard University Press, 1992).

15. UNCTAD, *World Investment Report 1993.*

16. Froot, *Foreign Direct Investment*, 192.

17. For a fuller discussion of the ideas discussed in this section, see Stephen H. Hymer, *The International Operations of National Firms: A Study of Direct Foreign Investment* (Cambridge, MA: MIT Press, 1976); and John H. Dunning, *Explaining International Production* (London: Unwin Hyman, 1981).

18. Raymond Vernon, "International Investment and International Trade in the Product Cycle," *Quarterly Journal of Economics*, 80 (1966):190–207.

19. The original formulation of this idea was put forward in F. T. Knickerbocker, *Oligopolistic Reaction and Multinational Enterprises* (Boston: Harvard Business School, 1973).

20. "The Die is Cast by Growth and Costs," *Financial Times*, 31 May 1994, 14.

21. One of the most sophisticated and balanced arguments in support of MNCs is made by Raymond Vernon, *Storm over the Multinationals: The Real Issues* (Cambridge, MA: Harvard University Press, 1977).

22. See Dicken, *Global Shift*, 388. Acquisitions are the more common form of FDI in developed countries, partly because such countries have a larger pool of companies available for purchase.

23. Reich, *The Work of Nations*, 146.

24. Andre Gunder Frank, for example, has argued that Brazil grew very fast during World War II because it was isolated economically from Europe. See his *Capitalism and Underdevelopment in Latin America: Historical Studies of Chile and Brazil* (New York: Monthly Review Press, 1969).

25. Recent studies show that none of the largest U.S. firms with direct investments in Latin America carries out any basic research in these countries. Robert Grosse, "Competitive Advantages and Multinational Enterprises in Latin America," *Journal of Business Research* 25 (1992):27–42.

26. Leslie Sklair, *Assembling for Development: The Maquila Industry in Mexico and the United States* (San Diego, CA: Center for U.S.-Mexican Studies, University of California, 1993), 244.

27. Graham and Krugman conclude, "Studies basically find that foreign-owned firms behave very similarly to domestically owned firms in the same industry. They pay similar wages, engage in similar amounts of R & D, and so on," in Froot, *Foreign Direct Investment*, 32. See also Dickens, *Global Shift*, for a review of the evidence.

28. The case is cited in Robert Gilpin, *The Political Economy of International Relations* (Princeton, NJ: Princeton University Press, 1987), 250.

29. Stephen Kinzer, *Bitter Fruit: The Untold Story of the Bitter Coup in Guatemala* (New York: Doubleday, 1982).

30. James Petras and Morris Morley, *The United States and Chile: Imperialism and the Overthrow of the Allende Government* (New York: Monthly Review Press, 1975).

31. "The Formula Crisis Cools," *Fortune*, 27 December 1982, 106.

32. For the best argument in support of this thesis, see Barry Bluestone and Bennett Harrison, *The Deindustrialization of America: Plant Closings, Community Abandonment, and the Dismantling of Basic Industry* (New York: Basic Books, 1982).

33. See, for example, Reich, *The Work of Nations*, chapter 17, and Barnet and Müller, *Global Reach*, 302.

34. For an example, see Leon Grunberg, *Failed Multinational Ventures: The Political Economy of International Divestments* (Lexington, MA: D.C. Heath, 1981), ch. 4.

35. "Everybody's Favorite Monsters: A Survey of Multinationals," *The Economist*, 27 March 1993, 9.

36. "Malaysia Urged to Boost GATT Role," *Financial Times*, 21 July 1993, 3.

37. Stephen D. Krasner, "Multinational Corporations," in Jeffrey A. Frieden and David A. Lake, eds., *International Political Economy: Perspectives on Global Power and Wealth*, 2nd ed. (New York: St. Martin's Press, 1991).

38. "Labour Pains," *The Economist*, 6 February 1993, 71.

39. UNCTAD, *World Investment Report (1993)*, 227.

40. Krasner, in *International Political Economy*, 174–175.

41. See Grunberg, *Failed Multinational Ventures*, for examples.

42. UNCTAD, *World Investment Report 1993*, 176 and 139.

43. "Cross-Border Linkups Bring Airlines Range But Uncertain Benefits," *The Wall Street Journal*, 7 June 1994, 1.

44. UNCTAD, *World Investment Report 1993*, 143.

45. Vernon, in *Foreign Direct Investment*, 73.

46. Paul Kennedy, *Preparing for the Twenty-first Century* (New York: Random House, 1993), 134.

17

The IPE of Energy and Oil

Dr. Timothy G. Amen

OVERVIEW

Energy, and especially oil, are inextricably bound into the fabric of the international political economy. Energy is wealth and it is power. Especially in an industrial world, to lack energy is to be dependent on others. The OPEC oil crises of the 1970s made clear that the world's unequal distribution of energy was a critical factor in international economics and politics. The impact of the 1970s oil crises was dramatic; the final consequences are as yet unclear. This chapter examines these two OPEC oil crises and the IPE of energy and oil in general as an example of the complex and dynamic economic and political relationships that characterize the world today.

Our survey of the history of the IPE of energy and oil reveals four tensions that are this chapter's themes. The first, which will be clear from the study of oil, is that the world is increasingly *interdependent*. Events in one part of the globe affect people everywhere. It is no longer possible to ignore "outside" forces or actors in making political or economic choices. A second and related theme is that politics and economics have become so tightly intertwined in many areas that it is useless to try to distinguish between them. The economics of oil influence the politics of oil, and vice versa.

A third theme is that political economy is increasingly not just international but *global* in scope, involving all nations at once, not just relations between them. To an important extent, the two OPEC oil crises have been responsible for the acceleration of this trend along with a proliferation of actors involved in the IPE of oil. Multinational corporations and international organizations, not just large nation-states, are important actors in this global arena. Furthermore, and the final theme of this chapter, is that neither states nor markets alone can determine outcomes in this interdependent, intertwined, global world. The case of oil demonstrates that IPE is a delicate balancing act, and that power often lies with those who have the potential to disturb that equilibrium. Thus a number of actors, including small nations or even terrorist groups, can greatly influence the IPE today.

In the last half of the chapter we examine some of the most frequent questions encountered in the study of the IPE(s) of energy and oil—and discuss the answers typically provided by the mercantilist, liberal, and Marxist-structuralist perspectives on international political economy.

Two particular commodities, coal and oil,[1] outline the story of the modern international political economy of energy. Of the two, coal has been the more significant in historic terms. Indeed, oil was discovered and developed as a commercial commodity only in the late 1800s, whereas coal was a "primitive modern industry"[2] well before the industrial revolution began in the late 1700s. In the twentieth century, however, oil clearly eclipsed coal as the star of the story, and the story itself became high drama. There is certainly a supporting cast in this story-turned-drama: natural gas, nuclear energy, and hydroelectric power are the most well-known "bit players." But oil and coal between them have long accounted for over two thirds of the total energy consumption of the world's industrial economies. And in 1990, oil by itself accounted for 22 percent more of total world energy consumption than did coal.[3]

Oil is also clearly the more important commodity in terms of the international political economy, so much so that some have dubbed the twentieth century "the oil century." The "Great Powers" of international politics have long had huge national supplies of coal, supplies which, in the abstract, could meet virtually all of their domestic needs for energy. Technology and considerations of national security and strategy are not abstractions, however, and early in this century these two forces combined to push oil to the forefront of the political economy of energy, both within the international system's key states and, inevitably, internationally as well.

The year 1973 was a turning point for the international political economy. By 1973, students of politics and economics—and viewers of TV news—*should* already have realized that the world had changed from the early days of postwar U.S. hegemony. The Vietnam War's prolonged conclusion showed the weakened resolve of the United States to fight communism everywhere and anywhere. The collapse of the Bretton Woods monetary system, built on U.S. financial hegemony, was complete when President Richard Nixon took the United States off the gold standard in 1971. U.S. dominance in business was openly challenged by the flood of cheap but sturdy Volkswagen, Toyota, and Datsun cars from abroad. The balance of wealth and power was shifting.

Many people, however, did not realize that fundamental change was under way. The shift in the global patterns of IPE were invisible to them as they concentrated on the details of everyday life, which seemed hardly changed at all. Suddenly, however, their lives were disrupted at every level of personal, business, national, and global relations.

War in the Middle East in 1973 suddenly brought home consequences that until this day have not yet been fully resolved. U.S. support of Israel in the Yom Kippur War with Egypt caused the Arab members of the Organization of Petroleum Exporting Countries (OPEC) to ban exports of petroleum to the United States and the other allies of Israel. In short order, gasoline prices skyrocketed and gasoline shortages appeared: plans to ration gasoline were made. Because energy is so vital to every aspect of an industrial society, every element of daily life was altered.

By the time the dust settled a year later, the world was truly changed. The world oil market was dominated by the OPEC cartel. Oil prices continued to rise and the changing pattern of world payments caused sudden and dramatic shifts in the global distribution of wealth. Individuals, industries, and nations that were once rich were suddenly heavily burdened by oil payments. Trade, finance, and security structures were all changed.

The OPEC oil embargo of 1973–1974 was an earthquake that rocked the international political economy—a short, sharp shock that shook institutional structures and changed the landscape for years to come. Like an earthquake, however, the *causes* of the OPEC oil shock had built up over many years. The sudden and dramatic shocks released pent-up pressures, but did not change them. The IPE of oil and energy traces a fault line; tensions build up over time, to be suddenly released. We must understand these continuing tensions as much as the quakes themselves.

As this chapter discusses the history of the IPE of oil and energy, four tensions will be examined. The first is the tension that arises due to *interdependence*. The overlapping structures of IPE means that states and markets are dependent on each other in ways that create tensions or pressures, giving perhaps one of the best illustrations of this condition. The second tension is created by the increasingly *intertwined nature of economics and politics* today. The tensions between states and markets that were highlighted in the first chapter of this book are magnified here as it becomes increasingly impossible to tell where politics leaves off and economic matters begin.

The third tension is created by the increasingly *global* nature of IPE structures. As problems and events become more global in scope, the role of the nation-state as the center of international relations is jeopardized. International organizations, including multinational corporations, seem to take on increasing importance.

Finally, the IPE of energy and oil demonstrate that *neither states nor markets alone* can determine outcomes in this interdependent, intertwined world. IPE is a delicate balancing act, and power often lies with those who have the potential to disturb that equilibrium. Thus, even relatively small actors, such as small nations or even terrorist groups, can have great influence in IPE today. This creates added tensions of risk and uncertainty. The shock wave of the two oil crises of the 1970s could occur again, profoundly disturbing the IPE but also shifting around wealth and power.

THE OPEC OIL CRISES OF THE 1970s: PRESSURES BEHIND THE SHOCK

The Organization of Petroleum Exporting Countries (OPEC) is an example of a **cartel**, or a producers organization.[4] Cartels typically attempt to organize production in ways that increase commodity prices and their profits. OPEC is unlike other cartels, however, in that it is composed of sovereign nation-states, not ordinary business firms. OPEC's actions are therefore conditioned by national desires for wealth, power, and security; politics lies at the very heart of OPEC.

The first oil shock occurred in late 1973, when another Arab-Israeli war was accompanied by a successful oil embargo imposed by Arab states within OPEC on countries supporting Israel in the Yom Kippur War. Witnessing the potential of "the oil weapon," OPEC as a whole then quickly increased the price of a barrel of oil in the international marketplace from $2.90 per barrel to $11.65—a jump of over 400 percent! The second oil shock occurred at the end of the decade, when Iranian nationalists finally succeeded in toppling the shah from his throne in Tehran. The ensuing panic in world oil markets pushed the price of a 42-gallon barrel of crude from $13 to $34 (by the early 1980s). In less than a decade, then, the oil-burning economies of the world saw their import bills for petroleum leap by almost 1,200 percent.[5]

One can trace the roots of either episode back through factors such as decades of building resentment over foreign control of vital national resources. The OPEC cartel was formed in 1960 when the major oil-exporting nations sought to gain more control over and profit from the oil located under their member nations. Up until then, the production, processing, and marketing of oil was dominated by seven major multinational oil corporations—the seven sisters—five U.S., one British, and one Anglo-Dutch company. The major oil companies blocked other companies from getting into the market, and effectively controlled the price, processing, and marketing of oil. The demand for oil was *inelastic*, which meant that there was no available substitute for it. Consumption rates did not decrease in the short run when oil prices went up, either. These economic conditions meant huge profits for oil companies, low consumer oil prices along with high consumption rates by consumers, but it meant also that host nations felt exploited and dominated by the oil companies and their client states.

Corporate control over oil was actively supported by the political and military power of the major industrialized powers. When Iran attempted to nationalize the assets of an oil company, Great Britain imposed an economic embargo on Iran. The United States helped overthrow the Iranian government and bring to power the shah, who supported U.S. oil companies. Meanwhile, host countries received only a small fixed royalty for their crude from the major oil companies.

In 1969, Colonel Muammar Gadhafi seized state power in Libya. Using the threat of nationalization, his new regime forced the oil multinational corporations (MNCs) operating in Libya first to cut production, and then to raise prices and accept an increase in taxes. For the first time, oil companies felt increasingly vulnerable to Middle Eastern states. Western governments did not take action against Libya.

How does one explain the changed, weakened positions of the heretofore dominant oil MNCs and the powerful states that were their "home countries"? The answers are complicated,[6] but a good starting place is a description of supply and demand curves in the world oil market in the years leading up to 1973.

Before World War II, dependence on oil was something the United States and other industrialized nations had not experienced because the United States had been the world's largest oil producer and exporter. Oil production in the Middle East was under the control of United States and European firms. Oil prices were relatively low. After the war, more inexpensive oil was imported from other countries, further driving down oil prices.

In response to the seemingly endless growth in the globe's thirst for oil, *new* production by *new* producers after World War II resulted in petroleum supply increases, which actually outdistanced the growth in world consumption by the end of the 1950s. The "annual rates of growth of the new foreign oil enterprises materially outstripped those of the seven largest companies. Indeed, they were twice as great in virtually every division of the industry. . . . [F]rom 1953 to 1972, the foreign oil industry passed from a position of very *high* concentration, with less than ten important participants, to one of *moderate* concentration, with at least fifty integrated multinational oil companies."[7] Clearly, with a multitude of new production companies having joined in the game, the majors found cooperation among producers much more difficult to arrange and maintain than in the past.

As industrialization gained a full head of steam after World War II, especially in the developed countries, their dependence on foreign oil increased as the demand for petroleum again accelerated. In the United States, Western Europe, and Japan, annual total oil consumption more than doubled: in Western Europe, consumption rose 270 percent; in Japan the figure was 500 percent! By the early to mid-1960s, Europe and Japan were fully recovered economically from the destruction of World War II—and ready to join the United States in increasing the demand on available world petroleum supplies. By 1973, then, generally rising demand plus increasing reliance on oil as a primary source of world energy,[8] coupled with specifically increasing demand for Middle East oil as the biggest, cheapest surplus pool of petroleum available, combined to make *countries* as vulnerable as *companies* to the growing assertiveness of Middle East statesmen.

Supply and demand curves, of course, do not tell the whole story of the West's inability to respond decisively to Arab oil producers in 1973. For instance, a full account of the year's events would delve into how the West's single strongest and richest state, the United States, had been thrown into ongoing turmoil and intermittent paralysis by both the unfolding of the Watergate scandal (the Watergate burglars went on trial in January) and the endgame in Vietnam (the U.S. Congress passed the War Powers Act over President Nixon's veto in November).

Corporate control over oil gradually weakened in the face of a variety of political and economic conditions. New companies finally got into the business, increasing competition among the oil companies. More oil was produced than could be consumed. Host governments increasingly found it easier to bargain with many of the new companies. Libya and Saudi Arabia, two of the largest producers, began to have more influence on oil prices. The five original members of OPEC increased to thirteen over the next decade and accounted for 85 percent of the world's oil exports. Yet OPEC failed to agree on a set price for oil and production levels.

The tone for a new relationship between host governments, the oil companies, and the industrialized nations was established in 1969, when Libya pressured Occidental Petroleum into new concessions. As it did, host countries were able to gradually wrangle bigger concessions from the oil companies. Libya demonstrated that revenue could be raised by increasing oil prices. OPEC as a whole, then, soon became more hawkish on questions of production and price levels and taxes. OPEC countries profited when the dollar was devalued in 1971 and the price of oil was increased to make up for this deficit. A year later, Western Europe, Japan, and the United States were quite dependent on oil as an energy resource and imported oil for that purpose, but this also made them more vulnerable to supply interruption.

That interruption came when the fourth Arab-Israeli war began on October 6, 1973. OPEC made a series of demands for the nationalization of oil and higher oil prices, and embargoed oil shipments to the West. In support of Arab states, the Organization of Arab Petroleum Exporting Countries (OAPEC) raised the price of oil from $2.29 per barrel to $5.12 to $11.65 per barrel by the end of the year. OPEC finally controlled both the price and supply of oil. Ownership of oil company subsidiaries went over to the oil producing states, effectively making the oil companies contractors of the oil producers.

The United States had tried to form an oil consumers "countercartel" at a conference held in Washington in early 1974, but the effort only demonstrated the inability of America, Japan, and Western Europe to respond collectively. The International Energy Agency (IEA), "the only common effort to emerge from the conference,"[9] certainly had developed no coordinated contingency plans to respond to the oil crisis. Most of the industrialized states counted on bilateral agreements with OPEC producers to solve their oil import problems. The oil companies went along with the price hikes because they could easily pass higher gas prices on to consumers.

At the level of the international system, OPEC "unilaterally" controlled prices throughout the mid-1970s. Its members did so by collaboratively determining both the price of oil and the production reductions necessary to limit supply and maintain the agreed-upon price. Saudi Arabia was the key to this process. It has long had the highest level of proved crude oil reserves of any state in the world.[10] OPEC's ability after 1973 to fix prices was due, more than any other single factor, to Saudi Arabia's willingness to restrict its own national production.

Saudi Arabia, the largest oil producer and exporter, and with its financial reserves, influenced OPEC's policies the most. Basically pro-Western, the Saudis were a steady, moderating voice, distinct from that of OPEC's more hawkish members. The Saudis made up for production cuts during times of recession and increased production enough to keep prices stable. Aside from their moderate political positions, Saudi Arabia and many of the richer OPEC members wanted to disrupt the international economy to some extent but not to the point of ruining their investment opportunities in the West. Other OPEC members, including Iran and Iraq, favored production cuts to drive up oil prices above the rate of inflation in the West.

Beyond Saudi moderation, conservation efforts and economic recession in the West led to a slackening of demand in world oil markets in the wake of the 1973 crisis. Recently discovered supplies of petroleum in the North Sea, Alaska, and Mexico were also finally coming on-line. The United States created a Strategic Petroleum Reserve that would release oil to the market in the case of another crisis. Ironically, then, the mid-1970s was a period of some stability in the international oil system.

Adding such "state-level" elements to the story is in fact the only way to understand fully why 1973 would not be the only crisis year in the oil decade. The story of the 1979 shock to the IPE of oil *is* very much more the tale of a single state than is the story just recounted of 1973. That state is Iran, and developments there ushered in the IPE of energy in which we have lived since.

In the late 1970s, demand for oil in the West continued to increase while Saudi Arabia lost interest in its management role in the cartel. The Saudis and Kuwaitis let production drop off. As at so many junctures in the past, political revolution precipitated the next great upheaval in the IPE of petroleum. Iran may have been number three in proved oil reserves in the mid-1970s, but as the Ayatollah Khomeini and his supporters took square aim at Shah Reza Pahlavi in 1978, the impact on international oil markets was global. One key to the eventual 1979 overthrow of the shah was the cutoff in late 1978 of all Iranian petroleum exports by the Ayatollah's supporters in the national oil industry. The subsequent general world price rise may not have been the immediate, fourfold increase of 1973, but a 260 percent jump in the aftermath of the revolution was nonetheless devastating. How was it that a full five years after the Arab embargo of 1973, one (non-Arab) country, accounting for less than 20 percent of all OPEC exports, could once again throw international economics—and politics—into such disarray?

The answer in the short term has to do with the psychology of panic, and the way in which the embargo of late 1978 revived unpleasant memories of 1973. A defining characteristic of any panic is a "Look out for number one," "Devil take the hindmost" inability to consider common benefits in the face of imminent threat to oneself. Panic, or at least the inability to cooperate in the short term, *had* characterized "the Western response" to the crisis of 1973.

Now a similar inability began to infect OPEC in general and Persian Gulf producers in particular. Oil producers sell their product to the world by way of two different (but related) markets. A long-term contract market accounted for most sales in the late 1970s: the contract, between oil company and producer, reflected the price set by OPEC. Oil not sold on this market was/is traded on spot markets, and such markets reacted swiftly to the withdrawal of Iranian oil in late 1978. As spot market prices shot up, the gap between these prices and long-term market prices widened. The primary beneficiary of such a gap was clear—the oil companies, whose long-term contracts gave them a supply of oil at a relatively cheap, stable price, which they could then sell at prices reflecting the spot market frenzy. OPEC states, remembering long years of perceived exploitation at the hands of the oil MNCs, now began to place their own surcharges on top of prices previously determined by OPEC. And many began to break long-term contracts in order to sell their oil on the more lucrative spot market. The Saudis tried to hold the line, but the momentum was inexorable.

In 1980, the Saudis and other moderate states regained control over the situation. But the outbreak of the Iran-Iraq war again destabilized oil markets. World production decreased by roughly 10 percent, driving up the spot market price of oil to $41 a barrel. The West responded by cutting consumption and trying to improve political relations with the oil producers.

REACTIONS TO THE OPEC OIL CRISES

The two OPEC oil crises changed and shaped the views of officials, experts, and the public about national security in several ways. For the first time since World War II, scarcity of natural resources and raw materials became a major problem. Many nations became dependent on energy and other resources. More important, however, they became vulnerable to oil-producing nations and their political objectives. Oil became more than just an economic problem. The economics of oil blended with efforts to use it as a political weapon to change the distribution of wealth and power in the international political economy. At first, U.S. military capabilities and political influence could not overcome OPEC's political and economic clout. The oil crises foreshadowed the North-South struggle that was to emerge between the developed and developing nations (see chapter 15 for more detail on North-South issues). The bipolar East-West conflict gave way to a multipolar struggle, one component of which was development problems between the rich and poor nations. Sandwiched in between these nations were the newly industrialized countries (NICs) who had successfully developed to some extent, but many of whom, like the West, were dependent on external sources of energy.

The oil crises also made it difficult to undo political and economic interdependence in the international political economy. States could no longer as easily insulate or isolate themselves from the international political economy in ways they could earlier. Trade had always made states interdependent with one another to some extent. Now most states needed energy and other resources if industrial development and economic growth was to continue. LDCs had been important to the United States as allies in its battle to contain international communism. LDCs would now be important for their markets but also for their resources. A nation's military power was now dependent on access to natural resources and raw materials to feed the economy's industrial base. The oil-producing nations were also affected by interdependence, as demonstrated by their efforts to charge more for oil but not at the expense of bankrupting the West.

As discussed in a number of other chapters, but pertinent here, is the accelerated pace of economic competition between states that emerged in the 1970s. Economic recession resulting from the two oil crises fostered efforts by states, in response to demands by groups and sometimes whole societies, to sustain or achieve more economic growth and higher standards of living. Many states found themselves caught between a rock and a hard place—between mercantilist and liberal forces. The economic health of a society became a matter of national security concern in a domestic and international environment where resources—natural or man-made—were increasingly viewed as scarce or becoming finite.

THE DEEPER ROOTS OF THE OIL CRISIS

The pressures that resulted in the oil crises of the 1970s were not just surface tensions, they derived from deep and long-standing conflicts and tensions. We can see how these pressures built and intensified by tracing briefly the fault line from World War I to the Yom Kippur War.

War-fighting coalitions obviously spring from a number of shared interests among partners. One important common denominator among the British (and Dutch), Russians, and French was reflected in the emerging—and converging—oil interests of actors such as Royal Dutch-Shell, the Rothschilds, and the czarist rulers of Russia. These interests had been in "together" on the ground floor, when European oil had been discovered in Russia in the 1870s, and when Dutch colonial possessions in Southeast Asia were first found to have the stuff in the 1880s—and had it shipped back to Europe through the British-controlled Suez Canal in the 1890s.

At the heart of the opposing coalition stood Germany, a country that had only become the modern state of this name in the year 1871—and which obviously had a lot of work to do if it was going to catch up to the Great Powers, which had been at the heart of international politics for centuries. Like Great Britain, Germany possessed impressive iron ore deposits, and the coal by which this iron could be turned into steel. What could then be done with the steel if a country were *really* interested in joining the older Great Powers in directing the show of international politics? Britain itself supplied the answer: build and operate a great navy.

The line connecting the international political economy of energy from World War I to the present is a startlingly clear one. The internationalization of this political economy was already obvious enough in the years before the war, but the war itself accelerated the process and shifted its geographic focus in ways dramatically familiar to us today. Indeed, World War I is much more important than World War II in focusing any picture of the contemporary IPE of oil. Events in Russia and the Middle East were (and are?) most important in this regard.

As a state, Russia did not survive the war. In 1917, Marxist revolutionaries completed the work of toppling the czarist state, installing a regime led first by Lenin and then by Stalin. Given its Marxist ideological base and Lenin's own analysis of imperialism (*Imperialism: The Highest Stage of Capitalism*), the fate of the Nobel and Rothschild—and all other foreign—stakes in the political economy of the new Soviet state was a foregone conclusion. Since the days of World War I, then, until the breakup of the Soviet Union in 1991, further development of "Russia's" huge oil reserves would be tightly, centrally controlled by the state, with its capital in Moscow.[11] Now, at the end of the century, that state and its control have disappeared, and the future of these vast reserves and production capacity is, of course, one of the most significant questions in the contemporary IPE of energy.

Even a cursory glance at a map of the world reveals the connection between Russian/"ex-Soviet" oil and the Middle East. The first significant Russian oil reserves were discovered in the late 1800s in Baku, in what is now (since the breakup of the U.S.S.R.) the independent state of Azerbaijan—and in what, during the life of the Soviet Union, was actually the "northern" Middle East. Indeed, one of the first great confrontations of the post–World War II Cold War arose over Moscow's attempts to turn part of northern Iran into an ostensibly independent republic of Azerbaijan. Much of what *was* the old Soviet Union *is* today the Middle East, complete with Muslim majorities—and large reserves of crude oil.

As might be expected, given Britain's concerns over secure supplies of petroleum with which to power the Royal Navy, this part of the world was of deepening interest to the British well before the World War I. In 1901, a British-born émigré to Australia, William Knox D'Arcy negotiated a "concession" from the Persian king (shah) to prospect for petroleum in Iran. By 1908, his efforts had brought in the first Middle East gusher, some six hundred miles south of Baku. In 1914, the year World War I began, the British government acquired 51 percent of the Anglo-Persian Oil Company, which had sprouted from D'Arcy's original concession from the Persian shah.[12] Mercantilist policies were clearly alive and well in London on the eve of World War I.

The war itself dispelled whatever doubts anyone might have had as to the significance of oil as the energy source of the future. Airplanes overhead and tanks on the battlefield guaranteed the primacy of petroleum in the military machines of the Great Powers at least as clearly as did the battleships of Churchill's navy. And beyond the war and the military machines, there was the automobile.

However, the very significance of oil itself now spawned new uncertainties. According to Daniel Yergin:

> A fear of imminent depletion of oil resources—indeed, a virtual obsession—gripped the American oil industry at the end of World War I and well into the early 1920s. The wartime experience—"Gasolineless Sundays" and the part played by oil in battle—gave a tangibility to the fear. When, in 1919, a retiring official wrote him that lack of foreign oil supplies constituted the most serious problem facing the United States, President Wilson sadly agreed: "There seemed to be no method by which we could assure ourselves of the necessary supply at home and abroad." The anticipated rapid depletion of American oil reserves was gauged against the rise in demand: American consumption had increased 90 percent between 1911 and 1918 and was expected to grow even faster after the war. America's love affair with the automobile was becoming ever more intense. The increase in the number of registered motor vehicles in the United States between 1914 and 1920 was astonishing—a jump from 1.8 to 9.2 million. The fear of shortage was such that one Senator called on the US. Navy to reconvert from oil back to coal.[13]

With Germany's challenge (at least temporarily) beaten back, but with new sources of insecurity quickly replacing it, it was perhaps inevitable that the allies of World War I—and the oil companies connected directly and indirectly to these states—would soon become competitors, and oftentimes colluders, in the IPE of oil.

The web binding states and oil companies together is perhaps nowhere better illustrated than in the case of the Turkish Petroleum Company (TPC) before and immediately after World War I. Turkey and Persia (Iran) shared (and still share) a border with each other—and with czarist Russia. The point where the three meet is less than three hundred miles from the Baku oil fields. The TPC was the result of a deal between its creators and the Ottoman Turkish Empire. Its purpose was to explore and exploit petroleum in "Mosul," which at that point was part of the Ottoman Empire and which today lies primarily in Iraq. TPC was as thoroughgoing a multinational corporation as can be imagined, even by today's standards. Created before the war, its owners were the German national bank (Deutsche Bank: 25 percent), Anglo-Saxon Petroleum Company (Royal Dutch: 22.5 percent), D'Arcy Exploration Company (Anglo-Persian, 51 percent of which was owned by the British government by early 1914: 47.5 percent), and its Armenian organizer (Calouste Gulbenkian: 5 percent).

Now the war was over, Russia was the Soviet Union, Germany and the Ottoman Empire were defeated (the latter state outright disappeared!), and the Middle East was threatening to burst into nationalist revolt(s) now that Turkish imperial control was defunct. What would become of TPC in particular—and the region's oil prospects in general? The French and British had actually signed secret agreements during the war that should have resulted in Mosul falling under French control, but with the value of the region's oil deposits now more apparent than ever, the British began to push quickly for readjustments. At the Paris Peace Conference which ended World War I, London and Paris addressed the issues head-on. The two states agreed to equally divide oil rights in Galicia (Poland), Romania, and Russia. Each agreed to allow the other to buy one third of the oil produced in their respective colonies. Further, France would get the German Deutsche Bank shares in TPC, while Britain in return would build pipelines from Mosul west across British-controlled territories to the Mediterranean Sea.

The United States, the third great victorious power at the Paris Peace Conference, was less than pleased with such cozy arrangements. Almost immediately, the United States began to agitate for access to the potentially lucrative Iraqi oil fields. Election of a Republican administration in 1920 increased the pressure from the western side of the Atlantic for American access to TPC territory. Commerce Secretary (and future president) Herbert Hoover argued and urged that a syndicate of American oil companies be formed to operate in the region. After six years of arduous negotiation, the TPC concession—and the TPC itself—was restructured. Anglo-Persian, Royal Dutch-Shell, the French Compagnie Française des Pétroles, and something called the Near East Development Corporation (NEDC) were accorded equal shares in the new TPC, with Gulbenkian retaining his 5 percent. And who was the NEDC? The Near East Development Corporation was a consortium extending American interests in the region, with Exxon, Mobil, Gulf, and ARCO being the ones easiest to identify. A red line demarcated the geography now open to the reconstituted TPC: "Within the red line were eventually to be found all the major oil-producing fields of the Middle East, save for those of Persia and Kuwait."[14]

Within this red line, then, lie states which seventy years later accounted for approximately 45 percent of total world petroleum reserves. Add Kuwait and Iran (Persia), and the figure jumps to over 60 percent! Little wonder, then, that the line from World War I to the present is so direct. Despite all the subsequent, significant discoveries in years since,[15] the Persian Gulf "end" of the Middle East remains squarely at the *center* of the supply equation in the international political economy of oil.

All of the "shocks" or crises in that political economy since World War I have been focused just as squarely in this same center of supply. Adolf Hitler's Nazi regime, in a determined effort to reduce German dependence on overseas oil, implemented a major domestic "synthetic fuels" program in the run-up to World War II. But just as certainly, the Nazis, whenever possible, cultivated economic and military ties to increasingly independent Middle East rulers. Such rulers would naturally seek aid wherever they could in their struggle to escape from British imperialism—and Hitler certainly *had* brought Germany back from its World War I defeat by Britain and its allies in spectacularly short order. Iran provides the clearest such case: there, British and American concern over the shah's growing regard for Hitler's "successes" led to the king's ouster in 1941.[16] Recall, too, that in this same year, only five months before Pearl Harbor and America's entry into World War II, the United States, Britain, and the Netherlands had embargoed oil shipments to Japan in retaliation for Japanese aggression in Southeast Asia. Britain's and the Netherlands' primary source of oil in 1941? Obviously and squarely it was the Middle East.

Following World War II, the Middle East was second only to Europe as a geography prompting earliest American involvement in the spreading Cold War. As already noted, the Soviet Union had sought to detach a large chunk of northern Iran in the earliest months after the war. When subsequent unrest in Greece and Turkey was judged to be the work of "armed minorities or . . . outside pressures," the U.S. president laid out the case for American aid to these states in his famous *Truman Doctrine* speech—and noted explicitly the threat that such pressures posed just slightly farther afield:

> It is necessary only to glance at a map to realize that the survival and integrity of the Greek nation are of grave importance in a much wider situation. If Greece should fall under the control of an armed minority, the effect upon its neighbor, Turkey, would be immediate and serious. Confusion and disorder might well spread *throughout the entire Middle East.*[17]

In a region where nationalist passions had been building since at least the end of World War I, "confusion and disorder" would soon become the order of the day.

President Truman's geography lesson would seem prescient just four years later, when a new, nationalist-minded prime minister in Iran would once again target British oil interests as he expropriated the Anglo-Iranian Oil Company. This time, American covert aid to the shah would be more important than British help in defeating the nationalist challenge to both the shah's royal rule and the foreign influence that supported it. Nationalist upheavals followed quickly in other key states throughout the region. Egypt, the world's most populous Arab state, saw its king deposed in 1953. Egypt was not a significant oil producer, but it was (and is) the geographic and population center of the Arab world—and also the location of the Suez Canal. Commerce, especially oil, shipped through the canal was of vital national interest to London and Paris.[18]

When the new Egyptian state nationalized this vital "international waterway," Britain, France, and Israel quickly used the question of the canal's security as a pretext for invading Egypt in 1956. The result was a temporary disruption in transshipment of Persian Gulf crude oil, and a second post–World War II oil crisis in the

IPE of energy. Shortly thereafter, a successful revolution occurred for the first time in an oil-*producing* Arab state: Iraq's monarchy was overthrown in 1958. Less than a decade later, when Israel fought the short, decisive "Lightning War" with its increasingly militant Arab neighbors, the canal was violently closed again, this time for eight long years. With three oil crises in less than twenty years, the stage was now set for the greatest oil shock of them all. Unwittingly, the international political economy of energy—and much, much more—now stood on the brink of the dramatic, transformative "oil decade."

OIL AND OPEC IN THE 1980s

The start of the Iran-Iraq War in August 1980 removed a little less than 10 percent of world oil exports from international markets, and OPEC and spot market prices soon reflected the diminished supply. But as the war dragged on and on, the long-term impact of changes in market conditions from 1973 to 1979 became dramatically apparent. When the war moved into the Gulf itself in the mid-1980s, and tankers and production and shipping platforms became the object of each side's attacks, no further run-up in oil prices occurred. In fact, as the war struggled on for eight long years, OPEC's ability to control world energy prices and markets all but collapsed. According to Joan Spero:

> OPEC's problems in the 1980s stemmed from its successes. The cartel's ability to increase the price of oil eventually transformed the world oil market. The demand for oil fell, non-OPEC production grew, and as a result, a long-term surplus emerged, putting sustained downward pressure on prices. Moreover, the excess supply made it more difficult, if not impossible, for OPEC to manage prices, as it had in the previous decade.[19]

In fact, in 1983, for the first time in OPEC history, the organization actually *reduced* the price of its "benchmark crude"—but still failed to halt OPEC's erosion as an effective, cooperative price-setting cartel. At the end of the Iran-Iraq War in 1988, oil prices in "real terms" were below their 1974 level.

With oil prices actually declining in the 1980s, the effect on demand, consumption, and international politics in the 1990s has been unsurprising. In 1990, as noted earlier, oil accounted for 22 percent more of total world energy consumption than did coal.[20] Iraq's invasion of Kuwait in August 1990—and the West's response to it—demonstrated how thoroughly the lessons of the 1980s had been learned: oil prices did spike up to $40 per barrel in the months following the invasion, but when U.S. warplanes began bombing Baghdad in January 1991, prices quickly retreated to half that level. Even without factoring in the effect of inflation, world oil prices dropped another 10 percent over the next three years.

The feud between Iraq and Kuwait had a long political history, of course (though not as long a history as the Iran-Iraq disagreement). Unsurprisingly, it was stirred into open warfare by events squarely within the changed IPE of oil. Iraqi President Saddam Hussein was particularly incensed by what he took to be Kuwaiti cheating on its oil production quotas as had been set by OPEC. Any such cheating, of course, would only further depress the price of petroleum, and Baghdad figured that Kuwaiti deceit had, by 1990, cost the Iraqi state treasury billions in lost oil revenues. Kuwait was also accused of duplicitously taking more than its share of oil from the neutral zone between the two countries, and with pushing too hard for repayment of loans made to Iraq during the Iran-Iraq War.

For all the sympathy Iraq's accusations provoked before the invasion, the act of sending in the tanks quickly cost Baghdad all but a handful of supporters. To oil consumers, the move was too reminiscent of 1980, when Iraqi troops had pushed toward the Iranian oil fields in the early days of that war. Had Iraq gained control of either the Iranian or the Kuwaiti oil fields, Iraq's influence as a regional—and world—power would have grown immensely. The addition of either neighbor's oil reserves to Iraq's own would have made Iraq a strong second to Saudi Arabia as the world's premier oil producer—and Saudi Arabia, of course, shares every bit as much of a border with Iraq as does Iran or Kuwait. This was a threat that consumer states, having grown used to a world of diminished "oil power" (and prices!) in the 1980s, could quickly come together to turn back.

While the long-term impact, if any, of the Gulf War on the IPE of oil remains to be worked out, the short-term effects appear to be stabilizing ones. The most notable such effect concerns the Arab-Israeli dispute. Upon invading Kuwait, Saddam Hussein had very few supporters in the Arab world, but one of the most vociferous was the Palestine Liberation Organization (PLO). With Iraq defeated, the PLO found itself with so few friends in the international system that it finally began to move in the direction of peace with Israel. With Arab-Israeli tensions generally appearing to decrease in the mid-1990s, a chief source of much of the turmoil in the international political system—and in the IPE of oil—over the last fifty years may at last be receding.

In the mid-1990s, then, an eerie stability characterizes the international political economy of oil. Demand for petroleum is up and doubtlessly heading higher, as is the demand for energy generally. While oil is not a renewable resource, ongoing discoveries of new pools of oil nonetheless are adequate to replenish current production. The World Energy Council estimates that there is enough oil in the ground today to last sixty years at current rates of consumption.[21] And in the Middle East, the source of so much of the international political and economic systems' turmoil over the last fifty years, an atypical peacefulness seems to reign.

THE IPE OF OIL AND ENERGY TODAY

Understanding where the IPE of oil and energy is going today depends on being able to recognize that there are several different actors to consider. Political scientists emphasize the *states* involved in this picture, and then quickly recognize the different categories of states on the contemporary stage. In the past, the primary distinction has been between increasingly assertive producer states and the oil-importing states that each year consume more and more petroleum. In the future, a further distinction—among types of oil-importing states—is likely to be just as important:

The shape and size of world energy demand is increasingly being determined not by rich countries but by the fast-growing developing countries of Latin America and Asia. Just as the oil producers in OPEC achieved sudden prominence after more than a decade of obscurity, so the full effect of the shift among consuming countries will not be felt for many years. But it is equally inexorable; and no less far-reaching.

By 2010 the share of total energy consumption accounted for by the rich countries will have fallen below 50% for the first time in the industrial era. . . . The growth in energy consumption in developing countries between 2000 and 2010 will be greater than today's consumption in Western Europe. By 2010 their emissions of carbon dioxide, the main contributor to global warming, will be almost as big as those of the whole world in 1970.[22]

As the industrial revolution continues to spread into the old third world, will states there behave as states have in the industrialized world over the last century? Will the newly industrializing countries have the same interests as industrial states have had historically? Will they have the same capacity to pursue such interests?

Economists emphasize the role of *markets* in this picture, and then quickly recognize how world energy markets have been shaped over the years, not just by disembodied laws of supply and demand, but by "corporate" actors operating well above the level of individual consumers. The big multinational oil companies are the first example of such, and over the years they too have changed dramatically: beyond "the majors," the private corporations of Rockefeller and D'Arcy fame, there are now the national oil companies operated by the governments of producing states to consider. These multinational corporations are not the only species of international organization in the picture. International government organizations (IGOs) such as OPEC (or the IEA or the Gulf Cooperation Council) further complicate and "distort" world energy markets.

Considering IGOs such as OPEC, of course, only brings us back to states and how states organize (or don't organize) to pursue what they see as their "national interest." Having come full circle in our inventory of actors, then, what does a student of IPE emphasize as she or he attempts to figure out where we go from here?

THE MERCANTILIST PERSPECTIVE

Students who diagnose the present condition and prescribe the future course of the IPE of energy from a mercantilist perspective are likely to be more worried about the state than either economic liberals or structuralists. Mercantilists generally perceive a strong positive role for the state in the IPE, but the shocks of the oil decade, and the portents for the future, combine to call such a role into doubt.

Surveying the transformation of the IPE of energy in the 1970s, mercantilists are struck by how the wealth and might of the international system's Great Powers were so successfully challenged by an actor that had only been created the decade before. Disturbing was the fact that the actor in question—OPEC—was not a state, but a collection of states. The government of the international system's wealthiest state, the United States, had been well aware before 1973 of increasing U.S. and Western reliance on overseas sources of oil, but it had been powerless to do anything effective to stop it. Then in 1973, with the wolf finally at the door, the state seemed even less able to respond. What, after all, was the policy reaction first to the embargo and then to oil price increases? Gas rationing and then acquiescence to a 400 percent price hike, indicated to many that the nature of power had changed in a fundamental way—and that states were ill-equipped to cope with such changes.

In the late 1970s, the U.S. embarked on a synthetic fuels program to try to wean the economy from its dependence on foreign oil. Alternative forms of energy were consciously cultivated through the state's exercise of fiscal policy. The result a decade later? As Yergin notes, in 1990 "United States oil imports were at their highest level ever, and still going up. The world was moving back to high dependence on the Persian Gulf."[23] Thus when Iraq rolled into the Kuwaiti oil fields, the United States apparently had no choice but to wage war to protect its national interest in Persian Gulf petroleum. Worse yet, the globe's only surviving superpower would now need the economic (if not the military) help of an international coalition to wage that war.

Now, near the end of the oil century, as new challenges appear, the state's capacity to respond constructively still seems very much an open question. If oil prices increase, as they seem likely to with demand from the third world increasing, the red ink in import-dependent states' trade balances seems guaranteed to grow. If states respond to this likelihood by successfully trying to decrease the use of imported oil in their overall energy mix, won't they only succeed in creating further problems? Looking at various energy scenarios for future energy consumption, it is striking to see how increased use of coal, natural gas, and nuclear power are projected to "balance" out against a decreasing role for oil in the twenty-first century IPE of energy.[24]

The Chernobyl disaster in the U.S.S.R. (and beyond) in 1986, and the Three Mile Island crisis in Pennsylvania in 1979 proved to many that even the strongest states were incapable of responsibly managing nuclear energy programs. Coal and natural gas as the policy choices for the future? The carbon dioxide emissions associated with these energy sources is certainly no less problematic for the environment than the CO_2 produced by the burning of oil.

Worse yet for proponents of the mercantilist perspective, what were once assumed by most to be the rightful prerogatives of state decisionmakers acting with sovereign impunity are now argued by many to be choices that no state acting independently has the right to make. Burn less oil but more coal and natural gas? Don't the global consequences of an overall increase of carbon dioxide emissions demand that states take such decisions cooperatively, and not as autonomous actors (see chapter 19)?

THE ECONOMIC LIBERAL PERSPECTIVE

At the end of the twentieth century, economic liberals are a good bit more sanguine than mercantilists as they look back and forward at the IPE of oil and energy. Fearing the heavy hand of government and believing in the guiding influence of free markets, liberals place states squarely at the heart of the crises of the oil decade—and free markets squarely at the heart of solutions to these shocks.

After all, in the United States, hadn't the government's Mandatory Oil Import Program of the 1950s begun the postwar process of distorting free market patterns of supply and demand? As a result, weren't prices higher in the United States than they would have been without such protection, and hadn't the political influence of domestic oil producers been artificially increased? Then, in 1971, hadn't government imposition of price controls on oil discouraged domestic production while simultaneously stimulating consumption? Was it really a coincidence that President Nixon then abolished oil import quotas and accelerated U.S. dependence on foreign oil just six months before the Arab oil embargo? In short there never really was a production shortage, only vulnerability to OPEC. The United States supported both Saudi Arabia and Iran in the 1970s because of the role they played in the U.S. campaign against communism.

If one really needed further proof of the malign effects of state intervention in free market transactions, didn't OPEC itself provide such? Here was a collection of individually harmless countries that by virtue of state-to-state collusion had managed within a decade to bring the "private" oil corporations to their knees, and then extort, from rich and poor alike, a fourfold increase in the price of petroleum—and kick the world economy into a prolonged global recession to boot.

From the liberal perspective, it was primarily the resilience of the free market that finally began to turn the situation around in the aftermath of 1973. Responding to classic laws of supply and demand, new non-OPEC sources of supply in Alaska, Mexico, and the North Sea came on-line and broke the grip of Persian Gulf producers. By the end of the 1970s, fresh, market-oriented governments in key countries such as the United States (the Reagan administration) and the United Kingdom (Prime Minister Thatcher) spurred the vital process of removing states farther from the marketplace. Not surprisingly, economic growth returned in the West in the 1980s, and even the withdrawal of Iran's and Iraq's oil from world pipelines proved incapable of disrupting global energy markets.

Now, in the 1990s, with economic growth returning to Latin America and Asia together with the North, liberals argue that the process should be allowed to continue without further government meddling. With the Cold War over, the productive capacity of the old Soviet Union can at last be reincorporated into the world energy market. The deadening hand of state control can be replaced with the entrepreneurial vigor of investors eager and capable of unlocking the energy riches of Siberia, Azerbaijan, and Turkmenistan.

If and when oil prices do again rise, economic liberals believe that rational—not national—economic actors are best equipped to calculate the appropriate response. If the price rises too high, too fast, alternative energy supplies are available. Even if increased coal and natural gas use do contribute to heightened CO_2 emissions (and it tends to be liberals who are most skeptical of a greenhouse effect), the market is more capable of responding innovatively and efficiently to such a development than even the most well-meaning government bureaucracy. An example of this argument is made by *The Economist*:

[T]he West's resolve to keep its own emissions to 1990 levels seems pointless. Even if this target is reached, it may secure few benefits for the climate. . . .

Forcing up efficiency in order to force down emissions is right only if governments are sure global warming is a grave hazard. Even then it would be foolish for the world to rush into cutting emissions. . . .

. . . So much more needs to be understood about global warming, that even small insights into the phenomenon could greatly cut the cost of coping with it. That is the paradox of climate change: it is too serious to panic about.[25]

For liberals, then, the future seems a less daunting place than it looks to those with a mercantilist perspective. Certainly the world has its share of problems. But, as with the great oil crises of the 1970s, the market can, if left sufficiently to its own devices, be counted upon to solve such problems with maximum efficiency.

THE STRUCTURALIST PERSPECTIVE

Structuralists have rich material to draw on when dealing with the IPE of energy and oil. Structuralism asserts that the institutions of global capitalism are inherently biased in favor of today's Great Powers, creating a web of dependency that mirrors in many ways the ties of nineteenth century colonial systems. With the IPE of oil itself rooted in that same nineteenth century, it is not surprising that structuralists would find IPE such a congenial object of study.

Structuralists note that within the Great Powers there are more than simply structural ties binding state and market together: statesmen themselves frequently have their roots directly in the capitalist marketplace. With the United States reeling from the first oil shock of the 1970s, who became the first vice president ever *appointed* to that office? It was Nelson Rockefeller, grandson of John D., the founder of the Standard Oil trust. Even when not directly involved at the highest levels of state in the world's dominant powers, the great international oil barons had direct and continuous access to such levels.

From this perspective, the great multinational oil companies in fact made Great Power foreign policy in the petroleum-rich Middle East well into the twentieth century. The West's ouster of the Persian shah in the early 1940s may have been precipitated by the king's enthusiasm for Nazi Germany's policies, but certainly the roots of Western distrust lie a decade deeper, when the shah had briefly nationalized the holdings of the Anglo-Iranian Oil Company. The message to all would-be independent rulers in this part of the world was clear: Establishing and maintaining their thrones would also require maintaining close and open ties to the international political economy of oil.

In only somewhat attenuated form, these ties survived World War II and persist to this day. The first direct step toward the 1973 Arab oil embargo was taken in the late 1960s, when the Libyan king was ousted from his throne, replaced by the vociferously nationalist Colonel Gadhafi. With monarchs in the Middle East becoming an increasingly endangered species with each passing decade, Saudi Arabia could not fail to take notice. How could the Saudis (and the Kuwaitis, and other conservative, "pro-Western" monarchies in the Persian Gulf) ensure that they would not be next? Taking a bold stand against the Jewish state of Israel in the early 1970s was a natural response, even if this meant (temporarily) challenging Western oil interests in the region.

Looking back over the last quarter century, structuralists see the 1973 crisis not as establishing some revolutionary new norm, but as one step in the gradual accommodation to an only slightly altered IPE reality. In that reality, "the majors" had in fact lost much of their oligopolistic clout. But just as surely, the health of OPEC states still depended on oil sales to the capitalist states of the West as much (or more) as Western economies depended on OPEC oil. What had been a relationship of dependency was now evolving into a relationship of limited interdependence, where strong ties between the West and a few friendly, "stable" Middle East regimes would ensure adequate foreign supplies of oil as the West weaned itself from its reliance on foreign petroleum. The West "understood" the pressures operating on friends such as the Saudis, and could live with occasional Saudi militancy as long as the pipelines remained open.

From the structuralist perspective, the Iranian revolution and its aftermath were more of a jolt to the IPE of oil than was the 1973 flare-up. After all, the Saudis *and* the shah of Iran were both firmly pro-Western in ideological terms, despite occasional differences with the West over the price of a barrel of crude. With the advent of Khomeini-style Islamic rule in Iran, however, a key term in the equation had shifted fundamentally. Here was a regime that not only cared little about ensuring adequate supplies of Persian Gulf petroleum to the West; it actively vilified the United States as a "Great Satan" for its crass materialism and continued oppression of third world peoples. When the Iranian revolution spread into the Iran-Iraq War, there would be little doubt, then, as to which side the U.S. and the West would take.

Politics, and economics as well, *do* make strange bedfellows, and in the 1980s, the U.S. became a de facto ally of Saddam Hussein and Iraq. A change in the structure of the Persian Gulf political economy drove the West into the arms of a regime that previously had been anathema. Even an Iraqi attack on a U.S. Navy gunboat in the midst of the Iran-Iraq War could not undercut the strange alliance forged by the Ayatollah's challenge to an American-led international order.

It would take an Iraqi challenge to that order—that structure—to undercut and eliminate the US.-Iraq alliance. When Saddam Hussein rolled Iraqi tanks across the border into Kuwait in 1990, he accomplished what an Iraqi air raid in 1987 on the U.S. naval frigate *Stark* (with the accompanying death of thirty-seven American sailors) had not. Baghdad's relationship with Washington could survive an "incident" such as the *Stark*. But the United States could not tolerate a redrawing of the energy map of the gulf in a manner that brought Kuwait inside the old "Red Line." Operation Desert Storm, with its dispatch of a 500,000-strong international military force to the Gulf, was the result. The structure of the political economy of the Persian Gulf—and of global energy—was restored.

To structuralists, what this portends for the future of the international political economy of energy is generally clear, even if the details are not. Changes in that IPE will be tolerated, as long as they do not threaten the basic structure of the international order. Even revolutionary challenges, such as Iran's under the Ayatollah (or the

Soviet Union's under Lenin and Stalin?), can be tolerated as long as they can be contained and isolated. But a "break-out," such as the spread of Islamic fundamentalism into the oil-rich reaches of the former Soviet Union, could well be another matter.

CONCLUSION

In the 1970s, two major oil crises shook the foundation of the international political economy. Under favorable supply and demand conditions, oil producers were able to use their new sources of wealth and power as a political weapon to bring about a significant shift in the international distribution of wealth and power. A series of political and economic events came together to foster an appreciation for the extent to which many nation-states had become dependent on natural resources and raw materials to sustain their wealth and power.

International political and economic conditions that made OPEC successful in the 1970s gradually shifted to weaken the cartel. However, the case of energy, and oil in particular, highlight the extent to which international interdependence, a tight connection between politics and economics, the global scope of the issue, and a delicate balance between power and wealth when it comes to determining policy outcomes have become regular features of the international political economy. The complexity of political and economic, and even social issues in some cases, has made it increasingly difficult to solve oil and other energy-related problems. In many cases, Great Powers have been brought to their knees by "small powers" or subnational groups. Mercantilists, liberals, and structuralists disagree as to which actors and issues should be dealt with in order to solve many of the problems associated with energy and oil.

Since the early 1970s, generating and sustaining national and international economic growth, and to some extent the ability to afford national security, have in some cases been constrained if not jeopardized by dependency on oil and other natural resources such as coal, which until then were still relatively cheap. The international political economy of the twenty-first century will more than likely face more oil and other commodity shocks related to the increasing scarcity and high prices of oil and other energy resources. These issues promise to become more than the high political economic issues that they have been since the 1970s. Because oil and other resources play such a vital role in the social, political, and economic fabric of all societies, they are likely to confront the public and government policymakers and business officials on a day-to-day basis, further transforming the international political economy.

Solutions to these problems will more than likely require a mix of market and state decisions. In some cases, markets will be vulnerable to political events and conditions that have little to do with markets but which can severely effect supply and prices. International interdependency and the proliferation of actors with a stake in these issues compels actors at all levels to cooperate with one another to solve these issues. However, as the Persian Gulf War demonstrated in the case of oil, but as we have also seen in other issues dealt with in this book, conditions that should promote cooperation often result in more intense conflict and often violence.

DISCUSSION QUESTIONS

1. Outline and discuss the role politics and economics played in events leading up to the two OPEC oil crises. (Note: Students may wish to go back in history as far as the material in the chapter allows them to.) Highlight the tensions and fault lines between these two academic dimensions of the crises.
2. Which factors—political or economic—played a larger role in ending the crises (or at least in weakening OPEC's power)? Explain.
3. Briefly outline and summarize the arguments made by each of the three major IPE approaches—namely mercantilism, economic liberalism, and structuralism—when it comes to explaining the IPE of oil and energy.
4. After reading the whole chapter, write your own assessment of what the international political economy of oil and energy is likely to be like in the early twenty-first century.

SUGGESTED READINGS

Abdulaziz al-Sowayegh. *Arab Petro-Politics.* Beckenham, Kent, England: Croom Helm Limited, 1984.

Simon Bromley. *American Hegemony and World Oil.* Oxford, England: Polity Press, 1991.

George Horwich and Edward J. Mitchell. *Policies for Coping with Oil-Supply Disruptions.* Washington, DC: American Enterprise Institute, 1982.

George Horwich and David Leo Weimer. *Responding to International Oil Crises.* Washington, DC: American Enterprise Institute 1991.

Neil H. Jacoby. *Multinational Oil.* New York: Macmillan 1974.

Merrie Gilbert Klapp. *The Sovereign Entrepreneur: Oil Policies in Advanced and Less Developed Capitalist Countries.* Ithaica, NY: Cornell University Press, 1987.

Roy Licklider. *Political Power and the Arab Oil Weapon.* Berkeley, CA: University of California Press, 1988.

R. K. Pachauri. *The Political Economy of Global Energy.* Baltimore: Johns Hopkins University Press, 1985.

Anthony Sampson. *The Seven Sisters: The Great Oil Companies and the World They Made.* New York: Viking, 1975.

Ian Skeet. *OPEC: Twenty-five Years of Prices and Politics.* New York: Cambridge University Press, 1988.

Joan Edelman Spero. *The Politics of International Economic Relations,* 4th ed. New York: St. Martin's Press, 1990.

Robert Stobaugh and Daniel Yergin, eds. *Energy Future.* New York: Ballantine Books, 1979.

Fiona Venn. *Oil Diplomacy in the Twentieth Century.* London: Macmillan, 1986.

Daniel Yergin. *The Prize; The Epic Conquest for Oil, Money, and Power.* New York: Simon & Schuster, 1991.

NOTES

1. Coal and oil are both fossil fuels, and as such are nonrenewable sources of energy. Crude oil is a mixture of petroleum liquids and gases in various combinations. Petroleum is a more general category than oil. In this chapter, we use the terms *oil* and *petroleum* interchangeably.

2. E. J. Hobsbawn, *The Age of Revolution, 1789–1848* (New York: Mentor Book, New American Library, 1962), 63.

3. "Energy Survey," *The Economist*, 18 June 1994, 4.

4. Not all oil-exporting countries are members of OPEC. Mexico and Great Britain, for example, are non-OPEC oil producers. The members of OPEC in 1973 were Iran, Iraq, Kuwait, Saudi Arabia, Venezuela, Abu Dhabi, Algeria, Libya, Qatar, the United Arab Emirates, Nigeria, Ecuador, Indonesia, and Gabon.

5. Assessing the transformation of the IPE which resulted, Robert Gilpin asserts that "World history records few equivalent redistributions of wealth and power in such a short period." Robert Gilpin, *The Political Economy of International Relations* (Princeton, NJ: Princeton University Press, 1987), 232.

6. See Joan Edelman Spero, *The Politics of International Economic Relations*, 4th ed. (New York: St. Martin's Press, 1990), 261–301, for an excellent general discussion of "Oil and Cartel Power." The account of the second oil crisis of the 1970s that follows draws heavily on Spero's analysis.

7. Neil H. Jacoby, *Multinational Oil* (New York: Macmillan, 1974), 172–173. The "seven largest," known variously as "the seven sisters" and "the majors," were/are Exxon, Chevron, Mobil, Gulf, Texaco, British Petroleum, and Royal Dutch-Shell.

8. Remember that in the early 1960s, coal still accounted for roughly 40 percent *more* of the world's *total* energy consumption than did oil. That is, coal represented 41 percent, and oil 29 percent, of total world energy consumption. "Energy Survey," *The Economist*.

9. Joan Edelman Spero, *The Politics of International Economic Relations*, 2nd ed. (New York: St. Martin's 1981), 258.

10. To put numbers one and two (and three and four) in perspective, Saudi Arabia (number one) in the mid-1970s had proved reserves two and one-half times greater than Kuwait's (number two). Number three, just slightly behind Kuwait, was Iran, and number four, Iraq, had reserves less than half of Kuwait's.

11. By the end of the "oil decade", the U.S.S.R. and its Eastern European satellites would annually account for slightly less than 20 percent of the world's total crude oil production. R. K. Pachauri, *The Political Economy of Global Energy* (Baltimore: Johns Hopkins University Press, 1985), 27.

12. Today's "BP"—British Petroleum—is a direct descendant of Anglo-Persian.

13. Daniel Yergin, *The Prize: The Epic Conquest for Oil, Money, and Power* (New York: Simon & Schuster, 1991), 194.

14. Ibid., 205.

15. For example, Venezuela (1922), Texas (1930), Algeria and Nigeria (1956), Libya (1959), Alaska's North Slope (1968), and the North Sea (1969).

16. It didn't help the shah's case that a decade earlier he had unilaterally canceled, if only temporarily, the British oil concession in Iran.

17. Thomas G. Paterson, ed., *Major Problems in American Foreign Policy*, vol. 2 (Lexington, MA: D. C. Health, 1978), 289–292 (emphasis added).

18. In the early 1960s, 15 percent of *all* world trade passed through the Suez Canal. Of that, petroleum from the Persian Gulf accounted for 75 percent of all Suez Canal business.

19. Spero, *The Politics of International Economic Relations*, 4th ed., 277.

20. That is, oil supplied 31.8 percent of world energy, while coal supplied 26.1 percent. Contrast this with the 1960 picture noted in footnote 8.

21. "Energy Survey," *The Economist*, 12.

22. Ibid., 3.

23. Yergin, *The Prize*, 770.

24. See, for example, the various scenarios in "Energy Survey", *The Economist*.

25. Ibid., 17–18.

Part V

Global Problems

It is increasingly clear that many IPE problems are more than international; they are *global* in nature. That is, these problems are not just conflicts or tensions between and among nation-states. They transcend the boundaries of nation-states and have become truly global in their impacts. The final part of this book looks at three aspects of these global problems. Chapter 18 examines the IPE of food and hunger, with special emphasis on the roles of states and markets as sources of the food and hunger problem. Chapter 19 presents an analysis of the IPE of the global environment, perhaps today's most serious global problem. Three case studies explore the IPE of the greenhouse effect, deforestation, and ocean nuclear waste dumping. Finally, chapter 20 looks at the United States in the context of its role and obligation as a key player in global events and presents four scenarios for the future of the United States in the IPE. A glossary of IPE terms follows Chapter 20.

18

The International Political Economy of Food and Hunger

OVERVIEW

The title of this chapter is purposely missing the word *world* because, technically speaking, the whole world is not hungry. Paradoxically, some countries are awash in a "sea of grain," while people in other parts of the world do not receive the daily required amounts of protein and calories necessary to fight off diseases usually associated with malnutrition and hunger, such as kwashiorkor and marasmus. One authority on the subject estimates that every day over one hundred million people on the earth are hungry or malnourished.[1]

Since World War II, media coverage and public attention to hunger in different places in the world has seemed greatest during or shortly after episodes of localized mass starvation brought on by drought or war. Yet malnutrition and even starvation remain permanent features of many countries, especially those designated by the United Nations as *most seriously affected* (MSA) countries. Why is this so? Can international political economy teach us anything about the causes of hunger and how it might be overcome?

This chapter makes two arguments. First, that an IPE of hunger incorporating the three traditional political economic perspectives of mercantilism, liberalism, and structuralism better explains hunger than the accepted dictum that hunger is chiefly the result of overpopulation and/or a lack of food production. Second, an IPE of hunger offers a variety of different views about the causes of hunger as well as solutions to the problem. An IPE of hunger points to *food security* as one of humankind's core values, which in the near future is not likely to be realized for all individuals, but which should become the focus of attention of those who desire to solve the hunger problem.

It is observed by Dr. [Benjamin] Franklin, that there is no bound to the prolific nature of plants or animals but what is made of their crowding and interfering with each other's means of subsistence. . . . Necessity, that imperious, all-pervading law of nature, restrains them within the prescribed bounds. The race of plants and the race of animals shrink under this great restrictive law; and man cannot by any efforts of reason escape from it. . . . When population has increased nearly to the utmost limits of the food . . . [v]icious habits with respect to the sex will be more general . . . [and] the probability and fatality of wars and epidemics will be considerably greater; and these causes will probably continue their operation till the population is sunk below the level of the food; and then the return to comparative plenty will again produce an increase, and, after a certain period, its further progress will again be checked by the same causes.[2]

Thomas Malthus (1798)

Until the 1970s, the dominant approach many scientists (especially biologists), commentators, and popular journalists used to explain *world hunger* was in terms of an imbalance between the amount of food produced in a particular geographic area in relation to the people that consumed it. In the eighteenth century, Thomas Malthus made popular the idea that food production increased arithmetically while human population grew exponentially, and so "man cannot by any efforts of reason escape" from hunger and famine. Malthus argued that because labor-intensive food production techniques did not lend themselves to producing surplus quantities of agricultural commodities, war, famine, and disease were left to check population growth rates.

In the 1930s and 1940s, the application of new technology such as tractors and other labor-saving devices, along with chemical fertilizers, eventually helped spur agricultural production to the point of huge surplus capacity in the United States, Canada, Western Europe, and Australia. Farm policies in these countries after World War II subsidized crop production, which led to huge surpluses of wheat, corn, and pork. In an effort to increase farm prices and income, many farmers in the United States, for instance, were even paid not to grow certain commodities.[3]

Before World War II was over, hunger became of major concern to the United States and its European allies that had incurred a good deal of damage to their economies during the war. President Franklin Roosevelt called a meeting in Hot Springs, Virginia, in 1943 to discuss hunger and the possibility of increasing world food supplies. This meeting produced the United Nations' first specialized agency, the Food and Agriculture Organization (FAO). The FAO studied the food situation in Europe and in the rest of the world, including the newly independent nations and colonies of the Western European nations, countries that collectively came to be known as the third world.

Many experts questioned whether food production in the developing areas of the world would be able to keep up with expected global population growth rates. The solution to the problem looked fairly simple: help less developed countries (LDCs) produce more food while encouraging them to lower their population growth rates. The tendency to view hunger as a lack of food production coupled with an overpopulation problem endemic to developing nations continued in the 1950s and 1960s. Some experts believed that assistance from an assortment of international organizations and individual countries, in particular the United States, was necessary if LDCs were to eventually overcome their hunger problems. During the 1950s and 1960s, food shortages in some developing nations were temporarily overcome when surpluses of U.S. commodities were distributed or "dumped" overseas in trade and aid channels. Public Law (PL) 480 and the U.S. "Food for Peace" program made food aid easily available to nations whose governments were also anticommunist and whose economies looked to be good markets for future sales of U.S. commodities and commercial products.

Many government officials and academics felt that hunger was likely to prevail in developing nations as long as "traditional" societies remained underdeveloped or "backward." LDCs were expected to eventually overcome their hunger problems as their economies developed and their governments and societies modernized. The World Bank and other financial institutions funded development projects that promoted the industrialization of underdeveloped economies along the lines of Western nations (see chapter 15).

None of these measures overcame the malnutrition and starvation that routinely occurred in India, parts of Southeast and East Asia, and in Africa. In many third world Asian and African nations, hunger continued to be attributed to either poor growing conditions, traditional farming techniques, and/or a lack of capital and economic infrastructure. Once again, overpopulation and rising birth rates were expected to wreck havoc on countries like India and China. Assistance from international relief agencies and financial institutions seemed to be too little, too late.

In the 1960s, a number of well-intentioned private foundations and nations financially supported the research and development of new varieties of wheat in Mexico and rice in the Philippines. The so-called *green revolution* produced grains that supposedly could be adapted and grown in LDCs that faced hostile growing conditions. Another technological solution to the hunger problem that gained popularity about the same time was the proposal to educate people in the third world about birth control. Stanford University Professor Paul Erhlich persuasively argued that the world's growing population was a time bomb waiting to explode.[4]

LIFEBOAT ETHICS

Other food and population experts were not so optimistic. Many of them painted a picture of a world fated to experience global starvation and wars if more commodities were not produced in time to feed growing numbers of hungry people in developing regions of the world. In the late 1960s, this view was made popular by biology professor Dr. Garrett Hardin. Hardin's views were well received in some official circles and by many food experts, religious groups, and well-intentioned concerned citizens.

Hardin used the analogy of overgrazing a commons to explain the relationship of population to the availability of food.[5] He argued that the world was much like a commons whereupon only so many animals could graze without eventually destroying it. The "tragedy of the commons" was that people acted in their short-term, rational interests by continually producing more livestock, which eventually used up the commons, dooming both them and society. Hardin argued that freedoms and liberties must be restricted or people would have too many children and destroy the global commons.

Based on this analogy, Hardin made popular a proposal to deal with overpopulation and the lack of food in third world nations. Given that the industrialized nations were not likely to transfer a sufficient amount of food and other resources to third world countries to stave off their hunger (because it was not in their political or economic interest to do so), it would be merciful if the donors instead practiced triage or "lifeboat ethics."[6] *Triage* is the medical practice of separating patients into three groups in an emergency situation when resources are limited. Some injured need only minimal assistance, some require attention and even surgery to survive, and some would die anyway, in which case it would be wasteful to use precious resources on them.

For Hardin, the world was like a lifeboat overcrowded with people and about to be pulled under as more and more survivors clung to the lifeboat. If the industrialized nations do not want to be swamped by the growing masses of people in the third world, it should cut them off and let those who were not going to make it on their own simply perish. In essence, Hardin argued that food aid was an unethical disservice to those whose life would end anyway after aid was discontinued.

In the early 1970s, this argument was well received by many U.S. aid administrators and other government officials who felt that assistance to third world countries was equivalent to pouring money down a rat hole.[7] These officials were already under attack from critics of U.S. aid programs and those who wanted to limit food aid because of the political strings attached to it. Coinciding with this development, in the late 1960s, U.S. foreign aid laws were changed as part of an effort to market grain to industrialized nations, or to at least earn some income from developing nations for the commodities they received.

LIFEBOAT ETHICS CRITIQUED

Some critics charge that Hardin's analogies of the world as either a commons or a lifeboat with limited resources are flawed. Even if the world does have a limited amount of resources, Hardin is wrong to suggest that the earth has reached the point where we can say that there are just enough resources available for a certain number of people to live comfortably while others should perish.

A question critics often ask is: must those in the industrialized nations live as lavishly as they do compared to people in developing nations? Might the rich still live relatively comfortably at a lower level of existence if it meant that more people could survive by consuming what the "haves" do not want to share with the "have-nots"? Likewise, is it fair that the United States, with 6 percent of the world's population, consumes 35 percent of the world's resources? How can the United States and other major commodity producers such as Canada and the European Union (EU), for instance, justify "mountains" of surplus wheat, butter, and cheese stored in the major food-producing nations, while so many people in the world are malnourished, hungry, and starving?

Hardin overlooks the distribution of the world's resources, including food. By some estimates, enough food is produced in the world to feed each person more than 2,700 calories a day. However, developing societies who need it the most lack the financial resources to purchase what they need. Many of them also lack the mechanisms and distribution channels necessary to ensure that individuals receive the daily minimum requirements of nutrients and calories. Hardin also overlooks the "pockets of hunger" in developed regions of the world. Living in an industrialized nation does not guarantee one an adequate diet.

Hunger, then, is a product of inadequate distribution mechanisms, but more important, a direct consequence of poverty. Poorer people anywhere in the world are likely to exhibit some of the characteristics of hunger. It is easy to understand why some critics of lifeboat ethics raise the issue of how much the relationship of the rich Northern industrialized nations to the poor Southern developing nations is responsible for poverty and, ultimately, hunger. The developing nations were relatively food self-sufficient before they were colonized by the West. Colonization or interaction with the industrialized nations via trade, aid, and investment in LDCs by Western banks and industries "immiserized" local economies. Those developing nations that overcame poverty and hunger, such as South Korea and Taiwan, were given huge amounts of aid because they were of strategic interest to the Western powers.

While only a small sector of a poorer economy profits from political and economic relations with industrialized nations, the great masses of people in large "underdeveloped" sectors of these economies become less capable of either producing the food they need themselves or purchasing it through trade channels. Hunger, then, is not endemic to LDCs, but is a by-product of their political and economic relationship to the industrialized nations. Many poorer nations have no choice but to become dependent on food and financial aid handouts to sustain their already low food-per-capita consumption levels. The relationship between the North and the South is defined by international *interdependence*, albeit one that is asymmetrical (unequal).

Finally, many demographers point out that Hardin's assumptions about population growth rates do not adequately reflect the history of population growth in the industrialized countries. Population growth rates went up in the Western developed nations when their economies were transformed from primarily an agricultural to an industrial base. Death rates gradually decreased due to improved hygiene and life-saving medical care. As people lived longer and per capita incomes increased, population growth rates naturally slowed. While there is evidence that the NICs are in the process of passing through the ***demographic transition***, many LDCs are poised but have yet to do so. Family financial security would take away the incentive to have more children that serve as laborers or secondary sources of income.

The point here is not to claim that (over)population is not a national problem with global dimensions. It is clear that in some societies the amount of food and other resources may be inadequate to meet the needs and demands of the population. Yet, it is not the case that overpopulation is a problem for all societies.[8] In some nations, sustaining the current population is a problem. Overpopulation alone does not cause hunger. Moreover, hunger is as much a matter of food availability and distribution as it is of production. The *rate* of population growth in many LDCs began to slowly decline beginning in the late 1970s. Yet 95 percent of the world's population increase in the next half century is expected to take place in the third world, where the vast majority of the world's poor live.[9]

If the hunger problem is viewed from a global perspective, it is still the case that there are more agricultural commodities than there are people to consume them.[10] Furthermore, as many critics of Hardin's ideas complain, even if population growth rates were to come under control at any time, more food would not necessarily be available to poorer members of society. Society's elites or the rich quite often control the nation's food distribution channels.

These criticisms of Hardin highlight the political, economic, and social conditions that contribute to hunger and that make the problem a multidimensional one. The application of IPE approaches to hunger became more fully appreciated in the early 1970s, when a world food crisis drew attention to the plight of people in developing nations faced with the prospect of the declining availability of food supplies through trade and aid channels.

THE WORLD FOOD CRISIS

In 1972, the FAO proclaimed a world food crisis[11] because the supply of world grain reserves reached record low levels and commodities of grain and feed grains usually available to food-import-dependent nations in the third world were no longer available to them. During this crisis, several events occurred almost simultaneously that resulted in a good deal of hunger and starvation in some of the poorer regions of the world.

The crisis began when the United States and Soviet Union experienced two consecutive years of drought in the major grain-producing regions of their countries. Before the Soviet shortfall became public information, the U.S. government purchased huge quantities of wheat from its producers and subsidized wheat and other grain sales to the Soviet Union. U.S. foreign policy officials used these grain sales, among other things, to promote a détente (relaxation of tension) with the

Soviet Union after the two countries signed the Strategic Arms Limitations Talks (SALT I) agreement in 1972. At first, U.S. farmers praised the deal because it would clear away surpluses that were holding down commodity prices. Soon, however, they felt cheated when the Soviet shortfall was made public and the price of grain shot up.

One consequence of the U.S. and Soviet shortfall and their grain deal was to reinforce the shift that had been occurring in the pattern of international grain trade since the late 1960s. Changes in the international production and finance structures, especially after the United States devalued its dollar in 1971, made U.S. grain exports more attractive to nations such as Japan and EU countries who wanted to "upgrade" their diets to include more wheat and meat products. Poorer nations who had relied on food imports to meet basic needs could no longer afford higher priced commodities of the major food exporters. Thus, many LDCs became even more dependent on food aid at a time when aid channels were drying up or grain corporations were more interested in selling grain than in getting rid of it through aid channels.

As grain stocks in the United States declined to record low levels, commodity prices shot up, resulting in food price inflation, which generated more demand by U.S. consumers to limit commodity exports and food aid. Commodities such as wheat and feed grains were rerouted away from LDCs to the industrialized nations who could more easily afford them at a time when poorer countries found themselves in great need of them.

Many developing nations also found themselves hostage to another political economic development that drained them of resources and limited their ability to pay for food imports. In 1973, the OPEC oil cartel embargoed shipments of oil to the United States and then dramatically raised the price of oil (see chapter 17). Many LDCs found it necessary to limit imports of food commodities and food products in order to pay their higher oil bills. Rather than remain dependent on food exporters for needed supplies, many LDCs reluctantly adopted food self-sufficiency policies.

On top of these political and economic conditions during the world food crisis, many LDCs were crippled by other routinely occurring natural events such as monsoons in Asia and drought in the Sahel region of Africa. Across the Sahel, almost a million people starved to death when food relief efforts were intentionally blocked.[12] Fertilizer production for many third world countries was also hurt by an unexpected shortfall in the anchovy catch off the coast of Peru.

After the world food crisis, hunger conditions did not improve that much for many people living in the poorer regions of many third world countries. Later in the 1970s, instances of mass starvation mounted because of civil war in Bangladesh and in many African nations; a drought in the Sahel region of Africa only served to make matters worse. Food was also intentionally used as a weapon in many wars, including Ethiopia and the "killing fields" of Cambodia.

Throughout most of the 1980s, the entire Sahel region of Africa experienced several more rounds of mass starvation and hunger. Ethiopia and the Sudan, in particular, seemed beyond help. Efforts by international food relief organizations and a multitude of private organizations and agencies did not halt the spread of hunger and starvation deep into the African continent. Interestingly, hunger gained some attention as a public policy issue in some of the industrialized nations that experienced two economic recessions.[13] Meanwhile, most major food-producing countries continued to produce surpluses of agricultural commodities. The occasion of the Persian Gulf War in 1991 once again demonstrated the connection between war and hunger when millions of Kurds were left stranded in a desolate region between Iran, Turkey, and the Soviet Union. The United States set a new precedent in 1992 by sending its forces (backed by a United Nations resolution) into Somalia to feed millions of starving people besieged by civil war and political strife.

The events of the world food crisis, along with numerous events and conditions that came after it, highlight the extent to which factors that routinely contribute to hunger and starvation are more political-economic in nature than they are biological or demographic. We will now lay out what IPE teaches us about hunger.

AN IPE OF FOOD AND HUNGER

Broadly speaking, an IPE of hunger accounts for the ways in which a combination of political and economic forces and factors generate hunger in different geographical areas of the world. Two important questions are: what is the connection between the acquisition of power and wealth and poverty and hunger?; and, what role does the international political economy play in preventing people from acquiring the food necessary to sustain themselves?

We can begin to answer these questions by outlining some basic features of the international political economy, especially the relationship of states to markets. The state (a collective set of each nation-state's governing institutions; see chapter 1) plays an important, if not the central, role in the international system today. International organizations such as the United Nations' FAO exist at the behest of nation-states that regulate both public and private international affairs. International organizations do not, as yet, have the authority to impose solutions to hunger on states or subnational actors. Officials of both nation-states and private nongovernmental organizations usually identify themselves as nationals from one country or another. Multinational corporations (MNCs) are not sovereign political entities either. That status is still accorded to the nation-state, which regulates the money supply and establishes the political conditions in which international corporate agribusinesses must operate.

Subnational groups may contend with the state for authority to govern a distinct territory or nation of people. These groups also play key roles when it comes to producing commodities or making any national or local food distribution system work. However, in most cases national governments adopt policies that, for good or bad, influence hunger and/or provide the resources necessary to overcome a myriad of hunger-related problems.

Interacting with states are markets (i.e., exchanges), which also take place within and among all nation-states at various levels of analysis. Markets, together with developments in the international production and finance structures directly influence hunger in a number of important ways. First, some agricultural commodities are routinely sold by the United States and other major commodity exporters to earn foreign exchange. Commodities are also purchased by nations unable to produce them for themselves or whose consumers desire to purchase items that cannot be grown locally. Actually, only about 10 percent of all agricultural commodities are exchanged via international commercial transactions. The rest are produced for domestic consumption and exchanged in local markets. However, for some groups and even entire nations, accessibility to that 10 percent of exchanged commodities can mean the difference between maintaining a healthy diet and slipping into a state of malnutrition and hunger.

Second, markets play a role in establishing agricultural commodity prices. In most societies, prices reflect the demand for goods related to their supply or availability. In cases of communist, socialist, or otherwise highly regulated societies, prices may be fixed according to some ideological principal. Prices can either deter or act as an incentive for farmers to produce and market their commodities. Furthermore, the price of commodities makes them relatively more or less available to certain individuals or income groups, thereby influencing the amount of hunger present in a society.

The third way that markets influence hunger is more generally in the way they condition the economic vitality of a particular nation-state or group of its people. A tension often occurs between states and markets when states attempt to regulate markets in order to accomplish a variety of national, political, social, and economic objectives. Both domestic and international markets—the latter more often—are looked to by groups and nation-states as sources of economic growth. The extent to which goods are successfully produced and marketed, either at home or in trade channels, can significantly influence the hunger problem. Those who profit from market transactions are less likely to go hungry, while those who do not are more likely to feel the effects of poverty, malnourishment, and even starvation.

Aside from international trade, agricultural commodities and food products are impacted by at least two other types of international economic transactions characteristic of the international finance structure. A good deal of controversy surrounds the issue of food aid or money that is donated or loaned to a group of people on a short- or long-term basis. Finally, international food production and distribution is effected by the international investment practices of different nations and MNCs. These businesses provide jobs for people, and in the case of agribusinesses, produce crops that are often sold abroad to earn foreign exchange. In many cases, crops grown specifically for export substitute for commodities that would be grown and consumed locally.

Each of the three traditional IPE perspectives—mercantilism, liberalism, and structuralism—locate the causes of hunger and solutions to the problem in a variety of relationships of states and other actors to the market. What follows is a brief discussion of how each ideological school of thought looks at agricultural trade, food aid, and agribusiness activity as specific causes and/or solutions to the hunger problem.

THE MERCANTILIST PERSPECTIVE

For mercantilists, food and hunger issues are tied up in considerations of national wealth and power. Mercantilists, or economic nationalists, view the world in ways similar to political realists (see chapter 9). Nation-states compete with each other for power and wealth in order to improve their relative position in a self-help international system where there is no sovereign political authority above the nation-state. Mercantilists emphasize how a nation's wealth and money ultimately contribute to its security.

For mercantilists, hunger is a regularly occurring condition related to a combination of physical and political-economic situations. Some countries are simply better endowed with a variety of natural resources, raw materials, and growing conditions that enhance food production. Mercantilists and realists consider food to be an essential ingredient of power.[14] Those states that are relatively food self-sufficient or that have the capacity to feed their population are less likely to be dependent on other states for food. Thus, they are less vulnerable to those who during a time of crisis or war would be likely to cut off their food supply. Many nations will go out of their way to enhance their food security. Japan, for instance, has always been very self-conscious about its dependency on other nations for raw materials and food supplies. Its desire to achieve food security in part explains its willingness to assist rice farmers with price and income support measures that have pushed the price of rice in Japan to as much as ten times higher than world market rice prices.

Nations with the capacity to produce large surpluses of commodities, such as the United States, Canada, EU members, Australia, and a few others, quite often benefit from the dependency of other nations for agricultural commodities and food products. Agricultural commodities sold abroad earned the United States a good deal of foreign currency after World War II. Agricultural trade accounted for as much as 26 percent of all U.S. exports in the 1980s. Many governments have also resorted to neomercantilist protectionist trade policies to insulate their farm support programs from international market forces and the protectionist policies of other countries. The major grain-trading countries use export subsidies and a variety of other measures to compete with one another for what have been declining shares of commodity export markets.

Agricultural trade enhanced U.S. power and its positions in the international security structure after World War II in other ways. A case in point is the power and influence the United States derived from supplying many of its allies with commodities through trade and aid channels. Along with loans and technical assistance, PL 480 food aid helped shore up pro–democratic-capitalist economies in the third world and helped the United States contain Soviet influence in those regions. Many recipients of U.S. food aid, such as South Korea, Taiwan, and Egypt, later "graduated" from U. S. assistance and became major purchasers of US commodities and food products.

At times, the United States has intentionally tried to use "food as a weapon." One case in point was in 1972, when the United States used a grain deal with the Soviet Union as a "carrot" to reward its arch rival for entering into an arms control agreement (SALT I) and pursuing détente with the United States. In 1980, the United States embargoed shipments of grain to the Soviet Union because it invaded

Afghanistan. In this case, the United States used its commodities as a "stick," not so much to change Soviet behavior as to embarrass it and force the Soviet people to reduce their consumption of meat—an unpopular policy, given that the government had recently promised Soviet citizens more meat.

Robert Paarlberg argues quite convincingly that food does not have a lot of political utility unless the supplier has a monopoly over food supplies.[15] In this case, the Soviet Union sought out other suppliers—and Argentina responded to the call. Argentina became a major grain producer and exporter, but also an export competitor of the United States. To some extent the use of food as a weapon backfired on the United States. U.S. farmers complained that the government played politics with U.S. trade policy. President Carter responded by raising government deficiency payments to farmers. President Reagan later rescinded the embargo, in part because U.S. officials feared that other importers of U.S. grains and foodstuffs would consider the United States an "unreliable supplier" in international grain markets. Many LDCs that formerly were willing to purchase agricultural commodities from abroad were no longer willing to do so and turned to self-sufficiency policies encouraging local farmers to meet consumer demand.

If anything, the case of the Soviet grain embargo demonstrates that the United States was discomforted as much as the Soviet Union: U.S. officials realized the extent of U.S. dependency on agricultural exports. More important, however, it demonstrated that regardless of who was most inconvenienced, nations are always *tempted* to use food as a weapon, even if only symbolically, if their political and military arsenals lack appropriate instruments.

As suggested above, mercantilists and realists consider foreign aid to be another tool of foreign policy. The United States employed PL 480 food aid quite effectively in its effort to contain the U.S.S.R. Grain shipments also benefited U.S. farmers and shippers, and helped hold down costs of government price and income support programs. Few experts would disagree with the argument that food aid provided to countries to deal with short-term emergencies benefited the aid recipient as much as it did the donor.

For mercantilists, agribusinesses operate at the behest of nation-states, who benefit from their investment and production of commodities. Most of the Western industrialized countries, along with international organizations, have chosen not to seriously restrict agribusiness practices in other countries. What regulations of agribusinesses and other transnational corporations there are originate with host governments.

Agribusinesses and other MNCs add to the wealth and power of both the host and country of origin. Aside from providing investment opportunities, from a mercantilist perspective they help transform the traditional agriculture sector of the economy from primarily labor to modern capital-intensive production techniques. They provide employment opportunities and infrastructure for people. They also benefit many of the LDCs in which they are located by transferring to them technology, managerial skills, and marketing and production techniques. MNCs also help LDCs earn foreign exchange, which, in turn, they can use to purchase needed commodities or consumer items (see chapter 16).

According to mercantilists, agribusinesses and other MNCs, then, earn income for the country in which they originated and help eradicate poverty in host nations. Higher income levels mean that locals generally eat more nutritious and larger quantities of food. Development also means that revolution is less likely and that governments that support MNC investment efforts in their country are likely to support the political and economic policies of the countries in which the enterprise originated.

In sum, to mercantilists, states regulate markets—employ trade, aid, and investment policies—in such a way as to attain state goals and objectives, which ultimately affect a state's ability to secure itself. Hunger is not likely to be overcome in any great measure unless it were in the national interest of states to overcome the problem. In the 1970s, it became clearer all the time that the distribution of financial resources and food was as much the result of how much power a nation had as it was a nation's ability to produce needed commodities. People in the industrialized-Western-developed nations were less likely to go hungry than their counterparts in developing nations. Mass starvation was more likely to occur in the politically weaker nations than in the more powerful countries.

In the past, the rule of thumb has been that, more often than not, food insecurity weakens some states and works to the advantage of food suppliers. On the other hand, economic interdependence among nations has made suppliers quite dependent on foreign markets to absorb excess commodity surpluses and food products. However, as long as nation-states compete with one another for limited resources, food is likely to serve as a symbolic, if not a real, weapon in national arsenals.

CASE STUDY: THE IPE OF FAMINE IN SOMALIA

Hunger, in its deadliest form, is often the result of political strife and war. Market forces in Somalia were disrupted by civil war and efforts to gain political control of the country. Nations that try to use food as a military weapon usually do so by withholding food from an enemy in order to extract concessions from them. In Somalia, however, food has been used as a peace-keeping tool, to overcome famine and starvation brought on by war as much as anything else.

In 1992, the United Nations peacekeeping operation in Somalia marked the first time UN or U.S. forces have intervened in a nation for the express purpose of humanitarian relief. The United States headed a United Nations multinational military contingency and rescue operation, used 12,000 of its own troops, and 13,000 troops from twenty other nations to distribute 100,000 tons of food supplies to millions of starving Somalis. The operation was also intended to settle political conflicts among a variety of clan leaders who controlled food supplies and distribution networks in Somalia.

Another objective of these combined forces was to reestablish some kind of national government in Somalia. Located on the "horn" of Africa's east coast, Somalia had recently been besieged by famine and civil war. Intense rivalry among six major clan families and, to a lesser extent, drought resulted in 300,000 people dead and another estimated 2 million facing starvation.

Continued

CASE STUDY: THE IPE OF FAMINE IN SOMALIA, *continued*

In 1992, the government of President Mohammed Siad Barre quit and went into exile, leaving local clan leaders to fight it out for control of the country. Refugees streamed into cities in search of aid and medical assistance. Clan members ambushed truck convoys and confiscated food supplies. Clans blocked and disrupted food distribution efforts in parts of the country they controlled and in many cities. They also blocked port facilities from receiving Red Cross and World Food Program food relief supplies. Many of the clans attacked officials and workers of the international food relief agencies who were conducting relief operations in cities and in rural areas.

Ironically, the roots of this internal strife and starvation can be traced to the geopolitics of the Cold War international security structure, namely the superpower conflict between the United States and the Soviet Union. Many of the clans acquired their weapons from both the Soviet Union and from the United States and its allies in the 1970s and 1980s, when the two superpowers competed for political influence in Somalia. The Soviets supplied the Somalis with AK-47 assault rifles and small weapons in the 1970s, as part of a program to expand communist influence within Africa. After Somalia invaded Ethiopia, a Soviet ally, in 1977, the U.S.S.R withdrew support. The shah of Iran, along with Egypt and other Arab nations, then supplied Somalia with weapons. From 1981 to 1989, the United States supplied the government of President Barre with $35 million worth of "lethal assistance" that included TOW antitank missiles and armored personnel carriers.

During the famine rescue operation, the U.S. and allied military forces tried to stay neutral among local clan leaders. Contrary to accepted military practice, the weapons of these groups were not quickly confiscated. After an ambush resulted in twenty-two dead Pakistani soldiers, however, efforts were made to roundup the larger weapons and to control the use of small rifles and other weapons.

In March 1993, a peace accord was signed by fifteen Somali chiefs, establishing a three-tiered, federal-style administration that would guide the country for two years, until elections could be held. Most of the U.S. and other forces were subsequently withdrawn from the country. The UN Security Council established a multinational force of 20,000 peacekeeping troops to replace U.S. forces. When a number of the clan leaders rejected the peace plan, military conflict returned.

Now that the Cold War seems to be over, some wonder if the United Nations should authorize a permanent multinational peace-keeping force to solve severe hunger problems such as those in Somalia. UN Secretary General Boutros Boutros-Ghali has proposed such an army under Article 43 of the United Nations charter. Whether such a force is created and can be effective is more a political issue related to the interests of the most powerful states in the international system than it is an economic matter.

THE LIBERAL PERSPECTIVE

Liberals look on the food problem in ways that mercantilists find politically naive, if not wishful thinking. For liberals, hunger is a problem that could easily be overcome if nation-states followed some basic economic principles and, for the most part, kept politics out of the hunger issue. For liberals, individuals or households *should* be the major actors who make economic and political decisions. Liberals prize efficiency, economic growth, and productivity beyond other values. When it comes to the relationship of food production to hunger, their outlook is simple: market forces should be allowed to set food prices, which—if governments did not interfere in markets—would result in enough food produced to meet even the tremendous demand in developing regions of the world.

States that cannot produce enough food locally usually import needed commodities from abroad. Liberals do not view imports as inherently bad, in and of themselves. If nations specialize in producing items for which they have a comparative advantage, and trade with other nations for what they need, both countries gain and increase the wealth of both nations. Imports, then, are justified if they comprise products that can't be efficiently grown domestically.

What bothers liberals more than anything else are trade problems that originate in national farm income and price support programs. When large surpluses develop, governments in the major grain-producing regions of the world distort market forces by paying farmers not to grow food. Governments may also pay farmers a deficiency payment to bring farm prices or farm income up to the level of nonfarm workers. Inflated or artificial prices merely generate more production, compelling governments to adopt an array of agricultural export enhancement and/or food aid measures to get rid of these surpluses. States will also often employ a variety of measures to limit agricultural imports to protect farmers.

Implied in a liberal argument about food and hunger is the assumption that many grain-exporting countries support their farmers because farm organizations are still very influential despite the declining numbers of farmers. In effect, state agencies are "captured" by farm groups and organizations when it comes to designing and implementing government farm policies and programs—extending the life of the farming vocation beyond its economic worth.

Recently, liberals have given quite a bit of attention to the Uruguay round of GATT negotiations held in Geneva, Switzerland. Agricultural import barriers and export subsidies were a major stumbling block in the multilateral negotiations among 108 nations to liberalize the international trade system. In 1993, the United States and EU nations, in particular, finally arrived at a timetable to eliminate these protectionist measures. Liberal trade experts blame national government farm support, self-sufficiency, and food security policies for failure to significantly reduce the level of trade protection for agricultural products and for failure to realize the goal of making more efficient the food production process.

The United States assumes that it is the world's most efficient commodity producer. So do Australia and many third world countries. It is not clear yet as to who might benefit the most and who will lose the most as a result of competition in agricultural trade. Nor are states ready to pay the costs of adjustments that will be made in different national economies as a result of less protection for farmers.

Liberals also have strong feelings about both trade and aid policies when it comes to LDCs and their efforts to overcome hunger. Hunger is not only the result of government intervention in markets in industrialized regions of the world, but also LDC mismanagement of their own economies. In the past, liberals have generally believed that the Western development model, emphasizing industrial productivity and economic growth, was applicable to developing nations. LDCs could grow out of and overcome their poverty and hunger problems if they imitated the West's approach to development. Trade was viewed as an "engine to growth." LDCs were to specialize in producing a few commodities, such as bananas, coffee, sugar, or tea, that could be exported abroad to earn foreign exchange. Food deficits would be made up by imports. This strategy required government to at first play a relatively strong role in the economy to ensure that market forces determined prices and that the growth of industry would be carefully coordinated and balanced with the extraction of resources from the agricultural sector of the economy.

Food aid was to help a government overcome the lack of infrastructure or a short-term capital deficit. Aid of all types would allow the government the opportunity to invest in industry and manufacturing. Food aid was supposed to give LDC governments some breathing room. Food aid would make up for agricultural production deficits and help governments overcome immediate hunger problems.

Liberals view dependency on long-term aid, and food aid in particular, as likely to distort local food production and distribution. Corrupt officials can always be counted on to misuse funds or sell food aid on the black market. Liberals also fault many governments for keeping food prices artificially low for consumers in urban areas, but taking away an incentive for farmers to produce more. Food aid is to be used only in short-term emergency situations and/or in consideration of efforts to correct market deficiencies.

Liberals generally view MNCs and agribusinesses as an asset to LDCs because of their economic effect on local economies. The positive economic effects of agribusinesses "spill over" and "trickle down" from the top to lower levels of the economy. What bothers liberals is when, for largely political reasons, agribusinesses do not realize their full potential. Local officials are either suspicious of them or tax them to the point of discouraging them from investing further in the local economy.

Recently a good deal of attention has been given to a second Green Revolution, furthered in part by MNCs and agribusinesses. This element of the information and knowledge structure centers around the use of biotechnology to create and engineer new varieties of plants and animals.[16] One of the most important figures associated with the Green Revolution is plant pathologist Dr. Norman Borlaug, who started the revolution in Mexico in 1944 with his work for the Rockefeller Foundation. Fifty years later, he was still working to apply the practical and scientific principles of the Green Revolution to 150,000 farms in Ghana, the Sudan, Tanzania, Togo, Nigeria, and Ethiopia. Dr. Borlaug cites China and other Asian nations as major success stories in the Green Revolution.

Growth hormones in cattle to produce more milk and genetic alterations to the reproductive cells of pigs, sheep, poultry, and other animals are expected to dramatically increase food production in both the developed nations and LDCs. Once again, new crops and virus- and insect-resistant plants are expected to revolutionize crop production. Liberals argue that many of these technologies will be developed and their benefits diffused throughout the world via MNCs. Furthermore, MNCs are expected to work closely with national and local governments to implement the technology and spread its benefits.

In sum, liberals emphasize that hunger results when governments intervene in markets and distort food production and distribution processes. The result is a glut of food in the major grain-producing countries of the world, most of whom are also Western industrialized nations. Meanwhile, demand for food in much of the developing but also overpopulated regions of the world goes unmet. Economic growth should help nations move through the demographic transition, bringing down birth rates, but also helping these countries overcome their hunger problems.

THE STRUCTURALIST PERSPECTIVE

For structuralists, the dominant actors are classes within a nation-state and classes of rich and poor whose interests cut across national boundaries. The nature of the relationship of rich classes and nations to poor ones is exploitation. Exploitation is a feature of the international production and finance structures that link rich with poor nations. While formal colonialism is supposedly a thing of the past, rich nations continue to subjugate dependent countries by practicing *neoimperialism*, that is, penetrating Southern economies via trade, aid, and investment policies and practices.

Similar to liberals, structuralists argue that markets fail due to government intervention in the economy. However, where the two perspectives differ is in the rationale for that interference. For structuralists, state policies reflect not so much protection of private (group) interests but the interests of a wealthy class of financiers, manufacturers, and businessmen. The rich became wealthy at the expense of the poor, both nationally and internationally. Rich nations continue to dominate poor ones, intentionally making them dependent on the rich for a variety of goods and services to develop their economies.

Hunger is the result of this exploitative relationship. Structuralists criticize mercantilists and liberals for not giving enough attention to factors and conditions that prevent food from being distributed more equitably in local, national, and international distribution systems.[17] Rich nations usually produce more food than its consumers can eat, yet millions of people in poor countries go hungry simply because surplus food is not redistributed to those who need it most.

Dependency theorists emphasize the negative consequences of the transfer of wealth and resources from Southern LDCs to Northern industrialized nations. Linkages between rich and poor nations "immiserize" the poor, who become worse off as a result of various transactions with the North. Most LDCs were relatively self-sufficient food producers until they were colonized by imperial powers. Exposure to the West brought about development of only a small sector of the economy, while in the larger poor enclave of the economy, the masses became impoverished and were more likely to be malnourished or even starve to death.

From the perspective of dependency theorists, trade is a weapon used by the rich to penetrate and make dependent poor countries. The *terms of trade* (value of trade exchanges) favor rich nations. Free trade policies benefit advanced industrial economies at the expense of the development of poorer economies. In the past, LDCs have produced mainly primary commodities that earned less income than the value-added products of a rich nation. Elites within developing nations joined with their counterparts in rich nations to establish and benefit from a local power structure that exploited the masses.

Instead of focusing on meeting the needs of its people, these governments adopted an array of policies that continued to benefit rich nations. Many LDCs specialized in producing one or two major export crops to earn foreign exchange. Quite often these crops are still financed and grown by large agribusinesses who were encouraged to invest in the country by the national power structure. These enterprises grow soyabeans (Brazil), vegetables (Mexico), beef (Costa Rica), or peanuts (Senegal), while the masses of people subsist on substandard diets and local staple crops.

There are two consequences of playing the development game. First, most of the masses never share in the income earned from trade. Trickle down does not work. Instead, the rich get richer and the poor get poorer. Second, governments of these countries are forced to import food they need to make up for food deficits created by an inappropriate development strategy that relies on trade.

In many cases, governments are simply too poor to purchase those commodities and instead become even more dependent on donations for food aid to make up the difference. Foreign aid usually has strings attached to it, such as requiring that payment be made in certain currencies. Governments are also known to resell aid to earn foreign exchange or to distribute aid to the middle class or to those groups, such as the police, it feels are likely to make a significant contribution to the economic development of society. Foreign aid, then, merely further entrenches poor countries in a vicious cycle of dependency, poverty, and hunger.

Agribusinesses and other MNCs also negatively impact LDCs in many ways. Their high-tech production methods displace local labor and small farmers, destroying the traditional agriculture or farm sector of local economies. Masses of people leave agriculture to find work in cities, putting pressure on urban centers for social services. Aside from producing inappropriate crops for export, agribusinesses use pesticides and insecticides that are outlawed in their home country. Many of them bribe local or national officials, complicate land ownership and reform programs, and disturb local food distribution programs. Structuralists are just as pessimistic about the benefits of biotechnology today as they were about the first Green Revolution. They worry that attempts to diffuse biotechnology throughout the third world will contribute to environmental damage and widen the income gap between rich and poor within developing nations as well as between the North and South. Structuralists also worry that those who support the Green Revolution or biotechnology in the third world overlook the food distribution system, land tenure system, and the fact that many LDCs grow cash crops for export instead of producing food for domestic needs.

Many **dependency** theorists would have LDCs cut themselves off from the industrialized nations and adopt either self-sufficiency or import substitution policies.[18] The development strategy China practiced before 1978 was often recommended by dependency theorists as a way for LDCs to eradicate poverty and hunger first before exposing the economy to outside political and economic influences. Poverty and hunger are wasteful and inefficient. Development experts should find ways to build an economy from the inside out rather than the outside in.

Other critics of industrial nation practices believe that the North and South can accommodate each other provided a new international economic order (NIEO) be worked out between them. So far, however, the NIEO movement that began in the 1970s has ground to a halt. The South simply does not have the political clout to demand and bring about reform of the entire international political economy.

The **modern world systems** approach focuses more directly on international structures of wealth and power that cause hunger in LDCs. Core rich states have dominated world trade networks since the sixteenth century. Peripheral regions were first colonized and then exploited for their resources and labor. Only semi-peripheral countries like the NICs have been able to develop successfully to any great extent. However, they did so because it was in the strategic and foreign economic interests of the United States to flood them with technical assistance, loans, food aid, and military security. As clients of the United States that border the Soviet Union, many of the NICs played a major role in helping the U.S. contain the U.S.S.R. From the perspective of modern-world-system scholars, conditions for the poorest countries are not likely to improve until or unless the international division of labor changes.

CONCLUSION

Since the early 1970s, studies of hunger have decidedly moved away from food production–overpopulation arguments to international political-economic explanations of the issue.[19] Hunger is a multidimensional problem. An IPE of food and hunger accounts for how food production and distribution is influenced specifically by international trade, aid, and investment practices but generally by the international production, finance, knowledge, and national security structures. Each traditional IPE perspective accounts for a piece of the hunger puzzle.

Given the variety of actors and their values, as well as the causes and possible solutions to the hunger problem, reconciling these interests seems unlikely. Therefore, we should expect continued incidents of malnutrition and even starvation given the relationship of states to markets and the distribution of wealth and power in the world. To permanently solve the hunger problem requires a task that has yet to be accomplished, linking *food security* for each and every individual with political and economic structures of wealth and power at the level of both the nation-state and the international system.[20]

Ironically, an IPE of food and hunger points to a possible economic solution to the hunger problem, given the desire of states and other actors to generate and sustain wealth. At times, the rich nations have found it to be in their interest to feed the poor, benefiting both rich and poor nations alike. However, long-term food and hunger problems associated with war and, especially, poverty are another issue. Overcoming these two problems requires a fundamental transformation and redistribution of wealth and power in the international system. At this point, it does not appear to be in the interests of those who benefit the most from the current distribution of wealth and power to do much more than deal with the immediate problem of starvation.

DISCUSSION QUESTIONS

1. Outline the overpopulation/lack of production thesis about world hunger and discuss some of the consequences of this argument for dealing with the hunger problem. Whose problem is it? What is and should be done about it?
2. Do the same for the political economic thesis about hunger as in question 1 above.
3. Outline the dominant themes and concepts applied to the hunger problem from the perspective of each of the major approaches to IPE: mercantilism, liberalism, and structuralism.
4. After reading the entire chapter, discuss the extent to which you feel that the hunger problem can be overcome. What are the major political ecomic fault lines or dilemmas one has to consider if the problem is to be solved.

SUGGESTED READINGS

David N. Balaam and Michael Carey, eds. *Food Politics: The Regional Conflict.* Montclair, NJ: Allenheld, Osmun, 1971.

J. I. Hans Bakker, ed. *The World Food Crisis: Food Security in Comparative Perspective.* Toronto, Canada: Canadian Scholars' Press, 1990.

Joseph Belden, ed., *Dirt Rich, Dirt Poor: Americ's Food and Farm Crisis,* Washington, DC: Institute for Policy Studies, 1986.

Alan Berg, *The Nutrition Factor.* Washington, DC: Brookings Institution, 1973.

Joseph Collins, *What Difference Could a Revolution Make?* San Francisco: Institute for Food and Development Policy, 1982.

Susan George, *How the Other Half Dies.* Montclair, NJ: Allanheld, Osmun, 1977.

———. *Ill Fares the Land.* Washington, D. C.: Institute for Policy Studies, 1984.

David Grigg, *The World Food Problem: 1950–1980.* New York: Basil Blackwell, 1985.

Betsy Hartman and James Boyce. *Needless Hunger.* San Francisco: Institute for Food and Development Policy, 1979.

Ray Hopkins and Donald Puchala. *Global Food Interdependence.* New York: Columbia University Press, 1980.

Francis Moore Lappé, and Joseph Collins. *Food First.* Boston: Houghton Mifflin, 1977.

Physicians Task Force on Hunger in America. *Hunger in America.* New York: Harper & Row, 1985.

Jack Shephard. *The Politics of Starvation.* New York: Carnegie Endowment for International Peace, 1975.

Mitchell B. Wallerstein. *Food for War—Food for Peace.* Cambridge, MA: MIT Press, 1980.

NOTES

1. Thomas Poleman, "World Hunger, Extent, Causes, and Cures," *Cornell International Agricultural Economics Study* (Ithaca, NY: Cornell University, A.E. Res. 82-17, 1984).
2. Thomas Malthus, *An Essay on the Principle of Population,* excerpted in Charles W. Needy, ed., *Classics of Economics* (Oak Park, IL: Moore Publishing, 1980), 48, 55.
3. See for example, Joseph Belden, ed., *Dirt Rich, Dirt Poor: America's Food and Farm Crisis* (Washington, DC: Institute for Policy Studies, 1986).
4. Paul Ehrlich, *The Population Bomb* (New York: Ballantine Books, 1971).
5. Garrett Hardin, "The Tragedy of the Commons," *Science,* 13 December 1968. A commons is an unfenced, communal grazing area.

6. Garrett Hardin, "Lifeboat Ethics: The Case Against Helping the Poor," *Psychology Today* (September 1974).

7. See, for example, William and Paul Paddock, *Famine—1975* (Boston: Little, Brown and Co, 1967).

8. Of course, it may be the case that, at some point in the future, farmers may not be able to produce enough food, given the population of the earth. When the "carrying capacity" of the earth will be reached is a hotly debated topic.

9. Paul Kennedy, *Preparing for the Twenty-first Century* (New York: Vintage Books, 1993), 32.

10. See "People May Be Starving But There's Food for All," *The Oregonian* (21, September 1993): A07.

11. For a more detailed discussion of the world food crisis, see Sartaj Aziz, ed., *Hunger, Politics and Markets: The Real Issues in the Food Crisis* (New York: New York University Press, 1975).

12. See Jack Shepherd, *The Politics of Starvation* (New York: The Carnegie Endowment for International Peace, 1975).

13. See, for example, the Physicians Task Force on Hunger in America, *Hunger in America* (New York: Harper & Row, 1985).

14. The classic statement to this effect is by the realist Hans Morgenthau, *Politics Among Nations* (New York: Knopf, 1948).

15. Robert Paarlberg, "Lessons of the Grain Embargo," *Foreign Affairs* 59: 1 (Fall 1980).

16. George Moffatt, " 'Super Rice' May Ease World Food Crisis," *The Christian Science Monitor*, 26 October 1994, 3.

17. See, for example, Betsy Hartman and James Boyce, *Needless Hunger: Voices from a Bangladesh Village* (San Francisco: Institute for Food and Development Policy, 1979).

18. Andre Gunder Frank, *Latin America: Underdevelopment or Revolution* (New York: Monthly Review Press, 1970).

19. Examples of two of the most popular studies that view the hunger problem from a political economic perspective are Frances Moore Lappé and Joseph Collins, *Food First* (Boston: Houghton Mifflin, 1977); and Susan George, *How the Other Half Dies* (Montclair, NJ: Allanheld, Osmun, 1977).

20. The issue of food security is discussed and applied in J. I. Hans Bakker, ed., *The World Food Crisis: Food Security in Comparative Perspective* (Toronto, Canada: Canadian Scholars' Press, 1990).

19

The Environment: The Green Side of IPE

OVERVIEW

Environmental issues have become increasingly important in recent years, as the pace of economic development and population growth has quickened and the limits of nature have been tested. Environmental problems have always existed, but they are different now. Today's ecological and environmental problems are increasingly *global* in nature. The problems of deforestation and global warming, for example, are much larger than any single nation's ability to solve them.

The problems of the environment involve states and markets throughout the globe. International political economy, therefore, must expand to accommodate the "green" issues of today and tomorrow. This chapter probes the frontiers of the green side of IPE.

In this chapter, we examine three cases of global environmental problems and discuss several international political and economic dimensions of these problems. We also examine a number of proposed global solutions to environmental problems. A conundrum has developed around the goal of "sustainable development." The primary question for an international political economy of the environment has become: How do nations and other political actors create wealth for today's generations without at the same time leaving a despoiled and depleted environment for future generations?

I wander thro' each charter'd street,
Near where the charter'd Thames does flow,
And mark in every face I meet
Marks of weakness, marks of woe.

In every cry of every Man,
In every Infant's cry of fear,
In every voice, in every ban,
The mind-forg'd manacles I hear:

How the Chimney-sweeper's cry
Every black'ning Church appalls;
And the hapless Soldier's sigh
Runs in blood down Palace walls.

But most thro' midnight streets I hear
How the youthful Harlot's curse
Blasts the new-born Infant's tear,
And blights with plagues the Marriage hearse.

"London," by William Blake[1]

Prophets proclaiming imminent catastrophe are nothing new in the history of Western culture. However, at no time in the past have predictions of global disaster achieved such wide currency and been given so much respectful attention by policymakers and the general public. The approach of inevitable doom has become the conventional wisdom of the late twentieth century.[2]

Ronald Bailey

The relationship between the environment and the international political economy is a two-way street with many twists and turns. Tensions among markets and political and economic actors impact the environment locally and, increasingly, globally. Likewise, environmental problems routinely influence the international political economy, yet increasingly more often in unexpected ways.

For instance, the two-way street between the international political economy and the environment was illustrated in chapter 12's discussion of the NAFTA agreement among Canada, the United States, and Mexico. Differences in domestic political economy concerns in these countries produced dramatically different environmental regulation regimes. The free trade agreement among them was possible only after a series of environmental side-agreements were reached that would minimize the impact of free trade on the environment.

This chapter focuses on the international political economy of the global environment. In it we discuss four aspects of environmental problems in general: the environment as a communal good, the increasing global scope of environmental problems, the proliferation of actors involved in these issues, and the multidimensional makeup and linkage between the immediate causes and effects of environmental issues. We then apply this general analysis to three cases of global air, land, and sea problems: the greenhouse effect, deforestation, and ocean disposal of nuclear waste. Finally, we explore a variety of proposed global solutions to environmental problems focusing on the role states and other actors, markets, technology, and even social and ethical values play in these solutions.

THE ENVIRONMENT AS A COMMUNAL GOOD

The fundamental dilemma that any IPE of the environment confronts is the "tragedy of the commons"[3] (introduced in a different context in chapter 18). The earth's stock of resources is limited—finite resources such as oil can be used up, living resources such as forests and fish runs can be overused and depleted. For the most part, the environment is a **collective good**, one that is shared by everyone but owned by no one. As the "tragedy of the commons" explains, such goods are prone to abuse because of the selfish character of human nature. Actions such as industrial production and the overconsumption of manufactured goods and services that abuse the environment benefit the individual, but may harm the community. Human nature, alas, drives us to seek individual benefit, even at the expense of the environment, if the costs are borne principally by others.

This tragedy can easily be seen in the current concern over the depletion of the atmospheric layer of ozone that protects the earth from harmful solar radiation (discussed in more detail below). Each time someone uses the chemicals that are responsible for ozone depletion—in a refrigerator,[4] for example, or in an aerosol spray—that person gets a direct and immediate benefit. Yet the harm to the environment is shared by all the inhabitants of earth, and may not become apparent for years to come. In weighing costs and benefits, we find that the benefits are clear and immediate while the direct costs (to the person making the choice) are negligible, diffused, and hard to evaluate. In effect, consumers get a "free ride" because there is no incentive for them to pay the costs associated with helping overcome the problem. So environmentally damaging activity takes place.

Many argue that the state *should* play a role in preventing or correcting the environmental tragedy of the commons. If society values the environment, but individuals abuse it, the state is left to take corrective action. State environmental regulations are, in fact, prevalent in many nations. In some nations, political Green parties have formed to influence state environmental policy in this direction. When environmental problems become *global*, however, the state's ability to deal with them breaks down. Even environmentally concerned governments fall victim to a **prisoners' dilemma** when it comes to global environmental problems.

The prisoners' dilemma occurs when self-interest becomes a barrier to the cooperation that is necessary to achieve collective benefits. (In chapter 8, we saw that the prisoners' dilemma prevented international banks from cooperating to provide LDCs with the debt relief that was necessary for their mutual success.) The environmental prisoners' dilemma is created by the nature of the costs of environmental improvements relative to the benefits.

Consider once again the example of global ozone depletion. Scientists are fairly clear about what is necessary to reduce or reverse ozone depletion: an expensive change in how some goods and services are produced. If *all* nations were to adopt policies to regulate ozone-depleting industry, the problem could be significantly reduced. Cooperation, with everyone sharing the costs, is necessary here.

Suppose that all nations have adopted the necessary regulation. What would happen if a single nation, say South Korea, were to "defect" from the group and begin once again to use cheaper industrial processes that harm the ozone layer? The effect on the global ozone problem would be small—no single country has that much impact on a global problem. The benefit to South Korea, however, would be relatively large and quite positive. South Korea would suddenly be relieved of a costly burden; its products, because they are cheaper, would have a competitive advantage on world markets. South Korea, the environmentally unfriendly defector, would gain wealth and perhaps power at the expense of other countries, while hardly harming the ozone layer at all.

If a nation can achieve competitive benefits with little cost from "defecting" from an environmental agreement, then some nations will be tempted to do so. If one nation defects, others may follow. The prisoners' dilemma explains why it is so much harder to address global environmental problems than those problems that are confined to a single nation or locality. This insight is critical because of the changing nature of environmental problems today. Because states are usually more interested in generating wealth and power than they are in saving the planet, many look past the nation-state for solutions to global environmental problems that are becoming more severe every day.

THE GLOBAL SCOPE OF PROBLEMS

Environmental and ecological problems have been around for centuries. Beginning in the seventeenth century during the industrial revolution, science and technology were harnessed to produce new labor-saving devices, industrial machines, and goods for mass consumption. Manufacturing industries were fueled by great quantities of inexpensive natural resources and raw materials, many of which were located nearby but the preponderance of which were located in colonial regions of the world. During the period of classic imperialism, the Europeans conquered and colonized "underdeveloped" territories, exploiting them for, among other things, their resources and raw materials. Meanwhile, on the European continent, air, water, and soil pollution spread beyond local areas. The development of the gasoline-driven engine at the end of the nineteenth century shifted demand away from coal and steam to oil and petroleum-based energy resources. Resources remained plentiful in supply and relatively inexpensive in cost—transportation being the biggest expense.

As industrialization spread throughout Western Europe and the United States, industrial pollution gradually became a bigger problem. Local authorities were primarily responsible for clean-up efforts. Many problems became transnational in scope, that is, problems spread over several nation-states. For instance, in the 1920s, the United States and Canada argued about the effects of lead and zinc smelting in British Columbia that carried down the Columbia River into the United States.

The global magnitude of environmental problems was not fully realized until the 1960s. In the United States, global resource depletion became one of the issues of the student movement, and the environmental movement that grew alongside of it. As the absolute amount of pollution discharged worldwide grew, so did scientific knowledge and public awareness.[5] In 1972, a Conference on the Human Environment was held in Stockholm, Sweden, and the United Nations instituted its Environment Program (UNEP). The OPEC oil embargo of 1973 and resultant high prices pushed the issue of energy resource scarcity onto the agenda of many nation-states but also onto the global agenda. Yet many LDCs viewed the attention the developed nations gave to the environment as an attempt to sidetrack discussion of LDC reliance on energy resources for the purpose of industrial and economic development.

The critical importance of the environment was further stressed in a shocking study done by the Club of Rome and released to worldwide attention in 1972. *The Limits to Growth*[6] provided a set of projections for the world based on postwar economic and environmental trends. The study argued that if previous patterns of economic activity and environmental abuse continued, it would be the *environment*, not land, food, or other factors, that would limit global progress. A rich future on an uninhabitable planet was the report's shocking prediction.

Oil supplies gradually increased in the 1980s, and oil prices declined or held steady, weakening interest in resource scarcity and environmental problems. Yet national and international attention to environmental problems reached new heights of intensity and worry in the 1980s, when a number of problems and events shifted attention away from pollution to broader issues of ecological (mis)management. Just some of these events included a major chemical spill at a Union Carbide plant in Bhopal, India; the acid rain debate between the United States and Canada; the Chernobyl nuclear reactor incident in the Soviet Union; discovery of a hole in the ozone layer over Antarctica; major drought and famine in Africa accompanied by drought in the United States; a chemical spill in the Rhine River; accelerated rates of deforestation in Brazil, the Ivory Coast, Haiti, Thailand, and other nations; the closing of many U.S. beaches due to toxic waste or spills; the tanker *Exxon Valdez* oil spill in Alaska; and the possibility of greenhouse warming effects on the Earth.

In 1987, UNEP published a report, entitled *Our Common Future*, that shifted more attention to the connection between the environment and the survival of developing nations.[7] Sometimes referred to as the Bruntland Report because the chair of the UN commission was Gro Harlem Bruntland (she later became the prime minister of Norway), the report was a best-seller outside of the United States. The report linked hunger, debt, economic growth, and other issues to environmental problems. A year later, British Prime Minister Margaret Thatcher and Soviet Foreign Minister Eduard Shevardnadze gave speeches that linked the environment to concerns about global security. According to Shevardnadze, the environment is a "second front" that is "gaining an urgency equal to that of the nuclear-and-space threat."[8]

Not all leaders and nations felt the way these leaders did. The Reagan and Bush administrations aligned themselves with many optimists about the environment and argued that more study needed to be done. Furthermore, they claimed, environmental measures were too costly, and unfairly penalized U.S. businesses. While the Western Europeans generally tended to be more willing to adopt new environmental policies, U.S. government officials argued that technology and markets could better solve these problems than coordinated efforts by nation-states in international forums.

At the 1992 "Earth Summit" in Rio de Janeiro, 178 nations signed the Convention on Biological Diversity that committed them to find ways to develop their economies while preserving the environment. The United Nations General Assembly created a 53-nation Commission on Sustainable Development (CSD) to translate the Rio accords into action (discussed in more detail below). Shortly before and at Rio, many nations became upset that the United States wanted to play only a minor role in managing the planet. Since then, the Clinton administration has announced that it will sign the Convention and promised to once again make the United States a major player in international negotiations to design and implement global environmental rules and regulations.[9] The Clinton administration also announced that it will reverse the course of the Reagan and Bush administrations and sign the Law of the Sea Treaty.[10]

THE PROLIFERATION OF ACTORS

In the three hundred years since the start of the industrial revolution, the problems of the environment have gone from being local and often temporary to global and possibly permanent. As these problems have expanded in scale and scope, they have encompassed an increasingly large number of *actors*, namely governments, business firms, international organizations, nongovernmental organizations (NGOs), and individuals. This has complicated both the analysis of environmental problems and the efforts to solve them.

Environmental and related groups in both developed and developing nations have moved beyond the goal of educating the public to affecting public policy. Mainly pessimistic in outlook, groups in the United States include the National Wildlife Federation, the Environmental Defense Fund, the Sierra Club, Friends of the Earth, the Public Interest Research Group, the Rainforest Action Network, and Public Citizen. Membership in most of these groups increased in the 1980s. Environmental groups such as Friends of the Earth have political or other connections with public interest and pressure groups in other nations. The size, cohesion, and effectiveness of these groups vary within different nations, depending on the extent to which environmental causes permeate not only politics but also popular culture, music, and even esthetics and religion. For many environmentalists, especially in developed regions of the world, the cause has become another basis upon which to attack the alienated individualism of a consumption-oriented capitalist society. Some environmental pressure groups, such as Poland's Ecological Club and Bulgaria's Ecoglasnost, have become political

(Green) parties. Many European Green parties have their roots in the environment-feminist-antinuclear movement of the late 1960s. Aside from winning as many as two thousand seats in national European elections, the Greens won 11 percent of the seats in the 1993 European Parliament election.

Nation-states have responded to environmental problems in different ways. In many LDCs, environmental issues often produce tension between the supporters of economic development and industrialization, and supporters of income redistribution, conservation, and sustainable development. In developed countries, this tension usually appears alongside such issues as public health, conservation, and even social engineering. One expert reports that in the mid-1980s, 110 LDCs and 30 developed nations had created environmental ministries or agencies to deal with an array of problems.[11]

Within the UN, the issue of the environment cuts across many different agencies and commissions. Only a few are: the Food and Agriculture Organization (FAO) and its subsidiary agencies, which monitor global hunger but also poverty and resource levels, especially in LDCs; the UN Population Fund, which supports population control programs in South Korea, China, Sri Lanka, and Cuba; and UN regional and global population conferences, which have been held in Rome, Belgrade, Bucharest, Mexico City, and most recently in Cairo in 1994. Other agencies have focused more directly on environmental problems. The UNEP came out of the UN Conference on the Human Environment, which adopted a "Only One Earth" theme. UNEP's "Earthwatch" network monitors atmospheric and marine pollution conditions all over the world. An International Referral System connects national information centers to a central data bank in Geneva. UNEP routinely spends millions of dollars a year on clean-up and management projects.

UNEP has focused on the issue of global warming (discussed below) as a major problem. Two other major UNEP environmental projects are water pollution and desertification. In an attempt to solve some of these and other problems related to human-settlements and refugees, conferences and conventions have been organized to produce studies, resulting in a number of treaties and protocols applicable to nation-states and businesses.

An increasingly large number of NGOs have made the environment their cause, the most notorious of which is Greenpeace. What started as a public awareness organization has become a proactive political organization whose goals vary from influencing national and international environmental legislation the world over to practicing civil disobedience on the high seas, for instance, when it comes to protecting whales or other marine life or protesting nuclear testing in the South Pacific.

International businesses have become increasingly more concerned about the environment. Until recently, the attitude of many of them has been that environmental rules and regulations were annoying and inefficient, to say the least. However, as environmental issues have become more pronounced, the definition of efficiency has come under attack for not including the cost of environmental damage. Deforestation (discussed below) is one such case. Many businesses have taken into account public interest and support for the environment. Many have changed the ingredients of some of their products, or in some cases eliminated the product altogether. Green products have become big business. Likewise, businesses that specialize in the production of environmentally friendly items have become big investment opportunities.

LINKAGES TO OTHER ISSUES

Despite these positive trends, nation-states continue to be pressed to deal with environmental problems. In the past, environmental issues were viewed as secondary to national security and economic growth objectives. Yet it has become clear that costs associated with a lack of resources and damage to the ecosystem add to the tension between nations when it comes to developments in the international security, production, and finance structures. Dependency on oil is a good case in point (see chapter 17 for more detail). Not only has the price of oil been raised and distorted, causing inflation, recession, and various other economic maladies, but nations have gone to war to preserve access to it. In 1991, the Persian Gulf War incalculably damaged Kuwaiti oilfields, as well as the region's water and air supply, climate, wildlife, and sea (see chapter 9).[12]

In the industrialized nations, economic growth, industrialization, trade, and investment combined have proved to be very costly to the environment. Growing international trade and investment means more industrially manufactured products and services that require vast amounts of energy resources. Trade protection in the case of production subsidies, which lead to the overproduction of agricultural and industrial goods, have been just as damaging as free trade to the environment. International economic interdependence, integration, and competitiveness have also compelled states to redefine national security in ways that better account for the environment (see chapter 9).

Many LDCs have not been as environmentally conscious as they could be, given their development objectives and strategies. Those strategies have recently come under a good deal of criticism for their failure to account for the environment. The socialist development model was as industrial-oriented as the Western liberal economic growth model. Many LDCs have debts to pay and must generate growth via trade or provide foreign direct investment opportunities to international businesses (see chapter 8).

The knowledge and information structure is also part of the global environmental balance. A nation's access to modern technology affects its environment in many ways. While high technology often involves the use of dangerous chemicals and potentially damaging processes, it has also helped cut down on pollution or solve any number of other problems.

CASE STUDY: THE GREENHOUSE EFFECT

Global warming and depletion of the stratospheric ozone layer are two interconnected problems that generate a great deal of controversy. Carbon dioxide, nitrous oxide, methane, chlorofluorocarbons (CFCs), ozone, and other infrared-absorbing gases are released by industrial, agricultural, and forestry activities. Greenhouse gases trap the sun's rays, contributing to a gradual warming of the earth's lower atmosphere. In theory, since recorded history the earth's temperature has gradually been rising, if only an average of a few degrees. The heavy concentration of industrial gases released into the atmosphere since the industrial revolution, and especially since the mid-1970s, has rapidly accelerated the rate of the earth's warming. Carbon dioxide makes up the largest concentration of these greenhouse gases, produced by the burning of fossil fuels, cement manufacturing, land deforestation, and the burning and clearing of land for agricultural purposes. Carbon dioxide emissions from fossil-fuel consumption between 1950 and 1987 alone totaled an estimated 130 billion metric tons.[13]

In dispute is the magnitude of a global warming trend and its consequences for the earth's natural and societal systems. Scientists have had difficulty measuring the earth's temperature. Their computer models cannot accurately account for such things as the interaction of oceans with atmosphere, cloud behavior, and the role of water vapor. Some believe that the earth's warming trend conforms to an expected variability in temperature patterns.[14] Still others boldly proclaim that "we cannot yet make useful predictions about climate, and that existing data show no evidence of the greenhouse effect."[15]

For a good many experts, global warming is real and has dire consequences for the earth. The atmospheric concentration of gases is expected to double the 1900 level between the years 2030 and 2080,[16] increasing the earth's temperature anywhere from 3.5 to 5 degrees Fahrenheit. The earth's warming is a global phenomenon that threatens natural ecosystems such as spruce and fir groves in Canada. The 1980s was one of the hottest decades on record. The decline in rainfall from time to time has threatened U.S. agricultural production in the western states and Great Plains region, all the while impinging on international food security. Some scientists also expect global warming to produce a rise in sea level of 0.2 to 1.5 meters on all coasts, damaging groundwater supplies, covering many island nations, and producing large numbers of refugees, especially from Bangladesh, China, and Egypt.

Some greenhouse gases—especially CFCs—have also eaten away at the earth's stratospheric ozone layer, which acts as a natural shield against the sun's ultraviolet rays. There is less controversy about the problem of ozone depletion than there is global warming. In 1975, scientists discovered a hole in the stratospheric ozone layer over Antarctica and for a good part of the year over nations in the region, such as Australia, New Zealand, and southern Chile. Many scientists believe that in the past twenty-five years, 2 to 10 percent of the stratospheric ozone layer over the northern hemisphere has disappeared. CFCs have contributed the most to the ozone layer problem. Used as refrigerants, aerosol propellants, cleaning solvents, and blowing agents for foam production, CFCs contain chlorine atoms that destroy ozone.

The effects of a depleted ozone layer around the earth are global in scope. They include a dramatic increase in the incidences of skin cancer, particularly melanoma—one of the most deadly varieties, more cataracts, damage to the body's immune system, as well as damage to crops and ocean phytoplankton. Scientists estimate that even if CFCs were to be completely banned, the ozone layer problem would last at least another one hundred years given the present level of atmospheric CFC concentration.

What has been done about the interrelated problems of global warming and depletion of the earth's ozone shield? In most instances, efforts to slow the production of greenhouse gases usually runs up against the issues of industrialization and economic growth. The regions of the world that produce the most greenhouse gases are Asia (minus Russia), North and Central America, and Europe, in that order—regions where large amounts of industrial activity have recently occurred.[17] In the industrialized nations, a number of approaches and policies have been adopted to deal with these problems. Most of them have been preventive in nature, such as efforts to cut auto and industrial plant emissions. Shifting from one type of fuel to another has been tried in some cases. New technologies have also helped local governments better monitor pollution levels and pinpoint polluters who can be held responsible for damages.

On the other hand, low oil prices have stifled interest in the development of alternative energy resources. In many cases, officials have had to trade off the effects of pollution for the benefits of the activity. A great deal of global warming is caused by forestry and agricultural practices. Cows, for instance, are a major source of methane gas. The point here is that cutting back on the production of greenhouse gases would mean major changes in the lifestyles of the industrialized nations. Estimated costs are $95 billion a year by the year 2000 to achieve a 20 percent reduction in U.S. emissions. Given these conflicting interests, it is easy to see why the policy approach of solving atmospheric problems at the local and national government levels has been incremental.

For LDCs, the situation is quite different. The issue primarily comes down to conserving energy resources, which translates into slowing down economic development and industrial activity. Yet most LDCs have not realized their development objectives, and in many cases have a great deal of debt to erase. For many LDCs, solving environmental problems must be subordinated to more immediate development objectives. When it is convenient, the industrialized nations blame the LDCs for atmospheric problems the industrialized nations have contributed the most to so far.

Some LDCs have come around to the perspective enunciated in the Bruntland Report that the problems of development and the environment are interconnected. Damage to the environment only worsens local economic conditions and frustrates growth strategies. In 1987, many countries signed the Montreal Protocol to Control Substances that Deplete the Ozone Layer. The industrialized nations agreed to cut ozone-depleting gases by 50 percent from the 1986 level, while LDCs are permitted to increase their output of gases for the time being. Measures such as phasing out old refrigerators and aerosol spray cans have been enacted in a number of countries. A number of nations have recently called for a change in the treaty to completely phase out CFCs by the year 2000.

A good many LDCs have begun to rethink their deforestation policies, as well as some of their agricultural practices. For the most part, however, these issues exhibit the same tendencies of most collective goods problems, namely free riders. It is not in the immediate interest of nations to pay the cost of trying to limit damage to the atmosphere. Those who do not pay are just as likely to enjoy the benefits of conservation and clean-up efforts should they decide not to pay. Yet in the last decade, as these problems have become more global in scope, they are being redefined as immediate threats to all levels of the international political economy, from nation-states all the way down to each citizen of the planet.

CAST STUDY: DEFORESTATION

Deforestation is such a case, the scope of which has until quite recently been viewed largely as a local problem. Scientists, national and international officials, and environmentalists almost overnight seemed to realize the severity of the problem. Many feel that the damage done to the earth by logging and cutting down the tropical rain forests might even be too late to overcome. Less controversy surrounds the causes of deforestation, compared with other environmental issues. Where most of the tension remains is between government and business practices, and proposed political and economic solutions to the problem.

Tropical rain forests now represent roughly 6 percent of the land surface of the earth, half of what they did fifty years ago. Since preagricultural times, they have shrunk by one third. Some 50 million acres of forest are cut down each year. Large tracts in the Ivory Coast, the Philippines, Thailand, and over thirty other developing and industrialized nations have been cleared for farmland, grazing, mining, and for fuel.

In nations such as Brazil, deforestation results, in part, from a government effort to resettle people away from urban areas into undeveloped jungle areas. Quite often huge quantities of wood are shipped overseas to earn foreign exchange. As many as thirty-three LDCs have been net exporters of wood, yet the 1990s have seen many of them actually become net importers of wood. Japan uses much of this wood to make cement foundation forms for its office buildings. After several uses, the wood is usually discarded, ending up in landfills. The United States also supplies Japan and a number of other Pacific Rim nations with logs and lumber from its ancient forests in the Pacific Northwest and Alaska.

Physically, deforestation threatens the earth's land, water, and air, making it a truly global problem in scope. In many cases, forest material is burned, releasing greenhouse gases that contribute to global warming. Deforestation has already wiped out countless species of plants and insects; scientists expect it to kill another one fifth of all species in the next ten years. The financial loss attributed to deforestation is incalculable because prices cannot be fixed for the losses of the many genetic codes in plants and insects, diversity that comes with organism mutation, and the 99 percent of naturally occurring species not exploited by man for food and medicines. Many of the tropical rain forests also contain plants that have proven to be effective in the fight against some forms of cancer and other diseases. The cases of Haiti, Brazil, and the Ivory Coast demonstrate that deforestation creates as many refugees as it resettles on land that has been stripped. Ecologically, the negative effects of deforestation include an increase in watershed runoff, which can result in either desertifying countries such as the Sudan or worsening flood conditions downstream in regions or countries such as Bangladesh, India, and Thailand.

What has been done about the problem of deforestation so far amounts to a resounding "not much" in relation to the severity of the problem. One estimate is that it would take 320 million acres (roughly twice the size of Texas) to begin to replace the rain forests that play such an important role in absorbing carbon dioxide[18] and perpetuating biodiversity. In many industrialized nations, conservation has a history of political support backed by national legislation. Even so, economic pressure to log timber continues in many regions within these nations. In some cases, environmentalists have successfully used legal tactics to slow up or even halt timber cutting and logging. Timber cutting remains a major public policy issue in places like the United States and Canada, where the economics of forestry come face to face with the conservation and environmental values and ethics of so-called "tree huggers." For the most part, the timber industry has found it economically and also politically profitable to invest in tree replacement and to employ a variety of new technologies and management techniques to stabilize the relationship between economic and ecological forces.

Forest replacement is not the objective of many environmental groups whose focus is the preservation of the tropical rain forests in developing nations. Until recently, LDCs have resisted the arguments of environmental groups, international organizations, NGOs, and others that campaigned for slowing down or even halting deforestation. From an LDC perspective, deforestation is not a cardinal sin; rather, it is a political and economic necessity. The forest helps pay off national debt and provides badly needed jobs. Many LDCs complain that the industrialized nations and international organizations are practicing "ecocolonialism" to the extent that they demand that LDCs shift their development objectives and strategies away from an emphasis on the extensive use of tropical rain forests and industrial activities.

Recently a number of LDCs such as Costa Rica have adopted forest conservation programs of their own. In an effort to pay off their bank loans, some LDCs have been willing to swap part of their debt for preserving a part of the rain forest. A number of NGOs, multilateral lending institutions, and international organizations have helped make these agreements. The U.S. Agency for International Development joined with a number of NGOs and public interest groups to sponsor a reforestation project in Haiti. Still many LDCs want more aid from the industrialized nations to replace what they would have earned through use of the forest. The United Nations reports that "tropical timber is worth $7.5 billion a year in an $85 billion-a-year global industry."[19] Many LDCs also complain that the industrialized nations have not done their fair share when it comes to slowing down timber cutting in their own countries.

On the agenda of the Rio Earth Summit in 1992 was a World Forest Agreement between the world's temperate timber exporters and importers and southern tropical exporters and importers. This agreement updated the 1987 International Tropical Timber Agreement that committed timber exporters to voluntarily try to balance exploitation of their forests with forest preservation. Tropical exporters now want to expand the agreement to include the United States and other temperate timber exporters such as Russia, Canada, France, and Germany, along with Japan, the world's biggest importer of timber.[20] Part of the agreement is that the temperate northern countries will provide LDCs with "appropriate resources" for conservation programs by the year 2000 in return for LDC efforts to adopt specific policies to help sustain their forests. Many environmental groups supported the treaty but were disappointed that it did not go far enough to solve many of the issues associated with deforestation.

CASE STUDY: OCEAN NUCLEAR WASTE DUMPING

Along with deforestation, the problem of ocean waste dumping has also climbed high on the international environment agenda. Like the other two cases, politics and economics play important roles as both causes and solutions to what many increasingly perceive as a severe global problem linked to many other issues. Aside from accidental oil spills that have become quite common these days, the United States, Great Britain, France, and the ex-Soviet Union have dumped large amounts of nuclear waste into different areas of the ocean since the mid-1940s.

In 1946, the United States began dumping low-level radioactive waste near the Farallon Islands west of San Francisco. Since then, the barrels have corroded and leaked. The International Atomic Energy Agency (IAEA) banned the dumping of high-level radioactive waste in the late 1950s. For the next twenty years, Belgium, France, Germany, Italy, Japan, South Korea, the Netherlands, New Zealand, Sweden, Switzerland, and Great Britain admitted to having dumped nuclear waste into the ocean. Up until 1970, the United States allowed dumping of radioactive waste at sites in the Pacific, Atlantic, and Gulf of Mexico. The practice was later abandoned, and in 1988, Congress enacted the Ocean Dumping Ban Act in an effort to end the dumping of industrial waste and sewage sludge at sea. The Soviet Union claimed never to have dumped radioactive waste at sea, but after the Soviet Union broke up, Russian officials admitted having done so. By some estimates, the Soviet Union dumped more nuclear waste into the ocean than the total of all other nations combined.[21]

As in the cases of greenhouse gases and deforestation, the issue of nuclear waste dumping is part of a broader set of environmental issues. Chemicals, solids, and nutrients from agricultural runoff, oil and gas development, logging, dredging, filling, and mining are routinely dumped directly into the ocean or otherwise end up in rivers and streams and make their way to the world's oceans.[22] Some of the effects of ocean pollution include: destruction of the world's fisheries, climate and sea level change brought on by changes in ocean temperature, and the destruction of salt marshes, mangrove swamps, coral reefs, and beaches, which means the loss of habitat and biological diversity.

The case of radioactive waste dumping in the ocean is as much if not an even greater threat to these ecosystems. Many assume that because oceans are so vast, they can absorb any amount of pollution. Radioactive waste tends to be absorbed by clay on the ocean floor and spreads easily through "ocean storms." Even if the effects on humans of radioactive waste in the ocean is not completely understood, the possibility always exists that localized concentrations of nuclear waste could cause cancers in humans and damage ecosystems in as yet unpredicted ways.

In 1972, the London Dumping Convention was formed with a membership of seventy-one nations. In 1983, its members agreed to stop putting even low-level radioactive waste into the world's oceans. In November of 1993, a new international convention was agreed to in London that permanently bans the dumping of radioactive waste at sea. Japan and the United States originally opposed the ban because they wanted to leave open the possibility of dumping low-level nuclear waste. Greenpeace and other environmental groups mounted a major campaign to support the ban. In October of 1993, Greenpeace observed a Russian navy ship dumping radioactive waste into the Sea of Japan. Since then, both Japan and the United States have reversed their positions. The Clinton administration declared that "the nuclear powers have a special responsibility to display leadership on sensitive ocean environmental issues."[23] Meanwhile Britain, France, and Belgium reserved the right to opt out of the agreement after fifteen years.

Britain, France, and China have no secure method of waste disposal. The United States has been forced to bury its contaminated submarine reactors in the sand at a site in Hanford, Washington, after moving the reactors by barge up the Columbia River. Many suspect that China dumps its waste down wells and mines or buries it in Tibet. Meanwhile, the Russians still have a total of 407 reactors that produce 26,000 cubic meters of liquid and solid reactor waste each year. Russia has asked the international community for aid in disposing of its nuclear waste, threatening to continue dumping in the ocean if it is not forthcoming. The United States has offered Russia $800 million to help deactivate its nuclear weapons as part of the Strategic Arms Reduction Treaty, but is cool about helping with the problem of naval waste.

SOLUTIONS: A GREEN IPE?

Global warming, deforestation, and nuclear waste dumping in the ocean all exhibit the tendencies of increasing severity, global scope, proliferation of actors, and linkages to other problems. Like so many other environmental problems, these three have been very difficult to solve. Yet the four characteristics of each problem we have discussed may actually force nation-states and other actors to compromise or otherwise find real solutions to them.

In considering solutions to these and other related issues, experts, officials, and activists must consider a number of questions. Who is most likely to pay the political and economic costs associated with solving these problems? Will new technologies help solve environmental problems or simply make them worse? Because issues are becoming more global in character, will solutions necessarily be most effective at the global or local level? Do international organizations have enough political authority and clout to design and implement global solutions? Or is attention on international organizations misplaced and better directed at nation-states—the basis of real political authority? And what about markets? Is there a positive role for the economy in solving environmental problems?

In an economic environment where pressure on the earth's resources is likely to continue to grow, will nation-states be willing to pursue objectives that do not require excessive amounts of natural resource consumption? This raises yet a more fundamental question: Can social values that emphasize economic growth and the consumption of industrially manufactured goods and services be replaced by values that are more environmentally friendly? We will try to briefly answer some of these questions, focusing on most often proposed solutions to environmental problems and on the role the international political economy plays in them.

Limit Population Growth

Population certainly plays a role in making demands on the environment. However, there is still no conclusive evidence that overpopulation itself is a global problem at this point (see chapter 18). Population growth patterns and forecasts are an aggregation of population growth trends in different nations and regions of the world. The claim that environmental problems result primarily from increased industrial activity that stems from population growth assumes that the growing number of people in the future will have the income to make demands on their economy for more energy and food resource products.

Most of the world's poor live in developing regions of the world and do not have that much economic influence. Reduced population in a society does not necessarily mean that people will consume fewer resources. In many cases increased industrial activity is a result of increased demand and consumption by a relatively wealthy minority. Some people in the newly industrialized countries (NICs) are beginning to demand more consumer goods. And of course, as economic development continues to spread, so will the ability of more people to consume the earth's resources.

The demographic transition promises that population growth rates will slow down naturally as people's income and standard of living increase (see chapter 18). From this perspective the population problem is actually a political economic problem of unequal distribution of wealth between the have and have-not nations of the world, and the unequal distribution of income within many developing societies. Many states in developing nations are quite authoritarian in nature and pursue development strategies that emphasize economic growth and the postponement of meeting people's basic needs (see chapter 15).

Ironically, it was the industrialized Western nations who promoted that model of development after World War II, for a variety of reasons related to national security and the preservation of capitalism (see chapter 9). Yet these objectives were attractive to many LDCs, not so much because they had to deal with an overpopulated society, but because they matched the political and economic interests of society's elite.

Does that mean that nothing should be done about current overpopulation problems in different nations? Not surprisingly, officials in some countries have tried to increase their population due to a lack of men for military service. Yet a good many nations still feel compelled to slow their population growth rate because of the economic burden more mouths make for society. Most have done this through education and providing people with birth control devices. In extreme cases, such as China and India, however, officials have forced some women to have abortions, be sterilized, use contraceptives, or inserted birth control devices into them without their knowledge.[24] For many humanists and culture experts, the empowerment of women and society's guarantee of political rights based on democratic principles are the best solution to the poverty and overpopulation problems.

Move Beyond the Nation-State:
International Organizations and Regimes

A popular recommendation is to shift political authority to bigger and more comprehensive units such as international organizations (IOs). The presumption is that these agencies will put cooperation and the interests of the globe ahead of national interests. The cases discussed above demonstrate that a number of IOs have indeed been quite busy when it comes to the environment. As yet, however, there is little evidence that they have been effective outside of the desire of their members to solve common problems. Most of the time, IOs lack funds and have served more as a forum for discussion than as an agent with real authority to assign costs or impose sanctions on those who damage the environment. This is not to say that IOs are not important. Rather, they are as yet at the mercy of their nation-state creators. This situation stands to change as problems become more severe and states are unable to solve them. Necessity being the mother of invention, IOs will continue to be looked to as cooperative ventures in the solution to many environmental issues.

There are variations on this theme. One is that the agent most likely to help solve environmental problems are **regimes**: norms, principles, values, and decision-making procedures that surround an issue.[25] Some believe that a number of regimes have already formed around a number of different environmental issues.[26] What is not clear, though, is how much regimes matter apart from the activity of nation-states that comprise them. Some believe that hegemons are necessary to promote cooperation and maintain regime institutions and procedures. Another problem is the extent to which linkages between issue areas make it difficult to separate one regime from another. For instance, should nuclear waste dumping be considered its own regime or part of the Law of the Sea regime? It is likely that the term *regime* will continue to be used in recognition of the many principles, norms, values, and political institutions that already deal with such problems as global warming or deforestation. However, the existence and analytical utility of regimes has yet to be firmly established.

It seems most likely that future solutions to environmental issues must account for political and economic structures of the international system as conditioned largely by the distribution of wealth and power in the world or by a hegemon (see chapter 9). At present, it appears that the international system is in between a Cold War structure and, for lack of a better term, a "new world order." It also appears that the United States does not want to be a hegemon, given the costs involved with that responsibility. On the other hand, President Clinton and his administration have suggested that the United States should play a more active leadership role in dealing with global environmental problems. This does not mean that the United States will not put some of its own economic interests before environmental interests, as it may have in the NAFTA trade talks (see chapter 12).

The fact that there is presently no firm international security structure in place may be good for the environment. At this time, environmental issues are more than likely to be high on the international agenda. The increasing severity and scope of environmental issues compel many states to redefine national security and economic growth. These older objectives will not be cast aside, but must be balanced with environmental considerations.

Markets for the Environment

Another solution to environmental problems is the market. Its supposed benefits are its flexibility over more rigid command and control policies of states. Many economists argue that some environmental problems should be "privatized" or assigned "property rights," which would help overcome the free rider problem. Many economists argue that government regulations do not work and that the market could be used as a mechanism to curb pollution by assigning permits to polluters. These permits could be sold to other businesses all the while lowering the level of acceptable pollution. Still another argument is that some problems are more costly to solve than others and that it would be more efficient to spend money on problems where the chances of achieving real success are greatest. Why spend billions on curbing greenhouse gases when it might be more efficient to purchase tropical forest reserves?

The market is usually not viewed as the best solution to environmental problems because economic costs of pollution are hard to calculate. Someone has to impose sanctions on violators or assign property rights, and that is usually the state. Once again, the economy does not operate in a political vacuum. Governments balance the costs and benefits of any environmental problem.

Despite the limits of the market, any realistic solution to the problem must include considerations about who pays and how far the money is likely to go to do what. Most experts want to use the market to stimulate people and nations to conserve resources or cut down on pollution.

A New Vision

This argument has received quite a bit of attention lately, and it takes many forms. Dennis Pirages made popular the idea of *ecopolitics.*[27] He argues that values associated with economic growth and technological fixes will not sustain the planet in the twenty-first century. Although not explicit as to exactly what objective should be pursued, Pirages argues that, along with literacy and democracy, the dominant social paradigm of the next century must reconcile limited energy resources with increasing demand for economic growth.

A number of critics have always been cynical about capitalism and its impact on the environment. Yet no comprehensive political economic systems have been developed so far as an alternative to what remains the most attractive economic system in the world. Others move further beyond discussions of the immediate political economy into the realm of religion and philosophy. A growing number of Christian communities emphasize the value of stewardship and trusteeship over the earth and its resources. Increasingly, more emphasis is put on sustaining the quality of life and replacing consumerism with an appreciation for respect and community with nature, instead of control over it.[28]

Sustainable Development

A general consensus has emerged that one of the most important goals of nation-states and international organizations must be the pursuit of sustainable development. As we enter the next century, the most often asked and pressing environmental question is: How do nation-states and other political actors create wealth for today's generations without at the same time leaving a despoiled and depleted environment for future generations?

The latest effort to answer this question was made at the UN Conference on Environment and Development (UNCED) that met in Rio de Janeiro in June of 1992. Dubbed the "Earth Summit," the conference created a Commission on Sustainable Development (CSD) to oversee provisions of Agenda 21, a 500-page blueprint for sustainable development. Some of the measures of Agenda 21 read like updated versions of the New International Economic Order (NIEO) provisions of the mid-1970s (see chapter 15) including: efforts to accelerate sustainable development through international economic policies that include LDC access of their exports to the industrialized nations and debt relief measures; and meeting basic human needs in the provision of food, clean drinking water, sanitation, and waste management. Agenda 21, though, blends these economic development measures with many provisions for protecting the environment including: promoting consumption and production patterns and the education of people in order to reduce environmental stress in national policies and strategies.[29] The Agenda seeks to accomplish these objectives through a combination of government designed and implemented programs complemented by market activities. Clearly, Agenda 21 reflects an accommodation of the interests of the Northern industrialized nations to the Southern developing nations.

Agenda 21 makes a decided effort to involve a wide range of actors in achieving sustainable development. These actors include the appropriate international organizations and nation-states, but also a large number of NGOs represented by some twenty thousand delegates at Rio. Some experts have come to believe that many environmental problems are best solved "at the most decentralized level of governance that is consistent with efficient performance of the task."[30] The intention is to involve as many people and grassroots groups as possible in solving environmental problems. Many international businesses have also made some commitment to sustainable development. Fifty chief executives of the world's largest corporations were active in the meetings preceding the Earth Summit. Although the Business Council for Sustainable Development opposed language in Agenda 21, it has advocated its own new standards to regulate international business and encourage the view that business practices should go hand-in-hand with environmental policies. Some lumber companies have made an effort to include environmental considerations and even the objective of sustainable development in their criteria for logging and other potentially damaging activities.[31]

Despite broad agreement as to the worthiness of sustainable development, actually achieving the objective is another matter. While a number of governments have adopted sustainable development as a national objective, Lester Brown and his associates at The Worldwatch Institute in Washington, D.C., argue that the world lacks the political will to formulate and follow through on the measures enunciated in Agenda 21.[32] Others argue that the Earth Summit might end up on the rocks of history if the political and economic relationships of the North to the South are not fundamentally transformed into a more cooperative and less polarized, confrontational relationship.[33]

And finally, three skeptical scientists argue that not enough is currently known to account for the normal fluctuations in nature to specify what a sustainable condition looks like. They suggest that

> science is probably incapable of predicting safe levels of resource exploitation. And even if accurate predictions were possible, . . . history shows that human shortsightedness and greed almost always lead to overexploitation, often to the point of collapse of the resource.[34]

CONCLUSION

Many environmental problems are becoming more global and more severe all the time, compelling nations and other political-economic actors to deal with them.[35] The international system is going through fundamental changes that require actors to broaden the conception of their interests to include those that are environmental in nature and scope. Despite the interest in new political, economic, and social values, there has yet to develop an alternative set of ideas that comfortably wed modern industrial society with the idea of preserving the environment. Efforts to deal with environmental threats to both nature and mankind are helping transform the international production, finance, security, and knowledge structures. Even if all the facts are not in, for the time being it would probably not hurt us to do as much as we can to limit damage to the environment—adopting a "no regrets" policy outlook.[36] Even if we cannot as yet determine how efficient or effective some environmental policies and programs are, their implementation will help limit damage to the environment.

The international political economy remains a source of many global environmental problems. It is also an integral part of any solution to those problems. While scientists have yet to completely understand and explain many of these problems, it is painfully clear that in the future the study of international political economy cannot ignore its green dimensions.

DISCUSSION QUESTIONS

1. Outline and discuss the "tragedy of the commons" and the "prisoners' dilemma." In what ways do these concepts contribute to our understanding of environmental problems?

2. The authors assert that environmental problems have become increasingly global in scope. What factors—political, economic, social—contributed most to this trend? Explain. (Note: The category economic includes such items as trade and finance but also the role of knowledge and technology.)

3. Examine each of the three case studies in terms of:
   a. the source of the problem—political, economic, social?
   b. the major actors and their interests in the problem
   c. potential solutions to the problem noting the tension between issues related to economic growth and the goal of sustainable development

4. After reading the entire chapter, discuss the assertion by Lester Brown that we lack the political will to solve environmental problems. Do you agree or disagree? Explain. What other things would you say that we lack or need in order to solve these problems?

SUGGESTED READINGS

Robin Brand and John Cavanagh. "Beyond the Myths of Rio: A New American Agenda for the Environment." *World Policy Journal* 10 (Spring 1993).

Frances Caircross. *Costing the Earth.* Cambridge, MA: Harvard Business School Press, 1992.

Lynton Caldwell. *International Environmental Policy: Emergence and Dimensions.* Durham, NC: Duke University Press, 1984.

Alfred Crosby, *Ecological Imperialism and the Biological Expansion of Europe, 900–1900.* New York: Cambridge University Press, 1986.

Thomas Homer-Dixon. "On the Threshold: Environmental Changes As Causes of Acute Conflict." *International Security* 16, (Fall 1991).

Jessica Tuchman Mathews. "Environmental Policy." In Robert J. Art and Seyom Brown, *U.S. Foreign Policy: The Search for a New Role.* New York: Macmillan, 1993.

Dorella H. Meadows et al. *The Limits to Growth: A Report for the Club of Rome Project on the Predicament of Mankind.* New York: Universe Books, 1972.

William Ophuls. *Ecology and the Politics of Scarcity.* San Francisco: W. H. Freeman, 1977.

Dennis Pirages. *The New Context for International Relations: Global Ecopolitics.* North Scituate, MA: Duxbury Press, 1978.

———. *Global Technopolitics: The International Politics of Technology and Resources.* Pacific Grove, CA: Brooks/Cole, 1989.

Michael Redclift. *Sustainable Development: Exploring the Contradiction.* New York: Methuen, 1987.

Scientific American. *Managing Planet Earth.* New York: W. H. Freeman, 1990.

NOTES

1. M. H. Abrams, ed., *The Norton Anthology of English Literature,* 5th ed. (New York: W. W. Norton, 1986), 42–43.

2. Ronald Bailey, *Eco-Scam: The False Prophets of Ecological Apocalypse* (New York: St. Martin's Press, 1993), 2.

3. See Garrett Hardin, "The Tragedy of the Commons," *Science,* 13 December 1968.

4. See John Holusha, "The Next Refrigerator May Take a Step Back," *The New York Times,* 4 March 1989.

5. See, for example, Rachael Carson, *Silent Spring* (Boston: Houghton-Mifflin, 1962).

6. Dorella H. Meadows et al., *The Limits to Growth: A Report for the Club of Rome Project on the Predicament of Mankind* (New York: Universe Books, 1972).

7. For more discussion of this report, see Jim MacNeill, "Strategies for Sustainable Economic Development," in Scientific American, *Managing the Planet Earth* (New York: W. H. Freeman, 1990), 109–124.

8. Cited in Jessica Tuchman Mathews, "Environmental Policy," in Robert J. Art and Seyom Brown, eds., *U.S. Foreign Policy: The Search for a New Role* (New York: Macmillan, 1993), 234.

9. See "Clinton Supports Two Major Steps For Environment," *The New York Times*, 22 April 1993, A1; and "Gore Promises U.S. Leadership on Sustainable Development Path," *The New York Times*, 15 June 1993, B6.

10. See "U.S. Having Won Changes, Is Set to Sign Law of the Sea," *The New York Times*, 1 July 1994, A1.

11. Jessica Tuchman Mathews, "Environmental Policy," 239.

12. See Michael G. Renner, "Military Victory, Ecological Defeat," *World Watch* (July/August 1991): 27–33.

13. See World Resources Institute, "Climate Change: A Global Concern" *World Resources 1990–91* (Washington, DC, 1990), 14.

14. For a more detailed discussion of this argument see Robert C. Cowen, "More Fuel for the Global Warming Debate," *The Christian Science Monitor*, 4 September 1990, 13. Cowen argues that El Niño's ocean currents account for as much as a third of the earth's warming.

15. Andrew R. Solow, "Pseudo-Scientific Hot Air," *The New York Times*, 28 December 1988, A23.

16. Stephen H. Schneider, "The Changing Climate," in Scientific American, *Managing Planet Earth*, 30.

17. World Resources Institute, "Climate Change," 15, Table 2.2. According to this report, the biggest contributors to the global greenhouse effect in 1987 were the United States, the former Soviet Union, Brazil, China, India, Japan, West Germany, and the United Kingdom.

18. Some Harvard University researchers have found that "temperate-zone forests may play a more important role in absorbing atmospheric carbon dioxide . . . than was previously believed." For a more detailed discussion of this finding, see "A Forest Absorbs More Carbon Dioxide Than Was Predicted," *The New York Times*, 8 June 1993, C4.

19. "Rich and Poor Nations Close to Agreement on Forest-Preservation Pact," *The Seattle Times*, 23 January 1994, A19.

20. "U.S. Cracks Door to World Forest Agreement," *The New York Times*, 13 April 1993, B8.

21. "Extensive Dumping of Nuclear Waste," *The New York Times*, 27 April 1993, A1.

22. "Most Ocean Pollution Starts on Land," *The Christian Science Monitor*, 29 November 1993, 17.

23. "Ban on Dumping Nuclear Waste at Sea," *The Christian Science Monitor*, 15 November 1993, 15.

24. "Third World Women Forced into Abortions, Sterilizations," *The Seattle Times*, 10 July 1994, A9.

25. See Stephen Krasner, ed., *International Regimes* (Ithaca, NY: Cornell University Press, 1983).

26. See, for example, Oran Young, *International Cooperation: Building Regimes for Natural Resources and the Environment* (Ithaca, NY: Cornell University Press, 1989).

27. Dennis Pirages, *The New Context for International Relations: Global Ecopolitics* (North Scituate, MA: Duxbury Press, 1978).

28. See "Environmental Legacy," *The Christian Science Monitor*, 1 December 1993, 22.

29. For a more detailed list of the items on Agenda 21, see "Agenda 21: The Cross-Cutting Edge of Sustainable Development," *The United Nations Chronicle* (June 1992): 49.

30. Hilary F. French, "Forging a New Global Partnership," in Worldwatch Institute, *State of the World 1995* (New York: W. W. Norton, 1995), 171.

31. See "Rio Condor, An Experiment in Ecology," *The Seattle Times*, 10 April 1994, B5.

32. Hilary French, "Forging a New Global Partnership," 171.
33. Robin Broad and John Cavanagh, "Beyond the Myths of Rio: A New American Agenda for the Environment," *World Policy Journal* 10 (Spring 1993): 72.
34. William K. Stevens, "Biologists Fear Sustainable Yield Is Unsustainable Idea," *The New York Times*, 20 April 1993, B10.
35. See, for example, the yearly publication, *State of the World*, by The Worldwatch Institute in Washington, DC.
36. For a more detailed discussion of this policy, see C. Boyden Gray and David B. Rivkin, "A 'No Regrets' Environmental Policy," *Foreign Policy* 83 (Summer 1991): 47–65.

20

The United States and the IPE

OVERVIEW

This chapter examines some of the domestic and international problems that confront the United States as it enters the IPE of the twenty-first century. The twentieth century was called by some the American Century. A U.S.-centered hegemonic system emerged after World War II that brought remarkable prosperity to the United States and a perhaps unexpected measure of peace and prosperity to the world. The virtuous cycles of earlier decades have seemingly collapsed, however, creating tension in all spheres of the IPE. To derive insights about the future of the United States and the international political economy, this chapter looks at a number of trends that have developed in recent years.

The United States continues to experience three fundamental tensions. First is the problem of reconciling domestic with international objectives. What choice is to be made when international obligations conflict with domestic needs? Second is the tension between the pursuit of political (security) and economic objectives. How is the United States to reconcile the liberal ideal of prosperity accompanied by the free movement of labor, technology, and capital, with the mercantilist tendency of states to compete for security and to restrict the economy in their favor at the expense of their political rivals? Third and finally is the tension between the tendency, on the one hand, for solutions to international problems to require a hegemon that imposes necessary costs on states and other actors, and the tendency for hegemons to weaken under pressure to solve problems in a more cooperative fashion. Simply stated, will Pax Americana continue in the twenty-first century, or will some viable structure replace it?

We focus on four scenarios for the future: Reemergence of U.S. hegemony; the rise of a pluralist cooperative international structure; a world of chaos and anarchy; and, finally, a scenario of surprises. The future is likely to display some aspects of all four outlines. Is optimism warranted? The question is important, since this book's readers by now understand how tightly they are connected to the events of the IPE.

In just twenty-five years we have gone from the American century to the American crisis. This is an astounding turnaround—perhaps the shortest parabola in history.[1]

Felix Rohatyn

The United States can easily remain the leading power in a more plural world but its leadership, to remain effective, needs a new formula. Taking on excessive responsibility for collective welfare is not a wise policy in such a world. Leadership requires a different style. It has to be based on a vivid sense of the limits of purely national power, and therefore the need for more plural management and a greater division of labor. . . . The task is to find a multilateral strategy that effectively engages the plural world's dispersed resources behind its common interests.[2]

David P. Calleo

In many ways, the twentieth century *has* been the "American century." The twentieth century witnessed the U.S. "rise to globalism" as one expert put it.[3] Many claim, however, that as the century ends, the United States is in a state of political and economic decline that makes it increasingly difficult to accomplish an array of domestic political and economic objectives. More important, decline in hegemonic wealth and power weakens the leadership's ability to solve a variety of international political and economic problems.

It is certainly not an exaggeration to claim that during this century, the United States—its values and its institutions in particular—have profoundly shaped the international political economy, more so than any other nation or set of liberal political, social, and economic values and institutions. For better or for worse, those values and ideas have been the major force behind political, economic, and social change in the industrialized nations and in less developed countries (LDCs).

Liberal values and institutions originated in Western Europe and developed over the last three centuries. England used its hegemonic wealth and power to promote free trade and democratic principles and processes. By the middle of the twentieth century, the United States was using its hegemonic political and economic wealth and power to carry on the British tradition throughout the world. During the postwar period, the primary international political struggle was between two conflicting outlooks about the world and how to organize it. Led by the United States, democratic-capitalist societies of the West sought to contain the socialist-communist societies of the East led by the Soviet Union and China.

In 1989, the **Cold War** between East and West appeared finally to end. The two Germanys were reunited two years later. As the Soviet Union encountered major economic difficulties, the Russian military empire continued to crumble. Many officials in the West, but especially in the United States, celebrated the political victory of the West over the East. One U.S. state department official went so far as to proclaim the "end of history" when he conjectured that democracy and capitalism appeared to be the choice of people everywhere in the world.[4]

Despite these successes, the world faced by U.S. officials in the 1990s does not leave them as encouraged as they were in 1989. Since the fall of the Berlin Wall in 1989, peace has not broken out all over. Democratic values and institutions are not easily adapted to many societies. In some cases, officials wonder whether such values and institutions are even appropriate, given some nations' history and current political and economic circumstances. In cases such as the republics of the former Yugoslavia, the end of authoritarian governance has provided many different ethnic groups the opportunity to "right past wrongs" through war, to make territorial gains, and in some cases to achieve "ethnic cleansing"—all in the name of nationhood and self-determination. Conflict and war in Bosnia and in other parts of Central and Eastern Europe has frustrated U.S. and European Union (EU) officials to the point that many of them agree with John Mearsheimer's ironic prediction that we "would soon miss the Cold War."[5]

Conditions have not improved since 1989 in many third world nations, either. In 1990, the United States sent 250,000 of its forces, in conjunction with U.N. allied forces, to liberate Kuwait from Iraq. Failure to dispose of Iraq's President Saddam Hussein made for a hollow victory but kept oil flowing to Western nations at relatively cheap prices. Shortly thereafter, U.S. and UN forces were sent to Somalia as part of a humanitarian effort to feed the people of a stateless country. President Clinton withdrew U.S. forces after efforts to establish a new government were met by local opposition that killed some fifty UN peacekeepers. In 1994, President Clinton sent 2,000 U.S. troops to assist in relief efforts for 1.2 million Rwandan refugees packed into several camps after a mass exodus out of Rwanda. Until then, an estimated 500,000 Rwandans were massacred by government forces after a military coup resulted in one ethnic group trying to eliminate another.[6]

When it comes to developments in the third world, in many ways the United States may face more anarchy in the twenty-first century related to, among other things, scarcity, tribalism, disease, and ethnicity, than it faces order predicated on capitalism and democracy.[7]

THE UNITED STATES IN THE IPE:
QUESTIONS, CHALLENGES, TENSIONS

These are just some of the challenges that currently preoccupy the United States and other nations. Alongside these issues, the United States must manage a number of domestic issues, many of them economic in nature. Many issues are no longer local but international or global in scope, and are also the concern of other actors such as international business enterprises and international organizations. The fundamental question for the United States is whether the liberal values, policies, and institutions, which have been so successful in this century, can successfully address these and other increasingly global problems.

This chapter examines the three fundamental tensions with which U.S. citizens and officials must deal.

- First is the problem of reconciling domestic with international objectives. What choice is to be made when international obligations conflict with domestic needs?
- Second is the tension between the pursuit of political and economic security objectives. How is the United States to reconcile the liberal ideal of prosperity accompanied by the free movement of labor, technology, and capital, with the mercantilist tendency of states to compete for security and to restrict the economy in their favor at the expense of their political rivals?
- Third and finally is the tension between the tendency, on the one hand, for solutions to international problems to require a hegemon that imposes necessary costs on states and other actors, and the tendency for hegemons to weaken under pressure to solve problems in a more cooperative fashion. Simply stated, will **Pax Americana** continue in the twenty-first century, or will some viable structure better serve U.S. and international needs?

In confronting these critical tensions, U.S. policymakers find themselves in a new domestic and global environment, and all four of the structures of the international political economy have been transformed in fundamental ways. This new environment presents new opportunities in some areas, but it also severely constrains policy options in other areas. This dilemma is perhaps best seen through an analysis of the tension between domestic needs and international responsibilities facing U.S. policymakers today.

PROBLEM #1: THE GROWING TENSION BETWEEN
DOMESTIC AND INTERNATIONAL PRIORITIES

In the years immediately following World War II, the United States seemed to have achieved a virtuous cycle of economics and politics. In an international political economy that was defined by the Cold War more than any other single factor, the United States benefited from a unity of purpose. Its domestic needs and international obligations worked together to strengthen power and achieve an unprecedented surge of wealth. U.S. policies regarding international trade, finance, security, and knowledge benefited itself while also creating a more stable and productive global IPE environment.

In the years since the collapse of the Bretton Woods system, this unity of purpose has withered. Increasingly, domestic needs and international obligations have come into conflict. There is perhaps no clearer symbol of this than the Vietnam War and its aftermath. Vietnam is just one example, however, of a pattern of stress and strain in the United States' political economy that affects the world as much as it impacts on the United States itself.

It is ironic that the tension between domestic and international priorities should be especially strong at the end of the century. When the Berlin Wall fell in 1989, many people wrongly assumed that the international obligations of the United States would disappear, or at least be noticeably reduced, making room for increased attention to the domestic agenda. There was even talk of a "peace dividend" because of reduced expenditures on national security, and television news show guests debated where and how this dividend should be spent.

Talk of a peace dividend was premature. The tension between domestic needs and international obligations has, if anything, increased since 1989. The fault lines can be seen along each of the main structures of IPE: national security, finance, production, and knowledge. Let us examine briefly the issues that strain each of these IPE linkages.

National Security: Problems Old and New

Many realists argue that even though the Cold War appears to be over, security is and must remain the primary objective of the United States. A few realists believe that until the Russian government is democratic and its economy completely capitalist, the Russians cannot be trusted. Most realists hold a more neutral view and argue that Russia is likely to remain one of the major powers in the world in the next century.[8] We should expect that its interests will always vary with U.S. interests. However, as the Russian economy slowly adopts capitalist institutions and practices, the government will more than likely be willing to institute democratic reforms that complement Western political and economic values.

For almost fifty years, U.S. officials were preoccupied with the Soviet threat to the territorial integrity of the United States and its allies. Today many of them appear to be operating on the assumption that most threats to the territorial security of the United States will come from third world leaders who have found it easier in a post–Cold War environment to pursue their national objectives. According to many political realists, the bipolar balance of power in the 1970s between the superpowers and their respective political and economic alliance partners began to break down and the national security structure became more multipolar in character. As other industrialized powers increased their economic wealth, they sometimes challenged U.S. objectives and leadership of the Western alliance. While continuing to be protected by U.S. "extended deterrence," Western Europe and Japan emerged as strong political and economic forces in the world. The People's Republic of China was gradually recognized as another global power because of its influence in East

Asia, but also because of its potential political and economic power. In many ways, China could simply not be overlooked. Many experts also included the newly industrialized countries (NICs) in Asia and other regions of the world as contending centers of political and economic influence and potential sources of conflict.

Less developed countries have become another threat to global security today. Many LDCs face drastic social and economic problems that incite domestic revolt and external aggression—recent events in Haiti and Somalia are examples of this condition. Many have authoritarian governments that adopt repressive measures to effect change in their domestic political economy. Some, such as North Korea, are frustrated and quite nationalistic in outlook. The global diffusion of military weapons and technology has made it easier for LDCs to acquire these means to threaten their neighbors. North Korea will probably soon join the club of nuclear nations. The industrialized nations continue to sell arms to many third world nations because it earns them foreign exchange and provides jobs for citizens. Many LDCs are now better able to purchase the great supply of arms that are shipped around the world each year.

The world remains a dangerous place and the international security responsibilities of the United States loom large. The days of unlimited defense budgets, however, are long gone for the U.S., and domestic problems require immediate attention. Public policies necessarily have taken on zero-sum characteristics when budgets are tight.[9]

An increased potential exists for conflict and war in the third world that could involve the United States. The Clinton administration followed in the footsteps of the Bush administration and cut defense spending between 3 and 4 percent per year. The emphasis within the U.S. defense establishment is to improve the readiness of the military and enhance the efficiency of its weapons. The United States may not be likely to fight a major war in the near future, but it could be involved in more Persian Gulf–type situations that require mobility and logistical capabilities. Some experts speculate that under these circumstances emphasis will be on the development of more sophisticated technologies, such as computer links, communications systems, satellites and sensors to improve the accuracy of precision-guided missiles and conventional weapons that will help destroy the enemy's systems and clear battle zones, cutting down on the number of U.S. casualties.[10]

On top of these issues, another complex matter continues to baffle U.S. officials, making it difficult for them to reconcile domestic with international security issues. As has so often been noted in this book, in an interdependent world, state efforts to promote and sustain economic growth have necessitated strategies to influence and control the international economy.

International Finance: The Dollar and the Deficit

The tension between domestic needs and international responsibilities is clearly illustrated in the finance structure by the problem of the dollar and the deficit. To the extent that U.S. policymakers in recent years have chosen the deficit over the dollar, they have chosen domestic interests over international obligations.

The deficit in question is the U.S. federal government budget deficit—the amount that the U.S. federal government must borrow because its outlays exceed tax revenues. In simple terms, this budget deficit exists because U.S. citizens and their representatives have voted for programs but not for the taxes to pay for them. Borrowing covers the cost of these unfunded programs. Because savings rates in the United States are very low, there are insufficient domestic funds to lend to the government and also satisfy other domestic needs, such as consumer and business borrowing. The extra funds to finance the deficit, therefore, must come from abroad: from Japan in the 1980s, and increasingly from third world countries in the 1990s. The deficit is thus an *international* political economy problem, since it draws resources from international financial networks. The amounts involved were (and continue to be) significant. In the course of the 1980s, the United States went from being the world's largest creditor nation to the world's largest net debtor nation!

As we saw in chapter 8, there are several implications of international borrowing. The first is that a capital account surplus results. That is, more funds enter the country for investment purposes than leave it, including deficit finance. This capital account surplus, however, must be matched by a current account deficit. The funds that the U.S. borrows from abroad, in simple terms, are ultimately used to purchase foreign goods and services, which are counted in the current account.

The U.S. current account deficit is thus at least partly the product of the U.S. government budget deficit. Economists sometimes talk of the "twin deficits" because they have been so closely associated in recent years. Table 20–1 provides data on the U.S. budget deficit and the current account deficit for selected years since 1980.

The deficit forced the United States into a position of having to choose between domestic and international interests. Domestic political interests have strongly resisted policies that significantly reduce the deficit, since this would require cuts in programs or higher taxes. Attention has thus focused on U.S. international obligations. In finance, the United States has an obligation, like other hard currency coun-

TABLE 20–1   U.S. Budget Deficits and the Current Account

YEAR	FEDERAL BUDGET BALANCE ($ BILLIONS)	CURRENT ACCOUNT BALANCE ($ BILLIONS)
1980	–$ 73.8	+$ 2.3
1982	–$128.0	–$ 11.4
1984	–$185.4	–$100.3
1986	–$221.2	–$150.2
1988	–$155.2	–$127.1
1990	–$221.4	–$ 91.8
1992	–$290.4	–$ 66.4

Source: Economic Report of the President 1994. Budget figures are for fiscal years, current account data are for calendar years.

tries, to work toward a stable but at the same time flexible system of foreign exchange, as discussed in chapter 7. A stable dollar is required to meet this responsibility. In trade, the United States has a long-standing policy of supporting the free trade policies of the GATT (see chapter 6 and the section below).

The information in Table 20–1 illustrates the choice that the United States made in the 1980s to sacrifice international financial concerns in favor of domestic needs. After 1986, the federal budget deficit continued to grow and the dollar began a long, erratic decline relative to other hard currencies. The dollar's depreciation reduced somewhat the current account deficit, but did not eliminate it. The domestic versus international tension of the dollar and the deficit remains in the 1990s. U.S. policymakers want to have *both* international stability *and* domestic prosperity, and seemingly cannot achieve either.

U.S. international obligations require that it reduce its deficit in order to eliminate international imbalance without currency instability or trade restrictions. But reducing the deficit in this case means putting international economics ahead of domestic politics. We do not yet know how this tension between domestic and international, between politics and economics, will ultimately be resolved.

The Tension Between Free Trade and Jobs

The United States' changing attitude toward international trade provides a third example of the rising tensions that characterize IPE for the United States. The apparent conflict between international obligations and domestic needs is perhaps nowhere clearer than in the area of international trade. The international responsibilities of the United States in the area of trade are clear, having been sharply defined over nearly half a century of policy and practice. Since the days of Bretton Woods, the U.S. has been a strong and vocal advocate of a liberal trading system. Free trade, open markets, global competition: these are the principles that have guided U.S. policy and, through its influence on the General Agreement on Tariffs and Trade (the GATT), these have been the watchwords of international economic policy.

The liberal policy of free trade has suited the United States in two ways for most of the twentieth century. Free trade fits the liberal philosophy of the United States; both the GATT and the Declaration of Independence have roots in the Scottish Enlightenment of David Hume and Adam Smith. More than philosophy, however, free trade was in the simple self-interest of the United States in the 1950s, just as it was in Great Britain's interest in the 1850s. Britain was the "workshop of the world" in those days, so free trade meant trade with Britain. The United States was the world's workshop in the early postwar years; free trade, then, was both good philosophy *and* good economics.

New tensions have slowly built as the U.S.-centered "workshop of the world" has been replaced with a "global production line" of which the United States is a key part, but not a dominating one. Increased world trade no longer necessarily means increased trade with the United States, breaking the link between domestic and international goals. And trade does not always take place on terms that favor U.S. firms or citizens. Some ships today arrive at West Coast ports to unload manufactured goods from Asia; they return with their cargoholds full of waste cardboard, to be recycled into new boxes abroad. This uncharacteristic "trash for cash" trade, whatever its origins or logic, seems an unlikely source of high-paying jobs for U.S. college graduates.

The advent of the World Trade Organization (WTO) presents the United States with potentially an even more powerful institution with which to advance its liberal trade philosophy. Changing terms and conditions in international trade, however, make many citizens uncertain about where free trade fits into national interest now. Neomercantilism and the rise of the "new protectionism" have been among the results. This tension has been seen in earlier chapters of this book, especially in the tensions over NAFTA (chapter 12) and those arising from the trade conflicts between the United States and Japan in the 1980s and 1990s (chapter 13).

There are many views about how the tension between trade and jobs should be resolved. One view holds that free trade and U.S. jobs are irreconcilable: the tradition of U.S. advocacy of free trade must be abandoned in the interests of domestic prosperity. This perspective has driven some of the more confrontational aspects of the U.S.-Japanese trade talks, for example. The state must step in to "manage trade" to keep jobs secure.

An alternative view holds that free trade and jobs *can* be reconciled, but only if the United States is willing to make the many changes and investments necessary to resume its position as a leading industrial nation. The United States would need to reduce its debts (especially the government budget deficit) and cut consumer spending to provide resources to invest in workers, factories, and technology. Proponents of this view call for an emphasis on "productivity" through investment, rather than "competitiveness" through trade barriers.[11]

Until the tension between free trade and domestic jobs is resolved one way or another, the United States faces a difficult dilemma. Both domestic *and* international policies are bound to lack unassailable credibility when their foundations are weakened by such fundamental fissures as these.

Knowledge and the National Interest

The structure of knowledge and technology (chapter 10) is also strained by the advent of the global economy, creating new tensions for the United States. Knowledge is power, it is said, and for much of the postwar period, one aim of the United States was to control access to knowledge in order to gain power. National security priorities thus dominated the agenda. U.S. policies aimed to develop science and technology that would serve national security interests. Access to this knowledge was strictly controlled to protect the national interest. U.S. business firms, of course, benefited directly from this emphasis, and were often able to profit as well by selling arms or technology to U.S. allies.

With the end of the Cold War, however, the technological emphasis has shifted from the generation of power to that of wealth. Weapons and technologies once protected as secret are now sold on open world markets. The inevitable question arises, what is in the national interest? This question was easily answered when the

Soviet bear lurked in the shadows; the answer is less clear in today's world, where the United States competes economically with nations with which it is allied militarily.

Realists would argue that it is in the national interest to limit access to scientific discoveries and technological advances. Liberals, however, respond that these know-how resources are not fundamentally different from other resources and that free and mutually beneficial exchange is the best course to take. The issue is clouded by several questions about the nature of international technological relationships.[12]

The first problem is that it is by no means clear that a policy of controlling technology would be in the self-interest of the United States—*if* such a policy was also adopted by others. As noted in chapter 10, the United States does not lead the world in many areas of science and technology, especially *process innovation*. A mercantilist technology regime could deny the United States access to advances in some important economic areas. A second problem is that technological change itself has reduced or eliminated any nation's ability to determine its own policies in the knowledge structure. Scientific and technical discoveries can be transmitted instantly around the globe via the Internet and other communications systems. The ability of individuals and firms to communicate is simply greater than the ability of governments and regulators to control the production, exchange, and distribution of technology.

The emergence of the global assembly line is another force weakening the ability to control access to technology. Global markets often give birth to global business organizations, MNCs, and transnational alliances, which necessarily share knowledge. Boeing commercial aircraft, for example, are now built for the global market. The aircraft are assembled in the United States, but components come from all around the world—even China. While it may still be possible to control some knowledge about design and construction of these aircraft—to protect U.S. wealth and power—it is unclear how long any lead can be maintained. Global markets mean global production, which, eventually it seems, means the global diffusion of knowledge.

Global markets for goods do not, however, mean global markets for knowledge. The liberal notion that free markets benefit everyone often breaks down in the case of science and technology because of the problem of intellectual property rights. Many countries do not honor U.S. patents and copyrights. U.S. firms see this as theft, but LDCs, viewing the problems mainly from the mercantilist and structuralist perspectives, see the use of U.S. technology as a basic right (an idea is not used up when it is used). So long as intellectual property rights are not well defined and enforced, the global assembly line threatens the interests of U.S. innovators.

In summary, the knowledge structure displays tensions of its own, which are compounded by changes in the other structures of IPE. The end of the Cold War terminated a period when U.S. interests were clear in these fields. Global forces make the domestic and international interests of the United States hard to reconcile, and perhaps even harder to clearly define.

PROBLEM #2: RECONCILING NATIONAL SECURITY
WITH ECONOMIC SECURITY

Many experts note that the forces of economic security and national security actively compete with one another in the international political economy today. In chapters 2 and 9, we discussed the age-old tendency for nations to feel insecure in a self-help international system where there is no single sovereign or global authority to ensure their security. Mercantilists and realists usually think of the production of wealth and other economic activities as subordinate to the state security drive. As we saw in the case of trade embargoes and boycotts, wealth is another tool states use to secure themselves. Economic liberals (see chapters 3 and 11) would argue that, at the same time, international forces reflected in economic interdependence and integration compel states not to interfere too much in their national or the international economy so as to realize the benefits of economic activity. How will the United States reconcile these two tendencies given not only the size of its economy and its economic interests, but also its national and international security interests, which often compel it to view the economy as another tool of foreign policy?

One way to answer this question is to focus on the characteristics that make a nation powerful. Many of the chapters in this book noted that increasing global political and economic interdependence in the 1970s brought about an appreciation for the extent to which national and international security and economic issues have become deeply intertwined with one another. Ideas about national security were dominated by realists who usually thought of security as an objective a nation achieved by converting its population, territory, natural resources, economic size, and military force into tools that helped it secure its borders or control others. These "hard" elements produced "command" power in that results were achieved by punishing or rewarding other states.[13]

Recently many experts have focused on "soft" power, which is composed of such things as technology, finance, a nation's position in the trade system, and even education. Their argument is that in today's international political economy, marked by a high degree of interdependence and integration, nations are often powerful to the extent that they use their wealth to gets others to do what they want them to do in a cooperative fashion. "Cooperative" power may involve providing collective goods and obtaining the consent of weaker states to accept a stronger state's agenda or ideas. We saw a good example of this in chapter 7: the extent to which the idea of a liberal trade system became "embedded" in the minds of those Western European officials who supported the U.S. objective after World War II. In the words of Joseph Nye:

> If a state can make its power legitimate in the eyes of others, it will encounter less resistance to its wishes. If its culture and ideology are attractive, others will more willingly follow. If it can establish international norms that are consistent with its society, it will be less likely to have to change. If it can help support institutions that encourage other states to channel or limit their activities in ways the dominant state prefers, it may not need as many costly exercises of coercive or hard power in bargaining situations.[14]

This kind of power is often used to account for Japan and the EU's status and influence beginning in the late 1960s. The increased presence of economic power, together with the attention states have given economic growth and other economic objectives, has led many experts to assert that economic activities and state objectives will increasingly replace national security and other political state objectives in the twenty-first century. The elements of power do shift around quite a bit. Meanwhile, security and economic objectives have indeed become intertwined. But it would be a mistake to argue that political considerations in the twenty-first century will become subordinate to economic concerns. Joseph Nye persuasively argues that Japan, for instance, is quite dependent on other nations for natural resources, which makes it vulnerable to the political objectives of its suppliers.[15] Economic interdependence produces asymmetrical advantages for some nations that soft economic power cannot easily fend off. Japan remains relatively weak militarily and still depends on the United States for its security. On the other hand, as noted in chapter 13, the United States has not been able to exploit these linkages very much because of its dependency on Japanese investment finance and markets for U.S. exports.

If anything, the twenty-first century promises to further intertwine security and economic issues, making it even more difficult for nations to sort out one set of problems from another. Mercantilists and realists are correct to stress the primacy of the nation-state as the major actor in the international system and its concern about territorial integrity in a self-help international system. Yet liberals are correct to emphasize the nation-state's drive for wealth, both as a necessity to acquire the weapons needed for security purposes, but also as another of the state's most important goals—raising national living standards. As noted above, economic policies designed to enhance the economic competitiveness of one nation often cancel out similar policies of another nation. And yet economic competition always stands a chance of generating hostility and even violent conflict.

When it comes to the clash between security and economic issues in the twenty-first century, one expert suggests that there are at least four instances where this tension will be felt. The first is the impact of national defense expenditures on the economic performance of the economy.[16] Contrary to what has become popular opinion, Aaron Friedberg argues that national defense expenditures can be a drain on the economy, but at times they can also stimulate economic growth in many ways, including investment in the development of new technologies that "spin off" to the private sector. Defense cuts initiated by the Bush administration and carried out in the Clinton administration cut defense expenditures as the percentage of GNP from 6 to 3 percent. Yet the U.S. economy has not doubled in growth, nor has the competitiveness of U.S. products improved that much. Further defense cuts would not necessarily mean more government spending in other parts of the economy. In short, the analysis of the relationship between defense expenditures and economic performance is something academics and policy officials have not as yet completely mastered.

Another area where the economy will affect national security is in the impact of economic change on the power and position of states in the international political economy. Many experts note that shifts in the distribution of wealth contribute to shifts in the distribution of military power and political influence. As the United

States grew economically after World War II, other industrial nations and some of the NICs expanded more rapidly, helping to transform the international balance of power from a bipolar to a multipolar configuration. Friedberg notes that the increased globalization of transportation, communication, trade, financial flows, technology development and transfers, and investment have produced changes in the security structure and processes of the international system. There are many more (nuclear) weapons producers and a willingness on the part of some countries to use them. Many LDCs are less dependent on the industrialized nations for weapons and security in the post–Cold War environment. Likewise, in the name of economic efficiency, many of the industrialized nations have adopted trade policies that make them dependent on other nations for some of their weapons. Tolchin and Tolchin argue that budget cuts for defense have made the United States dependent on Japan for semiconductors used in many of the more sophisticated weapons in its arsenal.[17]

The third area where we can expect tension between security and economic issues pertains to economic statecraft or in the use of the economy as a tool of foreign policy. We should expect weak states to try to control stronger states dependent on them for natural resources. The Persian Gulf War demonstrated continued dependency, especially of the industrialized nations, on the Middle Eastern states for oil (see chapters 9 and 17). Stronger states will be tempted to employ trade embargoes and other economic sanctions against weaker states, especially given public opposition to intervention in third world nations and the increasing disutility of weapons of mass destruction in these regions of the world. Economic sanctions continue to be used in an effort to get certain states to change their behavior. Finally, strong states may employ economic statecraft measures against other strong states. The United States has begun to prepare to retaliate against Japan for failing to bring down its trade surplus with the United States. These measures include forbidding Japan to bid on certain federal contracts. And as discussed in chapters 6, 10, and 13, Super 301 trade legislation has become a weapon the president and Congress have threatened to use if Japan does not change its trade practices. The tools of economic statecraft may not be as effective as military force, but they seem to be more appropriate and useful in a world where economic interdependence often precludes the use of more traditional means of trying to change a nation's behavior, namely through force.

National security and economics can be expected to produce tensions in the area of what Robert Gilpin refers to as "benign mercantilism." In an effort to preserve state autonomy, the United States and other nations have adopted measures that appeal to their "economic security." State assistance measures are intended to help some industries become or remain competitive in the international political economy. As discussed in chapter 2, these policies often offset those adopted by other states to accomplish similar domestic objectives. As a consequence, many states have shifted their role further away from liberal policies that indirectly help businesses, to consciously doing what they can to improve the economic climate for their nation and its businesses.

In the twenty-first century, the United States has available to it a number of economic and military instruments it can use to accomplish an array of economic and political objectives. What will be troubling will be the difficulties officials have prioritizing these objectives. As discussed in chapter 1, the China-MFN (most favored nation) issue is a case that demonstrates the complexity of issues at stake for the United States. MFN meant human rights to some groups, but it meant jobs and trade to others. The MFN issue also affected global security, because of China's military power and its ability to influence hard-line North Korea. MFN affects international investments and many other policies and activities. The MFN issue illustrates the usefulness of looking at a problem from different viewpoints, but it shows even more how various aspects of this issue are tied together, making a multisided study necessary. Given the complexity of this issue, it is not likely to be solved easily by adopting the policy recommendations of any one IPE approach.

Finally, still another set of economic issues are likely to butt heads with national security issues in the future, and those are environmental issues. To a large extent, environmental problems have been viewed as political and economic problems in a class of their own. Ironically, most officials (and academics) appear to be aware of the relationship of the environment to the traditional economic issues. Yet there remains a reluctance to integrate these issues directly into a discussion of their effect on the economy and national security issues.

PROBLEM #3: WITHER PAX AMERICANA?

The tension between domestic needs of the United States versus its international obligations inevitably leads to the question of the future of the postwar system of international political economy. Pax Americana is the name often given to this era of U.S. hegemony, an echo of the nineteenth century's **Pax Britannia**. Can the United States continue to lead if its domestic problems draw resources and attention away from its international responsibilities?

Can the United States continue to lead? This question has generated an active debate among scholars and public officials over the last twenty years. To a great extent, the debate has focused on two related questions. Is the United States strong enough to lead? And who will act as hegemon if the United States lacks either the strength or the will to lead in the future?

There are at least three sides to this debate over decline. Some scholars believe that the United States has entered a period of *absolute decline*, by which they mean that the United States is absolutely weaker than it was twenty or thirty years ago, and therefore too weak to be a global hegemon. Advocates of this view point to stagnating living standards in the United States and its rising international debt, discussed earlier in this chapter. They see the United States today as essentially similar to Great Britain a hundred years ago: well past its zenith, burdened by outdated roles and institutions, still influential, but not really powerful.[18]

A second and larger group of scholars believes that the United States is a victim of *relative decline*, not absolute decline. This is the notion that even if the United States has not lost wealth or power, other countries have caught up with it, creating a pluralist or multipolar international environment. Japan, Germany, and soon perhaps China stand with the United States today. The United States is still important in this environment, but its role is necessarily different from that of hegemon.

Evidence in support of the relative decline hypothesis is easy to find. Other countries now have incomes that equal or exceed the United States average. More important, perhaps, is evidence that the United States is no longer the dominant force in international trade and finance. Japan and the European Union seem able to compete with the United States head to head in these areas. Other countries have clearly caught up with the United States in some areas, if not all of them.

In his important book, *The Rise and Fall of the Great Powers*, historian Paul Kennedy argues that relative decline is perhaps inevitable. Hegemony is costly, and other nations take the benefits of a secure and prosperous world without necessarily paying their fair share of the costs. These other nations rise up and overtake the weary Titan. A more pluralist system necessarily emerges. What is important, then, is not that the hegemon withers away, which is nearly inevitable, but what sort of international structure replaces hegemony.[19]

Finally, a third group of scholars and policymakers insists that the U.S. is still the dominant force in the IPE today.[20] They make several good arguments. The first is that power in the IPE is both **soft power** (economics) and **hard power** (military power). No nation approaches the United States in its ability to mobilize hard power resources. Japan lacks military might; the European Union lacks the political consensus necessary to use their hard power. The Soviet Union is gone and China is as yet undeveloped. If hard power counts, then no country comes even close to the United States in overall strength.[21]

The antideclinists point to the 1991 Persian Gulf War and other recent military and humanitarian actions as evidence of continued U.S. hegemony. When real economic and political strength is needed, as in Kuwait or Rwanda, everyone looks to the United States. Finally, opponents of decline theories ask the question, if the United States is not the hegemon, who is? No nation seems to possess greater strength than the United States making it, perhaps, hegemon by default because of its great military power.

The decline debate is more than a battle of statistics and footnote references. If the United States does in fact remain a strong international force, then the liberal international regime that emerged from Bretton Woods may still be vital (although hegemony is no guarantee of peace and prosperity). If the United States is just one of many strong countries, however, then the future of IPE is even more uncertain and the very nature of the world order is doubtful.

THE FUTURE? FOUR SCENARIOS

The future is important: we will spend the rest of our lives in it. The future is also uncertain: what forces will emerge, how will institutions and structures adjust to them, who will benefit from these changes? It is impossible to know the future, but a good deal can be learned through mental experiments and thoughtful speculation about life's coming attractions. By now the readers of this book should be ready to think about the future in a knowledgeable and creative way. Here are four scenarios to stimulate thought and discussion.

Renewed Hegemony

Our first vision of the future imagines a return to the pattern of hegemony that characterized the prosperous years of Pax Americana. The richest, strongest nation will call a new Bretton Woods conference more than fifty years after the original meeting, and provide strong and decisive leadership in international economics and politics. Renewed hegemony is desirable, many scholars believe, because they hold that strong leadership is necessary to offset the natural forces of nationalism, regionalism, and class conflict that otherwise fragment and disrupt the IPE. The renewed hegemony scenario is haunted, however, by two unanswered questions: Who? and How? Who will be the new hegemon, and how will it lead?

Many nations have been nominated to be the new hegemon. The United States is often selected, for example, because of the history of Pax Americana, its undeniable military "hard power" dominance, and often for the simple reason that there is no better candidate. IPE abhors a hegemonic vacuum, some believe, and the United States will rush in to fill one when the time is right.[22] Other scholars, such as Lester Thurow, suggest that the European Union will lead the global IPE because of its large size and its proven ability, as a multinational consortium, to defuse nationalistic abuse and forge cooperative structures.[23] Japan is chosen by many, because of its economic "soft power" strength; in the post–Cold War world, it is said, Japan's soft power might be a more potent force than U.S. hard power.

If strong hegemony is renewed, how will the hegemon behave? What motives will the hegemon have in assuming leadership? Liberals believe in an unselfish hegemon, that provides the public goods of security and prosperity to the global community. Many who advance the United States as hegemon believe that it is in that country's interest to preserve and strengthen the liberal world order that grew out of the Bretton Woods conference. Others, however, take the realist view that hegemons are selfish and lead because that is the best way to advance national interest. Lester Thurow, for example, speculates a European leadership regime would benefit principally Europe; the leader would write the "rules of the game" and make others play a biased game. Finally, structuralists see a hegemon arising in order to preserve a stable core, so that the core's exploitation of the periphery can proceed smoothly.

Renewed hegemony is one scenario for the future, but strong hegemons have been the exception rather than the rule in modern history. What if no strong single leader appears?

Cooperative Arrangements

Another possible scenario is that of the United States working closely with many of its Cold War allies, consciously sharing power with them and with other nations to manage the international political economy in a cooperative fashion. There are several versions of this argument. One is that, in an interdependent international political economy with a multipolar balance of power, nations essentially "come to their senses" and rationally choose to cooperate with one another in order to manage the international political economy and solve other mutual problems.

Some scholars who study international organizations (IOs) believe that the international political economy is already headed in this direction. World Federalists, for instance, envision a world where IOs such as the United Nations gradually acquire more (sovereign) authority to produce international laws and regulations but also to impose sanctions to back up global legislation. Recently, many have looked more favorably at the tremendous amount of work being done by UN peacekeeping forces in places such as Cambodia and El Salvador. The UN, working in cooperation with many nongovernmental organizations (NGOs), has played a significant role in dealing with the increasing number of refugees in the world and combating AIDS and other terrible diseases. Why would nation-states be willing to give up some of their sovereignty to international organizations? The argument is that as problems such as international security, economic development, management of the international economy, and the environment have become more global in scope, fraught with complexity and costly for nation-states to solve individually, states will be more willing to look to international organizations and multilateral institutions and agencies for solutions.[24]

There are several problems with this argument. The first is the assumption that states will rationally choose to cooperate with one another. While states have found IOs, multilateral agencies, and regimes to be of some assistance to them, they are as yet unwilling to endow them with much more authority than they already have. As yet, the forces of integration work against the forces of national autonomy. In many cases, global problems have yet to be felt significantly at the national or local level; states resist payment to these organizations unless they directly benefit.[25]

Under another scenario, states will cooperate with one another simply as a reflection of the international distribution of wealth and power. In an interdependent world where the distribution of wealth and power has been sufficiently reshuffled since the 1970s, no one nation commands the hegemonic authority the United States did between 1945 and 1967. The United States has had to bargain with other nations over acceptable levels of trade protection in order to reach an agreement on new GATT trade rules. On most issues, the major powers must play a role or risk jeopardizing a solution to the problem. The environment summit in Rio in the summer of 1992 is a good case in point (see chapter 19). The United States did not officially participate in the conference, which weakened the adopted measures. However, the United States realizes that solutions to many of its own environmental problems will not be found unless it cooperates with other nations. Thus, the Clinton administration feels compelled to go back and sign some of the environmental agreements reached in Rio.

Interdependence may have a leveling effect on the distribution of wealth and power in the international system. However, it is still questionable to what extent nations will be willing to cooperate with one another under such conditions. Interdependence drives states apart as much as it pulls them together. It makes states, businesses, and even people feel vulnerable and *too* dependent on one another. One could look at the Rio summit and argue that the U.S. refused to support the measures at first because its leaders felt the summit was not in the political or economic interest of the United States. More important, the question is begged as to whether or not the summit will ultimately be successful if the United States does not participate in it.

In all cases where the United States might join in cooperating more closely with other nations on an equal basis, several questions are raised. Given the dynamics of global wealth and power, would a more equal distribution of power and wealth be anything more than a temporary condition? Would states realize it, and if they did, would they operate on that basis? Because, states have memories, and states have reputations, the experiences of the past necessarily condition the present. Cooperation is most likely when states find it in their interest to do so. We are left wondering, then, whether the issues states face will be serious enough to compel them to alter the tendency for certain states to lead and others to follow. So far, the threat to humanity stemming from nuclear weapons and the potential harm to all states from environmental damage have not compelled nation-states to overcome their decisive tendencies.

Anarchy and Chaos

Under some pessimistic scenarios, the twenty-first century will bring anarchy and chaos, along with diseases, such as the Ebola virus that promise to kill more people than AIDS in a shorter period of time. Overpopulation and ethnic conflict, especially in the poorest LDCs, promise to wreck havoc on national economies and to generate hostility if not warfare between ethnic groups and nations. Hunger is likely to continue unabated, especially in the Sudan region and parts of central and southern Africa. Not only will hunger be exacerbated by overpopulation but by increasing poverty and a bigger disparity between the world's rich and poor. These are some of the themes discussed by Robert Kaplan in his intriguing article "The Coming Anarchy." Although he focuses mainly on Africa, Kaplan implies that the overwhelming problems of poverty, overpopulation, and environmental damage are problems nations face in every region of the world in the next century.[26]

How would the United States deal with the anarchy or chaos that could become a major feature of the international political economy in the twenty-first century? Ironically, asking this question raises another question: could the United States insulate itself from these types of events? Most would answer no, because of the interdependence of nations and the high degree of globalization of political and economic structures. If this is the case, and we believe that it is, then states can be expected to have at least a long-term interest in solving these problems. Some states will have a greater capability of doing so than others and, depending on the immediacy of the problem, are likely to take the lead in solving it. Because the United States still has the preponderance of hard and soft power in the world and because its interests are still very much global, it can be expected to be out front on many of these problems, even if they seem only remotely of interest.

Many liberals worry that the further development of regional trading blocs will lead to a breakdown in international order. As we saw in chapters 6 and 11, these blocs may adopt liberal policies internally, by dropping trade barriers among their members; but they also employ discriminatory practices against nations outside the bloc. Some experts envision an international political economy composed of hostile trading blocs, each with a hegemon that defends its clients and competes with other blocs for unclaimed markets and territorial influence. The United States made moves in this direction when it promoted the North American Free Trade Agreement (NAFTA). Although by no means an integrated bloc in the sense of the EU, one purpose of NAFTA was to make the United States, Canada, and Mexico more competitive with Japan and the EU.[27]

There is one more source of breakdown or chaos facing the United States and any other nation in the twenty-first century, and that is a transformation of the international system itself. In other words, one must hold open the possibility that nation-states will no longer be the major political actors in the international system. In the 1970s, many speculated that sovereignty would be transferred to international businesses. More recently, some have speculated that more decentralized units such as city-states will come to hold people's loyalty. The mayors of some cities have circumvented their national governments to make trade deals with other nations. The argument here is that the nation-state will become passé, much like the city-state or empire did earlier. State security would give way to other objectives of other units.

Those who envision these dramatic changes see in the twenty-first century a fundamental shift away from the types of structures and practices that have defined IPE for at least four hundred years. They foresee a gloomy future, but they could be surprised.

A Surprise

We cannot find in the library the future of history, but we *can* look up the history of futures. Reading history, we can discover what people at different times expected of the future. The modern era has been filled with writers' dreams of what's to come, from Jules Verne to John Maynard Keynes.[28] What we learn from this study of the history of the future is that, when the future finally appeared, people were surprised by it. The future that appeared was different than the one they expected. Perhaps the best way to prepare for the future, then, is to prepare to be surprised![29]

Any number of unexpected events could change the course of history and turn the first three scenarios discussed here into just so much recyclable paper. Without going into too much detail, let us consider the possibility of a Surprise Scenario. One surprise, for example, would be the reemergence of a bipolar security structure such as the one that characterized the Cold War years. Contemporary writers frequently preface their remarks by saying, "Now that the Cold War is over . . ."— but what if it *isn't* over? The Soviet Union is gone, but Russia remains a potent force, with a large population, vast geography, and natural and human resources, and is still equipped with nuclear weapons. If not the Russia surprise, then perhaps a Chinese surprise could await us. If China's political and economic relations with the West deteriorated, then another Cold War stand-off could result.

The reemergence of OPEC or the rise of another resource-based cartel is another Surprise Scenario. OPEC's power has waned since the 1970s, as chapter 17 indicated, but dependence on oil imports is such today that just a few unexpected economic or political events might put OPEC in the driver's seat of IPE again. Who knows what group might set OPEC policy, and to what end?

Not all surprises are unhappy ones, however. Thomas Malthus, writing at the end of the eighteenth century, foresaw a world of overpopulation, starvation, and unrelenting violence. When it came around, however, the future was much different. The rising population, which Malthus saw as the main problem, was accompanied by technological improvements in farming, industry, and transportation. A number of relatively small improvements in science and industry combined to create something of a golden age. If peace and prosperity were not always and everywhere present, they were certainly far more prevalent than Malthus expected.

CONCLUSION: DAYS OF FUTURES PAST

At the Great Depression's darkest hour, John Maynard Keynes penned an essay called "Economic Possibilities for our Grandchildren," in which he speculated about the future of you who now read this book. Keynes wrote that the problem that preoccupied his times—the *economic* problem of unemployment—was temporary. Looking a hundred years ahead, he saw economic growth sufficient to meet the material needs of humans. With material want cured, he believed, we could turn our attention to more serious concerns about human existence.

> The *pace* at which we can reach our destination of economic bliss will be governed by four things—our power to control population, our determination to avoid wars and civil dissensions, our willingness to entrust to science the direction of those things which are properly the concern of science, and the rate of accumulation [saving]. Meanwhile, there will be no harm in making mild preparations for our destiny, in encouraging and experimenting in the arts of life as well as the activities of purpose.[30]

Keynes was an optimist. If he could look back today on this 1930 essay, he might well be surprised. The advance of science and technology has been impressive and is more important today than ever before. Hunger and population, war and revolt, and the problems of saving and debt remain, however, limiting progress toward "economic bliss." Even so, Keynes might remain a confident optimist, knowing that the enemies of progress are fear, uncertainty, and doubt.[31]

The future *is* uncertain, for the United States and for the world. Fear and doubt are justified. But it is still possible to be optimistic. The best way to prepare for an unknowable fate is with knowledge, and that has been the goal of this chapter and this book. We hope that this book has given you some tools you can use to grasp and understand some of the most important and vital issues of international political economy. The twentieth century has been a century of great change. One thing we are sure of is that change will continue even at accelerated rates.

The readers of this book have a personal stake in what happens in the IPE of the future. It is important that we continue to study the events, issues, and forces that shape the environment of our daily lives. It is critical to appreciate change and be able to interpret its effects. It is important that we have opinions—informed opinions—about these things. Armed with understanding, we can indeed be optimistic about the future possibilities of our grandchildren—and ourselves.

DISCUSSION QUESTIONS

1. The United States continues to experience a tension between its international objectives and its domestic needs. Discuss this tension, both in general and in terms of specific international and domestic concerns. Is it possible for the United States to choose one set of goals (either domestic or international) while ignoring the others? Explain.
2. The United States also must deal with a tension between economic security and political security. At some point, the values of the market come into conflict with the interests of the state. Explain the nature of this tension, citing specific examples and problems where possible. Are the goals of economic and political security *always* in conflict? Explain.
3. Is a hegemon necessary to create an environment conducive to international peace and prosperity? Discuss the theory of hegemonic decline—how hegemons tend to dissipate their strength. Is the United States a hegemon? A hegemon in decline? If the United States is unable to organize the global economic and political environment, what other country could perform this task? Explain.
4. This chapter ends with four scenarios for the future. Compare and contrast these different visions of the future. Which do you think is the most likely? Explain. Why does it matter which of these scenarios (or other set of conditions) actually occurs? How does what happens in the IPE affect you? Explain.

SUGGESTED READINGS

David P. Calleo. *Beyond American Hegemony.* New York: Basic Books, 1987.
———. *The Bankrupting of America.* New York: William Morrow, 1992.
Paul Kennedy. *The Rise and Fall of the Great Powers.* New York: Random House, 1987.
Henry R. Nau. *The Myth of America's Decline.* New York: Oxford University Press, 1990.
Susan Strange. "The Persistent Myth of Lost Hegemony." *International Organizations* 41 (Autumn 1987).
Lester C. Thurow. *The Zero-Sum Society: Distribution and the Possibilities for Economic Change.* New York: Basic Books, 1980.

NOTES

1. Epigraph quoted in David Halberstam, *The Reckoning* (New York: William Morrow, 1986), 63.
2. David P. Calleo, *The Bankrupting of America* (New York: William Morrow, 1992), 179.
3. Steven Ambrose, *Rise to Globalism: American Foreign Policy Since 1938* (New York: Penguin, 1988).
4. Francis Fukuyama, "The End of History," *The National Interest* 16 (Summer 1989): 3–35.

5. John Mearsheimer, "Why We Will Soon Miss the Cold War," *The Atlantic Monthly*, 226 (2 August 1990): 35–50.

6. See "First U.S. Troops Arrive in Rwanda for Relief Effort," *The Seattle Times*, 31 July 1994, A3.

7. For a detailed argument that supports this thesis, see Robert D. Kaplan, "The Coming Anarchy," *The Atlantic Monthly* 273 (February 1992): 44–76.

8. George Kennan is one advocate of this viewpoint.

9. See Lester Thurow, *The Zero-Sum Society* (New York: Basic Books, 1980).

10. See "Technology Spurs Changes in the Way We Fight Our Wars," *The Seattle Times*, 7 July 1994.

11. Paul Krugman is a leading advocate of this viewpoint. In his *Peddling Prosperity* (New York: Norton, 1994), he criticizes political entrepreneurs who "sell" trade policy as a patent medicine cure for economic woes.

12. For a more detailed discussion, see E. B. Kapstein, *The Political Economy of National Security: A Global Perspective* (New York: McGraw-Hill, 1992).

13. Joseph S. Nye, Jr., "The Changing Nature of World Power," *Political Science Quarterly*, 105 (Summer 1990): 177–192.

14. Ibid., 182.

15. Ibid.

16. Aaron L. Friedberg, "The Changing Relationship Between Economics and National Security," *Political Science Quarterly* 106 (Summer 1991): 195–212.

17. Martin and Susan J. Tochin, *Selling Our Security: The Erosion of America's Assets* (New York: Penguin Books, 1992). For a discussion of some of these same issues from a predominantly economic liberal perspective, see Ethan B. Kapstein, *The Political Economy of National Security: A Global Perspective* (New York: McGraw-Hill, 1992).

18. See Calleo, *The Bankrupting of America*. Calleo is more an advocate of the relative decline hypothesis, but in this notable study, he provides a good deal of evidence of decline.

19. Paul Kennedy, *The Rise and Fall of the Great Powers* (New York: Random House, 1987).

20. See, for example, Susan Strange, "The Persistent Myth of Lost Hegemony," *International Organization* 41 (August 1987): 551–574.

21. See Henry R. Nau, *The Myth of America's Decline* (New York: Oxford University Press, 1990).

22. Paul Kennedy comes to a conclusion much like this one in his *The Rise and Fall of the Great Powers*.

23. See Lester Thurow, *Head to Head: The Coming Economic Battle Among Japan, Europe, and America* (New York: William Morrow, 1992). Thurow actually advances a group of nations he calls the "House of Europe." He believes these nations will lead and dominate, although he does not go so far as to state that they will assume the mantle of hegemony.

24. For a detailed discussion of this argument, see Clive Archer, *International Organizations* (London: Allen & Unwin, 1983).

25. Senator Bob Dole makes an impassioned case for the United States not supporting UN peacekeeping efforts in "Peacekeepers and Politics," the *New York Times*, 24 January 1994, 15.

26. Robert Kaplan, "The Coming Anarchy."

27. For a more detailed discussion of regional block competition, see Thurow, *Head to Head*.

28. Indeed, thinking about the future is the essential aspect of the modern era. Premodern humans lived in a world of fundamental changelessness. For them, the future was the past, so they seldom imagined a different world.

29. This insight is due to Kenneth Boulding.

30. John Maynard Keynes, "Economic Possibilities for our Grandchildren," in *Essays in Persuasion* (New York: W. W. Norton, 1963), 373.

31. Keynes wrote about fear, uncertainty, and doubt as limits on self-interest action in his *General Theory of Employment, Interest, And Money* (New York: Harcourt Brace Jovanovich, 1964).

Glossary

Asia-Pacific Economic Cooperation Forum (APEC)   A forum for discussion and negotiation of trade and other issues among Asia-Pacific nations, including the United States, Japan, and China, and many other countries in this region. At the 1994 APEC meetings in Bogor, Indonesia, the group pledged to create a regional free-trade zone.

Autocracy   Government by a single person, who has ultimate power. Generally, autocracy refers to a system of highly centralized power in government.

Autonomous state   A state that is independent, not controlled by outside forces. Autonomous states have *sovereignty*.

Baker Plan   A plan to deal with third world debt problems proposed by U.S. Treasury Secretary James Baker.

Balance of payments (BOP)   A tabulation of all international transactions involving a nation in a given year, the BOP is the best indicator of a nation's international economic status. The most important parts of the BOP are the *current account* and the *capital account*.

Balance of payments deficit   This term usually refers to a *current account deficit* (see *current account*).

Balance of power   A concept that describes how states deal with the problems of national security in a context of shifting alliances and alignments. The balance system is produced by the clustering of individual national interests in opposition to those of other states. Peace among nations is usually associated with an approximate equilibrium in the distribution of power between nations in this system. Others argue that peace is enforced by a hegemon, not an equilibrium. See *hegemony*.

Bipolar system   An international security structure with two centers of power. The Cold War was a bipolar security structure, with hegemonic military power distributed between the United States and the Soviet Union.

Bipolycentrism   A configuration of power whereby global political, military, and economic power is distributed among two (bi) hegemons and any number of other major or rising powers. In the 1970s, the international security structure was said to be bipolycentric as a reflection of the continued superpower status of the United States and Soviet Union but also the growing influence of Japan, the EU, and the NICs.

Black markets   Illegal markets; markets that trade forbidden items, or legal items at forbidden prices. Many soft currency countries have black markets in currency, where exchanges are made at rates different from the official exchange rate.

Blocs   Groups of nation-states that are united or associated for some purpose. Examples of blocs are defense blocs, such as *NATO* and the *Warsaw Pact* and trade blocs such the *European Union* and *NAFTA*.

Bourgeoisie   In Marxian analysis, the bourgeoisie are the capitalist class who own the means of production. In everyday language, this term often refers to the middle class. See *proletariat*.

Brady Plan   A plan to deal with third world debt problems proposed by U.S. Treasury Secretary Nicholas Brady.

Bretton Woods   Bretton Woods is a place, a meeting, and a set of institutions and practices. Bretton Woods, New Hampshire, was the site of a series of meetings that took place in July 1944 among representatives of the Allied Powers of World War II (including the United States, Britain, France, Canada, and the Soviet Union, but also involving many smaller states). The Bretton Woods agreements created the International Monetary Fund, the World Bank, and the system of fixed exchange rates that prevailed in international finance until 1973.

Capital   "Stuff that is used to make stuff." Broadly speaking, capital is any long-lasting productive resource. Types of capital include physical capital, such as machines and factories; human capital, such as knowledge and learned skills; and financial capital, which is another term for money available for investment. The term *capital* is used in Marxist analysis to identify the owners of physical capital (capital vs. labor).

Capital account   The part of the *balance of payments* that records international borrowing, lending, and investment. If a nation has a capital account surplus, it means that it is a net debtor during a particular period.

Capitalism   Originally, the term described a political ideology that was identified with the capitalists, the owners of capital. Today, however, it usually refers to a market-dominated system of economic organization based on private property and free markets.

Cartel   A group of firms or nations that form a *bloc* to restrict supply of and increase profits from a particular product. OPEC is an example of an oil *cartel*.

Central bank   The chief monetary institution of a nation. Central banks regulate domestic financial institutions and influence domestic interest rates and foreign exchange rates. The central bank of the United States is the Federal Reserve System, which issues U.S. currency.

CFA Franc Zone   A group of African nations that are former colonies of France and that fix their exchange rate to the French franc.

Classical socialism   The economic system usually associated with communism. Classical socialism is a highly centralized system of production and distribution. The Soviet Union typified the classical socialist system prior to 1989.

Cold War   A phrase first used by Bernard Baruch in 1948 to describe the bipolar security structure that existed until 1989. The Cold War refers to the military and political confrontation between the United States and the Soviet Union and their allies.

Collective good   A tangible or intangible good that, once created, is available to all members of a group. The issue of collective goods raises questions about who should pay for these goods when they are to be provided to the entire group. No single person or entity has an incentive to pay for something everyone derives a benefit from. For example, cleaning up air pollution.

Common Agricultural Policy (CAP)   The system of agricultural subsidies employed by the *European Union*.

Communism   The system of political economy where control over state and market is centralized in a single, authoritarian party.

Comparative advantage   A nation has a *comparative advantage* in production of a good or service if it can produce it at a lower cost, or *opportunity cost*, than other nations. The theory of comparative advantage holds that nations should produce and export those goods and services in which they hold a comparative advantage, and import those items that other nations can produce at lower cost.

Consumer economics   An economic system organized primarily to satisfy consumer demands. See *Producer economics*.

Coordination mechanisms   Private and public institutions that organize the production and distribution of goods and services.

Core   A term used in the Modern World System analysis (core vs. periphery) in reference to the more-developed, capitalist part of the economic system, which interacts with the *periphery*, or less developed part of the system. These terms can refer to international geographic regions (e.g., *North-South*) or to sectors within a particular economy. See *Modern World System*.

Corn Laws Trade barriers that restricted agricultural imports into Great Britain from 1815 to 1846.

Counter trade A form of barter in international trade, where goods are paid for with other goods instead of money. *Counter trade* is most common in trade with *soft currency* nations, which often experience a shortage of *hard currency* funds with which to pay for imports.

Countervailing trade practices Defensive measures taken on the part of the state to counter the advantage gained by another state when it adopts protectionist measures. Such practices include antidumping measures and the imposition of countervailing tariffs or quotas.

Currency devaluation (or depreciation) By devaluing one's currency, exports become cheaper to other countries, while imports from abroad become more expensive. Currency depreciation thus tends to achieve the effects, temporarily at least, of both a tariff (raising import prices) and an export subsidy (lowering the costs of exports). Currency changes affect the prices of all traded goods, however, while tariffs and subsidies generally apply to one good at a time.

Current account A part of a nation's balance of payments that records financial flows due to international trade in goods and services and unilateral transfers (aid or gifts) between nations. A *current account deficit* means that a nation is paying out more for goods and services, etc., than it receives for the goods and services that it sells on international markets, which leads to rising international indebtedness.

Customs union A group of nations that agree to eliminate trade barriers among themselves and adopt a unified system of external trade barriers. The *Treaty of Rome* created a *customs union* in the form of the *European Community*.

Deflation A condition where the general level of prices falls over a period of time. Deflation (falling prices) is commonly associated with falling incomes, as during a *depression*.

Deforestation The destruction of forests, usually through excessive tree-cutting by humans.

Demographic transition The point where income growth exceeds population growth, making possible rising per capita income levels.

Dependency theory A theory of the relationship between industrialized (core) nations and less developed (periphery) nations that stresses the many linkages that exist to make LDCs dependent on richer nations. These linkages include trade, finance, and technology.

Depression A period of very significant decreases in incomes and employment in a nation as indicated by substantial decreases in gross national product and a high level of unemployment. A *depression* is more severe than is a *recession*.

Devaluation Also termed *currency depreciation*. A situation where the value of the domestic currency is reduced relative to foreign currencies. *Devaluation* increases the prices of imported goods, while making exports relatively less costly to foreign buyers.

Developmental capitalism Term used to describe the system of political economy of postwar Japan, where state policies are used to encourage industrial growth.

Direct foreign investment (DFI) Investments made by a company (often a *multinational corporation*) in production, distribution, or sales facilities in another country. The term *direct* implies a measure of control exercised by the parent company (U.S.-based IBM, for example) on resources in the host nation (e.g., Mexico).

Dual economy The theory of the *dual economy* is a liberal theory of economic development that views the world as having two sectors, a modern progressive sector and a traditional sector. Economic development and structural change take place as the progressive, market-driven sector interacts with and transforms the tradition-based less developed sector. Although the theory of the *dual economy* appears similar to the *core–periphery* interaction of the *Modern World System*, the nature of the interaction between sectors is distinctly different.

Dumping The practice of selling an item for less abroad than at home. *Dumping* is an unfair trade practice when it is used to drive out competitors from an export market with the goal of creating monopoly power.

Dynamic efficiency   An economic structure that produces high rates of economic growth.

Economic development   Increase in the level of economic activity in a nation, often measured by growth in GDP or per capital GDP. Generally, *economic development* involves structural changes, with populations moving from agricultural (primary sector) to manufacturing (secondary sector) to services (tertiary sector). The concept of *economic development* is rooted in the experiences of Western nations, especially Britain, the United States, and Germany.

Economic liberalism   The ideology of the free market. *Economic liberalism* holds that nations are best off when the role of the state is minimized. See *Laissez-faire. Economic liberalism* derives in part from fear of state abuse of power and the philosophy of individualism and liberty of the eighteenth century Enlightenment.

Economic nationalism   The ideology of *mercantilism. Economic nationalism* holds that nations are best off when state and market are joined in a partnership. The state protects domestic business firms, which become richer and more powerful, which in turn increases the power of the state. Alexander Hamilton and Friedrich List are two famous proponents of economic nationalism.

Ecosystem   An ecological community and its environment, considered as a single unit.

Embargo   A government prohibition of a certain activity. A trade embargo is a prohibition of trade with a nation.

Ethnic cleansing   The harassment, removal, or murder of citizens based solely on their ethnic or racial attributes, a term that emerged in the conflict following the breakup of former Yugoslavia.

European Coal and Steel Community (ECSC)   Organization established in 1952 to integrate the coal and steel resources of six European nations. Eventually evolved into the European Economic Community.

European Community (EC)   A creation of the *Treaty of Rome,* the *EC* was a group that eventually numbered twelve nations engaged in economic (and to a lesser extent, political) integration. Taken together, the EC member states formed the largest single market in the world. EC members were France, Germany, Italy, Belgium, the Netherlands, and Luxembourg (the charter members), plus Great Britain, Ireland, Denmark, Greece, Spain, and Portugal. See *European Union.*

European Economic Space (EES)   Group of nations that are not members of the *European Union* but that have negotiated free-trade or preferential trade agreements with the EU.

European Union (EU)   Successor organization to the *European Community* as defined by the *Maastricht Treaty.* As of 1995, the following countries were members of the EU: France, Germany, Italy, Belgium, the Netherlands, Luxembourg, Great Britain, Ireland, Denmark, Greece, Spain, Portugal, Austria, Finland, and Sweden.

Exchange rate   The ratio of exchange between the currencies of different countries (e.g., between the dollar and the yen). Changes in the *exchange rate* affect the prices of goods in international trade and, therefore, have important internal affects in nations. (See *Devaluation.*) The international system of *exchange rates* can be based on *Fixed (pegged) exchange rates,* as during the Bretton Woods period (1946–1973) and the period of the *gold standard* in the late nineteenth century, or *flexible (floating) exchange rate,* as during the period since 1946. *Fixed exchange rates* are determined by international agreements among states; *flexible exchange rates* are determined by market forces.

Export   A good or services that is sold to the citizens of another nation.

Export quotas   These international agreements limit the quantity of an item that a nation can export. The effect is to limit the number of goods imported into a country. Examples include orderly marketing arrangements (OMAs), voluntary export restraints (VERs), or voluntary restraint agreements (VRAs). The Multi-Fibre Agreement establishes a system of *export quotas* for less developed countries, for example.

Export subsidies   Any measure that effectively reduces the price of an exported product, making it more attractive to potential foreign buyers.

Feudal system   Medieval system of political economy organized around land holdings, or fiefs.

Finance structure   The system of institutions, practices, and arrangements that condition the use and exchange of financial resources. The international monetary system and the institutions that condition the distribution and payment of international debts are parts of the finance structure.

Fiscal austerity   Attempts to deal reduce current account deficits through measures including higher taxes, reduced expenditures and subsidies, privatization of state-owned enterprises, and monetary restriction.

Fixed (pegged) exchange rates   *Exchange rates* that are determined principally by state actions, not market forces.

Flexible (floating) exchange rates   *Exchange rates* that are determined principally by market forces, not state actions.

Free rider problem   Difficulty associated with *public goods*, where an individual is able to enjoy the benefits of a good or service without paying for them.

Free trade area   A group of nations that agrees to eliminate tariff barriers for trade among themselves, but which retains the right of individual nations to set their own tariffs for trade with nonmember nations.

GATT (General Agreement on Tariffs and Trade)   An international organization, based in Geneva, that negotiates reductions in trade barriers among its many member nations. GATT negotiations take place over a period of years and are termed "rounds," as in the Kennedy round and the Tokyo round, which reduced trade barriers for manufactured goods, and the recent *Uruguay round*, which aims to create freer trade in services and in agricultural goods.

Generalized system of preferences (GSP)   Regulations regarding tariffs set as part of the GATT.

Geopolitics   The combination of political and geographical factors that influence a nation within an IPE structure, especially the *security structure.*

Glasnost   A policy of openness, especially regarding public information.

Global warming   The increase in the temperature of the earth's atmosphere that results from the greenhouse effect.

Gold standard   A monetary system of *fixed exchange rates* where currency values are defined in terms of a fixed quantity of gold.

Great Leap Forward   A 1958 economic and social development program in China that organized a half-billion peasants into 24,000 "people's communes."

Green   The adjective *Green* often indicates an emphasis on environmental issues. The *Green* party in Germany, for example, is a political party devoted to furthering environmental and related positions.

Green revolution   Various scientific, technological, and economic programs that attempt to increase food production through introduction of advanced plant strains and farming techniques.

Gross domestic product (GDP)   Like GNP, GDP is a measure of a nation's economic production in a year. Unlike GNP, however, GDP measures only production that takes place within a nation. GDP is the accepted international measure of national economic performance. "Real" GDP adjusts GDP for changes in inflation. "Per capita" GDP is a measure of average income per person in a country.

Gross national product (GNP)   The total value of all goods and services produced in a country in a year. GNP is a measure of a nation's overall economic activity. "Real" GNP, which adjusts GNP for the effects of inflation, is a more reliable indicator of changes in a nation's production. GNP was the main measure of economic performance in the United States until 1991. Now the U.S. and most other nations rely on *gross domestic product* measurements.

Group of Seven (G-7)   The seven largest industrial democracies: the United States, Japan, Germany, France, Canada, Italy, and Great Britain. The leaders of the G-7 nations meet regularly to discuss common economic and political problems and to attempt to coordinate policies in some areas.

Hard currency   A currency of known value that can be readily exchanged on foreign exchange markets and is therefore generally accepted in international transactions. Examples of hard currencies today include the U.S. dollar, the Japanese yen, the German Deutschemark, and the Swiss franc. See *soft currency.*

Hard power   Military power. See *soft power.*

Hegemony   Dominance or leadership, especially by one nation over other nations. The theory of hegemonic stability holds that the international system achieves growth and stability only when one state acts as the hegemon, dominating the others but also paying the costs associated with counteracting problems in the international system.

Imperialism   Idea associated with the works of J. A. Hobson, V. I. Lenin, and R. Luxemburg. A superior-inferior relationship in which an area and its people have been subordinated to the will or interests of a foreign state. *Imperialism* is often associated with historical periods that correspond to conquest and colonization of developing territories by developed "modern" industrialized nations. Economic *imperialism* may result from a conscious policy or from the capital flows of private foreign investment. See *direct foreign investment.*

Import   A good or service purchased from citizens of a foreign country.

Import quotas   A limit on the quantity of an item that can be imported into a nation. By limiting the quantity of imports, the quota tends to drive up the price of a good, while at the same time restricting competition.

Import substituting industrialization   An economic development strategy that attempts to encourage industrial development, often by restricting imports of industrial productions or encouraging exports of these items.

Industrial revolution   The period from approximately 1780 to 1840, when an industrial sector developed in Europe, especially in Great Britain. This period is sometimes called the "first industrial revolution" to distinguish it from the "second industrial revolution" (approximately 1880 to 1910). The first revolution relied on mechanical innovations, while the second revolution was based on chemical and electrical innovations.

Inflation   A rise in the general level of prices in a country (as opposed to a rise in the price of a particular good). Hyperinflation is a condition where very high rates of inflation (1,000 percent per year price increases and more) are experienced.

Integration   In IPE, *integration* occurs when nation-states agree to unify or coordinate some political and economic activities.

Intellectual property rights   Patents, copyrights, and other rights to ownership or control of ideas, innovation, and creations.

Interdependence   Usually thought of as interconnectedness between nations and other actors in the international political economy conditioned by trade, aid, finance, and investment. Reactions to interdependence include the need to cooperate but also negative reactions related to the vulnerability and sensitivity it engenders.

International division of labor   The organization of global economic activity, often with special emphasis on the activities of *core* and *periphery.*

International Monetary Fund (IMF)   Created as part of the *Bretton Woods* system, the *IMF* is an organization of over 150 member states charged with stabilizing the international monetary system. The *IMF* makes loans to member states when they experience severe *current account deficits.* These loans are made subject to enactment of economic reforms, a practice called "conditionality."

Isolationism   The policy of withdrawing from world affairs, especially to prevent disruption or exploitation from external sources.

Keiretsu   Japanese "business families"; groups of businesses in different economic sectors that engage in cooperative strategic behavior—buying and selling goods within the group whenever possible, for example.

Keynesian theory   To be *Keynesian* is to be in agreement with the general thrust of the political economy of John Maynard Keynes (pronounced "Canes") (1883–1946). Because

Keynes's views were complex, original, and constantly changing, there is no precise definition of what it means to be *Keynesian*. A general definition is to believe that there is a positive role for the state to play in domestic affairs (fighting unemployment and poverty, for example) and in international affairs (the kind of role conceived for the *IMF* and the *World Bank*). Keynes's views were influenced by the catastrophe of World War I and the chaos of the interwar period.

Knowledge structure   The set of institutions and practices that conditions the production, exchange, and distribution of intellectual and technological goods and services, property rights, and their associated benefits.

Laissez-faire   A French term ("let be" or "leave alone") commonly associated with Adam Smith, the eighteenth century Scottish economist who advocated free market solutions to economic and social problems. Today, it refers to a view that individuals are best left to solve problems themselves through the "invisible hand" of market interactions, rather than through government policies.

Less developed country (LDC)   A nation with relatively low levels of income and industrialization.

Maastricht Treaty   This treaty creating the *European Union*, was ratified by members of the *European Community* in 1993.

Managed exchange rates   *Exchange rate* system where day-to-day FX (foreign exchange) changes are determined by market forces, but long-run changes are conditioned by state actions. Sometimes termed a "dirty float." See *flexible exchange rate*.

Maquiladora   Assembly plants in Mexico that use foreign parts and semifinished products to produce final goods for export.

Market   A form of social organization based on individual action and self-interest. Individuals exchange goods and services through market institutions. Markets are sometimes distinct physical places (such as the New York Stock Exchange or Pike Place Market in Seattle), but the term *market* generally refers to the broader market forces of profit and self-interest.

Market Leninism   See *Market socialism*.

Market socialism   A system of political economy that combines state ownership and control of some sectors of the economy with private ownership and market allocations in other sectors. See *classical socialism*.

Marshall Plan   Named for U.S. Secretary of State George C. Marshall, who proposed the program in 1947. A 1948–1951 U.S. postwar assistance program that provided $12 billion in aid to European countries. Also called the "European Recovery Program."

Marxism   An ideology that originated in the works of the German sociologist Karl Marx. There are many strains of *Marxism* that have evolved from Marx's works. Generally, *Marxism* is a critique of *capitalism* (as distinct from *economic liberalism*). *Marxism* holds that *capitalism* is subject to several distinctive flaws. *Marxism* tends to view economic relations from a power perspective (capital vs. labor) as opposed to the cooperative relationship implicit in *economic liberalism*. See *structuralism*.

Mercantilism   A seventeenth century idea that won't go away, *mercantilism* was an ideology that put accumulation of national treasury as the main goal of society. Today, it is an economic philosophy and practice of government regulation of a nation's economic life to increase state power and security. Policies of import restriction and export promotion (to accumulate treasure at the expense of other countries) follow from this goal. See *economic nationalism*.

Ministry of International Trade and Industry (MITI)   Japanese government ministry that deals most directly with trade issues. *MITI* has been credited by some for Japan's rapid industrialization in the 1960s and 1970s.

Mixed economy   An economy that combines important elements of *state* and *market* (although relative importance of these two elements may vary). Britain and France are both mixed economies, for example, although the state is relatively larger in France and the market relatively more important in Britain.

Miyazawa Plan   Third world debt plan proposed by Japanese Prime Minister Kiichi Miyazawa.

Modern World System (MWS)   A theory of economic development based on Marxist-Leninist ideologies. The *MWS* views economic development as conditioned by the relationship between the capitalist *core* and the less developed *periphery* nations. The historic mission of the *core* is to develop the *periphery* (often through the *semi-periphery*), but this development is exploitive in nature. The *MWS* therefore presents a theory that runs counter to liberal theories such as "hegemonic stability." See *core*.

Monetarism   A school of thought that focuses on the money supply as a key determinant of the level of economic activity in a nation. Monetarists tend to view state economic actions as likely to disrupt domestic and international affairs. Monetarists tend, therefore, to be closely associated with *economic liberals* in their dislike of state influences.

Monetary union   A group of nations that actively coordinate their monetary policies. Members of a *monetary union* might adopt a common currency, for example.

Most favored nation (MFN)   Trade status under GATT where imports from a nation are granted the same degree of preference as those from the most preferred nations.

Multinational corporation (MNC)   A business firm that engages in production, distribution, and marketing activities that cross national boundaries (see *direct foreign investment*). The critical factor is that the firm have a tangible productive presence in several countries. This factor distinguishes a *MNC* from an international firm, which produces in one country and exports to other countries. *MNCs* are sometimes called multinational enterprises (MNEs) or transnational enterprises (TNEs).

Multipolar system   A security structure with more than two centers of power.

Nation   A social group that shares a common identity, history, language, set of values and beliefs, institutions, and a sense of territory. Nations do not have to have a homogeneous ethnic culture but usually exhibit a sense of homogeneity. Nations may extend beyond states, be circumscribed by states or be coterminus with states. Since the seventeenth-century, the nation-state has been the major political (sovereign) unit of the international system.

Nation-state   Synonymous with the term "country," since the seventeenth century the nation-state has been the major political (sovereign) unit of the international system. The nation-state joins the nation—a group of people with a shared sense of cultural identity and territoriality—with the state—a legal concept describing a social group that occupies a territory—and is organized under common political institutions and an effective government. As sovereign entities, nation-states have the right to determine their own national objectives and to decide how they will achieve them.

New International Economic Order (NIEO)   A set of proposals made by less developed nations to reform international trade and financial structures.

Newly industrialized countries (NICs)   Nations that have achieved a large measure of industrialization in the second half of the twentieth century. Most lists of the *NICs* include South Korea, Taiwan, and Brazil, and sometimes Singapore and Hong Kong.

Nichibei economy   The economies of the United States and Japan considered as a single entity, not two separate units.

Nontariff barriers (NTBS)   Other ways of limiting imports include government health and safety standards, domestic content legislation, licensing requirements, and labeling requirements. Such measures make it difficult for imported goods to be marketed or significantly raise the price of imported goods.

North American Free Trade Agreement (NAFTA)   A free trade area among the United States, Canada, and Mexico, to be fully implemented by 2005. The NAFTA treaty was signed in 1992 and took force in 1994.

North Atlantic Treaty Organization (NATO)   International security organization founded in 1949 and based in Washington, DC. NATO served as the main western alliance during the Cold War. See *Warsaw Pact*.

North-South   The relationship between developed, industrialized countries (the North) and less developed countries (the South). This concept is often associated with *core-periphery* analysis, but can also be simply a descriptive device.

Oligarchy   System of government where control is held by a small group.

Opportunity cost   The value of the best foregone opportunity when a choice is made. See *comparative advantage.*

Organization of Petroleum Exporting Countries (OPEC)   Organization of nations formed in 1960 to advance interests of third world oil exporters. OPEC members include Saudi Arabia, Iran, Iraq, Kuwait, Qatar, Abu Dhabi, Algeria, Gabon, Libya, Nigeria, Indonesia, Ecuador, and Venezuela.

Path-dependency   The notion that future choices depend critically on the pattern of past choices and the sets of institutions and practices that developed previously.

Pax Americana   The period of U.S. hegemony following World War II. "Pax" means "peace."

Pax Britannia   The period of British hegemony following the Napoleonic wars. "Pax" means "peace."

Pax Consortis   A period of "universal peace" provided by a collective hegemon in a multipolar system.

Peace Dividend   Resources that become available for other uses during peacetime due to decreased expenditures on national defense.

Perestroika   Restructuring or reformation, especially the programs of governmental restructuring implemented in the Soviet Union in the mid-1980s.

Periphery   Nonindustrialized sector of the *Modern World System* that produces agricultural goods and natural resources. See *Core* and *Modern World System.*

Pluralism   Existence of many different ethnic, social, and political groups within society.

Political economy   The social science that examines the dynamic interaction between the forces of *Market* and *State,* and how the tension and conflict between these aspects of society affect the world. The term *political economy,* in certain contexts, has different meanings. In economics, for example, *political economy* is the name sometimes applied to Marxist analysis and sometimes applied to economic tools used to analyze political behavior.

Portfolio investment   Pattern of international investment where firms seek to acquire ownership in many industries or world regions in order to hedge investment risk.

Positive-sum game   Any human interaction that makes all participants simultaneously better off. See *zero-sum game.*

Prisoners' dilemma   Term coined by Princeton mathematics professor A. W. Tucker to describe a situation where best interests of persons in society taken individually are opposite from those of the same individuals taken as a group.

Process innovation   Inventions and improvements on producing existing goods, services, and techniques, but which do not result in new items. See *product innovation.*

Producer economics   An economic system organized primarily to generate sustained increases in production. See *consumer economics.*

Product cycle or **Product life cycle**   Terms coined by Harvard political economist Raymond Vernon to describe production and trade patterns stemming from product innovation and technological diffusion.

Product innovation   Pattern of inventions that focuses on creation of new goods and services, not refinements of existing items. See *process innovation.*

Production structure   The institutions and practices that condition the production, exchange, and distribution of goods and services in the IPE. International trade is a key component of the *production structure.* Essentially, the factors that determine what is produced, where, how, by whom, for whom, and on what terms. See *international division of labor.*

Productive power   Term used by Friedrich List to describe technology, education, and training, especially with respect to the industrial sector of the economy.

Proletariat   In Marxian analysis, the class of workers who do not own capital.

Property rights   A bundle of rights associated with ownership of a resource. Property rights include the right to use a resource and exclude others from its use, to gain from or control its use by others, and dispose of it. *Property rights* are defined by the state.

Protectionism   Theory of or belief in the advantages of restricting trade so as to encourage or benefit domestic producers.

Public goods   Goods or services that, once provided, generate benefits that can be enjoyed by all simultaneously. A lighthouse is the classic example of a *public good*.

Purchasing power parity (PPP)   An *exchange rate* such that a given amount of a currency will purchase the same amounts of goods and services at home as abroad.

Rational choice theory   A theory of *political economy* that focuses on the incentives facing individuals and states and how those incentives affect their behavior. The structure of incentives (costs and benefits) of the international system is seen as an important determinant of state behavior by *rational choice* theorists.

Realism   A theory of state behavior that focuses on national interest as a determinant of state behavior. States, like individuals, tend to act in their own self-interest, in the view of *realists*.

Recession   A decline in the overall level of economic activity in a nation as indicated by a decrease in real *gross national product*.

Regime   The environment in which a particular type of IPE activity takes place, including the various actors, institutions, and practices that exist to deal with a specific problem. The oil *regime*, for example, includes the nation-states, international organizations, private-sector firms, markets, agreements, and so on, that condition oil production, exchange and distribution, and related activities.

Rio Earth Summit   International conference held in Rio de Janeiro, Brazil, in 1992, to discuss global environmental problems.

Security structure   The sets of institutions, practices, and beliefs that condition international behavior as it relates to national security issues.

Semi-periphery   An intermediate zone between *core* and *periphery*. Korea and Taiwan might be considered part of the *semi-periphery* today in the *Modern World System* theory. See *core*.

Seven sisters   The seven largest international oil companies.

Social safety net   Social programs, such as old-age pensions and unemployment insurance, that provide for economically disadvantaged groups in society.

Soft currency   Currencies of uncertain value (due, perhaps, to high inflation rates) that are not generally accepted in international transactions. *Soft currencies* can usually be spent only within the nation that issues it, whereas a *hard currency* can be exchanged and spent in most nations. Some *soft currencies*, such as the ruble in the former Soviet Union, are called "inconvertible currencies" because it is illegal to convert them into *hard currencies*.

Soft power   Wealth, as used to influence the actions of foreign states. See *hard power*.

Solidarity   Polish labor union (and political party) founded in 1980 by Lech Wałesa.

Sovereignty   Independence from foreign control. See *autonomous state*.

Special economic zones   Regions of China where private ownership is permitted and market forces are used to encourage rapid economic growth. See *market socialism*.

Sphere-of-influence   The area or territory in which a hegemon or major state has interest and sustains either political, military, or economic influence. During the Vietnam War, it was common practice to refer to Southeast Asia as being in the United States' sphere-of-influence.

State   A legal concept describing a social group that occupies a defined territory and is organized under common political institutions and an effective government. A *state* has some degree of independence and autonomy. *States* are the primary units of the international political and legal community. As sovereign entities, *states* have the right to determine their own national objectives and the techniques (including the use of force) for their achievement.

Static efficiency   An efficient use of current resources, especially specialization according to the *comparative advantage*. See *dynamic efficiency*.

Statism   A trend whereby states subordinate economic policies to national and state political objectives. In more authoritarian or communist states, the state may restrict or otherwise heavily regulate market activities in favor of some ideological or nationalist objective.

Strategic Arms Limitation Treaty (SALT)   Arms control and reduction agreement between the United States and the Soviet Union, signed in 1972.

Strategic trade practices   Efforts on the part of the *state* to create *comparative advantages* in trade by methods such as subsidizing research and development of a product, or providing subsidies to help an industry increase production to the point where it can move down the "learning curve" to achieve greater production efficiency than foreign competitors. *Strategic trade practices* are often associated with state industrial policies, i.e., intervention in the economy to promote specific patterns of industrial development.

Structuralism   This theory accounts for the political-economic interconnectedness (structural relationship) between any number of entities: the *bourgeoisie* and *proletariat*, the *core* and *periphery*, the *North* and *South*. A number of ties bind these entities to one another, including trade, foreign aid, and direct investment. Much debate exists as to whether and how structural conditions can be changed or reformed. See *Marxism.*

Structures of IPE   Sets of institutions, practices, and beliefs that condition the international production, exchange, and distribution of production, finance, security, and knowledge.

Subsidy   Government payment to encourage some activity or benefit some group. See *common agricultural policy.*

Sustainable development   A pattern of economic development that is consistent with the goal of nondegradation of the environment.

Symbolic analysts   A term coined by U.S. political economist Robert Reich to describe a class of highly trained persons. To use the language of *Modern World Systems* analysis, *symbolic analysts* form the *core* of a knowledge-based global division of labor.

Tariff   A tax placed on imported goods to raise the price of those goods, making them less attractive to consumers. Though *tariffs* are used at times to raise government revenue (particularly in *LDCs*), they are more commonly a means to protect domestic industry from foreign competition.

Terms of trade   The value of a nation's exported goods relative to the value of the goods that are imported. A measure of the prices paid for imports relative to the prices received for imports.

Tragedy of the commons   Term coined by Garrett Hardin to describe situations where human nature drives individuals to overuse communal resources.

Treaty of Rome   A 1957 treaty among France, Britain, West Germany, Belgium, Luxembourg, and the Netherlands that established the European Economic Community in 1958.

Uruguay round   Set of negotiations of the members of the *General Agreement on Tariffs and Trade* (1986–1994) that focused on reducing trade barriers, especially regarding services and agricultural goods.

Vietnam syndrome   Essentially a lesson the United States supposedly learned from having lost the Vietnam War: essentially, don't intervene in other third world nations unless U.S. vital interests are at stake, the United States is assured of a quick and relatively inexpensive victory, and the U.S. public will support the operation.

Warsaw Pact   The Warsaw Treaty Organization (1955–1991) military and defense alliance among Albania, Bulgaria, Czechoslovakia, East Germany, Hungary, Poland, Romania, and the Soviet Union. See *North Atlantic Treaty Organization.*

World Bank   Officially called the International Bank for Reconstruction and Development, the *World Bank* is an international agency with over 150 members. Created by the Bretton Woods agreements in 1944, the *World Bank* originally worked on the reconstruction of Europe after World War II. Today, the *World Bank* makes low-interest loans to *less developed countries* to stimulate economic development.

World Trade Organization (WTO)   Successor organization to the *General Agreement on Tariffs and Trade* (GATT).

Yom Kippur War   The 1973 war between Israel and several Arab nations in the Middle East.

Zaibatsu   Large and powerful family-controlled financial and industrial organization of modern Japan. Among the leading zaibatsu are, Sumitomo Mitsubishi, Mitsui, and Yasuda.

Zero-sum game   An activity where gains by one party create equal losses for others. See *positive-sum game.*

Glossary of Acronyms

APEC	Asia-Pacific Economic Cooperation
BOP	Balance of payments
CAP	Common agricultural policy
DFI	Direct foreign investment
EU	European Union
EFTA	European free trade area
FX	Foreign exchange
GATT	General Agreement on Tariffs and Trade
GDP	Gross domestic product
GNP	Gross national product
GSP	Generalized system of preferences
IBRD	International Bank for Reconstruction and Development (also World Bank)
IMF	International Monetary Fund
LDC	Less developed country
MFN	Most favored nation
MITI	Ministry of International Trade and Industry
MNC	Multinational corporation
NAFTA	North American Free Trade Agreement
NATO	North Atlantic Treaty Organization
NIC	Newly industrialized country
NIEO	New International Economic Order
NTB	Nontariff barrier
OECD	Organization for Economic Cooperation and Development
OPEC	Organization of Petroleum Exporting Countries
PPP	Purchasing power parity
SALT	Strategic Arms Limitation Treaty
TRIPs	Trade-related intellectual property rights
WTO	World Trade Organization

Index